Memory and Cognition in its Social Context

Robert S. Wyer, Jr.
Thomas K. Srull
University of Illinois at Urbana-Champaign

90-1370

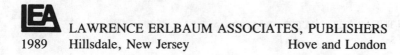
LAWRENCE ERLBAUM ASSOCIATES, PUBLISHERS
1989   Hillsdale, New Jersey   Hove and London

Lawrence Erlbaum Associates, Inc., Publishers
365 Broadway
Hillsdale, New Jersey 07642

Library of Congress Cataloging in Publication Data

Wyer, Robert S.
   Memory and cognition in its social context / Robert S. Wyer, Jr.,
Thomas K. Srull.
      p.   cm.
   Includes bibliographical references.
   ISBN 0-8058-0599-0 :
   1. Memory—Social aspects. 2. Human information processing—
-Social aspects. 3. Social perception. I. Srull, Thomas K.
II. Title.
BF378.S65W94   1989
153.1'2—dc20

                                                89-36227
                                                CIP

PRINTED IN THE UNITED STATES OF AMERICA
10 9 8 7 6 5 4 3 2

Dedicated to the Memory of
Darlene Goodhart

Contents

Preface

During the late 1970s, a small group of social psychologists began to meet in order to discuss their theoretical and empirical work in the largely uncharted waters of "person memory". One result was the preparation of a monograph, the objective of which was to report current research and provide a conceptual framework that would guide future efforts, not only in person memory but in social cognition more generally. The two authors of this volume were assigned the task of writing a capstone chapter that would bring together the ideas and research findings that emerged from the individual research programs of the other contributors.

We expected our task to be a simple one. In the time-honored tradition of information processing theory, we needed only to sketch out a flow diagram indicating the various stages of processing, identify where "memory" played a role, and our task would be complete. It did not take long for our naivete to become apparent.

In order to construct a flow diagram that would be compatible with the various phenomena our colleagues had uncovered, multiple memory and processing units were required. It also became clear that the information flowing through the system, even if it was just a skeleton system, had to be heavily cross-indexed. Moreover, provision had to be made for the different cognitive processes that were likely to occur when people processed information for different purposes. This led us to a very early recognition of the importance of information processing "goals" or "objectives." We were further surprised by the mounting evidence that, whereas some memory-based phenomena became less apparent over time, others actually increased in strength. In short, the social mind appeared to be much more complex than work from our cognitive colleagues had suggested.

Although our early objective was to integrate different streams of research, the model we developed had many empirical implications that were quite novel. Several of these were pursued and, much to our surprise, empirical support for the model began to accumulate steadily. We also found research from other laboratories that was quite consistent with implications of the model. In some cases, of course, modifications in the model were required to accomodate new data. However, these modifications had additional empirical implications, and these implications stood up quite well in the face of further study. We then began to monitor the journals more and more closely for findings that fell within the purview of the model.

The present book is the result of our efforts over the past seven years. It presents a substantially refined and elaborated conceptualization of social information processing that should be considered a new model rather than a simple extension of our initial effort (Wyer & Srull, 1980). Encoding, organizational, storage, retrieval, and inference processes are all specified in more detail. We also offer new conceptualizations of the representations that are formed from person and event information, and the way in which these representations are used to make judgments. The role of affect in information processing, and the content and structure of self knowledge, are also treated in some detail. Although the model is not without deficiencies, it nonetheless accounts for a wide range of phenomena and generates many nonobvious predictions that have been supported empirically. Thus, the model is both integrative and heuristic.

This book is genuinely collaborative. However, the collaboration extends far beyond the two coauthors. The University of Illinois Social Cognition Group, an exceptionally active consortium of faculty, postdoctoral fellows and graduate students from various social science disciplines, has met for many years to exchange ideas. Members of this group, both individually and collectively, have contributed in uncountable ways to nearly every aspect of our work. Their research is highlighted throughout this volume and their theoretical ideas (not always adequately acknowledged) are reflected in many aspects of the conceptualization we propose. In short, the entire book is largely a result of their effort and we are heavily in their debt.

Several people deserve special mention. Galen Bodenhausen, Bob Fuhrman, and Meryl Lichtenstein have been invaluable collaborators. In addition, Norbert Schwarz and Fritz Strack, colleagues with whom we have collaborated both at Illinois and in Germany, have had an enormous influence, as have Stan Klein and Leonard Martin who worked with us as postdoctoral fellows. Among the many individuals who have worked with us during their tenure as graduate students at Illinois, we are particularly indebted to Lee Budesheim, Gail Futoran, Lisa Gaelick, Sallie Gordon, Jon Hartwick, Janice Kelly, Alan Lambert, Steve Levine, and Victor Ottati. They are a terrific group of people and we were fortunate to have worked with them.

More senior colleagues have also influenced our theorizing. Don Carlston, Dave Hamilton, Reid Hastie, and Tom Ostrom were all members of the original "person memory" group and have continued to provide inspiration through both their own research and theorizing and their constructive criticism of our own. Equally valuable have been our interactions with John Bargh, Tory Higgins, and Jim Sherman. Although their influence may not always be readily apparent, it is broader and deeper than we sometimes admit.

The theoretical and empirical work that is represented in this volume was supported most recently by the National Institute of Mental Health (MH 3-8585, BSR) and, previously, by numerous grants from the National Science Foundation. Their continuing interest and support of our research is deeply appreciated. Much of the actual writing was done while the first author was an Associate of the Center for Advanced Study at the University of Illinois, with facilities provided by the University of Mannheim, Germany. Appreciation is extended to both.

We are also deeply indebted to Lawrence Erlbaum for his encouragement and for his patience in the delays that have occurred in submission of the manuscript. Larry's support, not only of our work but of cognitive and social psychology more generally, has been a major force in the development of social cognition. Like the rest of the field, we are greatly in his debt. There simply is no better publisher in the business.

Finally, we want to acknowledge the impact that Darlene Goodhart had on both our lives. In addition to making important contributions to social cognition, and serving as a uniquely competent and trusted critic of our ideas, Darlene was a valuable friend. Her support, tolerance, and love had a value that is impossible to express in words. She was married to one of us and an inspiration to both. Darlene's premature death was tragic, both for us and for the field. Our consolation is that we are much better people for having known her. We miss Darlene deeply, and it is to her that this volume is dedicated.

Robert S. Wyer, Jr.
Thomas K. Srull

Chapter 1
Introduction

This is a book about social cognition. Theory and research that fall under this rubric have captured the imagination and energies of many social and cognitive psychologists since the mid-1970s. Several other books on the topic have appeared (Fiske & Taylor, 1984; Hastie, Ostrom, Ebbesen, Wyer, Hamilton, & Carlston, 1980; Higgins, Herman, & Zanna, 1981; Cantor & Kihlstrom, 1981; Nisbett & Ross, 1980; Wyer & Carlston, 1979) and, more recently, two handbooks have emerged (Sorrentino & Higgins, 1986; Wyer & Srull, 1984). Moreover, a series of "advances" in the area has been established and several journals devote all or many of their pages to the topic. Given this flurry of activity, one might assume that the domain of inquiry is well defined and can easily be differentiated from others. Yet, "What *is* social cognition?" continues to be one of the most frequently asked questions we receive at colloquia and other speaking engagements. The question is frustrating, as there has never, to our knowledge, been a universally accepted answer. To convey both the objectives and limitations of this book, however, an answer must be provided.

The question actually has two more specific versions. First, what distinguishes social cognition from social psychology more generally? Second, what distinguishes social cognition from cognitive psychology? The answers to these two more specific questions are different. In combination, however, they not only provide a perspective on social cognition, but on what the present volume hopes to accomplish.

Social Cognition and Social Psychology

It can easily be argued that social psychology is the parent (or at least one of them) of contemporary cognitive psychology. The current focus of cognitive psychology on the processing of complex stimulus arrays, and the role that general world knowledge plays, was considered revolutionary when it occurred in the 1970s, replacing the more traditional concern with learning nonsense syllables and unrelated word lists. In social psychology, however, a concern with knowledge representation, and the influence it has on cognitive and social behavior, predates this "revolution" by more than a quarter of a century. A recognition that individual pieces of information are often represented as configural wholes, the meaning of which cannot be captured by examining the constituent elements, dates back to Soloman Asch's (1946) classic work on impression formation. An analysis of the memory organization of specific subsets of cognitions is reflected in the work of Fritz Heider (1946, 1958/1982), and was a major thrust of social psychological research for many years (cf. Abelson, Aronson, McGuire, Newcomb, Rosenberg, & Tannenbaum, 1968). More general characteristics of cognitive structure such as the differentiation and interrelatedness of the concepts that people have formed in different knowledge domains has its roots in the work of O.J. Harvey (e.g., Harvey, Hunt, & Schroder, 1961), William Scott (1963), and Milton Rokeach (1960). The research on communication and persuasion that was stimulated by Hovland and others in the 1950s (e.g., Hovland, Janis, & Kelley, 1953) was obviously concerned with the manner in which the information one receives affects judgments and decisions, as was research on attitude and belief change more generally (for summaries of the early theories and research, see Insko, 1967; Wyer, 1974). More recent work on impression formation (e.g., Anderson, 1971) and attribution (e.g., Kelley, 1967; Jones, Kanouse, Kelley, Nisbett, Valins, & Weiner, 1971/1987) was also concerned with the cognitive bases of social judgment.

In short, much of social psychology has been oriented around cognitive issues and questions. What, then, is new about social cognition? The answer, we believe, lies simply in the emphasis that social cognition theory places on *process* or, more accurately, processes. That is, social cognition, unlike cognitive social psychology of the type described above, takes as its objective a specification of the component cognitive operations that underlie the acquisition of social information and, along with preexisting knowledge, its use in making a judgment or decision.

To imply that the earlier research on impression formation, communication and persuasion, and attitude and belief change was *not* concerned with these matters may seem curious, if not contradictory. Any viable conceptualization of the manner in which information influences beliefs, attitudes, and behavior must make some assumptions about the cognitive processes that underlie these effects. In fact, however, the research that was performed seldom evaluated these assumptions directly, nor did it attempt to identify the particular point in the overall sequence of cognitive operations at which the observed effects were localized.

In contrast, the focus of social cognition is precisely on the cognitive mechanisms that mediate judgments and behavior. The sequence of these operations is usually assumed to be divisible into several component processing stages. These include:

1. the interpretation of individual pieces of information in terms of previously formed concepts or knowledge;
2. the organization of information in terms of a more general body of social knowledge, and the construction of a cognitive representation of the person, object, or event to which the information pertains;
3. the storage of this cognitive representation in memory;
4. the retrieval of the representation, along with other judgment- relevant knowledge, at the time a judgment is anticipated;
5. the combining of the implications of various features of the representation to arrive at a subjective inference; and
6. the transformation of the subjective inference into a response (e.g., judgment or behavioral decision).

The effect of a situational variable on an overt response could be localized in any one of these stages (or several of them for that matter). Moreover, the specific cognitive operations that are performed may differ in the type and amount of information that is acquired. They may also depend on the processing objectives of the individual and the time at which a response is required.

Although early social psychological research was often concerned with phenomena at one stage or another, the processing of information at this stage was seldom isolated, either theoretically or empirically, from the effects of processing at other stages. Nor was was an analysis provided for how the various processes operate in concert to generate a judgment or decision. For example, several principles of cognitive consistency (Abelson & Rosenberg, 1958; Festinger, 1957; Heider, 1958/1982; McGuire, 1960; Osgood & Tannenbaum, 1955) were postulated to govern the organization of beliefs and attitudes and the consequences of information bearing on one cognition on others that were related to it. However, it was never clear from the research whether the observed effects were the result of changes in the representation of interrelated beliefs and attitudes (which would presumably occur at the encoding and/or organizational stages) or the result of inferences that were made at the time of judgment.

Similarly, research on communication and persuasion was often concerned with the effects of the order in which arguments were presented (Miller & Campbell, 1959), the relative influence of emotional versus factual content (Janis & Feshbach, 1953), and the relative impact of informational variables versus source characteristics (Tannenbaum, 1967). However, whether these variables had their impact because they influenced the interpretation of information at the time it was first received, because they induced selective attention and encoding of the information, or because they affected the way that different pieces of information were combined to make a judgment was never established—or even pursued. Indeed, only William McGuire's (1964, 1968, 1972) work reflected a systematic attempt to understand the component processes that underlie responses to persuasive messages, to isolate the situational and informational factors that influence each process, and to specify how these processes act together to produce judgments.

Research in person impression formation has always been concerned with the manner in which different pieces of information combine to affect liking for the person. A conceptualization of these processes requires assumptions about the evaluative implications that are attached to each component piece of information and the relative importance (weight) that is given to each. Historically, however, the data used to evaluate these processes consisted only of liking judgments. These judgments were in turn based on factorially organized sets of stimulus adjectives, the weights and scale values of which (as well as the process for combining them) were inferred *post hoc* from the pattern of judgments that emerged (Anderson, 1965, 1970, 1981). Thus, no direct evidence was obtained for any of the processes that were postulated.[1]

In contrast to each of these traditions, social cognition theorists often design experiments that are intended to tap directly into one of the various stages of processing that underlie judgmental phenomena. In doing so, they recognize that a process cannot usually be isolated solely on the basis of judgment data. Just as the cognitive psychologist recognizes that behavior is only one link in a long chain of responses, the social cognition theorist recognizes that judgments (or behavioral decisions) are only the final link in a long psychological chain.

It is often important to understand the factors that affect the initial interpretation of information. To do this, one might obtain information about the types of concepts that subjects use to encode the stimuli into memory, as reflected in think-aloud protocols or open-ended descriptions of the objects. Alternatively, one might examine the time required to make concept-related judgments, or differences between the original information and later reports when subjects are asked to recall it.

Similarly, theorists are often concerned with the nature of the cognitive representations that are formed and the way they are stored in memory. Thus, they may examine the amount and type of information that is later recalled, as well as the order in which items are produced and the latencies between responses. Under some circumstances, it is likely to require an assessment of the cognitions (elaborations, counterarguments, etc.) that subjects generate in response to the information and are likely to include in its representation.

---

1. Alternative information integration processes are often evaluated on the basis of the accuracy with which algebraic models can describe the relation between stimulus input characteristics and the reported judgments. As we point out in Chapter 9, however, the same algebraic equation can be consistent with several different assumptions about the underlying integration process that subjects employ. Thus, these assumptions are impossible to distinguish on the basis of the quantitative of the equation alone.

Finally, an understanding of the factors that underlie the transformation of subjective inferences into overt responses may require not only knowledge of the response that is made to the particular stimulus, but also responses that are made to other, objectively irrelevant stimuli. These latter responses can provide evidence of the rules that subjects are using to transform their subjective judgments into overt responses.

It is sad but true: cut into a long chain of responses and the chain is destroyed. To put it another way, not all of the processes we have enumerated can be investigated in a single experiment. Thus, a research strategy must by developed that permits the processes at each stage to be identified and isolated. At the same time, however, a general conceptualization must be developed that will permit each of the component processes to be fit together into a functioning system. Such a conceptualization must specify, in general information processing terms, how the various processes interact. This is the ultimate objective of social cognition theory and research.

Social Cognition and Cognitive Psychology

The second issue to be raised is what distinguishes social cognition from cognitive psychology. At one level, both are concerned with the various stages of information processing we have outlined above. At another level, however, there are important differences.

One difference is that some cognitive processes are more important (i.e., capture more variance) than others in social interaction. While a cognitive psychologist may be very concerned about whether two meanings of a homophone can be activated simultaneously, or whether the stimulus suffix effect is due to a separate auditory store, or whether the time required to do mental rotation decreases with practice, social cognition theorists are relatively unconcerned with such matters (cf. Hamilton, in press). To the degree they shed light on how the cognitive system operates, they are, at some level, relevant. At the same time, however, their relevance is indirect and sometimes difficult to understand given our current knowledge.

Another difference is that cognitive psychologists are often concerned with the *capacity* of the cognitive system (cf. Holyoak & Gordon, 1984). How fast, how accurate, how far can the system be pushed before performance is destroyed? These are questions that are often pursued by cognitive psychologists, and some of the historical reasons for this have been outlined elsewhere (Lachman, Lachman, & Butterfield, 1979). The important point is that social cognition theorists are much more concerned with how the system actually operates within a given ecological context. To a much greater extent, we are concerned with what does happen rather than what can happen. Another difference between the two disciplines is that they focus on different end states. Although this is not an all-or-none issue, cognitive psychology gives much more emphasis to comprehension and learning. There is a much greater concern with sensory information, how it is picked up from the environment, encoded, comprehended, and ultimately represented within the cognitive system. In contrast, social cognition theorists give more weight to understanding how people make various judgments and behavioral decisions. Because of this, they are more concerned with specifying which aspects of the information that people receive are actually used, as well as how they are used.

These differences are important because they often produce differences in the task objectives that subjects are given in the research that is performed. This, in turn, produces differences in the results that emerge and the theories that are used to account for them. If there is one thing that we have learned from the past decade of social cognition research, it is that on-line processing objectives have an important impact on the interpretation that is given to information, the representations that are formed from it, and the features of the information that are most likely to be recalled (for a review of this literature, see Srull & Wyer, 1986). Because of this, there will often be differences in the paradigms used, the results obtained, and the theories developed by cognitive psychologists and social cognition researchers.

An Overview of Social Cognition Research

Many differences in task objectives occur at the input stages of processing. They are reflected in the initial interpretation of information, the subset of previously acquired knowledge that is used for organizing it and construing its implications, and the representation of it that is ultimately stored in memory. To the degree that theories in cognitive psychology fail to account for these effects, their relevance to social cognition is limited. While we believe that many of these factors have been ignored or deemphasized in cognitive psychology, we also believe that theories of information retrieval have highlighted many of the processes that occur in social settings. Thus, existing theories of retrieval processes (e.g., Raaijmakers & Shiffrin, 1980, 1981; Gillund & Shiffrin, 1984) may actually be of greater relevance to contemporary social cognition.

Some of these considerations are summarized in Figure 1.1. The figure indicates the relations among independent and dependent variables of concern in both cognitive and social psychology, as well as the hypothetical constructs that mediate their relation. Independent and dependent variables are enclosed in solid lines, and the hypothetical mediators in dashed-lines. Each pathway connecting two variables reflects a relation that must be specified by any theory of cognitive functioning. The diagram is obviously incomplete. As just one example, it does not

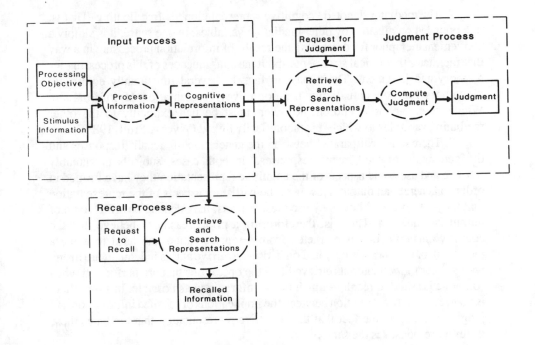

Figure 1.1 Relations among various components of social judgment. Observable (independent and dependent) variables are enclosed by solid lines, and mediating variables by dashed lines. Rectangles denote "states" and ovals denote "processes."

include the influence of general world knowledge. Several observations can be made with reference to the diagram:

1. The processing that occurs, and the mental representation that results from it, is a function of both the information presented and the goals of the person at the time the information is acquired. Moreover, the processes that occur may be idiosyncratic to a particular configuration of these variables. For example, subjects may encode and organize a set of traits and behavior descriptions differently if their goal is to form an impression of the person than if their goal is to learn and remember the information (Hamilton, Katz, & Leirer, 1980a, 1980b; Srull, 1983; Wyer & Gordon, 1982; Wyer, Bodenhausen, & Srull, 1984). By the same token, subjects with an impression formation objective may form a different type of cognitive representation from this sort of information than they would from an episodic sequence of observed behaviors (Allen & Ebbesen, 1981; Cohen & Ebbesen, 1979; Newtson, 1976; Wyer & Bodenhausen, 1985).

2. The mediator denoted "cognitive representation" is free floating. That is, it is bounded on all sides by other mediating variables. In one sense, it is simply a convenient metaphor for describing the results of information processing in a way that facilitates theoretical statements about the consequences of this processing for memory and judgment. There may, in fact, be several functionally equivalent metaphors for conceptualizing the cognitive representation of information. Whatever metaphor is chosen, however, must be tied explicitly to the other mediating variables to which it is theoretically linked (Wyer & Srull, 1988).

3. There is a clear parallel between the generation of "recall" responses and the generation of "judgment" responses.[2] In both cases, subjects presumably retrieve and use some aspects of the cognitive representation they have formed in order to generate an output. However, the particular aspects of the representation that they retrieve, and how they use these aspects, may depend on which type of output is requested. There is, therefore, no a priori reason to believe that the cognitive material that is extracted from a representation and used to make a judgment, or the way it is operated on in order to arrive at this judgment, are in any way similar to the material retrieved and the operations that are performed when someone is asked to recall as much of the information as possible. In short, there is no necessary direct relation between the implications of recalled information and judgments, despite the fact that the cognitive representation that mediates these different responses is the same.

More generally, Figure 1.1 divides the issues of social information processing into three general areas. These pertain to:

1. input—the way that information is encoded, organized, and stored in memory under different task objective conditions.
2. recall—the way in which the cognitive representation is accessed and used to recall past information when people are explicitly asked to do so.
3. judgment—the manner in which cognitive representations are retrieved and used to make different types of judgments.

The goal of the social cognition theorist is to articulate the relations among these components and to explicate the specific processes that are involved in each. As noted earlier, the theories that have been developed in cognitive psychology are most likely to be useful in conceptualizing retrieval processes. One strategy that is often productive is to apply these theories to patterns of recall data in order to infer the content and structure of the cognitive representations that are formed under different task objective conditions. Once the nature of these representations have

---

2. It is worth noting that it is important to distinguish between "recall" processes and the processes tapped by other memory indices. Recognition memory measures, for example, are often based on inferences about whether a stimulus item was or was not previously presented. Thus, under this scheme, they are more appropriately considered to be governed by "judgment" processes, as denoted in Fig. 1.1.

been established, the way in which they are used to make judgments can be conceptualized and empirically investigated.

The Objectives of this Book

General Objectives

We have noted several different stages of information processing that are involved in the acquisition and use of social information. A complete theory of social information processing must specify the cognitive mechanisms that operate at each stage. In addition, it must articulate how these processes function in concert to affect judgments and decisions. The objective of this volume is to outline a model of social information processing that may ultimately develop into such a complete theory.

The model we propose was guided by three interrelated sets of objectives referred to by Smith (1978) as *generality*, *extendability*, and *sufficiency*.

Generality. The theoretical vocabulary, the representational system, and the psychological mechanisms postulated in a model should not be specific to any single domain. The model should, for example, apply to the processing and representation of information about both individuals and groups. Similarly, it should apply to the processing of information about oneself as well as other people. The model should also be capable of accounting not only for controlled laboratory phenomena but also for more complex and naturalistic memory phenomena that are known to occur. Our intention is to demonstrate that the present model stands up quite well to all of these criteria.

Although several implications of the model are unique, others can (and *should*) be accounted for by other formulations as well. In most cases, however, these formulations apply to only a rather circumscribed set of phenomena, often involving only a single dependent variable. The proposed formulation purports to account for a much broader range of empirical findings than that to which other existing formulations are applicable. Moreover, it postulates a single set of cognitive mechanisms that govern the processing of information at several different stages.

Extendability. A model should be extendable in two ways. First, the processes it specifies should potentially subsume, be components of, or interface with those implied by other theoretical frameworks. Similarly, it should be able to account for the empirical phenomena investigated within these frameworks. The proposed model meets this criterion. That is, rather than being limited to a single aspect of information processing, it deals with encoding, storage, retrieval, judgment, and decision mechanisms. Moreover, it is sufficiently abstract that it can incorporate more articulated theories of specific processes. Its purpose is not to provide a final solution to all of the conceptual issues that have arisen in past work. However, the model specifies how one set of processes interfaces with another, and suggests when each set may be activated in natural social settings.

A second aspect of the extendability criterion is that a model must link the various processes to one another. Social cognition researchers are not only interested in social memory and judgment as independent entities, but also the relationship between them. No existing conceptual model attempts to analyze the nature of this relationship. Our attention to this aspect of the extendability criterion recognizes that any viable model must be able to be expanded, modified, and articulated at a more precise level as the relevant data base grows and becomes more diagnostic. The proposed model includes this feature of useful theory development.

Sufficiency. A model should obviously be logically coherent, internally consistent, and heuristically useful. We demonstrate the proposed model's ability to meet these criteria in several ways. First, we point out the model's consistency with past findings in the literature. Second we demonstrate its ability to generate several new predictions, some of which are quite counterintuitive and yet have received considerable empirical support. Third, we demonstrate how the model can be used to identify the psychological mechanisms that are responsible for complex social phenomena (e.g., affective reactions). Finally, we demonstrate how the model can be used to integrate what have often been considered "inconsistent" empirical findings.

There are, of course, inherent trade-offs among the three objectives noted above, and these have also influenced the development of the proposed formulation. The more general a model is, the less precise it can be. The more precise it is in accounting for any given phenomenon, the less extendable it will be into other domains. This is also a recognition of the fact that the model is only *a tentative* explanatory scheme for our current knowledge base. Nevertheless, integrating the current literature in social cognition into a single, unifying conceptual framework is a difficult and important challenge. But it is one we hope to meet in the present volume.

A Preview

Our discussion of the model and its implications for social information processing is organized as follows:

In Chapter 2, we provide a general overview of the model, describing briefly the functions of its various components and how they are theoretically interrelated. Chapters 3 and 4 describe in more detail our assumptions about the content and structure of memory. Then, in Chapter 5, we focus on the process of retrieving information from memory.

The next several chapters deal with specific processing components of the model. They concern the initial interpretation and encoding of information (Chapter 6), the more complex representations that are formed from this information (Chapters 7 and 8), the use of new and previously acquired information to make subjective inferences (Chapters 9 and 10), and the transformation of these subjective inferences into overt responses (Chapter 11).

The last two chapters of the volume focus on factors that enter into information processing at all stages, and therefore deserve consideration in their own right. Chapter 12 considers both the cognitive determinants and consequences of affect and emotion. Chapter 13 is concerned with the representation of self knowledge and its role in cognitive functioning.

We attempt in our discussion to be as explicit as possible about the cognitive mechanisms that operate at each stage of information processing, and in the way these processes interact. Formal postulates are often proposed and their empirical implications are explored. Throughout the volume we not only provide empirical support for unique predictions of the model, but also indicate the model's ability to account for a wide range of phenomena that have been identified. The model is admittedly incomplete. Readers will undoubtedly identify phenomena that have been neglected and processes that are not analyzed with a sufficient degree of precision. On the other hand, the conceptual integration that the model provides is substantial, as we hope to document in the remaining chapters.

Chapter 2
A General Model of Social Information Processing

Any viable theory of social information processing must account for a wide variety of social judgment and behavioral phenomena, including those that occur both in and outside of the laboratory. Moreover, the determinants of these phenomena must be conceptualized in terms of their mediating effects on specific stages of cognitive functioning. To accomplish this, the model must state how different phases of information processing interface, and how they operate in combination to produce judgments and behavior. In addition, the model must be able to incorporate precise but also more circumscribed statements of the cognitive mechanisms that operate at each stage of processing (encoding, organization, storage, retrieval, inference, etc.). In doing so, the formulation must also provide for the fact that the cognitive processes involved in any given instance depend substantially on both the goals toward which these processes are directed and the type of information that is available for attaining these goals.

The model of social information processing we outline in this volume fulfills these criteria. The model is admittedly metaphorical. For example, it postulates an interconnected system of "information storage" units and "information processing" units that appear to exist as separate entities. Moreover, long term memory is conceptualized as consisting of "bins," or storehouses of individual pieces of information about people, objects, and events. No pretense is made that these components of the model mirror the physiology of the human brain. There is nevertheless a correspondence between the functions predicated of the model's processing units and specific conscious and unconscious cognitive activities that humans appear to perform. Moreover, the content and structure of the information and storage units we postulate permit the model to account for numerous memory and judgment phenomena that alternative formulations have difficulty explaining.

The overall system we propose is conveyed in Figure 2.1. Storage units (the Sensory Store, Work Space, Permanent Storage Unit, and Goal Specification Box) are denoted by rectangles, and the processing units (the Executor, Comprehender,

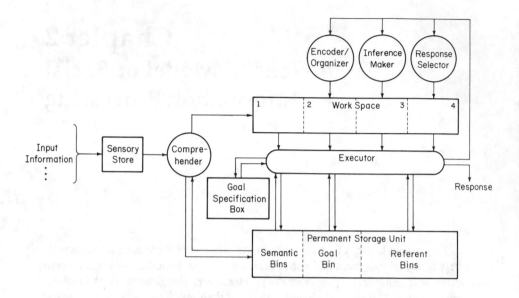

Figure 2.1. Metaphorical representation of the proposed model of human information processing. Rectangles denote storage units; ovals denote processing units. Arrows denote the direction of transmission of congitive material between units.

Encoder/Organizer, Inference Maker, and Response Selector) by ovals. The operation of the system is governed by the Executor, which transmits instructions to other processing units and controls the flow of information between these units and storage units. This information flow is conveyed in Figure 2.1 by directed pathways. The system bears some resemblance to general information processing models proposed by others (e.g., Bower, 1975; Hastie & Carlston, 1980) and also to ancestors of the present model (Wyer & Srull, 1980, 1986). However, it is much more precise than any of its predecessors with respect to its implications for both the characteristics of the storage and processing units and the rules that govern their operation. The model has a number of unique features that make it particularly applicable to issues of concern in social cognition.

    In this chapter, we briefly indicate the main features of each storage and processing unit, and provide a general description of information processing under conditions representative of those we consider later in this volume. Then, in Chapters 3 and 4, we turn to a more detailed discussion of two information storage units that are central to the proposed model and elaborate the implications of their postulated structure and function. The rules governing the storage and retrieval of information are stated more explicitly in both these chapters and also in Chapter 5.

Later chapters of the volume are devoted to the functions of the various processing units we postulate.

Storage Units

Sensory Store

Before information can be represented in terms of any mental code, it must be acquired by the various sense organs. In the present model, all external information, regardless of the sensory modality through which it is acquired, enters the system through a single Sensory Store. At any given moment, this unit holds the information impinging on all of the sense organs, and retains this information in roughly veridical form. The Sensory Store holds a large amount of information. However, the initial representation of it is assumed to decay extremely rapidly, usually in a matter of seconds.

The postulation of a Sensory Store is necessary for a complete conceptualization of information processing (cf. Sperling, 1960). However, this particular storage unit is relatively unimportant for an understanding of the social memory and judgment phenomena of concern in this volume. These phenomena typically occur because of much higher-level cognitive activity. Consequently, we do not devote much time to the Sensory Store in the discussion to follow.

Work Space

The Work Space is one of the central constructs of the proposed conceptualization, and its characteristics and implications are explored throughout this volume. It is conceptually analogous to working memory (Bower, 1975; Klatzky, 1975). However, its specific features and the role we predict it to have are unique in several respects.

Briefly, the Work Space is a temporary repository of all information that is operated on in the pursuit of a specific processing objective. Thus, at any given time, it typically contains both the input material to be processed and various concepts that are used in the processing of this material, as well as the results of this processing. Except under unusual circumstances, information may be retained in the Work Space indefinitely as long as it is relevant to a current processing objective. However, the capacity of the Work Space is limited. Therefore, if the processing objective to which information is relevant has been attained, or if further pursuit of this objective is not anticipated for some time, the Work Space may be cleared to facilitate the pursuit of more immediate goals. There are two implications of this assumption. First, inherent capacity limitations may lead information to be pushed out of the Work Space automatically as new information comes in. In addition, a volitional control mechanism exists that can also activate this clearing process. Once the Work Space has been cleared, any material that has not yet been transferred to permanent memory is lost from the system. The implications of this are more fully explored in Chapter 3.

Permanent Storage Unit

The Permanent Storage Unit is the long-term memory component of the system. It is a permanent repository of material that has, at one time or another, been the output of an Executor-controlled processing unit (i.e., all units except the Comprehender; see Figure 2.1). Its uniqueness lies in its structure and organization and in the search and retrieval processes that operate on it.

Specifically, we conceptualize Permanent Storage as consisting of a set of content-addressable *storage bins*. Each bin, which is of unlimited capacity, is designated by a header that identifies the nature of its contents. Three general types of bins are postulated. *Semantic* bins contain basic noun, action, and attribute concepts that can be used to interpret new information independently of its specific referent. In contrast, *referent* bins contain information about specific persons, objects, and events, as well as about general types of persons, objects, and events. Finally, a *goal* bin contains goal schemata and procedures for attaining different processing objectives. The information contained in a referent bin may vary in type, modality or code, and complexity. For example, it may consist of a proposition, a visual image, a personality trait description, an interrelated set of traits and behaviors, an event sequence, a concept associated with one's affective or emotional reactions, or some combination of these. Different types of representations may be deposited in the same bin. *Each representation is assumed to function as a single unit of information that may be stored and retrieved independently of other representations.* These storage and retrieval processes, along with other features of the Permanent Storage Unit, are elaborated in Chapters 4 and 5.

Goal Specification Box

The Goal Specification Box stores the immediate processing objectives of the system, along with appropriate sets of instructions ("goal schemata") for attaining them. The objectives may either be cognitive (e.g., to form a subjective impression of someone, to remember the information presented, to plan a future activity, etc.) or may pertain to generating an overt response. In either case, the instructions specified in the goal schema stored in the Goal Specification Box are reviewed by the Executor and used both: (a) to inform the relevant processing units which of several alternative procedures should be activated, and (b) to direct the appropriate flow of information between these units and storage units. The Goal Specification Box may contain more than one goal schema at a time, and so more than one goal can be pursued simultaneously. However, its capacity is limited. Therefore, as additional objectives and the procedures for attaining them enter the unit, others are displaced and consequently cease to affect any current information processing activity.

The limited capacity of the Goal Specification Box restricts both the number and the complexity of the goal-directed activities that can be performed at any one time. For example, as the complexity of the goal schema activated to attain a particular objective (i.e., the computational activity specified in the schema) increases, more space in the Goal Specification Box is required to store it. Therefore, fewer other goal schemata can be stored, and so the pursuit of other processing objectives is impaired. On the other hand, not all of the steps that are involved in attaining a particular objective need to be specified in the goal schemata used by the Executor. As we will note in more detail presently, the processing unit that performs each type of cognitive functioning (encoding, organizating, etc.) has a library of routines that have become "hard-wired" into the unit and, therefore, can be called and performed automatically. The steps involved in these routines do not need to be specified in a goal schema. When a particular task is unfamiliar, and relatively few existing routines in the library are applicable, the goal schema used by the Executor to direct processing must specify the various steps of processing in some detail. If a sequence of steps is performed frequently and in several different contexts, however, it may be added to the library of a processing unit along with a label that permits the sequence to be identified. Once this occurs, a new, simplified goal schema can be constructed in which the sequence is replaced by a simple "call" instruction. As a result, less space is required to store the new goal schema in the Goal Specification Box. Therefore, more room is available for other goal schemata that can be used in the simultaneous pursuit of other processing objectives.

This, of course, is a formal way of generating a self-evident prediction. That is, as activities become well-learned, they require fewer resources, and, therefore, the remaining capacity can be used to pursue other activities. As a common example, consider the different stages that are involved in learning how to drive a car. Initially, each step in the process of starting the car, getting it into gear, and ultimately negotiating it through traffic involve considerable cognitive effort and concentration. Eventually, however, these steps are performed with a minimum of cognitive involvement, and so one's cognitive resources can be devoted to other activities (e.g., talking with passengers, etc.). Although this and similar learning phenomena are commonplace, the model's ability to account for them is of theoretical importance.

In the conceptualization we propose, a heavy burden is obviously placed on the nature of the goal schemata that are activated and used to attain particular processing objectives. Unless the content of these goal schemata is known, the model is somewhat limited in the specific predictions it can make. Fortunately, much current theory and research on social information processing has implications for the nature of these goal schemata, as well as for the routines that make up the library of specific processing units. The model we propose is able to incorporate the implications of this theoretical and empirical work. In addition, it specifies when the cognitive processes implied by it are likely to occur.

Processing Units

In addition to the four storage units described above, the model postulates the existence of five processing units. One, the *Executor*, directs the flow of information to and from storage units and certain processing units, and transmits instructions to processing units concerning what specific routines to use. Each of the other processing units performs a different function. The functions range from low-level comprehension to higher-order decision making and overt response generation. The *Comprehender* enters into processing at an early stage and operates independently of the Executor. All other units (the *Encoder/Organizer*, the *Integrator*, and the *Response Selector*), and the flow of information between these units and the storage units, are activated by the Executor on the basis of instructions specified in a goal schema.

Executor

The Executor directs the flow of information between processing units and storage units. When a specific objective is activated, the Executor retrieves a copy of a goal schema that is relevant to the attainment of this objective from the goal bin in Permanent Storage, deposits it in the Goal Specification Box, and then uses the instructions specified in this schema to attain the objective in question. These instructions may include (a) the retrieval of prior knowledge from Permanent Storage, (b) the transmission of this information to a processing unit or, in some cases, a specified compartment of the Work Space, (c) the transmission of instructions to an appropriate processing unit concerning what library routines to use, (d) the retrieval of the results of processing from the Work Space, and (e) the transmission of these results to appropriate bins in Permanent Storage.

Many instances occur in which the Goal Specification Box is empty; that is, no specific processing objective is active. Under these conditions, the Executor initiates a "default program," which leads a relatively low level of comprehension and processing of information to take place continuously until such time as a specific objective is identified. The major function of this default program is to keep an updated internal representation of the environment and the world around us. A more detailed explication of this process, which permits the model to account for some data-driven or bottom-up processing, as well as the free association of ideas and the pursuit of internally-generated goals, is provided later in this chapter.

One important characteristic of the Executor should be emphasized. That is, the Executor does not have the capacity to *remove* individual pieces of information from a storage unit once the unit has been deposited there. Rather, it is equipped with a *copying* mechanism that permits it to retrieve and transmit a replica of the material contained in the storage unit, leaving its original position in the unit intact. This assumption proves to be central in understanding the implications of the formulation we propose, and many of our predictions are directly or indirectly based on it.

Comprehender

The Comprehender is an initial pattern recognition device. It interprets raw stimulus information in terms of previously acquired semantic concepts. Once attention is directed to particular events in the environment, these procedures are performed automatically. Like other theorists, (e.g., Lindsay & Norman, 1977; Reed, 1973; Rumelhart, 1977; Selfridge, 1959), we assume that visual input information can ultimately be processed in terms of both visual and auditory codes. Verbal information can similarly be represented in terms of several different memory codes. However, these encodings are at a much lower level of abstractness than those that occur at later stages of processing, in the pursuit of more complex processing objectives.

Thus, for example, the verbal statement "John hit the boy" is presumably interpreted by the Comprehender in terms of noun and action concepts. A more abstract encoding of this statement (e.g., in terms of a trait concept "aggressive") would *not* typically be performed by the Comprehender, however. Rather, it would be performed by the Encoder/Organizer in pursuit of a specific processing objective (e.g., forming an impression of the actor).

It is obviously important to explicate the specific processes employed by the Comprehender in performing the encoding of information. Much theoretical and empirical work in cognitive psychology, particularly in the areas of psycholinguistics and artificial intelligence, has been devoted to this matter. (In this regard, the Comprehender in our formulation is somewhat akin to the "Parser" in Schank and Abelson's, 1977, formulation of cognitive functioning.) Presumably, aspects of many conceptions of language comprehension could in principle be incorporated into a precise conceptualization of the routines employed by the Comprehender as we conceive of it. Although this is obviously important to do in developing a complete theoretical statement of the model we propose, it is outside the domain of social information processing per se. We therefore forego a detailed discussion of low level comprehension processes in this volume. This is not to say, however, that the general activities of the Comprehender are of little interest in the present context. Indeed, the role of the Comprehender is central to our conceptualization of many important social judgment phenomena. This becomes clear in Chapter 6.

Encoder/Organizer

The Encoder/Organizer is a higher level interpreter of material that has been transmitted to the Work Space by the Comprehender or, in some instances, has been retrieved from Permanent Storage and sent to the unit by the Executor. The Encoder/Organizer, unlike the Comprehender, *functions in pursuit of particular processing objectives*, using encoding and organizing operations that are specified in a goal schema. As noted earlier, these procedures are often included in the library of routines that the unit has available, and can be performed automatically once they are called. Consequently, a goal schema may only need to specify the name of any given procedure without reiterating the steps involved in it.

The Encoder/Organizer may be used to interpret individual items of information in terms of more abstract concepts. For example, it may encode a behavior ("stole the wallet") in terms of a trait concept ("dishonest"). In addition, it may be used to identify the referent of information as an instance of a more general concept or category based on several pieces of information in combination. For example, if a person's traits and/or behaviors are typical of an "extravert," or of a "good graduate student," the person may be encoded as an instance of this more general person category. A similar higher-level encoding occurs when interpreting individual episodes (ordering a meal, paying the waiter, etc.) in terms of a more general event sequence (eating at a restaurant).

The encoding and organization routines that are contained in the Encoder/Organizer's library may often be specific to the type and modality of the information that is transmitted to it. Moreover, the likelihood that they are called may depend on the particular purpose for which the information sent to it is being processed. Thus, for example, a woman who receives information about another's behavior may encode and organize this information quite differently if she is looking for a roommate or a dating partner than if she is looking for a graduate research assistant, or simply wants to describe the individual to a friend.

As the above discussion implies, the cognitive representation of input information that is constructed by the Encoder/Organizer may differ in several ways from the information itself. For example:

1. The encoding may be more general or abstract than the original information. A visual or verbal description of someone giving another an answer during an examination may be encoded as "cheating on an exam" or as "dishonest." Alternatively, it could be encoded as "helping someone out" or as "kind." Note that not all possible implications of the original information are necessarily contained in

the encoding of it by the Encoder/Organizer. Thus, if the behavior of giving another an answer during an examination is only encoded as "cheating," then its implications for helpfulness and kindness are lost.

2. The *organization* of features in a representation formed by the Encoder/Organizer may also differ from that of the information transmitted from the Comprehender. For example, the behaviors of a person that exemplify an extravert may be identified and grouped together in a single representation even though they were presented among other behaviors that are irrelevant to this representation. Similarly, the features specified in the verbal description of a human face, or of one's living room, may be organized spatially in the course of interpreting them in terms of a general representation of their referent. Or, a sequence of events may be organized temporally, even if they were not originally described in their chronological order.

3. Features that are not specified in the original information may be spontaneously added. These are typically features that must be assumed in order to interpret a configuration of known features as an instance of a complex concept. When this is done, the person may later be unable to discriminate the presented material from the spontaneous inferences.

We elaborate the nature of these and other differences, and provide empirical evidence for their occurrence, in our discussion of encoding and organizational processes in Chapters 6-8.

Inference-Maker

The attainment of a processing objective typically requires that a subjective inference be made, or conclusion be drawn, on the basis of either new information, previously acquired knowledge, or both. This inference may have the form of a judgment (i.e., the likableness of a person, or a particular attribute that the person possesses), a behavioral decision (to go to the movies), or a planned sequence of behaviors (what to do to get ready to leave for vacation). Sometimes, the inference may be made directly on the basis of the cognitive material that is brought to bear on it. (For example, if one's goal requires an inference of whether one has a meeting on Wednesday afternoon, and "2 p.m. appointment with Charlie on Wednesday" is included in the information available, the inference can be made directly, with little cognitive effort.) In many cases, however, information may bear only indirectly on a judgment or conclusion, and so some mental computation is required to generate an inference. This computation may be logical, causal, algebraic, or some combination thereof. For example, a woman may infer that she should vote against a political candidate based on knowledge that the candidate favors increased defense spending and the belief that people who favor defense spending should not be allowed to hold public office. Or, she may infer that someone is likely to be a good graduate student based on several different pieces of information that have different implications for this judgment (low grades, high GREs, and mixed letters of reference concerning the person's ability and motivation). In doing so, the person may attribute a reference's statement that the student was a poor research assistant to the particularly boring type of research the faculty member was doing and not to the student himself. The Inference-Maker performs these computations, the nature of which may vary with the amount and type of information available and the type of inference to be make.

Inference making, unlike other components of social information processing, has been the subject of substantial research in social psychology for many years. In some cases, formal algebraic, syllogistic or pseudo-logical inference rules have been proposed (cf. Abelson & Rosenberg, 1958; Anderson, 1971, 1981; Fishbein & Hunter, 1964; McGuire, 1960, 1981; Wyer & Carlston, 1979; Wyer & Hartwick, 1980). However, the rules for integrating the implications of information may not always be captured by such mechanistic rules. A case in point is when one is called upon to imagine a situation involving elements that have never before been considered in combination (e.g., a tiger shopping for a new suit at Brooks Brothers). Moreover, many inferences appear to be the result of applying simplifying rules of thumb, or "heuristics," that do not take into account all of the information available (for reviews, see Sherman & Corty, 1984).

Therefore, the inference rules that make up the Inference-Maker's library are quite varied, and the conditions in which they are applied are likely to depend considerably on both the particular goal being pursued and the type of information being considered. We discuss these matters in greater detail in Chapters 9 and 10.

Response Selector

The output of the Inference-Maker is a subjective judgment or decision that is internal to the information processor. The Response Selector comes into play when the subjective output must be transformed into an overt response. This response may be a value along a numerical scale, the answer to a yes/no question, a verbal description ("conscientious person"), a motor act (pressing a button), or an utterance made in the course of a conversation. The transformation rule involved depends on both the type of mental process and the type of response required.

The rules for transforming a subjective representation into an overt response have been studied extensively. For example, rules for representing subjective judgments along a numerical response scale have been proposed by Parducci (1965), Upshaw (1969; Ostrom & Upshaw, 1968), Wyer (1974; Wyer & Carlston, 1979), and Schwarz (Schwarz & Wyer, 1985; see also Strack & Martin, 1987). The rules of generating verbal outputs have been the subject of theorizing by Grice (1975) in the context of analyzing effective communication and by Higgins (1981; Higgins, McCann & Fondacaro, 1982; Kraut & Higgins, 1984) in the context of discussion and dynamics of social interaction. These rules, each of which may apply in different circumstances, are assumed to be contained in the Response Selector's library of procedures. The nature of these rules is discussed in more detail in Chapter 11.

General Systems Operation

The specific functions performed by different higher-order processing units, and the conditions in which they enter into goal-directed cognitive functioning, obviously differ considerably. However, a common set of rules are postulated to govern the flow of information to and from these units. That is, the mechanisms that govern the search and retrieval of information from memory units (the Work Space of Permanent Storage), the transmission of this information to a processing unit, and the subsequent storage of the results of processing, do not depend on which processing unit happens to be involved. In short, the model's assumptions concerning memory storage and retrieval, which we elaborate in the next three chapters, apply at all stages of information processing, and provide a common set of principles for use in conceptualizing the role of memory at each stage.

Before beginning our detailed discussion of the model, it may be useful to describe more generally the flow of information through the processing system en route to a judgment and decision. This is conveyed in general in the flow diagram shown in Figure 2.2. However, a more concrete, albeit oversimplified, example may be helpful to convey the link between the phenomenology of the human information processor in arriving at a judgment and the processes postulated by the proposed model.

Judgments Based on New Information

Suppose a woman is told that John (a) exercised daily, (b) gave Peter an answer during a Chemistry exam, and (c) worked overtime when his boss was away. If she later is asked, "Is John a kind person?", she may say something to the effect that "helping someone out is a kind thing to do, and that a person who performs this behavior is probably kind.

A social cognition psychologist who wishes to state these processes somewhat more formally might speculate that when the woman was asked whether John is kind, she recalled features of a "typical" kind person (i.e., trait adjective descriptions, prototypic behaviors, etc.) and determined if the individual pieces of information about John could be interpreted as exemplifying these features. Because giving someone an answer in an exam could be interpreted as an instance of "helping someone out," and because "helping someone" is an attribute of a kind person, the woman reported that John was likely to be this type of person.

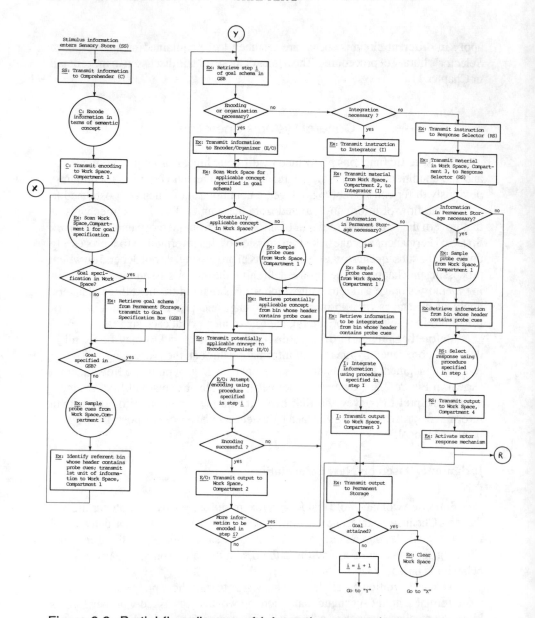

Figure 2.2. Partial flow diagram of information processing en route to a judgment or response. Rectangles denote transmissions of information from one unit to another. Circles denote the processing of information conducted by various processing units. Symbols preceding each step denote the processor involved: C = Comprehender; E/O = Encoder/Organizer; Ex = Executor; I = Inference Maker; RS = Response Selector.

Note that the woman's cognitive activities that are implicit in this description involve (a) the retrieval of a prototypic "kind" person from memory, (b) the encoding of the information presented in terms of features of this prototype, (c) an estimate of the likelihood that a person with these features exemplifies the prototype, and (d) a translation of this subjective estimate into an overt response. Considered in terms of the model we propose, these processes can be still further elaborated in a way that has additional implications. Specifically, the following processes are postulated:

1. The Comprehender encodes the features of each behavior (e.g., "John gave Peter an answer during an examination") in terms of low level semantic concepts ("examination," "gives answer," etc.), and then generates a mental representation of this behavior. The Comprehender also encodes the question ("is John a kind person?") and denotes it as representing a specific goal. It then transmits these two encodings to Compartment 1 of the Work Space (see Figure 1.1).

2. The Executor scans Compartment 1 of the Work Space for a goal specification. In the course of this search, it identifies the goal description that was transmitted from the Comprehender (i.e., to decide if John is a kind person). It then retrieves a copy of a goal schema pertaining to this objective (e.g., a specification of the steps involved in deciding if someone is a particular type of person) and deposits it in the Goal Specification Box along with a representation of the specific goal to be pursued.

3. The Executor examines the goal schema for the sequence of processing steps to be conducted. It then executes each of these instructions in turn by retrieving information from relevant storage units and transmitting it to the Work Space, and by directing the appropriate processing units to operate on it according to procedures contained in their libraries. In the present example, these activities would include the following:

a. The Executor samples a set of features from Compartment 1 of the Work Space that describes the object specified in the processing objective ("kind person"). It then uses these features as *probe cues* to identify a "kind person" bin in Permanent Storage. The Executor then searches this bin for a particular representation of its referent (i.e., the representation of a kind person). The features of the representation presumably include trait concepts (kind, helpful, considerate, etc.) and general behaviors ("helps people out," "compliments others," etc.). A copy of this representation is then made and transmitted to the Work Space.

b. The Executor identifies trait and behavior concepts contained in the "kind person" representation from the semantic bin in Permanent Storage. It transmits copies of these concepts sequentially to the Encoder/Organizer along with the input information about John and instructs it to determine if the information can be interpreted in terms of these concepts. Therefore, if "kind" or "helps someone out" is among the concepts contained in the "kind person" representation, and if "giving someone something" is one of the features of this semantic concept, then "giving someone an answer on an examination" will be encoded in terms of the concept. This encoding is returned by the Encoder/Organizer to Compartment 2 of the Work Space to await further processing.

c. The Executor returns copies of the features deposited in Compartment 2 of the Work Space to the Encoder/Organizer with instructions to determine whether these features *in combination* exemplify a person of the type specified in the processing objectives (i.e., a "kind person"). This is done by comparing the target's features with those contained in the representation of a prototypic "kind person" previously retrieved from Permanent Storage (step 3a). Based on this comparison, the Encoder/Organizer generates a result (i.e., a conclusion that the features either are or are not sufficient to instantiate the target as a "kind person"). This conclusion is transmitted to the Work Space, and the Executor is instructed that the objective has been obtained.

d. In this simplified example, only one relevant piece of behavioral information about the target was presented. Often, however, several pieces of information will be presented, and their implications will differ. When this is the case, the Encoder/Organizer may sometimes be unable to generate a result. That is, it may not clearly identify the target either as the type of person being considered or as *not* this type of person (cf. Ebbesen & Allen, 1979), and may notify the Executor accordingly. The Executor will then transmit copies of the encodings in Compartment 2 of the Work Space to the Inference-Maker with instructions to integrate them into a single subjective value according to a procedure in the Inference-Maker's library. This subjective value is sent to the Work Space (Compartment 3), and the Executor is informed that a subjective value has been obtained.

e. The Executor sends a copy of the output of Step 3c (or 3d) to the Response Selector with instructions to transform it into an overt response. If the response to be made is along a category response scale, the Response Selector may perform this transformation by positioning the scale in relation to a range of subjective values that are relevant to the judgment, and then mapping the particular subjective judgment onto this scale (cf. Ostrom & Upshaw, 1968; Parducci, 1965; Wyer, 1974). A similar mapping procedure may be used to generate "yes- no" or other verbal responses (cf. Wyer & Carlston, 1979). In any event, a representation of this response is transmitted to the Work Space (Compartment 4).

4. The Executor retrieves the output of the Response Selector and activates the motor mechanisms required to generate an overt response.

5. Upon completion of each stage of processing, the output of the processing involved that is returned to the Work Space by a processing unit is transmitted by the Executor to a referent in Permanent Storage. In our example, no previous bin existed pertaining to the target ("John"). Therefore, a new bin, with a header that specifies the name (or some other mental representation) of the target, is established, and the output of successive stages of processing is deposited in the bin as

it becomes available. Therefore, in the present case, the encoded representation of the target's behavior (the output of Step 3b) is deposited first, followed by the representation of the target as a kind person (Step 3c), and then the overt response that this generated on the basis of this representation (Step 3e).

6. When the processing objectives have been completed, the Executor clears the Work Space and removes the goal schema from the Goal Specification Box.

Judgments and Decisions Based on Previously Acquired Information

In our example, the information about John that formed the basis for judgments was the first and only knowledge available about this person. More typically, judgments and decisions about people and events are based on previously acquired knowledge about them that has already been stored in memory. Alternatively, it may be based on some combination of new and previously acquired information. Some of the more important implications of the model, which pertain to these situations, can be conveyed with reference to the example we outlined above.

Suppose that some time after she has concluded that John is a kind person, the woman in our example is asked if John is an *honest* person. It seems intuitively likely that she might respond to the question in one of two ways. On one hand, she might say that he is not honest, because he "cheated on an examination, which is a dishonest act." On the other hand, she might indicate that he is honest because "John is a kind person, and kind people are usually honest." The conceptualization we propose suggests the conditions in which each of these responses is likely to occur.

Specifically, the initial stages of processing involved in deciding if John is an honest person are identical to those outlined in Steps 1-5 above except that, in this case, the features of the target are compared to a representation of a prototypic "honest person." However, several additional considerations arise.

If the second judgment of John is requested shortly after the first judgment is made, the encoding of the original behavior (transmitted from the Comprehender) will still be in the Work Space at the time it is searched (Step 3b above). If this is the case, the behavior "gave an answer on an examination" may be encoded as "dishonest," or "cheats." These encodings, along with the features of the representation of John as a "kind person" may then both be contained in the set compared to a prototypic honest person in Step 3c. If, however, a period of time has elapsed, the Work Space will most likely have been cleared (Step 6). In this case, no information about John will be found in the Work Space, and only the most recent representation of him (retrieved from Permanent Storage) will be used.

This reasoning implies that, for a short period of time after the first judgment has been made, both the implications of the original information transmitted by the Comprehender and implications of the representation of John as a "kind person" may affect judgments of his honesty. After a lapse of time, however, only the "kind person" representation is likely to have an influence. Therefore, to the extent that the prototypic representation of an "honest person" contains favorable attributes (e.g., "kind"), John may be judged as honest despite the fact that the original information presented about him implied dishonesty. One implication of this is that the initial encoding of the information presented about a person, or inferences made about the person, will have an increasing effect over time in relation to the effects of the original information presented. A detailed analysis of this phenomenon, which has been empirically demonstrated (Carlston, 1980a,b; Wyer, Srull, & Gordon, 1984), is discussed later in this volume. The general point to be made here is that judgments of a person may depend substantially on both the nature of previous judgments made of this person and the time interval between judgments.

Non-Goal-Directed Information Processing

In many instances, information is acquired and processed without any specific goal in mind. In this case, no goal schema will be in the Goal Specification Box. Under these conditions, the system is assumed to enter a feedback loop that continues indefinitely until a specific goal is identified, either as the result of external information or information retrieved from Permanent Storage. The nature of this loop, indicated in Figure 2.2, can again be conveyed simply with reference to a concrete example. Imagine that the woman in our previous example is told that "John gave Peter an answer on an exam" *without* the accompanying request to make a judgment of John. The following steps are postulated to occur under such conditions:

1. The Comprehender encodes the statement in terms of the semantic concepts in the semantic bin ("gives answer," "exam," etc.) and transmits this representation to the Work Space, Compartment 1.

2. The Executor scans the Work Space for a goal specification. In the present case, none is found.

3. The Executor randomly samples a set of features or concepts from Compartment 1 of the Work Space. It then scans Permanent Storage for a bin whose header includes these features. In the present case, suppose two features are sampled: "exam" (a feature of the new information presented) and "psychology," which fortuitously happens to be in the Work Space as the result of prior cognitive activity. It then searches for a bin containing these features.

4. Suppose that a referent bin pertaining to "psychology examinations" exists. Then, the Executor retrieves a unit of information from this bin and transmits it to the Work Space, Compartment 1. This unit may consist of either a single event or a set of related events. For purposes of our example, suppose it is a propositional representation that "my final psychology examination is not until the end of exam week, and I cannot leave for Christmas vacation until December 22."

5. Steps 2 - 4 are then repeated. This time, "Christmas" may be among the two features that are sampled, and a bin associated with this concept will be identified. The unit of information on the top of this bin may be a propositional representation of the fact that "I need to buy a Christmas present for my boyfriend."

6. Again, Step 2 is repeated. This time, however, the search of the Work Space identifies a specific goal ("buy Christmas present for boyfriend"). When this occurs, the loop is left and the goal attainment subroutine is activated. That is, the Executor identifies a relevant goal schema pertaining to this objective and proceeds according to instructions specified in the schema, perhaps generating a tentative plan about what to buy and where to buy it.

A more explicit statement of these processes requires explicit assumptions about (a) the number of features contained in the set that the Executor uses to identify a bin from which to retrieve information, and (b) the likelihood that any given feature from the Work Space is sampled and included in this set. However, the general process outlined here permits the model to account for the free flow of thought, as well as the spontaneous initiation of goal-directed processing in the absence of external demands.

Conscious vs. Subconscious Information Processing

Considerable attention in the social cognition literature, and in cognitive psychology more generally, has been given to the difference between automatic and controlled information processing or, alternatively, between subconscious and conscious processing (cf. Bargh, 1984; Langer, 1978; Nisbett & Wilson, 1977; Schneider & Shiffrin, 1977). That is, certain well-learned cognitive activities are performed virtually automatically, without conscious awareness of the cognitive steps involved in them. The performance of these activities appears to place few if any demands on a person's cognitive system. Evidence of this comes from the fact that the introduction of these activities produces no decrement at all in other cognitive activities that are being performed simultaneously (Schneider & Shiffrin, 1977).

The automatic character of some types of information processing is implicit in the argument that people are often unaware of certain determinants of their behavior (Nisbett & Wilson, 1977; but see Ericsson & Simon, 1980). That is, the steps involved in automatic cognitive processing are not open to conscious introspection (Mandler, 1975). To this extent, people who are asked how or why they made a particular judgment or decision may be able to reconstruct only those components of the judgment or decision processes that were performed consciously and deliberately rather than automatically.

This hypothesis is also an implication of the model we propose here. Specifically, it follows from the distinction we make between (a) procedures that are contained in the libraries of processing units and procedures that are specified in the goal schema used by the Executor as a basis for directing goal-directed activity. The procedures in a processing unit's library are each identified by a name or other cognitive symbol. For example, the Encoder/Organizer may have a "trait encoding" routine that interprets behavioral information in terms of more basic personality trait concepts. It may have a second routine for interpreting a set of specific behaviors and traits as an exemplar of a particular type of person (e.g., "psychopathic"). A third routine may organize information in a way that facilitates its subsequent retrieval. These procedures are presumably acquired through learning. (In fact, the acquisition of a procedure may itself be a processing objective that is attained through a series of steps that are specified by a goal schema in Permanent Storage.) With time and repetition, however, the procedure may become part of the "hardware" of the system, and the goal schema in which it was originally contained may be replaced by one that simply calls the procedure in the processing unit's library without specifying the steps involved in it. In this sense, the learning of a procedure is somewhat analogous to the development of a "production system" that, once acquired, functions independently of the declarative knowledge base on which it originally rested (see Anderson, 1976, 1983; Smith, 1984).

The above assumptions permit the distinction between conscious and subconscious processes to be conceptualized. Specifically, we assume that *the "consciousness" of the system resides in the Executor*. That is, the information, goals, procedures, and other cognitive material that are transmitted from one part of the system to another are accessible to conscious awareness, and the transmission of this material is consciously directed. In contrast, the procedures that make up each processing unit's library, the use of which is *not* monitored by the Executor, are performed without conscious awareness of the cognitive steps involved.

Specifically, the information that is retrieved from Permanent Storage, instructions to processors about what procedures to activate, and the output of the processing units, are all subject to conscious awareness. Thus, for example, a woman who is asked how well she likes a person who "cheats on examinations" and "participates in anti-war demonstrations" may be aware that (a) she characterized the person as "dishonest and a social activist" on the basis of these behaviors, (b) she recalled an acquaintance who had these attributes, and (c) she based her judgment of the person on her liking for this acquaintance. This is because the output of each stage of processing (the encodings of the person's behavior in terms of personality traits, her interpretation of the person's encoded features as similar to those of a prior acquaintance, the retrieval of her liking for the acquaintance, and her use of this subjective judgment as a basis for her overt response) are all accessed by the Executor, and therefore are conscious. However, the woman will *not* generally be aware of the procedures for generating these outputs, which are typically contained in the libraries of the processing units involved. (For a similar distinction between the consciousness of the outputs of cognitive activity and consciousness of the processes that produce these outputs, see Ericsson & Simon, 1980; Mandler, 1975, 1984).

A related implication of this assumption comes into play in conceptualizing the distinction between the encoding processes performed by the Comprehender, on one hand, and by the Encoder/Organizer, on the other. The Comprehender is not under the control of the Executor. This means that the initial comprehension of input information in terms of low-level noun, action, and attribute concepts is automatic. Moreover, the concepts that are used by the Comprehender to perform its functions are retrieved without awareness. This makes intuitive sense. For example, consider the statement "John pounded the nail into the wall." It is impossible *not* to understand this statement. Its comprehension is virtually complete by the time we have read it. Moreover, we are not aware of having retrieved any particular semantic concepts for use in interpreting the statement. We are only aware of the *results* of this initial comprehension process, after they have been transmitted to the Work Space. However, now consider the statement "The nail pounded John into the wall." Although the noun concepts are easily interpretable, the action itself cannot be interpreted in terms of processes available in the Comprehender's library and semantic action concepts available to it in Permanent Storage. (For an elaboration of why this is so, see Chapter 3.) Such a statement is presumably transmitted to the Work Space and interpreted by the Encoder/Organizer, based on instructions transmitted to it by the Executor. The input and output of this latter comprehension process, which is monitored by the Executor, is subject to awareness, along with the output of various intermediate stages en route to the comprehension. (Thus, for example, we may interpret the statement by mentally constructing a bizarre Disney-like cartoon image of a large nail taking revenge on John by hammering him head first into the plasterboard. Or, we may simply assume that the statement contains a typographical error and may not try to interpret it at all.)

Our assumption that the consciousness of the system resides in the Executor, however, does not imply that the Executor is the "brains" and "motivation" of the system. In fact, the Executor in our system simply takes instructions from a goal schema, and itself has little independent decision-making capacity. Its "consciousness" comes solely from the fact that it can copy cognitive material from one location and transmit it to another, and that it therefore has access to the material it transmits.

Summary

In this chapter, we have provided a general overview of the components of our model and their functions, and have provided some examples of the general sequence of information processing steps that may exist in the course of both goal-directed processing and during the free flow of thought. At this level, the model is little more than a descriptive device for conceptualizing the points en route to attaining a processing objective at which different types of cognitive operations are performed. For the model to be useful, the operation of the various storage and processing units must be specified in much greater detail. The remaining chapters of this volume are directed to this end.

Chapter 3
The Structure and Function of the Work Space

The Work Space is a temporary repository of information that has been transmitted to it from either the Comprehender or (via the Executor) the Permanent Storage Unit. At any given time, it may contain both the input information that is used at various stages of processing and the output of these stages. Thus, it may contain (a) new stimulus information transmitted to it by the Comprehender and (b) previously formed knowledge representations drawn from Permanent Storage. It may also contain the output of various special-purpose processing units, including (c) more abstract encodings of information in terms of more general trait behavior and event concepts, (c) integrated representations of the information that have been formed with reference to a prototypic person or event, (e) subjective judgments of the person or event, and (f) episodic representations of overt responses to the stimulus (e.g., the representation of a judgment made along a category scale, etc.).

The Work Space is divided into four compartments. Compartment 1 contains the information transmitted to it from the Comprehender along with other previously acquired cognitive material that is sent to it by the Executor during the free flow of thought (see Chapter 2, pp. 28-29). This material is reviewed by the Executor for goal specifications, and generally provides the input to the Encoder/Organizer. The remaining compartments contain the output of special-purpose processing units along with any other cognitive material (concepts, knowledge structures contained in Permanent Storage, etc.) that was used to generate this output.

Therefore, suppose someone is asked to decide if a person who has performed several different behaviors would make a good graduate student. In such an event, Compartment 1 should contain the material transmitted to the Work Space by the Comprehender, that is, a representation of the processing objective and the low-level encodings of the person's behaviors. To the extent that the goal schema that is activated to attain this processing object requires that the behaviors be encoded

33

1	2	3	4
Behaviors	Behaviors	Trait Encodings	Inference
Goal Specification	Trait Encodings	Inference	Overt Response

Figure 3.1 Hypothetical example of material contained in four compartments of the Work Space following the processing of behavioral information for the purpose of deciding if the actor would be a good graduate student.

in terms of traits, copies of the behaviors may be transmitted by the Executor to the Encoder/Organizer, which encodes them in terms of trait concepts. These trait encodings, along with the original behavioral information, are returned to Compartment 2 of the Work Space. (Note that the representations of the behaviors are now in *both* Compartment 1 and Compartment 2.) Suppose a later stage of processing requires that the implications of the individual traits be integrated into a single value representing the quality of graduate student the person is likely to be.[1] Then, the Executor will transmit these encodings to the Inference Maker with instructions to compute this value. The output (an inference) along with the trait encodings is returned to Compartment 3. The inference will then be sent to the Response Selector, which will use it to generate an overt response in the language required to answer the specific question that was asked.

As a result of this cognitive processing the types of material contained in each compartment of the Work Space would be that shown in Figure 3.1. As this figure indicates, any given concept or piece of information may be represented more than once in the Work Space, depending on the number of times it has been involved in goal-direct processing. We discuss the implications of this presently.

Several additional assumptions are made concerning the characteristics of the Work Space. These assumptions, like others underlying the model we propose, are stated formally in terms of postulates. (For a complete listing of all of the postulates composing the model, see Appendix.)

Postulate 3.1. The Work Space is of limited capacity.

---

1. For simplicity in this example, we have bypassed an intermediate stage of processing, which may involve the retrieval of a prototypic representation of a "good graduate student" and a comparison of the set of trait encodings with the features of this prototypic. This activity, like the encoding of individual behaviors, is presumably performed by the Encoder/Organizer, and the results of this activity are returned to Compartment 2.

Consequently, the information contained in it is continually being displaced by other information. Whether a given piece of information is displaced is determined in part by the total amount of new information that enters the processing system and in part by the relevance of the information to the immediate processing objectives at hand. Postulates 3.2 and 3.3 elaborate this principle.

Postulate 3.2. The displacement of information from the Work Space may be either automatic or volitional.

Under conditions of high information load, the displacement of information is assumed to occur automatically. On the other hand, when a processing objective has been attained, or if the subject does not anticipate needing the information again for some time, the Executor may activate a "clear Work Space" routine to avoid unnecessary "clutter" and thereby to facilitate the processing of material relevant to other processing objectives. The clearing of the Work Space under these latter conditions is assumed to be the result of a control process (i.e., one over which the subject has some volitional control; see Atkinson & Shiffrin, 1968; Srull & Wyer, 1983). Empirical evidence bearing on this assumption is discussed later in this chapter.

Postulate 3.3. Under conditions of high information load, the material in the Work Space that has been least recently involved in processing (either as input to a processing unit or as output from the unit) is most likely to be displaced.

This is essentially a "first-in, first-out" principle. Note, however, that the likelihood of retaining information is determined by the recency of *using* it and not the recency of acquiring it. Thus, information transmitted from the Comprehender that is not involved in any additional processing is the most likely to be removed. Or, if several goals are being pursued, information that is relevant to the least immediate goal (the one with the lowest processing priority) is most likely to be displaced. In addition, when the attainment of a goal requires processing at several stages, the material involved at earlier stages of processing is more likely to be cleared than the material that is used at later stages. Thus, in our earlier example (Figure 3.1), a trait-based encoding of a person's behavior by the Encoder/Organizer (which is contained in both Compartments 2 and 3) may be retained longer than the representation of the behavior itself (which is contained in Compartments 1 and 2). Finally, the likelihood that information is displaced is obviously greater when processing demands are high (i.e., when several other processing objectives are being pursued simultaneously) than when they are low.

Postulate 3.4. Once the Work Space is cleared, any material that has not been transmitted to a bin in Permanent Storage is irretrievably lost.

This postulate derives its importance in part from the fact that the abstract encodings of the original information by the Encoder/Organizer may retain only a subset of its features. Similarly, the cognitive representation of a stimulus person or object that has been formed in the course of attaining a particular processing objective may not capture the implications of the original information for other objectives. On the other hand, the representation may contain features that were not described in the information but were inferred in the course of goal-directed activity. These inferred features are not distinguished in the representation from the ones that were explicitly mentioned.

The empirical implications of these considerations become clearer in the context of two additional postulates. These postulates are more appropriately included in the set we propose to govern information storage and retrieval, and we present and discuss them more formally in this context (see Chapter 5). However, their relevance to the present discussion requires that they be mentioned here as well.

Postulate 3.5. When information relevant to a processing objective is required, the Work Space is searched first, before goal-relevant information is retrieved from Permanent Storage.

Postulate 3.6. The search for information in the Work Space is random. The probability of retrieving a given unit of information from the Work Space increases with the number of times the unit is represented there at the time information is sought.

Thus, suppose information that has been originally processed for one purpose is relevant to a somewhat different processing objective that is introduced subsequently. Postulates 3.5 and 3.6 imply that as long as the Work Space has not been cleared, there is some probability that the original information transmitted from the Comprehender will be identified and used to attain this new objective. Once the Work Space is cleared, however, goal-relevant implications of the information that were not contained in the representation that was formed and sent to Permanent Storage will have no effect. Similarly, errors in memory for the original information presented (intrusions, distortions, etc.) are more likely to occur after the Work Space is cleared than beforehand. The likelihood that the Work Space is cleared generally increases over time, as new processing demands impinge on the system.

This means that once subjects have formed a representation of a person or object from information they have received, (a) the likelihood that they will use this representation as a basis for judgments and decisions rather than the original information itself, and (b) the likelihood that their recall of the information will contain distortions and intrusions, increases as time goes on.

Theoretical and Empirical Implications

Our conception of the Work Space and the postulates pertaining to it will play an important role in our theoretical discussion of cognitive processing throughout this volume. However, some rather unique implications of this conceptualization, many of which have received empirical support both in our laboratory and others', may be worth noting at this time. These implications are derivable from the six postulates noted above.

Effects of Amount of Processing on Recall and Judgment

As implied in our previous example, a given piece of information may be represented several times in the Work Space. Therefore, because the search of the Work Space for goal-relevant information is random (Postulate 3.6), the likelihood of retrieving a particular piece will increase with the number of times it is represented in the memory unit as a whole, or alternatively, the number of times it has entered into cognitive processing.

Therefore, suppose a person is asked to report his belief that there will be a nuclear war. To arrive at this estimate, the person may retrieve a subset of prior knowledge from a bin in Permanent Storage pertaining to nuclear war and may construe the implications of this knowledge for the judgment to be made. (This latter activity is presumably performed by the Inference Maker.) Each time a new piece of knowledge is considered, its implications are presumably integrated with the knowledge acquired previously to arrive at a judgment. The results of these computations, along with the material involved in performing them, are returned to the Work Space. Because this material is likely to include a representation of the proposition being evaluated (i.e., "there will be a nuclear war"), several different copies of this proposition may come to exist in the Work Space as a result of this cognitive activity.

The greater the amount of cognitive activity in which a particular piece of information or knowledge has been involved (or, more simply, the number of times it has been thought about), the more times it is represented in the Work Space. Consequently, the more likely it is that this information will be retrieved and used to attain a subsequent processing objective to which it is applicable. (This objective could be either to recall the information or to use it as a basis for making a judgment or decision.) The "amount of processing" effect on recall implied by the model is similar in some respects to that postulated by others (cf. Craik & Lockhart, 1972).

Indirect evidence that amount of processing influences both recall and judgments was reported by Wyer and Hartwick (1980) in a study of belief memory. Subjects were initially asked to report their beliefs in a series of propositions, some of which were plausible (e.g., "Vast oil resources lie under the frozen earth of Antarctica") and others of which were relatively implausible (e.g., "The all-volunteer army is accepting an increasing number of mentally-retarded recruits"). Each of these "informational" propositions, if true, had implications for a different target proposition ("The settlement of Antarctica will be greatly accelerated during the next few years," "The overall level of intelligence of Army personnel is declining," respectively). Later, subjects were asked to recall the informational propositions and also to report their beliefs in both these propositions and the target propositions.

Subjects were expected to think more extensively about implausible propositions than about plausible ones in the course of initially reporting their beliefs. They were therefore predicted not only to remember the implausible propositions better, but also to be more apt to recall and use them as bases for inferring the validity of the target propositions for which they had implications. Support was obtained for both predictions. That is, informational propositions were more likely to be recalled when they were implausible than when they were plausible. Moreover, subjects' beliefs in implausible propositions were more likely to influence their subsequently reported beliefs in the target propositions than were their beliefs in plausible ones.[2]

One thing should be noted in assessing the implications of these results. That is, the time interval between subjects' initial reports of their beliefs in informational propositions and their later recall and use of these propositions was too long to justify the assumption that the material was retained in the Work Space during this interval. Rather, one must assume that the greater cognitive activity involved in the initial processing of the implausible informational propositions led these propositions to be more frequently contained in the representations transmitted to Permanent Storage, thereby increasing the likelihood of retrieving and using them even after a long delay (for a more elaborate theoretical analysis of this possibility, see Chapter 5). On the other hand, the representations that are transmitted to Permanent Storage must theoretically have been retained at some earlier time in the Work Space. It therefore seems reasonable to suppose that a similar pattern of findings would have occurred after a short delay interval as well.

This ambiguity nonetheless calls attention to an important theoretical as well as empirical issue. That is, a *general* amount-of-processing effect is predicted only under conditions in which the processed material is still in the Work Space at the

---

2. These implications were determined on the basis of the Wyer-McGuire probabilogical inference model (McGuire, 1981; Wyer & Hartwick, 1980); see Chapter 9.

time of recall and/or judgment. Once the Work Space is cleared, any effect of amount of processing would need to be reflected in the extent to which the information was contained in the output of processing that is transmitted to various locations in Permanent Storage. Although the number of times that information is contained in the Work Space and the number of times it is transmitted to Permanent Storage may have been fairly similar in the conditions constructed by Wyer and Hartwick, this is not necessarily the case. In fact, the factors that govern the retrieval and use of information in Permanent Storage theoretically differ substantially from those that govern the retrieval and use of information in the Work Space (see Chapter 5). Consequently, amount-of-processing effects per se should generally be less evident a long time after information has been processed than they are after a short period of time has elapsed.

"Depth-of-Processing" Effects on Recall and Judgment

A related issue is raised by Postulate 3.3. That is, material in the Work Space that is less recently involved in processing is displaced first. This has two implications. First, the likelihood of recalling and using a given piece of information should increase with the number of *stages* of processing in which it is involved as well as the frequency of times it is used at any given stage. To the extent that the number of processing stages in which a piece of information is involved is an index of the amount of "cognitive elaboration" or "depth of processing" of this information, this increase would be consistent with the depth-of-processing effect on recall postulated by Craik and Lockhart (1972). In our conceptualization, however, this effect is confounded with a "recency of use" effect. That is, because the material used at earlier stages of processing is cleared from the Work Space before material involved at later stages, cognitions that have been used most recently in the course of attaining a processing objective (i.e., at later processing stages) should be better recalled than cognitions involved at earlier ones.

A more subtle implication of the model is worth noting, however. That is, the frequency with which information is involved in goal-directed cognitive activity will have less influence on its subsequent recall and use if this activity occurs at early stages of processing than if it occurs at later stages. Moreover, this difference should be particularly evident after a period of time has elapsed that is sufficient for some but not all compartments of the Work Space to be cleared. Although no existing evidence bears directly on this possibility, a thought experiment may help to convey the model's implications.

Suppose subjects are given a series of trait adjectives with instructions that whenever an adjective is followed by a star, they should generate a behavior that exemplifies it. Embedded in the sequence of stimulus adjectives presented are (a) 10 repetitions of adjective A, two of which are starred, and (b) four repetitions of adjective B, all of which are starred. According to the model, A should therefore be represented 10 times in Compartment 1 of the Work Space and B should be represented four times. However, A should be represented only two times in Compartment 3 (where the results of inference- making are sent) whereas B should be represented four times in this compartment. After engaging in the activity described above, subjects are asked to recall the trait adjectives they read. Alternatively, they are asked to make a judgment to which either A or B is potentially applicable. If this request is made a very short time after the inference task was performed, subjects should be more likely to recall and use A than to recall and use B. (This is because A is represented $10 + 2 = 12$ times in the Work Space whereas B is represented only $4 + 4 = 8$ times). After a longer delay, however, when Compartment 1 of the Work Space is cleared, subjects should be more likely to recall and use B than to recall and use A.

Other Effects of Time Delay

Although the above implications of our formulation have not been tested, other implications have received strong support. One of the more interesting of these implications derives from the assumption that the Work Space is the first area searched for goal-relevant information (Postulate 3.5). Therefore, if the Work Space contains this information, it is likely to be identified and used. Once the Work Space has been cleared, however, only those aspects of the information that were transmitted to Permanent Storage are available.

Several phenomena are predicted on the basis of this assumption. Imagine that one's objective is to judge a target person on the basis of certain behaviors the person is said to have performed. Several implications of these behaviors, although reflected in the material sent to the Work Space by the Comprehender, may not be captured by the more abstract (e.g., trait-based) representation that is formed of the target by the Encoder/Organizer. This will be particularly true if the person's behaviors have implications for several different trait concepts but have been encoded in terms of only one (cf. Carlston, 1980). Nevertheless, there will be a period of time in which the Work Space contains both the low level encodings of the behavioral information that were performed by the Comprehender and the representation of the target that is formed by the Encoder/Organizer. If the judgment is made during this time, it could be based in part on the implications of both sets of material. Once the Work Space has been cleared to make room for information relevant to other objectives, however, implications of the information that are not captured by the representation of the target sent to Permanent Storage are lost (Postulate 3.4). Consequently, they should have no influence on judgments. The likelihood that the Work Space is cleared typically increases over time. This means that the influence of the encoded representation formed of the target on judgments (relative to the influence of the original information presented) should generally increase with the time that has elapsed since the information was first presented and processed.

Support for this hypothesis has been obtained in several studies discussed in more detail later in this volume (Chapter 6). Two studies (Higgins, Rholes, & Jones, 1977; Srull & Wyer, 1980) investigated the effect of increasing the accessibility of a trait concept on judgments of a person whose behavior could be interpreted as exemplifying the trait. In Srull and Wyer's study, for example, subjects initially performed a task that required the use of concepts associated with hostility. Then, as part of a different experiment, they read a paragraph describing the behaviors of a target person. Some of these behaviors (e.g., "refused to pay the rent until the landlord painted his apartment") were ambiguous, that is, they could be either interpreted as hostile or attributed to other factors. Finally, either immediately, one hour, or one day later, subjects judged the target with respect to hostility. The trait concepts activated by performing the initial task were expected to lead subjects to interpret the target person's behaviors as "hostile," and to form a representation of the target as a "hostile person." Nonetheless, both these behaviors and others in the paragraph describing the target had implications that were not necessarily hostile. Thus, judgments made immediately after reading a stimulus paragraph were expected in some cases to be based on these implications as well as (or instead of) the target representation or the trait encodings of his behavior. After a delay, however, only the representation of the target as a hostile person was expected to be used. Consistent with this reasoning, subjects' ratings of the target's hostility increased over the time interval between information presentation and judgments. Analogous effects are obtained when other trait concepts are primed as well (cf. Higgins et al., 1977; Srull & Wyer, 1980).

In a somewhat different study (Carlston, 1980a,b) subjects first received behavioral information about a person that implied two evaluatively different traits (e.g., "kind" and "dishonest") and judged the target with respect to one of them. Either a few minutes or several days later, they judged the target with respect to the second trait. Presumably, subjects in the course of making their initial judgment interpreted the target's behaviors in terms of the trait they were asked to judge, and formed a representation of the target as someone who has this trait. This representation was then sent to Permanent Storage. Under long delay conditions, the original behavioral information had obviously been cleared from the Work Space by the time subjects made their second judgments. Under short delay conditions, this was less likely to have been the case. This means that the implications of the representation sent to Permanent Storage should have a relatively greater influence on subjects' judgments after a long delay. Consistent with this reasoning, the evaluative implications of subjects' first judgments affected their second judgments, and this effect increased with the time interval between the two judgments. These results are therefore also consistent with the model's predictions.

Automatic vs. Volitional Processes in Information Retention

Alternative interpretations of the effects described above are possible. For example, Higgins and his colleagues (cf. Higgins & King, 1981) have argued that *both* a representation of the stimulus details and the higher-level encoding of the material are transmitted to Permanent Storage (long term memory). However, the stimulus details (unlike the higher level encodings of them) decay over time, requiring increased use of the encoding both to reconstruct the original stimulus information (if one is asked to recall it) or to make judgments. In contrast, the proposed model does not postulate such a decay mechanism. Rather, it assumes that the detailed stimulus representation is never sent to Permanent Storage in the first place, and so the likelihood of its influencing judgments and recall depends solely on whether it has been cleared from the Work Space at the time the judgment and/or recall task is performed.

To distinguish between the conceptualization we propose and the interpretation given by Higgins et al. to the effects described above, it is necessary to manipulate factors that lead the Work Space to be cleared independently of the actual time interval between stimulus presentation and judgments (and therefore independently of the amount of decay of the original stimulus material). Two such factors were investigated in a series of studies reported by Srull and Wyer (1983). These studies also support our assumption that information may be cleared from the Work Space either automatically or volitionally (Postulate 3.2). Parallel studies were conducted to investigate the effects of clearing the Work Space on both the recall of information and judgments of a person described by it.

Recall. It is almost a truism that the ability to recall information decreases over time. In terms of the present model, this is due in part to the fact that when there has been only a short delay between the receipt of information and the time one is asked to recall it, representations containing this information may still be in the Work Space as well as in Permanent Storage. Thus, there may be several ways of identifying it. Once a longer period of time has elapsed, and the Work Space is cleared to make room for more immediate goal-relevant material, the information can only be retrieved by identifying representations in Permanent Storage that happen to contain it. Consequently, the likelihood of recalling the information should be less.

A more unique prediction of this conceptualization, however, is implied by Postulate 3.2. Specifically, the recall of information may also decrease with the *anticipated* time delay between the receipt of this information and its subsequent use. That is, if subjects after receiving information learn that they will not be called upon to use it to attain goals to which it is relevant for some time, they are likely to clear the Work Space *volitionally* to make room for information relevant to more pressing demands. Once this occurs, the likelihood of recalling the information

TABLE 3.1

Mean Number of Behaviors Recalled as a Function of Length of Actual Delay, Length of Anticipated Delay, and Point at which Subjects were Told About the Impending Delay

| | Subjects told about delay after behaviors were presented | | | Subjects told about delay before behaviors were presented | | |
	Short anticipated delay	Long anticipated delay	M	Short anticipated delay	Long anticipated delay	M
short actual delay	15.30	11.80	13.55	15.60	16.20	15.9
long actual delay	5.00	5.30	5.15	5.30	9.30	7.3
M	10.15	8.55		10.45	12.75	

should also decrease. In other words, the effect of anticipated time delay on information recall should parallel the effect of actual time delay.

This hypothesis was supported by Srull and Wyer (1983, Experiment 1). In some conditions of this study, subjects read a list of behaviors with instructions to learn them. Then, after reading the behaviors, they were told there would be either a short (5 minute) or long (45 minute) delay before being asked to recall them, and were given an unrelated task to perform in the interim. Independently of the anticipated delay, the actual delay before recalling the behaviors was also manipulated. Subjects who anticipated a short delay were expected to try to retain the information in the Work Space during the interim, whereas those who anticipated a long delay were expected to clear the Work Space intentionally to make room for material relevant to the interpolated task. However, when subjects were actually exposed to a long interpolated task, the demands of performing this task should have led the behavioral information to be displaced from the Work Space *automatically*, independently of subjects' attempts to retain it there. In summary, then, Postulate 3.2 implies that fewer behaviors should be recalled when *either* the anticipated or the actual delay interval is long than when both the anticipated delay and the actual delay is short. Results shown in the left half of Table 3.1 indicate that this was in fact the case.

An important contingency in these effects should be noted. That is, subjects under the conditions described above were not given an expectation concerning the delay interval until they had learned all of the target's behaviors. Consequently, the recall difference we obtained reflected differences in the likelihood that the behaviors were retained in the Work Space rather than differences in the processing of this information at the time it was received. In contrast, suppose that subjects are told of the impending delay between information presentation and recall *before* they receive the information. In this case, subjects who anticipate a relatively long delay may attempt to engage in relatively more elaborate encoding operations in an effort to retain the information. (Put another way, the anticipated delay may affect the goal schema that subjects activate for use in attaining the processing objectives at hand.) This more elaborate encoding may facilitate recall for reasons similar to those we discussed earlier in the context of amount-of-processing effects. If this is so, the effect of anticipated delay may often be opposite in direction to the effect we predicted and obtained in the first set of conditions we considered. This proved to be true in a second set of conditions run by Srull and Wyer (1983, Experiment 1). That is, subjects were told before reading the behaviors that there would be either a 5 minute or 45 minute delay before they were asked to recall them. Recall under these conditions (shown in the right half of Table 3.1) decreased as the actual time delay increased. In contrast to the first set of conditions, however, it was greater when subjects anticipated a long delay than when they expect a short one.

Judgments. If our interpretation of the recall data is correct, parallel effects of time delay variables should occur on judgments as well. Suppose subjects receive a series of behaviors that are either predominantly favorable or predominantly unfavorable and are told to form an impression of the person they describe. In the course of forming this impression, subjects should extract a general concept of the person that reflects the evaluative character of the presented behaviors (cf. Hartwick, 1979; for an elaboration of this assumption and evidence bearing on it, see Chapter 7). This evaluative person concept should be transmitted to Permanent Storage as well as returned to the Work Space along with the behaviors used in constructing it. However, some of the individual behaviors presented may either have unclear evaluative implications or implications that differ from those of the more general person concept. If subjects are later asked to judge the person and the Work Space has not been cleared, their judgments may be based on a sample of the material contained in the Work Space. This sample may sometimes include behaviors whose evaluative implications are less extreme than those of the person concept that subjects have formed. Consequently, subjects' judgments may often be less extreme than they would be if they were based on the person concept alone. In other words, they should be less extreme before the Work Space is cleared than afterwards.

We investigated this possibility using procedures analogous to those we employed in the recall study described earlier (Srull & Wyer, 1983, Experiments 2 and 3). That is, subjects read a series of behaviors that on the average were either slightly favorable or slightly unfavorable with instructions to form an impression of the person who performed them. After reading the behaviors, they were told there would be either a 5 minute or 45 minute delay before making their judgments. Then, they performed an interpolated task that in fact took either 5 minutes or 45

TABLE 3.2

Mean Likeableness of Target as a Function of Length of Anticipated Delay, Length of Actual Delay, and Favorableness of Behaviors Presented

	Favorable behaviors			Unfavorable behaviors		
	Short anticipated delay	Long anticipated delay	M	Short anticipated delay	Long anticipated delay	M
short actual delay	.40[a]	2.70	2.05	−.70	−1.80	−1.20
long actual delay	2.70	3.00	2.85	−1.70	−1.90	−1.80
M	2.05	2.85		−1.20	−1.85	

[a]Ratings, originally reported along a scale from 0 to 10, have been transformed for clarity to values along a scale from −5 (extremely dislikeable) to 5 (extremely likeable).

minutes, regardless of the time interval they had been told would occur. Subjects' judgments of the person's likableness, along a transformed scale from -5 (dislikable) to +5 (likeable), are shown in Table 3.2. As predicted, judgments were more extreme when either the actual delay or the anticipated delay was long than when both were short.

Effects of processing load. Additional studies by Srull and Wyer (1983, Experiments 4-6) investigated an additional factor that would influence the likelihood that the Work Space will be cleared automatically: specifically, the processing demands imposed on the subject in the period following information presentation. In these studies, the delay interval between the information presented and recall (or judgments) was held constant. However, some subjects were given a cognitively simple task (proofreading) to perform in the interim, whereas others were given a cognitively demanding one (solving a series of syllogistic reasoning problems). The Work Space is more likely to be cleared in the second case than in the first. Consistent with this prediction, the number of behaviors recalled by subjects in the "recall" experiment was less when the interpolated task was difficult, whereas ratings of the target by subjects in the "judgment" experiment were more extreme in this condition. A decay model of the sort postulated by Higgins and his colleagues would have difficulty in accounting for these differences.

This series of studies provides strong and consistent support for several aspects of the proposed conceptualization. First, they support Postulate 3.2, that displacement of information from the Work Space may be either automatic or volitional, and they identify several variables that determine which is the case. Second, they support the assumption that once the Work Space has been cleared, judgments are based upon an encoded representation of the target in Permanent Storage rather than the direct implications of the original behaviors represented. (If subjects' judgments were simply based on the implications of the behaviors that they could recall, the judgments would have been *less* extreme under those conditions in which the recall of behaviors was low. In fact, they were more extreme under those conditions.) Finally, the results demonstrate the model's ability to generate specific predictions of the effect of experimental variables on both the recall of information and judgments to which the information is relevant.

Concluding Remarks

Our conceptualization of the Work Space and the postulates surrounding its role in information storage and retrieval are central ingredients of the model we propose. As we have tried to convey in this chapter, the Work Space construct not only permits the model to account for a variety of phenomena that have been previously identified in the literature but generates unique predictions of phenomena that other conceptualizations have difficulty in accounting for. The conceptualization is of particular value in conceptualizing the factors that produce changes in information recall and judgments over time.

There are nevertheless problems surrounding our conceptualization and its applicability. The main ambiguity results from the model's inability to predict precisely how long information will remain in the Work Space in any given instance. For example, Srull and Wyer (1980) found that extending the time interval between stimulus encoding and judgments from one hour to one day further increased the influence of the encoding. To account for this change in terms of the model, one would have to assume that some small proportion of the original stimulus material was still present in the Work Space even after an hour's delay. This does not seem intuitively plausible. These matters must obviously be addressed in future refinements of the model and elaborations of its implications.

Despite this shortcoming, the Work Space construct, in the context of other components of the formulation we propose, is a powerful tool in both predicting and explaining a wide variety of memory and judgment phenomena. This will become increasingly clear in the chapters to follow.

Chapter 4
The Organization of Information in Permanent Memory

An adequate theoretical account of how social information is organized in long term memory must be able to accommodate the diversity of information that is stored. Some information we acquire consists of entire sequences of causally and temporally related events that we have either experienced personally or learned about from others. Our mental representations of such experiences may often be very complex. For example, a woman who is asked about a party she went to last week may be able to provide a detailed description of particular episodes that occurred (e.g., an incident in which a guest spilled a Bloody Mary on his girl friend's new white dress). The mental representation she retrieves and uses as a basis for this description may consist in part of a mental image of the people involved in it as well as the sequence of actions that took place (for discussions of visual representations of information in memory, see Klatzky, 1984; Kosslyn, 1980). In other words, it may consist of both verbally and visually coded features that are both spatially and temporally organized in relation to one another.

Other information we acquire may be quite different. Some of it may consist of single facts or propositions that we appear to retrieve independently of one another, in no particular order (cf. the information we have accumulated about World War II and the events surrounding it). Other knowledge we acquire may consist of simply a set of general attributes or (in the case of persons) trait descriptions. Or, it may simply be a memory of our general emotional reactions to a person or situation. Note that this latter knowledge pertains more fundamentally to ourselves. Representations of these reactions may nevertheless by stored at a memory location pertaining to the person or event that elicits them, independently of other information. As a result, we appear able to remember our feelings and thoughts about a person without being able to recall anything the person said or did that gave rise to them (Abelson, 1976).

A second consideration in developing a conceptualization of long term memory is that when people require information for use in making a judgment or decision, they do not recall all of the things they know about the person or event being judged. Rather, they are likely to retrieve only a small subset of this knowledge. Moreover, the particular subset that people recall and use may vary over time and situations. In some instances, it may be the subset they have most recently acquired or thought about. On the other hand, information about a person that has not been thought about in years may sometimes come to mind spontaneously as a result of chance events that cue its retrieval. Although an explication of these latter phenomena requires consideration of retrieval processes, it involves assumptions about the organization and storage of information in memory as well.

Most existing conceptualizations of memory, both in social and in cognitive psychology, have some difficulty in conceptualizing the entire range of knowledge structures that appear to exist and the processes that govern their retrieval. Many approaches have employed an associative network metaphor (cf. Anderson, 1976; Anderson & Bower, 1979, 1973; Collins & Loftus, 1975; in the area of social memory, see Carlston & Skowronski, 1986; Kihlstrom & Cantor, 1984; Wyer & Carlston, 1979). That is, concepts in memory are represented by nodes, and the associations among them by pathways. The length or width of the pathways may vary, depending on the strength of the association they represent (cf. Wyer & Carlston, 1979). According to some of these models, a stimulus event that leads a concept to be applied activates the node pertaining to the concept. Excitation that is generated at this node as a result of its activation then spreads along the pathways emanating from it to other nodes. If the excitation at these peripheral nodes reaches a threshold level, they are also activated and the concepts located at them are called to mind.[1]

An associative network metaphor can be quite useful for describing the manner in which specific subsets of information are organized in memory as a result of thinking about different pieces of this information in relation to one another (see, for example, Chapter 7). As a general conceptualization of how information is organized in memory, however, it is extremely unwieldy. (For an example of the complexity of an associative network model that would be required to account for even a small subset of the phenomena of concern in social memory, see Wyer & Carlston, 1979.) We point out specific problems that a network model has in accounting for several memory and judgment phenomena in the course of our subsequent discussion. Suffice it to say at this point that a more flexible conceptualization seems necessary to handle the diversity of the phenomena that exist. The conceptualization we propose provides this flexibility. At the same time, it has

---

1. Not all models that employ an associative network metaphor are "spreading excitation" models (cf. Anderson & Bower, 1973). In fact, our use of an associative network in conceptualizing the representation of person and event information (Chapters 7 and 8), as well as the structure of noun and attribute concepts in this chapter, does not make this assumption.

specific implications for memory storage and retrieval phenomena that are of considerable importance.

We begin by formalizing a basic assumption about the organization of information in the Permanent Storage Unit.

Postulate 4.1. The Permanent Storage Unit consists of a set of content-addressable storage bins. Each bin is identified by a header whose features define the bin and circumscribe its contents.

Three types of bins are postulated. One, *semantic* bin serves as a mental "dictionary." Its contents are usually used to interpret single pieces of information (or, in some cases, configurations) independently of the particular person, object, or event to which they refer. Other, *referent* bins are analogous to cognitive "encyclopedias." They contain one or more pieces of information about either a particular referent (Richard Nixon, last Saturday's cocktail party) or general ones (U.S. Presidents, cocktail parties). The third, *goal* bin is a specific type of referent bin. It contains various procedures (goal schemata) that specify the cognitive steps involved in attaining a particular objective. The content of semantic and referent bins, and their role in cognitive functioning, differ in important ways, and each type is worth discussing in some detail.

The Semantic Bin

The semantic bin, unlike referent bins, is directly accessible to the Comprehender (see Figure 2.1). Therefore, its contents often come into play at an early stage of processing, when the stimulus input information transmitted from the Sensory Store must be encoded. However, the concepts contained in this bin may also be retrieved by the Executor and sent to the Encoder/Organizer for use in performing higher order semantic encodings of information that are necessary in order to attain specific processing goals (e.g., deciding what traits are implied by a person's behavior, etc.).

In refinements of the model we propose, it may prove necessary to postulate different semantic bins for different types of concepts or different knowledge domains. For the present, however, we assume that all of the semantic concepts that are used to understand the denotative meaning of stimulus information are stored in a single bin. The concepts that are contained in this bin may vary in type and complexity. Here, we discuss four types that are of particular relevance to social information processing: *noun* concepts, *attribute* concepts, *action* concepts, and *propositional molecules*.

Noun Concepts

Noun concepts refer to general or specific entities (e.g., "doctor," "lawyer," "Ku Klux Klan," etc.). They may be conceptualized in network terms as each consisting of a central node that represents the concept itself and peripheral nodes depicting sets of features that denote this concept. These associated features may include (a) alternative names of the concept, (b) a general definition of it, and (c) prototypic representations of its referent, each consisting of a configuration of attributes in a specifiable relation to one another. Thus, the concept "person" might be represented in a manner similar to that shown in Figure 4.1a. Note that two alternative prototypic nonverbal representations are indicated. This recognizes the possible existence of two or more configurations of features that, although qualitatively different from one another, are equally "prototypic." In general, the features composing these configurations may be verbal (propositional), nonverbal (analogue), or both.

The stimulus information that is interpreted in terms of a noun concept may refer to the concept by name, or may consist of a configuration of defining and characteristic features. For example, the concept shown in Figure 4.1a could be activated by either the word "person" or by a physical stimulus whose features exemplify one of the prototypes. Thus, the comprehension of each type of input information may involve the use of the same mental concept. Three other observations are worth making at this point.

1. Our conceptualization recognizes the distinction between a concept itself and the name attached to it. In fact, a noun concept (as well as other types of concepts we will discuss) may have several different names. Each name functions as a feature that may activate the concept if it is contained in a communication. On the other hand, different concepts may sometimes have the same name, just as they may have other attributes in common. (For example, "strike" is the name of two different noun concepts, one of which refers to an action taken by workers in a labor dispute and the other of which refers to a pitch in baseball at which the batter swings and misses.) Consequently, a word that is presented out of context may activate any of several different noun concepts, depending on which one happens to be most easily accessible in the semantic bin. At the same time, applying a verbal label to a stimulus in one domain will not activate other concepts relevant to other knowledge domains that have the same name. Evidence reported by Tulving (1983) supports this implication.

2. The set of defining features that is located at one peripheral node of a noun concept is independent of the features at other nodes. This means that the use of the concept to interpret information containing one set of features does not necessarily lead other sets to be activated. One interesting implication of this is that a concept may sometimes be activated and applied to a referent without the name

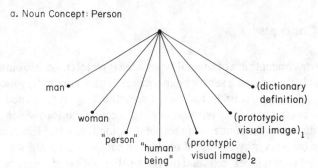

a. Noun Concept: Person

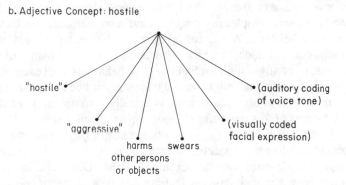

b. Adjective Concept: hostile

Figure 4.1 Network representation of (a) the noun concept person and (b) the attribute concept hostile.

of this concept ever coming into play. Phenomenologically, this means that a person may sometimes interpret information in terms of a concept without becoming aware of the name of the concept that was used.[2] Additional, more important implications of the assumption will become clear presently.

3. Noun concepts may sometimes refer to a type of person or object to which a referent bin also pertains. However, the cognitive representations that exist at these two memory locations, and their role in information processing, are quite different. We elaborate this distinction in the context of discussing referent bins.

---

2. This will theoretically occur when the concepts are applied by the Comprehender at the initial level rather than by the Encoder/Organizer. Thus, the activation and encoding of information in terms of the concept is presumably performed automatically, without conscious awareness (see Chapter 2).

Attribute Concepts

Attribute concepts are of several types. One type refers to attributes of objects that are closely tied to one's sensory experiences. These concepts, which may refer to colors, tastes, odors, sounds, and tactile sensations, are represented in a fashion similar to noun concepts. That is, they consist of a central node to which are attached alternative names of the concept and sets of defining features. However, several of the defining features may consist of one's own subjective sensations or reactions. Thus, both the verbal label "red" and the physical sensation of it may be understood in terms of the same attribute concept.

A second type of attribute concept refers to characteristics that are not directly related to sensory experiences. These concepts are typically abstract characterizations of actions and events that have previously been encoded at a lower level. The most obvious examples in the social domain are trait concepts that are used to characterize a behavior. A trait concept can also be conceptualized as consisting of a central concept node, to which are attached alternative names of the concept and alternative configurations of features (e.g., behaviors) that exemplify it. Thus, the trait concept "hostile" might have the form illustrated in Figure 4.1b.

A third type of attribute concept is actually a combination of the first two types. Concepts of this type refer to *emotional* or *affective states* ("happy," "sad," "angry," etc.). The features of these emotion concepts include alternative names of the concept and, like trait concepts, alternative configurations of semantic features (e.g., behavior descriptions) that exemplify them. Like concepts pertaining to sensations, however, their defining features include a cluster of one's own subjective (e.g., physiological) reactions. Each type of feature set may activate and be interpreted in terms of the same concept. Thus, for example, people may describe another person as angry because features of an overt behavior they observe correspond to those of a prototypic behavior that they use to define "angry." Alternatively, they may describe themselves as angry based on an observation of their *own* behavior (cf. Bem, 1967, 1972; Schachter, 1964; Schachter & Singer, 1962). On the other hand, people may also describe themselves as angry because they experience the particular subset of subjective reactions that they use to define the concept. As we will see, this interpretation of emotion concepts permits their role in cognitive functioning to be conceptualized in much the same manner as the role of other semantic concepts (for a similar view, see Bower, 1981). This proves to be a powerful tool in understanding the influence of affect and emotion at many stages of information processing. We return to this matter in Chapter 12.

Different attribute concepts (like different noun concepts) may have the same verbal label (name). Thus, "hard" refers to a different concept when it is used to describe a physical object than when it is used to describe a mathematical problem or when it is applied to a person.

Action Concepts

Concepts that refer to actions are more complex than noun or attribute concepts. This is because their definitions consist of sets of features that are in a specified a priori relation to one another. In the social domain, the action concepts of greatest interest pertain to behaviors. Like other semantic concepts, an action concept may be thought of as consisting of a central node to which alternative verbally and nonverbally coded configurations of defining features are attached, along with verbal or symbolic descriptions of the concept itself. However, the referent of these concepts cannot typically be conveyed by a single word. Rather, the specification of an action concept includes not only the action, but also the type of actor and, in some instances, the object toward which the action is directed and the type of implement involved (Rumelhart, 1984; Rumelhart & Ortony, 1977). Moreover, the actor, object, and implement are often in some specifiable spatial relation to one another. For this reason, a schematic representation of this sort of concept can be rather complex (for an example, see Rumelhart & Ortony, 1977). It will suffice for our purposes to view an action concept as simply an actor-action-object-implement configuration whose components (actor, object, etc.) are spatially and/or temporally related. Each component of the configuration functions as a *variable* that can be instantiated in terms of a specified range of *values*. The verbs specified in different action concepts may have the same name, and so other components are necessary to specify it completely. Thus, for example, different concepts are used to interpret "John hit the ball" and "the ball hit John." Similarly, different concepts are used to interpret "John broke the window," "John broke the bubble" and "John broke his promise."

Several alternative configurations of features may define a given action concept. These configurations may be coded either verbally or nonverbally. If the features of stimulus information provide a good instantiation of one of the configurations, they may be interpreted as exemplifying the concept. In some instances, however, input information (e.g., a verbal statement) may not specify all of the essential features of a configuration. "The boy hit the baseball," for example, does not specify the implement. This missing feature may therefore be assigned a "default value" (e.g., "bat") based on the prototype used to interpret it. Similarly, "She questioned the witness" may be understood in terms of a prototype that leads "she" to be assigned the default value "lawyer." When a verbal statement of this type is interpreted by the Comprehender, these default values are added to the encoding of the statement that is transmitted to the Work Space for further processing. Consequently, because only this latter representation is likely to be available later on, these additional features may subsequently be recalled as actually having been specified in the information. For evidence demonstrating this principle, see Barclay, Bransford, Franks, McCarrell, and Nitsch (1974).

Although the names of most action concepts contain a verb specification, the reverse is not true. That is, not all concepts whose labels contain a verb are action concepts. Many verb phrases are more appropriately conceptualized as referring to attribute concepts. For example, "behaves in a friendly manner," like "friendly," would presumably be encoded in terms of an attribute and not an action concept. "Keeps to oneself," "stutters," or "dresses sloppily" would also be attribute concepts despite the fact that they contain verbs. Therefore, the distinction between attribute concepts and action concepts is not simply one of whether the concepts are described by an adjective or a verb. As these examples indicate, the a priori classification of some concepts is inherently ambiguous. Fortunately, the validity of the proposed formulation does not depend on this classification.

Propositional Molecules

The fourth type of semantic concept is the most complex. Noun and attribute concepts are often used to interpret single words, or configurations of features that exemplify them, and action concepts are required to interpret single subject-verb-object sentences. In contrast, the fourth type of semantic concept we consider is typically used to interpret interrelated *sets* of statements. These concepts may be viewed as generalizations about ourselves, other persons, and events that constitute part of our general knowledge of how things function in the physical and social world in which we live. These generalizations may often pertain to temporal or causal relations among objects and events (e.g., "Smoking causes lung cancer," "What goes up most come down," "People with similar interests like one another," "People get tipsy if they drink too much") that can often be applied in interpreting particular events or situations that we encounter.

Perhaps the most formal conceptualization of the structure of these types of concepts and their role in cognitive functioning is provided by Abelson and Reich (1969; see also Wyer & Carlston, 1979; Wyer & Gordon, 1984) in the context of *implicational molecule* theory. Abelson and Reich note that many generalizations of the form noted above can be conceptualized as a set of interrelated statements that are "bound together by psychological implication." For example, the generalization "Smoking causes lung cancer" can be unpacked into a two-statement molecule of the form:

[A smokes; A has (or will get) lung cancer],

where A is a general class of persons to whom the statements pertain. Similarly, the generalization "People with similar interests like one another" could be unpacked into a three-statement *"similarity- attraction"* molecule of the form:

[A likes X; B likes X; A and B like one another],

where A and B are categories of persons and X is a category of persons, objects, or activities. Although the categories of people and objects to which the statements in a molecule pertain may often be large, they are not universal. Thus, the molecules do not necessarily apply to all statements that happen to have the form of those that compose them. ("Spinach," for example, would presumably be outside the range of values that X can take in the similarity-attraction molecule indicated above.)

The use of propositional (implicational) molecules to interpret information is similar to the use of action concepts. That is, if information one receives contains features that exemplify a sufficient number of the features of a molecule, the molecule is activated and applied. When not all of the features of the molecule are specified in the information, the unspecified features may be assigned "default values." This possibility is formalized by Abelson and Reich (1969) in terms of a *completion principle*. Specifically, if all but one statement in a molecule is instantiated in terms of the information presented, the molecule will be applied and, as a result, an instantiation of the remaining statements will be inferred. This latter instantiation is equivalent to a default value, and is presumably added to the cognitive representation of the information that is formed.

To give an example, suppose people have a "purposive behavior" molecule reflecting the generalization that people do things to get what they want. This molecule may have the form:

[A wants Y; X causes Y; A does X].

If the molecule is applied to information that Mary (an instance of A) wants to go to Europe (an instance of Y) and is saving money (an instance of X), the first and third statements in the molecule are instantiated. Consequently, applying the molecule to the information would lead to an instantiation of the second, unmentioned statement (i.e., to an inference that saving money will permit Mary to go to Europe). For similar reasons, information that Mary is saving money and that saving money will permit her to go to Europe should lead to the spontaneous inference that Mary wants to go to Europe.

Evidence that concepts akin to propositional molecules are applied in interpreting configurations of information has been obtained in a variety of research paradigms (cf. Bear & Hodun, 1975; Loken & Wyer, 1983; Picek, Sherman, & Shiffrin, 1975; Sentis & Burnstein, 1979; for a discussion of this research and its implications for implicational molecule theory; see Wyer & Gordon, 1984). A rigorous application of the theory is nonetheless difficult for several reasons. For one thing, individual differences in the number and type of implicational molecules that are formed, and in the range of persons and objects to which they apply, are undoubtedly much greater than the differences in the number and applicability of other semantic concepts we have discussed. Thus, although concepts resembling the similarity-attraction and purposive behavior molecules we used as examples are undoubtedly widely shared among members of our culture, considerable individual differences exist in the definitions of the noun and verb concepts involved in them, and, therefore, in the range of situations to which they are applied. Moreover, other molecules may be quite idiosyncratic to an individual or subculture.

Second, the application of an implicational molecule to the information presented in any given instance may depend on how specific features of the information happen to have been encoded in terms of noun, attribute and action concepts. For example, suppose Bob likes Led Zeppelin and Mary likes Bach's Brandenburg Concertos. Whether this information is interpreted in terms of a "similarity-attraction" molecule, and, therefore, whether Bob and Mary are inferred to like one another on the basis of this information, depends on whether "Led Zeppelin" and "Bach's Brandenburg Concertos" are encoded as instances of the same concept ("music") or different ones ("rock" and "classical music").

The encoding of the action concepts specified in statements may also determine which of several alternative molecules is applied. For example, people may have not only a "similarity-attraction" molecule of the sort noted above but also a "competition" molecule (exemplifying the concept that "people who want the same thing dislike one another") of the form:

[A wants X; B wants X; A and B dislike one another].

A person who is told that Art and Bill are both interested in Sharon might apply either of the two molecules in interpreting this information. Which one is applied may depend not only on whether "Sharon" is within the range of objects to which "X" is applicable in each molecule, but also whether "is interested in" is encoded in terms of the action concept "likes" or, alternatively, "wants."

These difficulties do not seriously detract from the value of propositional molecules as theoretical tools in conceptualizing the semantic concepts that compose our general world knowledge and how this knowledge may be used to understand new information we receive. In the formulation we propose, these concepts function much like other semantic concepts, and their use is governed by similar processes. This will become clearer as our discussion in this volume progresses.

Interrelatedness of Semantic Concepts

The concepts contained in the semantic bin are theoretically stored and retrieved independently of one another. However, these concepts are nonetheless related in terms of the sets of features that define them and the conditions in which they are applied. For example, attribute concepts are often defined in terms of behaviors that must themselves be understood in terms of an action concept. The definition of an action concept typically refers to persons and objects that must be understood in terms of noun concepts. Moreover, the application of a propositional molecule may require the prior encoding of information in terms of all three of these other types of concepts. Therefore, the comprehension of information may sometimes involve a series of steps, requiring the retrieval and use of concepts of more than one type.

The Role of the Semantic Bin in Cognitive Functioning

The unique role of the semantic bin in social information processing is elaborated in Chapter 6, where we deal specifically with the effects of activating semantic concepts on the interpretation of information. However, two postulates concerning this role are worth noting in the present context as well.

Postulate 4.2. The retrieval of information from the semantic bin is under the direct control of the Comprehender as well as the Executor.

Postulate 4.3. Semantic concepts are not applied to input information by the Comprehender unless they are necessary to understand the denotative meaning of this information.

Postulate 4.2 simply formalizes an assumption made earlier. It implies that in many cases, the initial comprehension of information in terms of semantic concepts occurs automatically. Put another way, the selection of concepts by the Comprehender to encode information is not affected by specific processing objectives that exist at the time the information is received. This, of course, assumes that the information presented *can* in fact be interpreted in terms of concepts that are available in the semantic bin. This may not always be true. In some cases, for example, information may be anomalous. Compare the statements "John pounded the nail with a hammer" and "The hammer pounded the nail with John." The first statement can be interpreted by the Comprehender because "John," "nail," and "hammer" occupy positions in the statement that are reserved for specifications of the actor, object, and implement, respectively, and each is within the range of values that these variables can be assigned in a definition of "pound." The automaticity within which the encoding is made is intuitively evident from the fact that it is impossible for native English speakers *not* to understand the statement at the time they read it. In contrast, two elements of the second statement ("hammer", and "John") fall outside the range of values that the actor and implement can take in the action concept denoted by "pound." Therefore, the Comprehender cannot interpret it. In such an event, the statement is presumably routed to the Work Space with an indication that it cannot be understood. Then, depending on processing objectives, the Executor may either ignore the statement or, if understanding it is necessary to attain some higher order goal, may transmit it to the Encoder/Organizer to be understood through the application of more complex encoding and organizational processes. The concepts used to attain this objective may also be drawn from the semantic bin. However, their use may be quite different. (For example, the Encoder/Organizer may construct a mental image of a Disney-like cartoon scenario of a hammer overthrowing its animate master and taking revenge by using him as a bludgeoning instrument.)

Postulates 4.2 and 4.3 in combination have important implications. Input information can often be interpreted at two different levels of abstractness. Two general conditions arise. First, suppose that encoding at one level is *required* before encoding at the other level can occur, and that the first level of encoding is *sufficient* to comprehend the information without any further higher-level processing. Postulate 4.3 implies that the higher level encoding will not occur spontaneously at the initial comprehension stage. Rather, it will occur only at a later stage of processing, in the course of pursuing additional processing objectives.

In the domain of social information processing, these implications have particular relevance to the interpretation of information in terms of personality trait concepts. Overt behaviors are generally interpretable in terms of action and noun concepts, and personality traits are higher level attribute concepts that are applied only after comprehension at a lower level has occurred. Consequently, Postulate 4.3 implies that *behaviors will typically not be spontaneously encoded in terms of trait (attribute) concepts unless more detailed processing objectives require it.* The relevance of this implication will become clear presently.[3]

Similar considerations come into play in interpreting information in terms of propositional molecules. Suppose people receive information that Bob likes tennis, Peter likes tennis, and Bob likes Peter. These statements exemplify the three propositions contained in the similarity-attraction molecule noted earlier. However, the individual sentences can be interpreted independently of one another, without recourse to this molecule. Therefore, according to Postulate 4.3, the molecule will not always be applied. Rather, it will be applied only if the recipient of the information has an implicit or explicit objective of forming an impression of the situation or the individuals involved in it at a level beyond that of the

---

3. This implication, which is potentially of great importance for an understanding of person impression formation as well as other social information processing goals, is in fact contrary to conclusions drawn by Uleman and his colleagues (Winter & Uleman, 1984). We believe, however, that this contradiction can be reconciled, and that Uleman's research findings are in fact quite consistent with the formulation we propose. We elaborate on this matter in Chapter 6.

sentence. For example, the molecule is more likely to be applied if the sentences are read in the context of a story than if they are presented out of context, in a list that people receive for the purpose of trying to remember them.

Different considerations arise when concepts at different levels of specificity can be used to encode information but encoding at neither level is a prerequisite for encoding at the other. Then, it is *not* necessarily the case that stimulus information will always be encoded in terms of concepts at the lowest level of abstractness. Indeed, a strong implication of the formulation we propose (elaborated in Chapter 5) is that when two alternative concepts can be used to interpret a given set of stimulus information, the concept that is most easily accessible in memory in the bin containing them will be the one that is applied. This concept is typically one that has been used most frequently or recently (Srull & Wyer, 1979). In the present context, it seems reasonable to suppose that social learning has led some concepts (e.g., "dog," "cat," "flower") to be applied more often to stimuli than others that are more specific ("collie," "Siamese," "petunia"), thus making them relatively more accessible in the semantic bin. The more abstract concepts are therefore more apt to be used. A similar observation has been made by Rosch (1973) in conceptualizing "basic level" categories. Unlike Rosch, however, our conceptualization provides more directly for individual differences in the nature of this "basic level," and for conditions in which concepts at this level will and will not be used. For example, animal lovers may more frequently use concepts associated with specific breeds of dog, and therefore may be more inclined to apply "collie" in encoding a stimulus, than other persons. Moreover, the relative accessibility of semantic concepts at different levels of generality should be affected by situational factors of the sort we discuss in Chapter 6.

Referent Bins

Referent bins contain the knowledge one has accumulated about either particular persons, objects, and events or prototypic ones. Whereas the semantic bin functions as a mental "dictionary" of words and phrases, referent bins, in combination, serve as an "encyclopedia" of stored knowledge about one's physical and social world. In this respect, these bins are somewhat analogous to the memory organization packets (MOPs) postulated by Schank (1982), and many assumptions about their formation and use are similar. However, the present conceptualization differs from Schank's in terms of the rules for storing and retrieving information (see Chapter 5) as well as in the diverse types of representations that are postulated.

The referents of bins may vary in both type and generality. The bins of primary relevance to social information processing pertain to either individual persons, groups of persons or events (Ronald Reagan, last night's dinner with Carol), or more general ones (U.S. presidents, eating at a restaurant, World War II, etc.). Moreover, bin referents may either be a single concrete instance (e.g., "eating dinner with Carol at the Four Seasons last Saturday") or be unrestricted as to time and place (e.g., "eating dinner with Carol"). Thus, some referent bins contain information about only one experience with the referent, whereas others contain information about several different experiences.

A referent bin contains all of the processing outputs pertaining to its referent that have been transmitted to it by the Executor. When the referent is a person, one output could be a visual representation of the person. Another could portray a specific event involving the person, including an encoding of one's own behavior or subjective reactions. An output might also consist of a cluster of traits and the behaviors that define them, a representation of a judgment one has made, or a representation of an overt response. A referent bin pertaining to an event may contain a representation of a general sequence of episodes that typically occur in succession. Alternatively, it can contain a representation of a specific event sequence that took place in a particular situation, along with a characterization of the persons involved in it. As these examples show, events can be represented in person bins, and specific persons can be represented in event bins. *The nature of the mental representation is determined early in the processing sequence, and is independent of where it is subsequently stored and how it is indexed in memory.*

Referent bins are activated independently of one another on the basis of features contained in their headers (for details, see Chapter 5). They are nevertheless interrelated by virtue of the fact that the information in one bin often has features that are contained in the header of another. For example, a bin pertaining to Sigmund Freud may come to contain the feature "psychoanalyst," which is a feature in the header of a more general referent bin pertaining to this type of person. Alternatively, a "psychoanalyst" bin may contain the names of particular individuals, such as Freud, who are psychoanalysts.

One effect of this interrelatedness is that the information used to attain a particular processing objective may sometimes be based not only on material in the bin pertaining to the particular referent to which this objective directly pertains, but also on information in other bins. Thus, the goal of describing Freud may lead to the retrieval of attributes of Freud from a "Freud" bin, one of which is "psychoanalyst." This in turn may lead the "psychoanalyst" bin to be identified and searched for attributes that characterize this general type of person ("curious," "relaxed," "distinguished," etc.). (The mechanisms that underlie this process are specified more fully later in this chapter and in Chapter 5.) Thus, one's description of Freud may be based not only on previously acquired knowledge about Freud per se, but also on more general attributes that pertain to the types of individuals he exemplifies.

Some Conceptual Distinctions

Although the general distinction we have made between semantic and referent bins may seem intuitively clear, certain similarities and differences between them should nonetheless be mentioned explicitly to avoid confusion in our later discussion.

First, a referent bin may refer to a concept (e.g., lawyer) that is also contained in a general semantic bin. However, there is a fundamental difference between the representation contained in the two types of bins. For example, the representation of "lawyer" in the semantic bin is restricted to a single set of features that *subjectively defines* what a lawyer is. A referent bin pertaining to "lawyers" may also contain these definitional features (particularly in the "header" identifying the bin; see below). However, it is not *restricted* to them. It may also, for example, contain the names of particular lawyers, personal experiences one has had with lawyers, visual images of lawyers and their behavior, and general characteristics that are assumed to typify lawyers (articulate, rich, slippery, etc.) but are not definitional in character.

The semantic bin and referent bins differ in function as well as in content. For one thing, they often come into play at different stages of processing. As we noted earlier, concepts in the semantic bin are often used by the Comprehender to encode individual pieces of information at a very low level. In contrast, the contents of referent bins are used primarily to attain more specific higher-level processing objectives.[4] A second difference in the functions of the two types of bins can be conveyed intuitively by comparing responses to the question "What is a lawyer?" with responses to the question, "What do you know about lawyers?" The answer to the first question is likely to be based on a noun concept in the semantic bin, whereas an answer to the latter is likely to be based on the contents of a referent bin pertaining to "lawyers." To this extent, the distinction being made here is similar to the distinction between "meaning" and "knowledge" noted by Kraut and Higgins (1984).

Trait concepts vs. person representations. The above differences between the semantic bin and referent bins calls attention to a more specific distinction between *trait* concepts (e.g., "hostile") and representations of *persons* who possess the trait (i.e., "hostile persons"). The former concepts are in the semantic bin. In contrast, the latter person representations are typically located in a referent bin pertaining to this type of person. (This assumes that persons have not learned an objective definition of a "hostile person" in the same way they have learned the definition of "lawyer.") The features of a trait concept "hostile" are restricted to those that descriptively imply this trait and therefore serve to define it. In contrast, the

---

4. The only exception to this occurs in the free flow of thought; see Chapter 2.

representations of persons who possess the trait may contain many evaluative and descriptive features (e.g., authoritarian, stupid, unpleasant, etc.) that have nothing to do with hostility per se but have been associated with prototypic or particular hostile individuals.

In the processing of information about people, trait and person concepts typically come into play at different stages. During impression formation, for example, trait concepts are invoked at an early stage of processing, when individual behaviors are interpreted in terms of these concepts or when explicit trait descriptions of a person are provided by others. Person concepts, however, become involved at a later stage, when encoded features of the person being described are compared to a prototype of (e.g.) a hostile person in order to determine if the individual is of this type, or when making inferences about other, unmentioned features of the person (i.e., other traits, likeableness, etc.) on the basis of this classification. This distinction proves to be extremely important in our discussion of several aspects of impression formation later in this volume.

Semantic vs. episodic memory representations. Although the content and function of semantic and referent bins is quite different, the distinction we have made is *not* simply a distinction between semantic and episodic memory as conceptualized by Tulving (1972; 1983). In Tulving's view, semantic memory constitutes knowledge that is not specific as to the time, place, and circumstances surrounding its acquisition, and does not include a representation of self as receiving agent. Semantic knowledge would therefore include the definition of "symphony orchestra," the knowledge that New York is east of Chicago, and the belief that Irishmen are heavy drinkers. In contrast, episodic memory consists of representations that include the circumstances in which the knowledge was acquired, and often one's own thoughts and behavior in the course of acquiring it. Thus, one's memory of the events that occur at a particular cocktail party, or in a laboratory experiment, would usually be episodic. Some knowledge could be either. For instance, the fact that the Empire State Building is south of 42nd Street would be semantic to the extent it is a fact that is represented in general world knowledge, but would be episodic to the extent that the building's location is computed on the basis of a personal memory of walking south from Times Square in order to get to it.

Although we recognize similar types of memories, we do not postulate separate episodic and semantic memory systems of the sort that Tulving assumes. Certainly the material contained in the semantic bin is a subset of the material that Tulving would consider to be in semantic memory. However, Tulving's distinction breaks down in our conception of referent bins. For example, the content of my "World War II" bin may contain a propositional representation of the fact that Hitler committed suicide along with many other individual facts that I have acquired over the years. These facts would constitute what Tulving would interpret as semantic knowledge. However, it may also contain a representation of my first visit to the

Anne Frank House in Amsterdam, which includes the emotional reactions I had while walking through the Franks' apartment and reading about the events that took place in the city during the war. Similarly, a referent bin pertaining to a personal acquaintance may contain not only personal experiences I have had with this person but also more abstract trait descriptions that are purely semantic in nature.

In short, a bin pertaining to a particular referent (e.g., "Paris," "football games," "my mother," "last year's New Years Eve party," etc.) may contain purely semantic memories as Tulving defines them, purely episodic memories, or some combination of both. In our conceptualization, the rules that govern the retrieval of information from a referent bin is the same regardless of the type of material contained in it. Thus, the proposed model actually argues against the existence of different memory "systems" as Tulving (1983) conceives of them.

This leads us to two matters that require elaboration. One is the organization and storage of information in referent bins. The second is the nature of the headers that identify these bins.

Organization and Storage of Information in Referent Bins

Three assumptions implicit in our previous discussion must now be formalized in terms of postulates. The first restates an assumption mentioned in our discussion of the Work Space in Chapter 3.

Postulate 4.4. Only the output of processing information in pursuit of a specific objective is transmitted to Permanent Storage.

In other words, if information is transmitted to the Work Space from the Comprehender but does not become involved in further processing, it is not permanently stored. This of course does not mean that fairly exact representations of stimulus input information never reach Permanent Storage. This is much more likely to occur, however, when the information processing load is low than when it is high. When several different pieces of stimulus information must be encoded or organized in order to generate an output of a particular processing stage, these pieces will often not be individually transmitted to Permanent Storage. Instead, only the representations that result from this higher-order, goal-directed processing will be sent. For this reason, it is crucial to understand the nature of the representations that are formed in the pursuit of different processing objectives if one is to predict both the amount and type of information that will ultimately be recalled about a referent and the influence it will have on judgments and decisions. Later chapters of this volume specifically address these questions.

Postulate 4.5. The output of processing at each stage is transmitted to and stored in a referent bin as a separate unit of information. The output of each stage is transmitted and stored in the order it is generated.

In other words, the representation of information that is formed at one stage of processing is stored (and therefore can subsequently be retrieved) independently of the representations that are formed of the same referent at other stages of processing or at other points in time. For example, suppose a subject is asked to rate the honesty of a target person based on information that (s)he gave someone an answer on an examination. The target's behavior may first be encoded as "cheated on an exam" or "dishonest." This may lead the subject to identify the target as a "dishonest person," and, finally, to assign the target a rating of -3 along a scale of honesty. Each of these outputs would be stored independently in a bin pertaining to the person, with the representation of "-3" on top, followed by a representation of the target as a dishonest person, and, finally, the encoding of the behavior itself ("cheated on an exam"). This postulate has obvious implications for the information that one is likely to recall and use at some later point in time.

Postulate 4.6. Information is transmitted to the bin pertaining to the referent to which processing objectives are relevant. If no previously formed bin pertaining to the referent exists, a new bin is formed.

This postulate has several implications. When stimulus information concerns several different referents, it could in principle be stored in a bin pertaining to each. In contrast, Postulate 4.6 implies that where the information is stored depends on the processing objectives that happen to exist at the time. Thus, for example, information that Mary slapped John at Sarah's dinner party refers to "Mary," to "John," and to "Sarah's dinner party." However, where the information is stored will depend on whether one's objective at the time the statement is processed is to form an impression of Mary, to form an impression of John, or simply to understand what went on at the party. In some instances, a person may pursue more than one objective simultaneously. However, if the person's objective in the above situation is only to form an impression of John, the information will only be transmitted to a "John" bin. Consequently, it is unlikely to be retrieved later on if the person is asked to recall information about Mary, and thus begins by searching the "Mary" bin.

Empirical evidence bearing on the validity of Postulates 4.5 and 4.6 is presented later in this chapter. However, a thought experiment may be useful at this point to convey some of their combined implications. Suppose subjects receive information that John slapped Mary at a dinner party in the context of four other pieces of information about John that did not involve Mary, four other pieces of information about Mary that did not involve John, and several additional pieces of information that involved neither John nor Mary. The information is ordered in such a way that the serial position of the target item, "John slapped Mary," is the same in all cases. For some subjects, however, this item is the first piece of information about John but the fifth (last) about Mary, whereas for others it is the first piece of information about Mary but the fifth about John. Subjects who receive this information with the goal of forming impressions of both John and Mary should form separate bins for John and Mary, and should store information in each bin that is specific to its referent. In contrast, subjects who receive the information with the objective of understanding what went on at the dinner party should form a single "party" bin. If the different pieces of information are stored independently of one another in the bins to when they are sent, the contents of the bins formed in each task objective condition should resemble that shown in Figure 4.2, where M refers to the pieces of information about Mary alone, J to the pieces of information about John alone, and JM to the target item concerning both John and Mary.

Note that subjects whose goal is to form impressions of John and Mary should store the target item in both the "John" bin and the "Mary" bin. However, its location in relation to other items contained in the two bins is different.

Therefore, suppose that subjects in each condition are later asked to recall either (a) information about Mary or (b) information about John. Assume that information is more likely to be retrieved if it is near the top of the bin being searched than if it is not (an assumption that we will formalize presently; see Chapter 5). Several predictions follow. For example, subjects who were originally told to form an impression of the party should recall the target item equally well, regardless of which person they are asked to recall information about and regardless of the position of the item in the sequence presented about this person. This is because the item is in the same position in the "party" bin in each condition.

In contrast, the recall of the target item by subjects who were asked to form separate impressions of the two individuals will depend substantially on *both* of these factors. Specifically, if the target item was the first item presented about John (but the last about Mary), they should recall it more easily if they are asked to recall information about Mary than if they are asked to recall information about John. However, if the target item is the last presented about John (and the first about Mary), the reverse should be true.

The predictions we have generated in our thought experiment are based on one somewhat tenuous assumption, namely, that the individual items of information presented under impression formation conditions are stored independently of one another. This assumption may hold when the information is acquired over a period of time, so that each piece has already been deposited in a bin pertaining to the person by the time the next piece is received. When information about a person

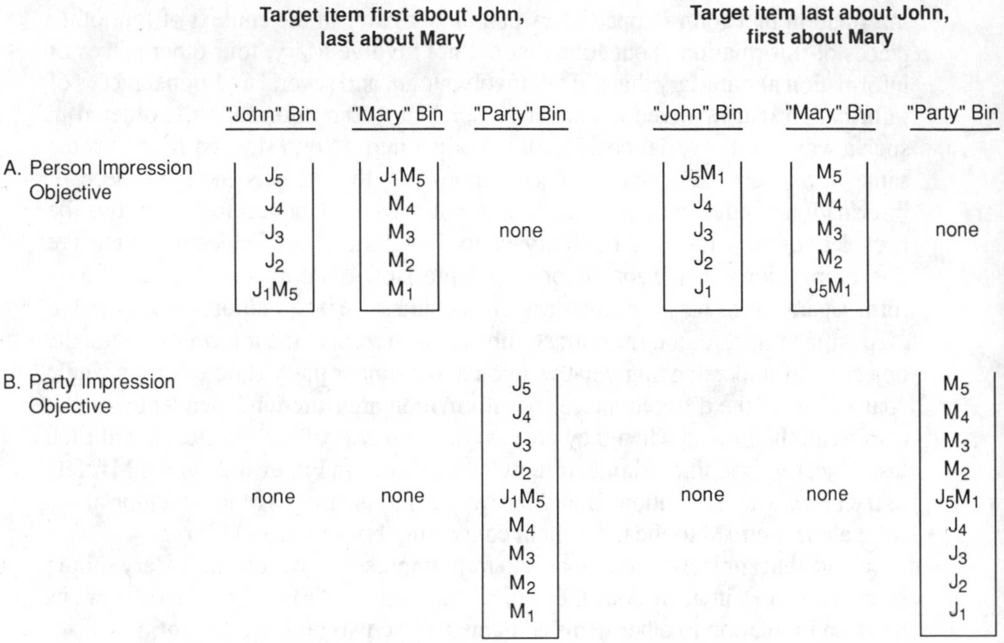

	Target item first about John, last about Mary			Target item last about John, first about Mary		
	"John" Bin	"Mary" Bin	"Party" Bin	"John" Bin	"Mary" Bin	"Party" Bin
A. Person Impression Objective	J_5 J_4 J_3 J_2 J_1M_5	J_1M_5 M_4 M_3 M_2 M_1	none	J_5M_1 J_4 J_3 J_2 J_1	M_5 M_4 M_3 M_2 J_5M_1	none
B. Party Impression Objective	none	none	J_5 J_4 J_3 J_2 J_1M_5 M_4 M_3 M_2 M_1	none	none	M_5 M_4 M_3 M_2 J_5M_1 J_4 J_3 J_2 J_1

Figure 4.2 Hypothetical bins formed by subjects with (a) the objective of forming an impression of John and Mary, and (b) forming an impression of the cocktail party, based on separate pieces of information about John and Mary. J and M refer to items about John and Mary, respectively. JM denotes the target item pertaining to both John and Mary. Subscripts denote the serial position of the item in the sequence of those pertaining to the person to whom the item refers.

is presented within a short period of time, however, subjects with an impression formation objective may construct a single representation of the individual that contains all of the presented behaviors and may store them in memory as a single unit. The order in which the items were originally presented may not be an important factor in locating the items within such a representation, and thus in the likelihood of remembering them. Therefore, the predictions outlined above may not hold in this case. This possibility is discussed in greater detail in Chapter 7.

Despite this qualification, our thought experiment makes salient an important point. That is, the *combination* of (a) subjects' initial processing objectives at the time they receive information (which affects where the information is stored) and (b) their objectives at the time of recall (which determines where the information is sought) potentially plays a vital role in understanding what material will actually be remembered and used as a basis for judgment.

Headers

Each referent bin is theoretically identified by a header that specifies the general nature of its contents. The features of a bin header determine what information is stored in the bin. They also determine whether or not the bin will be identified in the course of searching for information relevant to a particular processing objective.

Postulate 4.7. The header of a referent bin consists of (a) a name that specifies the referent and (b) a set of features that are strongly associated with it.

A bin's referent may be either a person or event in general or may be restricted as to time and place. For example, one might have a bin denoted "John" that refers to an acquaintance, but also more situation-specific bins that refer to "John in high school," "John at the office," or "John at the 1984 Rose Bowl game." These latter bins are presumably distinguished from the more general one by features other than "John" (e.g., "high school," "office," etc.) that are specified in their headers.

A bin header may contain either a nonverbally coded (e.g., visual) or propositional representation of what its referent looks like. It may also include general attributes that have become strongly associated with the referent, or even encodings of one's affective reactions. Thus, for example, the header of one's "Richard Nixon" bin might include the features "President" and "is dishonest" as a result of learned associations between these features and the referent. The strength of association of header features with the referent may vary. However, all header features are associated sufficiently strongly with the referent that they are attached to it without searching for additional information bearing on their applicability.

Postulate 4.8. The features of a bin header are applicable to all of the individual units of information contained in the bin.

A piece of information may sometimes contain all of the features specified in the header of a referent bin. However, this is neither a necessary nor a sufficient condition for the information to be stored in the bin. As implied in our discussion of Postulate 4.7, the storage of information in a particular referent bin is determined in part by the processing objectives that exist at the time the information is received as well as the features of the information itself. By the same token, a piece of information may be stored in a bin even if some of its features are irrelevant to, or even inconsistent with, header features, provided the features of the header are all *applicable* to the information being stored. As an example, the header of one's "Richard Nixon" bin may contain "President" and "dishonest." Nixon's establishment of diplomatic relations with China is irrelevant to the header feature "dishonest." A representation of the event may nevertheless be stored in the bin because the event occurred at the time the header features are applicable. Honest behaviors that Nixon performed during this period might also be encoded and stored in the bin despite the fact that "dishonest" is in its header. On the other hand, knowledge of Nixon's behavior as Vice President under Eisenhower, or when running for Governor of California, is less likely to be stored in this bin, as the feature "President" is not applicable to Nixon at these earlier stages in his political career. This should occur only if the knowledge about Nixon's earlier political behavior were considered in the course of attaining an objective that pertained to Nixon as President. Otherwise, it would be stored in a bin that refers to an earlier stage of Nixon's life, or in a general "Nixon" bin that is not restricted to his time as President.

As the above example implies, the features of different bin headers may overlap. That is, there may be a general bin pertaining to "Nixon," but also bins pertaining to "Nixon as President," "Nixon as Governor of California," etc. Analogously, the header of a general "restaurant" bin may contain "menu," "tip," "waiter," and other features that are associated with restaurants *in general*, and the bin itself may contain representations of events that occur in a typical restaurant (i.e., prototypic event sequences). However, the same features plus "dinner jacket" may compose the header of an "expensive restaurant" bin, which contains knowledge about events that are typical of this more restricted subcategory of restaurants (having wine served chilled in a bucket of ice, a chamber music ensemble, etc.).

Bins whose headers have features in common may nonetheless contain quite different types of information. This is because the processing objectives that lead information to be stored in the bins may differ. In many cases, the generality of the information stored in a bin is likely to correspond to the level of generality of its referent. For example, bins pertaining to "football games," "University of Illinois football games," and "the 1983 Illinois-Michigan football game" contain quite different representations at different levels of abstractness. Therefore, the question "Describe _____" is likely to elicit quite different responses, depending on which referent is specified in the request. The rules that govern which bin is identified under different conditions are stated more specifically in Chapter 5.

A question arises as to the conditions under which referent bins are formed about general types of persons or events rather than specific ones. Such bins are not formed automatically. Rather, their formation is governed by Postulates 4.6

and 4.8. That is, a general referent bin is formed only if an abstract concept of a referent is developed in the course of attaining a processing objective that requires it. Thus, for example, a person who meets her first two college professors may not spontaneously form a more general "college professor" bin. This will only occur if she has a processing goal (e.g., to decide what a "typical college professor" is like) that requires a general representation of a college professor to be constructed.[5] Moreover, when such a general bin is formed, it does not "erase" previously formed bins pertaining to specific instances.

When only one representation of a referent exists, there is little conceptual advantage in distinguishing between a bin containing this representation and the representation itself. The advantage of the bin construct is that it allows several alternative representations of the same referent to be stored in and retrieved from a single memory location.

Empirical Evidence

The most important implications of our conceptualization of permanent memory will become evident when we discuss search and retrieval processes in more detail. Before embarking on this discussion, support for several assumptions we have made is worth summarizing. These assumptions pertain to (a) the distinction between semantic bins and referent bins and the conditions in which they come into play in processing information, (b) the formation of separate bins for information about different referents, and (c) the fact that the units of information in a bin may be stored and retrieved independently of one another. We describe representative research bearing on each of these assumptions in turn.

The Distinction Between Semantic and Referent Bins

The semantic bin theoretically contains general noun, action, and attribute concepts that are used to interpret individual pieces of information independently of the particular referent to which the information pertains. In contrast, referent bins contain information about particular referents that have been stored as a result of pursuing some higher order processing objective. This distinction is supported by evidence that when semantic concepts are activated in the course of performing one task, they may influence the performance of subsequent tasks that are ostensibly unrelated to the first one. This may occur even when the specific events that took place in the first task cannot be remembered. Several experiments, which were

---

5. This assumption (among others) distinguishes the bin concept from that of a "memory organization packet" (MOP), which is apparently assumed to develop spontaneously (Schank, 1982).

originally designed to distinguish between semantic and episodic memory, bear on this implication of our model (for a more extensive review, see Tulving, 1983).

In a study by Jacoby and Witherspoon (1982), for example, subjects were shown a series of 60 words one at a time, and were asked questions that led them to focus on either the physical appearance of the words (i.e., "is the word written in capitals?"), its sound ("does it rhyme with chalk?"), or its meaning ("does it refer to a form of communication?"). Later, some subjects were presented the words again with instructions to indicate if they had been presented in the preceding task. Other subjects were shown the words tachistoscopically and asked to identify them. Subjects' performance on the recognition memory task was much better when they had previously considered the meaning of the words to be recognized than when they had responded to their sound or appearance. However, subjects' performance on the word identification task was high and independent of the sort of questions they had answered about the words.

In terms of the proposed conceptualization, this is precisely what we would expect. That is, performance on the initial task, regardless of the question asked, presumably requires the retrieval and use of a concept in the semantic bin. (This would be required simply to identify the stimulus as a word, which presumably was necessary in all conditions.) These concepts should therefore become more easily accessible and this increased accessibility should facilitate the later identification of words that denote them. (The processes that underlie this increased accessibility are described in the next chapter.) However, this does not mean that representations of these words, transmitted to the Work Space by the Comprehender, are transmitted to a *referent* bin in Permanent Storage pertaining to the "experiment." Thus, they may not be retrieved in a subsequent recognition task where performance is based on the representations contained in such a bin.

A similar interpretation can be given to a quite different study by Tulving, Schachter, and Stark (1982). Here, subjects first read a long list of words that were presented sequentially for five seconds each. Then, some subjects were given a recognition task, whereas others were given word fragments (e.g., A__A__IN, _E_D_L_M, etc.) and asked to complete the words to which they pertained. The tasks were performed either one hour or one week after seeing the original word list. Presumably, reading the original word list required the retrieval of concepts from a semantic bin by the Comprehender. Since these were uncommon words, redepositing them on top of the semantic bin should increase their accessibility. However, the representation of these words, transmitted to the Work Space, may not be stored in a referent bin, as their storage in such a bin is not relevant to any processing objectives that exist at the time. Therefore, subjects may not be able to retrieve them later, when information from referent bins is sought. Consistent with this reasoning, performance on the recognition task decreased substantially over the seven-day interval. In contrast, performance on the word fragment completion task was facilitated by reading the word list, and this facilitating effect was maintained over the seven-day interval.

An interesting parallel to the Tulving et al. study was performed by Warrington and Weiskrantz (1974) using both amnesics and normals as subjects. Again, subjects first studied a word list, after which they performed both a recognition task and a word fragment completion task similar to that described above. Normals far outperformed amnesics on the recognition task; the probabilities of a correct recognition response were 72% and 25% in the two cases. On the word fragment completion task, however, amnesics slightly outperformed the normal controls (34% vs. 25%). This suggests again that the activation of semantic concepts in the course of responding to the original word list increased the accessibility of these concepts in the semantic bin, and therefore facilitated performance on a task that required retrieval of the concepts from these bins. This was true for both amnesiacs and normals. However, only the normal subjects stored the words to be learned in a referent bin in Permanent Storage pertaining to the "experiment," and so only these subjects could subsequently recognize the words as having been presented.

The series of studies summarized above are obviously not relevant to *social* information processing per se. However, somewhat similar conclusions can be drawn from a social judgment study by Bargh and Pietromonaco (1982). In this study, subjects were initially asked to perform a "perceptual vigilance" task that required them to press a button whenever a light flashed on the screen. In fact, the "light" was a word that in some cases was semantically linked to hostility. In a second, ostensibly unrelated experiment, subjects read a paragraph describing behaviors of a person that could be interpreted as either hostile or nonhostile, and were asked to form an impression of this person. Subjects' later judgments of the person's hostility increased with the number of times that hostility-related words had been presented in the earlier vigilance task. Yet, in a subsequent recognition experiment, subjects were unable to distinguish between the words that had been presented during the task and other, nonpresented words. These results provide further evidence of the distinction between semantic bins and referent bins, and of the different conditions in which they enter into cognitive processing. The vigilance task presumably does not require higher order processing of the sort that is postulated to be performed by the Encoder/Organizer, and so it should not lead information to be transmitted to a referent bin. Subjects' inability to identify the words employed in this task is therefore not surprising. Nonetheless, exposure to the hostile trait words during the vigilance task increased the accessibility of hostility- related trait concepts in the *semantic* bin. Consequently, it increased the likelihood that a hostile trait concept was retrieved and used to interpret the target's behavior in the subsequent impression task.

The Independence of Referent Bins

The second assumption concerns the fact that information about different referents is stored in separate referent bins that operate independently of one another (Postulate 4.6). This assumption can be evaluated by determining the amount and type of information that can be recalled about the referents to which the information is relevant.

Specifically, the probability of retrieving any given piece of information should decrease, on average, with the total number of items contained in the same bin. This "set size" or "list length" effect, which is also implied by several other memory models (Anderson & Bower, 1973; Raaijmakers & Shiffrin, 1980, 1981; Rundus, 1971, 1973), is also an implication of the present formulation, as we indicate in our discussion of search and retrieval processes (Chapter 5). On the other hand, the likelihood of recalling a unit of information from a given bin should *not* be affected by the amount of information contained in *other* bins. Thus, if this reasoning is correct, the effect of the amount of information presented about one referent on the recall of information presented about both this and other referents provides a way of determining whether the information is stored in a single bin or in separate ones. This strategy was used in a series of studies by Srull and his colleagues.

1. In one study (Srull & Brand, 1983), subjects in one (memory set) condition read information about the behaviors of two persons with instructions to learn and remember as many of them as possible. Subjects in a second (person impression) condition were told they would later be interacting with one of the two persons and to form an initial impression of each. The number of behaviors attributed to each of the two targets was systematically varied. Subjects were later asked to recall all the behaviors presented. The likelihood of recalling a given person's behavior decreased with the number presented about this same person under both instructional conditions. However, it decreased with the number presented about the *other* person only under memory set conditions. This suggests that subjects with the goal of forming person impressions, unlike those with the goal of simply remembering the behaviors, formed a separate bin for storing information about each target person. Therefore, the amount of material contained in one bin did not affect the ability to recall information from the other.

In interpreting these results, it is important to ensure that the effects obtained under person impression conditions were not simply due to a greater tendency for subjects in these conditions to make semantic distinctions between the items presented. A second study provided this assurance. Here, subjects read information consisting of both nouns and trait adjectives, all of which described a single individual. If subjects engaged in more semantically-based organizational processes under a person impression set, their recall of one type of item should not be affected by the number of items presented of the other type. In fact, however, between-category set size effects occurred under *both* instructional conditions. Therefore, the critical variable determining organization of the information under person impression conditions is the *referent* to which the information pertains, and is not just the semantic category to which it belongs.

2. When separate referent bins are formed, the activation of features of a particular bin header should lead this bin to be identified and the information contained in it to be recalled. Therefore, suppose subjects receive information about several persons with instructions to form impressions of them. Here, subjects should form a separate bin pertaining to each person, presumably denoted by the person's name. If this is so, recalling the name of a person should lead the bin pertaining to this person to be identified and therefore should facilitate recall of the behaviors contained in it. However, suppose subjects receive the information with the goal of remembering it. In this case, as noted above, they may store all information (both person names and behaviors) in a single bin. In this case, remembering persons' names should *not* facilitate behavior recall.

A study by Srull (1983) supports these predictions. Subjects received information about the behaviors of several different persons, each identified by name. Some were told to form an impression of each person and others to remember the information. In some conditions, the behavioral information was blocked by person. (That is, all behaviors pertaining to one person were presented, followed by all behaviors pertaining to a second, etc.) Processing objectives did not affect the number of person names that subjects recalled; apparently, blocking the behaviors by person made the person names equally memorable in both conditions. However, the names should be used to identify different person bins in impression formation conditions, and therefore their retrieval should facilitate the recall of the behaviors associated with these persons. This should not be the case in memory set conditions. Consistent with these predictions, impression set subjects recalled more *behaviors per person* than did memory set subjects.[6]

Effects of Information Order on Bin Formation

The research summarized above shows that behavioral information is stored in either the same or different bins, depending on the processing objectives that exist at the time the information is received. The organization of information into bins may also be affected by the order in which it is received. A study by Anderson and Hastie (1974), although designed for a different purpose, is consistent with the

---

6. In additional conditions of this study, where the behaviors were not blocked by person when they were presented, subjects with impression formation objectives recalled both more referent names and more behaviors per referent than did memory objective subjects.

proposed model's implications for the nature of these effects. Subjects read a series of behavioral statements including some that referred to "James Bartlett" (e.g., "James Bartlett rescued the kitten") and some that referred to the "best lawyer in town" (e.g., "the best lawyer in town caused the accident"). In *Before* conditions, the behaviors were preceded by a statement that James Bartlett was, in fact, the best lawyer in town. In *After* conditions, subjects were not given this information until all the behaviors had been presented. After receiving the information in one of the above conditions, subjects were asked to verify the validity of (a) behavior statements that had actually been presented, (b) statements that were not presented but could be derived from the knowledge that James Bartlett was the best lawyer in town (e.g., "James Bartlett caused the accident," "The best lawyer in town rescued the kitten"), and (c) statements that were neither presented nor derivable. The time to verify each item, and the percentage of verification errors made, were recorded.

From the perspective of the proposed model, it is reasonable to assume that subjects in the Before condition stored all of the behavioral information in a single bin whose header contained both "James Bartlett" and "the best lawyer in town." In such a bin, the behaviors attributed to James Bartlett and those attributed to the lawyer are not distinguishable, and, therefore, the ability to verify them should not depend on whether they were actually presented or "derived." This was in fact the case. As shown in Table 4.1, both derived items and presented items were verified equally quickly, and the proportion of errors was low (approximately 10%) in all cases.

A quite different situation obtains in the After condition. Here, separate "James Bartlett" and "lawyer" bins need to be formed at the time of information acquisition. Moreover, the final statement, that James Bartlett is the bast lawyer in town, would in this case simply function as an additional item of information about Bartlett, and therefore would be stored in the "James Bartlett" bin on top of the other, behavioral items about this referent. As a result, the "best lawyer in town" bin may be identified as a result of considering the item describing this feature in the "James Bartlett" bin. However, the latter bin cannot be identified on the basis of any item contained in the former. If this is true, the verification of presented and derived items should depend on whether the items pertain to James Bartlett or to the lawyer.

To see this, first suppose that subjects are asked to verify a statement about James Bartlett. They will presumably begin by searching the "James Bartlett" bin for this item. In doing so, however, they are likely to encounter "is the best lawyer in town," which is the first item in the bin. This feature, which once identified is transmitted to the Work Space, may later serve as a retrieval cue that causes subjects to identify and search the contents of the "lawyer" bin without completing their search of the "James Bartlett" bin. As a result, the likelihood of verifying a derived item about Bartlett (which is stored in the "lawyer" bin) should increase. However,

TABLE 4.1
Response Times and Errors in Recall as a Function of the Type of
Statement being Judged and the Point at which Subjects are told that
James Bartlett is the Lawyer*

	Response Times		Errors in Recall	
	Statements about James Bartlett	Statements about the lawyer	Statements about James Bartlett	Statements about the lawyer
Before conditions				
Original statements	2.98	2.76	8.9%	6.8%
Derived statements	3.11	2.75	10.4%	12.0%
After conditions				
Original statements	3.67	2.31	26.6%	2.6%
Derived statements	3.23	3.99	5.7%	37.8%

*Adapted from J. R. Anderson & Hastie (1974).

the likelihood of identifying an item about Bartlett that was actually presented should *decrease*. Results support both of these predictions. The average time required to verify derived items about Bartlett was actually less than that required to verify presented items (3.23 vs. 3.67 seconds, respectively). Moreover, the percentage of errors was much less for the former items (5.7%) than the later (26.0%). Thus, derived items about Bartlett were verified both more quickly and more accurately than presented ones.

Now consider the verification of behavioral items about the lawyer. In this case, subjects begin by searching in the "lawyer" bin. However, because no item in this bin pertains to Bartlett, their search will not be diverted to the "James Bartlett" bin. This should increase their ability to verify an actually presented item about the lawyer. By the same token, it should *decrease* their likelihood of verifying a derived item about the lawyer (i.e., an item in the "James Bartlett" bin). The results summarized in Table 4.1 support these predictions as well. That is, the time required to verify derived items was much greater than that required to verify presented items (3.99 vs. 2.31 seconds), and errors were much more frequent for the former items (37.0% vs. 2.6%).

One further implication of the proposed conceptualization concerns shifts in verification times over trials. Once separate bins are formed for storing information, these bins should be retained in memory. However, once a behavioral item about a referent is verified, a copy of this item should be returned to the bin corresponding to its referent (i.e., the referent to whom the immediate processing objective is relevant) regardless of the bin from which it was drawn (Postulate 10). If this is true, then after a series of trials, each referent bin should contain both derived as well as presented items, and the differences in verification times described above should be eliminated. Anderson and Hastie's data also support this subtle implication of the model.

Organization of Information Within a Referent Bin

A third assumption underlying the proposed conceptualization is that the different units of information *within* a referent bin are stored independently of one another (Postulate 4.5). A unit of information may consist of either a single feature or several different features, organized in a way that is dictated by the processing objectives that exist at the time the information was encoded. In each case, however, the unit is stored (and subsequently retrieved) separately from other units of information that are contained in the same bin.

This assumption is central to the formulation we propose, and permits several otherwise impossible predictions to be generated. Evidence supporting the assumption and its role in accounting for a wide variety of phenomena is particularly relevant to our conceptualization of retrieval phenomena (Chapter 5) and also to a consideration of the sort of representations that are formed of persons and how they are used to make judgments (see Chapter 7). A study by Wyer and Bodenhausen (1985) on memory for social events helps to underscore the distinction between the organization of features within a particular unit of information and the organization of the units themselves in the bin containing them.

In this study, subjects read about the events that took place at a cocktail party. The party was described from the point of view of a person who attended it. The material included two unrelated target events, each consisting of four actions. The actions in each event were described either in chronological or counter-chronological order. For example, one event concerning a mishap at the party was described chronologically as follows (each action is denoted by a number preceding its description):

> As Bill made his way to the bar, (1) he saw John reach to get an hors d'oeuvre. (2) As he did so, a guest bumped his arm. (3) He spilled his Bloody Mary on Susan's new white dress. (4) Susan called John an idiot and stalked off to the kitchen.

In reverse order, the event was described:

There was a commotion. (4) Suddenly, he heard Susan call John an idiot and stalk off to the kitchen. (3) John had apparently spilled his Bloody Mary on Susan's new white dress. It was an accident. (2) A guest had bumped John's arm and spilled his drink. (1) John had been reaching to get an hors d'oeuvre.

In addition to the order manipulation, the first two and last two actions making up each target event were either separated by descriptions of two other, unrelated events or were presented together. Finally, the order in which the two target sequences were mentioned in the story was varied.

Under the conditions of primary concern, some subjects were instructed to remember the story as well as they could. Others were told to empathize with the person from whose perspective the story was written and to imagine their reactions to the events that occurred.

Later, after reading the story and either a 5-minute or 20-minute delay, subjects were asked to recall the actions described in the order they came to mind. Then, they were given a list of the actions and told to rank the order in which the actions had been mentioned in the story they read.

Subjects with the goal of empathizing with the person who attended the party were expected to form separate units of information pertaining to each of the events described and, in the course of comprehending these events, to mentally reconstruct their chronological order. However, they were expected to store each of these temporally-ordered representations as a separate information unit in a "cocktail party" bin, with the most recently formed representation on top. Consequently, the more recently constructed representation (the representation of the target event that was mentioned last in the story) was expected to be recalled first. Given that a representation was retrieved, however, the actions contained in it were expected to be recalled in the order they were encountered in the representation (i.e., chronologically). In other words, presentation order was expected to govern the recall of the target events themselves, whereas chronological order was expected to govern the recall of the actions composing these events. Results supported these predictions. That is, empathy set subjects were more likely than memory set subjects to recall the more recently mentioned target event before they recalled the earlier one. At the same time, empathy set subjects were also more likely to recall the specific actions making up the events in chronological order, regardless of their presentation order or whether they were separated or together in the presentation sequence.

A more subtle implication of the model was also supported by this study. That is, subjects may tend to use the mental representations they formed of the events described as a basis for recall a short time after the information was presented because these representations are most easily accessible in the Work Space (Postulate 3.5). As long as the stimulus material is also in the Work Space, however, subjects should be able to report the presentation order of the information accurately if they are explicitly asked to do so. In contrast, once the Work Space has been cleared and subjects must rely on the information transmitted to Permanent Storage alone, this should not be the case. As implied by these considerations, subjects' free recall of the information presented showed a similar pattern under both short and long delay conditions. In contrast, subjects' rank orderings of the actions in terms of their presentation order (a measure of their ability to reproduce this order) were relatively accurate under short delay conditions, whereas their rank orderings after a long delay showed the same pattern as their free recall.

On one hand, these results are not very surprising. On the other hand, the different patterns of effects on within-event organization and between-event organization, which are not directly implied by most alternative models of memory (cf. Baker, 1978), point out the need to postulate different rules for organizing and storing independent events and interrelated ones. (For other evidence of the need to make this distinction, see Smith, Adams, & Schorr, 1978). According to the present model, the critical factor is whether subjects have reason to think about the events in relation to one another, either in the course of comprehending them or in the course of pursuing some higher order processing objective. This latter contingency is evident in a third condition conducted by Wyer and Bodenhausen in which subjects were instructed to form an impression of the party as a whole. In attaining this objective, subjects may attempt to preserve the overall sequence of events that took place in the party. In fact, subjects under this condition were even less likely to recall the most recently presented event first than were subjects with a memory objective. More generally, the contingency makes salient the need to take into account the different cognitive activities that are apt to be involved in attaining different processing objectives—a need that will continue to be apparent throughout this volume (see also Srull & Wyer, 1986).

Concluding Remarks

Our conceptualization of long term memory has several implications, many of which will become more apparent once the postulates governing information retrieval are stated more formally. A major feature of the conceptualization is its ability to take into account several different types of knowledge about people and events of the sort we acquire in daily life, and differences in the way that features of this knowledge are organized in relation to one another. Visual representations of a person or event, interrelated configurations of trait and behavior descriptions, propositions, and memories of our own thoughts and feelings, each of which may have its own unique structure, can be accommodated. These different types of representations constitute different units of knowledge. Therefore, they may be stored at a single memory location (bin), and later retrieved, independently of other units. The content and organization of the features composing different types of knowledge units must ultimately be specified, as we attempt to do in later chapters.

However, the important thing to note here is that although the model is flexible with respect to the particular types of knowledge units that are formed and stored in memory, it postulates a common set of processes to govern the retrieval of this information that are independent of the specific type of knowledge unit involved. These processes are explicated in the next chapter.

Chapter 5
Retrieval Processes

Having discussed the general structure of the two main information storage units we postulate, we are now in a position to state more formally the rules that govern the search and retrieval of information from these units. As usual, we do this in terms of a series of postulates (for a complete summary, see Appendix). Once the postulates are presented, we discuss some of their implications and provide some empirical examples of their applicability.

Theoretical Considerations

Heuristic Postulate

The first, *heuristic* postulate has been implicit in much of our previous discussion. To state it formally:

Postulate 5.1. No more information is retrieved for use in attaining a processing objective than is sufficient to allow the objective to be attained. When this minimal amount of information has been retrieved, the search terminates.

In one sense, this postulate is self evident. That is, people are obviously unlikely to conduct an exhaustive search of memory for all of the knowledge they have accumulated that is relevant to a particular judgment or decision. Rather, they retrieve and use only a small subset of this knowledge, apparently assuming that its implications are representative of the implications of all the knowledge they have acquired.[1]

A potential ambiguity in applying Postulate 5.1 in a specific situation is the criterion for "sufficiency." When, for example, a behavior must be interpreted in terms of a trait concept, a single concept is clearly sufficient, and the first applicable trait concept that comes to mind is the one that is typically used. In other cases, a person must make a judgment or decision to which many different pieces of information are potentially relevant. In such cases, several pieces may be considered, the actual number of which depends on the diversity of their implications and the importance of the judgment or decision to be made. ("Importance," in our conceptualization, is presumably reflected in the goal schema that is used to attain the judgmental objective.) Nonetheless, one of the more striking general findings that has emerged from the social cognition literature is how little knowledge is actually brought to bear on a judgment or behavioral decision, regardless of its importance (cf. Taylor & Fiske, 1978). We provide several examples of this phenomenon throughout this volume.

Retrieval of Information from the Work Space

The next two postulates, which concern the retrieval of information from the Work Space, have already been mentioned, and are repeated here for the sake of completeness.

Postulate 5.2. When information relevant to a processing objective is required, the contents of the Work Space are searched first.

Postulate 5.3. The search for information in the Work Space is random.

---

1. To this extent, Postulate 5.1 is akin to the "availability heuristic" proposed by Tversky and Kahneman (1973) to underlie frequency judgments. They hopothesize that judgments of the frequency of occurrence of an object or event are based in part on how easily instances of its occurrence come to mind rather than on a subjective frequency count of the actual number of such instances one has experienced or learned about. (For a further discussion of this and other types of heuristics, see chapter 9.) We are arguing that the context and implications of the most easily accessible information are used as bases for judgment.

The Identification of Referent Bins

1. General Considerations

If the Work Space does not contain sufficient information to attain a processing objective, material must be retrieved from a semantic or referent bin in Permanent Storage. The first step is of course to identify a bin whose contents are relevant to this objective. This step is stated more precisely in terms of the next three postulates.

Postulates 5.4. The relevance of a referent bin to a particular processing objective is determined by comparing the features in its header with a set of *probe cues* compiled by the Executor. These cues are a subset of the features contained in Compartment 1 of the Work Space at the time the information is sought.

This postulate is similar in some respects to assumptions made in other theoretical formulations of retrieval processes (cf. Bobrow & Norman, 1975; Norman & Bobrow, 1976; Raaijmakers & Shiffrin, 1980, 1981). The nature of the comparison between probe cues and header features is conveyed by the next postulate.

Postulate 5.5. The bin identified for use in attaining a particular objective is the one whose header (a) contains all of the features specified in the probe set and (b) maximizes the quantity

$$\frac{\Sigma S_{h \cap p}(i)}{\Sigma S_h(j)}$$

where $S_{h \cap p}(i)$ = the strength of the association between the referent and the ith feature that is common to both the header and the probe set, and $S_h(j)$ is the strength of association between the referent and the jth feature of the header.

This postulate takes into account the strength of association between the features defined in the probe cues and the referent as well as the number of these features. The feature that is most strongly associated with the referent is generally the referent's name. Thus, "Nixon" is more likely to lead a "Richard Nixon" bin to be identified than is "President" or "dishonest." However, the general implications of this postulate can be seen most easily by assuming for simplicity that all associations are of equal strength. Then, the equation reduces to the ratio of (a) the number of features that the probe cues and the bin header have in common to (b) the total number of features contained in the header.

Therefore, the likelihood that a particular bin is identified increases with the number of features in its header that are also specified in the probe set. However, it decreases with the number of header features that are *not* contained in the probe set.

An example may convey these implications more clearly. Suppose the header of one bin contains only feature A (e.g., "football games"), whereas the header of a second contains A, B, and C (e.g., "Illinois vs. Michigan football games"). Then, Postulate 5.5 implies that if the set of probe cues compiled by the Executor consists of only feature A, the first bin will be identified rather than the second. However, if the probe set contains A and B, the second bin will be identified rather than the first. In other words, the request to "describe a football game" is more likely to lead one to retrieve and report information from the "football game" bin rather than the "Illinois vs. Michigan football game" bin, whereas the request to "describe an Illinois football game" is more likely to lead to the recall of information from the "Illinois vs. Michigan football game" bin than from the more general one. As we noted earlier, a general "football game" bin is likely to contain general characteristics of football games (the fact that there are eleven players on a side, that the game begins with a kickoff, etc.), whereas the "Illinois vs. Michigan football game" bin contains representations of events that are specific to this game (e.g., a Michigan player intercepting an Illini pass late in the fourth quarter and running 55 yards for a touchdown) and not more general facts about how football games are played. To this extent, our conceptualization provides an account of why people usually respond in different ways to the two questions despite the fact that, in principle, each type of response is an appropriate answer to both questions.

There are obviously times when no bin header contains all of the features that are specified in a set of probe cues. When this occurs, the following postulate comes into play.

Postulate 5.6. When no bin is found that contains all of the features in a set of probe cues, the set is randomly subdivided into smaller subsets, and the search is repeated using these subsets as probe cues until a bin is found.

This postulate takes into account the fact that in many instances, a processing objective may concern a hypothetical referent about which one has no specific prior information. For example, someone may be asked to imagine a tiger walking down Fifth Avenue. The initial set of probe cues that are used to retrieve relevant information might include both "tiger" and "Fifth Avenue." However, a previously formed bin whose header contains both of these features is unlikely to exist. In this event, the probe set will be divided into subsets (in this case, "tiger" alone and "Fifth Avenue" alone), and information will be retrieved from the separate bins. This information may then be combined into a single representation by the Inference Maker, using procedures specified in an appropriate goal schema.

2. Extraneous Influences on Information Retrieval

In trying to remember something, we sometimes recall information that, although not totally irrelevant to the goal we are trying to attain, is nevertheless not exactly what we are looking for. Often, what we recall is a surprise to us. For example, we may suddenly remember a past experience, or a person we have known that we have not thought about in years. More generally, the information we recall may be affected by fortuitous events that are objectively unrelated to the purpose for which the information is to be used. These possibilities are implied by an aspect of Postulate 5.4 that appears, at first glance, to be innocuous, but in fact has far-reaching implications. That is, the cues that govern the identification of a referent bin are a subset of the features contained in the Work Space at the time information is sought.

To understand the implications of this assumption, suppose that based on instructions specified in a goal schema, the Executor selects a sample of k features from the material contained in Compartment 1 of the Work Space and uses them as probe cues to identify an appropriate referent bin. When only one processing objective is being pursued, little information is contained in this compartment other than that to which objectives are relevant. Under these circumstances, the features selected as probe cues are likely to be restricted to ones that are directly relevant to the attainment of the objective. In some instances, however, two or more goals may be pursued simultaneously. Alternatively, the Work Space may not have been cleared of the information relevant to a previous processing objective at the time the probe set pertaining to a new goal is compiled. Yet another possibility is that information irrelevant to any processing objective is transmitted to the Work Space by the Comprehender at the time a set of probe cues is being compiled. For one or more of these reasons, some features may fortuitously be selected as probe cues that are *not* relevant to the objective at hand. These goal-irrelevant cues may affect the referent bin that is identified, and consequently, the nature of the information that is retrieved.

Many anecdotal examples of these effects can be generated. Empirical examples abound as well. One is a study by Bower (1981) on the influence of mood on memory for past experiences. Subjects who had been induced to feel either happy or sad were asked to recall their early childhood experiences. Happy subjects recalled more happy experiences, and fewer sad experiences, than sad subjects. In terms of the model we propose, this effect would be accounted for in terms of Postulates 5.4 and 5.5. Specifically, the procedure for inducing happiness or sadness presumably led concepts associated with this emotion to be transmitted to the Work Space. Consequently, happy subjects were likely to have happiness-related concepts in the Work Space, whereas sad subjects were more apt to have sadness-related concepts located there. If the Work Space is not cleared immediately after the mood-induction task is performed, several of these emotion-related concepts may still be there when subjects are asked to recall their childhood experiences. Therefore, these mood concepts may sometimes be fortuitously included in the set of probe cues along with "childhood experiences."

A similar interpretation can be given to the effects of thinking about oneself on information processing. Suppose one happens to have been thinking about oneself at the time one is asked for information about a particular acquaintance. Then, "self" may fortuitously be included in the probe set along with the name of the acquaintance. This may lead to the identification and retrieval of information from a bin pertaining to one's personal interactions with this individual rather than a bin containing more general information about the person. More generally, Postulates 5.4 and 5.5 have implications for several effects of objective self-awareness (Duval & Wicklund, 1972) on the recall and subsequent processing of information. We consider this possibility in more detail in Chapter 13.

Finally, these postulates account for the fact that under conditions of high information load (e.g., when many other objectives are being pursued simultaneously), information pertaining to a particular objective may be more difficult to retrieve. Material related to other objectives may exist in the Work Space under these conditions, and so the probe cues selected are more likely to contain irrelevant features that, in combination with goal-relevant features, do not compose the header of *any* existing bin. Alternatively, the probe set may fortuitously lead to the identification of a bin whose contents are quite irrelevant to the objectives at hand.

Thus, Postulates 5.4 and 5.5 have implications for a variety of phenomena that are not often considered in relation to one another. We refer to these postulates quite frequently throughout this volume.

Semantic Bases for Judgments and Decisions

The next postulate takes into account the fact that in many instances, the features specified in a bin header may be sufficient to attain processing objectives without examining any information contained in the bin itself.

Postulate 5.7. Once a bin is identified, the remaining features of its header are searched for information relevant to the processing objectives being pursued. If these features and their implications are sufficient to attain these objectives, they are used without retrieving any information from the bin itself.

Thus, if "dishonest" is a feature in the header of one's "Richard Nixon" bin, it may be considered a sufficient basis for judging Nixon's honesty and a search for further information may not be performed. Alternatively, if one is asked to describe Nixon, one might do so on the basis of the header features without considering the more specific contents of the bin itself (some of which may have quite different implications).

Episodic Bases for Judgments and Decisions

When header features cannot be used to attain processing objectives, the contents of the bin itself are searched for goal-relevant information. Postulate 5.8 governs this search process.

Postulate 5.8. When the contents of a bin are searched for information relevant to a processing objective, the search proceeds from the top down. A unit of information is identified as potentially relevant if its features include the probe cues governing the search. The probability of retrieving any particular unit, given that units stored on top of it have not been used, is a constant.

This postulate takes into account the fact that retrieval processes are imperfect. That is, information may be "missed" in a search of memory for goal-relevant material. The probability of retrieving a given unit of potentially relevant information is nonetheless an increasing function of its proximity to the top of the bin.

To see this, suppose that two potentially relevant units of information, A and B, are on top of a referent bin, and that each of these units is sufficient to attain the processing objective being pursued. The probability of using the unit on top of the bin, A, is simply the probability of retrieving it, or p. The probability of using the second unit, B, is equal to the probability that the first item is missed and the second is identified, or $(1 - p)p$. Thus, the probability of using the second unit will always be less than the likelihood of using the first. This of course assumes that each of the two units is sufficient to attain the processing objective at hand. If both are necessary, the likelihood of retrieving the second unit, B, is the same as the likelihood of retrieving the first (p).

1. Interference Effects in Information Recall

Two additional implications of this postulate should be noted. First, assume for the moment that the search for information in a bin continues until a sufficient amount of goal-relevant information is identified. Then, the likelihood of retrieving a relevant piece of information should not be affected by the amount of goal-*ir-relevant* information stored on top of it. That is, the relative probabilities of retrieving items A and B in the above example are the same, regardless of whether they are the first and second units of information in the bin or the ninth or tenth, provided the units of information on top of them are all goal-irrelevant. On the other hand, the *time* required to retrieve these items should differ in the two cases. Thus, *the factors that affect the likelihood of retrieving information and those that affect the time required to do so are not always the same.*

Second, the identification of a piece of information as *potentially* relevant to the attainment of a processing objective does not necessarily mean that it will actually be useful. This is because the presence of the probe cues in a representation does not guarantee that the representation has the specific features necessary for attaining the goal at hand. On the other hand, the search process implies that clearly irrelevant material (i.e., information that does *not* contain the features specified in the probe cues) is bypassed without any consideration whatsoever.

This difference makes salient an important implication of our conceptualization that has yet to be empirically evaluated. That is, the presence of obviously goal-irrelevant information in a referent bin (i.e., information whose features do not include the probe cues governing the search) should theoretically have no effect at all on the retrieval and use of relevant material. In contrast, the presence of potentially relevant information, to the extent it is retrieved but found to be inapplicable, may interfere with the recall of actually relevant material. The reason for this is implied by the next two postulates.

2. Recency and Frequency Effects on Information Retrieval

The likelihood of retrieving a piece of information depends on the recency and frequency with which it was acquired and used in the past. These possibilities are implied by the model we propose as a consequence of the following postulate.

Postulate 5.9 (Copy Postulate). When a unit of information in a bin is identified as potentially relevant for attaining a processing objective, a copy of this unit is sent to the Work Space. Thus, the original position of the information in the bin is preserved. When the use of the information is completed, the copy of it is returned to the top of the bin from which it was drawn.

Postulates 5.8 and 5.9 have important general implications. Specifically, once a piece of information (or a copy of it) has been retrieved for use in attaining a particular processing objective, it is redeposited on top of the bin. Therefore, it becomes more likely to be retrieved again when information from the same bin is sought. This implies a strong *recency effect* on the retrieval and use of information, and this is true even when the information is no longer in short-term memory (for evidence of this see Baddeley, 1976; Baddeley & Hitch, 1974, 1977; Bjork & Whitten, 1974; Tzeng, 1973; Watkins & Peynicrioglo, 1983). Note, however, that "recency" in this context does not necessarily pertain to the time at which information is *acquired*. Rather, it pertains to the recency with which it was *used* in the past.

In addition, Postulate 5.9 also implies a *frequency* effect. That is, only a copy of the information is retrieved from a bin. After it is used, however, this copy is returned to the bin as a separate unit of information. This means that the more often a unit of information is used, the more often it is represented in the bin. Therefore, the more likely it is to be retrieved as a result of the probabilistic search implied by Postulate 5.8. Consequently, although the model implies that recency of use is the predominate factor underlying the retrieval of information from Permanent Storage, frequency emerges as a strong secondary factor.

It is important to note that if processing objectives can be attained on the basis of information in the bin header, a search for information in the bin itself does not occur (Postulate 5.7). Under these conditions, judgments will be similar regardless of the frequency or recency with which specific information bearing on them has been stored.

3. Terminating the Search for Information

People obviously do not conduct an exhaustive search for all of the goal-relevant information they have acquired. Sometimes, such information simply does not exist. At other times, it may exist but be difficult to access, and so the search is terminated before the information is identified. In the present model, the termination of information search is governed by the following postulate:

Postulate 5.10 (Stopping Rule). A referent bin will be searched for goal-relevant information until either (a) information sufficient for attaining the processing objectives has been found, (b) a total of n units have been retrieved that are inapplicable for attaining these objectives, or (c) a total of k identical units of information have been retrieved, whichever comes first.

This postulate is similar in several respects to the stopping rules proposed by Rundus (1971) and by Raaijmakers and Shiffrin (1981). It implies that the search for information will terminate if a series of retrieval attempts either does not produce any goal-relevant information at all or produces relevant information that has already been retrieved. The values of n and k are theoretically specified in the goal schema governing processing objectives, and may vary with the objective and its importance.

The third criterion for stopping the search of memory is of particular relevance to a phenomenon we noted earlier in our discussion of evidence bearing on the separation of referent bins (Srull & Brand, 1983; see Chapter 4). That is, in combination with Postulate 5.9, it implies a decrease in the likelihood of recalling a particular unit of information as a function of the number of units contained in the bin being searched, or in other words, a "negative set size" effect. Specifically, the recall of a particular unit of information leads a copy of this information to be returned to the top of the bin from which it was drawn. This increases the likelihood that this same unit of information will be recalled again, and correspondingly decreases the likelihood that information located below it in the bin will be identified. If the unit is in fact identified again, yet another copy of it will be deposited on top of the bin. The greater the number of items in the bin, the less the likelihood that all of the items will be recalled before at least one item has been retrieved a sufficient number of times to reach the stopping criterion. More parsimonious theoretical accounts set size effects may exist (cf. Anderson & Bower, 1973; Collins & Loftus, 1975; Raaijmakers & Shiffrin, 1980, 1981; Rundus, 1971, 1973). These effects are nonetheless a direct implication of the present model under conditions in which the units of information are stored and retrieved independently of one another.

Summary: The Determinants of Information Retrieval

The postulates outlined in this chapter imply that several different factors may influence the retrieval of information: the amount of processing of the information at the time it is first acquired, the number and strength of associations that exist between attributes that happen to come to mind at the time information is sought and attributes of the referent to which the information pertains, and the frequency and recency with which the information has previously been thought about. These factors have all, at one time or another, been identified by other theorists and have been found empirically to influence information recall. The uniqueness of the formulation we propose lies in its implications for *when* these factors are likely to come into play.

Several of these implications can be conveyed through a simplified example. Suppose a subject learns about several specific behaviors of a past acquaintance, George, for whom a bin in Permanent Storage has already been established.

Suppose that some of the behaviors are "honest" and others are "dishonest," and that the initial processing of the behaviors has led each one to be interpreted in terms of the trait that it exemplifies. Then, these separate encodings are presumably sent to a "George" bin as well as being temporarily retained in the Work Space.[2] If the subject is asked to judge George's honesty a short time after the information is received, the likelihood of judging George as honest (rather than dishonest) should depend on the relative frequency with which honest and dishonest behaviors are represented in the Work Space (for a more detailed discussion of this contingency and the reasons for it, see Chapter 3). After a longer delay, however, this may not be the case. If judgment-relevant features (i.e., "honest" or "dishonest") are contained in the header of the "George" bin, judgments should be based on these features and the information about his specific behaviors should have no effect. More generally, this implies that when a strong association exists between the target and the attribute being judged, the effects of new judgment-relevant information will only affect judgments made a short time after the information has been received but not after a long delay. When only a weak association exists between the target and the attribute to be judged, new judgment-relevant information will affect judgments regardless of the time interval between information acquisition and judgments.

Moreover, the effects of new information may be different once it is transmitted to Permanent Storage than it is when it is still in the Work Space. Suppose, for example, that the order in which individual honest (H) and dishonest (D) behaviors are encoded and sent to Permanent Storage is HHHHHHDDDD. Before the Work Space is cleared, judgments are based on a random search of this memory unit, and so the more frequently represented behavior should be most likely to be retrieved and used as a basis for judgment. In other words, George should be judged to be "honest." In Permanent Storage, however, the four dishonest behaviors, which were transmitted last, should be on top of all six honest behaviors, and therefore should be more likely to be retrieved. Therefore, once the Work Space is cleared, George should be judged as "dishonest."

The contingencies outlined above have some more general implications. For example, Markus (1977; Markus & Smith, 1981) has argued that people will respond more quickly to questions about an attribute if they are "schematic" with respect to the attribute (i.e., if they both believe that the attribute applies to them and consider it to be important) than if they are not. Assuming that the attributes

---

2. When a person's behaviors are all learned within a short period of time, they may not be encoded and stored separately. Rather, the behaviors that exemplify each trait concept may be organized into a single "trait-behavior cluster" and stored as a single unit of information (Gordon & Wyer, 1987). This possibility is elaborated in Chapter 7, where we consider the representations formed from person information in some detail. For purposes of this example, however, we assume that each behavior and its trait encoding is stored as an independent unit.

for which people are "schematic" are contained in the header of their general "self" bin, our conceptualization would also predict this difference. Moreover, the frequency and recency of new self- relevant information that people receive and store in their "self" bin shall have less influence on self-judgments if the individuals are schematic with respect to the attribute exemplified by the information than if they are not. This should be true even though they can recall the information quite well when asked to do so. This is because recalling the information requires a search of the bin contents, whereas making self-judgments does not. This is one of numerous reasons why, according to the model, there is often very little relationship between judgments of a person or object and the implications of judgment-relevant information that one can recall about the object.

The retrieval postulates we have proposed come into play in discussing virtually all of the issues to be addressed in this volume. To provide examples of the range of their implications, we restrict our discussion in the remainder of this chapter to two quite different sets of phenomena. One set, which is implied by postulates surrounding the search for information within a referent bin, concerns the disproportionate influence of recently acquired and used information on judgments and decisions. The other set, which is implied by postulates concerning the identification of a referent bin, pertains to spontaneous and goal-directed reminding. Each body of literature is discussed in turn.

Recency and Frequency Effects on the Influence of New and Old Information

To reiterate, the search of a bin for goal-relevant information is top down (Postulate 5.8). Specifically, the Executor attempts to examine each unit of information in the bin, beginning with the unit on the top and working toward the bottom, to determine if its features include the set of probe cues that happen to be governing the search. If a unit of information containing these features is identified, the Executor copies it, sends it to the appropriate processing unit, and, when processing is completed, returns the copy to the top of the bin from which it was drawn. The search of a bin is imperfect, however. Therefore, the likelihood that the Executor actually identifies a particular potentially-relevant piece of information in the bin (given that any preceding units of information have been examined or passed over) is less than one. Nevertheless, the assumptions imply that the information that has been most recently deposited in a bin is more likely to be retrieved than information that has been deposited less recently.[3] In other words, recently acquired and/or used

---

3. These assumptions permit precise predictions to be made concerning the liklihood of identifying and retrieving a particular type of information as a function of its position in the bin, and also the time required to do so. We discuss these predictions in Chapter 6.

information will be the most likely to be retrieved and used again, albeit for a different purpose. This is true regardless of the stage of processing at which the information is involved (initial comprehension, inference, response generation, etc.). We review a representative sample of the research that bears on this general implication of the formulation for processing at these different stages.

Effects on Encoding

When the information transmitted to the Work Space by the Comprehender must be interpreted in terms of higher order semantic concepts in order to attain a particular processing objective, the Executor presumably retrieves copies of potentially applicable concepts from the semantic bin and sends them to the Encoder/Organizer with instructions to perform these encodings. When an applicable concept is found, the encoding is performed, and further attempts to interpret the information in terms of alternative concepts are aborted (see Postulate 5.10). This means that when a piece of information can be potentially interpreted in terms of several alternative concepts, the first applicable concept that is identified in a top-down search of the semantic bin will be the one that is used.

If this is so, factors that increase the recency with which a concept has been used in the past should increase the likelihood that a copy of this concept is near the top of the semantic bin. Therefore, they should increase the likelihood that the concept is used to interpret later information. Numerous studies of the effects of concept accessibility on the interpretation of information and judgments support this general prediction. Because this research is discussed in detail in Chapter 6 (for other reviews, see Bargh, 1984; Higgins & King, 1981), we restrict our discussion here to a brief example. Subjects in a study by Srull and Wyer (1979) initially performed a five-minute sentence construction task that required them in some instances to use an attribute or action concept associated with hostility. Then, as part of an ostensibly unrelated experiment conducted either immediately, one hour, or one day later, subjects were asked to form an impression of a person on the basis of descriptions of the person's behaviors (e.g., refusing to pay the rent until his landlord painted his apartment) that could be interpreted as either hostile or as conveying other attributes. Finally, they judged the target person with respect to hostility.

Subjects who had performed the initial sentence construction task judged the target to be more hostile than control subjects who did not perform the task. Moreover, the effects of the task on hostility judgments were still evident after 24 hours. Considered in isolation, there are a variety of alternative interpretations of these findings, the nature of which we consider in more detail in Chapter 6. In any event, the results are clearly consistent with the assumption that if concepts have recently been activated and used, albeit for a purpose that is totally unrelated to stimulus information that is presented subsequently, they may affect the interpretation of this information and judgments that are based on it.

Inference Making

People who are asked to make a judgment (e.g., to infer an attribute of a person, to report a belief that a proposition is true, etc.) presumably retrieve information from a referent bin that is relevant to this judgment. According to the formulation we have proposed, this is most likely to be the information they have acquired and/or used most recently. Several quite different types of studies support this general hypothesis. A representative sample of these studies, which reflect the range of phenomena to which the hypothesis is applicable, is provided below.

1. Effects of Making Initial Judgments on Subsequent Ones

When subjects who have received descriptions of a target person's behavior are asked to decide if the person has a particular trait, they may attempt to determine if these descriptions correspond to features of a prototypic individual who has the trait (drawn from a bin in Permanent Storage). In the process of making this comparison, the target's behaviors are presumably interpreted and organized in terms of the features of this prototype. An output of this process may be a representation of the target person that contains not only the trait being judged but other attributes of the prototype. This representation is then stored in a referent bin as a single unit. If additional judgments of the target are required later on, this representation is likely to be retrieved and its implications used as a basis for these judgments independently of the original information presented about the target.

A ground-breaking study by Carlston (1980a, b) bears directly on this hypothesis. Subjects received behavioral descriptions of a target person that had implications for two evaluatively different traits (e.g., kind and dishonest). The information was of two types. In some, single-implication conditions, a different set of behaviors had implications for each trait (i.e., some behaviors implied kindness and others implied dishonesty). In other, multiple-implication conditions, *each* behavior exemplified *both* traits. (For example, the same behavior, "giving someone an answer on an examination," could alternatively be interpreted as both kind and dishonest.) Subjects were first asked to judge the target with respect to only one of the two traits. Later they judged the target with respect to the second trait as well.

Single-implication conditions. At the time subjects read the behaviors presented under single-implication conditions, they presumably interpret the kind behaviors as "kind" and the dishonest behaviors as "dishonest." When they are asked whether the target possessed one of these traits, they may activate a prototype of a person with the trait, compare the encoded features of the target's behaviors with those of the prototype, and then, because a match occurs, respond affirmatively. In the course of this cognitive activity, however, a representation of the target as someone who has this trait, and also other features of the prototype, should be formed and stored in a referent bin pertaining to the target. Therefore, this representation should have the features of a "kind" person if subjects have been asked to judge the target's kindness, but should have the features of a "dishonest" person if they are asked to judge the target's honesty.

Now suppose these subjects are asked to judge the target with respect to the second trait. The behaviors that exemplify this trait and were previously encoded in terms of it may still be available in memory. Nevertheless, the unit of information that is on top of the referent bin pertaining to the target is presumably the representation that subjects formed of him in the course of making their initial judgments. Once the Work Space has been cleared, therefore, this representation should be used as a basis for their second judgments. Consequently, assuming that kind persons are believed to have favorable attributes that are shared by honest persons, the target should be judged to be relatively honest. Analogously, a target who was initially judged as dishonest should later be judged as relatively unkind. This is what happened. Subjects' trait judgments of the target with respect to the second trait were biased toward the evaluative implications of their first judgments. (For example, subjects judged the target to be more honest if they had first judged his kindness than if they had not. Correspondingly, they judged the target to be less kind if they had first rated his honesty.)

These data are therefore consistent with the assumption that subjects used their more recently constructed representation of the target person as a basis for judgments rather than conducting an exhaustive search for information that may have been more directly relevant. Two other aspects of Carlston's data strengthen this interpretation. First, there was no relationship between subjects' judgments of the target with respect to the second trait and the implications of the original behaviors that they could subsequently recall. Second, the effects of making initial judgments on final ones increased over the time interval between the judgments. As noted in Chapter 3, this is what one would expect on the basis of the assumption that the likelihood that the Work Space is cleared, and, therefore, the likelihood that judgments are based on information retrieved from Permanent Storage (i.e., the target representation), increases over time.

Multiple-implication conditions. When each behavior presented has implications for both of the traits being judged, some additional considerations arise. Here, as in single-implication conditions, subjects with the goal of forming an impression of the target person are likely to interpret the behaviors in terms of trait concepts at the time the behaviors are read, before they know what judgment they will be asked to make. In this case, however, the concept they use (either "kind" or "dishonest," in our example) theoretically depends on which one they happen to encounter first in the semantic bin. In the absence of any processing objective that calls differential attention to the two concepts, the use of one or the other concept may vary unsystematically over subjects. That is, some subjects who receive kind, dishonest behaviors may spontaneously interpret them as kind, and may form a representation of the target as a kind person at the outset. Others, however, may spontaneously interpret the behaviors as dishonest, and form a representation of the target as a dishonest person.

To see the implications of this, suppose subjects are asked initially to judge the target's kindness. Subjects who happen to have already encoded the behaviors as kind and to have formed a representation of the target as a kind person should, of course, judge the target as kind. Their later judgments of the target's honesty should, therefore, be evaluatively biased toward their initial kindness judgments, much as they were under single-implications conditions. However, consider those subjects who happen to have spontaneously encoded the behaviors as dishonest, and thus have formed a representation of the target as a dishonest person, before being asked to judge the target's kindness. The initial kindness judgments of these subjects, based on this representation, may be relatively neutral (or, at least, less kind than they would otherwise be). However, their later judgments of the target's honesty, which are also based on this representation, should be extreme (i.e., dishonest) and should be unaffected by their first judgments.

This was in fact the case. Subjects who had made extreme ratings of the target with respect to the first trait they were asked to judge (those who presumably had spontaneously interpreted the target's behavior as exemplifying this trait) made ratings of the second trait that were evaluatively biased toward their first judgments. This was not true, however, of subjects who had initially made neutral ratings of the target with respect to the first trait they considered.

Our discussion in this section does not begin to cover all of the theoretical and empirical issues surrounding the effects of making initial judgments of a person on subsequent ones. We return to this question in Chapter 7, where we discuss the cognitive representations formed of persons in considerable detail. However, Carlston's study demonstrates that the process of making initial judgments of a person leads to the formation of a representation that may come to influence later judgments of the person independently of the original information presented (for similar conclusions in a quite different paradigm, see Lingle & Ostrom, 1979).

2. Effects of Explaining Events on Predicting Them

The experiments described above concern the effects of a recently formed person representation on judgments of this person. Other types of cognitive representations should of course have similar effects. A compelling example is provided by Ross, Lepper, Strack, and Steinmetz (1977) in a study of the effects of generating an explanation for an outcome on predictions that the outcome will occur. Subjects read a case study of a man who had been in therapy. Then, they were arbitrarily asked to write a detailed explanation of either why the person might have committed suicide or, alternatively, why he might have donated a substantial sum of money to the Peace Corps. In some conditions, subjects were told explicitly that no one knew anything about what happened to the patient after leaving therapy. Moreover, little if any information in the case history had direct implications for either outcome. Later, subjects were given a list of events that might have happened to the person, including the one they had explained, and estimated the likelihood that each event had actually occurred. Subjects predicted that the outcome they had explained was more likely to have occurred than the outcomes they had not tried to explain.

This finding is implied by the proposed conceptualization. Subjects who are asked to explain an event retrieve prior knowledge about its possible determinants, and use this knowledge, in combination with other information available (e.g., aspects of the case study), to construct a plausible scenario of why the event might occur. This representation is then deposited in Permanent Storage in a bin pertaining to the target individual on top of the original information presented. When subjects are later asked to predict the likelihood of the outcome, this representation is more likely to be retrieved and used as a basis for predictions than the information presented, the implications of which, on average, may be less extreme.

Similar processes may underlie the effects of generating explanations of one's own behavior. In one study (Sherman, Skov, Hervitz, & Stock, 1981), subjects selected at random were arbitrarily asked to explain either why they might succeed on an anagrams task or why they might fail. Then, having generated an explanation of one or the other outcome, they predicted how well they would actually perform on such as task. As expected, their predictions were in line with the explanations they had generated. Subjects presumably retrieved self-knowledge that was consistent with the outcome they were asked to explain. This relevant subset of self-knowledge, redeposited on top of the relevant "self" bin, was more likely to be retrieved later and used as a basis for predictions than was other self-knowledge that had different implications.

This reasoning can be taken one step further. The predictions that subjects generate as a result of the activity outlined above are themselves outputs of processing that are presumably stored in memory on top of other information pertaining to the experiment and the type of task to be performed. Therefore, these predictions may have an effect on later task- related behavior. This proved to be the case in Sherman et al.'s study. Specifically, subjects, after generating predictions, actually performed the anagrams task. Those who had previously explained why they might succeed (and consequently had predicted success) actually performed better than those who had arbitrarily explained why they might fail (and therefore had predicted failure). Subjects' predictions apparently provided standards of performance that affected their later behavior on the task. This conclusion is strengthened by the results obtained under conditions in which subjects generated explanations for why they might succeed or fail on the anagrams task but did not predict their performance before engaging in it. These subjects performed well (relative to no-explanation control subjects) regardless of whether they had explained success or explained failure. The difference between these results and those obtained in the first set of conditions indicates that subjects' predictions *per se* affected their problem-solving behavior independently of the cognitions on which these predictions were based. (For other evidence that predictions of performance affect behavior independently of the considerations that underlie these predictions, see Goodhart, 1986.)

In the studies cited above, subjects' explanations for outcomes were explicitly requested. These explanations may sometimes be generated spontaneously. This is particularly likely when an unexpected event occurs. An interesting demonstration of this possibility was reported by Ross, Lepper, and Hubbard (1975). Subjects were given a series of suicide notes and asked to decide whether each note was real or bogus. They received trial-by-trial feedback that indicated that they were either correct the majority of the time or were incorrect the majority of the time. After completing the task, however, some subjects were told that the feedback they had received was false and bore no relation to their actual performance. The debriefing was quite convincing. Subjects were even shown a computer printout, obviously prepared before the experiment took place, that indicated the schedule of feedback they had been administered. Despite this debriefing, subjects who were told they had succeeded predicted they would perform better on a similar future task than those who were told they had done badly.

When considered in terms of the proposed model, the ineffectiveness of this debriefing is not surprising. Presumably, subjects spontaneously retrieved knowledge about themselves that would account for their success or failure on the task while it was being performed. This nonrepresentative sample of self-knowledge was then redeposited on top of the bin from which it was drawn. When subjects were later asked to predict their performance on the new task, they presumably recalled and used this biased sample of judgment-relevant information regardless of whether they had been told that the feedback was incorrect.

3. Effects of Previously Reported Beliefs on the Report of Subsequent Beliefs

When subjects are asked to report their belief in a proposition, they presumably retrieve a subset of relevant knowledge from a bin that refers to the domain of experience to which the proposition is relevant. Thus, subjects who are asked their belief that "there will be a nuclear war" may identify a "nuclear war" bin and search for information that has implications for the validity of this proposition. This information may itself have the form of a proposition (e.g., "America is rejecting

Russian appeals for disarmament," "Military defense spending is increasing," etc.). However, subjects are unlikely to perform an exhaustive search for all such "informational" propositions that bear on this belief. Rather, only the first judgment-relevant proposition they happen to identify may be used.

Some of the research bearing most directly on this possibility was conducted in the context of investigations of the interrelations among beliefs in syllogistically-related propositions (McGuire, 1960, 1981; Wyer & Hartwick, 1980). The beliefs in question typically concerned an informational proposition (A) and a target proposition (B) that in combination compose one premise and the conclusion of syllogism of the form "A; if A, then B; B." Henninger and Wyer (1976) found that if subjects are asked to report their beliefs in the conclusion B before reporting their beliefs in the premise A, these beliefs are inconsistent as defined by the probabilogical model of belief organization proposed by McGuire (1960, 1981) and Wyer (1974; Wyer & Goldberg, 1970).[4] On the other hand, if subjects report their beliefs in A before their beliefs in B, the consistency of these beliefs is much greater. This is true even when the belief propositions are separated by several other items in the questionnaire.

These data are in accord with expectations based on the formulation proposed here. Many alternative informational propositions could in principle be brought to bear on a given conclusion, each of which may have somewhat different implications. When subjects are asked to report their beliefs in the conclusion without having previously reported their belief in the particular informational proposition they were asked about in the questionnaire (i.e., proposition A), their search of memory for belief- relevant information may often lead them to retrieve and use an alternative proposition that happens to be nearer the top of the bin being searched. Therefore, their beliefs in the conclusion will appear inconsistent with their beliefs in A that they report later. In contrast, if A has recently been considered, and therefore a copy of it is near the top of the referent bin in which information is sought, it is more likely to be the informational proposition that is recalled and used as a basis for reporting beliefs in B. In this case, therefore, beliefs in the two propositions will appear consistent. These effects, incidentally, are evident even when several days have elapsed between reporting beliefs in A and reporting beliefs in B (Henninger & Wyer, 1976). Therefore, the effect appears attributable to the

---

4. According to this model, syllogistically related beliefs, defined in units of probability, are related according to the question

$$P(B) = P(A)P(B|A) + P(\overline{A})P(B|\overline{A})$$

where $P(A)$ and $P(B)$ are beliefs that the propositions A and B are true, respectively, $P(\overline{A}) = 1 - P(A)$ is the belief that A is not true, and $P(B|A)$ and $P(B|\overline{A})$ are the beliefs that B is true *if* A is and is not true, respectively.

increased accessibility of the informational proposition in Permanent Storage rather than in the Work Space.

An interesting phenomenon originally identified by McGuire (1960; see also Rosen & Wyer, 1972) is interpretable in light of these considerations. Specifically, when subjects report their beliefs in syllogistically related propositions in two experimental sessions one week apart, the beliefs they report in the second session are often more consistent than they were at first. This "Socratic effect" was originally interpreted as evidence that subjects actively attempt to reconcile logical inconsistencies among their beliefs once these inconsistencies are called to their attention. An alternative interpretation is possible, however. When subjects report their beliefs in a conclusion (B) before reporting their beliefs in a particular premise (A), these beliefs are likely to be inconsistent for reasons noted above. However, once beliefs in A are reported, a copy of this proposition (and the belief in its validity) is deposited on top of the referent bin from which belief-relevant knowledge is drawn. Consequently, if subjects are asked to report their beliefs in the conclusion in the second session, they are more likely to identify and use their belief in A as a basis for evaluating the conclusion than they were before. As a result, subjects' beliefs in the two propositions should be more consistent in the second session than they were at first.

The implications of this analysis were supported in the study by Henninger and Wyer (1976). Specifically, the "Socratic effect" identified by McGuire was evident only under those conditions in which subjects had reported their beliefs in conclusions before reporting their beliefs in premises during the first session of the experiment. When subjects had reported their beliefs in premises before their beliefs in conclusions, the consistency of these beliefs was high initially and did not increase further in the second session.

Other effects of knowledge activation on attitudes and opinions. A quite different study (Salancik, 1974) also supports the general hypothesis that subjects' beliefs and opinions are often based on the subset of judgment-relevant knowledge that they happen to be thinking about most recently. In this study, subjects near the end of a course completed a series of open-ended statements about their classroom behavior. In one condition, each sentence to be completed contained the stem "in order to" (i.e., "I raise my hand in class in order to..."). In the other condition, it contained the stem "because I" ("I raise my hand in class because I..."). Salancik reasoned that the completion of "in order to" statements would predispose students to think of extrinsic reasons for their behavior (i.e., "...in order to get a good grade"), whereas the completion of "because I" statements would predispose them to think of intrinsic reasons (i.e., "...because I want to understand what is going on"). Upon completing the questionnaire, students were asked how much they had enjoyed the course. These ratings were subsequently correlated with final course grades. As expected, this correlation was much higher in the "in order to" condition (i.e., when extrinsic considerations were presumably more accessible at the time subjects evaluated the course) than in the "because I" condition (when intrinsic factors were relatively more accessible).

Implications for communication and persuasion. The considerations outlined above have implications for a conceptualization of belief and opinion change. In many instances, the information we have accumulated has different and often contradictory implications for the validity of a particular position. In such instances, the influence of a persuasive communication may not result from the new information it provides, but rather, may occur because the communication calls attention to a selective subset of previously acquired knowledge that has implications for one position or another. For example, a communication that supports the proposition that abortion should be freely available to all may assert that a woman should have freedom of choice over whether she has children, thus reminding the recipients of their previously formed beliefs that this is true. In contrast, a communication that opposes abortion may assert that taking a life is immoral, thus directing recipient's attention to their previously formed beliefs in this proposition instead. People may already believe that both propositions are valid, and reading the communications containing them may not alter these beliefs. However, reading the first communication should move a copy of the pro-abortion proposition to the top of an "abortion" bin. The increased accessibility of this proposition should, therefore, increase the likelihood that the recipient subsequently infers that abortion should be freely available. Correspondingly, reading the second communication, which increases the accessibility of the anti- abortion proposition, should decrease this likelihood. This is true even if neither communication actually contains any information that its recipient did not already have.

Having said this, it is important to note that a representation of the content of the communication per se is unlikely to be the *most* accessible material in Permanent Storage that bears on the proposition to which the communication is relevant. Rather, recipients' cognitive responses to the communication in the course of reading it, which constitute outputs of higher order processing, are presumably stored in a bin on top of a representation of the communication content per se. These cognitive responses, which may consist of elaborations, counterarguments, or content- irrelevant thoughts, are more likely to be later used as a basis for reporting beliefs in the proposition to which the communication is relevant than is the content of the communication itself (cf. Greenwald, 1968). This possibility, which has been explored intensively by Petty, Cacioppo and their colleagues (for reviews, see Petty & Cacioppo, 1986; Petty, Ostrom, & Brock, 1981), provides an explanation for the typically low relation between the influence of a persuasive communication and the implications of the content of the communication that subjects can recall (cf. Greenwald, 1968; McGuire, 1968).

If this reasoning is correct, factors that interfere with subjects' higher order processing of a communication as it is presented (thus preventing material from being deposited on top of a representation of its content and implications) should increase the likelihood that the communication content itself is retrieved and used as a basis for judgments, and therefore should increase the apparent impact of this communication. The research on distraction effects on communication influence (for reviews, see Petty, Ostrom, & Brock, 1981; Wyer, 1974) can be interpreted in this light. In the earliest and still one of the most provocative investigations of these effects, Festinger and Maccoby (1964) found that fraternity members were more influenced by an antifraternity communication if they were distracted from thinking carefully about it than if they were not. In contrast, nonfraternity members were equally influenced under both distraction and no-distraction conditions. This suggested that nondistracted fraternity members generated counterarguments to the communication that were deposited on top of the message content in a "fraternity" bin, and that these counterarguments provided the basis for the attitudes they reported later. In contrast, distracted fraternity members, and nonfraternity members who were not motivated to counterargue, did not engage in this higher order counterargumentation. Consequently, their representation of the message content, which was still on top of their "fraternity" bin, had greater impact.

Effects of Overt Responses on Subsequent Judgments and Decisions

When an overt response is made to a stimulus, a cognitive representation of this response is presumably stored in a referent bin on top of the representation of the stimulus that led the response to be generated. Therefore, the response may often be retrieved and used as a basis for subsequent judgments or decisions independently of the factors that led to its occurrence. An intriguing demonstration of this was reported by Sherman, Ahlm, Berman, and Lynn (1978). Subjects were asked to judge the importance of recycling in the context of either very important social issues or very unimportant ones. Their ratings were more negative in the first condition than in the second. As shown in several other studies (Upshaw, 1969, 1978), this contrast effect does not indicate that the context stimuli affected subjects' underlying perceptions of the importance of recycling. Rather, subjects position their response scale differently in relation to subjective stimulus values, depending on the range of stimuli they are given to rate (for a more detailed discussion, see Wyer, 1974, and Chapter 11 of this volume). In other words, the contrast effect is the result of an output generation procedure that, in terms of the proposed model, is performed by the Response Selector. Nonetheless, when subjects were subsequently approached by a confederate and asked to help out on a recycling project, those who had rated recycling in the context of important issues volunteered less help than those who had rated it in the context of unimportant issues. Exactly the opposite effect occurred when subjects had rated context items but had not actually rated the target issue. Apparently, these latter subjects based their helping decision in part on social responsibility norms that were activated by the context issues. However, when subjects had actually rated recycling, they apparently retrieved this rating from the top of a referent bin pertaining to this issue, reinterpreted its implications in relation to a standard other than the one they had used to generate the rating initially, and used these implications as a basis for their behavioral decision.[5] Research with similar implications has been reported by Higgins and Lurie (1983) in a quite different research paradigm.

Summary

Evidence obtained in a variety of research paradigms converges on the conclusion that the knowledge we have acquired and used most recently has a disproportionate influence on judgments and decisions to which it is relevant. These recency effects appear to be evident at all stages of information processing, from the initial interpretation of information in terms of trait concepts to the generation of overt responses. Many of the phenomena we have mentioned are elaborated in much more detail in later chapters that are devoted to processing at these various stages. The point we wish to make here is that the storage and retrieval postulates we have proposed can be used to conceptualize phenomena that occur at all of these stages. The formulation is therefore useful in conceptually integrating a wide range of phenomena that are not often considered simultaneously in terms of a relatively small number of theoretical principles.

Spontaneous and Goal-Directed Reminding

One of the most common memory phenomena is also one of the least understood. That is, thinking about a person or event, either for some specific purpose, in the course of idle conversation, or when simply daydreaming, often leads us spontaneously to remember a person or event we have not thought about in many years. Sometimes, we may be vaguely aware of the factors that gave rise to this reminding. For example, walking around one's home town after an absence of many years and noticing a particular house may elicit memories of being a cub scout and playing on the swings in the yard of the "den mother" who lived there, and may even elicit more specific experiences that occurred during this period of early childhood. Other times, however, memories of past events appear to come out of thin air, and we are not at all aware of what cued their sudden retrieval.

Reminding phenomena have recently become of theoretical and empirical concern in cognitive psychology (Ross, 1984; Schank, 1982). Related issues have

---

5. This interpretation assumes that subjects did not store the procedure for generating their overt response in their "recycling" bin, but only the response itself. This is consistent with the assumption that the response selection procedures contained in the Response Selector's library are performed automatically and without conscious awareness.

been explored in the context of understanding how people retrieve information from "very long term" memory (Bahrick, 1984; Norman & Bobrow, 1979; Williams & Hollan, 1981). Schank (1982), while distinguishing between different types of remindings, nonetheless views them as instances of more general memory phenomena that are governed by a common set of processes. A similar view is inherent in the formulation we propose in this volume. That is, reminding phenomena are conceptualized in terms of the factors that lead different referent bins to be identified and the rules that govern the search for information contained in these bins.

Empirical work on reminding is obviously difficult. Remindings are inherently idiosyncratic to the individual, and the processes that underlie their occurrence must often be understood on the basis of qualitative analyses of individuals' free response protocols. Nonetheless, several bodies of research bear on the processes we postulate. We first outline briefly the nature of these processes within the framework of the model, and then describe representative samples of the research to which they are relevant.

General Considerations

To convey the implications of the proposed model for reminding phenomena, it is necessary to reiterate four sets of assumptions concerning the formation and use of referent bins.

1. Referent bins vary in their generality or abstractness. This generality is reflected both by the header specifying a bin's contents and the information contained in it.
2. A referent bin contains only information about referents to which the features of its header are applicable (Postulate 4.8).
3. The referent bin from which information is retrieved is determined by a set of probe cues. This set is compiled by the Executor by sampling the features contained in Compartment 1 of the Work Space (Postulate 5.4). It is not always restricted to features that are directly relevant to the processing objectives (if any) for which the information is being sought.
4. For a bin to be identified in a search of Permanent Storage, its header must contain all of the features specified in the set of probe cues that is currently governing the search (Postulate 5.5).
a. If the features in the probe set are all contained in the header of more than one bin, the bin identified is the one whose header contains the fewest number of features *in addition* to those in the probe set (Postulate 5.5).
b. If no bin has a header whose features include all of those in the probe set, a subset of the original probe cues may be sampled randomly, and the search

repeated with a smaller set of cues until a bin meeting the above criteria is found (Postulate 5.6).

The identification and retrieval of information from a bin may occur either in pursuit of a specific task objective, in the comprehension of new information, or spontaneously, in the free flow of thought (see Chapter 2). Thus, the processing outlined above theoretically applies both to goal-directed and nongoal-directed cognitive activity.

Spontaneous Remindings

Reminding is assumed to occur when a person, object, or event in one's immediate experience calls to mind another person, object, or event that has the same or similar features. Remindings may occur either in the course of goal-directed cognitive activity or spontaneously, without any specific objective other than to comprehend one's immediate experience. For example, a new acquaintance might spontaneously remind one of an old high school classmate, or an overheard comment about a lecture might remind one of the need to prepare a colloquium for the following week. Many interesting examples of this are provided by Schank (1982), as in the following:

> "X described how his wife would never make his steak as rare as he liked it. When this was told to Y, it reminded Y of a time, 30 years earlier, when he tried to get his hair cut in a short style in England, and the barber would not cut it as short as he wanted it" (p. 47).

In terms of the proposed model, a reminding occurs when the set of features compiled for use as probe cues match the features of a referent bin in Permanent Storage, leading information contained in this bin to be retrieved. Viewed in this light, there is no major difference between reminding and retrieval processes more generally. The distinction, if any, is more phenomenological than theoretical. That is, it lies in the extent to which the referent of the bin identified by probe cues (or the content of the information contained in it) is more or less similar to the one that is presently being thought about, and whether one is more or less "surprised" to think of the new information. Thus, for example, there may be nothing theoretically different between: (a) being reminded of McDonald's when making one's first visit to Burger King, and (b) being reminded of McDonald's when making one's tenth visit to McDonald's. In both instances, the person may retrieve information from a McDonald's bin that is identified by a matching of features in the immediate situation with those of the bin header.

Reminding may be conceptualized somewhat more formally using an example from Schank (1982). As a consequence of numerous visits to "sit-down" restaurants, one presumably has formed a general and abstract "restaurant" bin containing prototypic event sequences (e.g., one enters, is shown to a table, reads the menu, orders, eats, pays, and leaves). This bin is presumably identified by a header containing features typical of restaurants in general (e.g., "menu," "waiter," "tip," etc.). Consider a woman who, many years ago, had visited Legal Seafoods, a particular sit-down restaurant in Boston, where she was asked to pay before eating rather than afterwards. She may form a specific bin pertaining to this experience whose header includes this unique feature as well as ones that compose the more general "restaurant" bin header. Now suppose she enters a new restaurant that appears to have no distinctive features. The features she is likely to include in the probe set used to retrieve information necessary to understand this situation are likely to be a subset of those contained in her general restaurant bin header. They are, therefore, likely to lead the content of this general bin to be retrieved. In other words, she may not think of any other particular restaurant she has visited, despite the fact that many features of the present restaurant are shared by others.

Suppose, however, that after ordering her meal, she is unexpectedly asked to pay. She will presumably attempt to comprehend such an unexpected event in terms of prior experiences she has had. According to the model, the addition of the new feature to the probe set is likely to lead the "Legal Seafoods" bin to be identified. This is true even though many years have intervened. The retrieval of information from this bin may therefore be experienced as a "reminding." However, the processes underlying this experience are no different from those that underlie the retrieval of information from the more general restaurant bin. From a functional perspective, it would be very surprising if it were otherwise.

Additional implications of the model arise from the assumption that the features compiled by the Executor for use as probe cues may sometimes contain features that are not relevant to the goal being processed, but happen fortuitously to be contained in the Work Space as a result of either previous goal-directed processing or new stimulus input that has been transmitted to it by the Comprehender. The inclusion of these extraneous features along with goal-relevant ones may lead a bin to be fortuitously identified that has not been accessed for many years. Thus, a person who is asked to describe his home town may generally activate a general "Delhi, New York" bin containing general physical characteristics and general characterizations of the people who live there. However, suppose the individual had been engaged in a discussion of religion just before being asked for this information. The fortuitous inclusion of a religion-related feature (e.g., "church") in the set of probe cues may instead lead a more specific bin to be activated containing childhood experiences one had in churches (e.g., adjourning to the basement while the collection was being taken in order to avoid putting money in the plate, failing to show up to serve early morning mass, etc.) that had never been thought about in the 20 year interim.

Fortuitous remindings may also occur during the free flow of thought, in the absence of any goal-directed cognitive activity. The processing that is theoretically involved was described in Chapter 2. That is, in the absence of any specific processing objective (i.e., when the goal-specification box does not contain a goal schema), an iterative process is activated whereby the features of information contained in the Work Space are used to compile a set of probe cues, and information is retrieved from a bin in Permanent Storage whose header contains the features specified in this set. In some instances, the juxtaposition of features in the probe set may lead a referent bin to be spontaneously identified that has not recently been activated, causing one to be "reminded" of a person or event that has not been thought about in some time.

The header of a referent bin, and, therefore, the probe cues that lead to remindings, need not be verbal. The example given earlier, in which a new acquaintance reminds one of an old high school classmate, is presumably a result of the identification of a referent bin whose header features include visual codings of the acquaintance's physical appearance. A similar phenomenon occurs if one visits a town after an absence of many years, and finds that persons and events come to mind in the course of wandering through the town that had not been thought about either before or since (and perhaps *cannot* be recalled in the absence of the visually-coded features that compose the header of the bin in which they are contained).[6]

On the other hand, the proposed formulation calls attention to the important role of encoding in "reminding" phenomena. That is, a new experience will not lead a person to be reminded of a previous one unless the concepts that are used to encode it are similar to those that had been used to interpret the earlier one. In other words, these concepts must compose the header of the referent bin that contains the earlier experience. For example, consider Schank's "steak and haircut" anecdote noted earlier. For such a reminding to occur, the new event must be encoded in terms of features that are also contained in the header of the previously formed "English barber" bin. These features may either be abstract concepts (e.g., "never does what he asks despite repeated requests") or encodings of one's subjective reactions to the experience (e.g., "frustrated"). However, if the new event is interpreted in terms of a different set of concepts, the connection would presumably not be made. Another necessary condition is that the encoded features of the new experience identify a bin that pertains to the earlier experience *alone*. Presumably, if person Y in Schank's example had had experiences with several different persons who never did what he asked, his unique experience with the English barber would probably not have been retrieved.

---

6. Note that this, in effect, also provides an example of context-dependent learning (cf. Baddeley, Cuccaro, Egstrom, Weltman, & Willis, 1975; Davis, Baddeley, & Hancock, 1975; S.M. Smith, Glenberg, & Bjork, 1978).

Goal-Directed Remindings: Learning by Analogy

The point made above, that the nature of remindings depends on how the original information is encoded at the time of input, is equally relevant when remindings occur in the service of attaining some specific objective. Research of particular relevance to this phenomenon has focused on the role of remindings in the learning of cognitive skills (Ross, 1984) and learning by analogy (Gick & Holyoak, 1980, 1983; Ross, 1986). The general role of reminding in cognitive skill learning was demonstrated convincingly in a series of studies by Ross (1984), who monitored subjects' verbal responses as they learned how to use a computer text editor. Subjects in this study were trained to apply a particular principle in solving a problem (e.g., inserting a word). This was done using an example that involved a specific type of verbal material (e.g., a restaurant review). Later, the subjects' ability to solve the same problem was tested using material that was either similar to that of the training example (a second restaurant review), similar to that used to teach an alternative procedure for solving the problem (e.g., a telephone list), or unrelated in content. An analysis of subjects' verbal response protocols yielded several findings of interest. First, subjects generated remindings more frequently when they found it difficult to solve the problem than when they found it easy. (For example, in training text editing, subjects who were fastest generated fewer remindings than those who were slowest.) Therefore, reminding appears to be used as part of a conscious problem-solving strategy in the course of trying to perform the task at hand.

More important, when remindings occurred, they typically led subjects to employ the procedure they had learned using material of the same type as the test problem, rather than an equally appropriate procedure they had learned using material of a different type. Thus, suppose subjects had learned one procedure for inserting a word when typing a restaurant review and a second procedure when typing a telephone list. In the test phase, subjects' remindings typically led them to adopt the first procedure if they were typing another restaurant review, but to adopt the second procedure if they were typing another telephone list.

The importance of these findings derives from the fact that the utility or ease of applying the two procedures was not in any way dependent on the specific verbal content of the material being typed. Nevertheless, these content features affected subjects' likelihood of selecting these procedures. In terms of the conceptualization we are proposing, this suggests that the header of bins formed when learning the alternative procedures contained features that were specific to the verbal material to which the procedures were applied. Therefore, when content-related features were available at the time of test (along with a characterization of the problem), they were included among the probe cues governing the search and led to the retrieval and use of information contained in these content-restricted bins. Note that if this reasoning is correct, the priming of content features at the time of test should sometimes interfere with problem solution. This interference should occur when content features cue the retrieval of procedures that are inapplicable to the problem to be solved. A second series of studies by Ross (1986) demonstrated that this is indeed the case.

The general theme that emerges from Ross's work is that the initial problems that subjects are given tend to be encoded in concrete terms and that the rules of solving them are stored in a location that is defined in terms of the specific features of the situation. When subjects encounter a new problem solution, they encode the features of this situation in concrete terms as well and use the features as probe cues. Consequently, they may access the original situation and apply the rule learned in this situation to problem solution only if the content features of the two situations are similar. Moreover, they will apply the rule correctly only if there is a direct analogy between the features of one situation and those of the other.

An additional implication of the formulation we have proposed is based on considerations we raised when discussing the conditions in which new referent bins are formed (see Chapter 4). When people encounter two or more similar situations and have an objective of understanding their relationship, this goal-directed activity may lead them to extract features of the situations that can be encoded in terms of more abstract concepts that are applicable to both. They may then store the results of this activity in a new bin that is defined in terms of these abstract concepts. In the absence of these higher order processing goals, or when only a single situation is encountered, these abstract encodings may not be performed. In the present context, this suggests that a single concrete training problem may be insufficient to permit the principle involved in it to be encoded in a way that will lead it to be later retrieved and used as a basis for problem solution. Rather, two or more such problems may be required. Moreover, the problems must be presented in a way that stimulates thinking about them in relation to one another.

Evidence supporting these conjectures has in fact been obtained in a series of studies by Gick and Holyoak (1983) on analogical reasoning. In the paradigm employed in these studies, subjects are given a specific problem that can be solved in terms of a general principle. Then, they are given a second, analogous problem that can be solved in terms of the same general principle. The question is whether subjects will spontaneously recognize the analogy, and, therefore, whether exposure to the first problem will facilitate solution of the second.

More concretely, suppose subjects initially read a story about a general who wishes to conquer a fortress. There are many roads leading into the fortress. However, each one has been mined in such a way that only a small number of men can pass over it safely. Consequently, a full-scale attack along any given road is impossible. To attack the fortress successfully, the general divides his army into small groups, sending each to the head of a different road, and has them converge simultaneously on the fortress.

After reading this story, subjects are then given a problem faced by a doctor whose patient has a malignant tumor. A particular type of radiation will destroy the tumor. However, if it is applied from a particular direction with sufficient intensity to kill the tumor, the healthy tissue that the rays pass through will be destroyed as well. (At lower intensities, the rays will not harm the healthy tissue, but also will not kill the tumor.) How can the doctor destroy the tumor without risking the patient's life?

The solution, of course, is analogous to the general's solution to the military problem. That is, small amounts of radiation can be administered from different directions, all simultaneously converging on the tumor. Then, the tumor (like the fortress) will be destroyed, whereas the healthy tissue will remain undamaged. Despite the analogy between the two problems, subjects who had read the military problem and its solution were not appreciably helped in solving the radiation problem. In fact, only 30% of all subjects who read the military problem solved the radiation problem, as compared to 10% who solved it without exposure to the military problem. This low solution probability occurred even when the principle used by the general in the military problem was specifically stated (e.g., "The general attributed his success to an important principle: If you need a large force to accomplish something but are prevented from applying it directly, many smaller forces applied from different directions may work as well").

The reason is perhaps similar to that suggested by Ross's research. That is, subjects presumably encoded the military story (and also the principle, when it was explicitly stated) in concrete terms that were specific to the situation described and stored it in a bin that was defined in terms of these concrete features. When they later encountered the radiation problem, their search for a solution did not cue their recall of the first problem and its solution, even when they were looking for an abstract principle that would help them.

If this is the case, and if our argument is correct that situations are encoded in more abstract terms as a result of attempts to understand similarities among them, exposure to stories describing two or more analogous situations before being asked to solve the radiation problem should facilitate the solution of this problem. In fact, Gick and Holyoak (1983) found this to be the case. In evaluating their results, it should be noted that subjects who read two analogous stories rather than one were told at the outset to "study the two stories carefully for five minutes in preparation for answering questions about them." The introduction of this processing objective undoubtedly increased subjects' efforts to extract commonalities from the stories and to form a separate representation that was encoded in more abstract terms. Whether they would do this in the absence of such a processing objective is unclear.

Be that as it may, a consideration of the goal-directed reminding phenomena identified by Ross and by Gick and Holyoak within the conceptual framework we have proposed suggests several general conclusions. In the absence of any higher-order goal that leads people to perform abstract encodings of their experiences, these encodings may not be made, and the experiences may be stored in memory locations that are defined by rather concrete features. If these concrete features are present in the Work Space at the time the information is sought, the experiences may be recalled. The fortuitous presence of these features in the Work Space at the time information is sought may often lead to spontaneous remindings of the sort we described earlier. However, unless the information is encoded at a more abstract level in the process of pursuing some goal-directed activity at the time the information is received, it may *not* be later retrieved and used as a basis for attaining processing objectives to which it is relevant. In other words, goal-directed remindings of a sort that facilitate problem solving may not occur.

A Related Conceptualization

The conceptualization we have outlined is similar in many respects to a formulation proposed by Norman and Bobrow (1979) to account for the retrieval of information from "very long term" memory. In fact, a consideration of Norman and Bobrow's work raises some additional considerations that we have not previously addressed.

Norman and Bobrow (1979) postulate that when subjects require information for a particular purpose, they generate a "description," or set of concepts that describes the nature of the information required. This description may be at varying levels of specificity. Information is then retrieved at the level that meets this description and is evaluated in terms of its sufficiency for attaining the goal at hand. If the information is judged to be insufficient, the description is modified, and the search process is repeated until adequate information has been obtained.

Thus, for example, a person who wishes to decide where to eat may initially generate the description "restaurant." He may, therefore, retrieve the most readily accessible piece of information that fits this description (in this case, the representation of a particular restaurant), and may evaluate it in relation to a set of subjective decision criteria. If the restaurant meets these criteria, the search stops. However, in evaluating the restaurant, the person may note that the restaurant serves only steak, and that he is interested in seafood. The description is then modified to include this feature (e.g., "seafood restaurant") and the process repeats. This time, the restaurant retrieved may meet these specifications but be judged too expensive. If so, the description is made even more specific (e.g., "moderately priced seafood restaurant") and the process is repeated until an adequate restaurant is found. The interesting aspect of this example is that *not all of the criteria required to attain the processing objective are initially used as a basis for the memory search*. Rather, only a subset is used, with others coming into play only if the initial information retrieved fails to satisfy them.

In terms of the present conceptualization, each "description," as Norman and Bobrow conceptualize it, is equivalent to a set of probe cues, each set comprising the header of a different referent bin. Thus, in the above example, "restaurant," "seafood restaurant," and "moderately expensive seafood restaurant" may be headers of bins at different levels of generality, with each bin containing the names of restaurants that meet the header criteria. Given this assumption, the example given above has implications for the memory search processes initiated by the Executor to obtain information relevant to a processing objective. That is, it suggests that only a small number of features are initially selected as probe cues, and that this set is expanded only when the information retrieved does not lead to the attainment of the processing objectives at hand.

Thus, for example, when a person has the goal of deciding where to eat, some criteria for making this decision may initially be transmitted to the Work Space. However, not all of these criteria are initially selected as probe cues. For example, the initial search may be governed by a single cue, "restaurant," leading a general restaurant bin to be identified and the name of a restaurant, and its features, to be retrieved and compared to the selection criteria contained in the Work Space. If the representation of a moderately expensive seafood restaurant happens to be at the top of the restaurant bin, the restaurant will be identified without further processing. In contrast, when the initial search fails to meet the criteria, the search must be continued. However, in the process of determining that the first alternative is unacceptable, the criteria used (moderately expensive, seafood, etc.) are more extensively processed and therefore are more likely to be added to the probe cues that govern the subsequent search. This expanded set of probe cues (e.g., "moderately expensive seafood restaurant") may lead a more restricted referent bin to be identified, thereby avoiding the retrieval of other, equally unacceptable alternatives and increasing the likelihood that an acceptable referent will be quickly identified. This process suggests a more general proposition that may ultimately need to be incorporated into the set of formal postulates guiding search and retrieval processes. That is, the set of probe cues compiled to direct the retrieval of information from Permanent Storage is the smallest number that seems (subjectively) likely to attain the processing objective being pursued. The generality of such a principle remains to be explored.

Conditions may of course arise in which an acceptable candidate is not identified even with a fully expanded set of probe cues. In the above example, this would occur if a "moderately expensive seafood restaurant" bin did not exist. When this occurs, the probe cues may be *reduced* in number, as noted in Postulate 5.6. This leads a more general bin to be reidentified, and a more exhaustive search of its contents to be performed. For example, "seafood" may be dropped from the probe set, and a "moderately expensive restaurant" bin identified and searched for a place that does not specialize in seafood but is known to have it on the menu.

Phenomena such as these are obviously very difficult to investigate empirically. One study by Williams and Hollan (1981), however, provides support for the conceptualization we propose. Subjects in this study were asked over a period of several experimental sessions to recall the names of their high school classmates, and to think aloud while doing so. Their verbal recall protocols revealed strategies very similar to those suggested by the conceptualization outlined above. For example, a typical subject might begin by thinking about his "8th grade class" and, in doing so, recall the names of several classmates. Then, having exhausted the names easily retrievable through this strategy, he may progress systematically through specific classes (history, gym, etc.), retrieving additional names in each case. A more detailed example is provided by a subject who, having thought of a high school rock band, was able to generate the names of two players but not the third. The protocol then went as follows:

> ...I'm thinking about a time when they were playing over at our house...I was imagining the whole room and...the instruments set up and I'm trying to remember the name of this guy—who used to...Art! And he was also in our 10th grade art class... (Williams & Hollan, 1981, pp. 100-101).

In terms of the present conceptualization, this provides a nice example of the way in which expanding the number of probe cues can lead to the retrieval of additional information. That is, "high school rock band" presumably activated a bin that contained only representations of situations in which the name of the unidentified member was not encoded. However, based on information in this bin, the number of probe cues was further expanded to include features of particular situations in which the band had played. This led a more specific referent bin to be identified containing representations in which the person's name was a feature.

Concluding Remarks

At the beginning of this chapter, we presented a series of postulates concerning the processes underlying the retrieval of information from memory. These postulates, considered in combination with other aspects of the model, have broad implications, as we have attempted to convey in our discussion of recency effects and reminding phenomena. From the perspective of the model as a whole, an important feature of these postulates concerns their applicability at all stages of information processing and their independence of the particular processing objectives being pursued. In other words, a common set of rules governs the retrieval of information, regardless of whether one's objective is to comprehend the information one receives, to make a particular judgment or decision, or to recall the information one has acquired about a person, object, or event. The specific processing objectives obviously determine what sort of information is retrieved and how it is used. However, the search and retrieval processes per se are the same in all cases.

A second, related feature of the formulation lies in its specification of the sequence of steps involved in the search and retrieval of information in the course of pursuing a processing goal. That is, the Work Space is always searched first, before information in Permanent Storage. If information in the Work Space is irrelevant to the attaining of this objective and a referent bin is identified, the bin's header is searched for features that are sufficient to attain the goal at hand. Only if these first two sources fail to yield information sufficient to attain one's processing objective are the contents of the bin itself considered. To the extent that different factors affect (a) the presence of goal-relevant information in the Work Space, (b) the nature of the features that are likely to compose a bin header, and (c) the likelihood of identifying a piece of information within a referent bin, the model specifies the order in which these factors are likely to come into play in this retrieval process.

The research summarized in the last sections of this chapter provides some indication of the diversity of phenomena to which the retrieval postulates we propose are applicable. These postulates are obviously involved whenever previously acquired knowledge plays a role in comprehension, judgment, and decision making. Their implications continue to be evident throughout the remainder of this volume, where we discuss specific phases of social information processing in some detail.

Chapter 6
Encoding and Organization:
I. The Effects of Concept Accessibility
on the Interpretation of Information

The conceptualization we propose distinguishes among three levels of encoding and organization:

1. At a very early stage of processing, the Comprehender interprets input material in terms of low level noun, attribute, and action concepts drawn from the semantic bin in Permanent Storage. Comprehension at this level is postulated to occur automatically and independently of any higher order processing objectives for which the information is ultimately used.

2. A second stage of encoding occurs when a specific processing objective (e.g., to form an impression of someone, to explain the occurrence of an event, etc.) requires an interpretation of individual pieces of information in terms of more abstract goal-relevant concepts. Thus, people may encode a man's behaviors in terms of trait concepts in the course of determining whether they would like him, or deciding whether he has attributes that are suitable for a particular job. Or, they may interpret the things that occur in a particular situation as examples of more general, prototypic events in order to decide how to behave in the situation.

3. At the third, still higher level of encoding, individual pieces of information may be organized into a configuration of interrelated features that in combination function as a single unit of knowledge. For example, in the course of interpreting a number of individual actions, these actions may be organized into a single temporally or causally related sequence. Or, a set of behaviors or traits may be organized around a general concept of the person who possesses them to form a single representation of this person. This type of goal-directed encoding and organization, like the second type noted above, is performed by the Encoder-Or-

ganizer rather than the Comprehender, and is specific to processing objectives that exist at the time the information is received.

A detailed discussion of the encoding processes that occur at the first, initial comprehension stage, which is the focus of much theory and research in cognitive psychology (for a review, see Lachman, Lachman, & Butterfield, 1979) is beyond the scope of this volume. The next three chapters explicate the processes involved at the second and third stages. In the present chapter, we focus on the manner in which individual pieces of information are interpreted, and the effects of these interpretations on both the inferences that are made about the persons or objects to which the information is relevant and, in some cases, behavioral decisions. Chapters 7 and 8 discuss the processes of organizing these individual pieces of information into configural units, and the use of these *configurations* in making judgments and decisions.

Our separation of the last two encoding stages is somewhat artificial. For one thing, the processes that underlie the encoding of individual pieces of information may also influence the organization of this information, as we will point out in Chapter 7. It is therefore desirable to review briefly the processes we postulate to occur en route to making a judgment, focusing specifically on the role that the interpretation of the information at each stage of processing has on the representations that are formed from the information and judgments that are based on them. We use as an example the processes that underlie person impression formation, which has been a major focus of empirical research on the phenomena to be considered. However, similar processes clearly come into play in other types of goal-directed activity, as we will see. After providing this conceptual overview, we describe empirical studies that, in combination, give evidence of the general processes we assume to be operating. Then, we turn to several specific issues that are not only of theoretical importance in the context of the model we propose but also are of more general interest in understanding the factors that influence the initial interpretation of information and its ultimate effects. In the last section of this chapter, we provide examples of how the encoding phenomena we postulate can be applied in diagnosing the cognitive determinants of social behavior and judgments in situations both in and outside the laboratory.

General Considerations

Suppose people learn about a target person's behavior for the purpose of forming a general impression of this person. An initial step in this process is likely to involve an interpretation of the person's behaviors in terms of more general trait concepts that they exemplify. These trait encodings, which are performed by the Encoder/Organizer, are presumably based on the similarity between the features of each behavior to be encoded and the features of an attribute concept.[1] This concept is theoretically identified through the search and retrieval processes outlined in the last chapter. When an applicable trait concept happens to be in the Work Space at the time the behaviors are considered, this concept will usually be used to encode the behavior (see Postulate 5.2). Otherwise, the Executor performs a top-down search of the semantic bin until an applicable concept (i.e., a concept whose features are sufficiently similar to those of the behavior to justify the conclusion that it exemplifies the concept) is found. When two or more concepts are potentially applicable for interpreting a behavior, the first concept that is identified in the course of this top-down search is the one that is typically used.

Once the traits that are implied by the person's behaviors have been determined, people with an impression formation objective are likely to extract a general concept of the person as likeable or dislikeable based on the evaluative implications of these traits (Hartwick, 1979; for an elaboration of this assumption and evidence supporting it, see Chapter 7). This concept, along with features that have become associated with it in the course of forming it, is then transmitted both to the Work Space and also (via the Executor) to a referent bin in Permanent Storage.

Now suppose people are asked to judge the person's likeableness. The Work Space is the first area searched for judgment-relevant information. Therefore, if the judgment is requested a short time after the behaviors were learned and encoded, the Work Space may still contain both the concrete encodings of the behaviors that were sent there from the Comprehender and the representation formed from them, and so both may be used as bases for judgments. If a longer time has elapsed, however, the Work Space is likely to have been cleared, and so only the representation of the person that was transmitted to Permanent Storage can be retrieved and used as a basis for judgments. The initial interpretation of the person's behaviors in terms of trait concepts presumably influences the nature of this representation and its implications. Consequently, the particular concepts that are used to interpret the behaviors at the time they are first considered may have a substantial impact on the judgments that are ultimately made.

This possibility takes on added importance in light of the fact that the events that lead one or another applicable concept to be retrieved and used to interpret a person's behaviors may occur by chance, and may be totally irrelevant to the person or situation in which the behaviors take place. That is, they may simply be the concepts that were recently used for other, unrelated purposes, and therefore happen to be near the top of the semantic bin at the time the behaviors are learned. In other words, quite fortuitous events that lead a trait concept to be accessible in memory at the time behavioral information about a person is received may affect

---

1. Several rules have been postulated to underlie these similarity judgments (cf. Medin & Smith, 1981; Smith Shoben, & Rips, 1974; Tversky, 1977). Although a precise statement of these processes is ultimately important, they are beyond the scope of our discussion.

the interpretation of this information, and therefore may influence the impression that is formed of this person.

Although our description of these encoding processes and their effects seems straightforward, it makes several assumptions that require empirical validation. Moreover, a more rigorous analysis of these processes in terms of the proposed model leads to several specific predictions concerning when they will and will not occur and the factors that influence the magnitude of their effects. In the next section, we review a series of studies that bear on the validity of our description of the conceptualization outlined above and point out some additional implications of the conceptualization that have not as yet been tested.

Effects of Trait Category Accessibility on Person Impression Formation

The first study of the influence of trait concept accessibility on impression formation, which continues to be one of the most important, was conducted by Higgins, Rholes, and Jones (1977). Subjects read a paragraph describing a target person, Donald, as part of a study on reading comprehension. Before doing so, however, they performed a color-naming task as part of an ostensibly unrelated experiment. The task required them to learn 10 words, four of which were trait names. These trait names varied over experimental conditions in terms of both (a) their favorableness and (b) their applicability for encoding the behaviors described in the paragraph they were later asked to read about Donald. Specifically, under *Applicable Priming* conditions, the trait names activated concepts that were applicable for interpreting the behaviors to be presented but were either favorable (*adventurous, self-confident, independent, persistent*) or unfavorable (*reckless, conceited, aloof, stubborn*). In *Inapplicable Priming* conditions, they activated concepts that were also either favorable or unfavorable but were descriptively unrelated to the stimulus behaviors.

After completing the priming task, subjects then read the following description of Donald. (The applicable trait terms, which of course were not mentioned in the paragraph that subjects actually read, are indicated in parentheses following each behavior description.)

> Donald spent a great deal of his time in search of what he liked to call excitement. He had...risked injury, and even death, a number of times...He was thinking that perhaps he would do some skydiving or maybe cross the Atlantic in a sailboat (*adventurous/reckless*). By the way he acted, one could readily guess that Donald was well aware of his ability to do many things well (*self-confident/conceited*). Other than business engagements, Donald's contacts with people were rather limited. He felt he didn't really need to rely on anyone (*independent/aloof*). Once Donald made up his mind to do something, it was

as good as done...Only rarely did he change his mind, even when it might have been better if he had (*persistent/stubborn*). (Higgins et al., 1977, p. 145).

Subjects were then asked to describe Donald in their own words, and finally, to indicate how well they liked him.

When the trait concepts that were activated by the color-naming task were applicable for interpreting Donald's behavior, subjects' spontaneous descriptions of him often referred to attributes whose evaluative implications were consistent with these concepts. Moreover, their liking for Donald was biased toward the favorableness of the primed trait concepts. These effects were not evident in Inapplicable Priming conditions, where Donald's behavior could not be interpreted as exemplifying the concepts that were activated by the color-naming task. Here, the favorableness of these concepts had no influence on either subjects' descriptions of Donald or their liking for him.

The pattern of findings is not only consistent with the conceptualization we have proposed but eliminates certain alternative interpretations of "priming" effects. For example, one interpretation of the effects obtained under applicable trait priming conditions is that activating favorable (or unfavorable) trait concepts induces a general tendency to think positively (or negatively) about people in general, and, therefore, produces an evaluative bias in subjects' later descriptions and evaluations of the particular individual they were asked to consider. This bias could affect judgments independently of any effects that the primed concepts per se had on the interpretation of Donald's specific behaviors. If this interpretation were correct, however, subjects' judgments should have been affected when the primed traits were inapplicable as well as when they were applicable. The fact that this was not the case supports the contention that the effects of primed trait concepts on judgments were mediated by their effects on the interpretation of Donald's behavior, which in turn depended on their *descriptive* (denotative) applicability. Put another way, the initial encodings of the target's behaviors in terms of traits were based on purely descriptive considerations. Once these encodings were made, however, their evaluative implications provided a basis for forming a more general evaluative concept of Donald, and, therefore, influenced judgments of his likeableness.

The failure for judgments of Donald to be affected by priming inapplicable trait concepts is important for another reason. Our conception of the semantic bin assumes that concepts in this bin are stored and retrieved independently of one another, and that the retrieval and use of one concept does not increase the accessibility of others.[2] In contrast, other theoretical formulations of semantic memory assume that all trait concepts (as well as other concepts) are associated in

---

2. In fact, the activation of a concept, which results in a copy of the concept being deposited in the semantic bin on top of other concepts, should theoretically *decrease* the accessibility of the other concepts.

memory in a general associative network, based in part on their semantic similarity
(cf. Bower, 1981; Collins & Loftus, 1975; Wyer & Carlston, 1979). Bower (1981),
for example, assumes that evaluatively similar concepts are more strongly associated with one another than are evaluatively dissimilar ones (see also Rosenberg
& Sedlak, 1972), and that activating one concept therefore increases the accessibility of other, evaluatively similar ones. If this were so, however, the accessibility
in memory of applicable trait concepts should be increased not only by priming the
concepts themselves but also by priming other, inapplicable concepts that are
evaluatively similar. The failure for inapplicable trait priming to affect judgments
in Higgins et al.'s study disconfirms this prediction, and, therefore, is more
consistent with our conceptualization than with an associative network formulation
of semantic memory.

Frequency vs. Recency Effects

It seems intuitively obvious that the effect of priming a trait concept on the
interpretation of information will decrease with the time interval between the
activation of the concept and presentation of the information to be interpreted. In
terms of the proposed conceptualization, however, this is not a result of the time
interval per se. Rather, the decrease occurs because other applicable concepts are
likely to be activated in the interim, and copies of these concepts are redeposited
in the semantic bin on top of the explicitly primed concept. If subjects could be
prevented from engaging in cognitive activity that spontaneously activates other
applicable concepts in the time interval between their performance of the priming
task and the information they receive, the length of this interval should theoretically
have no influence on the likelihood of using the concept to interpret the information. (An alternative conceptualization that makes different predictions will be
considered presently.)

Our conceptualization also predicts a *frequency* effect. That is, the more often
a trait concept is primed, the more copies of it should be made and redeposited on
top of the semantic bin. Because the subsequent top-down search of the bin for an
applicable trait concept is imperfect, there is some probability that any given copy
of an applicable concept will be missed in this search. However, the more copies
of a concept that exist near the top of the bin, the more likely it is that a copy of the
concept will be identified and used. In other words, the likelihood of applying a
given trait concept should increase with the frequency of its prior activation as well
as the recency of its activation.

These basic predictions were confirmed in an early study by Srull and Wyer
(1979) that we described briefly in Chapter 5. Subjects initially completed a
sentence construction task that was ostensibly part of an experiment being conducted by an undergraduate honors student. Specifically, each item on the task
consisted of a set of four words, and subjects were asked to underline three of them

that could be used to make a sentence. In one, *hostility-priming* replication, the possible sentences constructed from some of the items (e.g., "hate her him I," "break arm his leg") presumably activated a concept associated with hostility. The sentences formed from other items (e.g., "paint box car the") were irrelevant to hostility. The overall number of items presented (30 vs. 60) and the proportion of hostility-related items (20% vs. 80%) varied over conditions. Thus, a total of either 6, 12, 24, or 48 hostility-related items were presented. A second, *kindness-priming* replication was similar except that the sentences that could be constructed conveyed kindness rather than hostility.

After completing the task, some subjects were immediately given an impression formation task in which they read a paragraph about a target person, Donald, and then rated him along a variety of trait dimensions. Other subjects were dismissed with the pretense that the materials for the other studies to be conducted were not ready. These subjects returned either one hour or one day later, at which time the impression formation task was performed.

The paragraph describing Donald contained several behaviors that were ambiguous with respect to the primed trait concept. That is, they could be interpreted as exemplifying this trait or another, unrelated one. For example, the paragraph administered in the hostility-priming replication was:

> I ran into my old acquaintance Donald the other day and I decided to go over and visit him, since, by coincidence, we took our vacations at the same time. Soon after I arrived, a salesman knocked at the door, but Donald refused to let him enter. He also told me that he was refusing to pay his rent until the landlord repaints his apartment. We talked for awhile, had lunch, and then went out for a ride. We used my car, since Donald's car had broken down that morning, and he told the garage mechanic that he would have to go somewhere else if he couldn't fix his car that same day. We went to the park for about an hour and then stopped at a hardware store. I was sort of preoccupied, but Donald bought some small gadget and then I heard him demand his money back from the sales clerk. I couldn't find what I was looking for, so we left and walked a few blocks to another store. The Red Cross had set up a stand by the door and asked us to donate blood. Donald lied by saying he had diabetes and, therefore, could not give blood. It's funny that I hadn't noticed it before, but when we got to the store, we found that it had gone out of business. It was getting kind of late, so I took Donald to pick up his car, and we agreed to meet again as soon as possible.

Mean judgments of Donald with respect to the primed trait are shown in Figure 6.1 for both replications. Judgments increased with the number of trait-relevant priming items contained in the initial sentence construction task and decreased with the time interval between the performance of the priming task and presentation of the stimulus information. Although this is hardly surprising, two aspects of the results are worth noting.

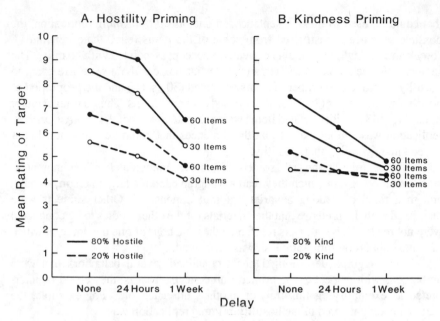

Figure 6.1 Mean ratings of the target person in terms of (a) hostility and (b) kindness as a function of the number of times the trait concept was primed and the time interval between priming and presentation of the stimulus information.

1. In the hostility-priming replication, only six priming items were sufficient to activate the trait concepts and, therefore, to affect subjects' ratings of Donald. (This is evidenced by the fact that ratings of Donald's hostility decreased over time under this condition. This would not have occurred if the priming items had not had some influence under "immediate" conditions.)

2. Although the effect of priming hostility decreased over time, it was still evident 24 hours after the initial priming task was administered. This seems counterintuitive. It is of course conceivable that many subjects did not activate and apply other judgment-relevant trait concepts during the 24 hours between experimental sessions, and so the primed concept was still near the top of the semantic bin despite the long delay. An alternative possibility, however, is that subjects who returned to the same experimental room 24 hours later spontaneously retrieved an episodic representation of their experience in the first session from a *referent* (i.e., "experiment") bin, and that features of this representation, once they were in the Work Space, were used as a basis for interpreting the stimulus information without accessing concepts from the semantic bin (see Postulate 5.2).

Note that these effects were not as evident in the kindness-priming replication. That is, more priming items were apparently necessary to produce an effect on the interpretation of the stimulus information, and the effect did not persist over as long a period of time. Perhaps the priming items used in this replication were not as clear exemplifiers of kindness, and, therefore, were less likely to activate a trait concept than were the priming items used in the hostility-priming replication. Moreover, the types of behaviors described in the stimulus paragraphs may have been more common. Consequently, alternative concepts that were applicable for interpreting these behaviors may have been more likely to be activated during the 24-hour delay.

Alternative Interpretations of Trait Priming Effects

1. General Considerations

Our interpretation of the results obtained by Higgins et al. and by Srull and Wyer assumes that the effects of priming trait concepts are mediated by the influence of these concepts on the interpretation of the information to which they are applicable. In addition, it assumes that the effects occur "on line," at the time the information is first presented. However, at least three other interpretations could be given to these results when considered in isolation.

1. Rather than interpreting the behavioral information in terms of trait concepts at the time it is received, subjects may read and store the information in memory in relatively unadulterated form. Then, when they are asked to make a particular judgment, they retrieve the information and interpret it in terms of whatever relevant concepts are most easily accessible at this time. In other words, the interpretative processes that underlie the effects observed in the earlier study could conceivably occur at the time of judgment and not at the time of information input.

2. Perhaps the effects are not mediated by the interpretation of the information in terms of trait concepts at all. Subjects who are asked to make a trait or evaluative judgment of a target may base their judgments on the implications of whatever they happen to be thinking about, independently of any specific information that is presented about the target. Thus, for example, people who have recently been thinking about favorable trait concepts may have a bias to make favorable judgments, whereas those who have been thinking about negative concepts may be disposed to make negative judgments, independently of the characteristics of the object being judged. As we noted earlier, this interpretation is called into question to some extent by Higgins et al.'s (1977) findings. That is, priming favorable and unfavorable trait concepts did not affect judgments unless these concepts were descriptively applicable for interpreting the behavioral information. Nonetheless, the interpretation would provide an alternative account of Srull and Wyer's results.

3. Despite attempts to dissociate the task in which trait concepts were primed from the subsequent impression formation task, it is conceivable that subjects had insight into their relatedness, and complied with implicit expectancies to use the

primed concept as a basis for judgments. Indeed, the frequency and recency effects observed by Srull and Wyer (1980) could simply reflect the effects of these variables on the salience of these experimental demands.

Fortunately, subsequent studies by Srull and Wyer (1980) argue against these alternative interpretations. Two sets of findings are important. First, if the interpretations outlined above were valid, priming effects should decrease with the salience of the primed concept at the time the judgments are reported or, in other words, with the time interval between the priming task and judgments. Moreover, this should be true regardless of whether this time interval occurs (a) between the priming task and presentation of the stimulus information or (b) between presentation of the information and judgments. In contrast, the interpretation we have proposed suggests that although priming effects should decrease with the time interval between priming and information presentation, it should *increase* with the interval between information presentation and judgments (i.e., with the likelihood that the Work Space is cleared of the original information). Figure 6.2 shows the results of a study (Srull & Wyer, 1980) in which either no time, one hour, or one day was interpolated between presentation of the priming task and judgments. In some cases, however, this time interval occurred between priming and information presentation, and in other cases between information presentation and judgments. Priming effects clearly decreased over time in the first case but increased over time in the second. (For additional evidence of an increase in priming effects with the time interval between stimulus presentation and judgments, see Higgins et al., 1977.)

The three alternative hypotheses are further called into question by the results of a second study (Srull & Wyer, 1980) in which the priming task was performed *after* rather than before the behavior information was presented. That is, subjects first read a paragraph about Donald, and then performed the sentence construction task. The frequency and recency of priming judgment-relevant trait concepts were manipulated as in the earlier studies. If the encoding of information in terms of a primed trait concept occurs at the time of judgment, the effects of these variables should be at least as great as they are when traits are primed before the stimulus information is presented. In fact, however, these variables had no influence on judgments whatsoever. Indeed, no priming effects at all were evident. These results confirm the assumption that the effect of priming concepts on the interpretation of information occurs at the time the information is first received. Once these interpretations have been made, their implications are used as a basis for later judgments, and the original information is not retrieved and reinterpreted in terms of concepts that become available subsequently.

There is one qualification on this conclusion, however. According to our conceptualization, behaviors are not encoded spontaneously in terms of trait concepts unless these trait encodings are relevant to a specific processing objective. In the studies we have reported, subjects received the stimulus information with

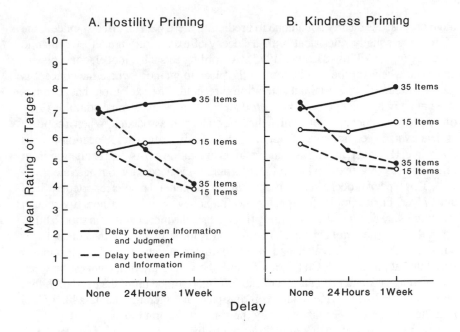

Figure 6.2 Mean ratings of the target person in terms of (a) hostility and (b) kindness as a function of the number of priming items, the length of the delay, and the type of delay. (Adapted from Srull & Wyer, 1980, pp. 846-847.)

instructions to form an impression of the person it described. The interpretation of the person's behaviors in terms of traits was presumably relevant to the attainment of this objective and, therefore, was performed "on line," as the behaviors were learned. In contrast, suppose subjects read the information with the goal of remembering it, or for some other purpose that does not require trait encodings. Then, they should not perform these encodings on line. Consequently, if they are *later* told to form an impression of the person, they must retrieve the unencoded behaviors from memory and interpret them in terms of whatever applicable trait concepts come to mind at the time these objectives are imposed. In this case, then, activating trait concepts after the information is presented (but before an impression formation objective is introduced) *should* have an influence.

2. A Theoretical Challenge

The results obtained by Srull and Wyer (1979) demonstrate that both the frequency and recency of activating a trait concept influence the likelihood that the concept will be used to interpret behavioral information. However, the model we have proposed is clearly not unique in predicting these general effects. Indeed, the effects are equally consistent with a "decay-of-excitation" model of semantic memory (e.g., Collins & Loftus, 1975). According to such a model, concepts are activated whenever the "excitation" at the place in memory where the concept is located exceeds some minimal activation threshold. The excitation that accumulates at a given concept location is produced either by an external stimulus or by other activated concepts with which the first concept is associated. When a concept is deactivated (i.e., no longer thought about), the excitation at its location decays over time. However, as long as some residual excitation exists, less excitation from other sources (e.g., external stimulus information) is necessary to reactivate it.

This type of model can clearly account for the general results reported by Srull and Wyer. For example, the greater the frequency with which hostility-related statements are contained in the initial priming task, the more excitation should build up at the "hostile" trait concept. Therefore, it is more likely that the concept will subsequently be reactivated and used to interpret the stimulus information presented about Donald. On the other hand, the longer the time interval between the priming task and presentation of the information, the more the excitation that was produced by the priming task will dissipate, and therefore the less likely it is that the concept will be reactivated by the stimulus information.

A refinement of such a model, proposed by Higgins, Bargh, and Lombardi (1985), leads to some interesting predictions. They propose that the frequency of activating a concept node has its primary effect on the *rate* at which excitation decays at the node once the concept is deactivated. Specifically, the excitation associated with frequently activated concepts decays less rapidly than the excitation associated with infrequently activated ones. This leads to an interesting prediction. Suppose two concepts are equally applicable for interpreting a particular piece of information. If the information is presented a very short time after one of the concepts has been activated, this more recently activated concept may be the one that is used to interpret it. However, if this concept has been used less frequently than the other one, it will ultimately lose its advantage, and the more frequently activated concept will be used.

To test this hypothesis, Higgins et al. initially exposed subjects to a 20-item sentence construction task similar to the one employed by Srull and Wyer. Five of the items (occupying positions 3, 7, 12, 15 and 20 in the sequence) contained a trait term that was necessary to use in order to construct a meaningful sentence. The five terms had similar descriptive implications. However, the first four denoted a concept that differed in its evaluative implications from the last one. In one condition, for example, the first four terms were synonyms of a favorable concept (e.g., *adventurous*, *bold*, *courageous* and *brave*) and the last one contained a term denoting an unfavorable concept with descriptively similar implications (e.g., *reckless*). In a second condition, the first four items contained synonyms of the unfavorable trait concept (*reckless*, *careless*, *foolhardy*, and *rash*) and the last item contained a term denoting the favorable one (*adventurous*). After performing the task, subjects were asked to count backwards for either 15 seconds or 120 seconds, after which they were given a statement with instructions to generate a single word that would describe the object to whom the statement pertained. In certain conditions, the statement described a behavior of a person that could be encoded in terms of either alternative trait concept (e.g., wanting to cross the Atlantic in a sailboat). Which concept—the one that was primed more recently (but less frequently) or the one that was primed more frequently (but less recently)—is more likely to be applied?

The results were quite clear. Under short (15-second) delay conditions, most subjects (21 of 30, or 70%) generated a concept that was either the same as or evaluatively similar to the more recently activated concept. Under long (120 second) delay conditions, however, most subjects (16 of 30, or 53%) generated a term that was synonymous with the more frequently primed concept. In other words, recency of activation predominated after a very short delay, whereas frequency of activation predominated after a long one.

These results are certainly consistent with the implications of Higgins et al.'s conceptualization. The question is whether the conceptualization we have proposed can account for them as well. The predominance of the more frequently activated concept under long delay conditions would be quite consistent with our formulation if the probability of identifying any given concept in the top-down search of the semantic bin (p) is rather low. Suppose that the order of priming favorable (F) and unfavorable (U) concepts if FFFFU. As a result of this priming, a copy of U should be at the top of the semantic bin, followed by four copies of F. Suppose that $p = .3$. Then, the probability of retrieving and applying the unfavorable (more recent) concept is

$$P(U) = p = .3.$$

However, the probability of retrieving the favorable (more frequent) concept is

$$P(F) = (1 - p)p + (1 - p)^2 p + (1 - p)^3 p + (1 - p)^4 p$$
$$= .7(.3) + .49(.3) + .343(.3) + .240(.3) = .531.$$

The strong recency effect of priming under 15-second delay conditions is more difficult for the proposed model to explain. Suppose the Work Space has already been cleared by the time 15 seconds had elapsed (which seems implausible). Then, the relative probabilities of activating the two alternative concepts should be the same as they are under long delay conditions. If, on the other hand, none of the Work Space has been cleared, subjects are most likely to apply the concept they identify in a random search of this area (Postulate 5.3). In this case, the more frequently activated concept should *also* be the more likely to be used, as more copies of this concept are represented there. The only way for the model to account for the effect is to assume that the cognitive activity required to perform the interpolated counting task leads part of the material to be cleared from the Work Space but not all of it. Because the least recently used material is the first to be removed (Postulate 3.3), a copy of the more recently used concept should be retained longer in the Work Space than copies of the earlier (more frequently used) ones, and this could produce the recency effect that Higgins et al. observed.

3. Some Additional Implications

Our interpretation of Higgins et al.'s results has additional implications that distinguish it from a decay-of-activation model.

1. The relative advantage of the more frequently activated and more recently activated concepts in Higgins et al.'s study should also depend on the difficulty of the interpolated task, and, therefore, on the likelihood that performing the task will displace information from the Work Space. Moreover, the effect should theoretically be nonmonotonic. If the task is simple and requires few cognitive resources, no material may be displaced from the Work Space. If this is so, the more frequently (less recently) activated concept should be represented more often in the Work Space and therefore should have the predominant influence. If the task is moderately difficult, the Work Space should be partially but not completely cleared, increasing the likelihood that the more recently activated concept will predominate. If the task is *very* difficult, however, the Work Space may be completely cleared, and so the concepts applied must be drawn from the semantic bin. If this is the case, the more frequently used concept should regain its advantage, as in long delay conditions of Higgins et al.'s study.

2. Higgins et al.'s conceptualization implies that frequency will always predominate over recency if a sufficient period of time has elapsed after the concept has been activated. The model we propose, however, predicts that in many instances, recency will continue to have the predominant influence. Reconsider the numerical example we provided earlier. This time, however, suppose that the more recently primed concept is activated twice rather than only once, and so the presentation sequence is FFFFUU. Then, assuming again that $p = .3$,

$$P(U) = p + (1 - p)p = .3 + .7(.3) = .51.$$

In other words, if U is activated twice at the end of the priming sequence, $P(U)$ is greater than .5, and so it should theoretically always have the predominant influence regardless of how many times F has occurred prior to it. More generally, the model we propose predicts that frequency will predominate over recency only if the number of times that the more recently primed concept is activated is less than some minimal value.

3. A related consideration is the *proportion* of times that two activated concepts are primed. Compare the effects of the priming sequence FFU with the effects of the priming sequence FFFFUU. The proportion of times that the two concepts are activated is the same in both cases. However, the proposed model predicts that the more recently activated concept will have a greater advantage over the frequently activated one in the second case than in the first.

4. More general and perhaps more interesting implications of the proposed conceptualization concern the nonparallel effects of priming on (a) the type of interpretation that is made of information and (b) the time required to generate this interpretation. Suppose two trait concepts, F and U, are each primed once. In one condition, this is done after presenting stimuli that require the activation of several other semantic concepts. In a second condition, it is done before presenting these stimuli. Later, a piece of stimulus information is presented that can be interpreted in terms of F and U but none of the other concepts that were activated. The relative likelihood of applying F and U should theoretically be the same in both conditions. However, the time required to retrieve and activate them should be greater in the second condition (where copies of other, irrelevant concepts are deposited on top of them in the semantic bin) than in the first.

As a second example, suppose F and U are either presented on successive trials, at the end of a priming stimulus series, or that several irrelevant semantic concepts are primed in between them. (That is, suppose the priming sequence is either XXXXFU or FXXXXU, where X is a statement that primes an irrelevant concept.) The model again predicts that the manipulation will not influence the relative likelihood of using F and U. Moreover, the response time of subjects who use the most recently primed concept (U) should also not be affected by the manipulation. In contrast, those subjects who use the less recently primed concept (i.e., those who have missed U in their top-down search of the semantic bin, and so identify F instead) should take longer to respond in the "separated" condition. The "energy cell" conceptualization proposed by Higgins et al. does not appear to predict these nonparallel effects on judgments and response times.

5. The model we propose generates quantitative predictions as well as qualitative ones. Theoretically, only one parameter, p, must be estimated from the data in order to determine the likelihood of retrieving and applying a concept under any given priming condition. In principle, therefore, a precise test of the model could be constructed by estimating the value of p on the basis of data obtained in one priming condition and (b) using this value to predict the likelihood of using the alternative concepts in other conditions. For example, suppose the concepts F and U are equally applicable for interpreting a piece of behavioral information, and that these concepts are primed in either the order (a) FFUFU, (b) FUFUF, or (c) UFUFF. The value of p should theoretically be the same in all three conditions.

Therefore, the value of *p* that is obtained by applying the formulation to the observed probabilities of using F and U in the first condition should effectively predict the relative probabilities of using these concepts in the other conditions as well.

Generalizeability of Priming Effects to Other Trait Judgments

The results reported by Higgins et al. (1977) indicate that the effects of priming trait concepts depend on the descriptive applicability of these concepts to the behaviors to be encoded. That is, the evaluative implications of trait concepts do not themselves affect the interpretation of behaviors that are encountered at the time that these concepts are activated. However, this does not mean that priming effects on *judgments* are restricted to the specific attributes to which the primed trait concepts are relevant. In fact, the effects may generalize to judgments of traits for which the primed concepts have no implications whatsoever.

The reason for this is implied by the account of impression formation processes we provided earlier, and the distinction we have made between *trait* concepts and *person* concepts (see Chapter 4). That is, once a target person's behaviors are individually interpreted in terms of trait concepts, subjects attempt to extract an evaluative concept of the *person* as likeable or dislikeable. After this person concept is formed, the target may be inferred to have attributes that are typical of the sort of person that he or she exemplifies (i.e., likeable or dislikeable) regardless of the descriptive relevance of these attributes to the one that was initially primed. Therefore, in the studies constructed by Srull and Wyer (1979, 1980), priming a hostile trait concept presumably led a target person's behavior to be interpreted as "hostile" based on a comparison of the features of the behavior with those that define this trait concept. The target was identified as a dislikeable person on the basis of this encoding. Once this is done, the target was inferred to have a variety of other negative attributes that are descriptively unrelated to hostility but are typical of dislikeable individuals (low intelligence, conceitedness, etc.). It is important to recognize the point in the overall impression formation process at which these various effects occur. The initial encoding of behaviors in terms of a primed trait concept is based exclusively on descriptive considerations. Only after this is done, and the target is identified as an instance of a general person concept, do evaluative considerations come into play. When they do, however, their effects can be quite far-reaching.

Automatic vs. Controlled Processes in Concept Accessibility Effects

The interpretation of behavior information in terms of trait concepts is postulated to be the result of higher order goal-directed activities that are performed by the Encoder/Organizer. However, this does not mean that subjects are always aware of *why* they happen to use particular concepts to interpret the information or of the conditions that led them to be accessible. This is because their accessibility is often the result of actions performed by the Comprehender, which functions independently of the Executor and is, therefore, not under conscious control. Only the *output* of the Comprehender, which is transmitted to the Work Space, is available to the Executor and, therefore, is subject to awareness; the cognitive processes that led the output to be generated are not.

As an example, a person who reads "the lawyer is hostile" is aware of having read the sentence and of its meaning. However, the person is not aware of the process of retrieving the noun and attribute concepts that were necessary to interpret it, or of any of the other cognitive mechanisms that were involved in understanding it. Moreover, unless that statement is relevant to some higher order processing goal, it may never be sent to Permanent Storage, and so it may be forgotten once the Work Space is cleared. Nevertheless, copies of the concepts that were used by the Comprehender to interpret the statement, which were drawn from the semantic bin, are then redeposited on top of it. Consequently, these concepts are more likely to be used to interpret subsequent information to which they are applicable.

In short, people may often interpret ambiguous information in terms of trait concepts without knowing why they happened to select these particular concepts and not others. This means that in the paradigm we have been considering, priming trait concepts may have an influence even though subjects are unaware that these concepts were activated in the course of performing the priming task, and cannot even recall having recently thought about them.

Research by Bargh and his colleagues (Bargh, 1984; Bargh & Pietromonaco, 1982) provides support for this contention. In one study, subjects were initially exposed to a perceptual identification task in which they were told that a flash of light would appear on a screen for a very short period of time and that their task was to press a button as soon as they saw it. In fact, the spot of light was a word that in either 0%, 20%, or 80% of the cases was hostility related. (In fact, the words were taken from the sentences used by Srull and Wyer in their sentence construction task.) Presumably, some of the flashes were in fact recognized as words, and were interpreted as such by the Comprehender in terms of a concept drawn from the semantic bin. However, the interpreted words are not ostensibly relevant to any higher order objective, and so they were likely to be cleared from the Work Space without becoming involved in any higher order goal-directed processing. (Consequently, subjects are unlikely to remember what those words were if later asked to recall them.) Subjects after performing this task were asked to read the Donald paragraph constructed by Srull and Wyer (1979, 1980) and to judge Donald's hostility. These judgments were more hostile in the 80% priming condition than in the 20% priming condition, and this was true despite the fact that subjects in a post-experiment recognition task showed no better than chance accuracy in identifying which words had been presented during the priming task. These results, which have been conceptually replicated in several studies since (e.g., Bargh, Bond, Lombardi, & Tota, 1986; Erdley & D'Agostino, 1988), are quite consistent with implications of the formulation we have proposed.

Assimilation vs. Contrast Effects of Activating Trait Concepts

The indication that priming effects can occur without awareness that trait concepts have actually been primed provides further evidence against a demand compliance interpretation of priming phenomena. In fact, if subjects *are* aware that the trait concepts they happen to think of when they receive stimulus information may have been activated by extraneous factors, they may intentionally avoid using these concepts to interpret the information. As a consequence, priming trait concepts under the latter conditions may sometimes have a negative, or contrast effect on judgments.

Indirect evidence that this may be true was obtained in a very provocative series of studies by Leonard Martin (1985, 1986). One particularly ingenious experiment (Martin, 1986) is illustrative. Subjects performed a series of ostensibly unrelated tasks. One, the priming task, required them to sort behaviors into two trait categories. In one case, the categories were "intelligent" and "adventurous," and in the other case, they were "intelligent" and "reckless." In *completed task* conditions, subjects were asked to sort eight behaviors, four of which exemplified each trait. In *uncompleted task* conditions, subjects were given 16 behaviors but were interrupted after sorting the first eight behaviors under the pretense that this was all the time available for the task. Therefore, all subjects actually sorted the same number of behaviors. The only difference was that some subjects thought they had completed the task whereas others thought they had not done so.

After performing several short interpolated tasks, subjects read a section of the "Donald" paragraph prepared by Higgins et al., describing a person who wanted to cross the Atlantic in a sailboat, etc. Under uncompleted task conditions, priming had the usual effect; that is, subjects' judgments of Donald along a reckless vs. adventurous dimension were biased toward the trait concept that was primed. In completed task conditions, however, *contrast* effects occurred. That is, subjects judged the target as less adventurous (or more reckless) if "adventurous" had been primed than if "reckless" had been activated.

Martin argued that in uncompleted task conditions, subjects did not associate the primed trait concept with the sorting task. Consequently, they assumed that the concept was activated by the information about Donald, and so they used it to interpret Donald's behaviors. Under completed task conditions, however, subjects more frequently connected the primed concept with the behavior sorting task, and so they consciously avoided using the concept to interpret the information about

Donald. Consequently, the alternative concept was more likely to be used, producing the contrast effect that Martin observed.

Martin's findings suggest that the effect of priming trait concepts on the interpretation of information may be evident only when subjects do not have insight into why the primed concepts come to mind, and, therefore, assume that they are activated by the stimulus material. (For a more recent study with similiar implications, see Lombardi, Higgins, and Bargh, 1987.) Ironically, this means that the introduction of experimenter demands into an experiment may decrease the likelihood of obtaining priming effects rather than increasing them.

An Alternative Interpretation

Although the above interpretation of Martin's results has some intuitive appeal, its implications may be somewhat embarrassing to the general formulation we have proposed. Specifically, the trait concepts that are used to interpret information are theoretically identified by the Executor and transmitted to the Encoder/Organizer for use in performing the encoding. Based on the assumptions we have made, there is no reason to suppose that the Executor transmits only those concepts that have not been consciously activated in the course of performing other tasks. To the contrary, the model assumes that the Executor sends the first potentially applicable trait concept it encounters in its search of the Work Space and (if no applicable concepts are found there) the semantic bin, regardless of why they were previously activated. Consequently, Martin's interpretation of these data is difficult for the proposed model to accommodate.

An alternative interpretation of Martin's data is possible and is more compatible with our formulation. This interpretation assumes that the positive effects of primed trait concepts obtained under incompleted task conditions are the consequence of encoding operations of the sort we have postulated. However, the contrast effects detected under completed task conditions are the result of comparison operations that occur at a later, response selection stage of processing. As we elaborate in Chapter 11, the generation of an overt response often involves the prior selection of a standard relative to which the element being judged is compared. In the present case, the target's adventurousness or recklessness may be evaluated in relation to a standard person that happens to be accessible at the time. Conceivably, subjects under completed task conditions of Martin's study, unlike those in incompleted task conditions, spontaneously formed a concept of a person who manifested the behaviors they had categorized, and later used this person as a standard of comparison in judging the target. Consequently, subjects who had categorized extremely reckless behaviors used a "reckless" person as a standard, and so they judged the target to be relatively less reckless (i.e., more adventurous) than did subjects who had sorted adventurous behaviors (and therefore used an "adventurous" person as a standard). These standards may not be applied when subjects have not completed the priming task, and, therefore, do not spontaneously form a concept of the person who performed the behaviors they sorted.

Assumptions similar to those we have made in interpreting Martin's results are also applicable to a study by Herr, Sherman, and Fazio (1983), who also found contrast effects of primed concepts on judgments. The priming stimuli used in their studies were names of animals that were either extreme or moderate in ferocity (in Experiment 1) or were extreme or moderate in size (in Experiment 2). These stimuli were primed with a color-naming task similar to that used by Higgins et al. (1977) to activate trait concepts. Then, as part of an ostensibly different study, subjects were given a series of animals and asked to judge them with respect to the attribute being considered. Included in the stimulus set were names of two fictitious animals ("jabo" and "lemphor"). When the priming stimuli had moderate values along the attribute dimension (e.g., they were either moderately ferocious or moderately unferocious), they had a positive influence on judgments of the fictitious animals along this dimension, but had contrast effects on judgments of the real animals. When the priming stimuli had extreme values along the attribute dimension, they had contrast effects on judgments of the stimulus animals regardless of whether they were fictitious or real.

The type of stimuli and judgments considered by Herr et al. are quite different from those employed in the study by Martin and other experiments we have reviewed. Similar processes may nevertheless operate. In fact, the contingency of priming effects on the ambiguity of the stimuli being judged was evident in the earlier study by Srull and Wyer (1979), who found that primed trait concepts had less influence on the interpretation of behaviors that were clear exemplars of these concepts (or their bipolar opposites) than on behaviors that were ambiguous. The contingency of priming effects on the extremity of the priming stimuli can be interpreted in much the same way we interpreted Martin's findings. Specifically, exposure to stimuli that are only moderately extreme with respect to an attribute may prime an attribute concept (e.g., "ferocious") without necessarily activating a concept of an object that has the attribute ("ferocious animals"). The attribute concept may then have an influence on the interpretation of ambiguous stimulus features, producing effects analogous to those observed in Martin's "incompleted task" condition. However, exposure to stimuli with extreme values along an attribute dimension may lead subjects to think about an *object* who has the attribute, and therefore may activate an object concept (e.g., "ferocious animal") as well as an attribute concept. If this occurs, the object concept may later be used as a standard of comparison, producing contrast effects analogous to those obtained in Martin's "completed task" condition.

Individual Differences in Concept Accessibility

In all of the studies we have described thus far, the accessibility of trait concepts was increased experimentally by having subjects perform a task that required their use. More general individual differences in concept accessibility may also exist that persist over time and situations. These differences in "chronic" accessibility may reflect differences in the frequency with which the concepts are typically used by people who occupy different social or vocational roles, have different recreational interests, or for other reasons make differential use of these concepts. In each case, those factors may affect the number of copies of the concepts that are located near the top of the semantic bin.

The effects of such individual differences were compellingly demonstrated by Bargh, Bond, Lombardi, and Tota (1986). The chronic accessibility of two trait concepts, kind and shy, was inferred from the frequency with which subjects had used the concepts to describe persons in a previous experiment. Then, in the main experiment, subjects for whom one of the two concepts was either high or low in chronic accessibility performed a priming task in which the situation-specific accessibility of this concept was manipulated using procedures similar to those employed by Bargh and Pietromonaco (1982). Later, subjects read a stimulus passage describing behaviors of a target person that were ambiguous with respect to the primed trait, and then judged the target with respect to both this and other, unmentioned traits that were either favorable or unfavorable.

Table 6.1 shows judgments of the target person (along a 0-10 scale) with respect to both the trait to which priming manipulations were directly relevant and unrelated traits. Experimentally-induced concept accessibility and chronic concept accessibility had independent and additive effects on judgments of the trait to which the primed concept was relevant. That is, both types of accessibility increased the extremity of ratings of the target person with respect to the trait. Moreover, in the "kind" trait replication, where the primed trait concept was favorable, ratings along unrelated trait dimensions were also affected. In contrast, in the "shy" replication, where the primed concept was evaluatively neutral, the effect of concept accessibility on judgments of unrelated traits was not evident. This latter contingency supports our interpretation of the conditions in which priming effects generalize over trait dimensions.

These data, therefore, provide evidence that individual differences in concept accessibility can have an important influence on the interpretation of information and on judgments based on this information. Moreover, these effects neither override, nor are they overridden by, more transitory, situationally-induced differences in the accessibility of the concepts.

Effects of vocational or social roles. Bargh et al.'s study is the most rigorous empirical demonstration of the effects of individual differences in concept accessibility that has been reported at this writing. However, the results of many studies

TABLE 6.1

Mean Trait Judgments of Target Person as a Function of The Chronic and Situationally-Induced Accessibility of the Trait Concept (adapted from Bargh, Bond, Lombardi, & Tota, 1986)

	"Kind" Trait Replication		"Shy" Trait Replication	
	High situationally-induced accessibility	Low situationally-induced accessibility	High situationally-induced accessibility	Low situationally-induced accessibility
1. Judgments along relevant trait dimension				
High chronic accessibility	7.8	7.2	8.0	7.5
Low chronic accessibility	6.9	6.7	7.7	7.4
2. Judgments along unrelated trait dimensions				
High chronic accessibility	6.6	6.1	5.1	4.7
Low chronic accessibility	5.8	5.6	5.2	5.3

are interpretable in terms of such differences. As noted earlier, it seems reasonable to suppose that individuals' social or vocational roles may often lead certain types of concepts to be more frequently (and recently) used, and therefore to be more chronically accessible. Therefore, they are more likely to be used to interpret new information.

An interesting example is provided by Anderson, Reynolds, Schallert, and Goetz (1976). Subjects in a classroom situation were asked to read the following story:

Every Saturday night, four good friends get together. When Jerry, Mike and Pat arrived, Karen was sitting in her living room writing some notes. She quickly gathered the cards and stood up to greet her friends at the door. They followed her into the living room but as usual they couldn't agree on exactly what to play. Jerry eventually took a stand and set things up. Finally, they began to play. Karen's recorder filled the room with soft and pleasant music. Early in the evening, Mike noticed Pat's hand and the many diamonds. As the night progressed the tempo of play increased. Finally, a lull in the activities occurred. Taking advantage of this, Jerry pondered the arrangement in front of him. Mike interrupted Jerry's reverie and said, "Let's hear the score." They listened carefully and commented on their performance. When the comments were all heard, exhausted but happy, Karen's friends all went home. [pp. 10-11]

The above paragraph is typically interpreted as concerning a group of friends who get together to play cards. However, it could also be about the rehearsal session of a woodwind ensemble. A second ambiguous paragraph was also constructed that could be interpreted as describing either a convict's attempt to escape from prison or a wrestler's attempt to break the hold of his opponent. Subjects after reading one of these paragraphs answered a series of multiple choice questions, each of which had two correct answers, depending on the interpretation given in the paragraph. (For example, a question pertaining to the paragraph described above concerned what the four people commented on, and the response alternatives included "the sound of their music" and "how well they were playing cards.")

Participants in the study were either female students who were planning a career in music education or students from a weight-lifting class in physical education. Music-related concepts are more likely to be chronically accessible to music education majors than to physical education majors, whereas sports-related concepts are more likely to be chronically accessible to physical education majors than to music majors. Consistent with this assumption, music majors gave more music-correct answers to questions about the first paragraph, but fewer wrestling-correct answers to questions about the second paragraph, than did the physical education majors.

There are some methodological ambiguities in interpreting these results. For example, the information was presented in classes that were either primarily for music education majors or primarily for physical education majors. It is quite possible that the different concepts that were used to interpret the information by students in these classes were activated by features of the immediate classroom situation and did not reflect differences in their chronic accessibility. The classroom context may also have induced expectations for subjects to select class-relevant alternatives to the forced-choice questions they were asked. These interpretative ambiguities cannot be dismissed. It nevertheless seems intuitively likely in light of Bargh et al.'s findings that similar results would occur even if they were eliminated.

Effects of general values. In fact, recognition of the possibility that individual differences in the chronic accessibility of concepts produce differences in the interpretation of information is not new. It stems at least from the New Look in perception (cf. Bruner, 1957). In one of several studies, Bruner (1951) exposed subjects to pictures that could be interpreted in two ways, each of which required the use of concepts associated with a different one of the six values measured by the Allport-Vernon Study of Values test: religious, economic, theoretical, social, political, and aesthetic. For example, one of the pictures could be interpreted as either a man bending over at work, or a man bending over to pray. Subjects with different value orientations were shown the pictures tachistoscopically and asked to describe what they saw. Subjects typically described the pictures in terms of concepts that were related to their values. For example, subjects with strong religious values tended to see the picture described above as a man praying, those with strong economic values tended to see it as a man working, and those who were not characterized by either of these values showed no consensus in how they perceived the picture. Comparable results were found with each of the other pictures.

Effects of Immediate Goals and Needs on the Interpretation of Information

A person who is pursuing a particular objective may activate concepts that are useful in attaining this objective. These concepts may affect the interpretation of both goal-relevant information and other, goal-irrelevant information, and these interpretations, once made, may influence judgments of the persons and objects to which the information pertains. Thus, for example, a man who talks with a woman for the purpose of deciding whether she would be a good graduate student may activate a set of concepts that are particularly relevant to this objective. Consequently, he may interpret the woman's behavior differently than he would if his goal were to decide whether to ask her for a date. This interpretation, once made, may influence the man's later judgments of the woman independently of the direct implications of her behavior for these judgments. The goals that seem likely to produce these effects may either be transitory and situation-specific or may be general and pervasive, occupying a large portion of a person's daily life activities over a period of days or even years.

The effect of transitory goals was examined in a series of studies on the effects of interpersonal communication conducted by Higgins and his colleagues. In an initial study (Higgins & Rholes, 1978), subjects were told they would read a paragraph describing a target person, and that they would then be asked to prepare a description of the person that would permit him to be identified by an acquaintance who either liked the target or disliked him. The paragraph that subjects actually read was similar to the "Donald" paragraph used by Higgins et al. (1977), containing behaviors that could alternatively be interpreted in terms of either favorable trait concepts or unfavorable ones. Subjects after reading the paragraph prepared their description of the target to be given to the intended recipient and then personally evaluated the target.

It seems reasonable to suppose that in writing their description of the target, subjects would encode the target's behavior in terms of trait concepts that were evaluatively consistent with those they expected the intended recipient would use, thereby increasing the likelihood that the recipient would be able to identify him on the basis of this description. Once these encodings are performed, however, they may provide the basis for subjects' own representations of the target, and thus may affect their personal judgments of the target. This appeared to be the case. Subjects who believed that the recipient liked the target used more favorable trait descriptions in their messages, and later judged the target to be more likeable themselves, than did subjects who believed that the recipient disliked the target.

Considered in isolation, the above results could simply be attributed to a tendency for subjects to conform to the apparent opinions of the message recipient. However, this interpretation is not viable. In a second set of conditions, subjects were told the recipient's attitude but did not themselves write a description of the target. These subjects' judgments of the target were unaffected by the recipient's apparent liking for him. It therefore appears that subjects did not spontaneously encode the target's behavior in terms of trait concepts unless they were required to do so in the course of writing a description of the target. Once these encodings were performed, however, they affected subjects' personal evaluations of the target person independently of the implications of the original information presented about him. Moreover, these effects appear to increase over time (Higgins & McCann, 1984). This latter finding provides further evidence that the influence of trait-based encodings of information on judgments increases once the Work Space has been cleared of the original information presented (see also Higgins et al., 1977; Srull & Wyer, 1980).

There are undoubtedly individual differences in the motivation to tailor one's communication to the views of one's audience, and, therefore, in the effects of those communications on one's own attitudes and opinions. One correlate of these differences was identified by Higgins and McCann (1984). Using a paradigm similar to that constructed by Higgins and Rholes, they found that highly authoritarian subjects were more inclined than nonauthoritarians to tailor their descriptions of the target person to the views of their audience, particularly if the audience was ostensibly higher in status than they were themselves. Correspondingly, authoritarian subjects' own reported judgments of the target person were relatively more influenced as well.

More pervasive differences in people's goals and needs may also produce differences in the encoding of information, and, therefore, in the influence of the information on later judgments and decisions. This possibility has recently been elaborated by Klinger (1975) in the context of analyzing the effects of individual's "current concerns." Klinger points out that these concerns, which may be either short-lived or enduring, may guide both thought and behavior. A person who suddenly loses his or her job will begin to think about virtually everything in terms of its implications for his or her financial status. Such a concern could last for years if the person's employment status does not change. A more transitory current concern is exemplified by job candidates who tend to think of everything (a dropped fork at dinner, a limp handshake at the airport, etc.) in terms of how it reflects on their chances of being offered the position. Klinger (1971) has shown that current concerns not only preoccupy thought content but also enter dream material. In general, the concepts they activate appear to break into consciousness forcefully, frequently, and in response to minimal cues from the environment.

Selective Encoding of Information

The concepts that happen to be activated at the time information is received may not only determine *how* information is encoded (i.e., the interpretation given to it) but also may influence *which* information is encoded and stored in memory. A large amount of information continually impinges on the human processing system, and the encoding of all of it in terms of higher order concepts may often exceed the system's processing capacity. This is particularly true when several different processing objectives are being pursued simultaneously. In such circumstances, information is more likely to be encoded into memory if it can be interpreted in terms of concepts that are easily accessible at the time it is received than if its interpretation requires concepts that come less easily to mind. Consequently, the former information is more likely to be recalled than the latter.

Goal-Directed Selective Encoding

The concepts that are most accessible in memory may often be activated in the pursuit of a specific processing objective to which the information being received is relevant. In some instances, people with a particular goal in mind may intentionally retrieve a set of concepts that are potentially useful for attaining this goal, and may actively search for aspects of the information that exemplify these concepts. Therefore, features that can be interpreted in terms of these concepts are more likely to be encoded than features to which the concepts are inapplicable. To the extent that only these higher order, goal-directed encodings are transmitted to Permanent Storage, this should bias the features of the information that can later be recalled.

Several indications of selective encoding have been obtained. A study by Wyer, Srull, Gordon, and Hartwick (1982) is illustrative. Subjects read a two-page passage constructed by R. Anderson and Pichert (1978) which described two boys' activities during an afternoon at one boy's home. Subjects in some conditions read the passage with the objective of either (a) someone who was interested in purchasing the home or (b) someone who was interested in burglarizing it. Later, subjects were unexpectedly asked to recall as much of the passage as they could. Not surprisingly, subjects were better able to recall features if they were relevant to their goal at the time they read the passage. (Thus, for example, subjects with a homebuyer objective were relatively more likely to recall that the basement had recently been repaired, whereas those with a burglar objective were more likely to recall that no one was ever home on Thursday and that the father had a coin collection.)

The effect reported by Wyer et al. could be due not only to the selective encoding of individual features of the information in terms of goal-activated concepts but also to the *organization* of these features in terms of a goal-related theme. This is particularly true if the goal- activated concepts bear some a priori relation to one another. In Wyer et al.'s study, for example, subjects with a burglar's objective may organize the material into broad categories that are relevant to their goal (e.g., indications of how easy the house would be to burglarize and how to do it, information about what to take and where it is located, etc.). The categorical organization of the information may also influence its later recall.

Some evidence of this organizational effect was obtained in a series of studies by Lingle and Ostrom (1979). In these studies, subjects were given information about a person with instructions to decide if the person was suitable for a particular job. When the information described both job- relevant and job-irrelevant attributes, subjects later recalled the relevant attributes better than the irrelevant ones. In other conditions, however, the attributes described in the information were either all relevant or all irrelevant. In these conditions, subjects also recalled more information if it was job-relevant. In other words, the encoding of the information in terms of goal-activated concepts facilitated its recall on an absolute basis, and not just because relatively more attention was paid to it than to the other information that accompanied it. (The manner in which the organization of information affects its recall is considered in more detail in Chapters 7 and 8.)

Nongoal-Directed Selective Encoding

The above studies suggest that the encoding of information in terms of concepts that are activated for the purpose of attaining a specific processing objective may increase the likelihood of recalling it. However, concepts that are easily accessible in memory for extraneous reasons may have similar effects. A series of studies by Bower, Gilligan, and Monteiro (1981) provides an indirect demonstration of these effects. Subjects were induced via hypnosis to feel either happy or sad before reading a story. The story described two persons, one of whom had a variety of positive life experiences and the other of whom had a series of unfortunate ones. Subjects later showed better recall of the experiences that were affectively congruent with the mood they were in at the time they read the story. Subsequent studies eliminated several alternative interpretations of the effect (for an elaboration, see Chapter 12). It therefore seems reasonable to suppose that subjects' induced mood states, or the procedures used to induce them (i.e., thinking about past personal experiences) activated concepts that were related to these states, and that subsequently subjects selectively encoded the information they read in terms of these concepts. As a result, the encoded information was better recalled than other material.

It is also possible that chronically accessible concepts, by virtue of increasing sensitivity to features of information that can be interpreted in terms of them, stimulate cognitive processes that *interfere* with the encoding of other information. A study by Erdelyi and Appelbaum (1973) supports this possibility. In this study, members of a Jewish organization were shown stimulus arrays for 200 ms and then were asked to recall the stimuli portrayed. The stimulus objects that subjects were told to consider were all neutral in emotional tone and were presented in a circular array. In the center of each array was an ostensibly task-irrelevant object. However, the nature of the object varied over conditions, being either a swastika, a Star of David, or a window. Relative to the window (control) condition, presenting the Star of David interfered with subjects' recall of the stimulus ojbects they were supposed to consider. Presenting the swastika interfered with performance to a still greater degree.

The Erdelyi and Appelbaum (1973) study is interesting for several reasons. First, it demonstrates how emotionally charged material can *automatically* capture the attentional resources one has available, so that less concurrent cognitive activity is possible. In other words, even though the specific goal of the subject was to ignore the center item and concentrate on the stimuli along the perimeter of the circle, this was not possible because of the automatic funneling of attention to the center item. This was true for both positively and negatively valenced stimuli. More generally, the experiment demonstrates how long-term personal values can often interfere with explicit, consciously directed processing objectives.

Postinformation Effects of Concept Accessibility

The effects of activating concepts on the interpretation and selective encoding of information at the time information is received are clearly substantial. Once these encodings have been performed, however, concepts that are activated subsequently should theoretically have very little influence on either the interpretation of the information or its recall. That is, subjects who have already formed a representation of a target that is relevant to their objectives will typically retrieve and use this representation, which is near the top of a referent bin pertaining to the target, as a basis for judgments and decisions concerning the target. In other words, they will not retrieve and reinterpret the original information in terms of concepts that happen to be accessible at the time of judgment. Several studies support this assertion.

1. Srull and Wyer's (1980) study, cited earlier, demonstrated that priming a trait concept before information about a person was presented substantially increased the likelihood that the concept was used to make judgments of the person. However, priming the same trait concept after the information was presented had no effect at all.

2. In a study by Massad, Hubbard, and Newtson (1979), subjects viewed a videotape showing the movements of a set of geometrical figures with instructions that it concerned either a guardian of treasure (a large triangle) against two thieves (a small triangle and circle) or a couple (the small triangle and circle) trying to flee

from a rapist (the large triangle). Then, after viewing the tape, subjects were told that an error had been made and that the tape had actually described the alternative situation. Subjects' later evaluations of the characters were minimally affected by the postinformation change in set unless they were given an opportunity to view the tape a second time from the new perspective they were given. In other words, once the information had been encoded in terms of concepts that were relevant to one perspective, these encodings were apparently stored in memory but the original material was not. Therefore, the information was not available to be reinterpreted in terms of concepts relevant to the second perspective unless it was presented a second time.

3. In the study by Bower et al. (1981), inducing a mood state in subjects before they read a passage had a substantial influence on the type of information that subjects recalled. However, inducing a mood state after the information was presented did not.

These studies argue strongly that the effects of activating concepts on the encoding of information occurs primarily at the time the information is first received, and that once these encodings have been made, concepts that are activated subsequently have little influence on either the interpretation of the information or the recall of it. Although some studies have purported to show postinformation effects of activating concepts on memory and judgment, a close scrutiny of these studies reveals that they do not necessarily contradict the conclusions we have drawn. In most of these studies, recognition procedures were used to infer memory for the information presented. Snyder and Uranowitz (1978), for example, found that when subjects were told after reading a passage describing the activities of a woman that she was either lesbian or heterosexual, their responses on a later forced-choice recognition task were biased in the direction implied by this postinformation characterization (see also Dooling & Christiaansen, 1977). However, these biases were probably the result of guessing strategies that were employed at the time the recognition task was administered and do not indicate a postinformation change in the memorial representation that was originally formed of the person (cf. Bellezza & Bower, 1981; Srull, 1984; Wyer & Srull, 1988).

Research using recall measures is hard to interpret for other reasons. In a study by Snyder and Cantor (1979), for example, subjects after receiving information about a target person were asked to evaluate the target's suitability for a job that required either introverted or extraverted personality characteristics. Before making this judgment, they were asked to write down everything they could remember that they considered relevant to the judgment they were asked to make. Subjects reported more information that confirmed the hypothesis they were asked to "test" (e.g., that the person was suited for an extraverted job) than information that disconfirmed this hypothesis. Moreover, their subsequent judgments reflected the implications of this bias. Although these results are provocative, the failure to obtain an indication of exactly how much information subjects were *capable* of recalling prevents one from drawing firm conclusions about the effects of post-information-processing objectives on retrieval processes per se. For example, subjects may have been able to recall all aspects of the information presented equally well but may have reported only those aspects that they believed to be relevant to the judgments they were asked to make.

R. C. Anderson and Pichert (1978) investigated the effects of both preinformation and postinformation processing objectives on recall. They used stimulus materials similar to those employed by Wyer et al. (1982) in the study described earlier in this section. However, the experimental procedure differed in several respects. Subjects in both studies read a story describing a house and its surroundings with the initial perspective of either a homebuyer of a burglar. In Anderson and Pichert's study, however, subjects after an initial attempt to recall the information were asked to think about the information they had read from a different perspective than the one they had been given before, being told explicitly that it might improve their memory for things they had not recalled earlier. These subjects recalled a greater proportion of the information relevant to the second perspective than they had at first, but they also recalled a lower proportion of information relevant to their original perspective than they had initially.

The generalizeability of Anderson and Pichert's findings is difficult to evaluate. For one thing, people very seldom receive information outside the laboratory for the explicit purpose of trying to recall it later. Perhaps more important, explicitly telling subjects to use the perspectives they were given as devices for recalling the information may have led them to infer that the investigator was more interested in their recall of perspective- relevant features than their recall of irrelevant ones, and this may have created a bias in their *reporting* of the information rather than in their actual ability to remember it.

In the study by Wyer et al. (1982), these problems were eliminated. That is, subjects read the passage with either the objective of a homebuyer, the objective of a burglar, or a more general comprehension objective, and made judgments relevant to the objective they had been assigned. Then, they reconsidered the information with either the same objective, a different specific objective, or a more general goal in mind, and made some additional judgments. Finally, they were given a surprise recall task, being asked to remember as much information as they could without being reminded of the objectives they had been assigned or their potential role in recall. As noted earlier, the type of information recalled was influenced by their preinformation processing objective but not by their postinformation goal. In fact, subjects' recall of *both* goal-relevant and goal-irrelevant material was slightly but significantly increased by reconsidering the information for a specific purpose, regardless of whether this purpose was the same as or different from the one they had had when initially reading it.

All things considered, it therefore seems reasonable to conclude that postin-formation processing objectives, unlike objectives that exist at the time information is first acquired, have very little influence on the interpretation and selective recall of this information once the information has been encoded and stored in memory.

A Theoretical Controversy: Are Trait Encodings Spontaneous?

According to Postulate 4.3, information is not interpreted by the Com-prehender in terms of any more abstract concepts than are necessary to understand its descriptive implications. More abstract encodings are only performed by the Encoder/Organizer in the service of higher order processing objectives. An im-plication of this assumption of particular relevance to social judgment is that people typically do not interpret a person's behaviors in terms of relevant trait concepts unless they have a higher order goal in mind to which trait-based interpretations are relevant. In most of the studies by Higgins, Srull, and Wyer, and others we have described, subjects received information about the target person's behaviors for the explicit purpose of forming an impression of this person, and so these trait encodings were performed. However, these encodings should theoretically not be performed spontaneously, in the absence of processing goals that require them.

This view has recently been directly challenged by Winter and Uleman (1984; Winter, Uleman, & Cunniff, 1985). They argue that spontaneous trait inferences do occur. Two quite carefully designed and imaginative studies were conducted to evaluate this possibility, the second of which (Winter et al., 1985) is particularly provocative. Subjects ostensibly participated in a study of digit memory. On each of 16 trials, subjects were given a sequence of five numbers and then, ostensibly as a distractor, were asked to read a sentence aloud before recalling these numbers. In fact, each "distractor" sentence described a behavior that was strongly associated with a particular trait concept. Later, subjects were unexpectedly asked to recall the behaviors and, in some cases, were given behavior-relevant trait names to use as retrieval cues. Recall of the behaviors was significantly greater when the traits were provided as retrieval cues than when other types of cues were given. Winter et al. argued that this effect would not have occurred unless the behaviors recalled had been spontaneously encoded in terms of traits at the time they were first learned.

In this study, subjects' processing objective at the time they learned the behavior statements obviously did not require them to encode the statements in terms of trait concepts. Therefore, acceptance of Winter et al.'s conclusion would create problems for the model we have proposed. Specifically, it would imply that behaviors are spontaneously encoded in terms of trait concepts by the Com-prehender and not by the Encoder/Organizer as a result of more specific goal-directed processing. More generally, their conclusion contradicts the implications of several other research findings in the area of person memory. For example:

1. The behaviors recalled by subjects who read about them with instructions to form an impression of the person they describe are clustered in terms of the trait concepts they exemplify (Hamilton, Katz, & Leirer, 1980a, b). (That is, behaviors that exemplify the same trait are recalled in closer proximity than those that exemplify different traits.) In contrast, the behaviors recalled by subjects who read the behaviors with instructions to remember them do not show evidence of this clustering. This suggests that subjects do *not* encode and organize behaviors in terms of trait concepts unless their goal at the time the behaviors are read (i.e., to form an impression) requires it.

2. In a study by Wyer and Gordon (1982), subjects read a set of trait adjective descriptions of a person followed by a series of behaviors that exemplify the traits described. When subjects received the information with an impression formation objective, their later recall of the trait adjectives appeared to cue the recall of the particular behaviors that exemplified them. When subjects received the same information with a memory objective, however, these trait cueing effects were not evident (Wyer & Gordon, 1982).

These findings suggest that subjects encode and organize behaviors in terms of trait concepts only when they receive information for the purpose of forming an impression of the person they describe. If the behaviors are spontaneously encoded and organized in terms of traits at the initial, comprehension stage, similar effects should occur when subjects have a memory objective as well. The question is how Winter et al.'s results can be reconciled with these findings as well as with the general model we have proposed.

In fact, there is a plausible alternative explanation for Winter et al.'s results. Winter et al. took great pains to insure that the stimulus behaviors they used in their study were strongly associated with the traits they later provided as retrieval cues. For example, "stepped on his girl friend's feet during the fox trot" was cued by "clumsy," and "paints a swastika on the synagogue wall" by "prejudiced." Conceivably, when subjects were asked to recall the behaviors but could not remember them, they used the trait cues they were given to generate typical behaviors that exemplified the concept, hoping that characteristics of these more general behaviors would remind them of the specific behavior that had actually been presented. (Thus, a subject who is given the cue "clumsy" may think of typical clumsy behaviors, such as "bumps into people on the dance floor," "steps on people's toes," etc., and these behaviors may have semantic features in common with the specific behavior presented.) These *behavioral* features may then cue the recall of the stimulus behavior even if the behavior had not been encoded in trait terms at the time it was read.

This alternative interpretation is plausible, and would be consistent with the implications of other evidence against the spontaneity of trait encodings. The mere existence of an alternative interpretation does not in itself invalidate the existence of the original one. Further research to clarify the issue is obviously necessary. Nevertheless, the weight of the evidence available at this writing seems consistent with the formulation we have proposed.

Effects of Concept Accessibility on Overt Behavior

Aside from their implications for the general theoretical formulation we have proposed, the phenomena identified in the research summarized in this chapter are of considerable importance. One general implication of the research is that quite fortuitous events that make one or another concept accessible at the time information is received may affect the interpretation of this information, and this interpretation may have enduring effects on judgments of people and objects to which the information is relevant. Moreover, these effects may actually increase over time. It is important to demonstrate, however, that the effects we have described are not restricted to pencil-and-paper judgments but rather, mediate overt behavior of the sort that is likely to occur outside the laboratory.

In fact, many of the phenomena identified in social psychological research can potentially be interpreted in terms of the effects of activating a concept or set of concepts on subjects' interpretation of the information that presumably mediates their behavioral decisions. Two quite different examples, one pertaining to the cognitive mediators of social behavior and the other concerning creative problem solving, may suffice to demonstrate this.

Cognitive Mediators of Social Interaction Behavior

Our behavior toward other persons depends in large part on our interpretation of their behavior toward us. Certainly our reaction to a colleague who says that he doesn't have time to talk to us depends in part on whether we interpret this rebuff as evidence of hostility and dislike for us or as too many demands on his time. Similarly, a female student's decision to accept a lunch invitation with a male faculty member may depend on whether she interprets the invitation as inspired by professional motives or social ones. It seems reasonable to suppose that concepts that happen to be activated at the time such events are experienced may influence the interpretation of the events and therefore may influence behavioral decisions.

1. Instigation to Aggression

Empirical evidence suggesting this possibility has been provided by several studies of the determinants of instigation to aggression. A classic study by Berkowitz and LePage (1967) is representative. Subjects ostensibly participated in a study on the physiological reactions to stress. In this context, they were told they would be participating with another person, and that they would be asked to evaluate one another's performance on a creative brainstorming task by administering electric shocks to one another. The subject was the first brainstormer, and received either a large or a small number of shocks from the other for his performance. The subject was then given the opportunity to evaluate the other's work, and was taken to the room containing the shock machine. In some conditions, however, a shotgun and a .38-calibre revolver were lying on the table, having ostensibly been left there by someone who was unconnected with the experiment. In other conditions, a badminton racket was lying on the table instead.

It seems reasonable to suppose that the guns, although ostensibly unrelated to the experiment, activated concepts associated with aggression. Because these concepts were activated *after* rather than before subjects received shocks from the partner, they should theoretically not affect subjects' interpretation of the partner's behavior per se (Srull & Wyer, 1980). It nevertheless seems reasonable to suppose that activating aggression-relevant concepts would lead subjects to interpret their *own* shock-administering behavior as conveying hostility. Consequently, it may lead them to base their decision about how many shocks to administer on how upset they were by having been shocked a large or small number of times by the partner. In contrast, subjects for whom hostile concepts were not primed may be more inclined to interpret the situation, and the implications of their behavior, as unrelated to hostility, and so their feelings toward their partner as a result of being shocked are less likely to influence their behavioral decisions. This is what Berkowitz and LePage's findings seem to suggest. That is, subjects in the "gun" condition administered more shocks to the partner who had previously shocked them frequently, but fewer shocks to the partner who had shocked them infrequently, than did subjects in the "badminton" condition.

More recent evidence suggests that simply the activation of hostility-related concepts may be sufficient to induce people to behave aggressively, even without being provoked. In a study by Carver, Ganellen, Froming, and Chambers (1983), subjects were asked to serve as a teacher in a study of "learning processes" in which their task was to administer shocks to a partner (the "learner") for making errors. Before serving in this capacity, however, subjects were asked to complete the scrambled sentence task used by Srull and Wyer (1980) to prime concepts of hostility. Subjects administered more intense shocks to the learner when 80% of the priming sentences were hostility related than when only 20% were hostility-related.

This result could actually create some problems for our interpretation of Berkowitz and LePage's results. To the extent that activating hostility related concepts leads subjects to interpret their adminstration of shocks on the learning task as conveying hostility, one would expect subjects to administer *less* intense shocks to the ostensibly innocent victim rather than more intense ones. Conceivably the activation of hostility related concepts led subjects to interpret the partner's frequent errors as stimulated by an unwillingness to cooperate, and, therefore, as hostile behavior, leading them to administer more intense shocks for this reason. A second possibility, however, is that priming hostility related concepts activates not only concepts associated with hostility per se but emotion-related concepts associated with *anger*. If this is so, the feelings associated with this emotion concept (Chapter 4) may stimulate hostile behavior independently of the actions of the persons toward whom it is directed. These alternative interpretations remain to be evaluated.

The preceding discussion makes salient the fact that the specific cognitive mediators of social behavior are often unclear. At the same time, a conceptualization of the effects in terms of the model we have proposed, or of concept accessibility effects more generally, suggests several alternative hypotheses concerning the determinants of these effects that might otherwise be overlooked.

2. Implications for Social Interaction

To the extent that concept accessibility influences overt behavior, it has obvious implications for the dynamics of interpersonal interaction. People may attempt to respond to one another in ways that are affectively similar to the way that they perceive others to respond to them. If this is so, factors that influence their interpretation of one another's behavior may have substantial influence on the character of the interaction that takes place between the persons involved. In an interaction situation, one's interpretation of others' behavior may be influenced in part by expectancies for how they will respond to one's prior behavior toward them. For example, if I expect another person to respond with hostility to a statement I make, concepts activated by this expectation may lead me to interpret the other's actual behavior as confirming it. This effect may be most likely to occur when the other's behavior is ambiguous.

Some indirect evidence of this, and more generally of the importance of taking into account the interpretation that people place on one another's behavior in accounting for interpersonal interaction phenomena, was obtained by Gaelick, Bodenhausen, and Wyer (1985) in a study of emotional communication. Marital couples engaged in a 10-minute videotaped discussion of a problem they were having in their relationship. In a later session, each partner reviewed the tape and rated selected statements that were made in terms of (a) the speaker's intentions to convey either love or hostility,[3] (b) the recipient's perception of these intentions, (c) the speaker's expectations for how the recipient would respond, and (d) the

3. These emotions were defined on the basis of a factor analysis of several different specific ratings of characteristics related to Leary's (1957) circumplex model of personality. For other evidence that positive and negative affect are independent dimensions, see Bradburn (1969), Diener and Emmons (1984), and Warr, Barter, and Brownbridge (1983).

recipient's actual response. People typically attempted to reciprocate the emotion that they perceived their partner to convey to them. However, they *actually* reciprocated this emotion only in the case of hostility. This was largely because partners' perceptions of one another's intentions to convey hostility were fairly accurate, but their perceptions of one another's intentions to express love were not. Rather, subjects' perceptions of love were guided primarily by their expectancies. One consequence of this is that communications of hostility were likely to escalate over the course of the interaction, whereas communications of love were likely to remain at their original level, independently of the other's response to them. It is interesting to speculate that a systematic activation of concepts associated with love and hostility prior to an interaction would have different effects on the quality of this interaction.

Creative Problem Solving

A quite different demonstration of the effects of concept accessibility on overt behavior was provided by Higgins and Chaires (1980) in an investigation of creative problem solving. In one of their studies, subjects were initially exposed to a series of pictures, each showing a container with its contents (e.g., a tray with candies on it, a bag containing potatoes, etc.). However, each picture was accompanied by a caption of one of two types. In some conditions, the name of the container and the name of its contents were connected by "of" (e.g., "tray of candies," "bag of potatoes," etc.). In the other condition, they were connected by "and" ("tray and candies," "bag and potatoes," etc.). Subjects in each condition were later asked to solve a task often used to infer creative problem solving ability. Specifically, they were given a box containing tacks and a candle, and were asked to mount the candle on a wall-board so that it could be lit without any wax dropping to the floor. A solution to the problem requires that subjects use the tack box as a basis on which to mount the candle, and then tacking the box into the wallboard. Recognition of this solution, however, requires that the tack box be dissociated from its function as a container of the tacks. Higgins and Chaires hypothesized that this insight would come more readily under "and" priming conditions than under "of" priming conditions. This was in fact the case. Under "of" conditions, 20% of the subjects solved the problem and the mean time required to do so was 9.1 minutes. (These values are virtually identical to those obtained under conditions in which no priming was administered at all.) Under "and" priming conditions, however, 80% of the subjects solved the problem and the mean time to solution was only 4.5 minutes. These results not only demonstrate the effects of activating concepts on problem solving behavior, but are of further interest in demonstrating that relational concepts can be activated as well as concepts that apply to individual referents.

Methodological Implications: Diagnosing the Cognitive Mediators of Judgments and Behavior

To reiterate, priming a concept increases the likelihood that the concept is used to interpret information to which it is applicable, and consequently influences judgments and behavior to which the information is relevant. If this is so, priming methodology can potentially be used to diagnose the specific cognitive mediators of behavior and judgments under conditions in which the nature of these mediators is unclear.

Specifically, several alternative concepts may often mediate a judgment, and the features that activate them may be inextricably confounded in either the information presented or the stimuli being judged. Therefore, the contributions of these alternative concepts cannot be separated by a systematic variation of the stimulus information itself. However, suppose a potential concept is among those that typically mediate judgments of a stimulus. Then, increasing its accessibility through priming procedures should increase the likelihood that the concept is actually applied. Therefore, it should influence judgments for which the concepts has implications. If, on the other hand, the concept is *not* among those that typically mediate judgments, increasing its accessibility should have no effect. This means that by selectively priming a concept and observing its effect on judgments or behavior, one can determine whether this is one of the concepts that mediates these responses. Two quite different applications of this logic are provided below.

Cognitive Mediators of Reactions to Rape

Exposure to pornography that portrays women as willing victims of sexual aggression often increases tolerance of rape (cf. Malamuth & Donnerstein, 1982; Zillmann, 1983). However, the particular concepts that are activated by pornographic material and give rise to this tolerance are not entirely clear. On the one hand, pornography could convey that women enjoy physical abuse, as suggested above. On the other hand, it could activate concepts that are associated with aggression per se, independently of the sexual content of the pornography. Or, it could activate general concepts about women (e.g., the concept that women are sex objects) that have nothing to do with aggression.

The possible influence of these and other concepts on the interpretation of rape incidents and judgments of the persons involved in them was investigated by Wyer, Bodenhausen, and Gorman (1985). College undergraduates were first exposed to a series of 12 slides with instructions to judge how objectionable it would be to show them in the public media. All slides showed pictures that were taken from popular magazines and photograph albums, and therefore were similar to ones that subjects were likely to have seen many times in the past. Therefore, we assumed that the pictures would activate previously formed concepts rather than creating new ones. Nine of the slides were fillers that had no relation to either sex or aggression. The others varied over conditions in ways that, based on normative data, selectively activated several different concepts. Some of these concepts and the slides used to activate them are as follows:

1. aggression is normal and socially sanctioned behavior (conveyed by showing police subduing a criminal; a boxing match, etc.)
2. people are cruel and inhumane, and social injustice is common (conveyed by slides showing a black man chained to a tree; a dead soldier with part of his head shot off, etc.)
3. close personal relations between men and women are desirable (conveyed by slides showing a couple holding one another, a couple lying fully clothed in a meadow, etc.)
4. women are sex objects who enjoy being dominated and are interested in sexual pleasure alone (conveyed by slides showing a stripper with legs spread, a cartoon of a woman "branded," etc.)

A set of slides that activated none of these concepts was presented under control conditions.

After viewing and rating the set of slides, which took less than 10 minutes, subjects were taken to a second room where an ostensibly unrelated experiment (run by a different experimenter) was being conducted. Here, they were given a questionnaire describing a series of rape cases which varied in terms of whether the victim and defendant were strangers or acquaintances, and whether or not the victim tried to resist. In each case, they made judgments of both the victim (her credibility, the likelihood that she was harmed, the degree to which she was responsible for the incident, etc.) and the defendant (whether he should have been convicted and the likelihood that he actually was convicted).

The effects of priming different subsets of concepts on judgments, and the conditions in which they occurred, provided insight into the concepts that may mediate reactions to rape, and when they are likely to be applied. To mention a few of the findings:

1. Priming concepts that people are cruel and inhumane and that social injustice exists increased subjects' beliefs that the defendant was actually convicted. However, it also increased their beliefs that the woman was responsible for the incident. In combination, these findings suggested that activating concepts associated with cruelty and social injustice increased subjects' need to believe in a just world (Lerner & Simmons, 1966), and therefore led them to interpret the rape incidents in ways that confirmed this belief. Consequently, they reported not only that the defendant was likely to have gotten what he deserved (i.e., to have been

punished) but also that the victim deserved what she got (i.e., that she was responsible).

2. Exposure to slides portraying women as sex objects generally increased males' beliefs that the victim was responsible for the incident. However, it decreased females' beliefs that she was responsible. Both effects were greater when the defendant was an acquaintance and the victim did not try to resist. Whereas presenting the priming slides to male viewers activated the concept that women are sex objects, presenting them to female viewers appeared to activate the concept that men think of women as sex objects. Consequently, they elicited a negative reaction in women that led to the opposite effect than they had on men's judgments. However, neither of the above concepts was considered applicable when the defendant was a stranger whom the victim resisted.

3. Priming concepts associated with close personal relationships between men and women increased both males' and females' beliefs that the rape victim was telling the truth and that she was harmed. However, it also increased male subjects' beliefs that the victim was responsible for her plight, while decreasing females' beliefs in her responsibility. This suggests that concepts associated with close relationships increased both men's and women's beliefs in the seriousness of the rape incident. However, whereas males attributed responsibility for the incident to the female victim, females attributed responsibility to the male defendant.

4. Although many different concepts appeared to underlie judgments of the rape victim, *none* of these concepts affected subjects' judgments that the defendant should be convicted. In other words, subjects believed that the defendant should be punished regardless of whether they considered the women to be partly responsible.

Independently of the specific implications of the results, the study provides a demonstration of the potential use of priming methodology to understand the cognitive mediators of judgments under conditions in which they are unclear.

Determinants of the Unwillingness to Express One's Views in Public

Germany has a law that is popularly known as the "Radicals decree." The legislation gives the government the right to deny civil service jobs to individuals who have participated in activities that are regarded as antagonistic to the national interest. In fact, Schwarz and Strack (1981) found that German college students were less willing to sign petitions opposing a government policy if they were seeking civil service jobs than if they were not. This suggests that people interpreted the petition as potentially antagonistic to government interests, and therefore those for whom the Radicals decree had potential implications were inhibited from signing it.

There is another interpretation, however. Specifically, people who are interested in obtaining civil service jobs may be *generally* more conservative than people who are not. Therefore, they may be relatively less willing to sign petitions independently of the Radicals decree. To this extent, the fear of negative consequences resulting from the Radicals decree may have little to do with their unwillingness to sign the petition. A second study by Schwarz and Strack (1981) evaluated these alternative possibilities using a using a priming methodology. Specifically, students in a dormitory were approached by an interviewer who was ostensibly seeking information about students' opinions on a variety of social issues. Some of the questionnaire items, although not mentioning the Radicals decree by name, were expected to activate concepts that were associated with it. One hour later, both these students and others who had not been interviewed were approached by a second individual who was collecting signatures on a petition concerning an issue of social importance. After either agreeing or refusing to sign the petition, subjects' intentions to seek a civil service job were determined.

The results of the study were very clear. Subjects who had not been interviewed (i.e., those for whom concepts associated with the Radicals decree had not recently been activated) were quite willing to sign the petition regardless of whether or not they were seeking civil service employment. Previously interviewed students who were not seeking civil service jobs were also willing to sign. In contrast, previously interviewed students who were seeking civil service jobs were unwilling to do so. In other words, activating concepts associated with the Radicals decree led subjects to interpret the request to sign the petition as an anti-goverment action. It therefore substantially reduced subjects' willingness to express their views publicly if they were seeking civil service jobs, but had no effect on their willingness to do so if they were not seeking these jobs.

It therefore seems reasonable to conclude that the Radicals decree did indeed have an inhibiting effect on people's willingness to express their opinions publicly, but only if the decree is salient to them at the time. Otherwise, the decree may have little influence.

Concluding Remarks

In this chapter, we considered a wide range of topics of both theoretical and practical interest. First, we analyzed in some detail the processes that underlie the interpretation of information in the course of pursuing higher order processing objectives, and have identified several factors that influence which of several alternative concepts is most likely to be applied. In the latter context, we considered (a) fortuitous situational factors that lead a concept to be more easily accessible, (b) the processing objectives to which the information to be interpreted is directly relevant, and (c) more general individual differences in the accessibility of concepts that might influence the likelihood of applying them. Regardless of why they happen to be accessible, concepts that are used to interpret information at the time it is first received appear to have a substantial and enduring impact both on judgments of persons and objects to which the information is relevant and on overt behavior toward them.

In this discussion, we focused primarily on the interpretation of specific pieces of information. We are now in a position to consider the organization of this information in the course of forming a more complex representation of the person, object, or event to which it is relevant. An understanding of these organizational processes, and how the representations that result from them are later used to make judgments and decisions, is of course of considerable importance. The next two chapters are devoted to these matters.

Chapter 7
Encoding and Organization: II. The Cognitive Representation of Persons

In the last chapter, we discussed how individual pieces of information (e.g., descriptions of different behaviors) are interpreted and how their interpretation affects judgments and behavioral decisions to which the information is relevant. A second consideration is how these separate pieces of information are organized into a mental representation of the person, object, or event to which they refer. The nature of such a representation, and the processes that underlie its construction, depend on both the type of information involved and the particular goals of the information processor. A person who receives information about someone's traits and behaviors is likely to construct a different mental representation if he is trying to form an impression of the person than if he is simply trying to remember the information. On the other hand, a person with an impression formation objective is likely to form a different sort of representation from behavioral information if the behaviors occur in many situations and at many different times than if they compose a single sequence of temporally or causally related activity. More specific objectives, such as deciding if someone has a particular trait or is suitable for a certain occupation, may lead to still other types of representations.

A complete understanding of the mental representations that are formed from social information and the processes that underlie their construction would therefore require knowledge of the contents of all cells of a two- dimensional matrix involving (a) goals and specific processing objectives on the one hand and (b) different types of information on the other. The currently available theoretical and empirical work on representational processes does not provide this knowledge. Therefore, we rely on only a few selected cells of the matrix to which a reasonable amount of research literature is relevant.

In the present chapter, we consider the manner in which information is processed for the purpose of forming a general impression of a person. This information typically describes a set of behaviors that a person has performed in different times and places. The behaviors are sometimes preceded by trait adjectives of the person, thereby providing general expectations for what the person may be like. In contrast, in Chapter 8 we consider the way in which causally and temporally related sequences of actions are represented in memory when recipients have the objective of understanding what transpired and why. The issues addressed in these two chapters are not entirely independent. Certainly a temporal sequence of behaviors that someone performs may convey an impression of this person. Moreover, a set of traits and behaviors may sometimes be used to construct a sequence of temporally-related events. (One such instance occurs in the courtroom, where jurors must piece together the information provided by different witnesses about a defendant's character and the circumstances of a crime to construct a scenario of what went on; see Pennington & Hastie, 1986a,b.) In general, however, a different body of research and theory bears on each set of issues.

The conceptualization of person impression formation we propose in this chapter has its roots in the pioneering work of Hastie (1980) and Hamilton, Katz, and Leirer (1980a,b), and is based on a large body of theory and research that has accumulated since. This literature has permitted us to develop a reasonably detailed theoretical model of the processes that underlie the formation of a person impression from trait and behavior information, the cognitive representations that result from this processing, and the way that these representations are later used to make judgments of the person to whom they refer. It is important not to overgeneralize the model we propose, for reasons noted above. Within its domain of applicability, however, the model generates quite precise predictions of both memory and judgment phenomena. Moreover, it can be used to conceptualize a variety of issues, including (a) the relation (or lack of relation) between the implications of information that people can recall about a person and judgments of this person, (b) the effects of instructions to disregard the information one has received about a person on both the ability to recall the information later on and the influence of this information on judgments, (c) the mental representations that are formed of individuals whose general traits conflict with the implications of stereotyped social groups to which they belong, and (d) the difference between impressions formed of individuals and impressions formed of groups of individuals.

An important feature of the model is that it generates predictions of both the recall of information about a person and judgments of a person under conditions in which they appear unrelated. In addition, the model can be used to conceptualize the priorities that govern the different goal-directed cognitive activities that are performed en route to forming an impression. To this extent, the model provides a basis for specifying in some detail the nature of a goal schema that is activated and applied when people have the objective of forming a person impression.

In this chapter, we first review the general processes we postulate to underlie person impression formation. Then, we present the theoretical formulation we propose in terms of a series of formal postulates that concern (a) the representations formed from trait and behavior information at the time it is first received, and (b) the process of retrieving the information contained in the representations. (The use of these representations to make judgments of the person to whom they refer is discussed in Chapter 10.) In the course of presenting this formulation, we point out many of its empirical implications and discuss the research bearing on their validity. Finally, we apply the formulation to specific issues to which the theory is potentially relevant, including several of those noted in the preceding paragraphs.

General Considerations

In the situations we consider in this chapter, people are usually asked to form an impression of someone on the basis of several different behaviors the person has performed in various situations and at various times. As people read through the various behavior descriptions with an impression formation objective in mind, they are hypothesized to engage in the following goal-directed activities:

1. They attempt to interpret individual behaviors of the person in terms of a more general trait concept. If they know which traits the person is likely to have before they learn about his behaviors, they typically encode his behaviors in terms of these traits. Otherwise, they interpret the person's behaviors in terms of whatever trait concepts happen to come to mind most easily (see Chapter 6).

2. Based in part on the trait inferences they have made, people form a general concept of the person as either likeable or dislikeable. If this evaluative concept can be formed easily on the basis of the initial (trait or behavior) information that is provided, the later information presented about the person may have little influence on the nature of this concept. In some cases, however, the traits that people use to interpret a person's behaviors may differ in favorableness, making a coherent evaluative impression of the person difficult to construct. When this occurs, and people are uncertain that their trait encodings of the behaviors are correct, they may review the behaviors they have interpreted in terms of each trait concept to determine whether a different, more evaluatively consistent set of traits is also applicable.

3. Once people have formed an evaluative concept of the person, they interpret the person's behaviors in terms of it. When a given behavior is evaluatively inconsistent with their concept of the person, however, they may think about it in relation to other behaviors the person has performed in an attempt to understand better why it occurred.

4. If some of the person's behaviors are inconsistent with the evaluative concept formed of him or her, people may review the person's other behaviors to confirm its validity. This leads them to think more extensively about the implications of those behaviors that are evaluatively *consistent* with the concept.

5. Now suppose that people who have received information about a person are later asked to make a specific judgment of the person. They will search memory for a trait and/or evaluative concept that is directly relevant to this judgment. If they find such a concept, they base their judgments on its implications without bothering to review the specific behaviors the person has performed. In other words, the person's behaviors are considered only if no general concepts of the person are directly relevant to the judgment to be made.

The cognitive representations that are theoretically formed as a result of the processing described above will be conveyed in terms of an associative network metaphor. That is, the features of the person are represented as nodes in memory, and the associative linages between them by pathways. It is crucial to remember when applying such a metaphor, however, that the *content* and features of the representations are the direct result of various cognitive *processes*. For example, an associative pathway between a trait concept and a behavior is usually the result of encoding the behavior in terms of the trait. A pathway between two behaviors is theoretically formed as a result of thinking about the behaviors in relation to one another. The strength of an association between two cognitive elements is assumed to depend on (a) the ease of establishing it (e.g., the number of features that are common to the two elements being associated), and (b) the amount of time spent thinking about the two elements in relation to one another. When subjects are either unable or unmotivated to perform certain of the cognitive activities noted above, the associative pathways that theoretically result from these activities are not established. In short, there is an intimate connection between the structure of the representations that we assume to result from impression formation and the cognitive processes that we assume to underlie their construction.

The complete formulation we propose consists of 14 postulates (for a complete listing, see Appendix). Twelve of these postulates concern (a) the encoding and organization of behaviors in terms of trait concepts, (b) the development of an evaluative concept of the person, (c) a consideration of the person's behaviors in terms of this evaluative concept, (d) the storage in memory of the representations that are formed as a result of this cognitive activity, and (e) the subsequent retrieval and use of these representations in recalling information. (Two additional postulates, discussed in Chapter 10, concern the use of the representations to make judgments.) We consider each set of postulates in turn.

The Cognitive Representation of Person Information

Trait Encoding and Organization

Suppose subjects are asked to form an impression of a target person on the basis of behaviors the person has performed. Some of the behaviors are likely to exemplify specific trait concepts, whereas others may have no clear trait implications. Moreover, some behaviors may be favorable, and, therefore, if considered in isolation, would lead the person to be liked. Others may be unfavorable and would normally lead the person to be disliked. We consider two general conditions. In one case, subjects have already formed a generalized expectation for what a person is like at the time they learn about the specific behaviors the person has performed. (This expectancy could result from knowledge of a stereotyped group to which the person belongs, from hearing an initial description of the person by another, from identifying the person as a well-known public figure, or from any number of other factors.) In the second case, subjects do not have any specific expectations for what a person is like, and so any inferences about the person must be based on the behavioral information alone (or on beliefs about what people are like in general).

According to the general formulation we propose in this book, the individual behaviors that subjects learn are initially encoded by the Comprehender in terms of low level semantic concepts. These encodings, which are performed independently of any specific processing objective, are then transmitted to the Work Space, where they are used to attain more specific goals to which they may be relevant (e.g., to form an impression of the person they describe). The first postulate pertains to the encoding of information at the latter, goal-directed stage of processing. Although the postulate is essentially a formal statement of the encoding process we discussed in Chapter 6, it is included here for the sake of completeness.

Postulate 7.1. People who learn about a person's behaviors for the purpose of forming an impression of the person will spontaneously[1] interpret these behaviors in terms of the trait concepts they exemplify.

---

1. Our use of the term "spontaneous" in this context should not be confused with "automatic." The latter term is typically used to refer to processes that take place without conscious awareness, and that place few demands on the human cognitive system (Bargh, 1984; Schneider & Shiffrin, 1977). By spontaneous, we simply mean that subjects consider the encodings of behavior in terms of traits to be an integral part of impression formation, and that they perform this activity without implicit or explicit requirements to do so.

a. These trait encodings are performed by the Encoder/Organizer by comparing the behavior descriptions with features of trait concepts that are stored in the semantic bin.

b. When a behavior can be encoded in terms of more than one trait concept, the concept that is most easily accessible in memory is the most likely one to be applied.

Many implications of this postulate, along with empirical support for them, have been elaborated in Chapter 6 and there is no need to repeat them. One additional implication of the postulate of particular relevance to the present considerations is worth noting, however. That is, when several different behaviors of a person are interpreted as exemplars of the same trait concept, an association is presumably established between the concept and each of these behaviors. In terms of a network metaphor, the result of this activity is a *cluster* of behaviors, each of which is independently linked to the trait concept by an associative pathway. If the behaviors of a person exemplify different traits, several such trait-behavior clusters may be formed. In other words, the encoding of the behaviors in terms of trait concepts also serves to *organize* them into different clusters. These representations may be independent of one another, and, therefore, may be stored and retrieved separately under conditions we elaborate presently.

Selective Encoding

The next postulate has specific implications for the influence of a priori expectancies on the selective encoding and organization of behavior.

Postulate 7.2. (a) If people do not have trait-based expectations for a person at the time they learn about the person's behaviors, they encode all of the person's behaviors in terms of trait concepts. (b) If people do have expectations for a person's traits at the time they learn about the person's behaviors, only the behaviors that exemplify these traits are encoded and organized in terms of them. However, behaviors with implications for other attributes of the person are not encoded in trait terms.

To see the implications of this postulate, suppose a target person performs some behaviors that are honest, some that are kind, and some that are intelligent. If no expectancies for the person's traits exist at the time these behaviors are learned, Postulate 7.2a implies that three trait-behavior clusters will be formed, one pertaining to each trait. However, suppose subjects are told before they learn about the person's behavior that the person is honest and kind without the person's intelligence being mentioned. Then, according to Postulate 7.2b, subjects will form only *two* trait-behavior clusters pertaining to "honest" and "kind" but will not form a cluster pertaining to "intelligent." To the extent that the organization of behaviors into clusters facilitates their recall (see e.g., Hamilton et al., 1980b; Srull, 1983; Srull & Brand, 1983), this implies that the intelligent behaviors would be recalled less well in the second condition than in the first.

Evaluative Concept Formation

The next postulate states the second objective of person impression formation, that is, to form an evaluative concept of the person being described.

Postulate 7.3. People who are asked to form a general impression of a person will attempt to construct a general concept of the person as likeable or dislikeable. This concept, although based on the trait concepts used to interpret the person's behavior, is primarily evaluative in nature.

Thus, for example, if an individual is described by behaviors that imply favorable attributes, people will form a general concept of the person as "likeable."[2] They often do this by comparing the individual's attributes with those of a prototypic "likeable" or "dislikeable" person. (For a discussion of the role of prototypes in person impression formation, see Cantor & Mischel, 1977.) This prototypic representation is drawn from a referent bin pertaining to these types of persons. The person concept that is formed, however, may also be influenced by the affective reaction that people experience in the course of thinking about the person's behaviors and traits. In fact, a cognitive representation of these affective reactions may often be a very important contributor to this concept (see Chapter 12).

On the other hand, it is important to note that several different prototypes of "likeable" and "dislikeable" persons may be contained in the bins pertaining to these types of persons. Therefore, although the central features of the person concept that is formed on the basis of one of these prototypes are evaluative, other,

---

2. The formation of this concept is restricted to conditions in which the subject's objective is to form a global impression of the person. If instead the objective is to form a more circumscribed impression (e.g., to decide if the person would be suitable for a particular job), descriptive as well as evaluative considerations may come into play.

more peripheral features of the concept may have implications for the specific traits that led to its formation. This means, for example, that the concept of a likeable person that is formed from a description of him as "warm and friendly" differs in some respects from the concept of a likeable person that is formed from information that he is "intelligent and witty." On the other hand, the person concept that is formed in each case may include additional features of a "likeable" person that are not descriptively related to any of the attributes on which the concept is based.

The assumption that the general concept formed of a person in the course of constructing an impression is evaluative may seem intuitively self- evident. However, it is central to many aspects of the formulation we propose. Support for the assumption has been obtained in a variety of research paradigms. A study by Hartwick (1979) is perhaps the most definitive. Subjects were given a series of trait adjective descriptions of a person with instructions either to remember the adjectives or to form an impression of the person they described. Later, subjects in both conditions were given a recognition memory test. Some of the recognition items were not in the original set but varied systematically in terms of both their descriptive and their evaluative consistency with the presented ones. Thus, if one of the original adjectives was "bold," the recognition items might include "adventurous" (both evaluatively and descriptively consistent with the presented one), "foolhardy" (descriptively consistent but evaluatively inconsistent), "cautious," (descriptively inconsistent but evaluatively consistent) and "timid" (both descriptively and evaluatively inconsistent). Subjects with an impression formation objective were significantly more likely than those with a memory objective to report that unmentioned adjectives had been presented when the adjectives were evaluatively consistent with the presented ones. This suggests that impression formation objective subjects extracted a general concept of the person described as likeable or dislikeable, and then used the implications of this evaluative concept as a basis for responding to recognition items when they were uncertain about whether the adjectives had been presented. In contrast, subjects with the different processing objectives were similar in their ability to distinguish between presented and unmentioned descriptively related adjectives. This indicates that the person concept that was formed under impression formation, but not memory objective, conditions was in fact primarily evaluative rather than descriptive in nature.

Further support for this conclusion comes from a study by Cohen and Ebbesen (1979), described in more detail in Chapter 8. In this study, subjects observed a videotape of someone with instructions either to form an impression of the person or to remember what occurred. Afterwards, all subjects rated the person they observed along a series of trait dimensions. Subjects who had viewed the sequence with an impression formation objective tended to make judgments that were evaluatively consistent with one another. This was much less true of subjects who had observed the person with a memory objective. This suggests that subjects with an impression formation objective extracted an evaluative concept of the person from the information they acquired and then used this concept as a basis for their specific trait judgments. In contrast, memory set subjects, who presumably had not extracted such a concept, based their trait judgments on a review of the individual behaviors they had observed, the implications of which were not always evaluatively consistent.

Which aspects of the information presented about a person are most likely to be used as a basis for the evaluative concept that is formed? A partial answer is provided by the next postulate:

Postulate 7.4. The evaluative concept of a person is typically based on only a subset of the information available about the person. This is most often the first subset of information that permits an evaluatively coherent concept to be formed.

Note that in many instances, Postulate 7.4 implies a primacy effect of information on evaluations of a person. That is, if the first information presented about a person has clear and consistent evaluative implications, the evaluative concept formed of the person will be based on these implications, and this concept may be later used as a basis for judging the person. Evidence that evaluative judgments of a person are primarily influenced by initial information presented about the person is provided by numerous studies reporting primacy effects (Anderson, 1965; Anderson & Hubert, 1963; Dreben, Fiske, & Hastie, 1979; Lichtenstein & Srull, 1987; Wyer & Unverzagt, 1985).

Caution must be taken about overgeneralizing these primacy effects, however. Postulate 7.4 implies that if the initial information acquired about a person is evaluatively neutral, or if its implications are unclear, it should have very little influence on the evaluative concept formed of the person relative to the later information (Wyer & Budesheim, 1987). Moreover, when the evaluative implications of the initial descriptions of a person are not entirely consistent, a substantial amount of information may be required before a general concept of the person is extracted (Srull et al., 1985).

Once an evaluative concept of a person has been formed on the basis of trait or behavioral information, subsequent descriptions of the person's behaviors are considered in relation to this concept. Postulate 7.5 formalizes this assumption:

Postulate 7.5. Once an evaluative person concept is formed, individual behaviors of the person are interpreted in terms of it. The ease of interpreting behaviors in terms of the concept, and therefore the strength of their association with it, is an increasing function of the behaviors' evaluative consistency with this concept.

In combination, Postulates 7.1-7.5 imply that a given behavior may often be contained in two different representations: a trait-behavior cluster and a representation that is defined in terms of the evaluative person concept. However, the basis for associating the behavior with the concept defining the latter representation is *evaluative*, whereas the basis for associating it with the concept defining a trait-behavior cluster is *descriptive*. Thus, for example, two honest behaviors might be associated equally strongly with the central concept of a trait-behavior cluster defined by "honest" even though one is favorable ("returned a lost wallet"), the other is unfavorable ("told the instructor that the student sitting next to him had cheated on the exam"). On the other hand, a favorable dishonest behavior ("told a lie to cover up for a friend") would be in a different cluster entirely. In contrast, all three behaviors would be represented in the evaluative person representation. Moreover, if the central concept defining this representation happens to be favorable, the favorable honest and favorable dishonest behaviors would both become more strongly associated with it than would the unfavorable honest behavior.

Responses to Inconsistency

Not all of the information we receive about a person is consistent in its implications. Three general types of inconsistency may arise. The first type occurs when the traits exemplified by a person's behaviors differ in favorableness, making a clear evaluative concept of the person difficult to extract. The second type of inconsistency occurs once this concept has been formed, when the behaviors the person performs are evaluatively inconsistent with the concept. A third type of inconsistency arises when a person's behavior in one situation has different trait and evaluative implications than the person's behavior in a second. (For example, a person may be friendly to colleagues at the office but a tyrant at home.) We consider this third type of inconsistency later in this chapter. The next postulates concern the manner in which people respond to the first two types of inconsistency.

1. Between-Trait Inconsistency

The behaviors performed by a person may exemplify traits that differ in favorableness. This often makes an evaluative concept of the individual hard to construct.[3] In such conditions, Postulate 7.6 comes into play.

---

3. Asch (1946) argued that people who are given evaluatively inconsistent trait descriptions of a person often reconcile this inconsistency by reinterpreting one trait as "general" and the other as "perhiperal." The information that a person is "kind and hostile" might therefore be interpreted as an indication that the person is fundamentally hostile but appears kind on the surface in order to disguise his basically malicious motives. In effect, this amounts to attributing different types of behavior to the individual traits that the person possesses. In the situation considered here, the individual's behaviors are described explicitly, and so the conflict may not be so easily resolvable.

Postulate 7.6. If a clear evaluative person concept cannot be formed on the basis of the initial information presented (e.g., if the initial implications of the information differ in favorableness), subjects who are uncertain about the traits of the person will review the behaviors they have encoded in terms of each trait to insure that they have interpreted these behaviors correctly. This cognitive activity leads associations to be formed among the behaviors that have been encoded in terms of each concept (i.e., the behaviors contained in each trait-behavior cluster).

In terms of the network metaphor we are using, this means that pathways will be established among the behaviors contained *within* each trait-behavior cluster that is constructed as a result of processes implied by Postulate 7.1. Note, however, that pathways are *not* formed between behaviors that are contained in one cluster and those that are contained in another, different cluster. Note also that the cognitive activity implied by Postulate 7.6 occurs only if subjects are uncertain about whether their trait encodings of the target's behaviors are correct. When explicit trait descriptions of a person are provided, subjects have less reason to question their interpretation of behaviors that exemplify these traits. In other cases, when the behaviors performed by a person exemplify traits that are evaluatively consistent, an evaluative concept of the person is easy to construct. In both cases, therefore, subjects may be relatively confident of their interpretation of the behaviors, and so the cognitive activity that underlies the formation of the associations among the behaviors within each cluster may not occur. In other words, this activity is most likely when (a) subjects do not have clear trait-based expectations for what a person is like *and* (b) the traits they have spontaneously used to interpret the person's behaviors differ in favorableness.

2. Inconsistencies of Behaviors with the Central Person Concept

The next postulate pertains to subjects' reactions to behaviors that are inconsistent with their evaluative concept of the person being described.

Postulate 7.7. Once an evaluative person concept has been formed, individual behaviors that are evaluatively inconsistent with the concept are thought about in relation to other behaviors that have evaluative implications in an attempt to reconcile their occurrence. This leads to the formation of associations among these behaviors. In contrast, behaviors that are either evaluatively neutral or evaluatively consistent with the person concept do not stimulate this cognitive activity.

Postulate 7.7 is similar to an assumption made by Hastie (1980) in an earlier model of person memory and impression formation. However, it differs in two important respects. First, it implies that the type of inconsistency that stimulates the formation of interbehavior associations is *evaluative* rather than descriptive. Second, it assumes that associations are formed only among behaviors that have clear positive or negative evaluative implications. Neutral behaviors are usually not relevant to the evaluative impression that subjects are presumably trying to form of a person, and so they are not considered when attempting to reconcile other behaviors that are inconsistent with this impression.

3. An Illustrative Example

The implications of Postulates 7.6 and 7.7 are best conveyed with an example. Suppose subjects learn that a man has performed three honest behaviors (bh), one kind behavior (bk), three stupid behaviors (bs), and two behaviors that have no evaluative implications (bo). Suppose further that these behaviors are presented in the order: $b_o\ b_h\ b_s\ b_k\ b_o\ b_s\ b_h\ b_s\ b_h$.

In the absence of any expectancies for the man's traits, subjects should form three trait-behavior clusters of the sort shown in Figure 7.1a, pertaining to "honest," "kind," and "stupid." Because the traits differ in their evaluative implications, however, a coherent evaluative concept cannot be extracted, and so an evaluation-based person representation is not constructed. On the other hand, subjects are stimulated to think about the behaviors within each cluster in relation to one another (Postulate 7.6), leading to interbehavior associations of the sort also shown in the figure.

Now suppose instead that subjects before receiving the behavior descriptions are explicitly told that the man is honest (T_h) and kind (T_k). In this case, only two trait-behavior clusters should be formed (Postulate 7.2). However, because the initial trait descriptions are evaluatively similar, a favorable person concept (P+) should be extracted, and the behaviors should also become associated with this concept, forming an evaluation-based person representation. These representations are shown in Figure 7.1b. Behaviors that are evaluatively consistent with the central concept defining the person representation are more strongly associated with it (as indicated by wider pathways) than other behaviors. However, evaluatively inconsistent ("stupid") behaviors are thought about in relation to other evaluatively related (i.e., consistent and inconsistent) behaviors, establishing associations to them (Postulate 7.7). (For simplicity in drawing the figure, each evaluatively inconsistent behavior (b_s) is assumed to become associated with the two evaluatively related behaviors that immediately precede it in the presentation sequence. However, if the inconsistent behavior is still in the Work Space at the time subsequent behaviors are read, forward associations may occur as well.)

A. Trait adjective descriptions not provided

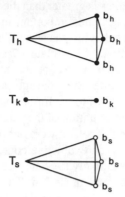

B. Trait adjective descriptions provided

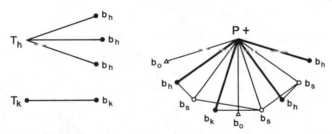

Figure 7.1. Trait-behavior clusters and evaluation-based person representation formed when (a) initial trait-adjective descriptions of the person
are not provided and (b) the target person is initially described as honest
(T_h) and kind (T_k). T_h and T_k are trait concepts associated with honesty and
kindness, respectively; P+ is a person concept with favorable evaluative
implications; and b_h, b_k, b_s and b_o are honest, kind, stupid, and evaluatively
neutral behaviors, respectively.

The representations shown in Figure 7.1b convey two general implications of
the formulation we propose. First, evaluatively neutral behaviors are not associatively linked to any other behaviors (Postulate 7.7). Therefore, except for their
association with the central person concept, they are totally isolated from other
behaviors in the representation.

Second, the cognitive activity implied by Postulate 7.7 is stimulated only by
the identification of evaluatively inconsistent behaviors. This means that, on
average, the number of associative pathways emanating from (and, therefore,

leading into) inconsistent items is greater than the number emanating from consistent ones. This difference becomes important in predicting the relative ease of recalling different types of behaviors, as we shall see.

An additional implication of Postulate 7.7 is not conveyed by our example. Specifically, behaviors of a person do not become associated with an evaluative concept of the person until after this concept has been formed. In other words, information that is acquired prior to the formation of this concept is not contained in the evaluation-based representation of the person. Suppose in our example that trait-based expectations for the person were not provided. Because the behaviors differ in their favorableness, an evaluative concept of the person is difficult to construct, and, therefore, is unlikely to be formed (if it is formed at all) until after several additional behaviors are presented. The behaviors that were presented before the formation of the concept should not be contained in the evaluation-based representation of the person. This has implications for the likelihood of later recalling these behaviors, as we note presently.

Bolstering

A major ingredient of a person impression is the evaluative concept formed of the person, which has implications for whether the person is likeable or dislikeable. It seems reasonable to suppose that once such a concept has been formed, subjects will not only respond to behaviors that are inconsistent with this concept by trying to reconcile their occurrence (Postulate 7.7). In addition, they will mentally review behaviors that are consistent with the concept in an attempt to confirm its validity. The effects of this "bolstering" are conveyed in an additional postulate.

Postulate 7.8. If people who have formed an evaluative concept of a person learn about specific behaviors of the person that are inconsistent with this concept, they will mentally review and think about other behaviors the person has performed that support its validity. This cognitive activity further strengthens the associations between the concept and behaviors that are evaluatively consistent with it.

Bolstering may have the same function as inconsistency resolution. That is, it permits the central concept of a person to be maintained. In this regard, inconsistency resolution and bolstering may be analogous to two cognitive responses to persuasion that have been identified in the area of belief and opinion change (for reviews, see McGuire, 1968, 1985). That is, attempts to reconcile behaviors that are inconsistent with one's concept of a person may be analogous to counterarguing (cf. McGuire, 1981; Osterhouse & Brock, 1970; Petty & Cacioppo, 1981, 1986), whereas bolstering is conceptually similar to an attempt to increase "consonance" with one's previously formed beliefs and attributes (cf. Festinger, 1957). The conditions in which these processes are postulated to occur in research and theory on attitude and belief change differ in important respects from those of concern here. The similarity in the cognitive responses being postulated is nonetheless worth noting.

Priorities in Impression-Directed Information Processing

The postulates we have proposed in this section recognize the possibility that people engage in several quite different cognitive activities en route to forming an impression. They encode behaviors in terms of traits, extract an evaluative concept of the person, and further encode the person's behaviors in terms of their evaluative consistency with this concept. In addition, they attempt to reconcile inconsistencies between the person's behavior and the implications of the concept they have formed of the person, and review beliefs that are consistent with this concept in an effort to confirm its validity. Each of these activities places demands on the human processing system. It therefore seems reasonable to suppose that when a large amount of stimulus information is presented in a short period of time, the simultaneous pursuit of all of the activities noted above may exceed people's processing capacity. In other instances, they may simply be unmotivated to engage in the cognitive effort required to attain all of the goals to which these activities are directed.

In such instances, therefore, it seems reasonable to suppose that subjects will not always perform all of the activities we have postulated, but will give some activities priority over others. This is particularly likely when processing demands are high. The failure to engage in one or more of the activities we have postulated should theoretically be reflected in the content and structure of the representations that are formed. For example, if subjects do not engage in bolstering, behaviors that are consistent with the concept defining the evaluative person representation should be less strongly associated with this concept. If inconsistency resolution is not performed, direct associative pathways between inconsistent behaviors and others contained in the representation should not be established. The model we propose has the capability of evaluating these possibilities, as will be shown.

Storage of Representations in Memory

The cognitive representations that are formed of a person are presumably transferred to long term memory (or, in terms of our model, Permanent Storage). The next postulate elaborates this assumption.

> Postulate 7.9. The trait-behavior clusters that are formed as a result of encoding a person's behaviors in terms of a trait concept, and the evaluation-based representation that is ultimately formed of the person, each functions as a separate unit of information. These representations are stored independently of one another in a referent bin in Permanent Storage that pertains to the person.

One implication of this assumption is worth noting. Specifically, many behaviors of a person may be represented at least twice in memory, once in a trait-behavior cluster (based on its descriptive implications) and once in the evaluation-based person representation (based on its evaluative implications). The importance of this dual coding will soon become obvious.

In combination, Postulates 7.1-7.9 provide a reasonably complete theoretical account of the mental representations that are formed of individuals on the basis of trait and behavioral information about them. (Extensions of the model that take into account the formation of role-specific and situation-specific representations will be considered later in this chapter.) We are now in a position to consider the use of these representations in recalling the information presented about the person. We now consider the matter.

The Recall of Trait and Behavioral Information About a Person

Suppose people who have received information about a person's traits and behaviors are later asked to recall the information they have read. They presumably identify the referent bin in Permanent Storage that contains information about this person and retrieve a representation from this bin. When more than one representation has been deposited in the bin, the most likely one to be retrieved is the one that is closest to the top (Postulate 5.8). This, in turn, is the representation that was most recently deposited (i.e., the last one formed, or the one that has been most recently used for another purpose).

This has important implications. Different representations contain quite different sets of behaviors. Moreover, although behaviors may be contained in more than one representation, these behaviors will be less accessible in some representations than they are in others, for reasons we indicate below. Therefore, situational factors that influence the accessibility of different representations will have an impact on the sorts of behaviors that subjects are likely to recall. Without knowledge of these factors, there is no a priori basis for assuming that one type of representation will be more accessible than another. Therefore, we will typically assume that the likelihood of retrieving any given representation is equal. One consequence of this assumption is that the likelihood of retrieving any particular representation is an inverse function of the total number of representations that have been formed.

To understand the more specific implications of the formulation we propose for the recall of information, it is necessary to state three additional postulates concerning the retrieval of specific features contained in a representation once this representation has been identified.

Postulate 7.10. The recall of the specific behaviors contained in a representation is the result of a sequential search process. The search begins at the central concept node and progresses along the various pathways in the network. Behaviors are recalled in the order they are activated in the course of this search.

a. When more than one pathway emanates from a particular node, the most likely path to be traversed is the one that reflects the strongest association between the nodes it connects.

b. When the only path emanating from a behavior node is the one by which it was accessed, the search is reinitiated at the central concept node.

Two other postulates are necessary to provide a complete account of memory retrieval.

Postulate 7.11. Traversing a pathway between two concept (or behavior) nodes increases the strength of association between them. It therefore increases the subsequent probability that recalling one of the concepts (behaviors) will cue the retrieval of the other.

Postulate 7.12. When a search activates n successive features, all of which have been retrieved previously, the search is terminated.

Postulates 7.11 and 7.12 are very similar to assumptions made by Rundus (1971) and others in accounting for category set size effects. That is, the more often a particular associative pathway has been traversed, the more likely it is to be traversed again in the future (for evidence of this, see Raaijmakers & Shiffrin, 1980, 1981). The greater the number of behaviors that are connected to a central concept, the more likely it is that the search process will become localized in an area of the representation that contains only a subset of the behaviors contained in it. Consequently, the remaining behaviors are less likely to be identified before the search is terminated (Postulate 7.12). When direct associations exist among the behaviors in a representation, the number of associations to any given behavior, and therefore the ease with which it can be accessed and recalled, may *increase* with the number of other behaviors that are contained in the representation. Holding constant the number of such associations, however, Postulates 7.11 and 7.12 imply that the likelihood of recalling a behavior will *decrease*, on the average, with the number of other behaviors contained in the representation.

The combined effects of a behavior's associations with both the central concept node and other behaviors on the likelihood of recalling it are captured by the following functional relationship:

$$PR(b_i) = f[S(C,b_i) + \Sigma S(b_j, b_i)]/N_b \qquad [7.1]$$

where $PR(b_i)$ is the probability of recalling behavior b_i, $S(C,b_i)$ is the strength of the behavior's association with the central concept C, $S(b_j,b_i)$ is the strength of association of b_i with a second behavior b_j, and N_b is the total number of behaviors that are contained in the representation.[4]

The general implications of these postulates can be seen with reference to the examples we provided earlier and conveyed in Figure 7.1. First, suppose subjects who expect a target person to be kind and honest receive information that the person has performed one kind of behavior, three honest ones, three stupid behaviors, and two evaluatively neutral ones. These subjects should form representations similar to those shown in Figure 7.1b. If they are later asked to recall the behaviors presented and happen to retrieve a trait-behavior cluster, they should recall the behaviors contained in this cluster together, before retrieving and recalling the behaviors contained in a second representation. Furthermore, assuming that both

---

4. As noted by Wyer et al. (1984; see also Raaijmakers & Shiffrin, 1981), an additional factor that must often be taken into account is the strength of association between these behaviors and contextual features of the situation in which the information is presented (i.e., characteristics of the experimental room, other participants in the experiment, etc.). For simplicity, however, we ignore this factor here.

the cluster pertaining to kind and the one pertaining to honest are ultimately retrieved, subjects should be more likely to recall the kind behavior than to recall any given one of the honest behaviors. On the other hand, subjects should recall *both* kind behaviors and honest behaviors better than stupid ones, because a cluster pertaining to stupid has not been formed.

However, suppose instead that subjects base their recall on the contents of the evaluation-based representation. According to Postulate 7.10, they should begin their search from the central concept node (P+), and progress down a pathway to a behavior that is relatively strongly associated with it. Therefore, the first behavior they recall will most likely be an honest one. If they continue their search along the pathways emanating from this behavior, however, the next one they will encounter is likely to be a stupid behavior. In general, because more pathways lead to stupid behaviors than to honest ones, the former behaviors should enjoy a recall advantage. Note further that *no* pathways lead to neutral behaviors. These behaviors can only be accessed from the central person concept node. Moreover, these behaviors are not represented in trait-behavior clusters. For both reasons, these neutral behaviors should be recalled very poorly.

Different predictions are made if subjects do *not* have trait-based expectations for what the target person is like at the time they learn about his behaviors. In this case, subjects theoretically form only the representations shown in Figure 7.1a. Therefore, they should recall honest and stupid behaviors equally well, provided they identify the trait-behavior clusters in which they are contained. Moreover, these behaviors may gain a recall advantage over the kind behavior. This is because the large number of interbehavior associations in the honest and stupid clusters may be sufficient to overcome the effects of differences in set size.

It is important to note that the search and retrieval postulates are potentially applicable regardless of the specific characteristics of the cognitive representations from which information is extracted. In fact, they are applicable to the retrieval of material from any cognitive representation that can be conceptualized using an associative network metaphor, whether or not the representation refers to a person. If these postulates are valid, they can be used to evaluate assumptions concerning the content and structure of the representations to which they are applied. We first consider evidence bearing on the nature of the trait-behavior clusters that are formed in the course of person impression formation. Then, we turn to the content and structure of the evaluation-based person representation.

The Recall of Information from Trait-Behavior Clusters

To reiterate, the interpretation of a person's behaviors in terms of trait concepts leads to the formation of trait-behavior clusters (Postulate 7.1). Each of these clusters is ultimately stored in memory as a single unit (Postulate 7.9). Several quite different sets of data provide converging support for these assumptions.

Clustering of recalled behaviors. To the extent that a trait-behavior cluster is retrieved and used as a basis for recalling the person's behavior, subjects should recall those behaviors contained in it before they identify and recall the behaviors contained in a second representation. A study by Hamilton, Katz, & Leirer (1980a,b) supports this prediction. That is, subjects who had read descriptions of a person's behaviors with instructions to form an impression of the person subsequently recalled behaviors in much closer proximity to one another if they exemplified the same trait than if they exemplified different ones. This clustering was *not* evident when subjects read the same behavioral descriptions with instructions to remember them. This suggests that subjects with an impression formation objective, unlike those with a memory objective, spontaneously encoded and organized the behaviors in terms of trait concepts, and that this organization affected their later recall of the behaviors.

Cued recall. If trait-behavior clusters are formed, recalling the trait concept that defines a given cluster should cue the recall of the behaviors that are contained in it. In other words, behaviors that exemplify a given trait concept should be more easily recalled if the trait concept is recalled than if it is not.

This prediction was confirmed by Wyer and Gordon (1982). Subjects were first given a set of adjectives that described several different traits of a target person, followed by a series of behaviors. Some behaviors exemplified each of the traits described, whereas others exemplified their bipolar opposites. Moreover, some of the behaviors exemplifying each trait were favorable and others were unfavorable. Thus, for example, if the target was described as "honest," some of the target's behaviors were favorable and honest (e.g., "returned a wallet containing money to the lost and found"), whereas others were either unfavorable and honest (e.g., "turned in a classmate for giving someone an answer in an exam"), favorable and dishonest ("told a friend he liked a gift that he actually thought was tasteless"), or unfavorable and dishonest ("sold a scratched record to a classmate after telling him it was almost new"). Subjects were told either to form an impression of the person described (impression formation set) or simply to remember the information presented (memory set). Later, they were asked to recall as much of the information (both trait adjectives and behaviors) as they could.

Subjects with an impression formation objective were more likely to recall behaviors exemplifying a particular trait concept if they had also recalled an adjective describing this trait (probability = .46) than if they had not (.20). This difference, which was independent of the evaluative similarity of the behaviors to the trait descriptions, suggested that the trait adjectives subjects remembered cued their recall of the associated behaviors. This is what one would expect if trait-behavior clusters were formed and later used as a basis for recall. In contrast, these cueing effects were not evident among subjects who had received the information with a memory set. These latter subjects recalled a given behavior with the same (low) probability regardless of whether they had recalled a trait adjective that could be used to describe it (.21) or not (.20).

In interpreting these data, it is important to note that the recall of a trait adjective did *not* facilitate the recall of behaviors that were descriptively inconsistent with it (i.e., behaviors that implied the bipolar opposite trait). Specifically, the likelihood of recalling a behavior (under impression objective conditions) was nearly the same regardless of whether an adjective with which it was descriptively inconsistent was recalled (.34) or not (.27). This confirms our assumption that the trait-behavior clusters *contain only those behaviors that can be interpreted in terms of the concept defining these clusters*, and not behaviors along the entire trait dimension.

Set size effects. The third type of data that bears on the existence of trait-behavior clusters requires a consideration of Postulates 7.11 and 7.12. These latter two postulates imply that if behaviors are organized into trait-behavior clusters, and if no interbehavior associations are formed among the behaviors within each cluster, the likelihood of recalling any given behavior in a cluster will decrease as the total number of behaviors in the cluster increases. Evidence that this is in fact the case was obtained in a series of studies by Gordon and Wyer (1987). Subjects with an impression formation objective read a description of 18 behaviors a person had performed. Three of these behaviors exemplified one trait, 6 exemplified a second, and 9 exemplified a third. Some subjects were told at the outset that the target possessed the three traits implied by the behaviors, whereas other subjects were not. Later, all subjects were asked to recall the behaviors they had read.

The likelihood of recalling a behavior is shown in Figure 7.2 as a function of the number of behaviors exemplifying the same trait. When the three trait concepts were similar in favorableness, the likelihood of recalling a behavior decreased as the number of other behaviors exemplifying the same trait increased, and this was true regardless of whether or not subjects had been given a prior indication of the nature of the person's traits. Note that the total number of behaviors was the same in all cases. Therefore, if subjects had not spontaneously organized the behaviors into different trait categories, but rather had treated them as a single undifferentiated list, these effects would not have occurred. The fact that these set size effects were similar regardless of whether a prior expectancy existed suggests that subjects *spontaneously* encoded the behaviors in terms of these concepts. This finding provides further support for our assumption that the encoding and organization of behaviors into trait- behavior clusters is an integral part of impression formation. Put another way, this organization does not appear to be an artifact of implicit task demands to interpret the behaviors in terms of trait adjectives provided by the experimenter.

Formation of interbehavior associations. The negative trait-category set size effects shown in Figure 7.2a suggest that the behaviors presented were encoded in terms of trait concepts without thinking about them in relation to one another, and

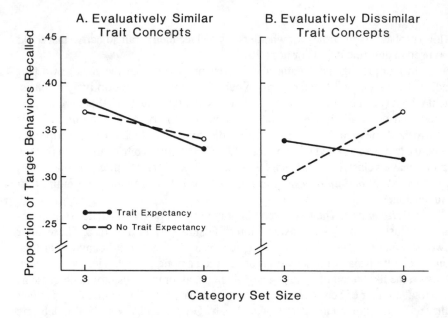

Figure 7.2. Proportion of behaviors recalled as a function of the number of behaviors presented that exemplify the same trait concept. (a) Trait concepts exemplified by the behaviors presented are similar in favorableness. (b) Trait concepts exemplified by the behaviors presented differ in favorableness.

that no interbehavior associations were formed. According to Postulate 7.6, however, this should be true only when subjects are relatively confident that their trait interpretations of the behaviors are correct. We speculated that this confidence is likely to be high if either (a) subjects are given an indication of the target person's traits before learning about the person's behaviors, or (b) the person's behaviors exemplify traits that are similar in favorableness, making an evaluative concept of the person easy to form. The conditions described above and shown in Figure 7.2a meet one or both of these criteria. Suppose, however, that subjects are not given a priori trait descriptions of a person, and that the person's behaviors exemplify traits that differ in their evaluative implications. Then, subjects may be less confident of their interpretation of these behaviors, and may reconsider the behaviors they have identified as exemplifying each trait in relation to one another to ensure that their interpretation of them is correct. If this occurs, associations may be formed among the behaviors in each trait-behavior cluster, the number of which may increase with the number of behaviors in the cluster. The facilitating effects of these associations on the accessibility of the behaviors may be sufficient to override the effects of set size per se. (In other words, the increase in $\Sigma S(b_j, b_i)$ in the numerator of Equation 7.1 may be sufficient to offset the increase in N_b in the denominator.)

Results obtained in other conditions of Gordon and Wyer's studies, in which the behaviors presented exemplified traits that were evaluatively heterogeneous, support this assumption. These data are shown in Figure 7.2b. When subjects were given explicit trait-based expectancies for what the target was like, the probability that they recalled a given behavior decreased as the number of other behaviors exemplifying the same trait increased, just as they did when the behaviors exemplified traits that were similar in favorableness. When the trait adjective descriptions were *not* provided, however, the probability that they recalled a given behavior *increased* with the number of other behaviors implying the same trait.

These results therefore provide strong support for Postulate 7.5. Note that the behaviors contained in a trait-behavior cluster should generally be easier to recall if associations have been formed among the behaviors themselves than if they have not. This hypothesis was also supported in Gordon and Wyer's study (see also Wyer, Bodenhausen, & Srull, 1984).

The Recall of Behaviors in the Evaluation-Based Person Representation: Responses to Expectancy-Inconsistent Behavior

Once an evaluative concept of a person has been formed, behaviors of the person are thought about in terms of this concept, and thereby become associated with it (Postulate 7.5). Moreover, behaviors that are evaluatively consistent with the concept, and therefore are easily encoded in terms of its features, become more strongly associated with the concept than do behaviors that are neutral or evaluatively inconsistent with it.

On the other hand, when subjects who have formed an evaluative concept of a person encounter a behavior that is inconsistent with this concept, two additional things may occur. First, subjects may think about the behavior in relation to other behaviors that have evaluative implications, leading interbehavior associations to be formed (Postulate 7.7). Second, they may mentally review and think more extensively about those behaviors that are consistent with the concept they have formed of the person to marshall support for its validity. This activity strengthens the consistent behaviors' association with the concept (Postulate 7.8).

Postulates 7.5 and 7.8 on one hand, and Postulate 7.7 on the other, have opposite implications for the relative ease of recalling behaviors that are evaluatively consistent or inconsistent with the central person concept. All other things being equal, consistent behaviors should have a recall advantage over inconsistent ones because of their stronger association with the concept (Postulates 7.5 and 7.8). However, the cognitive activity implied by Postulate 7.7 should lead more associative pathways to be formed to inconsistent behaviors than to consistent ones, and this should make the inconsistent behaviors relatively more accessible. These two factors should combine to give both consistent and inconsistent behaviors an advantage over neutral ones. However, the relative ease of recalling consistent and inconsistent behaviors depends on which of the two factors has the greater influence.

Most studies of person memory have shown a recall advantage of inconsistent behaviors over consistent ones, and an advantage of both types of behaviors over neutral behaviors (Bargh & Thein, 1985; Hastie & Kumar, 1979; Srull, 1981; Srull, Lichtenstein, & Rothbart, 1985; Stern, Marrs, Millar, & Cole, 1984; Wyer & Gordon, 1982). These findings suggest that under conditions similar to those that are typically constructed to investigate person memory phenomena, interbehavior associations have more influence on recall than does the strength of each behavior's association with the central concept. However, the proposed model implies many qualifications on this general conclusion, the nature of which becomes clear in the discussion to follow.

1. Evaluative vs. Descriptive Influences on Inconsistency Resolution

An important assumption of our formulation is that the general concept formed of a person in the course of forming an impression is fundamentally evaluative (e.g., either "likeable" or "dislikeable"). The inconsistencies that stimulate the cognitive activity implied by Postulates 7.7 and 7.8 are therefore evaluative and not descriptive. (Thus, for example, the activity results from a desire to understand why a likeable person might engage in dislikeable behaviors rather than why an honest person might do something dishonest.)

Support for this assumption comes from two types of studies. First, in the experiment by Wyer and Gordon (1982) noted earlier, behaviors were recalled better if they were evaluatively inconsistent with the trait adjectives than if they were consistent with them, and this was true regardless of whether the behaviors exemplified the traits described by these adjectives or their bipolar opposites. In fact, when their evaluative implications were controlled, behaviors were recalled somewhat better if they were descriptively *consistent* with the adjectives used to characterize the target than if they were descriptively inconsistent with them. As we suggested in the previous section, this latter difference presumably occurred because some subjects based their recall on trait-behavior clusters rather than on the evaluative person representation.

Other studies (e.g., Hastie, 1980; Wyer, Bodenhausen, & Srull, 1984; Wyer & Martin, 1986, Experiment 1) have also shown that behaviors are recalled better if they are evaluatively inconsistent with the trait adjectives used to describe a target person than if they are evaluatively consistent with these adjectives, regardless of whether the behaviors are descriptively related to these trait adjectives or pertain to totally unrelated attributes. These results also suggest that the factors that underlie inconsistency resolution are largely stimulated by evaluative considerations.

This does not necessarily mean, however, that descriptive factors play no role in inconsistency resolution. Their role may be most evident when the time available to think about the information presented is limited. In such instances, subjects may give higher priority to the reconciliation of evaluatively inconsistent behaviors that are descriptively related to the prototype on which their evaluative concept of the person is based. Some support for this possibility was obtained by Hastie (1980). In contrast to Wyer and his colleagues, he found that the recall advantage of evaluatively inconsistent behaviors over evaluatively consistent behaviors was greater when the behaviors were descriptively related to the trait adjectives used to characterize the target than when they were not. We elaborate on this possibility in more detail later, when we discuss the priorities that underlie the performance of different impression-directed cognitive activities.

In much of the research performed in the area of person memory, however, the evaluative consistency of the target's behaviors with the general person concept that was theoretically formed of him has been confounded with the descriptive consistency of these behaviors with the target's trait-adjective description. For example, if the person was described as honest, presumably leading a favorable person concept to be formed, the behaviors were either honest (favorable) or dishonest (unfavorable.) For the moment, therefore, we typically do not distinguish between these two types of relatedness. Rather, we focus on three general issues: (a) the existence of interbehavior associations and the conditions in which they occur; (b) the sequential search processes that govern the recall of behaviors that differ in their consistency with the person concept, and (c) the role of bolstering, and the conditions in which its effects on the recall of consistent behaviors are likely to override the effects of interbehavior associations.

2. The Formation of Interbehavior Associations

Many interpretations might be given to the relatively better recall of behaviors that are inconsistent with expectations for what a person is like. For one thing, expectancy-inconsistent behaviors may simply be more novel or distinctive (cf. Wyer & Gordon, 1982), and therefore may capture more attention. Alternatively, subjects may engage in more elaborate encoding of expectancy-inconsistent behaviors in an attempt to explain their occurrence (Hastie, 1984). This activity may lead these behaviors to become more strongly associated with concepts that compose subjects' general world knowledge, increasing the number of possible retrieval cues for these behaviors at the time of recall. Although both of these factors may conceivably contribute to the recall of expectancy-inconsistent behaviors, neither is postulated by the formulation we propose, and neither factor alone can account for many of the results we summarize below.

The recall advantage of inconsistent behaviors is theoretically due to the fact that when subjects encounter an inconsistent behavior, they think about it in relation to other behaviors that have evaluative implications. This leads direct associations to be formed between this behavior and the others. As a result, the number of access routes to the inconsistent behavior in the evaluative person representation is increased, and so the probability of identifying the behavior in the course of the sequential search implied by Postulate 7.10 is higher. Note that although this activity should produce the greatest increment in the recall of expectancy- inconsistent behaviors, it should also have a positive effect on the recall of expectancy-consistent behaviors, as some of these behaviors become associated with the inconsistent ones as a result of the cognitive activity we postulate to occur. In contrast, it should not have any influence on the recall of neutral or irrelevant behaviors, as these remain isolated from others in the evaluative person representation (Figure 7.1a). Studies by Srull and his colleagues (Srull, 1981; Srull, Lichtenstein, & Rothbart, 1985) provide support for these and other implications of the conceptualization.

Two sets of studies (Srull, 1981, Experiments 2 and 3; Srull et al., 1985, Experiment 3) are particularly informative as they support implications of the model that are nonintuitive. Note that if inconsistent behaviors stimulate the formation of interbehavior associations with other evaluative behaviors, the number of such pathways should increase with the number of inconsistent behaviors that are presented. This means that the addition of inconsistent behaviors to the set presented should increase the recall of *consistent* ones. Because consistent behaviors do not stimulate this cognitive activity, however, adding these behaviors to the set should *not* affect the recall of inconsistent ones. Srull (1981, Experiments 2 and 3) showed this to be true. Holding constant the total number of behaviors presented, the likelihood of recalling consistent behaviors was .28, .39, and .49 when 0, 6, and 12 inconsistent behaviors were contained in the list. In contrast, holding constant the number of inconsistent behaviors presented, the probability of recalling these behaviors was nearly identical (.62, .58, and .59) regardless of whether 0, 6, or 12 consistent behaviors accompanied them.

Note that although increasing the number of inconsistent behaviors should affect the recall of consistent behaviors, it should not affect the recall of evaluatively *neutral* ones. This is because interbehavior associations do not involve these behaviors. This hypothesis could not be tested in Srull's first (1981) study because the number of neutral behaviors was confounded with the number of inconsistent ones presented. In the later study (Srull et al., 1985, Experiment 3), however, the number of inconsistent behaviors presented was varied (0, 6, or 12) and the number of consistent and neutral behaviors was held constant (12 in each case). As in the earlier study, the proportion of consistent behaviors recalled increased with the number of inconsistent behaviors presented (.30, .39, and .47 when 0, 6, and 12 inconsistent behaviors were presented, respectively). However, the proportion of neutral behaviors recalled was nearly identical in each case (.29, .28, and .31, respectively).

In addition to supporting the implications of Postulate 7.7, the above results eliminate alternative explanations of the recall advantage of expectancy-inconsistent information. For example, if the effect were simply a result of expectancy-inconsistent behaviors being more distinctive, or being thought about more extensively, the differences in recall probabilities noted above would not be expected.

Interference effects on the formation of interbehavior associations. If the recall advantage of expectancy-inconsistent behaviors is due to the establishment of interbehavior associations, this advantage should be decreased or eliminated when subjects cannot engage in the cognitive activity that leads these associations to be formed. Two studies (Srull, 1981, Experiment 4; Srull et al., 1985, Experiment 1) support this hypothesis. In these studies, subjects were given a series of expectancy-consistent and expectancy-inconsistent behaviors with instructions to repeat each behavior aloud either 0, 1, 2, or 3 times immediately after it was presented. This "rehearsal" might be expected to increase the learning of these behaviors. However, it should also make it more difficult for subjects to think about a behavior in relation to the others. This difficulty should increase with the number of repetitions that subjects are required to perform. Consequently, the number of rehearsals should have a negative influence on the proportion of inconsistent items recalled. In addition, some of the associations that result from thinking about the target's inconsistent behaviors often involve consistent ones. Therefore, preventing this cognitive activity should decrease the number of retrieval routes to consistent behaviors, and should produce a decrement in their recall as well. This decrement should not be as great, however, as the decrement in recall of the inconsistent behaviors, because the number of associations formed to consistent behaviors is relatively less to begin with (see Figure 7.1). Furthermore, the number of repetitions should have *no* affect on the recall of neutral behaviors, which are not involved in the formation of interbehavior associations under any condition.

These implications of the model received strong support in both studies. The results of Srull's (1981, Experiment 4) study, shown in Figure 7.3, are illustrative. That is, the recall of inconsistent behaviors decreased substantially as the number of repetitions increased. Although the recall of consistent behaviors also decreased, this decrement was much less pronounced. As a result, when subjects were required to repeat each behavior 3 times, the recall advantage of inconsistent behaviors was either eliminated or, as in Figure 7.3, even reversed. In contrast, the recall of neutral behaviors was not affected at all by the number of repetitions. These results therefore provide strong support for our assumptions concerning not only the general role of interbehavior associations in recall, but also the specific types of behaviors involved in these associations.

Many other factors may of course decrease subjects' ability or motivation to perform the cognitive work that leads interbehavior associations to be formed. For example it may not be performed if the inconsistent behavior is apparently attributable to a situational factor rather than to the person who engaged in it

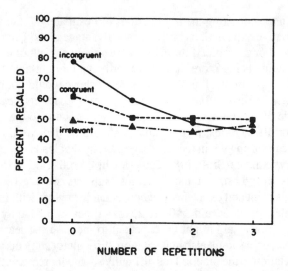

Figure 7.3. Proportion of inconsistent, consistent and neutral behaviors recalled as a function of the number of overt rehearsals required (reprinted from Srull, 1981, p. 455).

(Crocker, Hannah, & Weber, 1983). Still other factors that influence the formation of these associations are discussed in later sections of this chapter.

3. Sequential Search Processes in the Retrieval of Behavioral Information

A major strength of the formulation we propose is its ability not only to account for overall differences in the relative probabilities of recalling different types of expectancy-relevant behaviors, but also to generate predictions of both the order in which these behaviors are recalled and the time required to do so. Two additional studies by Srull investigated these implications. In the first (Srull, 1981, Experiment 1), subjects recalled the behaviors in writing and conditional recall probabilities were used as a basis for evaluating sequential search processes. In the second (Srull et al., 1985, Experiment 4), subjects recalled behaviors aloud and the difference in time required to recall successive behaviors was used as an additional index. The model's implications for these two measures are somewhat different.

Conditional recall probabilities. To see the implications of the model for the order in which different types of behaviors are recalled, suppose first that subjects have retrieved an evaluation-based person representation of the sort shown in Figure 7.1b as a basis for recalling behaviors. Postulate 7.10 implies that the search begins at the central concept node and proceeds along a pathway to a behavior that is most strongly associated with it. One immediate implication of this assumption, in combination with Postulate 7.5, is that the first behavior recalled is more likely to be consistent with the central person concept than to be inconsistent or neutral. In fact, this is the case. In an analysis of 288 free recall protocols, Srull (1981) found that the first behavior recalled was consistent with the person concept 55% of the time, with the remaining responses about evenly divided between inconsistent (25%) and neutral (20%) behaviors. These data suggest that inconsistent and neutral behaviors are associated about equally strongly with the central person concept. Note that these results are in marked contrast to the overall probabilities of recalling these different types of behaviors. (Overall, inconsistent behaviors are recalled much better than consistent ones, and neutral behaviors are recalled very poorly.)

Having identified the first behavior as a result of the processes described above, the subject typically proceeds along one of the associative pathways emanating from it to another behavior. If no such pathway exists, however, the subject is forced to return to the central concept node and reinitiate a search from that node. This assumption, in combination with Postulates 7.5 and 7.7, has several implications.

1. First, suppose subjects have recalled a consistent behavior. Because consistent behaviors are theoretically only associated with inconsistent behaviors, the likelihood of recalling an inconsistent behavior following a consistent one should be very high. In fact, this was the case in Srull's (1981) study; recall of a consistent behavior was immediately followed by the recall of an inconsistent behavior 90% of the time, whereas it was followed by the recall of another consistent behavior only 7% of the time and by a neutral behavior only 3% of the time.[5] Results of the later study, presented in the top half of Table 7.1, show an identical pattern.

2. Now suppose subjects have recalled an inconsistent behavior. This behavior may be associatively linked to either a consistent or an inconsistent behavior with about the same probability. Therefore, the recall of each type of behavior following recall of an inconsistent one should be relatively high and about equal, whereas the likelihood of recalling a neutral behavior should be low. In Srull's (1981) study, the recall of an inconsistent behavior was followed most often by the recall of a consistent one (47%), with inconsistent behaviors and neutral behaviors being recalled less frequently (20% and 32%). In the later study (see Table 7.2), the relative likelihoods of recalling consistent and inconsistent behaviors following the recall of an inconsistent one were reversed (25% vs. 45%). Most important, the

---

5. These probabilities are based on conditions in which the numbers of consistent, inconsistent, and neutral behaviors presented were the same (12 in each case). However, other conditions of the study, in which the numbers of each type presented were unequal, yielded identical conclusions.

TABLE 7.1

Conditional Recall Probabilities and Response Times Required to Recall
Different Types of Behaviors as a Function of the Type of Behaviors
Recalled Immediately Preceding Them

	Type of behavior previously recalled		
	Evaluatively consistent	Evaluatively inconsistent	Evaluatively neutral
A. Conditional Probability of recalling an			
evaluatively consistent behavior	.15	.25	.66
evaluatively inconsistent behavior	.69	.45	.12
evaluatively neutral behavior	.16	.29	.22
B. Time (in seconds) required to recall an			
evaluatively consistent behavior	7.9	5.6	9.1
evaluatively inconsistent behavior	5.4	6.1	8.7
evaluatively neutral behavior	9.4	8.8	9.3

likelihood that the recall of an inconsistent behavior was followed by the recall of a neutral one was fairly high in both experiments, contrary to expectations. We discuss this discrepancy from predictions presently.

3. Finally, suppose subjects have recalled a neutral behavior. This behavior is theoretically isolated from all other behaviors in the system. Therefore, subjects must return to the central concept node and reinitiate their search from that location. If this is the case, they should recall a consistent behavior with a high probability, for reasons noted earlier. This is in fact the case. In the 1981 study, the recall of a neutral behavior was followed by the recall of a consistent one 84% of the time. Results of the more recent study were similar (see Table 7.1a).

Thus, with one exception (the relative high probability of recalling a neutral behavior following the recall of an inconsistent one), these results are quite in line with the implications of Postulate 7.7, as well as other postulates bearing on the nature and type of the associations that are formed. It should also be noted that these predictions are extremely subtle and, to the best of our knowledge, no other existing model can make any predictions at all concerning these types of data.

Interbehavior response times. Now consider the implications of Postulates 7.7 and 7.10 for the time interval between the recall of successive behaviors. This interval should increase with the number of associative pathways that must be traversed in order to get from one behavior to the other. The interbehavior response times obtained in Srull's second study are presented in the bottom half of Table 7.1. These data are not completely parallel to the conditional recall probability data shown in the top half of the table. However, this nonparallelism is predicted by the model.

To see this, suppose a consistent behavior has been recalled. Then, the next item recalled should theoretically be an inconsistent behavior and the average time to identify it should be short, as the inconsistent behavior is often directly connected to it. However, consider cases in which the recall of a consistent behavior is followed by the recall of either a consistent or a neutral one. The time required to recall the second behavior should be long, because it can only be reached by returning to the central node and restarting the search. The results show this to be the case.

Alternatively, suppose subjects have recalled an inconsistent behavior. These behaviors are often connected directly to either a consistent behavior or another inconsistent behavior, and so the time required to identify these behaviors should be short. However, the time required to identify a neutral behavior following the recall of an inconsistent behavior should be long, because neutral behaviors are reached only through the central node. Again, this is what the results show.

The most interesting case arises when subjects have previously recalled a neutral behavior. Here, the parallel between conditional recall probabilities and interbehavior response times breaks down. Specifically, if subjects have recalled a neutral behavior, the likelihood that the next behavior they recall is a consistent one should be high, as noted earlier. To recall this behavior, however, subjects must still return to the central concept node. Therefore, the time to recall a consistent behavior following a neutral one should be long, and should not be appreciably different from the time required to identify other types of behaviors following a neutral one. This is again what the results show. That is, the probability of recalling a consistent behavior following a neutral one was very high, but the time required to do so was no different than the time required to recall other types of behaviors.

More generally, it not only takes a relatively long time to retrieve any behavior following the recall of a neutral one, but it also takes a long time to retrieve a neutral behavior itself, regardless of what other type of behavior was recalled just before it. This confirms the assumption that neutral behaviors are isolated from the others in the representation and do not enter into interbehavior associations. The only piece of evidence against this conclusion was noted above. That is, there is a relatively high probability of recalling a neutral behavior following the recall of an inconsistent one. Perhaps the best explanation for this is that some of the "neutral" behaviors are not entirely neutral with respect to their evaluative implications. Alternatively, the encoding of these behaviors may be biased in such a way as to make them appear consistent with the evaluative concept formed of the target person. In either case, such "neutral" behaviors might then be involved in the interbehavior associations that are formed during the encoding of an inconsistent item. Much more sensitive scaling procedures than we have used to date would be needed to pick this up.

4. Bolstering Processes

The results of the studies summarized above support our assumptions about the effects of inconsistency resolution on the formation of interbehavior associations and the influence of these associations on recall. According to Postulate 7.8, however, the evaluative inconsistencies between a person's behavior and the general concept formed of this person should often give rise to bolstering. That is, subjects may identify and think more extensively about behaviors that are consistent with their general concept of the person in an attempt to confirm the validity of this concept. This activity theoretically strengthens the associations that are formed between the consistent behaviors and the concept, and, therefore, increases the ease of recalling these behaviors. The typical recall advantage of inconsistent over consistent behaviors suggests that bolstering usually has less effect on recall than does inconsistency resolution. However, this may be partly because subjects have limited time available to process the information they receive, and so extensive bolstering does not occur. If this is so, giving subjects more opportunity to think about the information should increase the likelihood of bolstering, and this should be evidenced by an increase in the ease of recalling consistent behaviors. Such an increase might eliminate or even reverse the recall advantage of inconsistent behaviors that occurs when the opportunity for bolstering is more limited.

Several recent studies support this possibility. Wyer and Martin (1986, Experiment 1), for example, gave subjects a trait description of a person followed by behaviors that varied in their evaluative consistency with this description. In some conditions (comparable to those employed in previous impression formation research; see Srull, 1981; Wyer & Gordon, 1982), subjects after reading the behaviors performed a 5-minute distractor task before being asked to recall them. These subjects recalled inconsistent behaviors better than consistent ones. In other conditions, however, subjects were asked to think more extensively about the target person during the 5-minute period between information presentation and recall. These subjects recalled more consistent behaviors than inconsistent ones. One interpretation of this reversal is that the latter subjects took advantage of the 5-minute thought period to engage in bolstering, and that as a result, their recall of the consistent behaviors increased to a level that exceeded their recall of the inconsistent ones.

This interpretation is strengthened by the results of a more recent study by Wyer, Budesheim, Lambert and Martin (1989). In this study, the opportunities to engage in post-information bolstering (as in Wyer and Martin's study) and to engage on-line bolstering were varied independently. Specifically, subjects having

TABLE 7.2
Proportion of Consistent and Inconsistent Behaviors Recalled as a Function
of the Opportunity to Engage in On-Line and Post-Information Processing

Opportunity to engage in on-line processing	Opportunity to engage in post-information processing	
	Low (distraction conditions)	High (thought conditions)
Low (8 s)		
Consistent behaviors recalled	.406	.477
Inconsistent behaviors recalled	.458	.375
High (12 s)		
Consistent behaviors recalled	.511	.490
Inconsistent behaviors recalled	.448	.519

been given a trait-based expectation for a person were presented the person's behaviors sequentially for either 8 seconds each (comparable to the presentation time used in other studies; see Srull, 1981; Wyer & Gordon, 1982) or 12 seconds each. Then, both groups of subjects were either given an opportunity to think about the person described for five minutes or were distracted from doing so.

The proportions of expectation-consistent and expectation-inconsistent behaviors that subjects recalled are shown in Table 7.2 as a function of presentation time and the opportunity to engage in post-information processing of the information presented. When subjects had little opportunity to engage in either on-line or post-information processing, inconsistent behaviors were more likely to be recalled than consistent behaviors. However, when more opportunity was provided either while the behaviors were presented or afterwards, the recall of inconsistent behaviors remained the same or decreased whereas the recall of consistent behaviors increased to a level that exceeded the recall of the inconsistent ones. Unexpectedly, when subjects were given increased opportunity to engage in *both* on-line and post-information processing, the recall of inconsistent behaviors increased to a high level as well, and so the recall advantage of the consistent behaviors was once again eliminated. This suggests that subjects in these conditions were given more time than they needed to bolster and so they turned their attention once again to inconsistency resolution. The three-way interaction implied by these data was significant, $F(1,28) = 4.94, p < .05$, and was independent of whether the behaviors involved were descriptively or only evaluatively related to the initial trait descriptions on which the expectancies were based.

These data, therefore, indicate that the recall advantage of inconsistent behaviors is far from universal. Although this conclusion is not surprising, the model we propose localizes the processes that influence the recall of each type of behavior and, therefore, permits a clear a priori conceptualization of the factors that lead one type of behavior to gain a recall advantage over another.

The evidence that giving subjects a chance to think more extensively about the information they receive about a person increases their recall of expectancy-consistent behaviors has potentially important implications for impression formation in situations outside the laboratory. When we learn about a person who is important to us, or when we expect to interact with a person in the future, we may think more extensively about information about a person *after* we receive it. The aforementioned experiments suggest that this post-information processing may often differ from the processing that occurs at the time the information is received. That is, people may spend at least part of their time after the information is received trying to confirm the validity of the initial concept they formed of the person, and may not focus as extensively on behaviors that are inconsistent with this concept. Consequently, they may ultimately remember behaviors that are consistent with their general conception of the person as well as or better than inconsistent ones.

5. Inconsistency Resolution in the Absence of Trait-Based Expectations

In the situations described above, subjects were typically given trait adjective descriptions of the target person before learning about his behaviors, and the concept defining the evaluation-based representation formed of the target was presumably based on the implications of these trait descriptions. When no trait information is provided, however, subjects must form a general concept of the person on the basis of the trait implications of the behaviors themselves. When these behaviors vary in their evaluative implications, this may be hard to do. In fact, a series of studies by Srull et al. (1985, Experiments 5 and 6) suggest that a substantial number of behaviors may need to accumulate before a general concept of the person is extracted.

Subjects in these studies read a series of 50 behaviors with instructions to form an impression of the person they described. The list consisted of 10 blocks of five behaviors each, with each block containing two behaviors with positive implications for a particular trait (e.g., friendly), one behavior implying its bipolar opposite (unfriendly), and two behaviors that were evaluatively neutral. Thus, although the set of behaviors in each block was evaluatively biased, this bias was not great because contradictory information was also presented.

Postulates 7.5 and 7.7 imply that subjects will not attempt to reconcile evaluatively inconsistent information until they have extracted an evaluative concept of the person. Thus, the point at which subjects extract an evaluative concept of the target person can be inferred from the point in the series at which

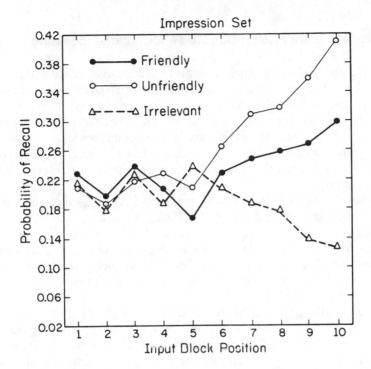

Figure 7.4. Mean proportion of evaluatively consistent, evaluatively inconsistent and evaluatively neutral behaviors recalled as a function of input
block position (based on data from Srull et al., 1985, Experiment 6).

inconsistent behaviors begin to show a recall advantage over consistent ones. These
data are presented in Figure 7.4 for one of the two experiments reported by Srull
et al. (The data from the other experiment are virtually identical.) Note that no
differences in recall occur until Block 5, and the recall advantage of inconsistent
over consistent behaviors is not appreciable until Block 7. Thus, according to the
logic outlined above, subjects did not form an evaluative concept of the person until
they had read at least 25 specific behaviors.

These data support the assumption that subjects will, in fact, spontaneously
extract an evaluative concept of the person even when a clear trait-based characterization is not provided. However, they also suggest that this concept is not
formed immediately unless the initial behaviors all have similar evaluative implications (see also Bargh & Thein, 1985).

Priorities in Impression-Directed Information Processing

The present model postulates a number of cognitive activities that are performed in the course of forming an impression of someone. For example, subjects (a) encode individual behaviors the person has performed in terms of the trait concepts they exemplify, (b) form a general evaluative concept of the person, (c) encode the person's individual behaviors in terms of this concept, (d) attempt to reconcile behaviors that are evaluatively inconsistent with the concept, and (e) review the behaviors that are evaluatively consistent with the person concept to confirm its validity.

Evidence that each of these various cognitive activities may occur has been summarized in the previous sections of this chapter. As we have noted, however, the performance of these activities makes considerable demands on the cognitive system. It is therefore likely that, in many situations, some of these activities will not be performed. Rather, a priority system may govern their performance, with low priority activities giving way to higher priority ones when information processing demands are particularly high.

The priorities that are given to certain activities are logically constrained. For example, one cannot reconcile inconsistencies between a person's behavior and a general evaluative concept of the person unless this concept has already been formed. Other, less obvious priorities are suggested by the results of studies we have described. For example, expectancy-inconsistent behaviors are recalled well when subjects have only a limited opportunity to think about the information they receive, whereas consistent behaviors are not recalled well until additional time is provided to think about them. This suggests that inconsistency resolution often takes priority over bolstering. In addition, Hastie (1980) found that the recall advantage of evaluatively inconsistent over evaluatively consistent behaviors was greater when the behaviors were descriptively related to the trait characterization of the target (on which the general concept of the person was presumably based) than when they were not. Perhaps subjects who engage in evaluative inconsistency resolution give higher priority to behaviors that are descriptively related to their prototype-based conception of a person than to behaviors that are only evaluatively related to this conception. Results reported by Wyer and Martin (1986, Experiment 2) also support this speculation.

These considerations suggest that the various impression-related cognitive objectives we have postulated, in order of decreasing priority,[6] may be as follows:

---

6. The priorities assigned to the first two objectives (trait encoding and evaluative concept formation) assume that initial trait descriptions of the target person are not provided. If these descriptions are given before any behaviors are presented, the evaluative concept may be formed at the outset, before any trait encodings of the behaviors are performed.

1. *Trait encoding* (Postulate 7.1)—the interpretation of the behaviors presented in terms of the trait concepts they exemplify.
2. *Evaluative concept formation* (Postulate 7.3)—the extraction of a general evaluative concept of the person.
3. *Evaluative encoding* (Postulate 7.5)—the interpretation of the person's behaviors in terms of their evaluative relatedness to the central concept.
4. *Inconsistency resolution* (Postulate 7.7)—the reconciliation of behaviors that are evaluatively inconsistent with the person concept;
   a. reconciliation of inconsistent behaviors that are descriptively related to the concept.
   b. reconciliation of inconsistent behaviors that are only evaluatively related to the concept.
5. *Bolstering* (Postulate 7.8)—a review of the behaviors that are evaluatively consistent with the central person concept in an effort to confirm its validity;
   a. bolstering with behaviors that are descriptively related to the central concept.
   b. bolstering with behaviors that are only evaluatively related to the concept.

Note that many of the goal-directed processes involved in this priority system theoretically affect the recall of a particular type of behavior. For example, evaluative encoding (goal 3) presumably leads associations to be formed between behaviors and the evaluative person concept, and these associations are stronger when the behaviors are evaluatively consistent with the concept than when they are not. Therefore, if only the first three cognitive objectives are pursued, evaluatively consistent behaviors should enjoy a recall advantage over evaluatively inconsistent ones. However, suppose inconsistency resolution occurs as well. The processes involved in attaining this objective have their greatest influence on the recall of inconsistent behaviors, and the magnitude of this influence may be sufficient to override the recall advantage of consistent behaviors that results from pursuing the first three processing goals. However, suppose all five goal- directed activities are performed. If bolstering, the lowest priority goal, is performed, it should increase the ease of recalling consistent behaviors, perhaps leading these behaviors to regain their recall advantage over the inconsistent ones.

Note that this priority system would account for several findings we have described. For instance, in Srull's (1981, Experiment 4) study, where subjects were prevented from thinking about the behaviors presented in relation to one another, only the first three processes described above may have been performed. Consequently, as Srull found, the recall of both consistent and inconsistent behaviors was relatively poor, with consistent behaviors having a slight edge over the inconsistent ones. In contrast, giving subjects a moderate opportunity to think about the behaviors in relation to one another should lead the fourth goal (inconsistency resolution) to be pursued. As a result, the recall of inconsistent behaviors should increase substantially in relation to the recall of consistent ones, as Srull's results also indicate. When subjects are given still more opportunity to engage in impression-directed processing, bolstering may occur. Consequently, the ease of recalling consistent behaviors may increase to a level equal to or greater than that of inconsistent ones, as research by Wyer and Martin (1986, Experiment 1) and by Wyer et al. (1989) (see Table 7.2) indicate. (When more time is available than is actually necessary for bolstering, subjects may return to inconsistency resolution, as the data in Table 7.2 also suggest.)

A more direct test of the priorities underlying impression-directed processing is provided in a second study by Wyer et al. (1989). In this study, subjects who had previously been given a trait description of a target person read a series of 36 behaviors of the person that were either (a) descriptively related to and evaluatively consistent with this description (D_C), (b) descriptively related to and evaluatively inconsistent with the description (D_I), (c) descriptively unrelated to the trait description but evaluatively consistent with it (E_C), and (d) descriptively unrelated to the trait description but evaluatively inconsistent with it (E_I). These behaviors were presented for either 4, 8, or 12 seconds each. Wyer et al. reasoned that if a certain type of goal-directed processing took priority over another, the recall of the type of behaviors involved in this processing should increase to asymptote more quickly with an increase in the processing time available than would the recall of behaviors involved in lower priority activities.

Results shown in the top half of Figure 7.5 provide some support for the priority system we have postulated. That is, the recall of behaviors that are descriptively as well as evaluatively inconsistent with trait-based expectations for the target increased to asymptote much more quickly than the recall of the other three types of behaviors. This suggests that reconciling inconsistent, descriptively related behaviors (goal 4a) took priority over either reconciling inconsistent behaviors that were descriptively unrelated to the concept of the person (goal 4b) or bolstering (goal 5).

A contingency in these results is noteworthy. Specifically, the data described above were obtained under conditions in which subjects believed they would receive only a relatively small number of behaviors (specifically, 20). In such conditions, subjects may believe they can easily assimilate all of the information they will receive, and therefore may decide to defer extensive processing of the information until it has all been presented. Therefore, they do not engage in low priority activities unless they have a large amount of time available with little else to do. If this is the case, different results should occur when subjects anticipate receiving more information than they can remember and therefore believe that they must evaluate its implications on line, at the time it is presented. This appears to be true. In other conditions of their study, Wyer et al. told subjects that they would be receiving 90 behaviors rather than only 20. (In fact, they read the same 36 behaviors presented in the first condition described.) Data obtained under this

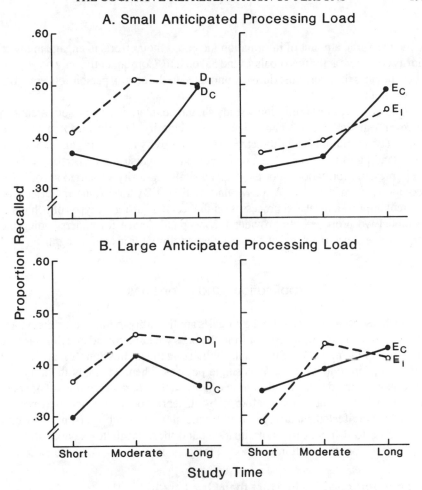

Figure 7.5. Proportion of behaviors recalled as a function of study time (short = 4 s, moderate = 8 s, long = 12 s) under conditions in which (a) subjects anticipated receiving a small number of behaviors and (b) subjects anticipated receiving a large number of behaviors. D_C and D_I denote behaviors that are descriptively related to the trait description of the person and are evaluatively consistent and evaluatively inconsistent with the central person concept, respectively. E_C and E_I denote behaviors that are descriptively unrelated to the trait description and are evaluatively consistent and inconsistent with the person concept, respectively.

condition are shown in the bottom panels of Figure 7.4. The recall of descriptive-ly-related consistent behaviors (D_C) and descriptively-unrelated inconsistent ones (E_I) both increased to asymptote quickly under these conditions, in contrast to the first set of conditions described. This suggests that subjects who anticipated receiving a large amount of information increased their efforts to engage in lower priority cognitive activities (goals 4b and 5a) on line. Consequently, only bolstering with behaviors that were descriptively unrelated to the central person concept (goal 5b) was not performed.

The results of this preliminary study should be interpreted with some caution. However, our findings do suggest the need to identify the priorities that underlie different types of impression-directed cognitive activity in order to gain a complete understanding of the results that are often obtained in research on person memory and impression formation. (For the use of a similar priority system to account for a complex set of data, see Wyer & Martin, 1986.) By specifying the effects of different impression-related processes on the recall of different types of behavior, the model we propose both provides a conceptual device for understanding the nature of these priorities and suggests a methodology for investigating them.

Applications and Extensions

In this section, we consider the model's applicability to impression formation phenomena in situations that differ from the ones we have considered thus far. We first consider the model's utility in conceptualizing the impressions that are formed of groups of individuals as well as single persons. Then, we apply the model to impressions formed under conditions in which general characterizations of a person are acquired after, rather than before, subjects learn about specific behaviors the person has manifested. Finally, we consider situations in which a person's attributes are specific to different roles or situations and these attributes have conflicting implications for an overall impression of the person.

Forming Impressions of More than One Person

Thus far, we have applied the model only to the impression formed of a single individual. A question arises as to whether similar processes are involved when subjects form impressions of more than one individual. Two conditions are of interest in this regard. One occurs when subjects attempt to form an impression of a group from information about its individual members. The second occurs when subjects receive information about several unrelated individuals at the same time, and attempt to form an impression of each person separately.

Forming impressions of groups. Suppose subjects wish to form an impression of a group of persons on the basis of information about its individual members. The processes that underlie these group impressions are theoretically similar to those that are involved in forming impressions of a single person. That is, subjects are likely to encode the behaviors in terms of trait concepts that are activated either by general expectancies or by the behaviors themselves. Moreover, they are likely to extract a general evaluative concept of the group and to interpret individual members' behaviors in terms of features of this concept. Thus, with one qualification, the representations formed of groups should be similar to those we have postulated to exist for individual persons.

The one qualification is important, however. It concerns the extent to which associations are formed among the behaviors that are attributed to different group members. The formation of these associations may depend on the particular type of group to which the information pertains. Some groups, such as fraternities and work groups, are highly cohesive, and their members must get along well with one another in order for the group to function effectively. In such cases, it seems likely that subjects will in fact attempt to reconcile the behavior of an individual member that deviates from the characteristics of the group as a whole (i.e., to understand how a person who behaves in an undesirable way can get along in a group that has generally desirable qualities, or how a person who behaves admirably can function in a group that seems to value socially undesirable characteristics). Under these conditions, interbehavior associations similar to those implied by Postulate 7.7 should be formed.

On the other hand, suppose the group being considered is one whose members typically have similar characteristics, but nonetheless do not necessarily interact and may not even know one another. Most groups about which people have stereotype-based preconceptions (e.g., Catholics, college professors, blacks, etc.) are of this type. In these cases, it is less likely that the behavior of a particular member will be thought about in relation to the behaviors of other members in order to reconcile its occurrence. Rather, the member who performed the behavior may simply be treated as an "exception," and no attempt at reconciliation will be made (cf. Weber & Crocker, 1983).

This analysis has obvious implications. When the group about which impressions are to be formed is a highly cohesive one whose members interact, the representations formed will be very similar to those postulated for single individuals, and these representations should affect recall in a similar way. Data reported by Srull (1981) suggest that this is the case. That is, behaviors attributed to individual members of a highly cohesive group were recalled better if they were inconsistent with the central concept of the group than if they were consistent with this concept.

When the group being described is one whose members do not interact, however, no associations should be formed among the behaviors of its individual members. In this case, the recall of individual behaviors should be primarily a function of the strength of their association with the central concept defining the representation. This means that *consistent* behaviors should be better recalled (Postulate 5.5). This prediction has also been supported, both in Srull's (1981) study and in a more recent study by Wyer et al. (1984).

A more subtle implication of our conceptualization should also be noted. If interbehavior associations are not formed among the behaviors of individual members of a loosely-organized group, these behaviors should be recalled less well *in general* than should either the behaviors of an individual person or the behaviors or members of a highly cohesive group. Results obtained in the two studies cited above confirm this implication of the model as well.

These studies therefore support our speculation that the model can be applied to groups as well as individuals. The results are of more general interest, however, in understanding the effects of group stereotypes on the recall of behaviors of persons who exemplify these stereotypes. Specifically, they imply that when a stereotype pertains to a general category of persons who do not necessarily interact, behaviors of stereotyped individuals will be better remembered if they conform to expectations based on the stereotype than if they deviate from these expectations. On the other hand, if the stereotype pertains to a cohesive group (e.g., a particular college fraternity), behaviors of individual members will be better recalled if they deviate from expectations based on the group stereotype than if they are consistent with expectations.

Forming individual impressions of several people at once. In many situations outside the laboratory (e.g., a cocktail party or a conference attended by people we have not met), we may be called upon to form impressions of several different individuals at the same time. It seems reasonable to suppose that persons in such a situation will form separate representations of each individual of the sort we have postulated, and will store these representations in memory at different locations that are specific to these individuals. The recall of these representations, and the behaviors contained in them, should be governed by processes similar to those we have postulated.

Some data bearing on impression formation under these conditions was obtained by Srull (1983) and by Srull and Brand (1983) in studies we described in Chapter 4. In the latter study, for example, subjects read descriptions of the behaviors of two different individuals with instructions either to form an impression of each person or to try to remember the behaviors they read. The number of behaviors attributed to each of the two persons was varied independently over experimental conditions. Subjects were later asked to recall the information they had read. Although the likelihood of recalling a given person's behaviors under impression set conditions decreased as the number of behaviors presented about this same individual increased, it was unaffected by the number of behaviors presented about the other individual. This means that separate representations were formed of each person (for an elaboration of this reasoning, see Chapter 4). These data do not indicate the precise nature of the representations that were formed. It seems reasonable to assume, however, that they are analogous to the representations that are formed when information about only one person is described.

To this extent, the present model is applicable when subjects form impressions of several persons simultaneously as well as when they form impressions of only one.

Results reported by Ostrom, Pryor, and their colleagues (Ostrom, Pryor, & Simpson, 1981; Pryor, Simpson, Mitchell, Ostrom, & Lydon, 1982) suggest some qualifications on these conclusions. Subjects in their research were given information that varied systematically in terms of both the persons to whom it pertained and the types of attributes it described. Unlike the conditions considered by Srull, however, subjects were implicitly instructed to make comparative judgments of these persons. Clustering analyses of subjects' recall data showed that when the persons described were unfamiliar, subjects appeared to organize the information in terms of attributes rather than in terms of the individual to whom it referred. When the persons described were well-known public figures, however, the opposite was true. These data suggest that subjects whose processing objective is to make comparative judgments of unfamiliar persons may not form general impressions of each individual separately, but rather may perform a feature-by-feature evaluation that leads these features rather than the person who possess them to be the basis for organization. When the persons being judged are familiar, however, and thus a prior representation of them exists, organizational processes similar to those identified by Srull are more likely to occur.

The Effect of Post-Behavior Trait Descriptions on Person Impressions

There are many instances in which we do not receive information about a person's general attributes (e.g., general characterizations by others, information about the person's membership in a stereotyped social group, etc.) until after we have learned specific behaviors the person has performed. For example, we may observe a person do things that we interpret as bright and insightful, and only later hear him described by a colleague as dull and obtuse. A question arises as to what effect these post-behavior characterizations have on the representations we form.

These effects can be theoretically derived from the model we propose. As an example, suppose subjects read a list of behaviors a person has manifested, some of which are honest and others of which are cruel. In the absence of a prior indication of the person's attributes, subjects at the time they receive the information presumably form two trait-behavior clusters, one pertaining to "honest" and the other to "cruel." Because the evaluative implications of these trait concepts differ in favorableness, subjects may also form associations among the behaviors within each cluster (Postulate 7.6). If the positive and negative behaviors are distributed randomly throughout the list, however, subjects will not be able to form an evaluative concept of the person, and so an evaluation-based representation of the person will not be constructed.

Now suppose that after reading the list of the person's behaviors, subjects learn that the person is considered by another to be cruel (or, alternatively, that the

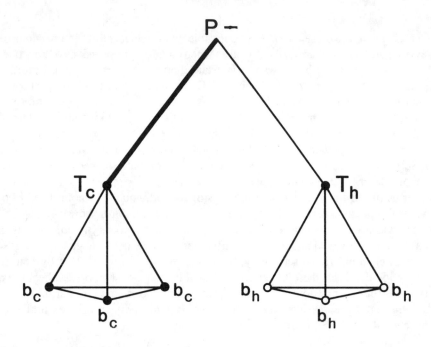

Figure 7.6. Evaluation-based person representation formed on the basis of a series of honest and cruel behaviors under conditions in which subjects are told after the information is presented that the target person is cruel. T_h and T_c denote honest and cruel trait concepts, respectively, P- denotes an unfavorable person concept, and b_h and b_c denote honest and cruel behaviors, respectively.

actor is Adolph Hitler, a person whom subjects believe a priori to have this attribute). Subjects should form an evaluative concept of the person on the basis of this general post-behavior characterization, which is the first clear basis for doing so. They may then think about the information they have received in relation to this concept. However, because the organization of this information into trait-behavior clusters has already been formed, no reorganization should occur (see Chapter 6). Rather, each cluster will become associated with the central person concept as a unit. Because the "cruel" cluster is evaluatively consistent with the central concept, it will be more strongly associated with the concept than will the "honest" cluster. The resulting representation should therefore resemble that shown in Figure 7.6. These assumptions imply that subjects should more easily recall the consistent (cruel) behaviors than the inconsistent ones. Note that this prediction contradicts the prediction made when the general characterization of the target is conveyed *before* the behavioral information is acquired.

The aforementioned study by Wyer, Bodenhausen and Srull (1984) supports this reasoning. Subjects were told to form an impression of someone who was either described by trait adjectives (intelligent or hostile) or identified as a well-known person who possessed the trait (Einstein or Hitler). This general characterization was given to subjects either before or after they read a series of behaviors that varied in both their evaluative and their descriptive consistency with the characterization. When the general description of the target was provided before the behavioral information was presented, subjects subsequently showed better recall of behaviors that were evaluatively inconsistent with the characterization, replicating earlier findings (Hastie, 1980; Srull, 1981; Wyer & Gordon, 1982). When the general characterization of the person was not conveyed until after the behaviors were presented, however, subjects showed better recall of behaviors that were evaluatively *consistent* with the general characteristics of the target. These results provide direct support for the conceptualization we have proposed.

Effects of Multiple Expectancies for a Person: General versus Situation-Specific Person Impressions

We often acquire different, and sometimes conflicting, information about what a person is like. This raises the issue of how we respond to such discrepant characterizations, and how we organize behaviors of a person in terms of them.

Data bearing on this question have been obtained in two different studies. In one (Wyer & Martin, 1986), subjects were given a set of adjectives describing a man's general attributes that were either favorable (e.g., kind or intelligent) or unfavorable (hostile or stupid). In addition, they were told that the man belonged to a group whose members had typically favorable attributes (Nobel Prize winners) or unfavorable ones (Nazis). Subjects then read a series of behaviors of the person, some of which referred to the person by name and others of which referred to him by the group to which be belonged. These behaviors varied in both their descriptive and their evaluative consistency with the attributes characterizing their referent.

The manner in which the behaviors were organized can be diagnosed most easily when the evaluative implications of the trait adjectives conflict with those of the target's ostensible group membership. Three possibilities were considered in evaluating the sort of representations that subjects form under these conditions.

1. Subjects may form a single concept of the person based upon the characterization of him "in general" (that is, on the basis of the trait adjective descriptions alone). If this is the case, behaviors should be recalled better if they are evaluatively inconsistent with these trait adjectives than when they are consistent with the adjectives. Moreover, this should be true regardless of whether the behaviors refer to the person by name or by his group membership.

2. Subjects may attempt to form an evaluative concept of the person that incorporates the implications of both the trait adjective descriptions and his group membership. In the conditions being considered, however, a clear evaluative person concept is difficult to extract (Burnstein & Schul, 1983). Consequently, no behaviors will be organized in terms of such a concept, and so the ease of recalling behaviors should not depend on their evaluative consistency with either the person's trait description or his group membership.

3. Subjects may form two separate evaluative concepts. One may refer to the person "in general" based on the trait adjectives describing him. The other may be a situation-specific concept of the man in his role as a group member. Subjects may then organize behaviors in terms of these two concepts, depending on whether the behaviors refer to the person by name or by group. If this is the case, behaviors that refer to the person by name should be better recalled if they are inconsistent with the evaluative implications of the trait adjectives describing him, whereas behaviors that refer to the person as a group member should be recalled better if they are inconsistent with the evaluative implications of the group stereotype (and, therefore, are consistent with the more general trait adjective description of the person).

In fact, Wyer and Martin's (1986, Experiment 2) results tend to support the third possibility. Behaviors that were both descriptively and evaluatively inconsistent with the characterization of their particular referent were recalled better than behaviors that were consistent with the characterization. (Thus, for example, if the target was described as kind but a member of the Nazi party, subjects recalled unkind behaviors better than kind behaviors if they referred to the person by name, but recalled kind behaviors better then unkind ones if they referred to the person as a Nazi.)[7]

Wyer and Martin's study suggests that subjects form situation-specific representations of a person that are distinct from their more general characterization of him. Further evidence for this was obtained in a study by Trafimow and Srull

---

7. When the behaviors were descriptively unrelated to the trait characterization of the person or his group membership, the opposite effects occurred. That is, behaviors that were evaluatively consistent with the characterization of the referent were better recalled. This contingency can be interpreted in terms of the priority system we described earlier. That is, the attempt to form two separate person concepts increases the cognitive resources that are devoted to evaluative concept formation (goal 2) and this may interfere with processing devoted to lower priority objectives. If goal 4a (the reconciliation of evaluatively inconsistent, descriptively related behaviors) is performed but not goal 4b (the reconciliation of evaluatively inconsistent, descriptively unrelated behaviors), Wyer and Martin's results can be explained. (For a more formal explication of this possibility, see Wyer & Martin, 1986.)

(1986). For example, when a target was simply described as "friendly," subjects recalled more unfriendly than friendly behaviors, and this was true regardless of whether they were performed at home or at work. In other cases, however, a situation-specific expectancy such as "friendly at home" was created. In this case, subjects recalled a greater number of unfriendly behaviors if they were performed at home, but an equal number of friendly and unfriendly behaviors if they were performed at work. Exactly the opposite was found when the target was expected to be "friendly at work."

The data obtained by both Wyer and Martin (1986) and Trafimow and Srull (1986) help to refine the general model. It appears that when the behaviors of a person in one situation (or role) tend to differ evaluatively from those performed in another situation (or role), people may not attempt to reconcile the differences, and may not even see them as inconsistent. Rather, they form multiple, situation-specific concepts of the person that guide their expectancies for what the person is like. (A conceptually similar process appears to occur in the domain of group stereotypes; see Weber & Crocker, 1983).

Concluding Remarks

The model of person impression formation outlined in this chapter specifies the nature of the cognitive representations that are formed from trait and behavioral information about the person and how these representations are later used to recall the information contained in them. As we have attempted to show, the model is consistent with a large body of empirical research, and is sufficiently flexible to address a wide range of issues. At the same time, it is sufficiently rigorous to generate detailed, subtle, and nonobvious predictions.

In this regard, the types of representations we have described in this chapter theoretically provide the basis for judgments of the persons to whom they refer. However, the way they are used to make these judgments differs from the way they are used to recall the information contained in them. Moreover, it often depends on the type of judgment to be made. This will become clear in Chapter 10, where we discuss in detail the principles we postulate to govern the use of person representations to make judgments and point out their implications for a variety of different inference phenomena.

Several different component activities underlie the formation of a person impression. One of the more important features of our conceptualization is its implications for the priorities that govern impression-directed information processing. If these priorities can be established, they would provide the basis for developing a rigorous statement of an impression-formation goal schema of the sort we have postulated to govern goal-directed cognitive activity. To this extent, the conceptualization exemplifies the manner in which a specific theoretical formulation of cognitive functioning can potentially be incorporated into the more general formulation we propose, thereby both (a) increasing the precision of the more general model, and (b) providing a conceptual framework for understanding when the processes implied by the more specific formulation are likely to be invoked, and the manner in which these processes interface with those that occur at other stages of processing.

We should nevertheless reiterate a note of caution that we expressed at the beginning of this chapter. The conceptualization we have outlined focuses on conditions in which a given type of information (trait and behavior descriptions) is presented in a particular way (in a randomly ordered sequence) and is considered for a specific purpose (to form an impression of the person it describes). A change along any one of these dimensions may radically alter the representation that is formed. Even the same type of information we considered in this chapter may be processed quite differently when it is communicated in a different format. For example, we are beginning to investigate the manner in which impressions are formed on the basis of information conveyed in informal conversations (Holtgraves, Srull, & Socall, 1989; Wyer, Budesheim, & Lambert, 1989). Wyer et al. found that people who listen to conversations that two persons have about a third tend to organize the behaviors described around concepts they form of the *speakers*, and these concepts are later used as standards of comparison in evaluating the person being discussed. Although the processes that underlie the representations that are formed under these conditions can be conceptualized and evaluated in terms of the model we propose in this chapter, the specific nature of these representations differs in important ways from the ones we have described.

In the area of political judgment, where people are asked to evaluate one or more political candidates on the basis of their party membership, stands on specific issues, and image-related characteristics (e.g., physical attractiveness), still other considerations come into play (Riggle, Ottati, Wyer, Kuklinski, & Schwarz, 1989; Wyer & Ottati, in press). Even more dramatic differences in the mental representations that are formed from information become apparent in the next chapter, where we consider sequences of events that people observe or read about, and that occur in a single situation or series of causally and temporally related ones.

Chapter 8
Encoding and Organization:
III. The Cognitive Representation of Social Events

By far the most common type of information we receive in the course of our daily lives is extracted from temporally related sequences of social events. The novels we read, the movies we watch, our personal experiences, and others' descriptions of their own experiences all include such sequences. Indeed, our mental life can be viewed as a continuous stream of temporally related episodes that we experience either as a participant or an observer.

Yet, our life experiences are obviously not remembered as a single, unending series of actions. Rather, we appear to categorize our memories of events in terms of the types of situations in which they occur (at school, at work, in social relations, etc.) or the individuals who are involved in them, and our memory for experiences in one life domain does not usually affect our memory for experiences in other domains. We may not even retain an accurate temporal record of the events that occur within a given domain or, for that matter, within a given situation. Thus, for example, we may be able to remember the people we met at a cocktail party but have extreme difficulty reconstructing the order in which we talked to them.

In this chapter, we provide a preliminary conceptualization of how sequences of social events are represented in memory, and how these representations are used as a basis for judgments. To do so, we first need to review in more detail the nature of the concepts and representations that compose our semantic and general world knowledge and that are used to interpret and organize the situation-specific events we encounter. Then, we describe the processes that theoretically underlie the representation of specific events, including (a) verbally described series of events of the sort we read about or hear described by others, (b) sequences of ongoing behavior that we happen to observe, and (c) personal experiences.

The Representation of Events in General Semantic Knowledge

Our general knowledge about actions and events is contained in three types of mental representations. Two of these are theoretically stored in the semantic bin. First, individual action concepts exist for use in interpreting "static" verbal or visual descriptions of a specific action (e.g., the statement "John hit the ball," or a photograph of John in the course of performing this activity). Second, more general semantic concepts referring to temporal or causal relations among actions may also be stored in the semantic bin in the form of "propositional molecules," (e.g., "A smokes; A gets lung cancer;" or "A harms B; B gets angry; B harms A").

The third type of representation consists of a prototypic *sequence* of temporally related events. This type of representation is usually stored in a referent bin. Thus, our knowledge of what usually happens at a restaurant may be stored in a general "restaurant visit" bin. Bins of this sort may contain information about not only the general types of events that take place (entering, ordering the meal, eating, etc.) but also the actions that are involved in them (looking at the menu, deciding whether to get an appetizer, telling the waiter, etc.). Still more specific behaviors that make up these actions may also be represented. In addition to descriptive knowledge about actions and events defined at different levels of specificity, the bin contains information about the order in which these actions and events are likely to occur. A conceptualization of the manner in which this general knowledge is represented in memory must therefore take into account both the descriptive and the temporal features of the events that this knowledge comprises.

Theory and research on the mental representation of prototypic event sequences have been stimulated in large part by script-processing formulations (e.g., Abelson, 1976, 1981; Bower, Black, & Turner, 1979; Graesser, 1981; Schank & Abelson, 1977). This class of theories typically assumes that the mental representations of prototypic event sequences are retrieved as conceptual units for use in interpreting specific occurrences, inferring their antecedents and likely consequences (Graesser & Clark, 1985; Read, 1987), and making behavioral decisions (cf. Langer & Abelson, 1972). We also borrow heavily from this class of formulations. However, to avoid confusion between the specific properties of scripts, plans, and goals as Schank and Abelson conceive of them and the properties of event representations that we postulate, we refer to these prototypic event sequences as simply event *schemata*.

We conceptualize an event schema as consisting in part of a series of "frames," each of which refers to an action concept that is contained in the semantic bin. As noted in Chapter 4, the features of such a concept include a set of *variables* (i.e., semantic concepts of person or objects) that are in specifiable spatial or functional relation to one another. For example, "orders the meal" is an action concept whose features include the spatially and functionally related variables "customer," "waiter," "menu," etc.[1] A clear conceptualization of the organization of the features that compose a particular action concept is obviously important (for one viable attempt to attain this objective, see Rumelhart & Ortony, 1977; Rumelhart, 1984). In this section, however, we skirt this issue. Here, we focus primarily on the manner in which action concepts are organized *in relation to one another* within the schema that contains them.

The organization of these concepts may be analogous in some sense to the organization of frames in a "comic strip," where each frame denotes a different action in a single, temporally ordered sequence (cf. Abelson, 1976). However, this analogy is not entirely satisfactory. As noted above, our concepts of the events that occur in a situation vary in specificity as well as in temporal relatedness. Certainly, if we are asked, we are able to describe a very detailed sequence of actions that are likely to occur in a restaurant (e.g., cutting the meat, sticking a piece with one's fork, lifting it to one's mouth, chewing, etc.). Yet, we typically do not plod through such a detailed sequence of actions whenever we think about what goes on in this situation. Rather, we appear able to think about the sequence of events that occurs at a given level of generality without progressing through a comic strip-like sequence of the individual, more specific actions that each event comprises. More generally, we can conceptualize prototypic events at any one of several different levels of abstractness, and can cognitively operate on them at this level without considering actions at either higher or lower levels. An adequate theoretical formulation of prototypic event schemata must permit this flexibility.

Wyer and Gordon (1984; see also Abelson, 1983) propose a hierarchical representation of action concepts at different levels of specificity, where concepts pertaining to actions at each level are nested within actions at a more general level. A simplified "restaurant" schema might therefore be conveyed in terms of an associative network metaphor as shown in Figure 8.1. Here, various concepts in the network are connected by pathways denoting the associations that have been formed by thinking about them in relation to one another at some point in one's life. One may progress through this representation either horizontally (temporally) or vertically (from one level of generality to another), depending on the purpose for which the representation is to be used.

An additional consideration, however, is raised by research on temporal order judgments of the actions that are presumably contained in such a representation.

---

1. The interpretation of imaginary events can be conceptualized within this framework as a process of inputing attributes necessary for the instantiation of a schema variable to entities that do not actually possess them. For example, "the Empire State Building told the Statue of Liberty what it wanted to eat" would be literally nonsensical, but could be interpreted as an imaginary event by assigning features to the two structures that would permit them to be interpreted as instances of "customer" and "waiter." This activity would presumably be performed by the Encoder/Organizer in pursuit of specific processing objectives that require it.

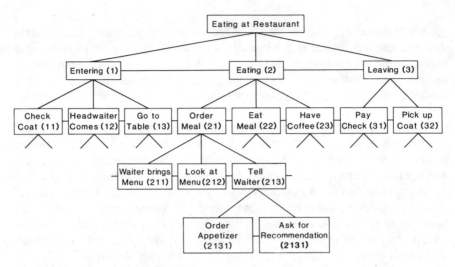

Figure 8.1. Hierarchical representation of a prototypic restaurant schema. Numbers in parentheses refer to temporal codes assigned to action concepts at each level of specificity in the hierarchy.

Suppose someone is given two actions at a particular level of the hierarchy, and is asked which one comes sooner. Will this judgment be made more quickly if the two actions being compared are close together (e.g., "entering the restaurant" and "ordering the meal") or if they are far apart ("entering the restaurant" and "paying the bill")? To make these judgments on the basis of the sort of representation we have proposed, a person would first need to identify the two actions to be compared in the hierarchy and then progress linearly along the pathways emanating from them until an intersection is reached, at which point their relative temporal location could be computed. This means that it would typically take more time to determine the order of two actions if they are far apart than if they are close together. Empirically, quite the opposite is the case. Temporal order judgments are *faster* when the actions compared are far apart (Galambos & Rips, 1982; Nottenburg & Shoben, 1980). This *"symbolic temporal distance* effect" is analogous to the effect that occurs when other types of objects are judged (e.g., when animals are compared in terms of size; see Banks, 1977).

To account for this result and still preserve the sort of hierarchical representation we have proposed, Wyer and Gordon (1984) assumed that the individual actions contained in such a hierarchy have temporally coded features that permit them to be directly compared, and that these features are more distinctive when the actions are temporally distant from one another. Specifically, each action concept at the highest level of the hierarchy is assigned a temporal code that distinguishes it from other concepts at the same level. Action concepts at more specific levels carry with them the temporal code assigned to the more general one(s) in which they are contained, but are assigned additional codes that distinguish them within this level, and so on. This sort of temporal coding scheme is shown in Figure 8.1, where the codes assigned to the components of a "restaurant" schema are indicated parenthetically beside the concepts to which they refer. Note that although the order of the actions defined at general levels are fixed, the order of the specific actions that compose them may sometimes be variable. In the restaurant schema, for example, ordering the meal almost invariably comes before eating it. However, certain actions involved in "ordering," such as "ordering an appetizer" and "asking for recommendations," may not always occur in the same sequence. These events are assigned the same temporal code at this level of abstractness. Consequently, their order cannot be determined.

Assume that when subjects are asked to decide the order of two actions, they identify the two concepts to which the actions refer and compare the first temporal codes in the series assigned to each. If these codes differ, subjects can make a decision immediately. If the codes are the same, subjects consider the second code in each set, and so on. The first (more general) codes assigned to two concepts are more likely to be the same if the concepts are close together in the sequence than if they are far apart. Therefore, more comparisons (and therefore more time) are typically required to distinguish them in the former case, as the results obtained by Nottenburg and Shoben (1980) and by Galambos and Rips (1982) both indicate.

This does not mean, however, that subjects will *spontaneously* think of actions more quickly if they are temporally distant than if they are close together. The opposite is the case. Suppose subjects are given an action (e.g., "eating the meal") as a stimulus and are asked to report the next action that comes to mind. They presumably identify the concept corresponding to this action in the hierarchy and then progress along a pathway emanating from it to another action concept. Therefore, the next action they report at the same level of specificity as the stimulus action should usually be one that is temporally adjacent to it. Evidence that this is true has been reported by Barsalou and Sewell (1985), who find that subjects tend to generate the actions in prototypic event sequences in temporal order rather than in order of typicality, importance, etc.

Correspondingly, when subjects spontaneously report an action at a different level of specificity than the stimulus action, this action should theoretically be one at an immediately adjacent level of specificity. Thus, subjects who are given the stimulus "orders the meal" should be more inclined to think of "reads the menu" than to think of "looks at the appetizers," which is at a more specific level than menu-reading.

Given the assumption of these temporally coded features, therefore, the hierarchical representation of the sort shown in Figure 8.1 is able to account for many of the general phenomena that intuitively and empirically result from the use of prototypic event sequences to make judgments. With these considerations in mind, we now turn to the way in which situation- specific sequences of events are represented.

The Representation of Specific Event Sequences: General Considerations

The representations we form of prototypic event sequences obviously play a role in the encoding and organization of new information we receive about specific sequences of actions and events. For this reason, the mental representations of prototypic and situation-specific sequences have many things in common. However, many differences arise as well. To mention two:

1. The representation of a prototypic event sequence comprises a circumscribed set of action concepts, each of which has clearly defined boundaries. In contrast, an everyday life experience often consists of an unending stream of events that are not so clearly demarcated. Moreover, an experience may consist of two or more conceptually unrelated series of events that are temporally overlapping. Thus, for example, a couple may initiate a conversation while eating at a restaurant and may finish it after returning home. The way in which these events are mentally combined to form a single, situation-specific event sequence is hard to conceptualize in terms of a hierarchical structure of the sort shown in Figure 8.1.

2. Subsets of actions that occur in the situations we observe or read about, and the order in which these actions occur, may exemplify prototypic event schemata or, in some cases, implicational molecules. The ordinal position of these subsets in relation to one another, however, often cannot be predicted on the basis of prior knowledge. For example, suppose we learn that John ate dinner at a restaurant and that upon returning to his car, he found he had a flat tire and had to change it. The two general events (eating at a restaurant and changing a tire) can each be understood in terms of a different prototypic event schema. However, the order in which the two events occurred is unpredictable.

The representation of event sequences of the sort one reads about (like the representation of person information of the sort we discussed in the previous chapter) may depend to a considerable extent on one's processing objectives at the time the information is received (Cohen & Ebbesen, 1979; Wyer & Bodenhausen, 1985). For the present, we focus on conditions in which one's processing objective is simply to comprehend the information. The representation of an event sequence that is formed under these conditions may often be preliminary to other, higher order representations that are constructed in the course of pursuing more specific goals (e.g., forming an impression of one of the individuals involved, making a particular judgment or decision, etc.) (For similar dual-processing models of the representations formed from event information, see Allen & Ebbesen, 1981; Cohen & Ebbesen, 1979.) The content of the event representation that is formed may vary with the nature of these more specific goals (cf. Cohen & Ebbesen, 1979; Massad, Hubbard, & Newtson, 1979; Wyer, Srull, Gordon, & Hartwick, 1982). However, the *structure* of this representation may be similar.

As we have noted, the features of an event sequence are of two types. *Descriptive* features refer to the individual actions portrayed, the people involved in them, and their situational context. *Temporal* features convey the order in which the actions occurred. Either or both types of features may be redundant with prior knowledge. For example, suppose John sat down, looked at a menu, ordered a meal, and ate it. Both the descriptive and the temporal features of the information are redundant with our general knowledge about what goes on in restaurants. However, suppose Susan went to the circus and saw a clown act, followed by a lion act, and then a trapeze act. In this case, the descriptive content of the information is redundant with general knowledge of what goes on at the circus, but the temporal order of the events is not. Or, suppose John was bringing a drink to Susan at a cocktail party when someone bumped his arm, and he spilled the drink on Susan's new dress. The descriptive content of this information is unpredictable. However, its temporal features are redundant with prior semantic knowledge about the causal relations between the types of described events. (That is, we know that getting bumped causes spilling, and therefore that *if* the events occur, they are likely to occur in the indicated order rather than the reverse.) In still other instances, of course, neither the descriptive content of events nor their temporal order can be predicted. A conceptualization of the representations formed of situation-specific event sequences must take into account both temporal and descriptive information.

Our conceptualization of how people with a comprehension objective represent social event sequences consists of four postulates.

Postulate 8.1. A person who learns about a specific sequence of actions or events with the objective of comprehending them divides the sequence into one or more units, each corresponding to a different action or event concept.

Thus, suppose a person reads that Willa gets out of bed, gets dressed and has breakfast, takes a plane to San Francisco, has three martinis on the plane and feels dizzy. The person may divide the event sequence into two units defined by the concepts "getting up in the morning" and "getting drunk on the plane."

It is of course obvious that any given action sequence may be potentially divided into different numbers of units, depending on the level of generality of the concept used to encode it. In the above example, each individual action could in principle be considered a separate unit. Alternatively, the entire sequence could be interpreted in terms of a single concept, "going to San Francisco." These considerations lead to a postulate that is actually a more specific version of Postulate 8.1.

Postulate 8.2. The number of subjective units into which a sequence is divided (a) increases with the level of detail at which one believes the sequence may later need to be reconstructed, and (b) decreases with the redundancy of the sequence with general world knowledge.

Thus, people will typically divide a sequence into more conceptual units if they believe they must remember it in detail than if they believe they only need to retain a general idea of what occurred. On the other hand, subjects are unlikely to treat individual actions as separate units if they can infer their occurrence on the basis of a more general concept to which they all pertain. In our example, therefore, the behaviors "gets out of bed," "gets dressed," and "has breakfast" are unlikely to be encoded as individual action units because both the actions and their order of occurrence can typically be inferred from the more general concept "gets up in the morning."

Situational and contextual factors also come into play. For example, information about a given action sequence will normally be divided into more units if it is presented in isolation than if it is presented along with information about other actions and events that occur over a long period of time. Thus, the sequence of actions described in our example is less likely to be encoded in terms of a single concept (e.g., "going to San Francisco") if this is the only information presented about Willa than if the sequence is described in the context of a story about Willa's experiences over the course of several months.

The implications of Postulate 8.2 become important when considered in combination with the next two postulates.

Postulate 8.3. Each action unit is assigned both (a) a descriptive code that identifies the concept used to interpret it and (b) a temporal code that denotes its time of occurrence in relation to that of other units.

Thus, in our example, the descriptive codes would presumably denote the concepts used to define the units ("gets up in the morning," "gets drunk on the plane," etc.). The temporal codes may be verbal or nonverbal time- related features ("early," "late," etc.) that denote the order in which the units occurred. (If more explicit temporal features are specified in the information, such as "morning," "afternoon," etc., these features may be used instead.)

Postulate 8.4. The actions contained in a unit become associated with the concept that is used to define the unit, but are *not* themselves assigned individual temporal codes.

This postulate recognizes that people are unlikely to perform spontaneously a detailed temporal coding of all the actions they observe or read about. In many cases, however, the order of such actions can be computed by consulting general knowledge about the causal or temporal relations between them. Thus, "gets out of bed" and "gets dressed," or alternatively, "has three martinis" and "feels dizzy," may not be assigned temporal codes. The order of the actions can nevertheless be computed if necessary on the basis of general knowledge that it is difficult to get dressed without first getting out of bed, or on the basis of a propositional molecule about the effects of drinking too much (e.g., "drinks too much alcohol; feels tipsy").

In some instances, of courses, the order of the actions contained in a unit *cannot* be determined on the basis of prior knowledge. In these instances, errors in reconstructing the action sequence are likely to occur. Postulates 8.1-8.4 permit the conditions in which these errors occur to be conceptualized. (Specifically, the particular actions contained in an event sequence are assigned temporal codes if they are interpreted as separate action units, but not if they are interpreted as parts of a more general unit.) Therefore, when the temporal order of the actions one observes cannot be inferred on the basis of general knowledge, one's ability to reconstruct their order later should depend on the size of the action units that were used to encode the actions at the time they were first learned.

A more general implication of Postulates 8.1-8.4 is that when people learn about a specific sequence of events, they are very unlikely to construct a detailed, temporally coded representation of it of the sort we postulate to exist in the case of prototypic event sequences. In fact, the representation they form may often be even simpler than the one we have used in our example. In constructing this example, we assumed that the recipient of the information about Willa had the goal of understanding the sequence of events as a whole. More generally, however, people learn about events in many different situations and at many different times, and these events are neither causally nor thematically related. Therefore, although people may interpret the subsets of actions composing such events in terms of previously formed action concepts, they may not always assign temporal codes to their representations of these events that permit the events to be temporally distinguished. Rather, they may store the representations as separate units of knowledge (cf. Wyer & Bodenhausen, 1985). We elaborate on this possibility in more detail presently.

We are finally in a position to consider the representation of different types of situation-specific event sequences in more detail. In our discussion, we focus on three types: (a) the representation of verbally described events that instantiate a prototypic event schema, (b) the representation of verbally described nonprototypic sequences, and (c) the representation of observed behavioral sequences. In addition, we consider the representations formed of personal experiences and how they may differ from the representations of other people's experiences that one reads about. Once we have discussed the nature of these representations, we consider more generally how event representations are used in interpreting information, in predicting and explaining events, and in making judgments and behavioral decisions.

Representations of Verbally Described Prototypic Events

Last Sunday, I went to Yeng Ching, a Chinese restaurant. I (a) saw a place in the corner and went to the table, (b) looked at the menu and pondered the house specialties, (c) used chopsticks to eat my meal, and (d) took out my Visa card and paid the bill. This mundane summary of my experience contains descriptions of two types of actions. Some, *generic* actions (i.e., going to a table, eating the meal and paying the bill) exemplify concepts in a prototypic event schema of visiting a restaurant. These actions could be predicted to occur on the basis of knowledge that I visited the restaurant alone, without any additional information at all. Other, *particularized* actions (finding a place in the corner, pondering the house specialties, taking out a Visa card) could not be predicted, but are nevertheless strongly associated with the generic ones and are immediately understood as components of these latter actions. The question arises as to which aspects of this information are likely to be retained in memory, and what processes underlie their retention. There are at least three hypotheses concerning this matter.

Complete representation hypothesis. The first hypothesis, which may seem unlikely in light of the considerations raised earlier, is that subjects (a) retrieve their prototypic "restaurant" schema, (b) instantiate its variables in terms of values specified in the set of information presented, (c) add frames describing actions that cannot be predicted a priori, and then store this entire representation in memory. Thus, assume for simplicity that the prototypic restaurant sequence used to interpret the information described above has the general form shown in Figure 8.2a. Then, the representation formed from this information would resemble that shown in Figure 8.2b, where A, C, and F (enclosed in solid lines) denote the concepts associated with the generic actions described in the presented information, a_1, c_1, and f_1 denote the particularized actions that are specified in the information and are associated with the generic ones, and B, D, and E (enclosed in dashed lines) are unmentioned generic actions that are contained in the prototypic event schema used to interpret the information.

Pointer hypothesis. A second possibility is suggested by the "schema pointer + tag" formulation proposed by Graesser, Gordon, and Sawyer (1979). Specifically, when subjects encounter a series of actions that are redundant with the ones

a. Prototypic Schema (General World Knowledge)

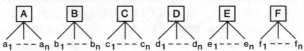

b. Complete Representation Hypothesis

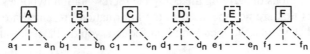

c. Pointer Hypothesis

d. Partial Copy Hypothesis

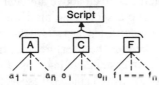

Figure 8.2. Representations of action sequences. The first panel (a) shows a prototypic schema composed of generic actions A-F along with particularized action features associated with them. Other panels show representations formed of situation-specific generic actions A, C, and F and their particularized associates a_1, c_1, and f_1, based on (a) the complete- representation hypothesis, (b) the pointer hypothesis and (c) the partial- copy hypothesis. In each case, concepts associated with the information presented are denoted by solid lines, and added or inferred features and concepts are denoted by dotted lines.

contained in a prototypic event schema, they store only a "pointer" to this schema along with instantiations of the schema variables in terms of values specified in the information. In terms of the conceptualization we propose, this "pointer" would be equivalent to a general concept (e.g., "visiting a restaurant") that is used to encode the event sequence as a whole. The generic actions specified in the information are not retained in the representation that is formed, and the particularized, nonredundant actions are appended as tags. Therefore, the stored representation of the action sequence would simply consist of the elements described in Figure 8.2c.

   Partial copy hypothesis. A third possibility is suggested by a more recent conceptualization proposed by Graesser and Nakamura (1982) known as the "script *copy* + tag" model. This model is most consistent with the conceptualization embodied in Postulates 8.1-8.4. That is, when the actions described in new information about a specific situation exemplify some of the concepts contained in a prototypic event sequence, copies of these concepts are extracted from the schema. The features of these concepts are then instantiated in terms of values specified in the information presented, and these instantiated concepts are then copied into the situation-specific representation being formed. However, in contrast to assumptions underlying the complete representation hypothesis, concepts about actions that are not specified in the information presented are not carried along. In other words, the representation formed would resemble that shown in Figure 8.2d.

Empirical Evidence

The three alternative hypotheses outlined above are somewhat difficult to distinguish, as several of their implications are similar. For example, suppose subjects who have read the information described above are later asked to recall this information. If this request is made a short time after the information is received, schema-irrelevant or schema-inconsistent aspects of the information may still be available in the Work Space. Moreover, these features may often be thought about more extensively in an attempt to interpret them in terms of the schema that is being applied. Therefore, for reasons noted in Chapter 3, these features may enjoy an initial recall advantage over schema-consistent features. If the schema-inconsistent features cannot be effectively integrated into the schema, however, they may not be included in the representation that is transmitted to Permanent Storage. This means that once the Work Space is cleared, schema-*consistent* information may have a recall advantage.

Results reported by Graesser, Woll, Kowalski, & Smith (1980) support this line of reasoning. Subjects read a story containing descriptions of events that were either typical of or atypical of those occurring in the type of situation described. (In other words, they were either predictable or unpredictable from the schema used to interpret the information.) Subjects who were asked to recall the information a short time after it was presented showed better memory for atypical actions than for typical ones. However, recall of the atypical actions decreased much more rapidly over time than did recall of the typical ones, with the result that the latter actions gained a recall advantage after a period of one week.

These results, unfortunately, could be accounted for in terms of all three of the hypotheses we have proposed concerning the content of the representation that was formed from the information presented. That is, the better recall of schema-consistent features after a period of time had elapsed could indicate either that these features were more likely to be retained in the representation (as implied by the complete representation and partial copy hypotheses) or that they were *inferred* from the content of the prototypic schema that was used to encode it (as implied by the pointer hypothesis). This exemplifies a general difficulty in using recall data to distinguish between the models. That is, it is hard to distinguish between the recall of information that is actually contained in the representation stored in memory and reconstructions of the original information, based on knowledge of the schema used to interpret it. The occurrence of intrusion or false recognition errors (e.g., reports of schema-consistent features that were not actually mentioned; see Bower, Black, & Turner, 1979; Graesser, Gordon, & Sawyer, 1979) can similarly be accounted for by all three models.

A different approach to investigating this question, taken by Fuhrman and Wyer (1989), provided indirect support for the partial copy hypothesis (Figure 8.2d). In this study, subjects read about a person named John in three situations that occurred over the course of a day (at work, at dinner, and at the movies). In one of the three situations, John was described as performing *generic* actions that were presumably redundant with those contained in a prototypic event schema pertaining to the situation, and therefore could be inferred to have occurred on the basis of the schema. (Thus, in the restaurant situation, John was described as going to a table, reading the menus, ordering the food, eating and paying the check.)

In a second situation, the protagonist was described as performing *particularized* actions that could not be predicted to occur on the basis of the schema. However, each particularized action was associated with a different generic action that could be predicted. (Thus, John in the restaurant was described as finding a place in the corner, looking for the house specialties, asking for chop suey, using chopsticks, and taking out his Visa card.) However, the generic actions with which the particularized ones were associated were not mentioned.

In the third situation, neither generic nor particularized actions were mentioned. (Thus, John was simply described as going to a Chinese restaurant for dinner.)

Each subject read about one situation that exemplified each of the three information conditions. (The situations in which generic, particularized, or no actions were described were counterbalanced over subjects.) After reading the passage, subjects were shown different pairs of the actions on a computer screen and were asked to judge their temporal order. They were told that some of the actions they would judge were ones they had read, but that others would need to be inferred from the information given. With this preamble, subjects judged both pairs of generic actions and pairs of particularized ones, regardless of whether or not the actions had actually been mentioned in the information. The time required to judge each pair was recorded.

No information conditions. Consider first the conditions in which subjects read no information at all about the actions that occurred. In this condition, their judgments of generic actions are necessarily based on a prototypic event schema pertaining to the situation that they had previously formed as part of their general world knowledge. Their judgments of particularized actions may be determined by identifying their generic counterparts in the prototypic schema and then basing their judgments on the order of these generic actions. To this extent, the patterns of response times to judge both generic and particularized actions should be similar to one another, and also similar to those observed when prototypic action concepts are judged out of the context of any given situation (Galambos & Rips, 1982; Nottenburg & Shoben, 1980). For example, if the generic actions are temporally coded in the manner shown in Figure 8.1, and these codes are used as a basis for judging temporal order, response times should decrease as the symbolic temporal distance between the actions increases. This was indeed the case, as shown in Figure 8.3a. Note that the effect of symbolic temporal distance is virtually identical for both types of actions. This supports the assumption that the particularized actions were based on criteria similar to the generic ones with which they were associated.

Generic-actions-only conditions. Now consider instances in which the generic actions were explicitly stated in the information but the particularized ones were not. The generic actions presumably exemplify some but not all of those that compose the prototypic event schema to which they refer. However, suppose subjects form a situation-specific representation that includes the unmentioned generic actions as well as the ones that were specifically stated, as implied by the complete representation hypothesis. Then, the pattern of response times to pairs of these actions should be very similar to the pattern that emerges under no-information conditions, when judgments were necessarily based on the prototypic event schema. Similar predictions would be made on the basis of the pointer hypothesis, which implies that the explicitly stated generic actions are not retained in the representation that is formed, and that judgments are therefore based directly on the prototypic event schema that the actions exemplify.

In fact, this was not the case. Figure 8.3b shows the time required to compare both generic and particularized actions under these conditions as a function of the symbolic temporal distance between them. The similar effects of symbolic distance on both judgments of the unmentioned particularized actions and judgments of their generic counterparts support our assumption that subjects inferred the order of particularized actions from the order of the generic actions with which they were associated. However, the effect of temporal distance on judgments of *both* types of actions was much less than its effect on judgments of these same actions when no information was presented. This indicates that the representation that underlies these judgments is not the same as the representation that underlies judgments of the same actions under no information conditions. This conclusion disconfirms both the complete information and pointer hypotheses.

In contrast, the partial-copy hypothesis can account for these results. If actions specified in the information presented are copied into the situation-specific representation formed, they are presumably closer together in this representation than they were in the prototypic schema from which they were drawn. They may therefore be less temporally distinctive in this new representation. (Put another

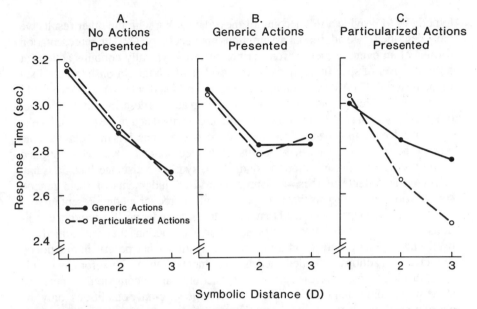

Figure 8.3. Mean time required to judge pairs of generic and particularized actions under different information presentation conditions as a function of the symbolic temporal distance (D) between the actions being judged.

way, they may be assigned less distinguishable temporal codes.) Consequently, the effects of symbolic temporal distance may appear to be less, as the results shown in Figure 8.3b indicate.

Particularized-actions-only conditions. Now consider conditions in which only particularized actions were mentioned in the passage. These actions are theoretically interpreted in terms of features of the generic action concepts with which they are associated. This process leads the relevant subset of generic action concepts to be activated. To the extent that these concepts alone are retrieved rather than the entire prototypic event schema in which they are contained, the pattern of temporal order judgments of these generic actions should resemble the pattern observed when the actions are explicitly stated. This appears to be the case. That is, the effect of symbolic distance on the time to compare the generic actions under particularized-actions-only conditions (Figure 8.3c) is very similar to its effect on judgments of the same actions under generic-action-only conditions (Figure 8.3b).

The problem arises, however, in interpreting data pertaining to judgments of the particularized actions that were actually presented. The effect of symbolic distance on the time to make these judgments is greater than its effect on the time to compare their unmentioned generic counterparts. If the particularized actions that were presented in this condition were interpreted and organized in terms of this subset of generic concepts, why should this be the case? For the partial-copy hypothesis to provide a full account of these data along with the other results we have described, two additional assumptions are necessary: (1) The representation formed of an event sequence from written material typically contains actions at only one level of specificity, namely, the level at which the actions are described in the material. (2) Additional features (e.g., interpolated actions) are more likely to be added to a representation that is formed from actions described at a high level of specificity than from corresponding actions described at a more general level.

In understanding the implications of these assumptions, it is important to note that in the two conditions in which particularized actions were not mentioned (generic-only and no-information conditions), symbolic distance had the same effect on judgments of these actions as it had on judgments of their generic counterparts. This suggests that both (a) the context-free scripted representation of the generic actions that was used to make judgments under no-information conditions and (b) the context-specific representation of the actions that was formed and used under generic-only conditions, contain features that permit unmentioned particularized actions to be identified as components of them. Therefore, once this identification takes place, the particularized actions can be compared in much the same way as the generic actions themselves. In generic-only conditions, only the actions mentioned in the story are contained in the representation that subjects form from it. This is because few if any additional actions need to be added in order to understand it at this general level. Therefore, the symbolic distance between the actions in the representation will be relatively small, as suggested above.

When only the particularized actions are stated, these same generic actions may be extracted from a script in long-term memory and used to interpret them. However, subjects may not include these general actions in the more detailed representation they form from the particularized ones. Rather, they may include *only actions at the same level of specificity as those presented.* In forming a representation at this level, however, subjects may need to add several unmentioned particularized actions, inferred on the basis of general world knowledge, in order to understand what took place at the same level of detail as the actions that were actually described. This may increase the effective symbolic temporal distance between these presented actions in the representation that is formed. As a result, the distance between any two context-specific particularized actions in this representation may be similar to the distance between comparable context-free actions in general world knowledge, and so symbolic distance effects on judgments of these actions may be similar to those obtained under no-information conditions.

Contingencies in the Use of Prototypic Event Schemata

The results in totality seem more consistent with the partial copy hypothesis than with the alternative hypotheses. In evaluating the generalizeability of these results, however, two important considerations must be raised. First, in this study, the actions that exemplify a prototypic event sequence were the primary focus of the stories that subjects read. In most stories one reads outside the laboratory, however, such actions are either not mentioned at all or, if mentioned, are used to provide a background for other events that the writer wishes to convey. For example, a storyteller may use a person's routine activities at a restaurant as an incidental context for describing other, nonprototypic actions that take place concurrently (e.g., the person's thoughts about a murder he is planning, a chance meeting with an old girl friend, etc.). In such conditions, the pointer hypothesis is more likely to apply. That is, readers or listeners may store only a reference to the prototypic context situation and may devote most of their cognitive resources to the more unique, nonprototypic events on which the story is focused. These considerations suggest an interesting hypothesis: *The more nonprototypic information that is contained in a written or oral description of the events that occur in a situation, the less detailed will be the encoding of any prototypic actions that take place.*

A second possible constraint on the use of prototypic event schemata to interpret new information is suggested by Postulate 4.3. According to this postulate, information is not interpreted in terms of any higher level concepts than are necessary to comprehend it. Although this postulate pertains to the activities of the Comprehender, similar considerations seem likely to govern goal-directed comprehension processes as well. That is, information will not be encoded or organized in terms of any more abstract concepts (or schemata) than are necessary to attain the processing objectives that exist at the time the information is received. This assumption was, in fact, implicit in our discussion of remindings and their role in analogical reasoning (Chapter 5).

The relevance of this assumption in the present context arises from the fact that in many instances, prototypic event schemata may exist at different levels of abstractness. The "visiting a restaurant" schema we have typically used in our examples is at a very high level of generality. More restricted prototypic schemata may also exist that pertain to particular types of restaurants (e.g., French, Japanese, fast-food, expensive, etc.). The features of these latter schemata may differ both from the general one and from one another. In these instances, what determines the level of specificity of the event schema that is activated and applied? One determinant is presumably the number and type of probe cues that direct the search for concepts that can be brought to bear on the interpretation of the information. That is, the prototypic schema associated with "Japanese restaurant" may be contained in a bin that is specific to this type of restaurant rather than in a more general "restaurant" bin. Consequently, the addition of "Japanese" to the probe cues may lead a schema to be retrieved from a "Japanese restaurant" bin rather than from the more general "restaurant" bin (Postulate 5.5). Therefore, it may influence the manner in which the information is encoded, what inferences are made about unspecified actions, and what aspects of the presented information are retained.

A related implication of this analysis is that an abstract prototypic event schema may sometimes not be activated at all for use in interpreting event information if this information can be interpreted in terms of more specific action concepts or schemata. Empirical support for this possibility is provided by Bower, Black, and Turner (1979), whose work remains among the most important and provocative of any performed on the role of prototypic event representations in memory and judgment. In the studies bearing most directly on the question at hand (Bower et al., 1979, Experiment 4), subjects read about either one, two, or three sequences of events, each of which exemplified the same prototypic schema. In one case, for example, the general schema referred to "visiting a health professional," and the specific exemplars concerned a particular individual's visit to a dentist, another person's visit to a doctor, and a third's visit to a chiropractor. Presumably, several events (feeling ill, entering the office, registering with the receptionist, etc.) are common to all three situations. Some of these actions were stated in all three situation-specific versions, whereas others were stated in only one or two versions and still others were not stated in any version. Subjects after reading the material were given a recognition memory task containing items that referred to all three types of actions.

If subjects activate a general "health professional visit" schema to use in comprehending the information as it is presented, this should not only facilitate their later recognition of schema-consistent actions that were actually mentioned but also lead them to make false recognition errors. That is, they should report unmentioned but schema-implied actions as actually having been stated. These errors did indeed occur. More important, the likelihood of making them increased with the number of situation-specific instantiations of the prototypic schema that subjects had read. This increase did not simply reflect subjects' confusion about which particular events were mentioned in each story; errors in responding to prototypic actions that were not mentioned in any of the stories also increased with the number of schema-relevant stories that were read.

Thus, the most reasonable interpretation of these data is that subjects who received several instances of the "health professional visit" schema were more likely to retrieve and use this schema to comprehend and organize the information than were subjects who received only one instantiation of it, and the greater number of recognition errors made by the first group of subjects resulted from their more frequent application of the schema. In short, several instances of the schema were required to activate it and to lead the information to be encoded in terms of it.[2]

---

2. This conclusion parallels the conclusion in Chapter 5 concerning the use of analogies (Gick & Holyoak, 1983). There, too, several instantiations of an abstract principle were necessary to lead subjects to encode the information at a level of generality that permitted them to see the principle's applicability to a new problem situation. Both quite different bodies of of research therefore are consistent in their implications that subjects do not spontaneously encode event information at higher levels of generality unless they need to do so to understand the information they receive as a whole.

The Representation of Nonprototypic Event Sequences

Encoding Processes

People's goals when they read about a sequence of events may often be to comprehend and remember it in sufficient detail to describe what went on to others, or to make a judgment on the basis of its general implications. When the sequence of events is prototypic, as in the examples we have considered so far, these goals are easy to attain. That is, the retention of only a few frames or action concepts is sufficient to permit the essential features of the sequence to be constructed.

When an event sequence is nonprototypic, this cannot be done so easily. Even here, however, it seems unlikely that subjects will normally perform a detailed encoding or organization of the sequence. Rather, they may adopt a strategy analogous to that implied by Postulates 8.1-8.4. That is, they may encode different subsets of these actions in terms of more general action concepts that they exemplify (Postulates 8.1). Because the events to which the concepts refer do not, in this case, have any a priori order, the concepts may be assigned a "temporal code" to denote their position in relation to one another (Postulate 8.3). However, the specific actions in the sets that are interpreted in terms of these concepts may not be assigned these temporal codes (Postulates 8.4).

Therefore, to modify our story about Willa,[3] suppose subjects learn that Willa is awakened by a telephone call from her brother. Her brother tells her that her father is dying. Willa quickly makes plane reservations to San Francisco and packs her bags. She is extremely upset on the plane, has three drinks, and feels dizzy by the time the plane lands. When she gets to downtown San Francisco, she finds that she cannot remember the name of the hospital where her father is staying, and cries on the streets of San Francisco.

According to Postulates 8.1-8.4, a person who reads this story will break it into broader action units, each defining a general concept (e.g., "learns that her father is dying," "gets drunk on the plane," "gets lost in San Francisco," etc.), and will assign each unit both a descriptive code that identifies the concept to which it refers and a temporal code that denotes its position. However, the individual actions that occur and become associated with these units may not be assigned such codes. Therefore, the representation that is formed may be conceptualized as similar to that shown in Figure 8.4. This representation is structurally similar to that suggested by the partial copy hypothesis concerning the way in which actions that exemplify prototypic event sequences are formed (see Figure 8.2d).

---

3. This version of the Willa story is similar to one employed by John Anderson (1980).

a. The telephone rings
b. Willa gets out of bed
c. Willa learns her father is dying
d. Willa gets on the plane
e. Willa has three drinks
f. Willa feels dizzy
g. The plane lands in San Francisco
h. Willa can't find the hospital
i. Willa breaks into tears

Figure 8.4. Theoretical representation of situation-specific action sequence formed from actions a-i. Each square in the diagram denotes an action unit formed from the specific actions connected to it by associative pathways.

Judgment Processes

The implications of this conceptualization were explored by Wyer, Shoben, Fuhrman, and Bodenhausen (1985) using comparative judgment methodology. Although the procedures used were similar to those employed in the studies described earlier, the nonprototypic nature of the event sequences permitted a more rigorous conceptualization of judgment processes to be applied. Wyer et al. postulated three components of the judgment process, each of which is relevant to a different stage of processing. Specifically, suppose a subject who has read our story about Willa is given two actions in the sequence and is asked either (a) which action occurred sooner or (b) which occurred later. To answer this question, three cognitive steps may be involved:

1. Identification. The subject identifies the more general action unit in which each action is contained. This is done by comparing its features with descriptive features of the concept that defines the unit. Thus, suppose the subject is asked which of the two actions, "the telephone rings" or "Willa has three drinks," occurred sooner. He would presumably identify these actions as contained in "learning that her father is dying" and "gets tipsy on the plane," respectively. This activity is presumably performed by the Encoder/Organizer.

2. *Comparison.* The subject compares the temporal codes assigned to the action concepts identified in step 1. If the codes differ (i.e., if the actions being compared are in different units), an immediate decision can be made. If the codes are the same (i.e., if the actions are in the same unit) the subject must compute the order on the basis of general world knowledge about their temporal or causal relationship. These comparisons and computations are presumably performed by the Inference Maker.

3. *Response generation.* The subject transforms the subjective judgment that results from step 2 into the response language necessary to answer the specific question asked (which comes "sooner" or which comes "later"). In terms of the proposed model, this is done by the Response Selector.

These cognitive activities are theoretically performed serially. Therefore, the time to generate a response should equal the sum of the times required to perform each of the component processes. Let t_I = the time to identify the concepts containing the actions to be judged, $t_{C,1}$ = *the time to compare the temporal codes assigned to these concepts,* $t_{C,2}$ = the time (if necessary) to compute the order of the actions on the basis of general world knowledge, t_R = the time to generate an overt response, and t_O = some baseline response time that includes comprehension of the question being asked, motor reaction time, etc. Then, the overall time to make a judgment, RT, is given by the equation:

$$RT = t_O + t_I + t_{C,1} + t_{C,2} + t_R \qquad [8.1]$$

An Empirical Test

To test the validity of this conceptualization of representational and judgment processes, Wyer et al. (1985) identified factors that they expected to influence specific stages of the judgment process and determined their effects on overall judgment time. Specifically, subjects read one of two versions of the Willa story. (A second story that provided a conceptual replication of the design was also used.) One version was similar to the one described in Figure 8.4, and could be encoded in terms of concepts that were *thematically related.* In the other version, the actions describing Willa's plane ride were the same, but these actions were preceded and followed by ones that exemplified *thematically unrelated* concepts (specifically, "getting up in the morning" and "going shopping"). Subjects read each story and then were asked to judge the order of all pairs of actions formed from the items composing it. Suppose subjects in the course of reading the stories encode and organize the event sequence in a manner similar to that described. Then, several factors should influence the overall time required to make these judgments through their mediating influence on the time to complete the various processes we have postulated.

Identification time. The time required to identify the units to which specific actions belong should depend on two factors. First, the unit memberships of actions should be easier to identify if the concepts defining these units are thematically unrelated than if they are related. Second, an action's unit membership should be easier to identify if the action is near the center of the sequence that defines a unit than if it is near the unit boundary, or the transition between one concept's range of applicability and another's. Results supported both of these hypotheses. That is, subjects took less time to judge pairs of actions from thematically unrelated sequences than pairs from thematically related ones. Moreover, they took less time to judge actions that were located near the middle of the units to which they belonged than actions that occurred near the boundaries of these units.

Comparison time. If the action units into which the sequence is divided are assigned distinguishable temporal codes, it should take less time to compare actions that are in different units than to compare actions that are in the same unit. This is because in the first case, $t_{C,2} = 0$. Results strongly supported this prediction. The time required to make between-unit comparisons was 216 msec faster than the time required to make within-unit comparisons. Moreover, the effect was statistically independent of the effects we attributed to differences in identification time (i.e., the effects of thematic relatedness or the positions of the actions within each unit).

Note that the difference between between-unit and within-unit comparisons provides an explanation of symbolic distance effects. Specifically, the probability that the actions being compared are in different units, and thus are judged quickly, increases with the distance between these actions. Therefore, averaged over the action pairs representing each level of symbolic temporal distance, response times should decrease as distance increases. In Wyer et al.'s (1985) study, the distribution of actions over the three action units (see Figure 8.4) was such that the proportion of between-unit comparisons reached asymptote at $D = 3$. Correspondingly, response times also decreased to asymptote at this point. Moreover, although overall response times decreased substantially over the first three levels of symbolic distance ($M = 2.908$ s, 2.825 s, and 2.739 s at $D = 1$, 2, and 3, respectively), these differences totally disappeared when only within-unit comparisons were considered ($M = 2.938$ s, 2.910 s, and 2.973 s at $D = 1$, 2, and 3, respectively).

Response generation time. The result of processing at the comparison stage is presumably an internally-coded concept of the order of the two events being considered. Overall response time is also a function of the time required to translate this subjective coding into the language that is necessary to respond overtly to the particular question being asked (t_R). Suppose the temporal codes assigned to the action units in which the sequence is divided are semantic, and that judgments that are based on a comparison of these codes are subjectively expressed in terms of them. Then, it should take less time to generate a response when the codes are semantically congruent with the attribute specified in the question ("which comes sooner?" or "which comes later?") than when it is incongruent and a language transformation is required. (For a similar conceptualization in other judgment domains, see Banks, 1977.) This implies that it should take subjects less time to judge actions at the beginning of the series (i.e., actions coded in terms of "soonness") if they are asked which action comes sooner, but should take less time to judge actions near the end (those encoded in terms of "lateness") if they are asked which comes later.

This semantic congruity effect is in fact evident in studies where the actions contained in prototypic action sequences are judged (Galambos & Rips, 1982; Nottenburg & Shoben, 1980). This is consistent with the assumption that the judgments are based on semantic temporal codes of the sort we have postulated (see Figure 8.1). In the present study, however, a congruity effect should occur only when subjects' judgments are based on the temporal codes that are theoretically assigned to action *units*. That is, it should be evident only when between-unit comparisons are made. The results of within-unit comparisons, which are computed on the basis of general world knowledge, may not be semantically coded. Consequently, within-unit congruity effects may not be observed. Because only three action units were presumably formed from the action sequence presented in Wyer et al.'s study, the existence of between-unit congruity effects could not be effectively evaluated. However, there was no evidence of a congruity effect when within- unit comparisons were made. In fact, there was no evidence of a congruity effect at all, regardless of what type of comparisons were involved. These data do not provide direct evidence that the action units used to encode the event sequence are assigned semantic temporal codes. However, they support the hypothesis that the individual actions that compose these units are *not*.

The evidence of congruity effects when prototypic action sequences are judged but not when situation-specific actions are judged may reflect a fundamental difference between the mental representations of these two types of sequences. This difference is implied by Postulate 8.4. That is, the actions contained in well-learned, prototypic sequences may be organized hierarchically, and may be assigned semantic codes at all levels of specificity in the hierarchy (Figure 8.1). In contrast, although the action units that make up situation-specific sequences of events may also be assigned semantic temporal codes, a more detailed temporal coding of the actions contained in these units is not performed.

The above conclusion may hold when the concepts used to interpret these actions are drawn from a prototypic event schema as well as when the actions are nonprototypic. In a second study reported by Wyer et al. (1985, Experiment 2), subjects read a story about a person's visit to a restaurant. The story described both prototypic events (looking at the menu, eating the meal, etc.) and specific actions that were associated with these events (considering a steak, salting the fries, etc.). Congruity effects occurred when generic actions were later compared but not when their particularized counterparts were judged. This suggests that the generic actions were judged on the basis of semantic temporal codes whereas particularized ones were not. The aforementioned study by Fuhrman and Wyer (1986) provided a further confirmation of this contingency.

Direct Associations Among Thematically-Related Events

The data reported by Wyer et al. (1985) do not necessarily indicate that situation-specific actions are actually represented in memory in a temporally organized sequence. The judgment processes we postulate assume that once the action units containing the actions being judged have been defined and temporally coded, the time required to compare the actions does not depend on how the units themselves are organized. In other words, results similar to those reported by Wyer et al. could occur regardless of whether the action units composing an event sequence are associatively linked in a linear (temporal) string and stored in memory as a single entity, or whether the units, once temporally coded, are stored in a referent bin as separate representations, independently of one another.

In fact, which is the case may depend in part on whether the processing objectives that exist at the time events are learned require that the events be thought about in temporal relation to one another. Some evidence of this contingency was reported by Wyer and Bodenhausen (1985) in a study we described in Chapter 5. Briefly, subjects read a story about the events that occurred at a cocktail party. Each event consisted of four specific actions that (a) were described either in chronological order or in the reverse order, and (b) were described either together or at different points in the story. Some subjects were told to form an overall impression of the cocktail party. Others were told to empathize with the person from whose perspective the story was written. Subjects with both objectives were expected to mentally organize the four actions composing each event in chronological order in an attempt to understand what went on, thereby forming direct associations between temporally adjacent ones. Consistent with this hypothesis, both groups of subjects (relative to subjects with a memory objective) later recalled the actions together and in chronological order regardless of how they were presented. These data indicate that subjects formed direct associations between the temporally related actions that composed each event, and that these associations led one recalled action to cue the retrieval of the next, much as the associated traits and behaviors in person representations cue the retrieval of one another (Chapter 7).

Impression objective and empathy objective subjects differed, however, in their recall of the events themselves. After a long delay (when the original material had presumably been cleared from the Work Space), subjects with the goal of forming an impression of the cocktail party tended to recall the events in the order they occurred in the course of the party. In contrast, subjects whose goal was to empathize with the protagonist tended to recall the second (more recently described) event before the first one. In other words, these latter subjects appeared to treat the action sequence defining each event as a separate unit of information and to store it in a referent bin independently of other sequences. Consequently, they later retrieved the more recently stored sequence first when asked to recall the information in the order it came to mind. In this regard, both impression objective subjects and empathy objective subjects ordered the events correctly when they were explicitly asked to indicate when they occurred in the passage. This means that the temporal codes associated with the action units defining the events, which were presumably similar in both conditions, were effective in determining the order of the events. However, only impression objective subjects formed direct associations between the action units that led one unit to cue the retrieval of the next one when they reported the actions in the order they came to mind.

The Representation of Personal Experiences

A Preliminary Study

The event sequences we have considered thus far pertained to unfamiliar persons that subjects read about. It seems reasonable to suppose that structurally similar representations may be formed of events in which one is personally involved. There are obviously enormous methodological problems involved in evaluating this possibility. This is because the representation one forms of a personal experience and another's representation of this experience may differ in content as well as in structure. However, an approach taken by Fuhrman and Wyer (1988) using comparative judgment procedures appears promising.

In one study, subjects first described both an experience they had in high school and one they had in college. Five actions composing each experience were then selected that were distinguishable and important for understanding what had occurred. Then, in a second experimental session, the subjects were presented all possible pairs of the 10 actions with instructions to judge either which action came sooner or which came later.

In addition, the list of 10 actions reported by each subject in the above group was given to a second, yoked subject with instructions to form an impression of the two experiences they described. These subjects were then also asked to judge the pairs of actions using procedures identical to those to which the first subjects were exposed. By comparing the pattern of response times for the first group of subjects with that of their yoked counterparts, we were able to infer similarities and differences between subjects' representation and coding of their own experiences and the representation and coding of these same experiences by subjects who had only read about them.

We assumed that both groups of subjects would subjectively divide the 10 actions into at least two units, one corresponding to each of the two experiences to which they were relevant, and would assign temporal codes to these units denoting the time period in which they occurred. (These codes may have been assigned a priori by the subjects who had actually experienced the events, and at the time of learning by the subjects who only read about them.) On the other hand, we thought that the two groups of subjects might differ in the number of additional units into which they typically divided the five actions composing each experience. This appeared to be the case, as will be seen.

Response times in this study were analyzed in terms of criteria similar to those used in the study by Wyer et al. (1985) described earlier in this chapter, and were evaluated in terms of their implications for identification, comparison, and response generation processes.

Identification time. To determine the order in which two actions occurred, subjects must first identify the action units to which they belong. In the study by Wyer et al., where all of the actions judged were part of a single story, an action was easier to locate when it occurred near the center of the unit to which it belonged than when it occurred near a unit boundary. In the present case, however, the two experiences to which the events were relevant were generally quite distinctive in terms of both content and of the time at which the events occurred. Moreover, the events had clearly distinguishable beginnings and ends. It therefore seemed likely that in this case, actions at the beginning and ends of these time periods might be more easily identified. This appeared to be true. Pairs of actions that occurred near the center of the experience to which they were relevant were judged more slowly than pairs of actions that occurred near either the beginning or the end. Moreover, this within-unit serial position effect did not significantly depend on whether the actions were judged by the person who experienced them or by someone else.

Comparison time. Subjects took less time to judge the order of two actions if they were relevant to different experiences than if they were both relevant to the same experience. This finding is consistent with the assumption that subjects had assigned distinctive temporal codes to the action units denoting these experiences, and subsequently were able to respond quickly when their judgments could be made on the basis of these codes alone. The magnitude of the difference was very similar for both subject groups.

This does not mean, however, that the two groups of subjects made similar encodings of the actions *within* each experience. Evidence that a difference did indeed exist was suggested by the effect of symbolic temporal distance (D) on response times. The results of Wyer et al.'s (1985) study suggest that a decrease in the average time to compare two actions with an increase in the distance between them is largely a function of the greater proportion of (fast) between-unit comparisons that occur at higher distances (see Figure 8.1). If this is so, however, and if the action sequence is divided into only two units (one pertaining to each experience), symbolic distance effects should be eliminated when only between-experience comparisons are considered. Data shown in Figure 8.5 indicate that this

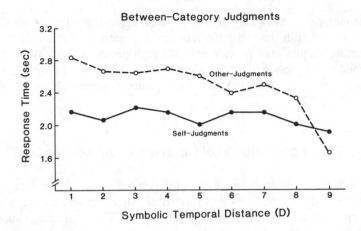

Figure 8.5. Mean response time to judge actions by (a) subjects who personally experienced them and (b) subjects who only read about them as a function of the symbolic temporal distance between them (from Fuhrman & Wyer, 1988).

was true when the actions were judged by the subjects who personally experienced them. It was not true, however, when the actions were judged by subjects who had only read about them. This difference suggests that the subjects who actually experienced the actions being judged treated the set that pertained to each experience as a single knowledge unit, and did not assign temporal codes to the individual actions contained in the unit. In contrast, the subjects who learned about the experience for the first time broke up the actions into smaller conceptual units in the course of understanding what went on, and assigned distinctive temporal codes to each.

Response generation. Subjects' use of *semantic* temporal codes as a basis for judgments should theoretically be reflected in semantic congruity effects. Suppose actions near the start of the series are coded in terms of "sooner." Then, they should be judged more quickly if subjects are asked which comes sooner than if subjects are asked which comes later. For similar reasons, actions near the end of the series should be judged faster if subjects are asked which comes later than if subects are asked which comes sooner. However, these effects should occur *only* if judgments are indeed based on semantic temporal codes. In fact, no clearly interpretable congruity effects were found in this study, regardless of which set of judgments were involved. This finding is consistent with that obtained by Wyer et al. (1985) when episodic event sequences were judged.

The study described above is encouraging in two respects. First, it suggests that the representations people form of their personal experiences are often similar to those that other persons would form as a result of reading about these experiences. The major difference may be that subjects break their own experiences into relatively larger units than they break others' experiences. Second, comparative judgment techniques may provide one (although not the only) way to attain an understanding of how self knowledge is represented in memory as well as knowledge about other people. We will discuss these possibilities further in Chapter 12.

The Representation of Observed Event Sequences

Fuhrman and Wyer's comparison of the representations formed of personal experiences and the representations formed of experiences by people who have read about them carries with it an implicit assumption. That is, the latter experiences were obviously described verbally. In contrast, subjects' personal experiences, at least at the time they occurred, may not have been verbally coded. Rather, they may have been coded in terms more appropriate to the sense modalities in which the events were actually experienced (cf. Kosslyn & Pomerantz, 1977). The broader question raised by Fuhrman and Wyer's (1988) study, and the assumptions underlying it, is whether the mental representation of events that one has actually experienced as a participant or observer is similar in content and structure to the representation of verbally described events that one reads or hears about.

In fact, our general hypothesis, that people do not perform a detailed coding of event sequences, seems particularly likely to be true when the event sequences are actually observed. The continuous stream of actions involved in an observed sequence of ongoing behavior is too complex and goes by too quickly to be coded and stored in detail. Rather, observers of an event sequence are likely to retain only those aspects of it that they believe will allow them to reconstruct it at a level of detail that is sufficient to attain whatever processing objectives exist at the time they observe it.

If this is so, the processes involved in the coding of an observed sequence of events should be similar in many respects to those that underlie the encoding and organization of sequences that are conveyed verbally. Suppose we see someone get up from his chair, walk to the refrigerator, get out a beer, open it and take a sip, and walk back to his seat. We are unlikely to retain this rather mundane sequence of actions as a continuous stream of motor acts. Rather, we may break the sequence into different action units, each exemplifying a different previously learned concept (e.g., "getting up," "walking to the refrigerator," etc.). We may then store representations of these concepts in memory along with rules for instantiating their features in terms of attributes of the specific situation observed. These representations may be sufficient to permit the sequence to be reconstructed in sufficient detail to permit our processing objective to be obtained.

The question is what these representations "look like." Two possibilities are suggested by Abelson's (1976) general conception of an event schema as analogous to a series of "pictures plus captions." One possibility is that we spontaneously assign verbal labels to the action units we identify ("gets up," "walks to the refrigerator," etc.), and then store these verbal labels. To this extent, the content of the representation formed from an ongoing sequence of events may not be appreciably different from the content of the representation we would form of the same events if we read about them or heard someone describe them.

As we indicated in Chapter 4, however, the application of an action concept to an event does not necessarily require that the event be assigned a verbal label. This may occur only if higher order processing objectives require it. That is, there is no reason to suppose that the cognitive activity required to transform a visually coded representation into a semantically coded one is spontaneously performed. Rather, we may simply retain a cluster of features that are coded in the same sense modality in which they are experienced, and that in combination serve to identify the action concept they exemplify. This cluster of features may often be a visually coded "frame," extracted from the ongoing stream of actions that we observe, that exemplifies the action concept to which it is relevant and that later permits the concept to be identified.

Thus, to return to Abelson's (1976) "pictures plus captions" analogy, the representation we store could consist of either a series of "captions" (verbal labels denoting the sequence of action concepts that make up the event sequence), or a series of "pictures" (the visual frames extracted from the sequence that exemplify these concepts). Each representation, however, may be used in much the same way to make judgments and decisions.

An Alternative Conceptualization

The above conceptualization, which is similar to that proposed earlier by Ebbesen (1980), is consistent with our general formulation of the manner in which event sequences are represented in memory. However, it is not universally accepted. In fact, most of the empirical work on the cognitive representation of ongoing event sequences, conducted by Darren Newtson and his colleagues (for reviews, see Newtson, 1976; Ebbesen, 1980; Wyer & Gordon, 1984) is based on a somewhat different set of assumptions.

Specifically, Newtson also argues that subjects who observe an ongoing sequence of behaviors divide it into subjective information units, and that each unit corresponds to an action concept at a higher level of generality. He further assumes that the representation that characterizes the unit is visually and not verbally coded. Finally, he argues that the particular visual frames that are extracted from the sequence to denote the action units are not based on their typicality per se. Rather, these frames occur at "breakpoints," or transitions between one action unit and the next. The nature of each unit can theoretically be reconstructed on the basis of the breakpoint frames that define its boundaries. The number and location of the breakpoints that subjects extract are determined by asking subjects to view the sequence and to press a button whenever one meaningful action ends and a second one begins. The number and location of these button presses is assumed to reflect the number and type of conceptual units into which the observed sequence is subjectively divided.

To the extent that Newtson's button-pressing task permits one to identify the frames that are actually extracted and retained in memory, it provides an invaluable tool for understanding the nature of subjects' memorial representations of events and the factors that affect them. For example, situational and individual difference variables that lead subjects to perform a more or less detailed encoding of a sequence of observed events (i.e., to interpret the sequence in terms of a greater or lesser number of specific concepts) should influence the number of breakpoints they identify. Moreover, factors that affect subjects' interpretation of the observed events should influence the locations of these breakpoints. Finally, to the extent that the number and location of breakpoints extracted indicate the number and type of concepts that are used to interpret an action sequence, they should be related to the manner in which subjects recall this sequence and the sorts of judgments that they make on the basis of it.

Some evidence supports these possibilities. In an early study (Newtson, 1973), subjects were explicitly instructed to divide a videotaped sequence of behaviors into either large or small units as they observed the sequence. These instructions not only affected the number of breakpoints that subjects extracted, but also influenced their judgments of the actor's traits and their confidence that these judgments were correct. (Specifically, subjects who were told to break the sequence into finer units reported greater confidence than those who were told to break it into larger ones.) In a second study, Newtson (1973) asked subjects to observe a videotape of a person engaged in building a model. In some conditions, the actor interrupted his model building, rolled up his pant leg, took off his shoe and put it on the table, and then went back to his task. In other conditions, this unexpected event did not occur. Subjects who observed the unexpected event subsequently extracted more breakpoints from the sequence than they had before the event had occurred, and extracted more breakpoints than control subjects who had not observed the event. Moreover, they made different trait and confidence judgments than did the control subjects.

Finally, Cohen and Ebbesen (1979) asked subjects to observe and extract breakpoints from a videotaped behavior sequence with instructions either to remember what went on or to form an impression of the actor. Subjects with an impression objective extracted fewer breakpoints than did subjects with a memory objective. Moreover, the former subjects' recognition memory for behavioral details was somewhat poorer. In contrast to Newtson's findings, however, subjects in the two task objective conditions did not differ appreciably in the extremity of their trait judgments of the actor or the confidence with which they made these judgments.

Cohen and Ebbesen (1979; see also Ebbesen, 1980) also compared the locations of the breakpoints that subjects typically extracted under the different task objective conditions. Only 25% of the breakpoint locations under impression objective conditions corresponded to any of the breakpoint locations under memory objective (small unit) conditions. This suggests that the concepts used by impression objective subjects to encode the behavior sequence differed qualitatively from the ones extracted by memory objective subjects and were not simply more general versions of them.

Similar conclusions are drawn from a study by Massad, Hubbard, and Newtson (1979). In this study, subjects identified breakpoints in a videotaped cartoon sequence in which the characters were portrayed by geometric figures. Some subjects were told that the cartoon concerned a guardian of a treasure against two thieves, whereas others were told that it showed a couple who was trying to escape from a rapist. The location of the breakpoints that subjects identified in the two cases differed considerably.

A Comparison of the Alternatives

In combination, the results of the studies cited above suggest that both processing objectives and a priori expectancies affect the number and type of action units into which an event sequence is divided, as defined by the Newtson procedure. Conditions that stimulate subjects to attend more carefully to the event sequence in an attempt to understand it (e.g., the occurrence of an unexpected event) may also increase the number of units into which the sequence is divided. It is, therefore, tempting to conclude that the effects of these factors on recall and judgments are mediated by their effects on the concepts subjects used to encode the sequence they observed as reflected by the breakpoints they identified. Unfortunately, however, such a conclusion may be premature. In fact, the aforementioned research does not provide evidence that Newtson's conceptualization is any more viable than the one we have proposed.

The problem in interpreting Newtson's research can be seen with reference to Figure 8.6. Figure 8.6a describes the sequence of processes that Newtson postulates to occur in response to a behavior sequence and the cognitive variables that are affected by these processes. As Ebbesen (1980) points out, this conceptualization is not necessarily implied by Newtson's data. Subjects are obviously able to perform the button-pressing task that Newtson developed to identify breakpoints, and situational and individual difference variables may affect the number and location of these breakpoints. But this does not in itself indicate that there is a direct relationship between these breakpoints and the content of the mental

A. Newtson's Conceptualization

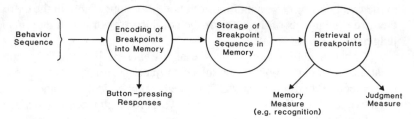

B. Ebbesen's Conceptualization

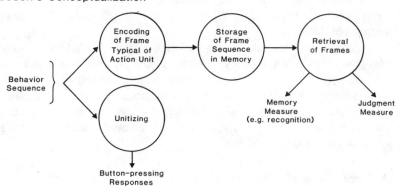

Figure 8.6. Sequence of cognitive processes mediating button presses, memory, and judgments implied by (a) Newtson's conceptualization and (b) Ebbesen's conceptualization of event memory.

representation that subjects actually construct from the event sequence they observe. Rather, the breakpoints that subjects identify may be an epiphenomenon that is produced by the task itself.

Ebbesen's alternative conceptualization is diagrammed in Figure 8.6b. In this diagram, the encoding of the event sequence and the button-pressing are independent responses to the stimulus event sequence, and the breakpoints inferred from button pressing neither reflect the memorial representation that subjects formed nor mediate the inferences they make.

1. Empirical Evidence

Two types of available evidence bear on the merits of the alternative interpretations outlined above. One concerns subjects' memory for various aspects of an observed sequence of behavior. The other pertains to the relation between unitizing indices and the memory and judgment variables that unitizing is theoretically supposed to mediate.

Memory for breakpoint and nonbreakpoint frames. Some of the most compelling support for a breakpoint conceptualization was obtained in a study by Newtson and Engquist (1976). The study compared subjects' memory for details of an event sequence that occurred at both breakpoints and nonbreakpoints. Specifically, subjects viewed one of two videotaped sequence of actions performed by a person in the course of everyday life (e.g., dancing, cutting a dress pattern, repairing a motorcycle, etc.). The locations of the breakpoints in each sequence were defined on the basis of normative data, and so subjects in the study itself were not required to press buttons to identify these breakpoints. Therefore, there is no reason to suppose that some aspects of the sequence would be remembered better than others simply because task demands led them to be thought about more extensively. Subjects were later shown static frames extracted from both sequences. These frames (a) occurred either at breakpoints or at nonbreakpoints, and (b) were either taken from the sequence that subjects had actually observed or from the sequence they had not seen. Subjects were asked in each case to indicate whether or not the frame had been taken from the sequence they had observed. Subjects were significantly more accurate in distinguishing between seen and unseen frames if the frames occurred near breakpoints than if they had occurred at nonbreakpoints. This is certainly consistent with Newtson's assumption that subjects' memorial representation of the event sequence contains the former frames but not the latter.

Ebbesen (1980), however, points out an ambiguity in interpreting these results. Breakpoint frames, which occur at transitions between one type of action and a second, may simply be physically more distinctive than frames that occur in the middle of an action sequence. In fact, evidence reported by Newtson, Engquist, and Bois (1977) supports this speculation. That is, a direct comparison of the features of breakpoint frames and nonbreakpoint frames showed that the former were physically less similar to one another than were the latter. If this is so, subjects in Newtson and Engquist's study may have been relatively more accurate in identifying seen vs. unseen frames when they occurred at breakpoints simply because these frames were inherently easier to distinguish, and not because of their location in the observed event sequence per se.

Relation to other memory and judgment indices. According to the conceptualization outlined in Figure 8.6a, memory and judgments should be a predictable function of the number and size of the units into which an event sequence is divided. Therefore, there should be a systematic relation between button-pressing indices of the breakpoints that theoretically define these units and memory and judgment indices. According to Figure 8.6b, this is not necessarily the case. That is, although some third variable may independently influence both button-pressing and memory/judgment measures, as found by Newtson (1973), there may be no *direct* relation between the two sets of indices. In fact, the weight of available evidence favors this latter interpretation. Cohen and Ebbesen (1979), for example, found that both the number of breakpoints identified by subjects who observed a videotaped behavior sequence and subjects' recognition memory for details of the sequence were less when subjects viewed the tape with the goal of remembering what went on. Within each task objective condition, however, the number of breakpoints that subjects identified was uncorrelated with their recognition memory. Nor was it correlated with either the extremity of subjects' trait judgments of the actor or their confidence in these judgments (Ebbesen, 1980). This suggests that both breakpoint identification and memory and judgment indices were independently influenced by a third variable (e.g., the attention that subjects paid to the behavior sequence they were asked to watch), and may both have been affected by situational or individual difference factors through the mediating influence of this third variable. However, the breakpoints identified using the Newtson procedure did not reflect the actual content of the cognitive representation that was formed from the sequence observed.

2. Overlapping Event Sequences: A Conceptual Ambiguity

In the majority of studies in which Newtson's procedures have been applied, the event sequences that subjects were asked to observe consisted of a series of relatively routine activities performed by a single individual. In contrast, the events that one often encounters outside the laboratory involve two or more people interacting with one another, and engaging simultaneously in different series of actions. Consider an argument between two individuals in which one person (A) begins to shout at the second (B), whereupon B starts to walk out of the room. At this point, A stops shouting, picks up a glass and throws it at B as he makes his exit. It is unclear whether such an episode would be represented in memory as two separate action sequences (one pertaining to each actor) that are encoded and stored independently, or as a single sequence of events that involves both persons in combination. In the former case, it would be impossible to reconstruct the nature of the interaction without some independent indication of how the sequences are temporally positioned in relation to one another. In the latter case, the assumption that successive breakpoints denote the boundaries of an interpretable event would not always be valid. (In our example, a breakpoint that denotes the onset of A's shouting at B might be immediately followed by a breakpoint that signifies the onset of B's walking out of the room rather than the end of A's shouting and the beginning of A's glass- throwing.)

These problems are avoided if the actions that compose an ongoing event sequence are each represented by a *single* frame that is typical of the concept it exemplifies. In our example, a frame pertaining to A's shouting at B, followed by a frame depicting B in the process of leaving the room and then a frame portraying A in the act of throwing the glass, could easily be used to represent the concepts pertaining to the three actions and, if retained, would permit the sequence to be easily reconstructed. For this reason, coupled with the problems created for Newtson's conceptualization by Cohen and Ebbesen's data, it seems most viable to assume that events in an observed sequence are represented by single frames rather than by breakpoint frames, consistent with the conceptualization we have proposed.

Which Specific Frames are Extracted?

The frames that are extracted from an ongoing event sequence at the initial stage of processing correspond to action concepts that are retrieved and used by the Comprehender at the initial encoding stage. These frames are then transmitted to the Work Space. Whether these frames are then encoded in terms of more general action or event concepts, and, therefore, whether they are actually retained in the representation that is ultimately transmitted to Permanent Storage, presumably depends on the observer's processing objective as well as other factors that may lead the observer to believe that he or she will need the frames to reconstruct the events in more or less detail. (When the observed events are prototypic, and their features can therefore be inferred on the basis of general knowledge, these encoding differences may actually not have much influence on subjects' ability to reconstruct accurately the events that take place.)

These considerations are related to Postulate 8.2. That is, the action concepts that are used to encode a behavior sequence (or, alternatively, the frames that exemplify these concepts) are unlikely to be retained in the representation that is formed and transmitted to Permanent Storage unless the concepts are relevant to the processing objectives that exist at the time the information is received. An observer whose goal is simply to obtain a general understanding of the behavioral events that occur may not consider many of the observed behaviors of sufficient importance to retain an encoding of them in the representation being formed. A more formal theoretical statement of this possibility, along with empirical data bearing on its implications, is provided by Lichtenstein and Brewer (1980). They assume that a person's behaviors are better remembered when they are interpretable in terms of event schemata that pertain to a plan or goal of this person. In other words, behaviors of a person that are not goal-relevant may not be considered important for understanding either the person or the situation, and so they may not be contained in the representation that is formed of the observed sequence.

To explore this possibility, Brewer and Dupree (1983) constructed videotapes of an actress engaged in a series of behaviors in her apartment. Under some conditions, certain "target" behaviors (e.g., taking a ruler from the drawer of a desk) were a means to attaining some higher order goal (using the ruler to set the hands of a clock). In other conditions, however, the frames of the sequence that conveyed this goal were omitted. Observers were later better able to recall the target behaviors if these behaviors had been originally seen as goal-relevant than if they had not.

Note that the aspects of the observed sequence that conveyed the goal-relevance of the target behaviors were not presented until *after* these behaviors had occurred. Thus, the better recall of goal-relevant behaviors cannot be attributed to differences in the attention paid to these behaviors or to the detail in which they were encoded at the time they were observed. Rather, the critical factor must be the extent to which the behaviors became associated with goals that subjects learned about subsequently. Note that the target behaviors in *both* goal-relevance conditions should still be available in the Work Space a short time after the sequence is observed. Therefore, the effect of behaviors' goal-relatedness on subjects' ability to remember them should be primarily evident after a long delay (when only the encoded representations transmitted to Permanent Storage are available). Recognition data collected by Brewer and Dupree support this implication. That is, the superiority in memory for goal-relevant target behaviors was much more evident in a delayed recognition task than in one that was administered a short time after the event sequence was presented.

The Role of Event Representations in Comprehension and Inference

In the examples we have used to convey the nature of event representations, the actions described in the information presented were usually sufficient to comprehend what took place and why. Often, however, this is not the case. That is, we must frequently make numerous inferences about actions and events that are not specified in the information we receive in order to understand what occurred. These inferences may concern things that happened either before, during, or after the events that are actually described. The question is what sort of action units are indeed inferred and added to the representation of an event sequence in such circumstances, and when these additions occur.

One answer to this question is suggested by Brewer and Dupree's (1983) research, described in the last section. That is, a central ingredient of the comprehension of social events may often be the ability to conceptualize them in terms of a causally and temporally related sequence of actions that is instrumental to the attainment of some higher order goal. This possibility has in fact been recognized in many conceptualizations of prose comprehension (cf. Mandler & Johnson, 1977; Schank & Abelson, 1977; Stein & Glenn, 1979; for specific applications to the organization of social information, see Black, Galambos, & Read, 1984; Read, 1987). These conceptualizations implicitly or explicitly assume that people who learn about an individual's behaviors attempt to interpret them in terms of the goals that stimulated their occurrence. Sometimes, however, these goals are not specified in the information. In such cases, people may try to identify a previously formed event schema, or set of schemata, whose central frames can be instantiated in terms of the behavioral information available, and whose other frames refer to the attainment of a goal that the protagonist might plausibly be pursuing.[4]

There are at least two general implications of this assumption. First, when a person cannot easily identify a goal-related event schema that permits behavioral information to be interpreted, the person may have difficulty interpreting, organizing, and ultimately remembering the information. Second, when more than one goal-relevant event schema can be used to interpret the behaviors presented, the specific one that is used may have considerable influence on the inferences that are made and the conclusions that are drawn. A substantial amount of research has been performed on these issues, and a complete review of it is beyond the scope of this chapter. An example of the work bearing on each issue may nonetheless be worth summarizing.

Schema Activation and Recall

Information about a person's behavior can often not be easily interpreted in terms of a goal-related event schema. When this behavior is peripheral to a more clearly interpretable goal-directed sequence of events that transpires in the situation, as in Brewer and Dupree's (1983) study, it may simply be ignored and ultimately forgotten once the Work Space is cleared. In other instances, however, a behavior may be central to an interpretation of the overall sequence of events. In this case, the failure to identify a goal-directed event schema that can be used to interpret the behavior may make the entire behavior sequence seem anomalous, and may have a major impact on recall of the information as a whole.

Perhaps the most dramatic examples of this have been provided by John Bransford and his colleagues. To provide but one example, based on a passage written by Nancy McCarrell (Bransford & Stein, 1984, p. 51), suppose subjects read the following excerpt from a letter:

> Remember Sally, the person I mentioned in my last letter? You'll never guess what she did this week. First, she let loose a team of gophers. The plan backfired when a dog chased them away. She then threw a party but the guests failed to bring their motorcycles. Furthermore, her stereo system was not loud enough. Sally spent the next day looking for a "Peeping Tom" but was unable to find one in the yellow pages. Obscene phone calls gave her some hope until

---

4. The goal-relevant event schemata postulated here should be distinguished from the goal schemata that we postulate to exist in the goal bin, which are used by the Executor to direct information processing. The latter schemata consist of *cognitive* procedures for retrieving and transmitting information and for instructing processing units what library routines to use in pursuit of a specific processing objective The event schemata considered here are simply descriptions of a sequence of social events, and are stored in a referent bin pertaining to the type of events involved rather than in the goal bin.

the number was changed. It was the installation of blinking neon lights across
the street that finally did the trick. Sally framed the ad from the classified
section and now has it hanging on her wall.

Individual actions described in the story, considered in isolation, could instantiate several different event schemata. However, few schemata that are spontaneously activated are likely to be able to account for all of the behaviors described
in combination. Thus, the passage as a whole seems nonsensical, and details of it
are unlikely to be retained. However, suppose subjects read the story with the
knowledge that the woman is trying to get rid of her neighbors. Behaviors and
events that initially made no sense suddenly become quite meaningful when
interpreted in terms of their relevance to this goal. Consistent with the implications
of this analysis, subjects who were given knowledge of this goal before reading the
passage had much greater recall of the material contained in it than did subjects
who did not have this knowledge.

Goal-Directed Event Schemata and Inferences

The important role of goal-related event schemata in the interpretation of
behavioral information is also shown graphically by Stephen Read and his colleagues (Read, 1987; Read, Druian, & Miller, 1985). To adapt an example from
Read et al. (1985), suppose subjects are given the following sentences describing
two persons, John and Mary, being told at the outset that the behaviors are in
random order:

John and Mary drove back to the apartment.
John gave Mary the money.
They walked out the door of the apartment.
John and Mary made love.
John picked Mary up on the corner near the drugstore.

Imagine that subjects after reading the statements with the objective of
understanding what went on are asked to make judgments of John and Mary. They
will presumably attempt to identify a goal-relevant event schema that will permit
them to interpret the information, and will then base their judgments on the
implications of this schema. However, at least two different schemata could be
applied, each of which implies a different sequence of events. One pertains to a
couple's attempt to obtain a contraceptive device in anticipation of making love:
"John gave Mary the money. They walked out of the door of the apartment. John
picked up Mary on the corner near the drugstore. John and Mary drove back to the
apartment. John and Mary made love." The second pertains to an individual's
interlude with a prostitute: "John picked Mary up on the corner near the drugstore.

John and Mary drove back to the apartment. John gave Mary the money. John and Mary made love. They walked out the door of the apartment." The impressions of the two individuals involved seem very likely to depend on which of the two event schemata is applied. Moreover, the underlying cognitive representation of many of the actions described (e.g., "they made love") may differ.

The event schema that is actually applied in such a situation may depend in part on which event or person concepts happen fortuitously to be most easily accessible in memory at the time the information is read. (This possibility could be investigated empirically using priming methodology similar to that described in Chapter 6.) Certain specific features of the information itself might also differentially activate these concepts and, therefore, influence the schema that is applied. It is interesting to speculate, for example, that ethnically prejudiced subjects would be more likely to interpret the interaction in terms of a "prostitute" schema if the characters were named "John Anderson" and "Maria Sanchez" than if they were named "John Montague" and "Mary DuPont."

The fact that the event schemata that are activated and used to interpret information may lead to the addition of unmentioned events that are necessary in order to apply it has implications not only for the recall of the information, but also for the sort of inferences that are made of the individuals who are involved in these events. Often, these inferences may not be at all implied by the information given. Rather, they may be based solely on the implications of the added frames. To borrow an intuitive example from Wyer and Carlston (1979), consider the following set of three statements, the first of which was borrowed from Schank and Abelson (1977):

> 1. John knew his wife's operation would be expensive. There was always Uncle Harry...John reached for the suburban telephone directory.

> 2. John could not face the thought of asking a friend to take out his girlfriend's ugly sister. There was always Uncle Harry...John reached for the suburban telephone directory.

> 3. John knew his wife's operation would be expensive. There was always Uncle Harry...John reached for the .32-caliber revolver he kept beside his bed.

Note that in each of the examples, information is provided about the situation confronting John and John's behavior, but no direct information is given about Uncle Harry. Nevertheless, a person who is asked to describe Uncle Harry's personality and physical attributes is likely to generate a quite different description depending on which passage is read. This is presumably because the context of each reference to Uncle Harry elicits a different event schema in each case, and the representation of Uncle Harry in each schema differs appreciably.

The Role of Event Representations in Higher Order Goal-Directed Information Processing

The comprehension of an event sequence may often be preliminary to many more specific processing goals that people perform. To this extent, the general sorts of event representations we have postulated may be constructed and used in a wide variety of situations. To conclude this chapter, we consider the use of event representations in the pursuit of three types of higher order goals: person impression formation and judgment, prediction and explanation, and behavioral decision-making. The issues that come into play are different in each case.

The Use of Event Representations in Person Impression Formation

Suppose subjects read or observe an event sequence with the objective of forming an impression of one of the protagonists. It seems reasonable to suppose that subjects with this objective will engage in many of the processes we have postulated to underlie person impression formation when trait and behavioral information is presented out of context (Chapter 7). In particular, they will encode the observed behaviors in terms of trait concepts (Postulate 7.1), and will attempt to extract a general evaluative concept of the person on the basis of these encodings and other behaviors they observe (Postulate 7.3). These representations are then deposited in a referent bin in Permanent Storage, presumably on top of the event representation on which they are based. These trait and evaluation-based concepts are, therefore, more likely than the event representation to be used to make judgments to which they are relevant.

Two studies by Ebbesen and his colleagues support the implications of this reasoning. In the study by Cohen and Ebbesen (1979) we described earlier, subjects who had viewed a videotaped sequence of an actor's behavior with an impression formation objective or a memory objective were later asked to judge the actor with respect to several different traits. Subjects' trait judgments were then intercorrelated under each task objective condition separately. These two sets of intercorrelations were then compared both: (a) to one another and (b) to normative estimates of how likely it is *in general* for a person with one trait to have the other one. These latter co-occurrence estimates are typically based on evaluative considerations; that is, traits that are similar in favorableness are judged more likely to occur together than traits that differ in favorableness (Rosenberg & Sedlak, 1972). The intercorrelations among subjects' trait judgments under memory set conditions were generally quite low and were unrelated to the intercorrelations of these trait judgments under impression formation conditions ($r = .08$). Moreover, the pattern of intercorrelations under impression objective conditions was significantly related to the pattern of normative co-occurrence estimates ($r = .48, p < .01$), whereas the pattern of intercorrelations under memory objective conditions was not ($r = .30$,

$p > .10$). In combination, these data suggest that subjects with an impression formation objective extracted a general evaluative concept of the person on the basis of their observations, and later used the implications of this concept as criteria for making judgments (see Postulate 7.3). In contrast, subjects with a memory objective, who had not formed an evaluative person representation at the time their observations were made, based their judgments on a review of the event representation itself. As a result, their trait judgments, based on different aspects of the representations, were unrelated to one another.

A question that arises in this latter condition is precisely how the event representation is used to arrive at trait judgments. This question was investigated in a later study by Allen and Ebbesen (1981; see Ebbesen, 1980). In this study, subjects were shown behavior sequences of different lengths (specifically, sequences that were either 30s, 60s, 90s, or 180s in length) with instructions to remember what occurred. These sequences were constructed so that pooled over subjects, each action was presented the same proportion of times in each tape length condition. Subjects after viewing the segments were asked to verify certain behavioral details (e.g., "Did she hold the spoon in her hand?") and also to judge several different traits of the person (e.g., "Was she critical?"). The time required to respond to these questions was recorded and analyzed as a function of tape length. First, consider the verification of behavior details. On the average, the distance of any given behavior detail from the beginning of the segment that subjects observe should increase with the length of this segment. Therefore, suppose subjects' representation of the events portrayed in the segments consists of a series of temporally ordered frames, as we proposed in the preceding section, and subjects review this representation sequentially in order to find the behavioral detail they are asked to verify. Then, the time they take to do this should increase on the average with segment length. This was in fact the case.

The effect of segment length on the time required to make trait judgments is more complicated. This is because more than one event in the segment may have implications for the trait being judged. Assume that any given frame of the event representation is equally likely to contain judgment-relevant information. Then, the average distance of the first relevant information from the beginning of the representation should be similar regardless of the overall segment length. Therefore, if observers only search the event representation until they find the first relevant piece of information, and use this information as a basis for judgments without looking further, response time should not be a function of segment length. On the other hand, suppose subjects perform an exhaustive search, attempting to identify all relevant information before making an inference. Then, an increase in response time with segment length should occur.

It seems intuitively reasonable that whether the search is partial or exhaustive will depend on the type of trait being inferred. Based on normative data, Allen and Ebbesen were able to distinguish between (a) "concrete" traits that could typically

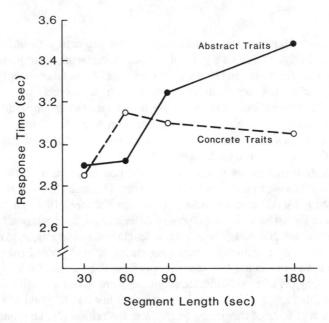

Figure 8.7. Mean response time to judge abstract and concrete traits as a function of segment length (adapted from Allen & Ebbesen, 1981).

be inferred from a single behavior (e.g., argumentative, cheerful, etc.) and (b) "abstract" traits that require many samples of behavior to verify (e.g., objective, noncommittal, etc.). The mean time to judge each type of trait is shown as a function of segment length in Figures 8.7. As expected, the time to infer abstract traits increased markedly with segment length, whereas the time to infer concrete traits was quite independent of segment length.

Although the above pattern of data can be interpreted in other ways (cf. Allen & Ebbesen, 1981; Wyer & Gordon, 1984, p. 110), it is nonetheless consistent with the formulation we have proposed. Moreover, it indirectly supports our assumption that the frames of an event sequence are often stored as a single, temporally ordered unit of information rather than as separate units. One implication of our conceptualization remains to be tested, however. That is, suppose subjects in Allen and Ebbesen's study had viewed the event sequence with the goal of forming an impression of the person described. In this case, they should form an evaluation-based concept of the target person at the time they initially view the sequence, and their later judgments should be based on this concept (see Chapter 7). In this condition, the time required to make trait judgments should not depend on tape length regardless of the type of trait being judged.

The Role of Event Representations in Prediction and Explanation

According to the formulation we proposed in Chapter 7, subjects with the goal of forming an impression of someone attempt to construct trait-based and evaluation-based representations of the form described in Figure 7.1. This may be true regardless of whether the information they receive is an ordered list of traits and behaviors or a temporally ordered sequence of events. In the latter case, subjects may use a causally and temporally related sequence of events to construct a categorical (trait- and person-based) representation that is relevant to the attainment of their higher order processing goal.

In many situations that people encounter, however, the reverse is true. That is, people's processing objectives may *require* the construction of a temporally or causally related sequence of events, but the information they receive is organized categorically, and, therefore, is not in a form that facilitates the construction of this sequence.

For example, processing objectives may require one to predict a future event or to explain an event that has already occurred. In both cases, people may actively attempt to organize the information they receive in a way that permits it to be understood in terms of a previously formed event schema. When this is accomplished, they may generate a prediction by accessing a frame of the event schema that comes after the ones to which the information is directly relevant and instantiating its features. Similarly, the individual may generate an explanation by accessing and instantiating an earlier frame of the schema.

1. The Use of Event Representations in Jury Decision-Making

Evidence that these processes do occur in the course of goal-directed comprehension and explanation has been obtained in a series of studies by Pennington and Hastie (1986a, b) on the cognitive dynamics of juror decision-making. In these studies, subjects are typically given courtroom testimony concerning a criminal case with the objective of deciding the defendant's guilt or innocence. Some of the testimony typically favors each alternative verdict. Pennington and Hastie propose a "story model" of decision-making whereby the recipient of the information first attempts to construct alternative stories concerning the sequence of events that took place and why they occurred. Different stories may be constructed, based on the testimonies of different sets of witnesses. Once the stories are constructed, the recipient evaluates their plausibility, based on the credibility of the witnesses and an evaluation of the inherent likelihood of the sequence of events implied by them. The recipient's verdict of guilty or innocent is a result of these mediating evaluations.

Although the story model is inherently sensible, and is consistent with the general formulation we propose, it is obviously not the only possibility. It is conceivable, for example, that subjects in a jury situation consider each piece of evidence separately as it is presented, evaluative its probable validity based on the witness's credibility, and ultimately arrive at a judgment by aggregating the implications of the various pieces of evidence, each considered as a separate entity in isolation from others (cf. N. Anderson, 1981).

Pennington and Hastie attempted to distinguish between these alternative accounts of decision-making processes, and obtained strong support for the story model. In an initial study (Pennington & Hastie, 1986a), subjects who had read a trial transcript were later asked to recommend a verdict (first degree murder, second degree murder, manslaughter, not guilty, etc.), and to talk aloud as they thought about their decision. A content analysis of these protocols, based on criteria used by Schank (1972, 1975; see also Graesser, 1981), conformed more closely to a "story" structure than to alternative, categorical structures.

A second series of studies (Pennington & Hastie, 1986b) examined the implications of the story model more directly. Subjects in one experiment listened to the transcript of a murder trial containing some statements that favored the defense and others that favored the prosecution. In story order conditions, the events were described in the order they actually occurred (e.g., testimony about events that preceded the incident was first, followed in order by testimony about the incident itself, the arrest, the autopsy, etc.). In witness order conditions, the testimony was organized by the witness who provided it, and presented in the order it was given in the original trial. This was done in a 2x2 design so that the order of presenting prosecution items (story vs. witness) and the order of presenting defense items (story vs. witness) was varied independently. Subjects after receiving the testimony reported their verdict and their confidence in it.

When the evidence favoring one verdict was presented in story order and evidence favoring the other verdict was not, 73% of the subjects recommended the first verdict. When the evidence favoring both verdicts was presented in the same way, the percentage of subjects who favored a guilty verdict was similar regardless of whether the presentation of evidence was in story order (57%) or witness order (63%). However, subjects reported substantially greater confidence in their judgments when the information was conveyed in story order. Therefore, the ease of constructing a story from the evidence presented clearly biased subjects' judgments. More generally, these data confirm the hypothesis that subjects attempt to construct causally and temporally related sequences of events to use as a basis for their decisions, and that when they can do this easily, they are more confident of the decisions they make. There are many implications of this conclusion.

1. If jurors actively construct causally related event sequences from the evidence they receive, they may base their judgments on the plausibility of the event sequences as a whole rather than on the credibility of the particular pieces of evidence that are involved in its construction. In other words, evidence given by

noncredible witnesses from which a plausible event sequence can be constructed may have more influence than evidence from highly credible witnesses that implies an implausible sequence of events.

2. To expand on this possibility, suppose the prosecution evidence can be used to construct an intuitively plausible account of the crime, but that to do so, one must accept the evidence from a disreputable witness. In contrast, suppose the defense testimony is based on evidence from universally reliable witnesses, but that the sequence of events implied by the testimony as a whole is intuitively implausible. The question is which body of evidence will have greater influence on verdicts, and whether its relative influence will depend on how the evidence is presented. It seems reasonable to suppose that if the information is presented in "story" order, thus making the event sequences easy to construct, decisions will be influenced by the plausibility of the sequence of events as a whole independently of the credibility of the individual pieces of evidence that led to its construction. If, however, the evidence is presented in "witness" order, thus making the story more difficult to construct, the credibility of the individual pieces of testimony may be more influential. One practical implication of this reasoning is that a lawyer who has weak witnesses but can build a convincing story would be most effective by presenting the evidence in story order. In contrast, a lawyer with strong witnesses but a weak story line would do best by presenting the evidence in witness order.

3. Jurors who actively construct a causally and temporally related event sequence from the testimony they receive may often need to infer the occurrence of events that were not mentioned in the testimony but must have occurred if the "story" is to be valid. If this is so, and if the event representation they construct is then stored in memory as a single knowledge unit, the inferred events may be indistinguishable from those that were actually mentioned, and thus they may be later recalled as actually having been stated in the information presented. In other words, intrusion errors will occur in jurors' recall of the information. Moreover, statements referring to these unmentioned events may be falsely recognized as having actually been contained in the original testimony.

A study by Pennington (1986; Pennington & Hastie, 1985) supports these latter predictions. That is, subjects who had heard testimony about a court case and had arrived at a verdict were then given a recognition memory test. Some recognition statements had not actually been mentioned in the testimony but were implied by one of the possible causal scenarios that could be constructed from it. Subjects were more likely to report these statements as having been mentioned in the testimony if the statements pertained to the story on which subjects' personal verdict was presumably based than if they pertained to the story supporting the opposite verdict. (Actually mentioned statements were also reported more often in the first case than in the second.) These effects could of course reflect a guessing bias that occurred at the time that recognition judgments were reported and may not reflect the content of the underlying memorial representation (cf. Bellezza & Bower, 1981; Wyer & Srull, 1988). Nonetheless, the results are consistent with the conceptualization proposed.

Construction of event sequences in other domains. The explanatory event representations constructed in the research by Pennington and Hastie were in the service of a very specific goal (deciding someone's guilt or innocence). They may also be constructed, however, to attain more general processing objectives. For example, we may try to explain a person's behavior in a situation in order to decide how we should respond to the person in this situation or a subsequent one. Or, we may attempt to account for unexpected happenings that we believe to be relevant to some later judgment or decision we may have to make.

Indirect evidence of the role of event representations in these more general goal-directed activities was reported by Spiro (1977). In this study, subjects received information about an engaged couple with instructions that the experiment was concerned with either memory or with "reactions to situations involving interpersonal relations." In some versions of the story, the man informs the woman that he doesn't want children, where upon the woman experiences considerable upset and a bitter argument ensues. Subjects who believe they will need to report their reactions to the situation may interpret this information in terms of a previously formed event schema about people who fall in love but who then find themselves in disagreement on matters of great importance. Later frames of such a schema may typically convey the couple being unable to reconcile the difference and ultimately deciding to separate.

After reading this story, subjects engaged in routine activities unrelated to the experimental task. During this period, the experimenter, who ostensibly knew the couple, "incidentally" noted that they eventually married and were still happily together. (In other conditions of the study, the stated outcome was consistent with the event schema that was presumably used to interpret the situation.) The experimenter's remark should have little effect on subjects whose goal is to remember the original material. In contrast, subjects whose objective is to interpret and react to interpersonal relations may try to construct a scenario of how this unexpected outcome might have occurred. In doing so, they may speculate that one or the other partner had a change of mind, that the woman found that she couldn't have children, or that some other event might have led the couple to avoid the conflict that would otherwise have led to their separation. This inferred event may then be added to the representation that subjects construct and store in memory.

Subjects after completing the activities they were performing were dismissed. However, they returned either a few days or several weeks later, at which time they were asked to recall the story they had read in the first session. They were explicitly told to report only things that were mentioned in the story and *not* to include any personal reactions or inferences they may have made. In fact, subjects under memory-objective conditions recalled the material with reasonable accuracy, and errors in their recall were not systematically affected by the additional information they received about the outcome of the couple's interaction. In contrast, subjects whose original objective was to interpret the interpersonal relationship made frequent errors, the number of which increased over time. These errors were typically of the sort one might expect as a result of attempts to reconcile the ancillary material with the original information. For example, one subject recalled that "the problem was resolved when they found that (the woman) could not have children anyway." Another reported that although one person thought the matter was important, the other did not (for other concrete examples, see Spiro, 1977, pp. 144-145).

These results are, therefore, consistent with Pennington's (1986) finding that people construct event sequences to use in explaining information that requires the inference of other unmentioned events, and that these inferred events become part of the representation they form. Note that these missing inferences are unlikely to be made unless they are necessary in order to attain an immediate or anticipated higher order processing objective. They also may not occur if the available information can be interpreted in terms of a single prototypic schema. As implied by the partial-copy hypothesis noted earlier, subjects in the latter condition may simply copy those action concepts from the schema that are instantiated by the presented information and form a representation based on these concepts alone, without adding unmentioned events to the representation. Additional data reported by Spiro (1977) support this latter contingency. Specifically, subjects made many fewer intrusion errors when they received incidental information that was consistent with the prototypic event schema they had presumably used to interpret the original story (e.g., when they were told that the couple separated and never saw one another again).[5]

2. The Use of Event Sequences in Behavioral Decision-Making

People are called upon to make numerous decisions in the course of their daily lives. Some of them occur in familiar situations and others occur in quite novel ones. According to the conceptualization we propose, the process of arriving at these decisions is similar in each case. Suppose a goal is identified that requires a behavioral decision. The Executor, based on information contained in a goal

---

5. Intrusion errors of the sort we postulate to result from forming event representations are much less likely to occur when subjects form person representations based on sets of unrelated behaviors of the sort we considered in Chapter 7. This is because the comprehension of these behaviors typically does not require the inference of the other, unmentioned behaviors in order to form a goal-relevant representation on the basis of them. In fact, the number of intrusion errors (e.g., the recall of behaviors that were not mentioned in the information presented) is extremely low in the studies performed in the person memory paradigm (Srull, 1981; Wyer & Gordon, 1982; Wyer et al., 1984). This suggests a fundamental difference in the sorts of representations that are formed in the two types of situations and the cognitive processes that underlie their construction.

schema, retrieves information from a referent bin pertaining to the goal (or to the person or object to which the goal is relevant). It then transmits this information to a processing unit with instructions to generate an output that can be used as a basis for deciding what to do. In many instances, this information may consist of an event schema that describes what typically occurs in a situation and its likely consequences. Note that this schema may be the same representation used to attain other processing objectives (e.g., the comprehension and organization of new information, generating predictions or explanations, etc.).

To use a mundane example, a man who enters a restaurant must understand the events that occur and how to respond to them. He may accomplish this by activating a "visiting a restaurant" schema, and by instantiating it in terms of other general features of the restaurant being visited. Once this is done, the instantiated representation may be used by the Inference Maker and the Response Selector as a guide in inferring what sort of responses should be made at different points in the sequence and in ultimately generating these responses. In some cases, the responses may be generated without cognitive activity, based on output routines that are hard-wired into the Response Selector's library. In other cases, a more deliberate decision process may be involved. Which is the case presumably depends on the novelty of the situation with which the decision-maker is confronted.

Although this conceptualization seems rather unexciting, it has several implications in the context of the overall formulation we propose. The accessibility of event sequences, like the other units of knowledge that are stored in referent bins, depends on the frequency and recency with which they have been formed and used in the past. Moreover, conceptually related event sequences may be stored in different referent bins, depending on the processing objectives that existed at the time they were formed. When more than one event schema can potentially serve as a guide to decision making, the one that is actually used may depend on (a) the particular set of probe cues that happen to be selected for use in identifying a referent bin, and (b) which of several applicable event schemata contained in the bin happens to be nearest the top, and thus is most likely to be retrieved.

Research performed by Ellen Langer and her colleagues (for a review, see Langer, 1978) is worth noting in this regard. In one study (Langer & Abelson, 1972), shoppers were approached outside a supermarket by a woman who had ostensibly hurt her leg, and were asked by the woman for help. In some cases, the request was to call her husband and tell her to pick her up. This request was likely to be considered legitimate under the circumstances. In other cases, she asked the customer to call her boss and tell him she would be late—something that ostensibly was not very important and therefore was not the sort of thing one would normally ask a stranger to do. The other variable manipulated in the study was the order in which the woman (a) described her adversity and (b) made her request. Specifically, under *request-first* conditions, the woman said: "Would you do something for me? Please do me a favor and call my husband to ask him to pick me up. My knee is killing me. I think I sprained it." In contrast, under *need- first* conditions, the woman's words were: "My knee is killing me. I think I sprained it. Would you do something for me? Please..."

Thus, the descriptive content of the woman's statements were identical in the two cases, with only the order of the two components varying. The question is which appeal would be most effective in soliciting aid, and whether its effect would depend on the legitimacy of the request.

Several alternative predictions might be generated on a priori grounds. The one that provides the best account of the results is the following. Consider request-first conditions. Here, the woman's initial statement, which focuses attention on the subject, may predispose the subject to seek and retrieve information from a "self bin" that contains information about oneself as a person who helps others. Specifically, it may contain an event sequence implying that one is a socially responsible person who helps others when asked to do so. The legitimacy of the request may not be a central feature of this event schema, and so people who apply it may provide help with similar likelihood regardless of the legitimacy of the request.

In contrast, suppose the victim's statement of need is conveyed first. The features of this initial statement, if used as probe cues, may lead an event schema to be retrieved from a bin containing information about people in need of help rather than from a self bin. The event schemata stored in this sort of bin may be more likely to have implications that people who make legitimate requests should be helped, whereas those who make unnecessary requests should be refused. In this condition, then, subjects' helping decisions may be more likely to vary with the legitimacy of the request.

Langer and Abelson's results are consistent with this interpretation. That is, subjects' likelihood of helping the victim increased with the legitimacy of the request in the second condition but not in the first. In evaluating our interpretation of these results (which is similar to that given by Abelson, 1976), it is important to bear in mind that no direct evidence is available on the sort of cognitive representations that actually provided the basis for behavioral decisions made in these conditions. Moreover, the model we propose clearly does not generate a priori predictions that the particular pattern of results obtained would occur. Be that as it may, the results clearly indicate that the order in which requests and statements of need are communicated activate different cognitive representations that lead different criteria for behavioral decisions to be applied. It seems reasonable to speculate that these representations may sometimes be event schemata.

Concluding Remarks

In this chapter, we have attempted to identify several issues surrounding the representation of social events in memory, and to provide a tentative conceptualization of the nature of these representations and how they are used. The conceptualization is admittedly incomplete and undoubtedly deficient in many respects. However, it provides a framework upon which future research and theorizing can be built. It seems clear that an adequate account of the construction and use of event representations is central to a complete formulation of social information processing. Providing this account is a major objective of our future work.

Chapter 9
Inference Making: I. General Processes

The last several chapters have been concerned with the sorts of mental representations that are formed from social information. These representations are of limited interest, however, without an accompanying understanding of how they are used to arrive at judgments and behavioral decisions. This task is theoretically performed by the Inference Maker (see Figure 2.1), based on rules that, although typically acquired through social learning, have become hard-wired into the unit's library. These rules depend on the type of judgment to be made and the type of knowledge available. They may also depend on the information-processing demands that are placed on the judge or decision-maker. One must, therefore, not only be able to circumscribe the alternative rules that may potentially be used to make a particular type of inference. In addition, one must be able to specify the conditions in which each of these rules is likely to be applied.

It is perhaps obvious from the above comments that a comprehensive view of inference processes is hard to acquire. Some general conclusions nevertheless emerge from a consideration of the different types of inferences that people are often called upon to make, the rules that appear to govern them, and the conditions in which these rules are likely to be invoked.

An obvious limitation of our discussion should be noted. In this single chapter, we cannot hope to do justice to the extensive literature on human inference, judgment, and decision-making that has accumulated over the past two decades. This research and theorizing has been reviewed extensively elsewhere, both by the present authors (e.g., Wyer & Carlston, 1979) and others (Anderson, 1981; Hastie, 1983; Kahneman, Slovic, & Tversky, 1982; Nisbett & Ross, 1980; Revlin & Mayer, 1978; Sherman & Corty, 1984). Although the inference phenomena we consider are only representative of those that exist, they are sufficient to convey the nature of the framework that must be developed for understanding inference and judgment in general. We focus on three types of inferences, concerning (a) the membership of objects in social categories, (b) the validity of belief propositions, and (c) the use of cognitive "heuristics" (Kahneman et al., 1982; Sherman & Corty, 1984). In this latter context, we propose a general principle that appears to govern inferences

255

in a variety of situations in which heuristics are used. After considering these
general issues, we turn in Chapter 10 to a discussion of inferences in a specific
judgment domain, namely, that of persons.

Inferences of Category Membership

Many inferences we make about our social environment concern the membership of an object in a social category. These inferences are typically made with
some subjective likelihood, or probability. The category involved may be of several
types. For example, we may infer whether a person is a liberal or a conservative,
is likely to be successful in a particular job, or is generally likeable. We may infer
whether a person's behavior is due to some general aspect of the person's personality or to external, situational factors. Moreover, we may judge whether a
particular statement is true or false. All of these judgments can be conceptualized
as inferences about the membership of a stimulus in a category ("liberal," "good
for the job," "true," "personally responsible," etc.). Judgments along a response
scale can also be conceptualized as subjective "expected values," or inferences of
the scale category that the object best exemplifies, based on an underlying distribution of beliefs about the object's membership in each of the categories available
(Wyer, 1973; Wyer & Carlston, 1979).

In fact, many of the inferences we discuss throughout this chapter may be
conceptualized as inferences about category membership. This does not imply,
however, that the processes that underlie these inferences are the same. In the
present section, we restrict our attention to a particular type of categorical inference.
Specifically, we are concerned with inferences of the likelihood that a person or
object belongs to a social category, or group (e.g., "liberal, "salesman," etc.).
Several of the considerations we raise also come into play in a conceptualization
of inferences more generally.

The particular rules that govern the assignment of an object to a category are
discussed in considerable detail by Lingle, Altom, and Medin (1984; see also Smith
& Medin, 1981), and we do not repeat their penetrating analysis. Generally, such
assignment involves a comparison of the features of the object to be categorized
with those that either define the category itself, that characterize a prototypic
member of it, or that characterize a particular exemplar. It is obviously important
to know which of these criteria is actually used and when. For simplicity, however,
we typically ignore this question in our present discussion.

When one's knowledge of the object's characteristics does not permit it to be
unequivocally identified as a category member, this is done with some subjective
probability. In principle, three factors are relevant to the mental computation of
this probability. One is the likelihood that the object actually has the particular set
of features that are being considered as a basis for categorizing it (F). The second

is the likelihood that an object with these features belongs to the category (C). This latter inference may be conceptualized as a conditional probability $P(C|F)$. The third factor is the likelihood that an object would belong to the category even if it did not have this set of features, or $P(C|\overline{F})$. When these two conditional probabilities are not the same, the overall likelihood that the object belongs to the category C, or $P(C)$, may lie somewhere between them, depending on the judge's belief that the object actually has the features that are being considered. This possibility can be described more formally by the following equation

$$P(C) = P(F)P(C|F) + P(\overline{F})P(C|\overline{F})\qquad\qquad[9.1]$$

where $P(F)$ and $P(\overline{F}) = 1 - P(F)$ are the subjective likelihoods that the object being judged does and does not have the subset of features F, respectively. This equation has the character of weighted average. That is, $P(F)$ and $P(\overline{F})$, the relative weights attached to the two conditional beliefs, sum to 1.

If the components of Equation 9.1 were true probabilities, the equation would be a mathematically correct statement of the relations among them. Because they are not, but are subjective *estimates* of the probabilities, the validity of the equation is an empirical question. Moreover, as a characterization of the cognitive processes that underlie subjects' categorical inferences, the equation calls attention to several additional questions.

1. The equation leaves open the fundamental issue of *how* the component inferences are made. What is the process whereby people estimate the likelihood that an object belongs to the category C given that it has the set of features F that are being considered?

2. The set of features that subjects actually use to infer an object's category membership is very unlikely to include all of the ones they could potentially consider. What factors determine how many features are contained in this set, and how are these features selected?

3. Equation 9.1 assumes that people who wish to make a categorical inference take into account both the likelihood that the object belongs to the category given that it has the features specified and the likelihood that the object would belong to the category even if it did *not* possess these features. It is conceivable that subjects do not consider this latter probability.

We discuss each of these matters in turn.

Conditional Inferences of Category Membership from Feature Information

It may seem intuitively obvious that a person who wishes to decide if an object belongs to a particular category will attempt to decide if the object has features that are typically possessed by category members. This could be done in two ways. First, the person may first activate a set of features that characterize members of the category being considered and determine if the object possesses them. Alternatively, the person may identify features of the object to be categorized and determine if these features are typically possessed by category members. In each case, the person's inference that the object belongs to the category is likely to increase with the number of common features that are identified.

It should be noted, however, that the inferences that result from these two processes are not always the same. The first inference is essentially the likelihood that a category member has the features that are possessed by the particular object to be categorized. This conditional inference is, in effect, $P(F|C)$. The second inference is the likelihood that an object belongs to the category if it has the particular set of features possessed by the object, or $P(C|F)$. This latter probability, which of course is the one that is required (see Equation 9.1), is not necessarily the same as the first. In fact, if the two conditional inferences were indeed true probabilities rather than subjective estimates, they would be related according to the equation

$$P(F)P(C|F) = P(C)P(F|C),$$

or,

$$P(C|F) = \frac{P(C)}{P(F)} P(F|C) \qquad [9.2]$$

In other words, although the conditional inferences are related positively, one is an accurate estimate of the other only if $P(C) = P(F)$, that is, only if the likelihood that an object is in the category (C) and the likelihood that it has the particular set of features being considered (F) are the same.

Many instances can be found in which this is not the case. For example, the number of university faculty members who are short, have black hair, are quiet and read poetry (F) is undoubtedly greater than the number who are Chinese studies professors (C); that is, $P(F) > P(C)$. Consequently, the likelihood of being a Chinese studies professor if one is short, has black hair, is quiet and reads poetry, or $P(C|F)$, is objectively much less than the likelihood that one has these attributes if one is a Chinese studies professor, or $P(F|C)$. To this extent, the use of the first probability to infer the second would be a bad strategy.

Despite this fact, the preponderance of evidence suggests that subjects do indeed employ this strategy. That is, they mentally compute an estimate of $P(F|C)$, and then use this as an estimate of $P(C|F)$. Some of the more provocative indications of this tendency have been reported by Kahneman and Tversky (1973) in the context of their research on the "representativeness" heuristic. To cite a well-known example from their work, subjects were given personal descriptions of an individual who was ostensibly drawn at random from a group of 100. Some subjects were told that the group consisted of 70 lawyers and 30 engineers, whereas others were told that these frequencies were reversed. The different base rates theoretically affect the subjective probability of being in the category given characteristics of the individual being judged, or $P(C|F)$. Nevertheless, subjects' estimates of the likelihood that the individual was a lawyer, or, alternatively, an engineer, were similar regardless of the base rate information they were given.

There are undoubtedly some constraints on the generality of this finding. If subjects had been told that the group consisted of 100 lawyers and no engineers (or, alternatively, 100 engineers and no lawyers), it seems unlikely that they would not have taken this information into account. Nevertheless, there appear to be a large number of instances in which subjects do infer the likelihood that an object with certain features belongs to a category from their belief that a member of the category would have the features they are considering, without evaluating base rate differences at all.

This conclusion is consistent with the conceptualization we have proposed. That is, we have assumed that the process of judging a person as being of a particular type (likeable, honest, etc.) often involves the identification of a prototypic representation of this type of person and a comparison of the person's features to those of the prototype, with an affirmative response resulting if the match is sufficient. "Base rates" are not involved in this process.

A theoretical issue is nevertheless raised by the analysis provided above. That is, do people equate the two conditional probabilities because they ignore base rates, based on the erroneous assumption that the two unconditional probabilities are equal? Or, as implied in the above paragraph, do subjects ignore the implications of base rate information because they invoke an inference process to which this information is irrelevant? In fact, the tendency for subjects to infer $P(C|F)$ from $P(F|C)$ may be one reflection of a much more general tendency to treat conditional relations as biconditionals, and, therefore, to infer that if one situation or condition implies a second, the second also implies the first. This possibility has far-reaching implications that we consider in the final section of this chapter.

Criteria for Inferring Category Membership: Which Features are Considered?

There are other implications of the categorization process we have proposed. To reiterate, subjects who wish to decide if an object belongs to a category theoretically search for features of the object that either define the category or are believed to characterize its members. In other words, they look for evidence that confirms the object's membership in the category. Features of the object that are not possessed by category members, or that suggest that the object belongs to a different category than the one that is being considered, are generally not involved in this process, and, therefore, may often be ignored.

To see the implications of this tendency, suppose that a person has three attributes that are typically possessed by extraverts but not introverts and three others that typically characterize introverts but not extraverts. If subjects are given information about all six attributes and are asked if the person is an extravert, they should theoretically activate features of an extravert, search for and identify three of these features in the information about the target, and respond affirmatively. However, suppose subjects are instead asked if the person is an introvert. In this case, they should activate features of an introvert, find three of these features in the target information, and again respond affirmatively. In each case, the disconfirming features are not involved in the inference process. This process therefore produces a bias to conclude that the person belongs to the category being considered, regardless of which category this happens to be. Two quite different types of research bear directly on this possibility.

1. Confirmatory Hypothesis Testing

Snyder and his colleagues (Snyder & Swann, 1978; Snyder & Cantor, 1979) also postulate that when people wish to establish an individual's membership in a social category, they actively seek evidence that confirms this membership to the exclusion of evidence that disconfirms it. This search process may govern not only the acquisition of new information but also the recall and use of knowledge that has already been acquired and stored in long term memory.

To examine the first of these possibilities, Snyder and Swann (1978) told subjects that they would be asked to determine whether a person they would be interviewing was suitable for either a job that required introversion or a job that required extraversion. Subjects then selected from a list of questions the ones they would like to ask the candidate. Some of the questions in the list presupposed extraversion (e.g., "What do you like about parties?"), thus eliciting responses that necessarily would be interpreted as implying this attribute. Other questions in the list presupposed introversion (e.g., "When do you feel like being alone?"). Subjects tended to select questions whose answers presupposed the existence of the attribute they were attempting to verify, virtually guaranteeing that the candidate's response would appear to confirm his or her suitability for the job they were asked to consider. Similar conclusions were drawn from a later study (Wyer, Strack, & Fuhrman, 1988) in which subjects were asked to choose from a list of questions that required yes-no answers (e.g., "Do you like parties?", or "Do you sometimes feel like being alone?"). In this case, subjects showed a general tendency to select questions about attributes that were typically possessed by members of the category they were considering (i.e., questions that, if answered affirmatively, would provide confirming evidence of category membership). In both studies, therefore, subjects selected questions about features that were possessed by members of the category they were considering rather than features that would, if possessed, call membership in the category into question.

The search of memory for previously acquired information seems to be governed by similar processes. Snyder and Cantor (1979) asked subjects to read a fairly lengthy passage describing a woman's attributes and behavior in several different situations. Some of the information conveyed extraverted tendencies and other information conveyed introverted tendencies. Subjects' objective at the time they read the passage was simply to comprehend it. Later, however, some subjects were asked whether the person was an extravert whereas others were asked if she was an introvert. The first group of subjects judged her to be more extraverted, and less introverted, than the second group. Moreover, when they were asked to list the aspects of the passage that were most relevant to their judgments, both groups of subjects tended to list characteristics of the protagonist that were possessed by typical members of the category they were asked to consider rather than characteristics that were usually not possessed by category members.

2. Feature Positive Effects

A related phenomenon is the tendency for subjects to use the presence of features as positive evidence of category membership but not to use the absence of features as evidence. In a study by Newman, Wolfe, and Hearst (1980), for example, subjects were given pairs of complex stimuli and were asked in each case to predict which stimulus was the "good" one. Subjects were much better at learning to identify "good" stimuli when these stimuli were distinguished by the presence of a feature that the others did not have than when they were distinguished by the absence of a feature that the others possessed. This indicates that subjects tend to search for concepts that are defined in terms of attributes that its exemplars possess rather than attributes that its exemplars do not possess.

An interesting investigation of "feature-positive" effects in a quite different situation was constructed by Fazio, Sherman, and Herr (1982). Subjects in an initial experimental session rated the funniness of a series of cartoons. In a second session, they were exposed to cartoons they had originally rated as fairly neutral. Some subjects were told to press a button if they thought the cartoon was funny (doing nothing if it was not). Others were told to press a button if they thought the cartoon was not funny (doing nothing if it was). After performing this task, all subjects again rated the cartoons along a scale identical to the one they had used in the first session. Note that a "positive" (button-pressing) response to a cartoon in the first condition indicates a belief that the cartoon was funny, whereas a similar response in the second condition conveys a belief that it was unfunny. Subjects' ratings of "funny" cartoons were more extreme (funny) in the first condition, whereas their responses to "unfunny" cartoons were more extreme (unfunny) in the second condition.

The authors concluded that subjects' ratings were influenced by their previous behavior in a manner implied by Bem's (1965) earlier findings and general theory of self-perception (Bem, 1972). However, positive instances of behavior were considered more informative, and therefore had more influence on their later inferences, than negative instances (nonbehaviors).

A somewhat different interpretation of these findings is possible that is more directly implied by the conceptualization we have proposed. That is, subjects who are told to make a response when a cartoon is funny search for features that characterize funny cartoons, pressing a button if they find a sufficient number of them. However, characteristics of unfunny cartoons are not involved in this process. By the same token, subjects who are told to press a button when the cartoons are unfunny look for features that characterize unfunny cartoons, responding affirmatively if they find a sufficient number of these features without considering "funny" aspects of the cartoons. As a result of this process, "funny" features of all cartoons should be more salient to subjects in the first condition than in the second, regardless of whether subjects pressed a button in response to the cartoons or not. Therefore, they should all be judged as funnier in the first condition. This, in effect, is what Fazio et al. found. That is, "funny" cartoons were judged as funnier, and "unfunny" cartoons were judged as less unfunny, in the first condition than in the second. These data are therefore quite consistent with the confirmatory bias postulated by Snyder and his colleagues and with the categorical inference process we have proposed.

3. The Role of Noncommon Features

The above discussion is of course oversimplified. One should not conclude from it that features that do not confirm an object's membership in a category have no influence at all on categorical judgments. Even though subjects may search for positive features, they encounter disconfirming ones in the course of their search, and may therefore take them into account as well as the confirming ones. These disconfirming features may simply be given relatively less weight than the confirming ones.

The processes that underlie the use of disconfirming features have been explored by Tversky and Gati (1978) in an analysis of similarity judgments (see also Tversky, 1977). They also assume that when subjects are asked to decide whether one (target) stimulus is similar to a second (referent) stimulus, they identify features of the referent and determine whether the target also has them. Noncommon features have a negative influence on the judgments they make. However, features of the target that are not possessed by the referent have relatively more negative influence than do features of the referent that are not possessed by the target.

One implication of this is that asymmetries often occur in judging similarities. To see this, suppose that A has five features, four of which are common to B. However, B has 10 features (the four that are shared with A and six others). If subjects are asked how similar A is to B, they should theoretically activate the 10 features of B and determine whether A's five features are included among them, finding that they are in 4 of the 5 cases. However, suppose subjects are asked how similar B is to A. Then, they should activate the five features of A and determine whether B's features are included among them. This is true in only 4 of 10 cases. This analysis implies that B should be judged less similar to A than A is to B.

Tversky and Gati's analysis was restricted to similarity judgments. However, to the extent that categorization processes and similarity judgments both involve a comparison of the features of one entity (e.g., a category or an exemplar of it) to those of the second (the object to be classified), it seems reasonable to suppose that similar considerations operate here as well (cf. Lingle et al., 1984). For example, suppose feminists have few features that are not also possessed by liberals, whereas liberals have a relatively large number of features that are not possessed by feminists. It follows that subjects are less likely to judge liberals to be feminist than they are to judge feminists to be liberal.

Some additional implications of this analysis arise in considering the inferences that a particular target stimulus belongs to a category. That is, holding constant the number of features that the target and the category have in common, the likelihood that the target is judged to belong to the category should decrease with the amount of knowledge that one has about the person to be categorized (and therefore the number of features of the target that are not shared by the category). It should also decrease with the detail with which the category is characterized (i.e., the number of features of the category that are not shared by the target). In other words, the more one knows about either a target or a category, the less likely it is that the target will be assigned to the category.

4. Effects of Feature Accessibility on Categorical Judgments.

There is an important qualification on the above analysis. A fundamental assumption of the general model we propose is that people do not perform an exhaustive review and analysis of all of the knowledge that they could potentially bring to bear on a judgment. Rather, they consider only a subset of this knowledge that happens to be easily accessible at the time. In the present context, it is very unlikely that people use all of the information they have received about a person or object in deciding the person's category membership. Nor do they consider all of their knowledge about the category or its exemplars. Thus, the considerations raised above are more appropriately applied to the number of features that people happen to access and use under the conditions in which the categorization is to be made, rather than to the number they actually have knowledge of and, in other conditions, might happen to recall.

Both characteristics of the judgment task, and recent experiences that make one or another subset of concepts and attributes accessible in memory, may influence the particular features that subjects consider. An indirect indication of this influence is provided by Salancik's research on the determinants of self-judgments (Salancik & Calder, 1974; Salancik & Conway, 1975). In Salancik and Conway's study, subjects were asked to judge their religiousness. Before doing so, however, they were asked to indicate their agreement with several statements about their religious and nonreligious behavior. In some instances, religious behavior statements contained the phrase "on occasion" (i.e., "I go to church on occasion"), whereas nonreligious statements contained the word "frequently" (i.e., "I frequently swear"). In a second condition, the terms used in these two types of statements were interchanged ("I frequently go to church," "I swear on occasion," etc.). Subjects who responded to the first set of statements later reported themselves to be more religious than subjects who responded to the second set.

Although there are several possible interpretations of this finding, one is particularly congenial to the categorization processes we are considering. That is, statements containing "on occasion" are able to be verified with only a few positive instances of the behavior described. Therefore, subjects who consider these statements are more inclined to search for and identify such instances, and therefore to respond affirmatively. In contrast, statements containing "frequently" take many positive instances to confirm but are easily disconfirmed by a few negative instances. These latter statements may therefore bias subjects to search for negative instances, find them, and respond negatively. This means that subjects in the first condition described above are likely to have positive instances of their religious behavior and negative instances of nonreligious behavior accessible in memory, whereas subjects in the second condition are likely to have negative instances of their religious behavior and positive instances of their nonreligious behavior accessible. If subjects then use this subset of behavioral "features" as bases for inferring whether they belong to the category "religious," they should be more likely to confirm their membership category in the first case than in the second.

A quite different demonstration of the effects of attribute salience of category-related judgments is provided by Tversky and Gati (1978) on similarity judgments.

The study shows that the stimuli being judged may themselves activate different criteria for comparison, and therefore may affect the conclusions that are drawn. Subjects were given sets of four countries—one referent and three targets—and were asked to rank order the targets in terms of their similarity to the referent. The referent and two of the target countries remained constant over experimental conditions. However, the third varied in ways that were expected to make different dimensions of comparison salient. In one case, for example, where the referent was Israel, the targets in one condition were England, Iran, and Syria, and the targets in the other condition were England, Iran, and France. Tversky and Gati reasoned that in the first condition, the most salient basis for comparing the countries would be their religious orientation (Moslem vs. non-Moslem). Along this dimension, England is more similar to Israel than is Iran. When Syria is replaced by France, however, the most salient dimension of judgment is geographical (European vs. non-European), and along this dimension, Iran is more similar to Israel than is England. Results were completely in accord with the implications of this analysis; that is, England was judged more similar to Israel than Iran in the first condition, but less similar to Israel than Iran in the second. (Results using different stimulus sets and alternative dimensions of similarity were comparable.)

The Role of Negative Conditionals

All of the research described thus far concerns factors that underlie subjects' estimates of $P(C|F)$, or the positive conditional inference defined in Equation 9.1. The third issue made salient by our conceptualization of categorization processes concerns the extent to which subjects take into account not only this probability but also the probability that an object would belong to the category even if it did *not* have the subset of features that are being considered.

Data bearing on this matter are limited. The available evidence, however, suggests that subjects do in fact take into account *both* conditional inferences, and that they combine their implications in the manner that Equation 9.1 suggests. In one study (Wyer, 1975), subjects were given information about the frequency with which people possessed a hypothetical gene (A) and the frequency with which people who had and did not have the gene possessed an attribute (B). These frequencies were conveyed verbally in statements of the following form:

> Persons frequently (sometimes, rarely) have gene A.
> Persons with gene A frequently (sometimes, rarely) have attribute B.
> Persons who do not have gene A frequently (sometimes, rarely) have attribute B.

Twenty-seven sets of statements, conveying all combinations of frequencies, were presented. After reading each set, subjects estimated the likelihood that a

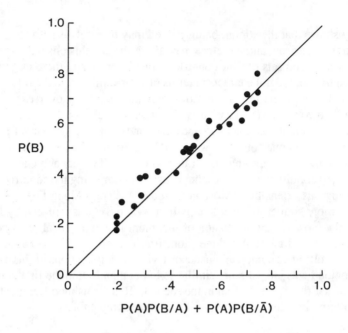

Figure 9.1. Mean estimates of the likelihood that a person has an attribute B, or P(B), as a function of mean predicted values based on Equation 9.1. (Adapted from Wyer, 1975.)

particular person would have the attribute [$P(B)$], followed by the likelihood that the person would have the gene [$P(A)$], and the likelihood that the person would have B given that he did or did not have A [$P(B|A)$ and $P(B|\bar{A})$, respectively]. These estimates, reported along a scale from 0 (not at all likely) to 10 (extremely likely) and divided by 10 to convert them to units of probability, were used to compute predicted values of P(B) for each subject separately for each of the 27 sets of stimulus statements. A plot of the mean obtained estimates of $P(B)$ as a function of the mean predicted values, shown in Figure 9.1, indicates a very close quantitative fit of the model. In fact, the standard error of the difference between predicted and obtained values, without the use of any ad hoc curve-fitting parameters to maximize goodness of fit, was .048 (less than half a scale unit). Perhaps more important, functional measurement analyses (cf. Anderson, 1970) showed that all three model components combined in precisely the manner implied by the equation (cf. Wyer, 1975). In other words, both conditional probabilities had exactly the influence they were predicted to have.

To the extent that subjects' inferences of the likelihood that the persons had attributes in the above study are equivalent to inferences of category membership (i.e., inferences that they belonged to a class of persons who had the attribute), these results support our assumption that the negative conditional is involved in categorical inferences. The stimulus materials used in the study, and the procedures employed, are very artificial, thus raising questions about the generalizeability of the conclusions drawn. Studies in more naturalistic situations also provide some support for the conceptualization, however. A study by Wyer (1972) is representative. Subjects, run in pairs, first described to their partner a particular attribute they personally possessed. (Each member of the pair described a different attribute.) Then, each subject received bogus feedback that the other perceived them to be either similar or dissimilar with respect to the attribute they had described. Both before and after receiving this feedback, subjects estimated their belief that they would like their partner (i.e., that the other was in the category "likeable"), followed by their belief that the partner possessed the attribute that the subjects had personally described and their conditional beliefs that they would like the partner if he or she did or did not have this attribute. Although Equation 9.1 was not as successful in describing the relations among these beliefs as it was in the previous study described, it was sufficiently accurate to justify its applicability in accounting both for subjects' postfeedback beliefs that they would like the other and for changes in these beliefs relative to prefeedback estimates.

Summary and Conclusions

In this section, we have discussed the processes that may underlie inferences that an object belongs to a social category. In doing so, we have skirted several fundamental questions concerning the nature of these inferences. In particular, we have ignored the question of whether these inferences are made by comparing the features of an object with (a) features of a prototypic member of the category, (b) features of a category exemplar that happens to be accessible in memory, or (c) features that characterize the category as a whole. Fortunately, detailed analyses of this matter are provided elsewhere (Lingle et al., 1984; Smith & Medin, 1981). The issues we have addressed are relevant regardless of which categorization criterion is used.

There is, of course, another aspect to the role of categorization processes in inference making. Once an object's category membership is inferred, the category may be used as a basis for further inferences about characteristics of the person or object that has been categorized. We consider this question in chapter 10, in the context of person judgment.

Belief Formation and Change: Inferences of the Validity of Propositions Based on General World Knowledge

A second common type of inference concerns the likelihood that a statement is true or false. The statement may refer to a specific person or event (e.g., "My girl friend is in love with another man") or to people or events in general ("Women are underpaid"). It may pertain to the past ("Shakespeare's plays were written by Frances Bacon"), present ("The depletion of the ozone layer is increasing the incidence of skin cancer") or future ("There will be a nuclear war within the next 10 years"). Moreover, it may pertain to a matter of fact, such as most of the examples above, or may be an evaluation or expression of opinion (e.g., "Ronald Reagan was a worse actor than he was a President," "The federal government should spend less money on defense and more on education"). Beliefs in all of these assertions, some of which are objectively verifiable and others of which are not, are essentially estimates of the likelihood that the assertions are members of the category "true." For this reason, these inferences are likely to bear some resemblance to inferences of category membership more generally. (For a more detailed discussion of the equivalence of the two types of categorical inferences, see Wyer, 1973, 1974; Wyer & Carlston, 1979). There are some important differences, however, which surround the type of knowledge that is brought to bear on these inferences, the factors that affect the accessibility of this knowledge, and the actual processes that govern its use.

For example, the criteria that are used to infer membership in social categories of the sort we considered in the last section ("conservative," "good graduate assistant," etc.) involve the comparison of an object's features with those that define the category or characterize its exemplars. In contrast, the criteria for inferring the truth of assertions of the sort described above may be beliefs in other propositions, stored as part of general world knowledge, that have causal or logical implications for them. For example, we may believe that there will be a nuclear holocaust in the next 10 years because we believe that the number of nuclear power plants being built is escalating, and that if this increase continues, the likelihood of a serious malfunction will increase correspondingly. Or, we may believe that Ronald Reagan had no understanding of what was going on in the country because he denied knowledge of the sale of arms to Nicaraguan rebels, and that if this is so, he must generally have been oblivious to the policies carried out by his subordinates.

A more formal statement of these inference processes, which is quite similar in form to that provided in the previous section for categorical inferences more generally, was proposed by Wyer and Hartwick (1980). They postulated that when people are asked to report their belief in a target proposition, B, they identify a referent bin containing information about the general issue to which the proposition is relevant and search the bin for knowledge that has implications for the validity of this proposition. The most easily accessible piece of knowledge that meets this criterion is likely to be used. In some instances, this knowledge may consist of a previously formed belief in the proposition being evaluated. Then, subjects may simply retrieve and report this belief without searching for additional knowledge. Often, however, a previously formed belief in the proposition either does not exist or is not easily accessible. Then, subjects identify another, "informational" proposition, A, that has implications for the target's validity, and mentally compute the likelihood that the target would be true if this informational proposition were true. They may also construe the likelihood that the target would be true even if the informational proposition were not true. In neither case is this conditional inference made on the basis of extensive deliberation. Rather, it is itself based on a small subset of semantic or general world knowledge about the causal, temporal and logical relations among the types of events to which the two propositions pertain. In many instances, for example, these inferences may be based on propositional molecules of the sort discussed in Chapter 4. (For an application of implicational molecule theory to belief inference processes, see Loken & Wyer, 1983.)

Finally, subjects theoretically arrive at an overall belief in the target by subjectively averaging the two conditional inferences, weighting each by their belief that the informational proposition is or is not true, respectively. This estimate may be described by the equation

$$P(B) = P(A)P(B|A) + P(\overline{A})P(B|\overline{A}) \qquad\qquad [9.3]$$

where $P(B)$, in units of probability, is the belief that target proposition B is true, $P(A)$ is the belief in the informational proposition A, $P(\overline{A}) = 1 - P(A)$ is the belief that A is not true, and $P(B|A)$ and $P(B|\overline{A})$ are conditional beliefs that B is true if A is and is not true, respectively. This equation is identical in form to Equation 9.1. In this case, however, the conditional inferences are not based on a comparison of features of a category with those of the object to be categorized. Rather, they are based on general world knowledge about the *causal* relations between the events described in the two propositions, A and B.

Perhaps the most theoretically important aspect of this analysis lies in its implications that subjects who are asked their belief in a proposition do not perform an exhaustive search of memory for knowledge that bears on its validity. Rather, they search for an "informational" proposition in a referent bin pertaining to the knowledge domain to which the target proposition is relevant, and use the first such proposition they encounter in the course of this search. The question that arises, therefore, is what factors determine the proposition that happens to be accessed. After presenting briefly some data bearing on the general validity of Equation 9.3 as a description of conditional inference processes, we turn to this issue in some detail.

Empirical Evidence

Numerous studies have examined the implications of Equation 9.3 as a description of how some beliefs are used to infer the validity of others. As this research has been summarized in detail elsewhere (McGuire, 1981; Wyer, 1974; Wyer & Carlston, 1979; Wyer & Hartwick, 1980), only one example is provided here. In this study (Wyer, 1970c), subjects read nine stories, each describing a different hypothetical social situation of the sort they were likely to encounter in daily life, either from newspapers or informal conversation. Each story was in two parts. The first part led subjects to believe that a particular event (A) was unlikely to occur, and also affected their beliefs that a second event, B, would occur if A did and did not take place. The second part of the story provided further information about the situation that increased subjects' belief that A would occur without affecting their perception of A's implications for the likelihood of B. In neither part of the story, however, was the target event itself explicitly mentioned. One story, for example concerned the likelihood of a student riot taking place at a particular university (A) and the likelihood that the university president would be fired (B). The first part of the story described the president as coercive and intimidating, thus establishing a low initial belief that a riot would occur. However, the second part provided new information that substantially increased this belief without affecting subjects' perceptions of its implications for whether the president would remain in office.

After reading each part of the story, subjects reported their belief that event B would occur, followed by their belief that A would occur and their conditional beliefs that B would occur if A did and did not occur. These estimates, reported along a scale from 0 (not at all likely) to 10 (extremely likely), were divided by 10 to convert them to units of probability. The last three probabilities were then combined in the manner dictated by Equation 9.3 to provide a predicted estimate of $P(B)$, for each subject separately, for each of the nine stories. Subjects' estimates of $P(B)$ after reading each part of the story are shown as a function of mean predicted values in Figure 9.2. Mean changes in $P(B)$ are shown as a function of predicted changes in the first panel of Figure 9.3.

The quantitative accuracy of the model is obviously very high. In fact, the standard error of the difference between mean predicted and mean obtained values of $P(B)$ was in each case less than .05 (i.e., less than half a scale unit), without the use of any ad hoc curve-fitting parameters.

Evidence that both conditional inferences played a role in subjects' overall beliefs in the target proposition is provided in the second panel of Figure 9.3, where predicted changes in $P(B)$ are plotted as a function of changes in only the first component of the equation. This component alone obviously cannot account for the results we obtained.

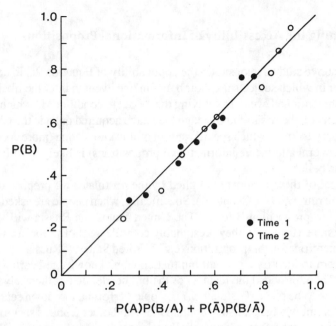

Figure 9.2. Mean beliefs in a target proposition B, or P(B), as a function of mean predicted values based on Equation 9.3. (Adapted from Wyer, 1970c.)

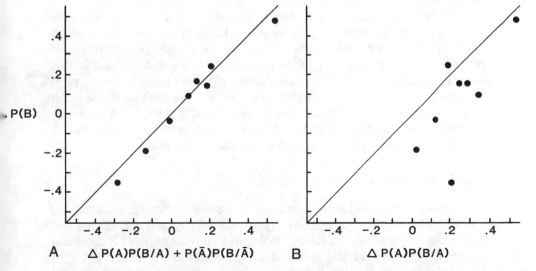

Figure 9.3. Mean changes in beliefs in proposition B as a function of mean predicted changes based on (a) Equation 9.3, and (b) beliefs associated with the positive conditional inference alone. (Adapted from Wyer, 1970c.)

Determining the Accessibility of Informational Propositions

The above study demonstrates the applicability of Equation 9.3 in describing the manner in which subjects use their belief in one event to infer the likelihood of another, unmentioned event. In applying the model to conditions in which subjects report beliefs on the basis of knowledge they have acquired outside the laboratory, it is necessary to know which specific subset of this knowledge (more specifically, which of several alternative informational propositions) is likely to be brought to bear on the belief.

Several of these factors are implied by the postulates we propose to govern information retrieval (see Chapter 5). Specifically, when people are asked to report their belief in proposition B (e.g., "The United States and Russia will go to war within the next 10 years"), they presumably compile a set of probe cues from the concepts mentioned in this proposition (e.g., "United States," "Russia," "war", etc.) and use them to identify a referent bin that contains knowledge bearing on these concepts. Then, provided the features of the bin header do not themselves permit the inference to be made (Postulate 5.7), people perform a top-down search of the bin itself for knowledge units that contain these and other features specified in the proposition and, therefore, are potentially relevant to the inference. To the extent that a knowledge unit contains an informational proposition with implications for the judgment, this proposition will be used and other, alternative informational propositions (contained in other knowledge units) will not be considered.

These considerations imply that at least three factors should affect the likelihood that an informational proposition will be identified: (a) the recency with which the proposition has been activated and used in the past (and, therefore, its proximity to the top of the bin), (b) the frequency with which the proposition has been thought about (and, therefore, the number of knowledge units in which it is contained), and (c) the strength of its association with features of the target proposition that is being judged (and, therefore, the likelihood that the representation containing it will be identified by the probe cues that govern the search). Data bearing on each of these factors are described briefly below.

1. Recency

Several experimental demonstrations that recently acquired concepts and knowledge are the most likely to be brought to bear on judgments were summarized in Chapter 5. More direct evidence that activating informational propositions affects subjects' beliefs in target propositions was obtained by Henninger and Wyer (1976). Subjects reported their beliefs in propositions composing 16 different pairs corresponding to A and B in Equation 9.3 (e.g., "The army is recruiting persons with below average intelligence," "The quality of the peace-time army is deteriorating," etc.). Conditional beliefs corresponding to $P(B|A)$ and $P(B|\bar{A})$ were also reported. The belief propositions associated with any given A-B pair were separated by at least 16 others in the questionnaire form. However, the order of these propositions was varied. When subjects reported their beliefs in B after reporting their beliefs in A and the conditional propositions, Equation 9.3 described the relations among these beliefs quite accurately. This suggests that subjects used their beliefs in A and its implications to infer the likelihood of B in the manner implied by this equation. When subjects reported their beliefs in B first, however, the descriptive accuracy of Equation 9.3 was poor. This indicates that when A had not been recently activated by reporting beliefs in it, subjects typically based their beliefs in B on some other informational proposition that happened to be more accessible.

The most interesting results reported by Henninger and Wyer were obtained in a second session one week later, when subjects reported their beliefs a second time. In this session, Equation 9.3 described the relations among their beliefs very well regardless of the order in which they were reported. As noted above, subjects who reported their belief in A last in Session 1 apparently based their beliefs in B on other criteria. Their consideration of A nevertheless led this proposition (or a copy of it) to be deposited on top of the bin from which knowledge about B was drawn. This apparently made it more accessible when subjects reported their beliefs in B in Session 2, and increased the likelihood that it was used. As a result, Equation 9.3 described the relations among subjects' beliefs accurately in the second session even when beliefs in B were reported first.

Effects of time delay. Considering an informational proposition at one point in time should affect target beliefs reported later only if other belief-relevant information has not been activated and used in the interim. In Henninger and Wyer's study, the issues to which the belief propositions were relevant were not ones that subjects considered every day, and other belief-relevant information was therefore unlikely to have been thought about in the one-week interval between experimental sessions. If the issue is one that subjects frequently consider in their daily lives, the effects of activating an informational proposition on beliefs in a target proposition should not persist over time.

An unpublished study by Wyer and Hartwick suggests that this is so. Subjects in this study first read over a series of belief propositions for the ostensible purpose of insuring that they were understandable. This "comprehension" task had the effect of activating the propositions without requiring that subjects report their beliefs in them. Included in the series were two pairs of propositions that occupied the positions of A and B in Equation 9.3. In one case, B was the proposition "Drinking coffee is desirable," that subjects continually receive relevant information about as a result of either drinking coffee themselves or observing others do so. The informational proposition, A, had either positive implications for it (i.e., "Drinking coffee keeps you alert"), or negative implications ("Drinking coffee gives you insomnia"). In the other case, B was a proposition, "Student use of (the university) health center will increase," that subjects were not expected to think about frequently, and A's implications for it were again either positive ("Dental services are scheduled to be provided at the health center") or negative ("Some doctors at the health center are about to loose their licenses"). After reading the "comprehension" list, subjects reported their beliefs in the target proposition (B). These beliefs were influenced by the implications of the particular informational proposition (A) that had been mentioned in the comprehension list, and this was true regardless of which issue was involved. When subjects again reported their beliefs one week later (without first performing the "comprehension" task), their beliefs about the use of the university health center were similar to those they had reported in Session 1, suggesting that they continued to base their inferences on the particular informational proposition that was activated in the earlier session. In contrast, although exposure to informational propositions had had a substantial effect on subjects' beliefs that drinking coffee was desirable in Session 1, these effects were not apparent in the second session. This suggests that in this case, other judgment-relevant information had been activated during the time interval between sessions, and that this information was used instead.

Individual differences. The tendency to think about judgment-relevant information may depend on the nature of the information itself, and the likelihood of activating and thinking about it spontaneously, as well as the likelihood of encountering it in daily life. One indication of this is provided by Goodhart (1985). Subjects in an initial session completed a questionnaire that assessed individual differences in the tendency to think positively or negatively about themselves and their abilities. Then, they completed several questionnaire indices of subjective well-being. They again reported their well-being one month later, without having first completed the measure of positive and negative thinking.

The well-being that subjects reported immediately after completing the positive and negative thinking measures was correlated positively with their tendency to engage in positive thinking but negatively with their tendency to engage in negative thinking. However, only negative thinking was related to subjects' reports of their well-being one month later. Apparently the differences in positive thinking that were measured in Session 1 did not reflect general tendencies to engage in this type of thinking spontaneously. Therefore, the positive thoughts that were activated by completing the initial questionnaire were used as a basis for inferring well-being shortly afterwards, but their effects were quite transitory. In contrast, the amount of negative thinking that was assessed by the questionnaire in Session 1 reflected a more pervasive tendency to engage in this thinking spontaneously. Therefore, it indicated the likelihood that negative thoughts would be generally accessible in memory, and, therefore, would be used as a basis for well-being judgments regardless of whether they had recently been reported in the experiment.

2. Frequency

The effect of differences in the frequency of activating a belief statement on its use as an informational proposition has not been directly investigated. To the extent that the individual differences in positive and negative thinking assessed in Goodhart's study reflected differences in the frequency of these thoughts (or copies of them) in memory, her study provides indirect evidence of this effect. A study by Wyer and Hartwick (1980), mentioned in Chapter 3, is also relevant. Briefly, subjects initially reported their beliefs in pairs of propositions occupying the positions of A and B in Equation 9.3. The informational proposition was in some cases plausible and in other cases implausible. In a second experimental session, subjects first recalled the propositions they had considered earlier. Then, they reported their beliefs in the target proposition (B) followed by their beliefs in the informational proposition (A), and its implications for B [$P(B|A)$ and $P(B|\bar{A})$]. Implausible informational propositions are more likely to stimulate thought than plausible ones in the course of reporting beliefs in them, and are likely to enter into a greater number of newly formed knowledge units as a result of this cognitive activity. If units that are formed are deposited in Permanent Storage in a bin pertaining to the issue at hand, the relatively greater frequency of units containing implausible propositions should make these propositions more likely to be retrieved and used. Consistent with this reasoning, subjects were more likely to recall informational propositions if they were implausible than if they were plausible. Moreover, Equation 9.3 was relatively more accurate in describing the relation between subjects' beliefs in implausible informational propositions and their beliefs in the target.

3. The Effects of Previous Cognitive Activity on the Associations Formed Between Informational and Target Propositions

When subjects search a referent bin for judgment-relevant information, they obviously do not retrieve and evaluate the implications of every piece of information they encounter in the course of this search (See Chapter 5). Rather, they identify a set of features that are likely to characterize the knowledge that is relevant, and consider only representations that contain these features. Thus, suppose a person is seeking information bearing on the likelihood that American industrialists are producing substandard merchandise. The person may compile a set of the key concepts mentioned in this statement (e.g., "American," "industrialists," "substandard merchandise," etc.) and may search for representations that contain them, passing over other representations that may also be contained in the bin being searched. If this is so, the person's retrieval and use of a particular informational proposition depends in part on whether it, or the knowledge unit that contains it, has features in common with the target proposition. In our example, therefore, it depends on whether the informational proposition in question either refers to concepts such as "American," "industrialists," or "substandard merchandise", or else is associated with other propositions (e.g., the target proposition itself) that do. These latter associations may have been formed as a result of previous experiences that led the subject to think about the concepts, or the propositions containing them, in relation to one another.

Some of the conditions in which these associations are formed were investigated by Wyer and Hartwick (1984). Subjects initially read a series of randomly ordered propositions for the ostensible purpose of deciding if they were understandable. (This "comprehension" task presumably made the propositions more accessible in memory.) These propositions included 16 A-B pairs, constructed such that one proposition in each pair (A) had implications for the second (B). One set, for example, was similar to the one described above; that is, A was the proposition "American industrialists are only concerned with making a profit," and B was the proposition "American industry is producing substandard merchandise." After reading the "comprehension" list, subjects reported their beliefs that 16 of the propositions were true, and reported their attitudes toward each of the remaining ones (i.e., how desirable it would be *if* the proposition were true). The 32 propositions were distributed over the two questionnaires so that subjects reported either (a) their beliefs in both propositions in a pair, (b) their attitudes toward both, (c) their belief in A and their attitude toward B, or (d) their attitude toward A and their belief in B. Then, in a later experimental session, subjects recalled as many of the propositions as they could. Finally, they reported their beliefs in all 16 of the target propositions, followed by their beliefs in the informational propositions and the two relevant "conditional beliefs", $P(B|A)$ and $P(B|\bar{A})$. Subjects in some conditions were expected to form an association between the two propositions (A and B) during the first session of the experiment, leading them to recall and use A in the second session when they were asked to think about B. In what conditions is this most likely to occur?

To answer this question, consider the types of information that subjects are likely to seek as bases for reporting beliefs and attitudes. Subjects who are asked to report their beliefs in a proposition are likely to search memory for information about an *antecedent* condition that has causal implications for its validity. Thus, in our example, subjects who are asked to report their belief that American industry is producing substandard merchandise may search for a proposition about a factor that affects the extent to which this is true. The informational proposition that was made salient by the initial familiarization task ("American industrialists are only concerned with making a profit") describes one such factor. Therefore, this proposition is likely to be identified and used. As a consequence, an association is established between the two propositions, and this knowledge unit (i.e., an A-B pair) is then transmitted to Permanent Storage.

In contrast, suppose subjects are asked to report their *attitude* toward the target proposition. In this case, they are unlikely to search for antecedents. Rather, they are likely to search for undesirable or desirable *consequences* of the situation described in the proposition (e.g., a consequence of American's producing substandard merchandise, such as "America's status as a world economic power will decrease"). In this case, the informational proposition activated by the familiarization task will not be considered, and, therefore, will not become associated with B. In summary, then, this reasoning implies that A will become more strongly associated with B if subjects have reported their belief in B in Session 1 than if they have reported their attitude toward it.

Quite the opposite effects should occur, however, when subjects consider the informational proposition. That is, if subjects in the first session are asked to report their belief in this proposition, they should search for an antecedent condition with implications for it (i.e., reasons why American industrialists are only concerned with profit). The target proposition that is activated by the familiarization task does not specify such a condition, and so it should not be considered. On the other hand, subjects who are asked to report their attitudes toward A should search for possible consequences of A's being true. The target proposition (that American industry produces substandard merchandise) describes such a consequence. Therefore, it may be identified and used, leading it to become associated with A. This means, then, that subjects who are later asked to report their beliefs in B will be more likely to recall and use the informational proposition A if they have previously reported their attitudes toward A during the first session of the experiment than if they have previously reported their beliefs in it.

These predictions were supported in Wyer and Hartwick's study. First, subjects' later recall of the target proposition (B) was more likely to cue the recall of the informational proposition that had implications for it (A) if subjects had previously reported their belief in B than if they had reported their attitude toward it. On the other hand, B was also more likely to cue the recall of A when subjects had previously reported their attitude toward A than when they had reported their belief in it. Moreover, an application of Equation 9.3 to the beliefs that subjects subsequently reported indicated that they were more likely to use A as a basis for reporting their beliefs in B when they had previously reported their belief in B, or their attitude toward A, than under other conditions.

Additional Considerations: Models vs. Processes

The processes we have postulated to underlie inferences of the validity of belief statements are quite consistent with the general formulation we have proposed. Moreover, Equation 9.3 appears to capture the nature of these processes. An application of this equation requires the assumption that one and only one informational proposition is applied in evaluating a target. (The implications of other propositions may sometimes be taken into account indirectly through the estimate of the negative conditional, $P(B|\bar{A})$.) There are limits to the generalizability of this assumption. There are certainly many instances in which more than one piece of information is taken into account. Nonetheless, the accuracy of Equation 9.3 in describing belief formation and change under the conditions in which it has been applied (for reviews, see Wyer, 1974; Wyer & Carlston, 1979) suggests that the assumption is quite reasonable a good proportion of the time.

An additional assumption underlying the applicability of Equation 9.3 has more general implications. We have assumed that this equation describes a conditional inference process, whereby subjects first mentally compute their beliefs that a target proposition, B, is true if an informational proposition, A, is and is not true, and then subjectively average the results of these two computations (weighting them by their beliefs that A is and is not true, respectively). In principle, however, this same equation could also describe two other, quite different cognitive processes.

One is suggested by the fact that Equation 9.3 would be a tautology if its components were true mathematical probabilities. Suppose, as Wyer and Goldberg (1970) originally assumed, that humans are intuitive probability theorists. If this were so, the success of Equation 9.3 in describing the relations among subjects' probability estimates would reflect a more general tendency for people to apply the laws of probability in inferring one belief from others.

A second conceptualization is suggested by McGuire's (1960, 1981) model of belief organization. He proposes that beliefs are organized in memory syllogistically, and subjects use syllogistic principles to infer the implications of one belief for another. Note that the first term on the right side of Equation 9.3 refers to subjects' beliefs in two premises of a syllogism ("A; If A, then B."), the conclusion of which is "B." The other term refers to beliefs in a second, mutually exclusive set of premises ("not- A; if not-A, then B."), the conclusion of which is also "B." Conceivably, subjects arrive at their beliefs in B by applying syllogistic reasoning, and these beliefs are predictable from the sum of their beliefs in the two mutually exclusive sets of premises that imply it.

Thus, three quite different processes—algebraic, probabilistic, and syllogistic—could potentially underlie the relation between the beliefs composing Equation 9.3. As we have noted, this equation often does an excellent job of describing both the qualitative and the quantitative relations among the beliefs that compose it. Even if the equation fit perfectly, however, it would not distinguish between the three alternative conceptions of the processes that underlie it. To make this distinction, one must apply criteria other than the fit of the equation per se.

When these other criteria are considered, the algebraic, conditional inference interpretation we proposed in this chapter seems most viable. If, for example, the fit of the model were a manifestation of a more general tendency for subjects to think probabilistically, other equations based on the laws of probability would also describe the relations among their beliefs and their inference of one belief from another. In fact, Equation 9.3 is the only equation based on the laws of mathematical probability that accurately describes social inference processes (cf. Wyer, 1976).

The evidence against its interpretation as a description of the general tendency for subjects to organize their beliefs syllogistically is more circumstantial. However, the "hydraulic" model of syllogistic belief organization initially proposed by McGuire (1960) suggests that activating one's belief in a conclusion should influence one's beliefs in the premises that logically imply it as well as vice versa. Data reported by Henninger and Wyer (1976) suggest that this is not the case.

Be that as it may, it is important to recognize that a model that describes the relations among beliefs, or the effects of information on judgments, is only as good as the conceptualization of the cognitive processes that it describes, and that its quantitative accuracy is a necessary but not a sufficient basis for inferring its validity. The attractiveness of Equation 9.3 lies in its consistency with the more general theoretical formulation of social information processing we propose, and not in its quantitative precision alone.

Heuristic Principles of Social Inference

As our discussion in the last two sections testifies, the processes that underlie inferences may often be idiosyncratic to the type of object being judged and the type of judgment being made. This is primarily because these processes are partly the result of social learning, and this learning is often domain specific. However, just as it would be ludicrous to assume that a single set of inference processes underlies all types of judgments in all stimulus domains, so would it be ludicrous to assume that all inference rules are domain- and judgment-specific. Anderson (1971, 1974, 1981) showed that algebraic principles of information integration may apply in a variety of different situations.

An important class of inference rules has been identified by Tversky, Kahneman, and their colleagues in their research on cognitive *heuristics* (for reviews, see Kahneman et al., 1982; Sherman & Corty, 1984). Heuristics are cognitive rules that people use to simplify difficult judgments. The application of such rules does not always produce correct judgments. However, it requires far less extensive processing than would be necessary to arrive at a judgment through other, more guaranteed procedures.

There have been many excellent reviews of heuristic principles (Kahneman et al., 1982; Sherman & Corty, 1984), and we do not duplicate these efforts. One observation is worth making, however. Specifically, a large number of the principles that have been uncovered by Tversky and others, as well as some principles that have not yet been conceptualized within this framework, may be the result of applying a single assumption, either implicitly or explicitly. In our discussion of categorical inferences, we noted the tendency for people to infer (a) the likelihood that an object belonged to a category if it possessed a particular set of features from (b) the likelihood that an object would have the features if it belonged to the category. This tendency may be a reflection of a much more general disposition to treat conditional relations between objects and events as biconditionals, and, therefore, to infer that if one condition A implies a second, B, then B implies A as well.

Empirical Evidence

There is, in fact, evidence to support this assumption. In a study by Wyer (1977), subjects were given a stimulus sentence of the form "Xs are Ys" (e.g., "businessmen are conservative") and were told to assume that the statement was true. Then, based on the statement, they inferred the likelihood that each of several "test" statements was true. The test statements included all possible relations between membership (or nonmembership) in one category and membership (or nonmembership) in the other. Thus, for example, if the test statement was "businessmen are conservative," subjects inferred the likelihood that a businessman is a conservative (*X is Y*) and also that a conservative is a businessman (Y is X), a nonbusinessman is not a conservative (*not-X is not-Y*) and a nonconservative is not a businessman (*not-Y is not-X*). These inferences were made in several stimulus domains that varied in terms of whether the categories were described in abstract terms (denoted by symbols) or were familiar. In the latter case, the stimulus statements were either likely to be true on a priori grounds (e.g., "businessmen are conservative") or unlikely to be true (e.g., "feminists are apathetic persons"). The results were very clear and generalized over the various types of stimulus statements we considered. That is, the test statement that was identical in form to the stimulus statement (*X is Y*) was judged most likely to be true (averaged over stimulus replications, $M = .971$). However, the statement that was judged next most likely was the statement of the form *Y is X* ($M = .706$), followed by *not-Y is not-X* ($M = .660$) and *not- X is not-Y* (M = .642). Thus, the test statement that was inferred to be most likely to be true was the one that directly implied the stimulus statement. However, the statement that was inferred next most likely was not its logical equivalent (*not-Y is not-X*) but rather, was the reverse conditional, *Y is X.*

Indirect evidence that subjects treat conditional relations as biconditionals was obtained in a quite different study of problem-solving by Wason (1968). Subjects in this experiment were given four cards. Each card contained a letter on one side and a number on the other. Subjects were asked to determine the validity of the proposition "All cards with a vowel on one side have an even number on the other side." They could do this by turning over any or all of the cards. In one case, for example, the cards given subjects showed the symbols A, B, 2 and 3. In this case, the proposition would be verified most easily by turning over the A and determining if it had an even number on the other side (i.e, by verifying the conditional statement "if a vowel, then an even number") and by turning over the 3 and determining if it had a consonant on the other side (i.e., verifying the logical equivalent "if not even, then not a vowel"). A much greater number of subjects, however, turned over the "2" card rather than the "3" card. In other words, they apparently attempted to verify the statement "if even, then a vowel," although the validity of this statement does not actually bear on the validity of the test proposition.

In combination, these two quite different studies support the assumption that subjects treat conditional relations as biconditionals. We are sufficiently confident of this inference rule to treat it as a formal postulate.

> Postulate 9.1. Subjects who infer that a stimulus condition implies another (that X implies Y) will also believe that the second implies the first (that Y implies X) and, therefore, will infer X from the existence of Y.

Applications

If Postulate 9.1 is valid, it has numerous implications for the inferences that people tend to make in a variety of situations. Numerous examples of this tendency pervade the literature, several of which are provided below.

1. Representativeness

The first example has already been noted in our previous discussion of categorical inferences. That is, people often believe that members of a particular social category have certain attributes. Consequently, they may infer that people who have these attributes belong to the category. Empirical examples of this tendency, noted earlier in this chapter, are described by Kahneman, and Tversky (1971) as applications of a representativeness heuristic. That is, subjects appear to base their inferences of a person's membership in an occupational group on attributes that are typical of group members independently of the a priori likelihood of belonging to the group.

2. Availability

Most people believe that if a particular type of stimulus has occurred very frequently, it will be easy to remember. Based on this belief, they may assume that if something is easy to remember, it is likely to have occurred frequently. Consequently, they may infer the frequency with which events have occurred from the ease with which instances of them come to mind. This rule, denoted by Tversky and Kahneman (1973) as an availability heuristic, has been demonstrated in numerous types of research (for a review, see Sherman & Corty, 1984). For example, people typically infer that more English words begin with k than have k as the third letter, although the reverse is actually true. This is presumably because it is relatively easier to think of words that start with k. In a more graphic example, 80% of subjects infer that death is more likely to occur as the result of an accident than as the result of a stroke. In fact, strokes cause far more deaths than do accidents (Lichtenstein, Slovic, Fischoff, Layman, & Combs, 1978). Accidents, however, are more often written up in vivid detail in newspapers and are portrayed more often on television. Thus, instances of them come to mind more easily.

3. Time Estimation

People typically find that events are easy to remember in detail if they have occurred recently. Consequently, they may infer that an event has occurred more recently if they can remember a lot about it. Thus, for example, they infer the relative recency of two events from the relative amount of information they can recall about them. The use of this heuristic was demonstrated by Brown, Rips, and Shevell (1985). Specifically, subjects' judgments of the temporal order of social events (e.g., the death of John Lennon vs. the eruption of Mt. St. Helens) were predictable from the relative amounts of knowledge they could retrieve about the events in question.

4. Simulation

People undoubtedly believe that events are easier to imagine happening if they are extremely likely to occur than if they are improbable. Consequently, they may infer that events are relatively more likely to occur if they are easy to imagine. Many demonstrations of the use of this "simulation" heuristic and its implications have been reported (cf. Kahneman & Tversky, 1982). For example, people believe that a disease with easy-to-imagine symptoms is more likely to affect them than an equally prevalent disease with hard-to-imagine symptoms (Sherman, Cialdini, Schwartzman, & Reynolds, 1982).

The effects of generating explanations of an event on predictions of its occurrence (cf. Ross, Lepper, Strack, & Steinmetz, 1977; Sherman, Skov, Hervitz, & Stock, 1981) provide additional examples. That is, subjects were asked to explain a hypothetical event involving either themselves or another, and then to predict the actual likelihood of its occurrence. The process of generating an explanation for the hypothetical event presumably made the occurrence of the event easier for subjects to imagine, and this increased their predictions of its likelihood.

A widely cited application of this principle is based on the further assumption that people will generally be more upset by the occurrence of an undesirable event if they can easily imagine how it might have been avoided (making it seem more likely that it *could* have been avoided) than if they cannot. In a study by Kahneman and Tversky (1982), subjects were asked to consider two persons who are caught in a traffic jam and arrive at the airport 30 minutes late for their scheduled departure. One person finds that his flight left on time, whereas the other learns that his flight was delayed and actually left only five minutes before he arrived. Which man is more disappointed by missing his flight? It is easier to imagine how five minutes could have been saved (by not stopping to buy a paper, by not having had a second cup of coffee, etc.), than to imagine how 30 minutes could have been saved. Consequently, the second passenger is more likely to believe that he could have made his flight, and so he is more disappointed by failing to do so.

5. Beliefs in a Just World

As a result of either personal experience, reading Horatio Alger, or religious training, people may often believe that persons will be punished or will otherwise experience adversity if they are bad, but that they will have joy and success if they are virtuous. Consequently, they may infer that people are likely to be bad if something terrible happens to them but are virtuous if they experience joy and success. This principle was first proposed by Lerner and Simmons (1966) as the "just world" hypothesis. That is, subjects who witness someone experience pain (for reasons that are ostensibly beyond the person's control) evaluate the person more negatively if they believe that the pain will continue than if they believe that the pain will be terminated or will be offset by positive experiences (Lerner & Simmons, 1966). More generally, subjects' disparagement of a sufferer is directly proportional to the amount of pain they believe that he or she has to endure.

6. Similarity and Attraction

People usually learn from experience that people like one another if they have similar attitudes or interests. Consequently, they may infer that people have similar attitudes or interests if they like one another. This of course is an implication of cognitive balance theory (Heider, 1958). (For reviews of empirical evidence, see Insko, 1984; Wyer, 1974).

7. Salience and Perceptions of Influence

People find from experience that they pay more attention to participants in a social interaction, and have better memory for what they say and look like, if the participants are influential, or if they dominate the interaction, than if they do not. Consequently, they may infer that a participant in an interaction has been more dominant or influential if they recall having paid more attention to him or her, or if they have better memory for what the person looked like. Several quite different studies support this possibility. For example, in a study by Taylor, Fiske, Close, Anderson, and Ruderman (1974), subjects observed a group discussion in which one person was rendered unique, either by virtue of his or her gender, race, or clothing. The unique participant was later judged to be more influential in the group discussion than persons who were similar to one another in these respects. Other studies show that subjects attribute more responsibility in conversations to people (themselves or others) who are in their real or imagined line of vision as they observe the conversation (Regan & Totten, 1975; Storms, 1973). These studies converge on the conclusion that salient aspects of a person, which may have nothing to do with the person's actual responsibility for what occurred in a situation, are likely to capture subjects' attention, and, therefore, to be contained in the representation of the situation that is stored in memory. Consequently, the person is likely to be attributed influence and responsibility for what went on in the situation when this representation is retrieved and used as a basis for judgments.

The above summary provides a sample of the variety of inferences that potentially result from general tendency to treat conditional relations as biconditionals, and therefore to infer one condition from a second based on general knowledge that the second is caused by the first. Many of the judgmental heuristics that have been identified can be interpreted as manifestations of this general tendency. To the extent Postulate 9.1 is valid, it can be used to generate several new hypotheses concerning the inference rules that people apply in various circumstances. We leave these hypotheses to the imaginative reader.

Chapter 10
Inference Making:
II. Judgments of Persons

In discussing inference processes in Chapter 9, we made few specific assumptions about the nature of the cognitive representations upon which these inferences were based. Inferences of category membership were assumed to involve a comparison of one set of features with another, without regard for how the features composing each set were organized in relation to one another. Our conception of inferences about the validity of belief propositions assumed that, for the most part, the cognitive basis for these inferences was another proposition that was often stored in a referent bin independently of other relevant knowledge about the issue of concern. More generally, however, inferences may be based on features of a more complex representation of a person, object, or event, the implications of which may sometimes conflict. In such instances, an understanding of inference processes requires knowledge of not only the content and structure of this representation, but also how this representation is used.

The need to acquire this knowledge is painfully evident from the typical lack of a systematic relation between the judgments that one makes and the implications of judgment-relevant information that one can recall. This evidence is apparent in research on person impression formation (Anderson & Hubert, 1963; Dreben, Fiske, & Hastie, 1979), communication and persuasion (Greenwald, 1968), attribution (Fiske, Taylor, Etcoff, & Laufer, 1979), and attitude-behavior relations (Loken, 1984). Several attempts have been made to specify the conditions in which a relation between recalled information and judgments does and does not exist (cf. Hastie & Park, 1986; Lichtenstein & Srull, 1985; 1987; Sherman, Zehner, Johnson, & Hirt, 1983). The results of these efforts converge on the conclusion that when people have a judgmental objective at the time they acquire information, they form a judgment-relevant concept of the target "on-line," as the information is received. Then, they use this concept as a basis for their judgments without reviewing the individual pieces of information that led to its formation. In this case, there is little relation between these judgments and the implications of the information that subjects can recall. In other cases, subjects' only objective at the time they receive information is to comprehend it. In such instances, they may store each piece of information in memory separately, and may retrieve it later, piece by piece, regardless of whether they are required to recall it or to use it to make a judgment. Under these circumstances, a relation between judgments and the implications of recalled information is more evident.

The research and theorizing to date, however, typically does not provide insight into precisely how the cognitive representations that have been formed from information are actually used. In most instances, this is understandable, because a precise conceptualization of the content and structure of these representations is not available. An exception, however, occurs with respect to the representations that are formed of persons. The nature of these representations is reasonably well established (see Chapter 7). In this domain, therefore, we can begin to examine judgment processes in some detail.

We begin by stating two postulates concerning the way in which person representations are used to make judgments. We then apply these postulates, in combination with the representational model we outlined in Chapter 7, to several issues, including (a) primacy vs. recency effects in recall and judgments and the relation between the information that is recalled about a person and judgments of this person, (b) the effects of making initial judgments of a person on later ones, (c) the effects of instructions to disregard information about a person on later judgments of the person, and (d) the role of stereotypes in person judgment. We also consider situational and individual differences in the use of person representations. A consideration of these issues provides insight not only into which aspects of a cognitive representation are used to make judgments, but also when and how they are used.

General Considerations

Imagine once again a situation in which subjects are asked to form an impression of someone on the basis of a series of different behaviors the person has performed. As we noted in Chapter 7, two types of representations are theoretically formed from this information. First, the behaviors are encoded in terms of trait concepts that they exemplify, leading trait- behavior clusters to be formed. Second, subjects extract an evaluative concept of the person (if possible, based on the first information presented about the person) and encode and organize the person's behaviors in terms of this concept as well.

Once formed, these representations are presumably transmitted to a referent bin in Permanent Storage, where they become available both for recalling the behaviors that were presented and for judging the person to whom they refer. However, the way that the representations are used to attain these two (memory and judgmental) objectives may differ considerably. Moreover, the use of these representations to make judgments theoretically depends, in part, on the type of judgment to be made.

Two postulates are proposed to govern the priorities with which representations are selected and their features used to make inferences.

Postulate 10.1 People who are asked to judge a characteristic of a person will search memory for a person representation whose central concept specifically pertains to this characteristic. If such a representation is found, they base their judgments on the implications of this concept, without a review of individual behaviors.

Postulate 10.2. If a representation whose central concept has direct implications for a judgment cannot be found, people will retrieve and use a general evaluation-based person representation as a basis for the judgment. This judgment will be based on both (a) the evaluative implications of the central person concept defining the representation, and (b) behaviors contained in the representation that have direct implications for the judgment.

Several implications of these postulates can be seen with reference to an example. Suppose subjects receive information consisting of several kind behaviors (b_k) followed by a series of dishonest ones (b_d). Based on assumptions outlined in Chapter 7, subjects should encode the two sets of behaviors as "kind" and "dishonest," respectively, forming two trait-behavior clusters pertaining to these traits. They should also extract an evaluative person concept based on the initial (favorable) behaviors (P+), and organize the behaviors around this concept as well. Because the last (dishonest) behaviors are evaluatively inconsistent with the concept, interbehavior associations should be formed between these behaviors and others (Postulate 7.7). The resulting representations should, therefore, resemble those shown in Figure 10.1.

Now, suppose subjects are asked to judge the target's kindness, honesty, likeableness, and intelligence. According to Postulate 10.1, subjects will judge the person's kindness and honesty by searching for and identifying the trait-behavior clusters whose central concepts bear directly on the judgments, and basing their judgments on the implications of these concepts. Therefore, they will report that the person is "kind" and "dishonest." Similarly, to judge the target's likeableness, they will retrieve the evaluative person representation and will use its central concept as a basis for their judgment, therefore reporting that the person is "likeable." Suppose, however, that subjects are asked to judge the person's intelligence. No representation exists whose central concept has direct implications for

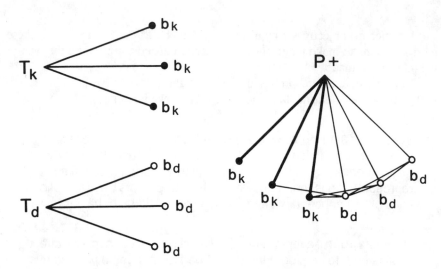

Figure 10.1. Trait-behavior clusters and evaluation-based person representations formed from three kind behaviors (b_k) followed by three dishonest behaviors (b_d).

this attribute. Therefore, according to Postulate 10.2, subjects will base their judgments on the evaluative implications of the person concept, P+, and the descriptive implications of any behaviors they identify in a partial review of those that have become associated with the concept. Because no intelligence-related behaviors are contained in the representation, this review will not yield any additional judgment-relevant information. Consequently, subjects will judge the target to be "intelligent," based on the evaluative implications of P+.

It is important to note the role of Postulate 7.4 in the formation of these representations and the predictions that are made. If the behaviors in our example had been presented in the reverse order, the two trait-behavior clusters would be the same, but the concept defining the person representation, which is based on the first behaviors presented, would be unfavorable. In this case, therefore, the target would theoretically be judged as stupid rather than intelligent. Alternatively, suppose the kind and dishonest behaviors were distributed haphazardly throughout the list that subjects read. The trait-behavior clusters would again be the same. However, because no clear evaluative concept can be formed from either the first behaviors or the later ones, an evaluative person representation would not be constructed. In this case, subjects who are later asked to judge the target's likeableness would be unable to base it on a previously formed evaluative concept of the person. Therefore, they must combine the evaluative implications of the two trait-behavior representations. We consider this process later in this chapter.

Postulates 10.1 and 10.2 obviously do not provide a complete account of interpersonal judgment. For one thing, they do not take into account the possible effects of information and general knowledge that is not contained in the representations formed of the particular person being judged. For example, subjects appear to use the transitory affective reactions that they happen to be experiencing at the time they judge an object as information about how they feel about this object, and therefore as a basis for judging the object's likeableness (cf. Griffitt & Veitch, 1971; for similar effects on self-judgments, see Schwarz & Clore, 1983). Moreover, people may sometimes assume that others are similar to themselves, and therefore use self-knowledge as a basis for judgments of others (cf. Ross, Greene, & House, 1977). We discuss these and other judgment phenomena in later chapters.

Nevertheless, the judgment postulates presented here, considered in combination with aspects of the model that concern the representation of person information in memory, are able to account for a wide variety of judgment phenomena identified in several research paradigms, and they generate several nonintuitive predictions that have empirical support. Moreover, they permit a conceptualization of these effects of person information on both recall and judgments under conditions in which judgments and the implications of recalled information appear unrelated or even inconsistent. These features of the model are conveyed in the examples provided below.

Primacy vs. Recency Effects in Recall and Judgment

Postulate 10.1 implies that when a representation has been formed whose central concept has direct implications for a judgment, this concept will be used as a basis for the judgment without reviewing the specific behaviors that also have implications for it. Therefore, although some of these behaviors may have implications that differ from those of the concept itself, these implications will not be reflected in the judgment that is made.

The results of several studies are interesting to consider in this light. These studies appear to show that the first information about a person has the primary influence on judgments, whereas the last (more recently acquired) information is better recalled. In a typical study using this paradigm (e.g., Dreben et al., 1979; Lichtenstein & Srull, 1987; Wyer & Unverzagt, 1985), subjects receive either a set of favorable behaviors describing a person followed by a set of unfavorable ones, or a set of unfavorable behaviors followed by a set of favorable ones. Their liking for the person described is influenced primarily by the initial behaviors presented, consistent with Postulate 7.4. However, the more recently presented behaviors are evaluatively inconsistent with the person concept that is formed on the basis of the initial behaviors, and, therefore, should stimulate the formation of interbehavior associations (Postulate 7.7). Thus, the behaviors may be better recalled for this reason and not because of their recency per se.

Suppose, however, that behavioral information is presented under conditions in which subjects do *not* have the goal of forming an impression, and, therefore, are unlikely to form a central evaluative person concept at the time the information is presented. In this event, subjects are forced to compute their evaluation of the person at the time they are asked to report it. To do this, they must use specific behaviors that they are able to remember. In this case, subjects' judgments and the implications of the behaviors they can recall should be more highly correlated.

A study by Lichtenstein and Srull (1987) supports this reasoning. In some conditions of this study, subjects read a series of behaviors with instructions to form an impression of the person who performed them. In other conditions, subjects read the behaviors with instructions to correct grammatical errors. Results obtained under impression formation objective conditions replicated previous findings. That is, subjects judged the target person on the basis of the first behaviors presented, whereas the most recent behaviors were better recalled. Moreover, the correlation of judgment with the evaluative implications of recalled behaviors was low. In contrast, judgments by subjects with the "comprehension" objective were based on the most recent behaviors presented, and these judgments were correlated positively with the implications of the behaviors that subjects recalled.

Effects of Predicting a Person's Behavior on Subsequent Trait Judgments

To reiterate, Postulates 10.1 and 10.2 imply that if subjects have formed a representation of a person whose central concept is directly relevant to the judgment they are asked to make, they will base their judgment on this concept without reviewing any more specific information. In some instances, however, none of the concepts defining subjects' representations of the person may have direct relevance for the judgment they wish to make. In these instances, subjects theoretically revert to their evaluation-based representation of the person and base their judgments on both (a) the evaluative implications of the central concept, and (b) behavioral features of this representation that have descriptive implications for the judgment.

Support for these hypotheses was obtained by Wyer, Srull, and Gordon (1984). Their study investigated the effects of predicting a person's behavior on judgments of the trait implied by this behavior. Subjects read a set of trait adjectives describing a particular attribute of the person. Then, they were asked to predict whether the person would perform a series of behaviors that implied not only this trait but also a second trait that had either similar or different evaluative implications. Thus, for example, subjects under some conditions were given trait adjectives describing a person as "honest," and then predicted whether the person would engage in either honest, kind behaviors (e.g., returning a lost wallet) or honest, unkind behaviors (e.g., telling a girlfriend that her hairdo was ugly). Finally, subjects judged the target with respect to both the original trait and the other trait implied by the predicted behaviors.

According to the proposed conceptualization, subjects should form an evaluative concept of the person on the basis of the trait adjectives describing him. When they are later asked whether the person would engage in the behaviors they are asked to consider, they presumably base their predictions on the descriptive consistency of these behaviors with the trait that led the evaluative person concept to be formed. Therefore, they should (and do) predict that the person would in fact perform these behaviors. During the course of making the predictions, however, the behaviors presumably become associated with the central person concept.

Therefore, suppose subjects are later asked to judge the target with respect to the trait implied by both the predicted behaviors and the trait adjective descriptions. These judgments should be based directly on the concept pertaining to this trait (Postulate 10.1), and, therefore, they should not be affected by the predicted behaviors. However, suppose instead that subjects are asked to judge the trait implied by the predicted behaviors alone. Because this trait is *not* directly implied by the central person concept, judgments of it will be based partly on the evaluative implications of this concept and partly on the descriptive implications of the predicted behaviors that have become associated with it (Postulate 10.2). These judgments, therefore, should be influenced by *both* sets of implications.

The results obtained by Wyer et al. (1984) show this to be the case. That is, subjects' judgments of the trait that were directly implied by the trait adjectives were based solely on the implications of these adjectives, and the implications of the behaviors subjects had predicted had no influence whatsoever. In contrast, subjects' judgments of the trait implied by the predicted behaviors alone were influenced by *both* the evaluative implications of the trait description and the descriptive implications of the behaviors. These data provide strong support for Postulates 10.1 and 10.2. (For further support of these conclusions in a different research paradigm, see Carlston, 1980a,b.)

Effects of Instructions to Disregard Information on the Later Recall and Use of this Information

A direct application of the proposed formulation to judgment processes involves our assumptions about the organization of information in Permanent Storage as well as the judgment postulates we have proposed here. These studies (Wyer & Budesheim, 1987; Wyer & Unverzagt, 1985) investigated conditions in which subjects' judgments are influenced by information that subjects have been told to disregard. This research is of particular interest as it bears on our assumptions concerning the independence of trait- behavior clusters and evaluation-based representations (Postulate 7.8) as well as on Postulates 10.1 and 10.2. The design of the studies is complex. Therefore, we first convey the essential features of the Wyer and Unverzagt study through an example, and then discuss general implications of this study in terms of the model we propose.

Reconsider our earlier example, in which subjects are asked to form an impression of someone on the basis of a series of kind behaviors followed by a series of dishonest ones. As shown in Figure 10.1 (and repeated for convenience in Figure 10.2a), subjects should form (a) a trait-behavior cluster associated with "kind," (b) a trait-behavior cluster associated with "dishonest," and (c) an evaluation-based representation of the person as "likeable" (based on the first information presented) that contains *both* kind and dishonest behaviors. All three representations are then stored in a referent bin pertaining to the person. If subjects, after receiving this information, are asked to judge the target's honesty, kindness, and likeableness, they should judge him as kind, dishonest, and likeable based on the central concepts of the representations that have direct implications for these judgments.

Now, however, suppose instead that subjects are told to disregard some of the behaviors that were initially attributed to the person. When will the implications of these behaviors persist to affect judgments despite these instructions, and how well will the behaviors be recalled? The answer to these questions depends in part on whether the behaviors to be disregarded occur first or last in the sequence of those presented, and when subjects are told to disregard them. These contingencies are described below.

1. Effects of Instructions to Disregard the First Information Presented Immediately After it is Received

First, suppose that immediately after receiving the initial (kind) behaviors, subjects are told that a mistake has been made, that the behaviors actually do not pertain to the person they are being asked to judge, and to disregard these behaviors. According to the formulation we propose, material that has been transmitted to Permanent Storage cannot be "erased." However, subjects in this condition should nonetheless be able to "restart" the impression formation process. Specifically, they may relabel the bin containing the representations they formed from the initial information as "to be disregarded." They may then construct new representations on the basis of the remaining information, and store these latter representations in a "judgment-relevant" bin. Therefore, in our example, they should form a trait-behavior cluster defined by "dishonest," and a new evaluation-based person representation, defined by a concept of the person that is unfavorable (P-), that is based on the last behaviors presented. The representations contained in the "to-be-dis-

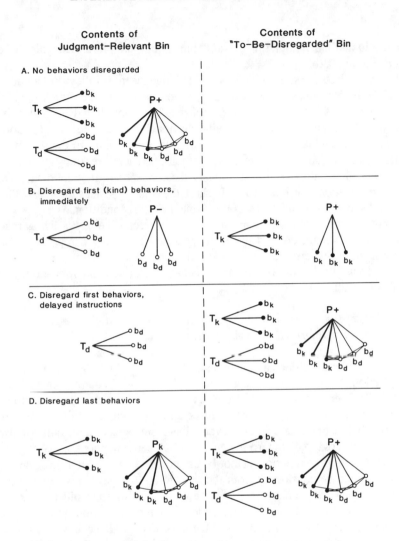

Figure 10.2 Trait behavior clusters and evaluation-based person representations contained in judgment-relevant and to-be-disregarded referent bins. Figures are based on the assumption that a series of kind behaviors is followed by a series of dishonest behaviors and (a) all behaviors are considered in making judgments, (b) subjects are told to disregard the first (kind) behaviors immediately after they are learned, (c) subjects are told to disregard the first behaviors after the remaining (dishonest) ones are presented, and (d) subjects are told to disregard the last (dishonest) behaviors. T_k and T_d represent kind and dishonest trait concepts, respectively, $P+$ and $P-$ represent favorable and unfavorable person concepts, and b_k and b_d represent kind and dishonest behaviors.

regarded" bin and the "judgment-relevant" bin should, therefore, resemble those shown in Figure 10.2b.

If these subjects are subsequently asked to judge the target, they should judge him to be both dishonest and dislikeable, based on the concepts defining the two representations contained in the judgment-relevant bin. They should also judge the target to be unkind. This is because no trait-behavior cluster has direct implications for this judgment, and no behavior with descriptive implications for the judgment is contained in the evaluative person representation. Therefore, the judgment is based only on the evaluative implications of the concept defining the evaluative person representation (Postulate 10.2). In short, the behaviors that subjects are told to disregard should have little effect on judgments in this condition.

However, suppose subjects are now asked to recall the to-be-disregarded behaviors. They should do this by identifying and retrieving a representation contained in the "to-be-disregarded" bin. Because both of the representations stored in this bin contain only to-be-disregarded behaviors, these behaviors should be recalled quite well.

2. Effects of Instructions to Disregard the First Information Presented After the Remaining Information has been Received

Now consider conditions in which subjects are also told to disregard the first set of behaviors, but this is not done until all of the remaining behaviors have been presented. Different considerations arise in this case. Under these conditions, subjects have formed all three of the representations shown in Figure 10.2a (i.e., the two trait-behavior clusters and the evaluation-based person representation) by the time they are told to disregard the behaviors. Because the contents of the bin containing these representations cannot be erased, the only way to segregate the representations to be considered from the ones to be disregarded is to copy the judgment-relevant representations into a new bin, labelling the old one "to be disregarded." In this case, the central concept of the evaluation-based person representation was defined on the basis of the to-be-disregarded behaviors. Therefore, the only representation that is relevant to judgments is the trait-behavior cluster that is formed from the last behaviors presented. Consequently, the two bins should contain the representations shown in Figure 10.2c.

If subjects are asked to make trait and likeableness judgments of the target under these conditions, they will presumably base both types of judgments on the implications of the concept defining the trait-behavior cluster they formed from the last behaviors. Consequently, as in the first condition we considered, neither trait nor likeableness judgments should be influenced by the to-be-disregarded behaviors. Suppose, however, that subjects are asked to recall the behaviors they were told to ignore. Again, they should do this by searching the contents of the to-be-disregarded bin for these behaviors. Because all of the initially-formed representations are contained in this bin, the particular behaviors to be disregarded will be difficult to identify. Therefore, unlike the first condition we considered, the to-be-disregarded behaviors will be recalled relatively poorly.

3. Effects of Instructions to Disregard the Last Information Presented

Finally, suppose subjects after receiving all of the target person's behaviors are told to disregard the last set of behaviors presented. Again, all three representations have been formed by the time these instructions are given. In this case, the concept defining the evaluation-based person representation as well as the judgment-relevant trait-behavior cluster should be copied into the judgment-relevant bin, as shown in Figure 10.2d. Note that the to-be-disregarded behaviors are contained in the representation, and cannot be segregated from the other behaviors in the representation.

Therefore, suppose subjects are asked to judge the trait implied by the behaviors they have been told to disregard. As in the previous case, they will not base their judgments on the contents of the trait-behavior cluster they are supposed to ignore. Instead, they will revert to the evaluation- based representation, and will base their judgments on: (a) the evaluative implications of the central concept, and (b) a partial review of the behaviors contained in the representation for some that have descriptive implications for the judgment (Postulate 10.2). Because the behaviors to be disregarded are contained in the representation, these behaviors will influence trait judgments despite the instructions to ignore them. Note, however, that these behaviors should *not* influence judgments of the target's likeableness. This is because the evaluative person concept is based on the first behaviors presented. Therefore, subjects' liking judgments are uninfluenced by the last behaviors in the series, regardless of whether or not subjects are told to ignore these behaviors.

If subjects are asked to recall the behaviors they were told to disregard, however, they should retrieve material in the to-be-disregarded bin to attain this objective. Therefore, for reasons noted earlier, these behaviors should be recalled poorly despite their influence on trait judgments.

The recall and judgments predicted under the three conditions described above are summarized in Table 10.1. Considered in combination, these predictions are complex but interesting. That is, behaviors at the beginning of the series that subjects are told to disregard should have little influence on either trait or likeableness judgments, and this should be true regardless of whether subjects are told to disregard these behaviors immediately after they are presented or not until the remaining ones have been learned. However, subjects' recall of the to-be-disregarded behaviors will be better in the first condition than in the second. In contrast, behaviors at the end of the series that subjects are told to disregard *should*

TABLE 10.1

Predicted Effects of To-Be-Disregarded Behaviors on Trait Judgments,
Likeableness Judgments, and Recall

	Predicted effect of to-be-disregarded behaviors on		
	Judgments of trait implied by to-be-disregarded behaviors	*Likeableness judgments*	*Recall of to-be-disregarded behaviors*
Instructions to disregard first behaviors immediately after they are presented	None	None	High
Instructions to disregard first behaviors after the remaining behaviors are presented	None	None	Low
Instructions to disregard last behaviors presented	Positive	None	Low

affect trait judgments but not likeableness judgments, although subjects' recall of the behaviors is poor.

Results reported by both Wyer and Unverzagt (1985) and Wyer and Budesheim (1987) confirm these predictions. In doing so, they not only support Postulates 10.1 and 10.2 but, more generally, indicate that different criteria are used as a basis for different types of judgments. Moreover, these judgments can neither be predicted directly from each other, nor can they be predicted from the specific information that subjects could recall at the time the judgments were made.

There are nevertheless many contingencies in the generalizeability of the effects reported above. The study by Wyer and Budesheim (1987) examined these contingencies and, in the process, identified an additional factor that must be considered in understanding judgment processes under the conditions we have constructed. These matters are described briefly below.

4. Effects of Behavior Relatedness

The behaviors that subjects were told to disregard in Wyer and Unverzagt's study (see also Wyer & Budesheim, 1987, Experiment 1) were descriptively unrelated to the behaviors they were supposed to consider. That is, the two sets of behaviors had implications for traits along two totally different dimensions. Different considerations arise when the two sets of behaviors imply values along the same trait dimension.

First, suppose the to-be-disregarded and not-to-be-disregarded behaviors imply opposite poles of the same dimension (e.g., the first behaviors are honest and the last ones are dishonest). In this case, the representations formed, and where they are stored under various conditions, should be analogous to those that were formed and stored when the two sets of behaviors were descriptively unrelated (see Figure 10.2a). (Note that two different trait-behavior clusters are formed, one pertaining to "honest" and the other to "dishonest.") However, two important considerations alter the predictions that are made concerning the effects of these representations on judgments.

Suppose subjects are told to disregard the last (dishonest) behaviors presented. In this case, the concept defining the remaining (honest) trait- behavior cluster, which is transferred to the judgment-relevant bin, has descriptive implications for the same trait to which the to-be-disregarded behaviors were relevant. Therefore, according to Postulate 10.1, judgments of this trait will be based on the implications of this concept rather than the evaluation-based person representation. Consequently, the to-be-disregarded behaviors should have no influence on trait judgments under this condition. This is in contrast to the analogous condition in which the two sets of behaviors are descriptively unrelated.

Trait judgments should also be based on the trait-behavior cluster containing the not-to-be-disregarded behaviors when the to-be-disregarded behaviors are first but subjects are not told to ignore them until after the remaining ones are learned. An additional consideration arises here, however. That is, when the first and last behaviors presented exemplify traits along the same dimension, subjects may try to interpret the last behaviors in a manner that is consistent with the earlier ones. For example, they may interpret dishonest behaviors as less dishonest when the behaviors that precede them imply honesty than when they do not. This means that under conditions in which subjects are not told to disregard the first behaviors until after the later ones have been presented, the first behaviors may indirectly affect trait judgments that are based on the remaining (last) behaviors.

Finally, consider conditions in which the behaviors to be disregarded are descriptively *consistent* with the remaining ones; that is, they imply the same trait as the ones to be considered. The major difference between this condition and the others we have described is that in this case, subjects should form only one trait-behavior cluster rather than two. Therefore, under conditions in which subjects are not told to disregard any behaviors until all of them have been presented, only one trait-behavior cluster exists. If subjects do not transfer this (biased) cluster to the bin containing judgment-relevant information, this means that trait judgments will be based on (a) the implications of the evaluation-based person representation and (b) a review of the behaviors contained in it. Because the to-be-disregarded behaviors are contained in this representation, they may have an influence on judgments. This means, then, that trait judgments in this condition *will* be influenced by behaviors that subjects are told to disregard after all of the information is presented, regardless of whether these behaviors were first or last in the series.

Although these predictions seem complex, they can be summarized fairly easily:

1. When the behaviors that subjects are told to disregard are descriptively unrelated to the behaviors they are supposed to consider (as in Wyer and Unverzagt's (1985) original study), they will have an influence on trait judgments only when they are presented last.

2. When the behaviors that subjects are told to disregard are descriptively inconsistent with the remaining ones, they will have an influence on trait judgments only when they are presented first and subjects are not told to ignore them until after the remaining behaviors have been presented.

3. When the behaviors that subjects are told to disregard are descriptively consistent with the remaining ones, they will influence trait judgments under both of the above conditions.

Wyer and Budesheim's (1987) results were perfectly in line with these predictions.

5. Adjustments for Bias

An additional factor that is necessary to consider in the present context should be mentioned. That is, subjects who are told to disregard information they have received may be aware that this information may have influenced their impressions of the person being described. Therefore, they may attempt to adjust the judgments they *report* in order to compensate for this possible bias. (For evidence of adjustment processes in other research paradigms, see Schul & Burnstein, 1985; Thompson, Fong, & Rosenhan, 1981.) This may be partly the result of an intrinsic desire to respond correctly, and partly the result of applying general rules of communication that emphasize informativeness and accuracy (Grice, 1975; Higgins, 1981; Kraut & Higgins, 1984; for a more complete discussion of response generation processes, see Chapter 11).

Subjects are most likely to believe that their subjective judgments are biased under those conditions in which a bias actually exists. These are presumably the conditions in which to-be-disregarded behaviors are predicted to have an influence based on the theoretical considerations outlined above. However, the *magnitude* of the bias that subjects perceive to exist, and, therefore, the magnitude of their adjustment, may depend on the consistency of the implications of the biasing information with general world knowledge. In the present context, subjects may be predisposed to assume on a priori grounds that a person is likeable and engages in favorable behavior (Kanouse & Hanson, 1971; Wyer, 1970a). If this is so, subjects may perceive themselves to be less influenced by favorable information than by unfavorable information. Consequently, they may adjust less to compensate for the influence of favorable information that they are told to ignore. This implies that under those conditions in which to-be-disregarded behaviors are predicted to have an influence, this influence will appear to be greater when the behaviors are favorable than when they are unfavorable.

In fact, this was invariably the case in both Wyer and Unverzagt's (1985) study and Wyer and Budesheim's (1987). That is, in all conditions in which subjects' judgments were predicted to be influenced by to-be-disregarded behaviors, the magnitude of this influence on reported judgments was greater when the to-be-disregarded behaviors were favorable than when they were unfavorable. In fact, when the to-be-disregarded behaviors were unfavorable, they sometimes had a negative, or *contrast* effect on reported judgments. This suggests that in this condition, subjects attempted to adjust too much for the bias of the to-be-disregarded information.

The judgment phenomena we have discussed in this section are admittedly complex. However, the complexity is inherent in the phenomena themselves. To understand judgment processes, one must not only know the nature of the cognitive representations that are formed on the basis of the information that bears on the judgment, but also how these representations are used. Moreover, as implied by our discussion of adjustment processes, one must also understand the factors that determine how subjective judgments, once they are computed, are transformed into an overt response (see Chapter 11). The theoretical formulation of person impression formation we have proposed, when considered in the context of the overall model we have presented in this volume, appears useful in conceptualizing these judgment phenomena.

The Role of Stereotypes in Person Concept Formation and Judgments

Postulates 10.1 and 10.2 imply that subjects base their judgments whenever possible on the implications of the central concept they may have formed of the person at the time they receive the information. They revert to specific information about the person only if a judgment-relevant concept cannot be identified. Factors that determine the nature of this central concept are, therefore, likely to have a profound influence on the judgments that are made later. One of the major determinants of this concept, implied by Lichtenstein and Srull's (1987) research, is the processing objective that subjects have at the time the information is received. Another consideration may be the amount of cognitive effort that subjects anticipate having to expend in order to attain their judgmental objective (cf. Fiske & Pavelchak, 1986). Subjects who have two alternative criteria available for forming a general judgment-relevant concept of a person may be inclined to choose the alternative that is easier to apply. This is particularly true when they expect the judgmental task confronting them to place considerable demands on their cognitive resources. The judgments they ultimately make of the target, based on the concept they form, may be correspondingly influenced.

These considerations have implications for the role of stereotypes in judgment. People may often form prototypic representations of persons who belong to different social, ethnic, or occupational groups. Each such representation is presumably defined by a central concept similar to those that characterize the representations of individuals. If a particular person's membership in such a group is known, it provides a possible basis for forming a central concept of this person, much as do personality trait adjectives in the typical person impression paradigm. (For evidence that trait adjectives and group stereotypes can have similar effects on the person representations that are formed, see Wyer & Martin, 1986.) Moreover, it is much easier to use this criterion than it is to extract a person concept from several different pieces of specific information about the person. Therefore, when subjects anticipate having to make a judgment that requires substantial cognitive work, they may be inclined to use this stereotype-based concept as a theme to organize the specific pieces of information about the person rather than attempting to derive a concept through a more analytic assessment of the diverse implications of this information. This means that judgments of the person will be more influenced by the stereotype in the former conditions than in the latter.

Empirical Evidence

Research by Galen Bodenhausen and his colleagues (Bodenhausen, 1987; Bodenhausen & Lichtenstein, 1987; Bodenhausen & Wyer, 1985) provides strong support for these assumptions. In one study, (Bodenhausen & Wyer, 1985, Experiment 2), subjects reviewed the case file of a criminal for the purpose of making a parole recommendation. The criminal was assigned a name that identified him as Hispanic ("Carlos Ramirez"), white Anglo-Saxon Protestant ("Ashley Chamberlaine"), or ethnically nondescript ("John T."). Moreover, the crime the person had committed was stereotypic of either lower-class Hispanic criminals (assault in a bar) or of upper-middle class, white-collar criminals (forgery and embezzlement). Finally, the material in the case file itself, which contained indications of the target's background and behavior in prison, alluded in some cases to possible mitigating life circumstances surrounding the particular crime that was committed, suggesting that it was unlikely to recur. In other cases, this latter information was not provided. Subjects after reading the information first made a recommendation for parole, and then were asked to recall the information contained in the case file.

Table 10.2 shows parole recommendations as a function of the implications of the mitigating life circumstances information (presented or not) and whether the target's name activated a stereotype that was consistent with the crime committed, a stereotype that was inconsistent with the crime, or no stereotype at all. The

TABLE 10.2
Effects of Stereotyped Activation and Mitigating Life Circumstances
Information on Parole Recommendations (adapted from Bodenhausen
& Wyer, 1985)

	Type of stereotype activated		
	Consistent with crime	Inconsistent with crime	None
Mitigating life circumstances information presented	5.93	7.50	8.36
Mitigating life circumstances information not presented	5.64	8.43	5.79

implications of these data are very clear. First, consider conditions in which no stereotype was activated. Here, subjects recommended parole more strongly when the case information suggested that mitigating circumstances surrounded the original crime. When a stereotype was activated, however, the influence of this information disappeared. Instead, subjects were less inclined to recommend parole if the target's crime was stereotypically consistent with the ethnic group to which he belonged than if it was inconsistent. This was true regardless of whether mitigating life circumstances information was provided.

In interpreting these results, it is important to consider subjects' recall of the information as well. If subjects had simply ignored the case file information when a stereotype was activated, their recall of this information should have been generally less than it was when no stereotype was activated. This was not the case. In fact, subjects' recall of the case information was often an interactive function of the implications of the life circumstances information presented and the consistency of the crime with the stereotype. (For example, subjects recalled crime-relevant life circumstances information less well, but other background information better, when the crime was stereotypically consistent with the target's group membership than when it was not.) In combination, these data suggest that when the target's group membership activated a stereotype, subjects formed a concept of the person based on this stereotype. They then processed the information in the case file with reference to this concept, leading them to remember some aspects of this information better than others (for a detailed discussion of these effects and their implications, see Bodenhausen & Wyer, 1985). Despite this processing, however, subjects based their parole recommendations on only the implications of their stereotype-based central concept of the target without reviewing features of the representation itself. Thus, as in many other studies we have cited, there was little relation between the effects of stereotype and case information on judgments and their effects on the type and implications of the information that subjects could recall.

Considered in isolation, Bodenhausen and Wyer's results would suggest that the use of stereotypes to make judgments takes priority over the use of more specific information about the person. In other words, individuating information about the target had an influence only when a stereotype was not activated. This conclusion must be evaluated in the context of results reported by Locksley, Hepburn, and Ortiz (1982). In this study, subjects were given information about a target person's gender and also specific information that the person's behavior was either assertive or unassertive. In this case, subjects based their judgments almost entirely on the behavioral information, and the stereotype-based conception of females as less assertive than males had no effect. These results may appear contradictory to Bodenhausen and Wyer's conclusion. That is, they suggest that the use of individuating information about a person takes priority over the implications of stereotypes.

There is a very good explanation of this difference, however. Bodenhausen and Wyer note that the judgment task constructed by Locksley et al. was a very simple one, in which the traits being judged could be directly inferred from the behavioral information presented without much additional thought. In contrast, the judgments made by Bodenhausen and Wyer's subjects were potentially much more complex in principle, requiring an evaluation and integration of several different types of information. As suggested earlier, subjects may use stereotypes as a basis for forming their general concepts of a person, and ultimately for making judgments of this person, primarily when they expect the judgment task to be complex and processing demand to be high.

A subsequent study by Bodenhausen and Lichtenstein (1987) clearly demonstrates that this is the case. In their study, subjects read a trial transcript concerning a person who was accused of assault in a bar. Some subjects read the transcript with the expectation that they would be asked to decide the defendant's guilt. Others read it with the expectation that they would be asked to judge his aggressiveness. The material contained evidence that the defendant was either generally aggressive or generally non-aggressive. Moreover, the defendant was identified by a name that was either Hispanic or nondescript. After receiving the information, subjects were asked to make both guilt and aggressiveness judgments (that is, both the judgment they expected to make and the one they did not expect). Based on the considerations raised above, it seems reasonable to suppose that subjects who anticipated making an aggressiveness judgment would use the individuating information about the target that bore directly on this attribute to form their concept of the target. In contrast, subjects who anticipated making a (complex) guilt judgment should be more likely to organize the information around a concept based on the stereotype. These concepts, once formed, should be used as bases for judging the target. Moreover, this should be true regardless of which judgment is ultimately made.

TABLE 10.3
Judgments of Defendant's Aggressiveness and Guilt as a Function of
Defendant's Ethnicity and Type of Judgment Anticipated (adapted from
Bodenhausen & Lichtenstein, 1987)

	Defendant's ethnicity	
	Hispanic	Nondescript
Aggressiveness judgment anticipated		
Agressiveness judgment	5.09	4.73
Guilt judgment	4.70	4.97
Guilt judgment anticipated		
Aggressiveness judgment	5.12	4.48
Guilt judgment	5.27	3.38

Data pertaining to both types of judgments, summarized in Table 10.3, unequivocally support this reasoning. Subjects who had anticipated judging the target's aggressiveness based their judgments on the individuating information contained in the case file, and the defendant's ethnicity had very little effect. This was true both when subjects judged the defendant's aggressiveness and when they judged his guilt. In contrast, subjects who had expected to judge the defendant's guilt based their judgments on the stereotype that was activated by his name (replicating Bodenhausen and Wyer's results), and this was also true regardless of which judgment they actually made.

Note more generally that the influence of stereotypes depended on subjects' processing objective at the time information was received (which presumably affected the nature of the central concept that was formed of the target), and not the type of judgment they ultimately reported. These results are therefore quite consistent with the more general conceptualization we propose concerning the use of person representations in making judgments.

A Note of Caution

Bodenhausen and Lichtenstein's results exemplify a more general point, namely, that it is impossible to make universal statements concerning whether stereotypes will or will not influence judgments of individuals. A person's social or ethnic group membership may enter into judgments in a variety of ways that depend not only on the type of judgment being made but also the judge's attitude toward and relation to the stereotype group. Two further examples from our own laboratory are representative (see Hamilton, 1981, for a more extensive summary of stereotyping research).

Effects of gender stereotypes on occupational suitability judgments. Futoran and Wyer (1986) found that information about a job candidate's gender combined additively with the effects of information about attributes of the candidate to affect judgments of the candidate's suitability for a gender-stereotyped occupation. In particular, candidates' gender had the same effect on judgments of their suitability regardless of whether the candidates were explicitly described as having attributes that were stereotypically associated with males or females, and regardless of whether these attributes were relevant or irrelevant to performance in the job. This means that the effect of gender on job suitability judgments was not mediated by subjects' inferences that a candidate had judgment-relevant attributes that were typical of males or females. Rather, subjects considered "male" and "female" to be attributes in their own right that were relevant to performance in jobs that were typically filled by men and women, respectively, and, therefore, they used gender in much the same way they used other job-related attributes (assertiveness, intelligence, sensitivity, etc.).

A possible reason for this is suggested by Hong and Wyer (1989): when a target's membership in a stereotyped group is conveyed along with information about other attributes of the target, it may not become conceptually separated from these attributes. If this is so, the influence of a stereotype should be more apparant when subjects learn about the target's membership in the stereotyped group some time before other information is conveyed, and, therefore, are likely to form an initial concept of the target on the basis of its group memberhsip alone.

There is no evidence of this in the stimulus domain considered by Futoran and Wyer. However, Hong and Wyer's (1989) study of the effects of country of origin on product evaluations, is suggestive. Specifically, subjects learned that a product was made in a country with a reputation for manufacturing either high quality or low quality merchandise. They also received information about specific attributes of the product that were either favorable or unfavorable. When the product's country of origin was conveyed in the same experimental session as the attribute descriptions, both types of information affected judgments, and these effects were similar regardless of which type was presented first. In this case, therefore, the product's country of origin was simply treated as one of several attributes. When the product's country of origin was conveyed in a different experimental session, 24 hours before the attribute information, however, it not only had a greater direct impact on evaluations of the product but it influenced the interpretation of the later attribute information and, therefore, affected the impact of this information as well. As we mentioned, it is hazardous to overgeneralize the effects of stereotypes over judgment domains. These results nevertheless raise the possibility that introducing a time delay between gender and attribute information in Futoran and Wyer's study might have increased the likelihood that a stereotype was activated and used as a basis for judgments here as well.

Effects of stereotypes and prior attitudes on judgments of sorority members. In a study of the effects of stereotypes on judgments of sorority members, Lambert (1987) gave subjects a passage describing behaviors and attitudes of a target person that suggested that she was either gregarious (an attribute that was stereotypic of sorority members) or nongregarious (nonstereotypic of sorority members). In addition, the target's membership (or nonmembership) in a sorority was indicated unobtrusively by providing background information that indicated her campus living accommodations. Subjects who were themselves sorority and fraternity members (and had favorable attitudes toward sorority members, as determined by data collected in an earlier experimental session) rated the target more favorably if she ostensibly belonged to a sorority than if she did not, and this was true independently of information bearing on her gregariousness. In other words, these subjects used membership in a sorority as an independent basis for judgments in much the same way that Futoran and Wyer's subjects used gender to judge occupational suitability.

In contrast, subjects who did not belong to sororities and fraternities (and had negative attitudes toward sororities), did not judge the target on the basis of her group membership alone, but took the implications of her behavior into account as well. Specifically, they based their judgments on how *typical* the target was of sorority members, evaluating her favorably (relative to nonsorority members who behaved similarly) if her behavior was atypical (nongregarious) and unfavorably if it was typical (gregarious). There are several possible interpretations of these findings.[1] The general point, however, is that although ingroup and outgroup members had descriptively similar stereotypes of sorority members, they nevertheless used the stereotype differently in making judgments of the person to whom it pertained.

Thus, there are no simple answers to the question of how group stereotypes affect judgments of individual persons. Their influence depends heavily on the type of judgment being made as well as on the particular characteristics of the stereotype. It may, therefore, be more fruitful to focus attention on the particular types of judgments and to specify the role of group membership information (along with other types of knowledge) in the context of conceptualizations that underlie these judgments, rather than attempting to develop broad-based generalizations (or more accurately, overgeneralizations) about the influence of stereotypes per se.

Dual Processing Approaches to Person Inferences

The complexity of the information processing demands that subjects anticipate being placed on them may be only one of several factors that influence the

---

1. One plausible account of these findings is that pro-sorority subjects, who either belonged to sororities themselves or were closely affiliated with them (i.e., belonged to fraternities), perceived sorority (in-group) members to be more heterogeneous than did non-sorority (out-group) subjects (Park & Rothbart, 1982). Therefore, they may have been less likely to consider the target's typicality for this reason.

cognitive basis for forming concepts of a person, and ultimately, the judgments that are made of them. Additional considerations are raised in the context of two recent formulations of person judgment proposed by Fiske and Pavelchak (1986) and Brewer (1988). Both models assume that people who anticipate judging a person sometimes use a general concept of the person as a basis for their judgment, but at other times combine the implications of specific pieces of knowledge they have about the person's behavior and attributes. The models differ in the factors they postulate to influence the adoption of these two judgmental strategies. Fiske and Pavelchak (1986) focus on characteristics of the information presented that lead subjects to use one or the other strategy. Brewer (1988) focuses to a greater extent on motivational and individual difference variables. The conceptualizations are not incompatible (but see Fiske, 1988), and both are generally consistent (in spirit, if not in detail) with the more general conceptualization we have proposed.

Informational Determinants of Category-based Judgments (Fiske & Pavelchak, 1986)

Fiske and Pavelchak (1986) restrict their attention to conditions in which a subject is asked to make an evaluative (i.e., likeableness) judgment of a person on the basis of information about the person's membership in a social category, the person's behaviors and specific attributes, or both. The processes they assume to occur under these conditions, which are shown pictorially in Figure 10.3a, are summarized as follows:

1. The assignment of a target to a social category may result from either (a) an explicit statement that the target belongs to the category, or (b) attributes and behaviors of the target that are strongly associated with the category or its exemplars and, therefore, lead the category to be activated spontaneously.
2. If a target has been assigned to a category and if other attributes of the target are compatible with it (i.e., either consistent with or unrelated to those that characterize category members), subjects base their evaluation of the target on their liking for the category as a whole, without considering implications of the target's attributes and behaviors.
3. If a target has not been assigned to a category, or if a category assignment has been made but the target's other attributes (i.e., those that were not used as a basis for category membership) are inconsistent with those of other category members, subjects engage in "piecemeal" processing. That is, they consider the target's individual attributes and integrate their implications to arrive at a judgment.

This conceptualization has many implications in common with Postulates 10.1 and 10.2. We also assume that when subjects have formed a general evaluative concept of a person (based on either the person's social category membership or

A. Fiske and Pavelchak (1986)

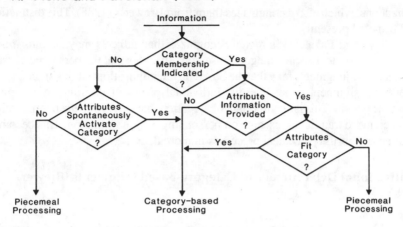

B. Brewer (1988)

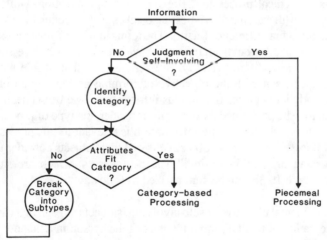

Figure 10.3   Conditions leading up to category-based and piecemeal processing implied by formulations proposed by (a) Fiske and Pavelchak (1986) and (b) Brewer (1988).

other criteria), they use its implications as a basis for inferring the person's likeableness (Postulate 10.1). If no such person concept has been formed, however, subjects resort to a more analytic process that involves an integration of the implications of the target person's behaviors, the traits they exemplify, or other information available. There is, however, one difference between the two conceptualizations, which also distinguishes them from Brewer's (1988). This distinction will be noted presently.

Fiske and Pavelchak's model recognizes that subjects may *spontaneously* assign a person to a social category based on attributes that the person possesses, and that their judgments may then be based on the implications of this spontaneous category assignment rather than the individual pieces of information presented about the person. This is an important observation that enters into the interpretation of other, more traditional research on person impression formation. This becomes clear as we discuss piecemeal processes in more detail.

Motivational Determinants of Category-based Judgments (Brewer, 1988)

Fiske and Pavelchak's dual-processing conceptualization focuses primarily on characteristics of the information presented that predispose subjects to engage in categorical vs. piecemeal processing. Brewer's conceptualization, while not denying the effects of these characteristics, also takes into account the role of motivational and individual difference factors. The terms in which Brewer presents her model are somewhat different from those we have used. However, its essential features can be summarized fairly readily. Brewer assumes that people receive information about a person with the objective of forming an impression of the person. After the individual pieces of stimulus information have been encoded at a level we postulate to be performed by the Comprehender, the type of processing that ensues depends on whether (a) the information is relevant to this processing objective and, if it is, (b) whether the objective is one that subjects consider to be personally important, or "self involving." These processes, which are shown schematically in Figure 10.3b, can be summarized as follows:

1. If their judgmental objective is self-involving, subjects engage in a careful analysis and integration of the individual features of the person in a manner akin to that considered by Fiske and Pavelchak to be piecemeal. This is done without considering the person's membership in a more general category.

2. If their judgmental objective is not self-involving, subjects attempt to assign the object to a social category that it explicitly or implicitly exemplifies.

a. If the target's attributes are consistent with the characteristics of the category as a whole, subjects make a category-based judgment comparable to that proposed by Fiske and Pavelchak.

b. If the target's attributes are inconsistent with the trait characterization of other members, subjects subjectively divide the category into subclasses, designate the target as one of these subclasses, and base their judgment on the features of this subclass.

Brewer's conceptualization brings together several theoretical and empirical issues in the area of person impression formation that have seldom been considered in combination (cf. Brewer, 1988). In its present form, however, some problems are encountered in applying it rigorously. One problem surrounds the a priori specification of what sorts of judgments are self-involving and what sorts are not. The conditions investigated by Lambert (1987) provide a convenient example. To reiterate, subjects with either very favorable or very unfavorable attitudes toward sororities judged a target person who was or was not identified as a sorority member. Are these judgments "self-involving" or not? On the one hand, subjects with extreme attitudes toward sororities are likely to be ego-involved in evaluating individual members of this liked or detested group. On the other hand, the person judged was not someone that subjects knew or expected to meet. Lambert's finding that pro-sorority subjects made category-based judgments of sorority members suggests that the judgments may *not* have been self-involving. Had the results come out differently, however, the opposite argument could be made just as plausibly.

With one exception, Brewer's conceptualization is compatible with both Fiske and Pavelchak's and the one we have proposed, at least insofar as it applies to evaluative (liking) judgments. The exception concerns an assumption that differentiates all three formulations, and surrounds the processing that occurs when a person is identified as member of a social category but nevertheless has attributes that are incongruent with category membership. In such instances, Fiske and Pavelchak assume that subjects default to piecemeal processing. Brewer, on the other hand, assumes that subjects continue to engage in category-based processing, but that they assign the target to a subcategory of the more general one that is more compatible with the person's attributes. Finally, Postulate 10.1 implies that neither of these things occurs. That is, to the extent that subjects have formed an evaluative concept of the target on the basis of his or her category membership, and this concept has direct implications for their judgment, they should base this judgment on the concept without performing any more detailed processing.

A definitive evaluation of these three assumptions must await the results of further research. However, Lambert's (1987) results are worth reconsidering in this context. To reiterate, subjects with extremely favorable attitudes toward sororities evaluated a target person more favorably when she belonged to a sorority than when she did not, regardless of whether the attributes implied by her behavior were stereotypically consistent with the category (sociable or dependent) or inconsistent with it (independent or aloof). This finding is consistent with the implications of Postulates 10.1 and 10.2. However, it seems contrary to either the assumption that subjects default to piecemeal processing when the target's attributes are inconsistent with those that characterize the category as a whole, or that they differentiate the category into subtypes under these conditions. On the other hand, anti-sorority subjects took into account *both* the target's category membership and her behavior, basing their judgments on her typicality rather than on either type of information alone. This finding is not directly implied by any of the three formulations. However, "atypical sorority members" may function as a subcategory of the more general category of "sorority member" that antisorority subjects evaluate favorably. To this extent, the finding is most congenial with Brewer's model.

The Nature of Category-Based and Piecemeal Processing

The research bearing on the validity of Postulates 10.1 and 10.2, coupled with the considerations raised by Brewer and by Fiske and Pavelchak, provide potentially important insights into the components of a person representation that are likely to enter into judgments and when these components are likely to be used. At the same time, these conceptualizations do not specify precisely *how* these components are used. Different considerations surround the way in which category-based judgments are made and the way in which individual pieces of information are combined in the course of piecemeal processing.

1. Category-Based Inference Processes

There are three ways in which a person may arrive at an inference on the basis of a person or object's category membership. Which process is used depends in part on the particular type of inference to be made.

Attribute judgments. One type of category-based inference concerns the extent to which a person has a particular trait. These inferences may be based on the extent to which the attribute is typical of members of the category to which the individual has been assigned. Thus, if "conniving" is associated with subjects' concept of a lawyer, and if these subjects are asked whether a particular lawyer has this attribute, they are likely to respond affirmatively. The magnitude of this inference may be determined by the strength of association between the concept of lawyer and the attribute being judged. Alternatively, it may depend on the ease with which particular exemplars (i.e., lawyers) who have the attribute come to mind (Tversky & Kahneman, 1973). (We discuss this latter possibility in more detail later in this chapter.)

Evaluative judgments. A second type of inference is evaluative rather than descriptive. That is, subjects may be asked to infer their liking for a person they are considering. This may typically be interpreted as a request to assess one's internal affective reactions toward the person. To the extent that the category to which a person has been assigned elicits positive or negative affect, this reaction may determine the evaluation that is made. We discuss this possibility, and empirical evidence bearing on it, in Chapter 11.

Inferences of past and future events. Still a third process may be involved when subjects are asked to make a judgment that requires an inference of a person's past or future behavior. In this case, subjects may activate a prototypic or particularized event sequence (i.e., a sequence of behaviors and their consequences that typify members of the category or, perhaps, were experienced by a particular exemplar). This possibility is discussed in some detail by Abelson (1976) in his general analysis of script-based inference processing. To borrow his example, a faculty member who looks over a graduate school application may note two or three features that, in combination, elicit an episodic event schema of a former student who hung around the department for eight years without ever writing up his dissertation. The faculty member may base his admissions recommendation on the implications of this scenario rather than upon the presented information per se. Or, a graduate school applicant who comes from Chicago's south side and got Ds in physical education may activate a "self-script," leading the evaluator to predict that the applicant will get off to a slow start but will ultimately get his act together and wind up on the faculty of a major university.

Two aspects of these examples are noteworthy. First, the features that activate one or another scenario may not themselves have direct implications for the judgment. Second, although several pieces of information may sometimes come into play in initially categorizing the person being judged, their individual implications are not considered. Rather, once an existing event schema is activated on the basis of the category to which the person is assigned, inferences are made by simply "reading off" those frames of the representation that are relevant and instantiating them in terms of the features of the particular person being judged. (For further discussion of the use of event sequences to make judgments, see Chapter 8.)

2. Piecemeal Processing

To the extent that the separate implications of individual pieces of information about a person are combined to form a single judgment, how is this done? The most formal theoretical statement of piecemeal processing is provided by Norman Anderson (1965, 1971, 1981). He postulates that when subjects are required to consider several different pieces of information, they construe the implications of each piece separately. Once this is done, they average these implications (along with a neutral "initial impression"), assigning a weight to each that corresponds to its relative importance. The judgment that emerges can theoretically be described by the equation

$$J_0 = \frac{\sum_{i=0}^{n} w_i s_i}{\sum_{i=0}^{n} w_i} = \frac{w_0 s_0 + w_1 s_1 + w_2 s_2 + \ldots w_n s_n}{w_0 + w_1 + w_2 + \ldots w_n} \qquad [10.1]$$

where s_i is the scale value of the ith piece of information, and w_i is the weight attached to it. (w_o and s_o are the weight and scale value of an "initial impression" of the stimulus that exists before any specific information about it is presented.)

This equation and its implications have been evaluated in a variety of stimulus and judgment domains (cf. Anderson, 1971; 1974; 1981), and have often provided a very good quantitative account of the manner in which different pieces of information combine to affect judgments. Several assumptions surrounding the applicability of the equation should be noted, however. Perhaps the most important is the assumption that subjects construe the implications of each piece of information separately rather than as part of a more general conceptual theme. Suppose subjects are told that a man both helped an elderly woman across the street and stole a purse. They are likely to react differently to the information if they assume that the two behaviors occurred in different situations than if they assume that the person stole the purse from the woman he was ostensibly helping. In the latter case, a scenario is constructed in which helping is a ploy that facilitates the crime, and loses its positive evaluative character. In this case, Equation 10.1 is inapplicable.

Wyer and Carlston (1979) list several conditions in which subjects are in fact likely to consider the implications of information as separate entities:

1. Information is more likely to be analyzed into discrete units when it (a) is of different types, (b) comes from different sources, or (c) concerns different objects or elements. Thus, a photograph of a person and a description of her personality are more likely to be combined algebraically than two verbal descriptions. Or, descriptions of a person provided by two different acquaintances are more likely to be considered separately, and their implications combined algebraically, than are similar descriptions of the person from the same source.

2. Instructions to treat each piece of available information as equally important may predispose subjects to think about it in a piecemeal fashion, and may correspondingly decrease the likelihood of its being considered with reference to a prototype or schema. Moreover, when a large number of different sets of information are judged in succession, subjects may often default to a more mechanistic integration rule that can be applied routinely to all sets rather than engaging in schema-based processing that is unique to each.

3. Pieces of information are more likely to be treated as separate units, and their implications to be combined algebraically, if their implications are inconsistent, or for other reasons are difficult to integrate in terms of a single prototype. When one person says that John is kind and another says that he is cruel, both assertions cannot be correct. The recipient is therefore likely to arrive at a compromise between the implications of the two assertions, weighing each by its subjective credibility or importance. The inconsistencies that give rise to piecemeal processing need not be so pronounced, however. This processing strategy may be adopted whenever a subject has difficulty imagining the sort of person who would

have the characteristics attributed to him (or her). It is neither necessary nor sufficient that the characteristics have different evaluative implications for this to occur. A person who is described as adventurous and cautious is hard to imagine, although both attributes are favorable. On the other hand, the description of someone as friendly and deceitful, two attributes that differ in favorableness when considered in isolation, may spontaneously activate a prototype of a "back-stabber," and therefore may elicit a response that cannot be predicted from the separate implications of "friendly" and "deceitful."

These considerations are worth noting in the context of Fiske and Pavelchak's (1986) formulation. These authors point out that although subjects may often engage in piecemeal processing when a target's category membership is not explicitly stated, particular configurations of attributes may spontaneously activate a category to which the target is likely to belong, and thus may instigate category-based processing instead. Early investigations of the applicability of Equation 10.1 to impression formation processes are useful to consider in this light. In much of this research (for a summary, see Anderson, 1971), subjects were asked to estimate their liking for persons who were described by sets of personality trait adjectives. The adjectives used to construct these sets were typically selected randomly from pools that represent different levels of normative favorableness, and therefore they were unlikely to match features of a previously formed person category. In these conditions, an averaging process of the sort implied by Equation 10.1 is quite likely to occur. Under some conditions, however, the adjectives presented may fortuitously activate an existing prototype or person concept. Under these conditions, category-based processing may occur, and judgments may deviate from those implied by an averaging model.

Two studies reported by Birnbaum (1974) provide examples of this possibility. In these studies, subjects made judgments of people who were described by adjective pairs constructed in the manner described above. In general, these judgments increased with the favorableness of the adjectives composing the pairs in a manner that was quite consistent with the implications of Equation 10.1. However, some consistent deviations from predictions occurred. For example, one stimulus person was described as "studious" and "refined," both favorable adjectives when considered in isolation. This person was evaluated less favorably than persons who were described by one of these adjectives in combination with a less favorable one (e.g., "studious" and "unpredictable," or "refined" and "impulsive"). Apparently, the combination of "studious" and "refined" spontaneously activated a prototype of a polite but uninteresting grind, and such a person was considered less likeable than someone who showed a bit of spontaneity (e.g., unpredictability or impulsiveness).

3. Processing of Behavior Information

In the impression formation conditions in which Equation 10.1 has typically been applied, the information presented has usually consisted of personality trait adjectives (for an exception, see Lampel & Anderson, 1968). Piecemeal processing may also occur when subjects must review behavioral information about a person to arrive at a judgment. Or, as implied by Postulate 10.2, it may occur when subjects need to combine the implications of behavior information with those of a more general concept they have formed of the person they are judging. Equation 10.1 may often describe the integration processes that occur in these instances. Certain configurations of behaviors, like certain configurations of adjectives, may spontaneously activate a general concept, and, therefore, may instigate category-based processing. In this case, however, the concept that is activated may be an event schema of the sort described in Chapter 8 rather than a person concept. That is, the individual behaviors may be interpreted as a temporally or casually related sequence of events, and the implications of this *sequence* may be used as a basis for judgments rather than the behaviors' individual implications. (The tendency for subjects to construct event sequences spontaneously may be reflected by differences in memory for the behaviors as well as in judgments; see Smith, Adams, & Schorr, 1978.)

4. Alternative Piecemeal Processing Rules

Equation 10.1 has been very successful in accounting for information integration processes under conditions in which piecemeal processing is likely. Some caution should be taken, however, in accepting it as a general account of this type of processing. Other piecemeal processing rules may sometimes be invoked. For example, subjects may *sum* the implications of the individual pieces of information they receive rather than averaging them. The extremity of judgments generally increases with the number of presented pieces of information that have similar implications for the judgment (cf. Anderson, 1965; Fishbein & Hunter, 1964). (Thus, a person described by three favorable adjectives is liked better than a person described by only one.) Although these set size effects can theoretically be accounted for by an averaging model (Anderson, 1965), this does not mean that summation *processes* are not involved. This is certainly the case when attributes other than likeableness are judged. For example, a person whose sole material possessions consist of a $5000 car and a $1000 stereo will undoubtedly be judged wealthier than a person whose sole possession consists of only a $5000 car. Regardless of whether Equation 10.1 can describe the relation between this judgment and characteristics of the stimulus information, it is clear that the underlying *process* is summative. This is because we have learned that a person's wealth is determined by summing up the person's material assets rather than averaging them. The more general point of this example is that the type of information integration process that people apply is likely to depend to some extent on socially learned rules that may often be specific to certain stimulus domains or types of judgments.

These considerations return us to an observation we made earlier in this chapter. Although quantitative and qualitative accuracy is a necessary condition for the validity of a theoretical model of cognitive functioning, it is by no means sufficient. In the case of Equation 10.1, as in the case of the equation we used to describe conditional inference processes (Equation 9.3), different processes may underlie its accuracy. In fact, the processes underlying Equation 10.1 could in principle be summative.

A simple example makes this clear. Assume that two pieces of information, A and B, activate concepts that each consist of 10 features, and that the evaluative implications of these features sum to 6 and 2, respectively. Assume further that a judge sums the implications of the favorableness of the features he considers to arrive at a judgment of the object described, but that his information processing capacity is limited to a maximum of 10 features at a time. When either A or B is presented in isolation, all 10 features of the concept it exemplifies can be processed, and so judgments based on them are 6 and 2, respectively. However, when both pieces of information (a total of 20 features) are presented in combination, the judge's information processing capacity is exceeded. If the judge samples randomly five features of the concept activated by each piece, and then combines their implications additively, the resulting judgment may approximate the average of the judgments based on each piece separately. Nevertheless, the underlying integration process is summative.

Summary and Conclusions

In this chapter, we have provided a detailed account of the processes that underlie inferences about persons. In doing so, we considered (a) *what* aspects of the cognitive representations formed of persons are used to make different types of judgments, (b) *when* these aspects are used, and (c) *how* they are used. Our conception is not intended to be complete, either in terms of the types of inferences that are often made or the processes that underlie them.[2] Nonetheless, the issues

---

2. For example, we have intentionally ignored inferences of the causes of a person's behavior. This is partly because these inferences are implicit in our discussions elsewhere in this volume (see, for example, the discussion of implicational molecules in Chapter 4, or of event schemata in Chapter 8), and partly because these inferences are discussed extensively in many other places (cf. Harvey, Ickes, & Kidd, 1976; Hastie, 1983; Jones & Davis, 1965; Kelley, 1967, 1971/1987; Kruglanski, 1980), and we have nothing particularly novel to add.

we have discussed, and the approach we have taken, provide the building blocks of a more complete conceptualization and suggest the issues it must address.

As we noted at the outset, any conceptualization of inferences about a particular type of stimulus object or event must be preceded by a conceptualization of the cognitive representations that are formed from information about these stimuli. Because we have been able to develop such a conceptualization in the person domain, our understanding of inference processes is correspondingly advanced. As our understanding of the representational processes becomes further refined and modified, however, corresponding modifications of our assumptions about inference processes may be required. At this writing, however, the processes we have postulated seem viable.

Chapter 11
Response Generation

The output generated by the Inference Maker is an internally coded judgment or decision. In many instances, this output must be transformed into an overt response. The response may be a motor behavior or a sequence of related acts, a verbal statement about an object (made orally or in writing), or a rating along a category scale. In all cases, the output is theoretically produced by the Response Generator, based on procedures contained in its library.

Many response generation procedures are highly idiosyncratic and context dependent. This is evident from the enormous diversity of behaviors that are performed by different people in a given situation and by the same person in different but related situations. Because the procedures contained in the Response Generator's library are performed without being monitored by the Executor, the transformation of a subjective inference into an overt response may often occur automatically, without conscious awareness of precisely how it was done. In one sense, this simply recognizes that people acquire well-learned responses to different configurations of stimulus features, some of which may be internally generated and others of which may pertain to the situational context in which the response occurs.

In research on social judgment, it is particularly important to understand the response generation rules that govern the transformation of a subjective inference into a rating along a category scale of ordered alternatives. Many of the data we have discussed in this volume have consisted of responses along such scales. To simplify our discussion of these data, we have usually assumed an isomorphic correspondence between subjects' internal codings of their inferences and the category ratings they make. However, this assumption is frequently not correct. When it is not, situational and individual differences in the judgments that subjects report may sometimes be attributed to differences in subjects' inferences when, in fact, they only reflect differences in the criteria that are used to report these inferences. A major focus of this chapter is on the processes that govern the use of category rating scales to report subjective judgments. However, the assumptions underlying the processes we postulate often apply to the generation of other types of responses as well.

General Principles of Interpersonal Communication: Politeness, Informativeness, and Accuracy

Our discussion in this chapter is guided by an obvious but important observation. That is, social behaviors, regardless of whether they are motor acts, verbal utterances, or category ratings, are essentially interpersonal communications. That is, they are generated with the intention of conveying information to another. In the social psychology laboratory, many of the communications that occur are between the experimenter and the subject. The experimenter's communications to the subject include instructions about the objectives of the experiment, descriptions of what to do and how to do it, the type of stimuli presented, and the questions that are asked. The subject's communications include behaviors that are performed in response to the experimenter's instructions and answers to the experimenter's questions.

It would be surprising if the processes that govern communications between participants in an experiment (e.g., the experimenter and the subject) did not bear some resemblance to the processes that govern social communication in other interpersonal interactions. Three factors are particularly relevant in both the psychology laboratory and more generally: politeness, informativeness, and accuracy.

Politeness

People in a social interaction usually attempt to convey information in a way that the other participant(s) will consider inoffensive. I am certainly likely to express my views differently if I am asked what I think of Ronald Reagan by someone who belongs to the Christian Anticommunist Crusade than if I am asked by a member of the American Civil Liberties Union. This is particularly true if I have just met the individual. This does not necessarily imply that I intentionally engage in dishonesty. Rather, I attempt to convey my actual opinion, but in terms that will not offend the recipient.

Similar tendencies may exist in experiments. In fact, they may be quite pervasive. Experiments are social situations in which subjects often have little personal investment. Participants usually try to understand what the experimenter wants and expects in these situations, and then, to be cooperative, may generate outputs that conform to these desires and expectancies. The cues that subjects use to infer the experimenter's wants and expectancies may sometimes be rather subtle, and may often not be intended (Orne, 1962; Rosenthal & Rosnow, 1969). For example, imagine that subjects are asked by an experimenter to write an essay in support of a particular position. If they are offered money to do this, they may infer that the experimenter expects most people to disagree with the position and to be unwilling to advocate it without pay. If, on the other hand, they are asked to advocate the position without any pressure or monetary inducement, they may infer that the experimenter expects most people to agree with the position and to find it both easy and desirable to advocate.

Suppose, therefore, that subjects in each condition are later asked by the experimenter to report their attitudes toward the position advocated. If they try to generate responses that conform to the experimenter's expectations for what is "normal," they may report stronger agreement with the position in the second condition than in the first. This, of course, is also a well-known implication of cognitive dissonance theory (Festinger, 1957) and has often been found empirically (cf. Festinger & Carlsmith, 1959; for a review, see Wickland & Brehm, 1976). Several other well-known social psychological phenomena may be conceptualized similarly. (For an analysis of experiments in several different research paradigms that can be interpreted in terms of subjects' attempts to generate responses that the experimenter wants or expects, see Wyer, 1974.)

Informativeness and Accuracy

A formal statement of communication processes has been provided by Grice (1975). He proposes a number of "communication axioms" that theoretically govern both the generation of communications to others and the interpretation of these communications by the recipient. The implications of several of these axioms for social communication have been elaborated by Higgins (1981; for other elaborations and extensions, see Clark, 1985). Although many of Grice's axioms appear self-evident at first glance, they have far-reaching implications. Two principles are particularly germane to the issues of concern in this chapter. Specifically, communications are intended to be both (a) informative and (b) accurate. To the extent that these criteria are applied by both the generator of a communication and its recipient, these principles lead to two general hypotheses:

1. People generate communications that they believe will be informative to the intended recipient, and do so in a language that they believe will permit their implications to be correctly interpreted.

2. Recipients of a communication will assume that the communicator has, in fact, attempted to be informative and accurate in generating the communication, and will interpret its implications on the basis of this assumption.[1,2]

These hypotheses apply to question-and-answer situations as well as to other forms of interpersonal communication. Specifically, the person who is asked a question typically assumes that the questioner is requesting information that he or she does not already have,[3] and attempts to generate a response that provides this information. Moreover, the respondent attempts to do so in a way that the questioner will understand and interpret correctly. Perhaps the most common and intuitively obvious example of this occurs in responding to the question "Where do you live?" If I am asked this question by someone I meet while vacationing in Greece, I am likely to say that I live in America. If I am asked by someone I meet on a business trip to New York, I am likely to say that I live in Illinois. This is because I believe that the second questioner already knows that I live in America, and that this response would be uninformative. In neither case, however, will I respond by giving my street address in Urbana. This is because this extra detail conveys no meaningful information to anyone who is not familiar with the small town in which I live.

Intentions to be informative and accurate govern interpersonal communications in general. However, to the extent that experimental subjects consider the responses they generate to be communications to the experimenter, these intentions should operate here as well. Strack and Martin (1987) provide a detailed and provocative analysis of the role of these factors in responding to questionnaire

---

1. Perhaps the most interesting intuitive application of the second hypothesis arises in the interpretation of communications that would normally go without saying. The recepient of such a communication may attempt to make the message informative by constructing conditions in which it would have information value. Suppose a person sees a newspaper headline to the effect that a U.S. Senator is not a member of the Ku Klux Klan. This would normally go without saying. Therefore, to make this headline newsworthy, the reader may speculate that there was some reason to believe that the Senator did belong to this group at one time, or that he has been accused of prejudice against minority groups. One consequence of this is that the reader, having read the headline, may increase his belief that the Senator is prejudiced rather than decreasing it.

2. There are undoubtedly instances in which these axioms do not apply. We certainly expect a used-car salesman to be somewhat less than accurate in describing the virtues of a car he wants to sell. In heterosexual interactions, we often attribute compliments to impression management. Nonetheless, the axioms apply in a large number of situations, including the ones we consider in this chapter.

3. An obvious exception arises in "test-taking" situations, where the questioner knows the answer and is evaluating the recipient's knowledge. These conditions may sometimes arise in informal interactions as well as formal ones. The dynamics of these situations are of psychological interest, but we forego a discussion of them here.

surveys, and many of the ideas presented in this chapter are similar. In our discussion, we begin by considering the processes that underlie subjects' responses along category rating scales of the sort that are typically used to report judgments of attributes and abilities (e.g., honesty, likeableness, self-esteem, etc.). We first describe the procedures that may underlie the use of such scales, and discuss factors that may affect subjects' assumptions concerning the stimulus values to which they apply. Then, we provide examples of how responses made along these scales may influence subsequent judgments and overt behavior.

Following this discussion, we consider other types of categorical responses that subjects are often called upon to make. Although the informativeness and accuracy principles are of considerable relevance in each case, the manner in which they come into play is somewhat different. Finally, we turn briefly to some methodological implications of the theoretical analysis we have described, and discuss possible ways of separating the effects of experimental variables on subjective inferences from their effects on the language used to report them.

The Use of Category Response Scales

To reiterate, people try to convey information to others in a way that will permit it to be interpreted correctly. This implies that when people are asked to make a judgment, they often attempt to construe the perspective, or frame of reference, of the person to whom they are communicating, and generate a response that they believe will be accurately understood by someone with this perspective. Often, communicators assume that the recipient's attitude is similar to their own, being determined by their common experience with the types of stimuli being judged. Thus, I may refer to a newborn baby as "big" but to a one-bedroom house as "small," despite the fact that the house is much larger than the baby.

In other instances, however, communicators recognize that their own ex-perience, and therefore their perspective, may differ from the recipient's. In such cases, they may modify the labels they would normally use to denote their subjective judgments in order to permit these judgments to be correctly interpreted from the perspective that they assume the recipient to have. Thus, I am much more likely to describe myself as a "good" racquetball player to someone who is just beginning to play the game than I am to a former champion. This is because I infer that the first person has primarily been exposed to novices, and would consider me to be better than most of the players he has seen, whereas the national champion would consider me to be a pushover. For similar reasons, I am likely to describe my hometown in the Catskill Mountains as "beautiful" to a lifelong resident of Champaign, Illinois, but as only "pretty" to a native of Switzerland.

These intuitive examples testify to the fact that people who communicate a subjective judgment to another typically do not employ a standard set of labels that are invariant over time and situations. Rather, they construe the labels that the intended recipient would use to describe their judgment and respond in these terms.

This fact is of considerable importance in understanding the process that underlies subjects' reports of their judgments in experiments. In many laboratory situations, the terms that subjects can use to report their judgments are not self-generated, but rather, are limited to a set of alternatives provided by the experimenter. Often, they consist of ordered categories along a semantic differential, with each category representing a different amount of the attribute to be judged. The categories are often denoted only by numbers, with only the scale endpoints assigned verbal labels (e.g., "very dishonest" vs. "very honest," "dislike very much" vs. "like very much," etc.). Even when verbal labels are assigned to these categories, their referent is often not clear. (Does "very dishonest," for example, refer to the amount of dishonesty manifested by someone who cheats on his wife, or the amount manifested by Al Capone?) When communicators (subjects) are asked to report their judgments along such a scale, they must first make an assumption about the nature of the referents to which the recipient (experimenter) believes the scale is applicable, and, therefore, the range of stimulus values that the scale is supposed to include. Then, once this is done, they must map the particular judgments to be made onto this scale. We consider these two component processes in turn.

Positioning the Response Scale

It is conceivable that subjects who are asked to report a judgment along a scale of ordered categories will typically think of the most and least extreme stimulus values they can imagine, and will use these values to define the most and least extreme scale categories, regardless of the nature of the stimuli rated or their perception of the recipient's perspective. However, both empirical evidence (cf. Parducci, 1965; Upshaw, 1969) and intuition argue against this possibility. To modify slightly an earlier example, suppose some subjects are asked to rate babies along a scale from (very small) to (very large) and others are asked to rate a set of houses along this same scale. It is obvious that some of the babies rated by the first group of subjects will be assigned higher values than some of the houses rated by the second group. This would not occur if subjects always anchored the scale similarly. Clearly, subjects position the scale to include different ranges of stimulus values, depending on the type of object they expect to rate. As we will see, other factors may influence response scale position as well.

Formal theoretical statements of the manner in which subjects use a response scales to report a judgment, and the factors that affect it, are provided elsewhere (cf. Ostrom & Upshaw, 1968; Parducci, 1965; Upshaw, 1965, 1969; see also Wyer, 1974). However, the essential features of these formulations can be conveyed fairly simply. Each formulation assumes that when subjects are asked to evaluate a

A. Subjective Continuum of intellectual ability

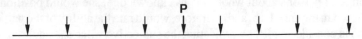

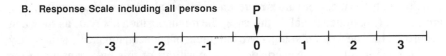

B. Response Scale including all persons

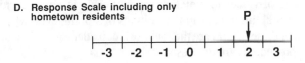

C. Response Scale including only
   university professors

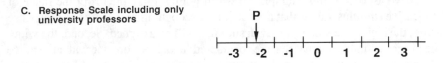

D. Response Scale including only
   hometown residents

Figure 11.1 (a) Locations of known persons along a subjective continuum of intellectual ability, and positions of a category response scale to include (b) the full range of known persons (c) only university professors, and (d) only residents of one's home town. Arrows denote the projected rating of a hypothetical person P onto these scales.

stimulus along a response scale, they identify what they believe to be the most and the least extreme stimulus values that the experimenter considers to be relevant. Then, they subjectively position the response scale they are given so that its endpoints correspond to these values. Once this is done, they map the subjective value they have assigned to the stimulus they are asked to judge onto this scale. (A more detailed analysis of this mapping procedure is provided later.)

As an example, suppose a woman is asked to judge the intellectual ability of an acquaintance who comes from the same small mining town in Ohio in which she herself grew up and, like herself, became a university professor. Suppose further that she is asked to report this judgment along a scale from -3 (very low) to +3 (very high). The woman may have encountered people over the course of her life that vary widely in their intellectual skills. A representative sample of these individuals might be located along a subjective continuum of internally coded stimulus values as shown in Figure 11.1a. If the woman were to consider the entire range of persons about whom she has knowledge, she would position the scale as shown in Figure 11.1b, and, therefore, would rate the ability of the particular person she is considering (P) by projecting the subjective value she has assigned to P onto this scale. However, suppose the woman believes that the scale is meant to pertain only to stimulus values that are typical of university professors. Then, she might position her response scale as shown in Figure 11.1c. Alternatively, she may consider only the range of values represented by people from her home town, who are generally nonintellectual. In this case, she might position her scale as shown in Figure 11.1d. The woman's subjective judgment of her acquaintance's ability may be the same in all cases. Nevertheless, the positions of this judgment along the response scale, and the ratings made of the person, differ considerably.

Two aspects of this example are worth noting. First, the lower the range of subjective stimulus values that are taken into account in positioning the response scale, the higher the value any given stimulus will be assigned. Second, the wider the range of stimulus values that are considered (and, therefore, the wider the range of values that are included in any given scale category), the more likely it is that any two stimuli will be assigned the same rating. Thus, factors that affect subjects' assumptions about the range of values to which a response scale is supposed to pertain may produce substantial differences in their ratings of stimuli, even when their subjective judgments of these stimuli are the same. We consider some of these factors after the mapping procedures are discussed.

Mapping of Stimulus Values onto the Response Scale

In conveying the general effects of differences in response scale position (Figure 11.1), we assumed that once subjects have positioned their response scale to include a particular range of subjective stimulus values, they determine the response category to which any given stimulus belongs by projecting its value directly onto the scale, thereby preserving its position in relation to other stimuli within the range being considered. This assumption, which is made by Upshaw (1962, 1965, 1978) and others (Wyer, 1974), is useful in conceptualizing the effects of situational and individual difference variables on the judgments that subjects report. However, the assumption may not be strictly correct. At least two additional factors may influence the mapping of subjective judgments onto a category response scale.

1. The Frequency Principle

Parducci (1965) postulated that when subjects are asked to judge several different stimuli along a response scale, they assume that the experimenter intends them to distribute their judgments of these stimuli fairly evenly over the set of categories available. Moreover, they attempt to comply with the implications of this assumption. The effect of this may be conveyed with a simplified example. Imagine that three subjects are asked to rate a test stimulus, X. Each subject, however, is exposed to a different set of context stimuli whose actual values are distributed over a subjective continuum of judgment in the manner shown in Figure 11.2. Because the most and the least extreme context stimuli have the same subjective values in all three cases, the three subjects should position their response scales similarly. However, suppose that subjects attempt to distribute their responses evenly over the response scale. Then, the second subject should assign X to a more positive scale category than the first. Considered in isolation, this might also be predicted on the basis of a simple contrast effect of context stimuli on the subjective perceptions of the test stimulus (cf,, Helson, 1964). However, subject 3, according to the frequency principle, should *also* judge X more positively than subject 1, although the context stimuli to which this subject is exposed are extremely positive as well as extremely negative. Thus, the frequency principle generates unique predictions of context effects that cannot be attributed either to differences in response scale position or to differences in subjective perceptions of the stimuli being judged. (For a more formal statement of the combined effects of the frequency principle and response scale positioning, see Parducci, 1965.)

2. Anchoring and Adjustment

A quite different procedure for mapping stimulus values onto a response scale is suggested by Tversky and Kahneman's (1974) analysis of anchoring and adjustment processes. Their conception of these processes is broader than we convey here. One implication of their analysis is that when subjects who are given a stimulus to rate along a response scale, they focus on one of the two scale endpoints and use it as an "anchor" relative to which the presented stimulus is compared. That is, they first estimate the value of the anchor, and then adjust their rating of the target stimulus either upward or downward in a way that reflects the difference between its value and the anchor value. However, they do not usually adjust enough. Because of this, subjects will typically make "higher" estimates if they use the "high" end of the scale as an anchor than if they use the "low" end.

When subjects vary unsystematically with respect to which scale endpoint they use as an anchor, the effects of this adjustment bias are likely to cancel when responses are averaged over subjects within a given experimental condition. Consequently, they may not influence the conclusions drawn from between-condition comparisons of subjects' ratings. In some cases, however, experimental manipulations may produce systematic biases to use one endpoint or another as an anchor. A factor with surprisingly interesting implications was identified by Schwarz and Wyer (1985). Their studies concerned the effect of using different procedures for rank ordering stimuli on subsequent magnitude ratings of these and

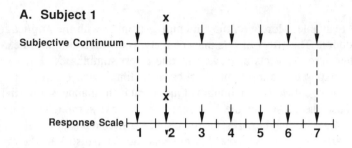

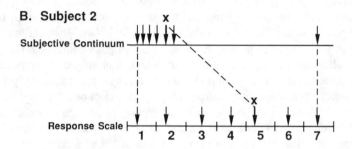

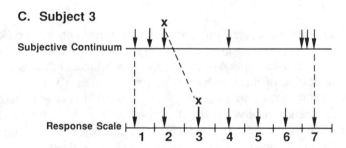

Figure 11.2 Subjective distribution of stimulus values presented to three hypothetical subjects and the mapping of these values onto a seven-category response scale, based on Parducci's frequency principle.

other stimuli. Subjects first rank ordered a series of environmental issues from "most important" to "least important." They did this by first identifying the stimulus that was "most important" and assigning it a "1," then selecting the next most important stimulus and assigning it a "2," and so on. Using analogous procedures, other subjects ranked the issues either from "least important" to "most important," from "most trivial" to "least trivial," or from "least trivial" to "most trivial." Then, all subjects rated the stimuli they had ranked, as well as environmental issues they had not previously considered, along a rating scale from 0 to 100, using 50 as the scale midpoint. This scale was in some cases defined in terms of importance, with high values indicating greater importance. In other cases, it was defined in terms of triviality, with higher values indicating greater triviality. In summary, the conditions of the study composed a three-factor design consisting of two rating criteria (importance or triviality), two ranking criteria (importance or triviality), and two ranking procedures (from "most" to "least" vs. from "least" to "most").

The results were unequivocal. Subjects who rank ordered issues from "most" to "least" assigned higher ratings to both these and other environmental issues than subjects who had ranked them from "least" to "most." This was true regardless of either the rating criterion or the ranking criterion. Thus, for example, subjects who had ranked the stimuli from most to least important subsequently assigned higher ratings to stimuli along a dimension of importance, but also higher ratings along a dimension of triviality, than did subjects who had ranked stimuli from least to most important. Moreover, subjects who had ranked stimuli from most to least trivial also rated them higher (regardless of the rating criterion) than subjects who had ranked stimuli from least to most trivial.

Although these findings seem bewildering at first glance, there is a quite reasonable interpretation of them. The rank ordering task may lead subjects to use different ends of the response scale as an anchor, depending on the procedure that is used. Specifically, subjects who rank order from "most" to "least" acquire a bias to use the high end of the response scale as an end anchor, whereas those who rank order from "least" to "most" develop a bias to focus on the low end. Therefore, because subjects fail to adjust enough, they may assign higher values to stimuli in the former case than in the latter, and this may be true regardless of the specific ranking or rating criteria that are employed.

A further study by Schwarz and Wyer (1985) provided additional support for this interpretation. This study showed that subjects also rated environmental issues as more important (or trivial) if they had previously ranked qualities of a marriage partner from "most" to "least" important (trivial) than if they had ranged them from "least" to "most." Thus, the effects occur even when the stimulus domain to which the ranking and rating tasks pertain are totally unrelated.

The effect identified by Schwarz and Wyer is quite transitory. For example, when subjects were asked to report their beliefs in propositions about the need for environmental reforms before performing the magnitude rating task, the effect of rank ordering was eliminated. Be that as it may, the theoretical importance of Schwarz and Wyer's research for our present purposes lies in its evidence that anchoring and adjustment processes do occur, and that the linear mapping of subjective stimulus values onto response scales may therefore not be as straightforward as Upshaw and others initially assumed. The linear mapping assumption is nevertheless a useful one in conceptualizing the effects of situational and individual difference variables on the responses that subjects make along the scale. With this in mind, we return to a consideration of some of the factors that may influence subjects' decisions about the range of stimulus values to which a response scale pertains and the implications of these decisions for an understanding of the responses they generate.

Determinants of Response Scale Position

To reiterate, subjects who are given a category response scale to use in reporting their judgments position it to include the range of stimulus values to which they believe the experimenter intends it to apply. This permits them to transform their subjective judgment onto the scale in a way that the experimenter will interpret correctly. But what factors affect judges' perceptions of the range of stimulus values to which a response scale is applicable? Several factors and their possible effects may be worth describing briefly.

A determination of the range of values to which a response scale applies is likely to be a two-stage process. First, subjects identify the category, or domain of stimuli, to which the scale is applicable (e.g., whether it pertains to babies, to persons in general, to houses, etc.). Then, they infer the subset of stimulus values to which the scale is relevant within this domain. We discuss each stage in turn.

1. Type of Stimuli to be Evaluated

A major determinant of the range of stimulus values to which a response scale is considered to be applicable is the type of stimulus (or stimuli) to be judged. A person who is asked to judge the size of babies along a scale of heaviness is likely to assume that the scale is restricted to babies and not to people in general or to all physical objects (e.g., houses).

Although this example is intuitively obvious, the general principle that underlies it is less so. Why is it, for example, that subjects do *not* assume that the response scale along which they are asked to judge babies applies to people (or physical objects) in general? Stimulus objects often belong to several different categories, and the range of values of the stimuli contained in them varies. Moreover, these categories are not always hierarchical; that is, one category is not always a subset of another. This is particularly true of social stimuli such as persons, who may be categorized on the basis of gender, social or occupational role, age, or many other criteria that are often independent of one another.

In some cases, of course, the nature of the category is stated explicitly by the experimenter. For example, an experimenter who tells subjects that their task is to judge the size of "babies" is likely to assume that the scale provided pertains to members of this particular category, whereas subjects who are told that their task is to judge "persons" are likely to assume that the scale pertains to this broader category instead. Often, however, the category membership of the stimuli to be judged is not clearly specified. Under these circumstances, what determines which of the several categories to which a stimulus belongs is the one to which the response scale is applicable? Four factors are worth noting.

Diversity of the stimuli to be rated. When a subject is asked to judge more than one or more stimuli, the category to which the response scale is relevant is obviously one that includes all of these stimuli. It seems reasonable to postulate the following principle to govern the selection of this category: *The stimulus category to which a response scale is assumed to be applicable is one that (a) all stimuli to be judged exemplify and (b) is no more abstract than is necessary to include these stimuli.* This principle applies both when several stimuli are judged and when only one stimulus is rated. In the former case, it implies that a woman who is asked to report her liking for beans, peas, and corn may infer that the scale provided her pertains to "vegetables." In contrast, a woman who is asked to judge her liking for beans, steak, and apple pie may infer that this pertains to "food," and a person who is asked her liking for beans, Mozart, and Chicago may conclude that it pertains to "things in general." To the extent that the range of stimulus values contained in these categories differs, the ratings of any given stimulus (e.g., "beans") along the scale may correspondingly differ.

To apply the principle to single stimulus judgments, return to our earlier example. Suppose a person is asked to judge the size of a *particular* baby. This stimulus is an instance of the more general category "baby." This category, which is sufficient to include all of the stimuli being judged but is less abstract than "person" or "inanimate object," is therefore likely to be taken as the category to which the "size" scale is relevant. On the other hand, suppose the subject had been asked to judge the size of "a baby," considered without regard to any particular referent. In this case, "baby" may be treated as an instance of "person," which includes other exemplars at the same level of abstractness ("adult," "teen-ager", etc.) but is itself not as abstract as other categories to which "baby" may belong. Therefore, "person" may be the category to which the scale is applied. Although this analysis seems rather mundane, it accounts for the fact that subjects may assign "baby," considered out of context, a low value along a scale of size, but may assign a particular baby a high value along this same scale.

A somewhat more interesting application of this principle can be made in accounting for results reported by Wyer (1970b) in a study of evaluations of social role occupants. He found, for example, that although "mother" was evaluated as more likeable than "druggist," "unkind mother" was evaluated as less likeable than an "unkind druggist." In other words, the addition of a negative attribute often reversed the relative favorableness of the two types of persons being judged. This phenomenon cannot easily be accounted for by a simple information integration model, which assumes judgments to be composites of the component features of the stimuli being judged (Anderson, 1971; see Chapter 10). It is easier to conceptualize in terms of the considerations raised above. Subjects who evaluate "mother" and "druggist" are likely to interpret them as instances of the category "persons," and along this scale, "mother" has a higher subjective likeableness value than "druggist." However, subjects who consider an "unkind mother," or "unkind druggist," may interpret these stimuli as instances of the more circumscribed categories "mother" and "druggist," respectively. Therefore, because "unkind mother" has a lower subjective likeableness in relation to other types of mothers than "unkind druggist" has in relation to other types of druggists, the first stimulus is rated less favorably along the "mother" scale than the latter is rated along the "druggist" scale. (For a related conceptualization of this phenomenon and data supporting its validity, see Higgins & Rholes, 1976.)

An alternative to the postulate we propose should be noted, however. When the stimulus is of a type about which the communicator and recipient are likely to have real-world knowledge, the category to which the stimulus is assigned may be the one that is most commonly used in communicating about objects of this type. This category may be at a "basic" or intermediate level of generality (Rosch & Lloyd, 1978). Thus, for example, we typically refer to objects out of context as "chairs" rather than as "pieces of furniture" or as "straightback kitchen chairs," and we refer to "babies" when we see instances of this category rather than to "people" or "six-month old infants." These "basic level" categories may serve as default options in inferring the domain of stimuli to which a response scale is relevant when no other cues are provided concerning the experimenter's intentions.

In social stimulus domains, however, the concept of a "basic level" category may be inapplicable. For one thing, the nature of a "basic level" assumes a nested hierarchy of objects at different levels of abstractness. Many social stimuli are overlapping, and do not fit readily into a hierarchy (cf. Lingle, Altom, & Medin, 1984). For example, a subject may be asked to indicate his liking for a black female college professor. In this case, the person could be categorized as "black," as "female" or as "college professor," none of which is any more "basic" than another. Under these conditions, the principle we have postulated is also insufficient to infer the category to which the response scale is applicable, and so inferences about the nature of this category must be guided by other considerations of the sort described below.

Communication context. When the experimenter does not state explicitly the category of stimuli to which a response scale is relevant, the communicator may infer it indirectly from characteristics of the situation in which the judgment is reported. These characteristics may include both (a) aspects of the recipient's apparent background and knowledge, and (b) features of the situational context in which the judgment is requested. Reconsider the woman who is asked to judge the university professor from her home town. She may classify the target as a university professor if the questioner is one of her own university colleagues, or if she is asked to judge the person in her office at the university. However, she may classify him as a "person from my home town" if the questioner is someone she meets during a return to her place of origin. In short, the social judgmental context, as determined by attributes of either the questioner or the situation in which the question is asked, may lead the respondent to infer the perspective of the questioner and, therefore, the class of persons or objects to which the response scale is applicable.

These considerations sometimes become important in interpreting the results of experiments in which people are asked to evaluate themselves, other subjects, or even fictitious persons. These studies are typically conducted using college students as subjects, in a university setting, by a person who is associated with the university. It seems reasonable to suppose that in the absence of other cues, subjects are likely to infer that the response scale they are given pertains to "college students" and position it to include a representative sample of this population, rather than applying it to a more broadly defined class of persons. Thus, they may rate a person who snubs them as "extremely dislikeable" along a scale of likeableness despite the fact that they do not consider this person nearly as despicable as a Nazi war criminal.

Category accessibility. The factors discussed above come into play as a result of subjects' conscious attempts to construe the category of objects to which the experimenter intends a response scale to apply. There are instances in which no cues are available concerning this matter. In this case, factors that are extraneous to the judgment task itself may affect the accessibility of judgment-relevant categories, and thus may influence the likelihood that these categories are applied. To continue with our example, the woman who is asked to judge her home town acquaintance's intellectual ability may be more likely to classify him as a "university professor" if she has recently participated in a promotions committee meeting than if she has recently thought about visiting her parents for Christmas. These priming effects may be overridden, however, by conscious attempts to be informative and accurate, and thus by providing more direct indications of the domain of stimuli to which the experimenter intends the scale to be relevant.

2. Within-Category Variability in the Stimuli to be Judged

Once the domain of stimuli to which a response scale is relevant has been inferred, the scale must be positioned in relation to a particular range of values that are possessed by the stimuli within this domain. The most obvious determinants of subjects' perceptions of this range, and also the most widely investigated, are the values of stimuli to which the subject is actually exposed in the course of performing the judgmental task. That is, a person who is asked to judge a series of weights will perceive that the scale pertains to a higher value if the weights are all heavy than if they are all light. Consequently, a moderately heavy stimulus will typically be mapped onto a lower value along the scale (i.e., judged as lighter) in the first case than in the second. This "contrast" effect of "context" stimuli on judgments of "target" stimuli is well established, and several interpretations of it have been proposed (cf. Helson, 1964; Sherif & Hovland, 1961). However, the weight of available evidence favors an interpretation along the lines presented here. This is true both in psychophysical judgment (Parducci, 1965) and social judgment (Ostrom & Upshaw, 1968; Upshaw, 1978).

A psychophysical judgment experiment by (Brown, 1953) is particularly noteworthy. In this study, subjects were asked to judge a series of weights. In one condition, the test weights that subjects were asked to judge were each preceded in the series by a context weight that was either heavier or lighter. Exposure to the context weight had contrast effects on subjects' ratings of the test weight that followed it. In a second condition, subjects before judging each test weight were asked to hold a metal tray of weights that, in its totality, weighed exactly the same as the context stimuli that were used in the first condition. However, they were told that the tray of weights was one of the series of stimuli to be judged. The tray had contrast effects on judgments of the test weight similar to those observed in the first case.

A third condition was the critical one. Here, subjects were also given the tray of weights to hold before rating the test stimuli. However, they were led to believe that it was not part of the stimulus series, and that they were holding it as a favor to the experimenter while he set things up for the next stimulus trial. If exposure to the interpolated weight affected subjects' actual perceptions of the test weights (cf. Helson, 1964), it should have influenced their ratings of the test stimuli in the same way it affected them in other conditions. In fact, it had no effect at all on these ratings. This finding is quite consistent with the conceptualization we have outlined. That is, subjects who were led to believe that the tray was part of the stimulus series took it into account in deciding the range of values to which the response scale pertained, positioning the scale to include higher values when the tray was heavy than when it was not. In contrast, subjects who believed that the tray was irrelevant to the judgment task did not consider it when deciding the range of values to which the response scale pertained, and therefore positioned the scale similarly regardless of its weight. Therefore, the effect of the tray on ratings of test stimuli was eliminated.

3. The Role of Self-Perceptions in Judgments of Social Stimuli

When subjects make psychophysical judgments, they are likely to infer the range of relevant stimulus values primarily from the range of values of the stimuli to be judged. When they judge characteristics of persons (e.g., personality attributes, the favorableness of opinions toward various social issues, etc.), an additional factor comes into play. That is, subjects may perceive themselves to be in the same category as the person whose attributes are being judged. To this extent, they may infer that the value they assign to themselves (a relevant part of the judgment situation) should be considered in deciding the range of stimulus values

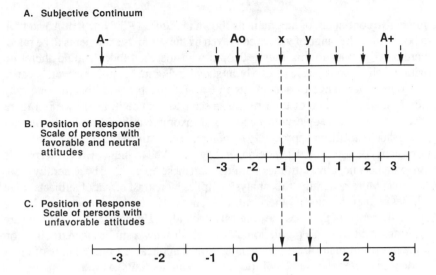

A. Subjective Continuum

B. Position of Response Scale of persons with favorable and neutral attitudes

C. Position of Response Scale of persons with unfavorable attitudes

Figure 11.3 (a) Location of persons with Favorable (A+), neutral (Ao), and unfavorable (A-) attributes, and location of stimulus statements, along a subjective continuum of favorableness. (b) Position of response scale used by persons with favorable and neutral attitudes. (c) Position of response scale used by persons with an unfavorable attitude. X and Y denote the values of two representative stimulus items and their projections onto these response scales.

to which the response scale is applicable. Therefore, they may spontaneously take this value into account when positioning the scale. If subjects' self-judgment is within the range of values that they are actually asked to judge, it should not, of course, affect subjects' positioning of the response scale. Suppose, however, that their self-judgment is outside this range. Then, this judgment, rather than the subjective values they have assigned to the stimuli being rated, may be used to define one of the scale's endpoints. Consequently, it may influence the ratings that subjects make along the scale.

A provocative demonstration of this possibility is provided in a series of studies by Upshaw (1962, 1965) on the effects of subjects' own attitudes toward a concept on judgments of others' attitudes. Although the design of the studies is complex, their essential features can be conveyed in a simplified example. Suppose people with either positive (A+), neutral (Ao) or negative (A-) attitudes toward minority groups are asked to judge the favorableness of attitudes conveyed by opinion statements that range from neutral to favorable. (In the actual study, this range was varied systematically over conditions.) Assume that the stimulus statements, and the positions of the three subject groups' attitudes, are positioned along a subjective continuum of judgment as shown in Figure 11.3. Note that Ao and A+ are both within the range of values conveyed by the stimulus statements to be rated, whereas A- is outside this range. People with these attitudes should therefore position their response scale similarly, as shown in Figure 11.3b. However, because A- is outside the range of statements to be rated, people with this attitude may extend the negative end of their response scale to include it, as shown in Figure 11.3c. As a result, people with neutral and favorable attitudes toward minority groups should not differ appreciably in their reported estimates of the favorableness of opinions conveyed by the statements they are asked to judge. However, people with extremely negative attitudes should report these opinions to be generally more favorable. More generally, this analysis implies a contrast effect of subjects' own attitudes on their ratings of others' attitudes, but only when their own attitudes are outside the range of the ones they are asked to judge. Upshaw's (1965) results are quite consistent with this prediction. Although Upshaw's studies were focused on judgments of attitudes, the conceptualization is applicable to judgments of other personal characteristics (e.g., abilities and personality traits) as well.

Assimilation vs. Contrast Effects of Context Stimuli

The use of context stimuli to determine the range of subjective values to which a response scale applies typically produces a contrast effect of the stimuli on ratings of test stimuli. The effect should be viewed in light of other considerations that would seem to imply a *positive* effect of context stimuli on judgments. As we noted in Chapter 6, features of the situation in which judgments are made (which include, of course, other stimuli to be judged) may activate concepts that are used to interpret the stimuli to be evaluated. Later judgments are based on these concepts, and, therefore, are affected positively by their descriptive and evaluative implications. These "assimilation" effects of context on *subjective* judgments of a stimulus, which presumably occur at a relatively early stage of information processing, are opposite in direction to the contrast effects on *reported* judgments that are produced by the influence of context on response scale positioning. It is conceivable that these two opposing effects often offset one another, yielding little net effect of context stimuli on judgments at all.

The question therefore arises as to when one type of context effect is likely to be observed and when the other type will predominate. One factor is suggested by the fact that assimilation effects are the result of encoding the test stimuli in terms of semantic concepts that are activated by the context stimuli and are descriptively applicable for interpreting them (see Chapter 6). To this extent, context stimuli are more likely to have positive encoding effects when these stimuli, and the criteria for judging them, are based on semantic considerations than when they are not. A study by Wyer and Schwartz (1969) provides evidence of this contingency. Subjects were asked to judge a target stimulus following exposure to context stimuli that had either favorable or unfavorable implications along the dimension of judgment. The semantic content of the stimuli and its relevance to judgment varied over experimental conditions. In one (no semantic content) condition, the stimuli were photographs of either high or low quality. Here, strong contrast effects occurred; judgments of the quality of the target stimulus were substantially lower when the quality of the context photographs was high than when it was low. In a second, (high semantic content) condition, the stimuli were statements about blacks and the context stimuli were either favorable or unfavorable. In this case, context effects were strongly positive; the target statement was rated as more favorable when the context statements were also favorable than when they were unfavorable. In two other (moderate semantic content conditions), the stimuli were cartoons that were rated in terms of their funniness, or social issues that were judged along a dimension of liberalness or conservatism. In these cases, context effects were not particularly strong in either direction. Wyer and Schwartz concluded that when the stimuli had no semantic content, the context stimuli were used as standards of comparison in judging the target stimuli, producing contrast effects for reasons noted earlier. When the stimuli being judged had semantic content, subjects attempted to interpret the test stimuli in a manner that was consistent with the semantic implications of the context statements that preceded them, leading to assimilation effects.

This, of course, is not the only factor that is likely to determine the relative magnitudes of assimilation and contrast effects. A second factor, suggested by research on the influence of category accessibility on judgments (Herr, Sherman, & Fazio, 1983; see Chapter 6), may be the extremity of the context stimuli in relation to the test stimuli. Additional research is obviously necessary, however, to circumscribe more clearly the conditions in which these two effects occur.

Effects of Overt Responses on Later Behavior and Judgments

The research described in previous chapters provides examples of how the *process* of generating a response to a stimulus may affect subsequent judgments of the stimulus and also overt behavior toward it. (See, for example, the effects of predicting one's performance on a task on actual task performance; Dweck & Gilliard, 1975; Goodhart, 1986; Sherman et al., 1981.) However, an additional implication of the general model we propose is that an overt response per se, independently of the processes that led it to be generated or the cognitions that were involved in this processing, may affect later behavior and judgments. A representation of one's overt response to a stimulus is theoretically deposited in a referent bin pertaining to the stimulus. As a result, it becomes an available piece of information about the stimulus that can be retrieved and used independently of other knowledge. However, the rules for generating an overt response, which are often irrelevant to knowledge about the stimulus per se, are typically not stored in this bin. This means, for example, that although a response that subjects report along a category scale may be influenced by contextual factors that affect its relation to the subjective inference it represents, the response may be later retrieved and used as a basis for judgments and decisions independently of contextual factors.

Perhaps the most compelling demonstration of this phenomenon was constructed by Sherman et al. (1978) in a study we mentioned in Chapter 5. Subjects in this study, ostensibly run in pairs, were asked to judge the importance of a series of social issues that in some cases were normatively very important and in other cases were rather trivial. In one condition, "recycling" (an issue of moderate importance) was included near the end of the questionnaire, whereas in a second condition, this issue was not mentioned. Upon completion of the questionnaire, and while the experimenter was out of the room, one subject (who was actually a confederate) "spontaneously" indicated that she happened to be a volunteer worker on a recycling project and, on this pretense, solicited help from the other (real) subject. The question was how much help the subject would be willing to provide.

Subjects who had not responded to the recycling item in the questionnaire volunteered more help when the context issues they had rated were important than when they were trivial. Under this condition, subjects appeared to base their helping decision on a general social responsibility norm that was activated by thinking about the important social issues but not by thinking about the trivial ones. When subjects had rated recycling in the questionnaire, however, this was not the case. These subjects rated recycling as less important when the context issues were important than when they were trivial, presumably because they inferred that the response scale was applicable to a higher range of stimulus values in the former condition. Their later helping decisions were then in line with their ratings; that is, they also helped less when the context issues were important.

The context issues apparently had little effect on participants' *subjective* perceptions of the importance of social issues at the time the questionnaire was completed. (If it had, contrast effects on helping behavior would have occurred even when recycling had not formally been rated.) Rather, the context issues only affected subjects' transformation of their subjective judgments of recycling onto the scale. Once this was done, the rating was stored in memory. Later, when help was requested, the rating was retrieved out of the context of the issues in which it

---

4. These effects occurred only under conditions in which the confederate, in making her request for help, explicitly mentioned the presence of the recycling item in the questionaire, thus calling subjects' attention to it and the response they made. Under conditions in which the confederate requested help without mentioning the item, subjects' helping behavior was similar to that under no-judgment conditions. This simply indicates that subjects' responses to the item, made in the context of many other items, were not sufficiently noteworthy to be retrieved from permanent memory without the presence of situational factors that made it prominent.

was originally embedded, its implications were evaluated in relation to a set of standards that was similar in both experimental conditions, and these implications were used as a basis for helping decisions.

Sherman et al.'s study is particularly impressive because it shows that category ratings may ultimately come to influence social behavior toward the person or object being rated independently of the subjective judgment to which the rating initially pertained. A quite different study by Higgins and Lurie (1983) has conceptually similar implications. Subjects were given a description of the sentences imposed for various criminal offenses by both a target judge, Jones, and three "context" judges. The context judges' sentences were either longer or shorter than the ones that Jones imposed. Subjects were asked to judge Jones along a scale from "lenient" to "harsh." As expected, they rated Jones as more lenient when the context sentences were long than when they were short, suggesting that they positioned the "harshness" response scale to include longer sentences in the former case.

The critical aspect of the study took place a week later. Here, subjects were given a sample of sentences recommended by a *different* group of context judges that again were either long or short. They were then asked to recall the sentences that Jones imposed in the first session. Higgins and Lurie hypothesized that subjects, having assigned a category rating to Jones along the harshness scale in Session 1, would remember this rating better than the sentences on which it was based. Therefore, they were expected to retrieve the harshness rating they had made, reinterpret its implications in terms of the sentences imposed by the context judges in session 2, and use these implications as a basis for "recalling" Jones's sentences. This means that Jones should be recalled as having imposed longer sentences when the context judges in Session 2 advocated long sentences (thereby leading harshness ratings to be associated with longer sentences) than when they advocated short sentences. This was also the case; subjects reported Jones as having made much longer sentences in the first case than in the second, and this was true regardless of the sentences imposed by context judges in Session 1.

Effects of Verbally-Coded Responses

The two examples above concern the effects of category ratings on judgments and decisions. The tendency to retrieve previous responses out of context and use them as bases for later judgments and decisions is a more general phenomenon, however, that pertains to other types of responses as well. Verbal labels that one assigns to a stimulus may have similar effects. For example, although I subjectively judge a colleague's new hair style to be "ugly" when I first see it, I may convey this opinion in much more diplomatic terms. Later, I may retrieve my verbal description of her hair and interpret its implications in terms of the concepts to which I usually apply this description. Consequently, I may "remember" her hairdo as less hideous than I had subjectively judged it to be when I saw it.

These processes have been investigated in the laboratory by Higgins and his colleagues (Higgins & Rholes, 1978; Higgins & McCann, 1984). In the first study, subjects were told that their task would be to read a paragraph describing a target person's behavior, and then, based on this description, to prepare a written characterization of the person that would permit an acquaintance to identify him. They were further told that the acquaintance either liked the target or disliked him. The behaviors that were mentioned in the paragraph (e.g., wanting to cross the Atlantic in a sailboat, being well aware of his ability to do things well, etc.) could be interpreted as exemplars of either favorable traits (adventurous, self confident, etc.) or unfavorable ones (reckless, conceited). Some subjects after reading the paragraph actually prepared a written description of the target to be given to the recipient. These subjects chose trait terms to use that were evaluatively consistent with the recipient's attitude toward the target, presumably because this would facilitate the recipient's identification of him. (Politeness norms may have operated as well; see previous discussion.) Moreover, their subsequent evaluations of the target were evaluatively consistent with the description they had written. Other, control subjects were told the intended recipient's attitude toward the target and read the paragraph describing him but did not actually prepare a written description of him. These subjects evaluated the target similarly regardless of how well the recipient liked him. This means that subjects did not simply base their judgments on the recipient's apparent attitude toward the target. Rather, they were influenced by their verbal description of the target in the communication they had generated. This description was retrieved and used as a basis for their judgments independently of the factors that gave rise to its initial construction.

Higgins and Rholes' findings have important implications for the effects of informal communication of the sort that occurs in daily life. That is, they suggest that our personal opinions may sometimes be more influenced by the verbal labels we have used to express them to others than by the information we have acquired that is relevant to these opinions. Thus, conditions that lead people to express publicly more extreme points of view than they would normally (or, alternatively, that lead them to express more moderate opinions than the information actually warrants), may have important influences on issue-related behaviors they perform, and judgments they report, in other situations later on. Self-judgments may have similar effects. A person who is inclined to be self-deprecating when describing his ability to others may subsequently come to believe that he actually has low ability, and this perception may influence his performance in areas to which the ability is relevant.

Additional Considerations

In the studies described above, the responses that subjects generated were later retrieved from memory and used out of context as information that was relevant to judgments and decisions. One other way in which one response may affect another is indirectly implied by the informativeness axiom. The judgments that people are asked to make are often conceptually related and are based on similar subsets of knowledge. For example, they may be asked to estimate someone's ability to get along with co-workers, and also his ability to get along with people in general. The two items are obviously related. However, people who are asked to respond to both questions in succession may infer that the questioner wants to obtain different information from each question, and therefore expects them to distinguish between the criteria for responding to the questions. Therefore, if people have responded to the first item, they may intentionally exclude the factors that underlie this response from consideration when responding to the second. This may introduce a systematic bias in responses to the second item.

Evidence of this phenomenon was reported by Strack, Martin, and Schwarz (1987). Subjects were asked to report their happiness with dating followed by their happiness with their life in general. In one condition, the two questions were on different pages and were not explicitly related. In this condition, the two measures were correlated .55. In a second condition, however, the two questions were presented on the same page and were preceded by a statement that the experimenter was interested in "two areas of life that may be important for people's overall well-being...." In this condition, the correlation between the two judgments was only .26. This suggested that many subjects in the latter condition intentionally excluded their dating behavior as a basis for evaluating their general happiness in an attempt to distinguish between the two judgments they were asked to report. Additional studies by the authors provided further support for this interpretation.

A perhaps more dramatic demonstration of this effect is provided in a study of political judgment by Ottati, Riggle, Wyer, Schwarz, and Kuklinski (1989). In this study, subjects reported their agreement with a variety of propositions pertaining to civil liberties. In conditions of primary relevance to the issues at hand, propositions that applied to people in general (e.g., "People should have the right to express their views in public") were each preceded in the questionnaire by a related one pertaining to a particular social group that was either positively regarded (e.g., "The American Civil Liberties Union should have the right to express their views in public") or negatively regarded ("Members of the American Nazi Party should have the right to express their views in public"). However, the specific proposition either immediately preceded the general one to which it was related or was separated from the general proposition by at least six other, unrelated items.

The results were quite dramatic. When the two related propositions were separated in the questionnaire, subjects reported greater agreement with the general proposition when the specific proposition that preceded it referred to a favorable group ($M = 2.56$ along a scale from -5 to +5) than when it referred to a unfavorable one ($M = 1.76$). This suggests that the particular subset of social knowledge that was activated by responding to the specific proposition was used as a basis for evaluating the general proposition as well, and therefore had a positive influence on judgments for reasons elaborated in Chapter 9. In contrast, when the specific proposition immediately preceded the general one, agreement with the general proposition was *less* when the group mentioned in the specific proposition was favorable ($M = 2.09$) than when it was unfavorable ($M = 2.91$). Thus, when the two propositions were together, subjects in responding to the general proposition appear to have intentionally excluded from consideration both the group mentioned in the specific proposition and the knowledge that was used to evaluate it, responding to it as if the general proposition were worded "Except for (e.g.) the American Nazi Party,...." In fact, contrast effects occurred, suggesting that the juxtaposition of the two propositions led subjects to use their attitude toward the specific proposition as a standard of comparison in evaluating the more general one.

Direct Estimation of Subjective Stimulus Values

The above discussion has focused on conditions in which the scale categories that subjects are required to use to report their judgments are not well defined, and, therefore, the stimulus values to which the categories apply are not clear. Not all response scales are of this type. Often, subjects are asked to report judgments in units that are familiar to them. For example, they may estimate the weight of an object in pounds, or may indicate the number of times that a particular type of event has occurred. This is often done by checking one of several choice alternatives, each of which specifies a particular range of physical stimulus values. The choice alternatives are typically worded in such a way that all possible stimulus values are taken into account. Thus, for example, a person who is asked to estimate the frequency with which (s)he goes out on dates might be given a set of choice alternatives such as:

a. less than once a month
b. 1-2 times a month
c. 3-6 times a month
d. 7-15 times a month
e. over 15 times a month

These alternatives cover all possible frequencies, and the meaning of each alternative is clear. Thus, the problems of construing the range of stimulus values to which the scale pertains, and the subjective values corresponding to any particular alternative, are eliminated. Some additional factors arise, however, that may affect not only how subjects respond along these scales but also how they construe the implications of these responses for other judgments they make. These effects are partly the result of subjects' application of the informativeness principle. However, other considerations come into play as well.

To see this, compare the set of response alternatives noted above with a second set:

a. less than once a week
b. 1-2 times a week
c. 3-5 times a week
d. 6-10 times a week
e. over 10 times a week

This set of alternatives, like the first set, covers all possible dating frequencies. There is an important difference between the two sets, however, which arises from their implications for what frequency is "typical." It seems likely that people who are given a set of response alternatives of this sort are likely to infer that the administrator considers the middle category to denote what the average person is likely to do. Therefore, they may infer that the dating frequency the experimenter considers "typical" is about 3-5 times a month in the first case, and is about 3-5 times a week in the second.

This may have two effects. First, subjects may have only an approximate idea of their own dating frequency. Moreover, they may not do an exhaustive search of memory in order to compute it. Rather, they may base their frequency estimate on not only a partial search of memory for instances of dating that come easily to mind (Tversky & Kahneman, 1973; see Chapter 9), but also their perception of what is "typical," assuming that others' behavior is a good predictor of their own. Therefore, if subjects assume that the center category of the scale they are asked to use is an indication of what is typical, their personal frequency estimates may be biased toward this value. In our example, this means that they will report a higher dating frequency when they use the second scale than when they use the first.

At the same time, because subjects also take direct knowledge of their behavior into account, their estimates may often differ from the value they infer to be typical on the basis of the scale they are given. They may, therefore, evaluate themselves differently, depending on whether it is above or below what they perceive to be average. In our example, subjects are more likely to infer that they are below average in dating frequency when they are given the second (high frequency) scale than when they are given the first. Suppose they use these perceptions as bases for evaluating themselves, and consider dating to be socially desirable. Then, they may see themselves as more deficient, and, therefore, may be more dissatisfied with their dating behavior, when they have been given the high frequency scale than when they have been administered the low frequency one.

A series of studies by Schwarz, Hippler, Deutsch, and Strack (1985) supports this reasoning. In one study, subjects estimated the amount of time they spent watching television. In one (high frequency scale) condition, the choice alternatives ranged from "up to 2 1/2 hours" to "more than 4 1/2 hours." In a second (low frequency scale) condition, the alternatives ranged from "up to 1/2 hour" to "more than 2 1/2 hours." After responding along one of the response scales, subjects reported how satisfied they were with their leisure time.

If subjects base their frequency estimates in part on their perceptions of what they think is typical, they should report watching more television if they are administered the first (high frequency) scale than if they are administered the second one. At the same time, they are more likely to perceive themselves as watching less television than average in the first condition. Consequently, because excessive television watching is considered undesirable, these subjects should evaluate their use of leisure time relatively more favorably than subjects who are administered the second (low frequency) scale. Schwarz et al.'s findings confirmed these predictions.

An interesting extension of this idea was provided by Schwarz and Scheuring (1986). In this case, the dependent variable concerned subjects' satisfaction with their current sexual relationships. One experiment was conceptually similar to the one described above. That is, subjects were asked to indicate either (a) the frequency with which they masturbated or (b) the frequency with which they had intercourse. In each case, the response alternatives provided them ranged either from "less than once a week" to "more than once a day", or from "never" to "more than once a week." Subjects who made estimates along the first (high frequency) scale reported higher frequencies of engaging in the activity to which it was relevant (masturbation or intercourse) than subjects who were administered the second (low frequency) scale. However, subjects who were administered the high frequency scale reported greater satisfaction with their sexual relationships when the scale pertained to masturbation (and leading them to infer that their masturbation frequency was below average) than when the scale pertained to intercourse (leading them to infer that they had intercourse less frequently than average). Correspondingly, subjects who were administered the low frequency scale reported less satisfaction when the scale pertained to masturbation (leading them to infer that they masturbated more frequently than average) than when it pertained to intercourse.

The effects of the different frequency scales on subjects' judgments described above presumably result from their effects on subjects' perceptions of themselves as more or less deviant from what is "typical," as inferred from the frequency specified in the center scale category, and their evaluation of themselves as more or less discrepant from this external standard. The most theoretically interesting results obtained by Schwarz and Scheuring were obtained in a second study in which subjects were asked about their frequencies of *both* masturbating and having intercourse, and the types of scales administered were varied independently. In this condition, unlike the one in which only one attribute was assessed, subjects could make a direct comparison of their intercourse frequency estimate and their masturbation frequency estimate. Because of this, subjects' satisfaction with their sexual relationships may not depend on their evaluation of themselves in relation to others. Instead, it may be determined by their perception of the relative frequencies with which they personally have intercourse and masturbate, independently of these external standards. As noted above, subjects infer that they engage in each activity more often when they are administered a high frequency scale than when they are administered a low frequency scale. Therefore, they should be more satisfied with their sexual relationships when they have reported their intercourse along a high frequency scale, but more satisfied when they report their masturbation along such a scale. Note that these predictions are precisely the opposite of those that occur when subjects were administered a single scale. Schwarz and Scheuring's results supported these predictions as well.

These findings are of general importance in demonstrating that the response alternatives one happens to use may have quite different effects when subjects are predisposed to evaluate themselves in relation to an internal standard than when they are inclined to use an external standard. Further investigation of the conditions in which different standards are applied may be worth investigating, and their effects may be evaluated using procedures analogous to those described above.

Methodological Implications

Independently of their theoretical interest, the rules that are used by subjects to transform subjective judgments into overt responses must be understood in order to interpret data of the sort collected in many social psychology experiments. Both verbal responses and category ratings that are observed in different experimental conditions may be affected not only by the subjective implications of the cognitive representations on which these responses are based but also by the way in which these implications are transformed into overt behavior. Unless these effects can be separated and their independent contributions established, the interpretation of data may be misleading. A few representative experiments may suffice to convey this fact.

Interpretation of Open-Ended Responses

1. Attributions of Behavior to Dispositions and Situations

One of the better known phenomena identified in research on social attribution is the apparent tendency for subjects to attribute their own behavior to characteristics of the social environment but to attribute others' behavior to characteristics of the actors themselves. Although this tendency undoubtedly occurs (cf. Jones & Nisbett, 1971), it is by no means as universal as psychologists initially assumed. (For a theoretical analysis of the conditions in which the tendency is and is not likely to occur, see Monson & Snyder, 1977.) Moreover, early investigations of the difference may well have been misinterpreted as a result of a failure to take the informativeness principle into account.

In one study (Nisbett, Caputo, Legant, & Maracek, 1973), for example, subjects were asked to explain either (a) their own choice of major or (b) a friend's choice of major. These open-ended responses were coded in terms of whether they referred to a dispositional characteristic of the decision-maker or to a situational characteristic. Subjects' explanations for their own behavior were often phrased in terms of the object (e.g., "because it is interesting"), whereas their explanations for the other's behavior referred to the other person as well (e.g., "she thinks it is interesting"). Nisbett et al. interpreted the first type of response as an attribution to a situational factor (i.e., a characteristic of the curriculum) and the second type as an attribution to the actor (the person's idiosyncratic attitude toward the curriculum). Based on this interpretation, they concluded that people were likely to attribute their own behavior to external situational factors but to attribute other's behavior to internal, dispositional factors.

A consideration of subjects' verbal responses in terms of the informativeness principle, however, suggests that such an interpretation may be misleading. To continue with our example, people may consider the statements "I think it (the curriculum) is interesting" and "it is interesting" to be synonymous when they are used to explain their personal choice of major. A person would not say that something was interesting unless he personally thought it was, and the insertion of "I think..." into the verbal explanation goes without saying. In explaining another's behavior, however, there is a difference in meaning between "it is interesting" (which implies that the speaker personally thinks the curriculum is interesting) and "he thinks it is interesting" (which does not have this implication). In fact, what the speaker happens to think is irrelevant to the other's choice. Therefore, subjects may be more inclined to use the phrase "he(she) thinks..." in reporting their explanations of others' behavior than explanations of their own. To this extent, the difference in verbal responses obtained by Nisbett et al. would not reflect a fundamental difference in the type of attributions that subjects make. Fortunately, not all research on self vs. other attribution differences is susceptible to this interpretable problem. (But see Wyer, 1981, for additional ambiguities associated with the interpretation of data bearing on this difference.)

2. Insight into the Determinants of One's Own Behavior

A provocative article by Nisbett and Wilson (1977; see also Wilson & Nisbett, 1978) argued that people have little insight into the determinants of their behavior.

In one of the experiments used to support this argument, subjects in a supermarket were asked to evaluate the quality of different pairs of socks. The socks were aligned in a row on the counter, and subjects considered them in order, from left to right. Although the socks in each position were identical in quality, subjects tended to choose the most recently considered pair (i.e., the one on the right) as the one they preferred. Thus, the position of the socks on the table affected subjects' choices. Nonetheless, subjects when asked to explain their choice never cited its position as a basis for their decision. Nisbett and Wilson interpreted this as an indication that subjects had little insight into the determinants of their choice.

A consideration of this finding in terms of the informativeness principle suggests an alternative interpretation, however. When asked to explain their choice, subjects are likely to assume that the questioner is seeking information about factors that are directly related to the decision and not remote determinants that are separated from the decision by several interpolated causal steps. (Thus, for example, if I am asked to explain a hostile remark to my secretary, I may cite her failure to get a paper typed as fast as I would like, and may not report the fact that I had a fight with my wife this morning and my car broke down on the way to work. This may be true even though I am quite aware that these other factors contributed to my frustration and irritability.) Strictly speaking, subjects in Nisbett and Wilson's study did *not* choose the socks *because* they were on the right. Rather, they chose the socks because of the quality as they perceived it. The quality of the more recently considered pair of socks was more salient than the quality of other pairs, and this may have affected their perceptions. However, the recency of considering the socks was not a direct basis for choosing them. Therefore, subjects are unlikely to consider sock position as a factor that the experimenter is interested in knowing about.

Some more general considerations are raised by this example. To answer a question of the sort Nisbett and Wilson's subjects were asked, one must infer the standard relative to which the behavior should be considered. Suppose a person who buys a pair of green socks in a particular store is asked why he purchased them. To answer this question, the person must make an implicit assumption about the alternative the information-seeker is thinking about when he asked the question. For example, the questioner may be asking whether the person bought the green socks rather than blue ones, in which case an appropriate response might be "green goes with my eyes." Or, the questioner may be asking why the person bought socks rather than some other article of clothing. In this case, an appropriate answer might be "I have plenty of shirts, but all of my socks have holes in them." Or, the questioner might be wondering why the person bought socks in this particular store rather than another, in which case "they were on sale" might be an appropriate answer. Note that some of these explanations would qualify as dispositional attributions, whereas others would be classified as external or situational. Therefore, once again, the conclusion drawn about whether a particular behavior is attributable to situational or dispositional factors may depend in part on the recipient's assumption about what, specifically, the questioner has in mind.

Category Ratings

As the preceding examples suggest, an appropriate interpretation of subjects' verbal responses to a question requires knowledge of their assumptions about the standard of comparison that the questioner wants them to use. Similar considerations obtain when interpreting a respondent's rating along a category scale. When the range of stimuli to which the scale is relevant is not stated explicitly by the experimenter, the subject must infer it indirectly on the basis of factors similar to those we discussed earlier. However, to interpret the subject's responses, the experimenter must also be aware of these factors. Otherwise, inappropriate conclusions may be drawn.

Although several indications of such interpretations exist in the literature, a second study reported by Nisbett and Wilson (1977) is representative. In this study, subjects judged the emotional impact of a communication that either did or did not contain a particularly emotion- provoking passage. Although subjects who read the passage reported that it had a considerable effect on their judgments, their actual ratings of the communication did not differ from those of the subjects who had not read the passage. Again, Nisbett and Wilson concluded from this that subjects are insensitive to the factors that determine their responses. As we have argued at length in previous sections of this chapter, however, subjects are likely to use the stimuli they are asked to rate as indications of how to position their response scale. In particular, they are likely to position their scale to include a more extreme set of subjective stimulus values when they are asked to judge an extreme (i.e., emotional) stimulus than when they are asked to judge a moderate one. Consequently, the projections of these judgments of the stimuli onto the scale may not differ despite the fact that they differ subjectively. Note that if this interpretation of Nisbett and Wilson's study is correct, it implies, somewhat ironically, that the *experimenters*, not the subjects themselves, had little insight into the determinants of the subjects' behavior.

Separation of Effects on Subjective Judgments and Effects on Response Language

The question arises as to how to separate the effects of situational and individual difference variables on the subjective judgment of a stimulus from their effects on the language used to report it. There are at least three possibilities. One, of course, is simply to provide all subjects with explicit standards to use as scale anchors. A second possibility is suggested by Upshaw (1978). To use Upshaw's example, suppose two scales associated with criminal punishment pertain to the severity of the punishment and to the length of the recommended sentence. Responses along both scales may be mediated by subjective judgments of a single underlying attribute (severity) and thus, within a given experimental condition, may be highly correlated. Then, if an experimental manipulation influences judgments along one scale without influencing judgments along the second, one can conclude that its influence is due to its effect on the positioning of one response scale but not the other, and is not due to its effect on subjective inferences of the attribute being measured (which should be reflected in differences in ratings along both scales).

Upshaw found this to be true in a study of social influence. Specifically, subjects read about a court case in which a criminal was convicted of manslaughter, and were told that the judge recommended a sentence that varied over experimental conditions between 1 and 31 years. Subjects then gave their own recommendation of the sentence to be imposed, and also estimated the sternness with which the criminal should be dealt. Within each experimental condition, subjects' estimates of sternness were highly correlated with the length of sentence they recommended, indicating that the two scales assessed the same underlying attribute. Nonetheless, subjects' estimates of the appropriate sentence to be administered increased with the length of the sentence the judge imposed, whereas their rating of sternness did not. This indicates that subjects used the judge's sentence as a standard in positioning their "length of sentence" response scale, and that this affected the transformation of their subjective judgments of the severity with which the criminal should be punished onto this scale. However, it did *not* influence subjects' inferences of severity itself.

Still a third procedure for evaluating the magnitude of response language effects is possible. This possibility arises from the fact that if an experimental manipulation affects the manner in which subjects position their response scale in relation to the range of subjective values of the attribute being judged, it should influence subjects' judgments of all objects along the scale to an approximately equal degree. This should be true even if these objects are objectively irrelevant to the manipulation. Thus, if a manipulation affects ratings of one stimulus to a greater degree than it affects ratings of a second, objectively irrelevant stimulus, the difference between the two ratings may indicate the extent to which the manipulation influenced the subjective judgment of the first stimulus over and above its effects on the language used to report it.

A study by Steiner (1968), on the effects of evaluations by another on self evaluations, is interesting to consider in this light. In this study, subjects completed a personality inventory that they were told would be evaluated by a senior undergraduate student. They then rated themselves with respect to the attributes being assessed along a series of semantic differentials, and also rated the "average

TABLE 11.1
Change in Reported Judgments of Self, the Average Person, and the Evaluator
as a Function of the Evaluator's Feedback (adapted from Steiner, 1968)

	Change in semantic differential ratings			Change in judgments of evaluator's competence
	of self	of the average person	difference	
Positive feedback	1.71	.48	1.23	1.36
Negative feedback	1.16	1.01	.15	0

Note: Changes are scored in the direction of the feedback administered.

person" along the same scales. Finally, they estimated the ability of the senior student to evaluate them accurately.

In a second experimental session, subjects received bogus feedback about the senior student's ratings of them along the same semantic differentials they had used to make self-ratings in the first session. These ratings were systematically either higher or lower than subjects' initial self-ratings. Subjects then rerated both themselves and the average person along the scales, and reassessed the senior student's ability to evaluate them accurately.

Subjects' mean ratings of themselves and the average person are shown in Table 11.1 under positive and negative feedback conditions. Because the "average person" is objectively irrelevant to the feedback that subjects received about themselves, it seems reasonable to attribute changes in these ratings as a result of feedback to shifts in subjects' positioning of the response scales they used to report these judgments. If this assumption is made, the differences between self-ratings and average person ratings, shown in the third column of the table, indicate the actual changes in subjective self-judgments that were produced by the feedback. Viewed in this light, the results are quite interesting. That is, subjects appear to have accepted positive feedback about themselves and changed their subjective self-judgments accordingly, as indicated by a positive difference between the change in self-ratings and the change in average person judgments under positive feedback conditions. However, they attributed negative feedback to the fact that they had been using the response scale differently than the evaluator, and, therefore, they changed their own positioning of the scale in a manner that eliminated this difference. As a result, both their self-ratings and the average person ratings were affected similarly, but little change in subjects' actual perceptions of themselves occurred.

The plausibility of this interpretation is strengthened by subjects' ratings of the evaluator. These evaluations, of course, were made along a different scale than the ones to which feedback was relevant, and so changes in judgments along this scale should not be influenced by changes in response language. Subjects' judgments of the favorable evaluator increased from the second session to the first, as would be expected if subjects interpreted the evaluator's ratings as evidence of a true positive evaluation. However, their judgments of the unfavorable evaluator did not correspondingly decrease but instead, remained unchanged. This would also be expected if subjects did not interpret the negative ratings they received as actually unfavorable, but rather, attributed them to a difference in the way they and the evaluator had used the response scales.

Concluding Remarks

In this chapter, we have not attempted to consider all of the theoretical and empirical issues that surround the transformation of subjective judgments into overt responses. Rather, we have tried to provide an appreciation for the nature of these issues and their implications for a general understanding of social information processing. The role of informativeness, accuracy, and politeness, and how they combine to influence communication phenomena both in and outside of the laboratory, has only begun to be understood. We believe that research on the determinants and effects of response generation processes is one of the more neglected areas of social cognition, and we encourage future work on this important component of information processing.

Chapter 12
The Role of Affect and Emotion in Information Processing

The last several chapters have each focused on the structure and function of a different storage or processing unit. It has often been impossible, of course, to consider in isolation the processes that are theoretically associated with any particular unit. A person's response to a stimulus situation is almost always mediated by cognitive processing at several different stages, and data bearing on the effects of processing at one stage cannot usually be interpreted independently of assumptions about the processing that occurs at other stages.

In addition, several situational and individual difference variables may affect processing at more than one stage. One example was noted in the last chapter. That is, context stimuli may affect not only the interpretation of information presented about a test stimulus (a function that is theoretically performed by the Encoder/Organizer) but also the positioning of the response scale that is used to report judgments of the stimulus (a function that is performed by the Response Generator). The next two chapters focus on the effects of two factors that potentially play a role in virtually all phases of social information processing: (a) the affect or emotion that one experiences at the time information is processed and a judgment or decision is made, and (b) the "self."

The two factors are obviously related. One's affective reaction to a stimulus is basically an attribute of oneself. Moreover, the affect or emotion that one experiences may be both a determinant and an effect of one's self-perceptions and the thoughts that one has about them. However, several theoretical and empirical issues are unique to each factor. In this chapter, we consider both the cognitive determinants and the cognitive consequences of people's emotional experiences. Because our discussion cuts across almost all of the types of processing we have considered in previous chapters, it incidentally provides an integration of many of the issues we have addressed earlier.

The Cognitive Representation of Affect and Emotion

Single stimuli or configurations of stimuli that we encounter in daily life often elicit configurations of subjective, physiological reactions. These reactions may either be innate, unconditioned responses to stimuli or may have become conditioned to stimuli through learning. Although we are typically unable to isolate the particular reactions that make up any given cluster, we are conscious of their occurrence and experience them as either pleasant or unpleasant. Moreover, we distinguish qualitatively between different clusters of pleasant (or unpleasant) reactions, and consequently come to assign them different verbal labels. This is presumably also a result of social learning. A mother who hears her child cry or observes other manifestations of an internal state that she personally labels as "sad" may tell the child "Don't be sad." This may lead associations to be formed between the label "sad," the cluster of internal reactions the child experiences, and overt behaviors (e.g., crying) that the child is aware of manifesting. The resulting configuration of associations among subjective physiological reactions, behavioral manifestations, and verbal labels comes to function as a concept that is stored in memory, where it can be retrieved and used to process information and knowledge in much the same way as other concepts.

In addition, associations are formed between features of the emotion concept and elements of the situation in which they occurred. Consequently, the cognitive representation of the situation may include these features. In this way, certain configurations of situational features may become associated in memory with different affective reactions and with the concepts that denote these reactions. Our conceptualization of the cognitive representation of affect and emotion is based on these general assumptions.

The Representation of Emotion in Memory

Semantic representations. Concepts of different emotions or affective states ("angry," "sad," "happy," etc.) are a subset of the attribute concepts that are contained in the semantic bin in Permanent Storage (see chapter 3). These emotion concepts, like trait concepts, can be conceptualized metaphorically as consisting of a central node to which different configurations of defining features are attached. These features may include verbal labels (e.g., names of the concept) and representations of overt behaviors. In addition, they include a cluster of internal subjective (e.g., physiological) reactions. A simplified representation of the concept "angry" might therefore resemble that shown in Figure 12.1.

Some conceptualizations (cf. Isen, 1984; Schwarz & Clore, 1987) distinguish between "affect," "mood," and "emotion" in terms of the duration with which they are experienced, the specificity of the object toward which they are directed, and subjects' awareness of the factors that give rise to them. Although these distinctions

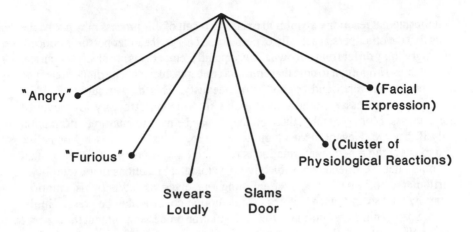

Figure 12.1 Hypothetical cognitive representation of the emotion concept "angry."

may be useful in some contexts, we do not consider them in the conceptualization we propose here. Rather, we use the terms interchangeably throughout our discussion. We recognize, of course, that concepts may exist at different levels of generality, and that "good" and "bad" may refer to general emotion concepts that are each instantiated by several more specific ones ("happy," "sad," etc.). However, the role of these various concepts in cognitive functioning is theoretically similar.

An emotion concept of the sort shown in Figure 12.1 may be activated and used by the Encoder/Organizer to interpret subsets of stimulus information to which it is applicable. Moreover, once such a concept is applied, it may be used by the Inference Maker to infer other, unspecified features of the stimulus object. Thus, if we personally experience the cluster of internal reactions that define the concept "angry," we may interpret these reactions in terms of the concept and, therefore, infer that we are experiencing anger. On the other hand, we may also apply the concept to ourselves if we observe ourselves perform behaviors (e.g., swearing loudly, slamming the door, etc.) that exemplify it. To the latter extent, our conceptualization accounts for phenomena similar to those implied by the James-Lange theory of emotion. (That is, we infer that we are angry because we observe ourselves curse or slam the door, rather than cursing or slamming the door because we are angry.) However, our conceptualization also explicitly allows for inferences of emotions based on unique subsets of internal physiological reactions.

The same emotion concepts that are applied to oneself are also applied to others. Therefore, if we hear another person describe himself as "angry," or observe his facial expression, we may apply an "angry" concept to the person and, as a result, infer the presence of other features, such as the person's internal reactions. This permits the model to account for empathy. It is important to note, of course, that the internal reactions we infer to exist as a result of this process may not be the ones that the other person actually experiences. That is, the other person's concept of "angry" may differ from our own. Consequently, empathy is not always accurate.

It is also important to note that emotion concepts, like other attribute concepts, may not be activated and applied spontaneously. This may occur only if the concepts are necessary to encode stimulus information at a very low level of abstractness. More generally, these concepts may be used to interpret information only if they are relevant to the attainment of a higher order processing objective that exists at the time the information is received (see chapter 4). This means that we may often experience the subjective physiological reactions that exemplify a particular emotion without ever labeling ourselves as having this emotion. Moreover, these and other features of an emotion concept may be present in the Work Space, and, therefore, may affect information processing without the concept itself being activated. Recognition of this fact becomes important in understanding some of the effects we discuss later in this chapter.

Representations of affect in referent bins. Emotion concepts and their associated features are also found in referent bins. These bins may pertain either to particular persons, objects and events, or to prototypic ones. In some cases, emotion concepts may be included among the features of a bin header, and, therefore, they may affect the likelihood of identifying and retrieving information from the bin. In addition, emotion concepts or their features may be part of one or more of the representations that are contained in a bin. Therefore, if our representation of a personal experience contains the features of an emotion concept, the recall of this representation and a review of its contents may lead these features to be identified. If the features include a cluster of subjective physiological reactions, we may therefore reexperience these reactions. Put more simply, thinking about an experience that made us sad at the time it occurred may make us feel sad again.

This is not *necessarily* the case, however. That is, emotional reactions to a past experience may occur only if they are among those features that happen to be identified in the course of mentally perusing the cognitive representation we have formed of it. One obvious implication of this is that the longer we think about a past event, the more likely it is that we will encounter features in our cognitive representation of it that correspond to the subjective physiological reactions we had to the event at the time it occurred, and, therefore the more likely it is that we will subjectively reexperience these reactions.

The representation of affect in the goal bin. Finally, emotion concepts and features may be part of a goal specification. That is, they may identify a goal schema that indicates the cognitive steps involved in attaining a particular processing objective. If the physiological reactions that are associated with a particular emotion are experienced as unpleasant, a goal may be to eliminate these reactions, and a goal schema may exist for doing so. This latter assumption permits the model to account for the role of affect in the stimulation of goal-directed cognitive activity (e.g., activity directed toward the elimination of a particular emotional state).

One general implication of this analysis is that emotions, or the concepts associated with them, have no special role in social information processing. Rather, they function in much the same way as other concepts. They may influence the encoding and organization of information in memory, and the storage and retrieval of information. Moreover, they may themselves be used as informational bases for judgments to which they are relevant. Finally, they may stimulate goal-directed cognitive or motor behavior. We elaborate on these various effects, and empirical data bearing on them, later in this chapter.

Alternative Conceptualizations

Our conceptualization should be evaluated in the context of other contemporary theories of the relation between affect and cognition. These theories often differ considerably in their implications, as exemplified by the formulation proposed by Bower (1981) and Zajonc (1980). Bower's conception is more similar to our own. He also postulates the existence of emotion concepts in memory, and assumes that these concepts operate in much the same way as other concepts in the processing of information. Unlike our formulation, however, Bower assumes that emotion concepts are embedded with all other concepts in a general associative network. Thus, the two formulations differ, not in the nature of emotion concepts per se, but rather, in the assumptions they make about the memory structure in which the concepts are contained and the specific cognitive processes that underlie their influence.

Zajonc's (1980) conceptualization (see also Zajonc & Markus, 1984) is far less congenial to our own. Zajonc postulates that cognitive and affective responses to stimuli are the result of two independently functioning systems. Whereas nonaffective responses to stimuli are the result of a cognitive analysis of their descriptive features ("discriminanda," in Zajonc's terms), affective responses are based on features ("preferanda") that are not captured by these descriptive stimulus features. Moreover, affective responses to stimuli are not cognitively mediated.

Although there is little direct empirical evidence against Zajonc's claim, neither is there much evidence to support it. Most of this evidence comes from studies of the effects of frequency of exposure to a stimulus on judgments of liking for the stimulus (cf. Kunst-Wilson & Zajonc, 1980; Moreland & Zajonc, 1977; Wilson, 1979). In these studies, subjects are typically exposed to novel stimuli (e.g., Chinese characters) different numbers of times. Later, subjects are asked to estimate their liking for the stimuli, to judge how familiar they seem, or in some cases, to indicate whether they ever saw the stimuli before. These studies typically show that liking for stimuli increases with the frequency with which they were presented, even when differences in subjects' estimates of their familiarity are partialled out (cf. Moreland & Zajonc, 1977). Moreover, when stimuli are tachistoscopically presented for very brief periods of time, subjects' liking for the stimuli significantly increases with exposure frequency even though subjects' recognition memory for the stimuli is low and is not significantly affected by the frequency of their presentation (cf. Kunst-Wilson & Zajonc, 1980; Wilson, 1979). Zajonc concludes from these data that subjects' liking judgments are based partly on their affective reactions to the stimuli (which increase with frequency of exposure) but are not mediated by cognitive responses (e.g., subjective familiarity, as reflected in recognition accuracy).

As Birnbaum (1981; Birnbaum & Mellers, 1979a,b) points out, however, this conclusion is somewhat suspect. The model proposed by Zajonc, shown in Figure 12.2a, assumes that two mediators, "subjective familiarity" and "subjective affect," mediate the affective (e.g., liking or pleasantness) judgments that subjects report. To conclude that this model is valid, one must establish that reported affect is correlated with exposure frequency over and above the effect of subjective familiarity. To do this on the basis of a single *index* of rated familiarity, 100% of the variance in subjective familiarity must be captured by this index. It seems very doubtful that this is the case (no single measure of any construct is likely to capture 100% of the variance in the construct). If it is not, the residual correlation of liking judgments with exposure frequency (over and above the effect accounted for by the recognition measure) could be attributed to differences in the proportion of variance in subjective familiarity that the measure of rated familiarity does not capture.

In fact, Birnbaum (1981; Birnbaum & Mellers, 1979a,b) has shown in a reanalysis of Zajonc et al.'s data that a single-mediator model of the sort noted in Figure 12.2b can provide as good an account of the results as a model that postulates two independent (affective and cognitive) mediators (Figure 12.2a). As Moreland and Zajonc (1979) point out, Birnbaum's reanalysis does not demonstrate that a two-mediator model (or, for that matter, a 20-mediator model) is invalid. However, in the absence of empirical evidence suggesting that a second mediator is necessary, the more parsimonious model would seem preferable.

The assumption that affective responses are not always cognitively mediated is also suggested by the observation that these responses may sometimes be faster than responses to the specific descriptive features that compose the stimulus that elicits them. Moreover, these affective responses may remain strong even when the descriptive features of the stimulus cannot be retrieved. Thus, for example, we can sometimes decide that a person who passes us on the street is attractive (or unattractive) much more quickly than we can identify any particular physical attribute of the person that we regard as relevant to this decision (hair color, body build, complexion, etc.). Moreover, we may later feel very confident of our judgment even though we do not remember clearly what the person's specific characteristics were.

A. Two-mediator Model

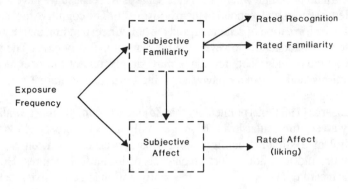

B. One-mediator Model

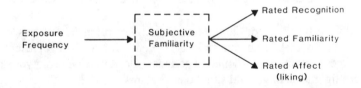

Figure 12.2 Alternative models proposed to describe the observed relations between frequency of exposure to a stimulus and reported liking for the stimulus, based on (a) the two-mediator model proposed by Zajonc, and (b) the one-mediator model proposed by Birnbaum.

To the extent that this phenomenon occurs, it suggests that affective responses to the stimuli are not mediated by a piecemeal analysis of their constituent elements. However, this conclusion does not mean that the responses are not cognitively mediated. The phenomenon may simply exemplify a more general capacity to respond holistically, or "schematically," to configurations of descriptive stimulus features without having to analyze them piecemeal. To provide a trivial example, it takes more time to determine whether the letter sequence PQXNSO is the same as or different from PQXSNO than to decide whether R is the same as S. This is because we have no schema for the first letter string, and must process it letter by letter. However, it takes no more time to decide whether BREAK is the same as

BRAKE than to decide whether R is the same as S, because we have a schema for these letter strings and respond to them holistically. The cognitive mechanisms that underlie the formation of schemata, and the holistic responding that results, are not completely understood. However, the mechanisms clearly exist. The speed with which affective judgments are made may simply reflect the operation of these mechanisms and may not convey anything particularly unique about affective responding per se.

Lazarus (1982) has pointed out that Zajonc's argument may be valid (if at all) at only a very molecular level. More generally, affect is preceded by a cognitive appraisal of a stimulus configuration. This appraisal may itself be holistic or schematic, and may not require an analysis of individual features. However, the holistic meaning that is assigned to the configuration is a cognitive precursor to the affective reaction that is experienced. This view is more compatible with our own conceptualization than is Zajonc's. Lazarus's conception, however, calls attention to the need to specify precisely the types of stimulus situations that are likely to lead to different types of cognitive appraisals, and therefore to activate different types of emotion concepts. The next section addresses this matter.

Cognitive Determinants of Affect and Emotion

As we have noted, emotion concepts may often be features of an event representation that is contained in a referent bin. Such a representation may sometimes pertain to a particular experience. Or, it may be prototypic, consisting of a configuration of general situational features with which the emotion concept has become associated through learning. When subjects encounter a situation whose features exemplify a prototype with which an emotion concept is associated, they may interpret the situation in terms of the prototype. In so doing, other features of the prototype may be activated. If one of these latter features is a cluster of the subjective physiological reactions that characterizes an emotion, subjects may experience these reactions (or, more simply, may experience the emotion).

To the extent this is true, an important objective of research on cognition, affect and emotion is to identify the configurations of situational features with which different types of emotion concepts become associated. The attainment of this objective is a formidable task. People appear to experience a very large number of different emotions, as evidenced by the number of words that they use to describe them (cf. Ortony, Clore, & Collins, 1988). In addition, to the extent that the associations formed between these emotional reactions and situational charac-teristics are socially learned, many of the associations may be idiosyncratic.

There are nevertheless many commonalities in the emotions that are likely to become associated with different general types of stimulus situations. The ease with which motion picture directors can manipulate the emotional responses of their audiences testifies to this fact. Within a given culture, it may therefore be possible to circumscribe at least partially the type of situations (or, more accurately, cognitive representations of the situations) with which different types of emotion concepts become associated. Several attempts to do this have in fact been made (cf. Abelson, 1983; Higgins, 1987; Ortony et al., 1988; Roseman, 1979). Although our own analysis differs to varying degrees from each of these conceptualizations, it borrows ideas from them all.

In this regard, we do not pretend to provide a complete theoretical account of the determinants of emotion. Rather, our intention is to outline a general approach that may be useful in conceptualizing the cognitive bases of emotion that is compatible with the general theory of information processing we are espousing, and that has the potential to be refined and expanded into a more rigorous and complete theoretical formulation.

Our conceptualization distinguishes between the intensity of emotional reactions, their pleasantness and, within each general category of pleasantness, their quality. These various characteristics of an emotion may have different determinants, as indicated below.

Determinants of Pleasantness and Emotional Intensity

1. The Interruption and Completion of Goal-Directed Activity

According to the general model we propose, most cognitive activity is goal-directed. That is, judgmental or behavioral goals are activated by either internal or external stimuli (see chapter 2). These goals, in turn, activate goal schemata that are used by the Executor to direct the flow of information between processing and storage units. In many instances, this cognitive activity results in the generation of a behavior, or sequence of behaviors, that is expected to lead to the attainment of the goal. Whether this behavior sequence actually leads to goal attainment, and the consequences of its success or failure to do so, will be considered in detail presently.

The activities that are required to attain a particular goal may be conceptualized as a sequence of more specific behavioral objectives, or subgoals. For example, a superordinate goal may be "to see a play," and the subgoals that are involved in attaining it may be "arrange for tickets," "get to the theater," etc. The sequence of subgoals, considered in combination, constitute a *plan* (for similar conceptualizations, see Miller, Galanter, & Pribram, 1960; Schank & Abelson, 1977). The subgoals that compose a plan may each be broken down into a sequence of more specific subgoals (a subplan), and each of these subgoals into a sequence of still more specific ones, and so on.

The hierarchy of goals and subgoals of the sort described above compose a prototypic event schema of the sort we discussed in Chapter 8 (cf. Figure 8.1). As we noted in the course of this earlier discussion, event schemata have multiple functions. That is, they can be used to interpret new information, to explain present events, or to predict future ones. In addition, they may be retrieved and used by the Executor (along with a goal schema that specifies the sequence of cognitive activities that underlie the behavioral decisions to be made) to instruct the Response Generator as to what behaviors should be generated to attain the desired end state.

A simplified example of an event schema that might serve as a basis for goal attainment is shown in abstract form in Figure 12.3, and a specific instantiation of it, pertaining to seeing a play, is shown in Figure 12.4.

In this example, the general goal (G, or "see a play") is broken into two behavioral subgoals, g_1 and g_2 (i.e., "arrange for tickets" and "get to theater on time") that constitute a plan for attaining it. Each subgoal is further broken into sequences of more specific behavioral objectives, each of which constitutes a plan for attaining the subgoal. At very low levels in the hierarchy, the plan associated with each subgoal (e.g., "look up phone number") consists of specific, well-learned behavioral acts or routines that, once initiated, are performed with a minimum of effort or cognitive monitoring. These routines are presumably stored in the library of the Response Generator, and therefore may be generated automatically. At higher levels, however, the subgoals are more abstract, and the plans for attaining them usually require conscious decisions.

One aspect of the example shown in Figures 12.3 and 12.4, which was not considered in our earlier discussion of event schemata, is quite important in the present context. That is, *alternative* plans, or behavior sequences, may be available for the attainment of a particular goal. Thus, in our example, g_1 ("arrange for tickets") may be attained through the plan consisting of g_3 and g_4 ("drive to the ticket office" and "buy the tickets") or the plan consisting of g_5 and g_6 ("call the theater" and "make reservations"). Which alternative is selected in a particular instance is determined by how closely the features of its cognitive representation match the features of the particular situation with which the decision-maker is confronted. When alternative plans exist, conditions that prevent the use of one alternative (conceptualized as conditions in which there is an insufficient feature match) may lead to the activation of the second. When only one alternative plan exists, of course, the inability to implement the behavior sequence involved will prevent the superordinate goal from being attained.

These considerations become important in the discussion below. We first consider the effect of goal blocking, or interruption, which we postulate to generate negative (unpleasant) emotions. Then, we consider the effects of goal attainment, with which positive (pleasant) emotions are theoretically associated.

Emotional consequences of goal blocking and interruption: negative affect. We assume that when a series of goal-directed activities has been initiated, an interruption of these activities elicits an unpleasant emotional reaction. This assumption is hardly novel (see, for example, Mandler, 1975). In the context of the

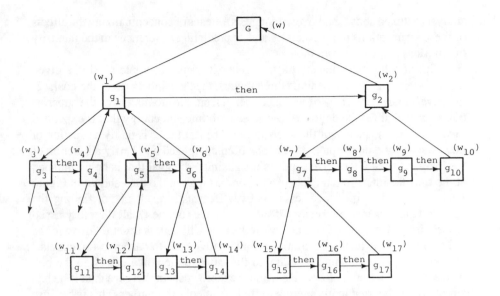

Figure 12.3 Representative event schema used as a basis for attaining goal G. In the figure, g_1, g_2, etc. refer to subgoals, or events, that are instrumental to the attainment of a more general goal in the hierarchy, and w_1, w_2, etc. are weights that represent the amount of time and effort expended in attaining the subgoal.

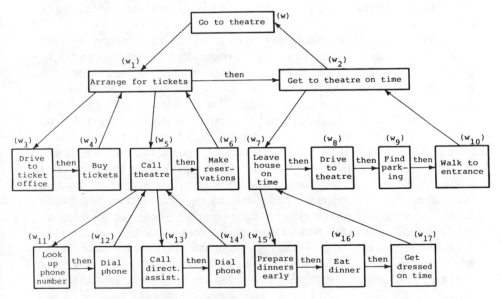

Figure 12.4 Instantiation of the general event schema described in Figure 12.3, pertaining to the general goal of seeing a play.

analysis outlined above, however, it suggests a means of conceptualizing the effects of these interruptions more precisely and of predicting differences in the intensity of emotions that result from them.

Specifically, the intensity of the affect experienced by interrupting a given routine seems likely to depend on three factors: (1) the *importance* of the goal, (2) the *psychological distance* of the interruption from the attainment of the superordinate goal, and (3) the degree of *investment* of time and energy that is expended in vain as a consequence of the interruption. The last factor is partly a function of how much of the interrupted routine has been completed and partly a function of the availability of alternative routines for attaining the goal that is being pursued at the time the interruption takes place. For example, in the plan shown in Figure 12.4, a man will experience less negative affect as a result of not finding the theater's number in the directory if the alternative routine ("call directory assistance") is available than if it is not. Moreover, he will be less upset if "drive to the ticket office" is available to him as an alternative way to "arrange for tickets." However, suppose the man had chosen the latter routine, had driven to the box office, and had found it closed. He would be more upset in this case than if he had simply been thwarted in his attempt to find the telephone number. This is because the person's investment of time, at the point of interruption, is greater in the former case than it is in the latter. The greatest negative affect is experienced from an interruption that occurs close to the attainment of the goal and when no alternative plan is available for attaining it. For example, if a couple, having driven to the theater, finds that they have forgotten to bring the tickets and they have no money to purchase additional ones, the negative affect they experience is likely to be considerable.

Although the foregoing analysis involved a relatively mundane goal, a similar approach can be taken in conceptualizing the consequences of interruptions in the pursuit of more general life goals that take place over a long period of time. For example, imagine an undergraduate who has a plan of becoming a clinical psychologist. The subgoals in this plan include (1) taking a psychopathology course from the great Professor X, (2) getting high scores on the GRE, (3) going to Harvard for graduate training, and (4) getting a job at a major university. If the student attempts to enroll in Professor X's psychopathology course and finds it is closed, the negative affect experienced may be relatively low, particularly if there are other psychopathology courses available, or if X will offer the course again. On the other hand, if the student is rejected by Harvard, the negative affect will be greater because (a) the interruption is closer to the superordinate goal, and (b) there is a greater commitment to the plan for attaining it. Even in this case, however, an alternative routine may be available (e.g., the student may have been admitted to other universities). In contrast, if the student is convicted of a felony during his or her first year of graduate work, such an interruption would presumably eliminate all alternative pathways to the attainment of the superordinate goal. In this case, the affective reaction may be extremely intense.

The preceding analysis can be formalized in a way that allows specific predictions to be made of the intensity of affect one experiences as the result of an interruption. Such predictions require that the event schema that guides behavioral decisions be specifiable a priori, and that the relative amount of time and effort required to attain the subgoals that compose the various plans can be estimated. For purposes of our example, assume that the schema conveyed in Figures 12.3 and 12.4 is essentially complete, and that the relative magnitudes of the time and effort required to attain each subgoal in the hierarchy are estimated by the weights shown in Figure 12.3. Note that the weight attached to a particular subgoal is equal to the sum of the weights of the subgoals comprising the plan required to attain it (or, if two or more alternative subroutines are available, the *minimum* of the summed weights computed for each plan). Thus, for example:

W (the total time and effort required to attain G) = $w_1 + w_2$,
where
$$w_1 = \min(w_3 + w_4, w_5 + w_6), \text{ and}$$
$$w_2 = w_7 + w_8 + w_9 + w_{10}.$$

Given these assumptions, the factors that determine the amount of negative affect that is generated by an interruption can be quantified. For example, the *distance* of an interruption from a goal (D) is simply the difference between W and the sum of the weights associated with the subgoals that were attained prior to the interruption. Thus, suppose that an interruption occurred between g_8 and g_9 (i.e., between "drive to theater" and "find parking"). Then,

$$D = W - (w_1 + w_7 + w_8).$$

The *investment* in the interrupted plan (I) is reflected in the sum of the weights of the subgoals that would have to be retraced in order to initiate a new plan that would permit the superordinate goal to be attained. To this extent, one's investment depends on whether alternatives to the interrupted plan in fact exist. In our example, suppose an interruption occurs between g_{11} ("look up the phone number") and g_{12} ("dial phone"). Then, $I = w_{11}$, because only g_{11} would have to be retraced to initiate an alternative plan that would permit the same subgoal (g_5, or "call the theater") to be attained. On the other hand, suppose the interruption occurs between g_8 and g_9. In this case, the investment ($I = w_1 + w_7 + w_8$) is much greater, because no alternative routine for attaining the superordinate goal is available.

The negative affect that results from an interruption is postulated to be a positive function of investment (I) and a negative function of the distance to the goal (D). However, these effects should be systematically greater when the importance or value of the goal (V) is high than when it is low. Therefore,

Negative affect = $V(k_1 I - k_2 D)$.   [12.1]

Our analysis has been restricted to interruptions in the pursuit of goals that have not already been attained. However, it may also apply to the effects of disrupting a state of affairs that already exists. Ortony et al. (1988) recognized the existence of *preservation* goals (e.g., keeping one's job, preserving the life and health of one's family, or maintaining one's personal property) that do not typically require conscious, goal-directed activity unless an event occurs that makes them salient (one gets fired, one's mother dies, or one's home is burglarized). When such an event occurs, however, the negative affect experienced may be considerable.

The effects of disrupting a preservation goal may also be conceptualized in terms of Equation 12.1. In this case, the distance of the disruption or interruption from the goal (D) is of course zero, since the goal has already been obtained at the time of the disruption. The negative affect experienced is likely to be substantial for this reason alone. However, according to Equation 12.1, this negative affect should increase with (a) the importance of the goal (V) and (b) the investment in the goal I. Note that investment depends partly on the availability of alternative plans for regaining the disrupted goal state. This means, for example, that the death of one's mother is likely to be extremely debilitating because the disrupted goal state is impossible to reestablish. Losing one's job may also be traumatic if one is financially dependent on it and no alternative plan exists for regaining it or an equivalent goal state. However, it may be relatively less devastating if one is independently wealthy or if one has several alternative job opportunities.

The emotional consequences of goal attainment: positive affect. Whereas negative affect results from the interruption of goal-directed activity, positive affect is postulated to result from its successful completion. Although this seems self-evident, few cognitive theories of purposive behavior have adequately addressed this possibility. For example, Mandler's (1975) assumption that affect is generated by the interruption of a plan seems inapplicable to the generation of positive affect; it is difficult to imagine any interruption of plan that would lead to a positive affective state. Other conceptualizations of the dynamics of positive affective states (e.g., Berlyne, 1967, 1971; Csikszentmihalyi, 1975; Csikszentmihalyi & Bennet, 1971; Deci, 1975; D. W. Fiske & Maddi, 1961; Klinger, 1975, 1977; Solomon & Corbit, 1974) have provided important theoretical insights into these phenomena, but a general conceptualization of the determinants of positive affect in goal-directed activity remains elusive.

With some auxiliary assumptions, the general analysis we have proposed can be applied to positive affective states as well. That is, the positive affect that one experiences from attaining a goal, like the negative affect that results from failure to attain it, is presumably a function of the subjective importance of the goal. In addition, it seems reasonable to suppose that reactions such as "pride," "satisfaction," and "joy" resulting from successful completion of a plan will be (a) a positive function of the time and effort expended and (b) a negative function of the subjective likelihood (i.e., expectancy) that the goal will actually be attained. Thus, the positive affect experienced at any point along the path to a goal is given by

Positive affect $= V(1 - P)D_b$,

where V is the subjective value of the goal, P is the subjective likelihood of attaining it, and D_b is the subjective distance from the *beginning* of the plan at which the affect is being assessed. Thus, if the main goal is completed, D_b is simply the sum of the weights of the various subgoals involved in attaining it. On the other hand, the equation may also be applicable in predicting the positive affect experienced in attaining various subgoals themselves.

One attractive feature of the formulation we have outlined is its ability to predict both the negative affect that results from failure to attain a goal and the positive affect that results from success in terms of an overlapping set of parameters. At the same time, the formulation is incomplete. Although the intensity of positive and negative emotions may be a result of the factors identified in our analysis, the *type* of emotion that is elicited is not accounted for. This may depend on the particular type of goal being sought, and one's perception of why the goal was or was not attained. Before discussing this matter, however, two other factors that may influence emotion intensity are worth mention.

2. Deviations from Expectations

Our examples of the effects of goal interruption and goal attainment have focused on material goals that require overt motor behavior. The interruption or completion of cognitive goals may operate similarly. A person whose goal is to understand the implications of research reported in a journal article is likely to experience negative affect if this goal is blocked. Moreover, the intensity of the affect is likely to be greater if the person has already spent considerable time and effort reading the paper when the confusion occurs. Thus, the person's negative emotions may be less intense if his/her understanding is thwarted at an early point in the introduction than if s/he has waded through the entire introduction and method, only to find that the results reported are inexplicable.

Comprehension goals may also come into play in the effects of a deviation from expectations on emotional reactions. One of the major analyses of these effects is provided by McClelland (see McClelland, Atkinson, Clark, & Lowell, 1953). He postulated that the relation between affect and deviation from expectations follows a "butterfly curve." That is, affective reactions to an experience become more positive as its deviation from expectations increases to a moderate level. As the deviation from expectancies becomes still greater, however, affective reactions to the experience decrease in positivity, and may in fact be quite negative when the deviation is very large.

This conceptualization has numerous interesting implications. For one thing, it explains why complex stimuli that seem quite unpleasant when they are first experienced increase in attractiveness after repeated exposures to them, and often become pleasant after a sufficient number of repetitions (i.e., when they become less deviant from expectations). At the same time, simple stimuli (which may be only moderately deviant from expectations when one is first exposed to them) may be pleasant initially but may become less so as the number of repetitions becomes greater. (Note, however, that this latter prediction seems at odds with Zajonc's, 1980, hypothesis that liking increases linearly with exposure frequency.)

It is interesting to speculate that the effects of deviations from expectancies can be conceptualized as special cases of the effects of goal interruption and goal attainment. If people have a general comprehension goal when they are exposed to stimuli, they presumably experience negative affect if this goal is thwarted, but experience positive affect if it is attained. Suppose subjects have sufficient knowledge to comprehend a stimulus event. Then, the more cognitive effort they expend in doing so, the more positive affect they should experience (see Equation 12.2). If stimuli that are moderately deviant from expectations can be comprehended but require effort to do so, this could account for the positive affect they elicit. On the other hand, stimuli that are extremely discrepant from expectancies may not be able to be understood at all, and this goal blocking leads to negative affect. These assumptions permit many features of the butterfly curve proposed by McClelland to be accommodated within the conceptual framework we have proposed.

3. Consequences of Goal Conflict

The applicability of the conceptualization outlined above is limited to conditions in which a single goal is pursued. In many conditions, people desire two or more goals simultaneously, and the behavior that facilitates the attainment of one goal may interfere with the attainment of the other(s). The conflict that arises between these mutually incompatible alternatives may itself generate affect over and above the effects of any goal blocking that is created by the conflict.

The clearest theoretical statement of the nature of these goal conflicts and their effects was provided many years ago by Neil Miller (1959). The basic types of conflicts that Miller identified are well known. However, their characteristics are worth reviewing briefly as a preface to considering the effects of conflicts in more complex goal-directed activity of the sort that often arise in social decision making.

Approach-approach conflicts. These conflicts arise when two equally attractive goals cannot both be pursued simultaneously. Such conflicts, which occur frequently in everyday life, may involve goals that are either of little consequence (e.g., "Should I read *Psychological Review* or the *New Yorker*?") or of extreme importance (e.g., "Should I sign a pro football contract or accept admission to Harvard Law School?"). As the absolute value of the two alternative goals increases, the amount of negative affect that is experienced will also increase. However, relative to other types of conflicts, the persistence of this affect is low. This is because the conflict is usually resolved as soon as one begins to lean in favor of, or even think about, one of the alternatives rather than the other. Moreover, the negative affect generated by the conflict itself is rarely of sufficient magnitude to override the positive affect that is experienced by anticipation of the goals themselves.

Avoidance-avoidance conflicts. These conflicts arise when one is confronted with two equally unattractive situations and the avoidance of one requires experiencing the other. For example, a woman who is unhappily pregnant may be morally opposed to having an abortion, or a person with a toothache may be terrified of going to the dentist. Such conflicts are intense and difficult to resolve. They produce considerable stress, not only because they are unavoidable but because their resolution necessarily requires exposure to an aversive situation.

Approach-avoidance conflicts. These conflicts arise when a single object or or outcome has both attractive and unattractive features. Therefore, exposure to the positive features requires exposure to the aversive ones as well, and avoidance of the undesirable aspects requires giving up the positive ones. A child who is forced to finish his spinach to have dessert, a teenager who is sexually curious but morally inhibited, and a coauthor who objects to certain statements in a paper but does not want to offend his colleague, all experience such conflicts. Miller (1959) pointed out that as one approaches the object or situation, the unpleasant aspects of it become more prominent. The ultimate result is a vacillation between approach and avoidance. Such a conflict is difficult to resolve and consequently generates considerable negative affect.

Multiple-conflict situations. Although it is useful to analyze the dynamics of conflict situations into the three types identified by Miller (1959), many conflicts that one encounters in the real world do not have the "pure" forms we have described. For example, a man who must choose between taking a job at University A or remaining at University B may see both attractive and unattractive features of each alternative. Such a situation is actually a composite of all three types of conflict, and which type the person experiences at any given time may depend on which aspects of the choice alternatives he happens to think about. For example, attention to only the attractive features of the two alternatives may elicit an approach-approach conflict. However, a comparison of only the unattractive features of the two alternatives may elicit an avoidance-avoidance conflict. Finally, a consideration of each alternative in isolation, taking into account both its attractive and its unattractive features, may elicit an approach-avoidance conflict.

This analysis has implications for conflict resolution. As we have noted, approach-avoidance conflicts are the most difficult to resolve and avoidance-avoidance conflicts are the most aversive. Thus, to the extent that a decision maker wishes to eliminate the conflict and to minimize the negative affect associated with it, he or she should conceptualize the choice situation in a way that produces an approach-approach conflict rather than one of the other types, thereby facilitating its resolution and maximizing the positive affect that results. This means, in effect, that the person should focus on the positive attributes of each choice alternative and should ignore the negative attributes. It is interesting to speculate that people who are confronted with a given choice will experience different amounts of affect, and will resolve the conflict more or less easily, if they are led via various experimental manipulations (e.g., cognitive priming) to conceptualize the situation in each of the three alternative ways.

Changes in the features that people consider over the course of conflict resolution can also be predicted. If subjects who are first confronted with a decision are asked to reflect on the considerations surrounding it, they may often report negative features of each choice alternative as well as positive ones. After a period of time has elapsed, however, and subjects have had a chance to reconceptualize the situation as an approach-approach conflict, they should be more apt to report positive features of each alternative, but less apt to report negative features, than they were originally.

A problem in resolving conflict situations results from the fact that the attractive (or unattractive) features of choice situations cannot always be compared along the same dimensions. For example, how much is a high salary (available at University A) worth in terms of the quality of students (available at University B)? In resolving such conflicts, one is often forced to use a weighting scheme that is difficult to justify on purely rational grounds and the validity of which may be questioned by the decision maker, even after the choice is made. Because of these ambiguities, the affect generated in the course of resolving a conflict may linger for some time after the resolution. Indeed, the manner in which this affect is eliminated following a decision has been the focus of much research and theory, notably in the area of cognitive dissonance (Festinger, 1957; Wicklund & Brehm, 1976).

Qualitative Differences in Emotional Reactions

The particular type of positive or negative emotion that is likely to result from the successful completion or interruption of goal-directed activities presumably depends on the situational conditions that surround these activities. It may also depend on the particular type of goal that is being sought, and the reason why the

TABLE 12.1
Representative Emotional Reactions as a Function of Perceived Characteristics of the Situation in Which They Occur (based on Abelson, 1983)

| Predicted Emotion | Recipient | Perception of situation | | | | Cause of Actual and Imagined Outcomes |
| | | Imagined Outcome | | Actual Outcome | | |
		Agent	Value	Agent	Value	
Gratitude	Self	—	Negative	Other	Positive	—
Pride	Self	Self	Negative	Self	Positive	Different
Joy	Self	—	Neutral	—	Positive	—
Anger	Self	Self	Positive	Other/self	Negative	Different
Disappointment	Self	Self	Positive	Self	Negative	Same
Sorrow	—	—	Neutral	—	Negative	—

goal is either blocked or attained. A person who believes that he failed to get a good examination grade because he went out on a date the night before and didn't have the time to study may experience a different emotion than someone who attributes his failure to the fact that he loaned a friend his classnotes and the person did not return them.

Several approaches have been taken in conceptualizing the situational factors that give rise to different emotions. A particularly detailed account of the effects of these factors is provided by Ortony et al. (1988). However, a somewhat simpler conceptualization by Abelson (1983), which is based in part on an earlier analysis by Roseman (1979), is more obviously congenial to the general theoretical framework we propose.

Abelson identifies six factors that, in combination, affect the type of emotional reactions that one has to an event and its outcome: (a) the recipient of the outcome (oneself or another person), (b) the favorableness of both the actual outcome (positive, neutral or negative) and the outcome that the perceiver had imagined or expected to occur, (c) the causal agents of both the imagined and the actual outcome (self, another person, or the situation), and (d) whether the determinants of the imagined and actual outcomes are perceived to be the same or different. Table 12.1 shows the possible reactions that result from a few representative combinations of these variables. For example, "gratitude" arises when one receives an unexpected positive outcome as a result of another person's actions. "Anger" arises when a positive event is expected to result from one set of circumstances, but a negative event actually occurs as a result of a different set of circumstances. Note that this anger may be directed toward either oneself or another, depending on the perceived causal agent of the actual event.

Many emotions can be conceptualized in terms of the six variables shown in Table 12.1. It is unclear whether all can be. It is also unclear whether each combination of these variables elicits one and only one unique emotion. A total of 324 possible combinations of values can be specified by the 2 (recipient) x 3 (agent of imagined goal) by 3 (agent of actual goal) by 3 (value of actual goal) x 2 (perception that the causes of the imagined and actual goals are similar or different) configuration of variables. Although not all variables are relevant to each emotion (see Table 12.1), this is nevertheless a considerable number of possibilities. Moreover, both Abelson (1983) and Roseman (1979) point to additional variables that may influence emotions in some instances.

In this regard, two emotion-eliciting conditions that are not usually considered within the framework proposed by Abelson have been identified by Higgins (1987) in an analysis of emotional responses to self-perceptions. He notes that people often evaluate themselves in relation to either an internal standard, or ideal self (i.e., attributes and behaviors that they would personally desire to manifest) or an external standard (characteristics that other persons believe they should have). He postulates that a discrepancy between one's actual self-perception and one of these standards may elicit goal-directed behavior that is designed to eliminate the discrepancy, and that a failure to do so (goal interruption or blocking, in the terms we have used earlier) may lead to a negative emotion. The nature of this emotion depends on the type of discrepancy that is involved. Higgins hypothesizes that a discrepancy between one's self-perception and one's ideal indicates a failure to attain positive outcomes, and that this leads to dejection-related emotions (disappointment, sadness, etc.). In contrast, a discrepancy between one's self-perceptions and an external standard signifies the possibility of receiving negative outcomes, and this elicits agitation-related emotions (fear, tenseness, etc.).

It is conceivable that the conditions that give rise to these different reactions can be conceptualized in terms of the variables proposed by Abelson and indicated in Table 12.1. For example, Abelson's analysis assumes that emotions arise from discrepancies between actual outcomes and imagined outcomes. These discrepancies may be somewhat analogous to discrepancies between one's actual self and one of the two types of imagined selves identified by Higgins. Be that as it may, more work must obviously be done at both the conceptual and the empirical levels to determine the necessity and sufficiency of these variables in specifying the type of emotions that are likely to be elicited in different situational contexts.

An important feature of both Abelson's and Higgins' conceptualizations arises from the fact that the variables they postulate to activate different emotions are *perceptual*, and do not necessarily reflect reality. This means that the emotions that are theoretically elicited in a particular situation may vary, depending on subjects' interpretation of both the values of the outcomes that occur and reasons for their occurrence. When a person is uncertain about the appropriate interpretation of a particular situation, the person's emotional reactions may vacillate, depending on which interpretation he happens to be thinking about. More generally, several factors that we have postulated earlier in this volume to affect the accessibility of concepts in memory may influence the interpretation that is given to features of an ambiguous situation and, therefore, may affect a person's emotional reactions to the situation in ways that are potentially accounted for by the sort of conceptualization we have outlined.

Cognitive Consequences of Affect and Emotion

Having discussed the cognitive determinants of emotional reactions, we now turn to their cognitive consequences. As we have already noted, it is often difficult to localize empirically the effects of situational and individual difference variables in a particular phase of cognitive processing. The model we propose is nevertheless quite clear as to how affect and emotion should theoretically operate at each stage. We consider each stage in turn and outline briefly the model's implications for the role that affect may play. Then, we present data that bear on this role. As will be seen, the data concerning the effects of affect at several phases of information processing (in particular, encoding and retrieval) are quite mixed. Perhaps not surprisingly, the most convincing evidence comes from the use of the emotions one experiences at the time one thinks about a stimulus as information about one's feelings toward the stimulus, and, therefore, as a basis for judgments to which these feelings are relevant.

To establish the causal effect of different emotions on cognitive functioning, it is of course necessary to induce differences in emotional states experimentally.[1] An inordinate number of procedures have been employed. These include (a) having subjects describe personal life events in which the emotions to be induced had been experienced, (b) asking them to make statements that are typically associated with different moods (e.g., "I feel great!" "I want to go to sleep and never get up," etc.), (c) playing up-beat or gloomy music, (d) giving subjects small gifts, or alternatively, exposing them to uncomfortable physical surroundings, (e) giving subjects feedback that they have done well or poorly on a test, (f) manipulating their facial expressions, and (g) capitalizing on naturally occurring events (e.g., the weather). Although most of these procedures are successful in eliciting the emotions they are intended to influence, there are often problems in interpreting their effects on specific aspects of cognitive functioning. In particular, most procedures that are

---

1. A considerable amount of research on the role of affect in cognitive functioning has involved a comparison of depressed subjects with nondepressives (for a review, see Blaney, 1986). Although this research is of importance, its implications for the *causal* influences of affect are often hard to assess. Differences in the past experiences of depressive and nondepressive subjects may systematically affect the encoding, organization and retrieval of information in these studies for reasons that are not a result of the affect they are experiencing per se. Therefore, we do not consider this literature in the present chapter.

used to induce differences in affect may also influence other variables that could plausibly account for the phenomenon being investigated.

The nature of these confounds varies with the procedure and with the situational conditions in which it is employed. In such instances, it is usually necessary to demonstrate that several different operationalizations of an independent variable have the same influence on the dependent variables one is investigating. Unfortunately, the research on affect and cognition is characterized by a tendency to confound differences in the mood-induction procedure that is used with differences in the processes being investigated and in the dependent variables that are used to infer their existence. (Indeed, a skeptical reviewer of the literature in this area would be tempted to speculate that mood-induction procedures are often selected strategically to maximize, rather than minimize, the likelihood that they will influence the particular dependent variable one is assessing for reasons that have little to do with affect per se.) This confounding often makes the generality of the conclusions drawn hard to assess. These matters should be kept in mind in evaluating the research summarized below.

Initial Encoding and Interpretation of Information

Emotion concepts that exist in the semantic bin may theoretically be activated and used to interpret information to which they apply. This information may concern either oneself, another person, or, in some cases, an animal or even an inanimate object. The conditions in which any particular concept is used to encode stimulus information are theoretically identical to those in which other attribute (e.g., trait) concepts are applied. These encoding effects can be investigated empirically in ways that are analogous to those that are used more generally to establish effects of concept accessibility on encoding phenomena (see chapter 6). That is, subjects are induced to experience a particular emotion, thereby activating concepts that pertain to this emotion. Then, they are exposed to information that is evaluatively ambiguous, and the extent to which the activated emotion concepts affect their interpretation of the information is inferred.

Three theoretical and empirical contingencies in the occurrence of these effects, noted in earlier chapters, bear repeating in this context:

1. Concepts affect the interpretation of information only if their features are descriptively applicable to this information (Higgins, Rholes, & Jones, 1978). That is, the interpretation of information that is only evaluatively related to activated concepts should not be influenced by them. This means that it may often not be sufficient to lead people to experience positive or negative affect in general to detect an encoding effect. Rather, the activated concepts must pertain to a particular emotional state, and the information presented must be interpretable in terms of descriptive features that are associated with these concepts.

2. Encoding effects occur only at the time information is received (Srull & Wyer, 1980). Once information has been encoded in terms of one set of concepts, it is unlikely to be retrieved and reinterpreted in terms of concepts that are activated subsequently. This means that inducing an emotion at the time information is presented to subjects may affect its interpretation, but inducing a mood at the time of judgment will not.

3. Attribute concepts are typically not applied automatically to the interpretation of information. Rather, they are applied only if an encoding of the information in terms of these concepts is relevant to some higher order processing objective (e.g., impression formation).

In fact, very little research bears directly on the effects of affective or emotion concepts on the interpretation of ambiguous information. Subjects in a study reported by Bower (1981) were induced to feel either happy or angry. This was presumably done by having them recall a past event in which they had experienced the emotion. (In fact, the mood induction procedure is not explicitly stated in Bower's summary of the study.) Then, while they were in this emotional state, subjects told stories in response to a number of TAT cards. Happy subjects were more likely to interpret the cards as conveying happy situations than were angry subjects.

To the extent that our assumption about the mood induction procedure is correct, however, the study does not rule out the possibility that the procedure primed not only emotion concepts but also descriptive concepts that were sufficiently applicable to the situations portrayed in the TAT cards to influence their interpretation. In addition, there is no direct evidence that specific features of the TAT card content were actually interpreted differently in the conditions being compared. Rather, subjects may simply have made up stories independently of the card content, based on their past experiences with persons and objects of the type portrayed. To this extent, the results would reflect the influence of emotion concepts on the retrieval of prior knowledge rather than on the encoding of new information.

An unpublished study by Kelly and Wyer (1987) circumvented some of these problems. In some (*mood-before*) conditions, subjects were first induced to feel either happy or sad by recalling a past experience that elicited this emotion. Then, as part of an ostensibly different experiment, they read a story about a target person that was ambiguous with respect to the emotion the target experienced. (In one story, for example, a person's grandmother dies but her insurance money permits him to attend the college of his choice; in another, a young person finds and cares for a lost pet but ultimately has to return it to its owner.) In other (*mood-after*) conditions, subjects were not induced to feel happy or sad until after they read the story. Finally, subjects in both conditions judged the feelings that were experienced by the target person in the story they had read.

According to the considerations indicated above, an effect of emotion concepts on subjects' interpretation of the story content would be evidenced by an influence of the mood manipulation on their judgments under mood-before conditions but not under mood-after conditions. This was, in fact, the case. Subjects generally judged the target to feel less happy than sad, as evidenced by a negative difference between their ratings of the target's happiness and their ratings of his sadness (each along a 0-10 scale). When subjects' own emotional state was induced before they read the story, however, this difference was less negative when subjects themselves felt happy ($M = -.99$) than when they felt sad ($M = -5.76$). In contrast, when subjects' emotions were not induced until after they read the story, their judgments of the target's emotional state did not appreciably depend on which type of emotion they were personally experiencing (-3.61 vs. -4.76 under happy and sad mood conditions, respectively).

The absence of mood induction effects in mood-after conditions suggests that subjects did not simply use their own emotional state as a direct basis for inferring the target's. Consequently, the data support the hypothesis that the feelings subjects were experiencing at the time the information was presented activated emotion concepts that influenced their interpretation of the target's affective reactions. Unfortunately, however, a second study performed by Kelly and Wyer, using different stimulus materials and induced mood states, did not produce comparable results. Therefore, in the absence of other corroborative evidence, conclusions concerning the role of emotion concepts in the interpretation of new information should be treated with some caution.

Selective Encoding and Organization

Subjects are more likely to include features of information in the representations they form from it if these features can be encoded and organized in terms of concepts that come easily to mind. In the present context, this means that if an emotion concept happens to be in the Work Space at the time subjects receive information, features of the information that are interpretable in terms of this concept are particularly likely to be encoded. As a result, these features are more apt to be included in the cognitive representation that is formed, and therefore more likely to be recalled later, than are other features of the information.

1. Selective Encoding of Story Content

The most successful attempt to investigate this possibility was reported by Bower, Gilligan, and Monteiro (1981) in a study we mentioned earlier in this volume. To reiterate, subjects were hypnotically induced to feel either happy or sad. Then, they were given a posthypnotic suggestion to reexperience this mood as they read a prose passage describing the interaction between two friends. Some experiences were of the sort that would make a person happy, whereas others were of the sort that would make someone upset and depressed. Subjects were later asked to recall as much of the story as they could. As predicted, subjects recalled more happy events, and fewer sad events, if they were happy at the time they read the story than if they were sad. In a second study, in which subjects were not induced to feel happy or sad until after they read the story, the type of information they recalled was unaffected by their mood. This confirms the fact that the effects were a result of selective encoding at the time of information acquisition and were not a result of selective retrieval of information that was consistent with concepts activated at the time of recall.

2. Selective Encoding of Unrelated Words and Phrases

A second approach that has been taken in investigating selective encoding effects involves asking subjects to recall a list of words, some of which are affectively positive and others of which are affectively negative. According to the conceptualization we propose, this procedure should generally be less effective in demonstrating selective encoding than the procedure used by Bower et al. (1981). As noted earlier, activated concepts are likely to affect the encoding of information only if (a) features of these concepts are descriptively applicable for interpreting the information, and (b) an encoding of the information in terms of higher order attribute concepts is relevant to the attainment of a processing objective. Assuming that subjects who are told to read a story about an interpersonal interaction have an implicit impression information objective, both of those conditions existed in the aforementioned study by Bower et al. However, *neither* condition typically obtains when subjects are simply asked to learn a list of words.

It is therefore not surprising, from the perspective of the model we propose, that the results obtained in this paradigm are inconclusive, and, in fact, rather chaotic. Blaney (1986) reviews numerous studies performed using a variety of mood-induction procedures. Many of these studies are difficult to interpret because the same mood that was induced at the time subjects read the stimulus materials was reinduced at the time of recall. Studies in which recall mood was manipulated independently of presentation mood, or was not manipulated at all, typically show little evidence for selective encoding effects on the recall of single words and phrases.

Two exceptions are worth noting in the context of the theoretical contingencies described above. In both studies, a processing objective was induced that presumably led subjects to encode the information they received in terms of higher order attribute concepts. The study of potentially greatest relevance was performed by Forgas and Bower (1987). To induce emotions, subjects were given positive and negative feedback about their performance on a personality test. Then, they received information about several hypothetical persons as part of a study on impression formation. Each target person was described by some favorable behaviors and some unfavorable ones. Subjects, after reading the descriptions, made evaluative judgments of the persons being described, and finally, recalled the information they had read.

It seems reasonable to suppose that in this study, as in other studies of impression formation (cf. chapter 7), subjects with the objective of forming an impression encoded the behaviors in terms of concepts that were accessible in memory and, in addition, attempted to extract an evaluative concept of the person being described (Postulate 7.3). Consequently, subjects who had positive (or negative) emotion concepts accessible in memory were more likely to encode the behaviors that exemplified these concepts, and were more likely to include these behaviors in their representation of the target persons, than behaviors to which the concepts were inapplicable. These representations and the behaviors contained in them were then used as a basis for both recall and judgments, producing the effects that the authors observed.

Unfortunately, an ambiguity in the study results from the fact that the task used to induce different mood states was a personality test. It seems likely that positive feedback on such a test is likely to activate favorable *trait* concepts, whereas negative feedback is likely to activate unfavorable ones. The descriptive features of these trait concepts, rather than the emotion concepts associated with subjects' mood, may have been used to encode the behavioral information about the target persons. This could also account for the effects observed.

In a quite different study by Ingram, Smith, and Brehm (1983), subjects' affective state was manipulated by giving them success or failure feedback on a test of "social perception." Then, subjects were given a series of words that were affectively positive or negative and were asked to respond to them in one of several ways. In "self-referent" conditions, subjects were asked if each word did or did not apply to themselves. In "semantic" conditions, they indicated whether each word meant the same as a second, referent word. In still other conditions, they were asked questions that had nothing to do with the personal relevance of the words or their semantic meaning.

The dependent variable was a composite index that reflected the net unfavorableness of the words that subjects later recalled. Of the task conditions investigated, the only one that seems intuitively likely to lead subjects to encode the words in terms of affect-related concepts rather than descriptive ones is the self-referent condition. Consistent with this speculation, only under self-referent conditions was the net unfavorableness of the words recalled greater for subjects who did poorly on the self- perception test than for subjects who succeeded.

Although these results, like Forgas and Bower's, are suggestive, similar problems occur in interpreting them. That is, success or failure on a social perception test is likely to activate not only emotion concepts but also positive and negative self-relevant trait concepts. The words presented under self-referent conditions may have been selectively encoded in terms of these trait concepts rather than the emotion concepts that accompanied them. Therefore, these results do not provide unequivocal evidence of the effect of emotion concepts on the encoding and organization of individual pieces of information. On the other hand, they do suggest that whatever effects may occur are contingent on higher order processing objectives that require the use of the particular concepts that are activated by the mood-induction task.

Retrieval Processes

1. Theoretical Considerations

The influence of affect-related concepts on the retrieval of information is implied by Postulate 5.4. Briefly, if emotion concepts happen to be in the Work Space at the time information in Permanent Storage is sought, these concepts or their associated features may fortuitously be included among the probe cues that are compiled to govern the selection of a referent bin. Consequently, information may be retrieved from a bin whose header contains these emotion-related features rather than a more general one. This may produce a bias in the sort of information that is retrieved.

Thus, for example, a person who is asked to recall experiences he has had with his father may normally identify and retrieve information from a general "experiences with father" bin, some of which may be pleasant and others of which may be unpleasant. Suppose, however, that the person is feeling "happy," and that an emotion concept associated with these feelings is in the Work Space. If features of this concept are fortuitously selected as probe cues, the person may identify and retrieve information from a "happy experiences with father" bin rather than the more general one, and this may bias the quality of the experiences the person recalls.

Therefore, the model we propose predicts that affect-related concepts that are activated at the time of retrieval may influence the type of information that is retrieved. At the same time, it circumscribes the conditions in which these effects will occur. Specifically, they occur *only* when the information to be recalled is stored in a bin whose header includes features of the emotion concept that has been activated. Put more simply, emotion concepts that are activated at the time of recall will influence the type of information retrieved only if this information was organized in terms of these same concepts at the time it was first acquired (or if it has since been thought about in terms of these concepts for some other reason). The studies that have been conducted to investigate the effect of emotion on information retrieval (for a review, see Blaney, 1986) have yielded very mixed results. In fact, many of the apparent inconsistencies that exist in the results obtained can be understood in terms of the considerations raised above. There is some question, however, as to whether these effects are due only to the cueing properties of the verbal labels that are attached to the emotions that subjects experience at the time of recall rather than to other features of the emotion concepts that have been activated.

2. Retrieval of Newly Acquired Information

To reiterate, activating concepts at the time of retrieval will theoretically affect the recall of information only if this information was encoded and organized in terms of these concepts at the time if was first learned. This contingency is evident in the study by Bower et al. (1981). Briefly, subjects read a story describing the experiences of two persons. If subjects were in a happy or sad mood at the time they read the story, they tended to recall information that was affectively congruent with this mood. In contrast, if subjects read the story in a neutral mood and were not put into a happy or sad mood until the time they were asked to recall the information, the type of information they recalled did not depend on the mood they were in.

On first consideration, this may seem surprising. It seems likely that subjects spontaneously encoded the happy or sad experiencing in the story in terms of emotion concepts at the time they read about them. If this is so, emotion concepts that are activated by the mood induced at retrieval might be expected to cue the recall of these experiences. According to the model we propose, however, the critical factor is not how individual pieces of information are encoded, but rather, whether the *bin in which they are stored* is identified by an emotion concept or its associated features. As noted by Wyer and Bodenhausen (1985), subjects who read a thematically integrated story with an impression formation objective may not encode it as individual pieces of information. Rather, they may store it as a single event sequence, in a bin whose header pertains to the story as a whole. In Bower et al.'s study, this header is unlikely to have contained features that were specific to only one of the two emotions conveyed by the story material. Consequently, the retrieval of information from this bin is unlikely to have been systematically affected by the activation of these features at the time of recall.

A series of list-learning studies by Bower, Monteiro and Gilligan (1978), performed in a quite different research paradigm, has similar implications. In one of these studies, subjects were asked to learn a list of words in either a (hypnotically-induced) happy mood or sad mood. Later, they recalled the words in a mood that was the same as or different from their mood at learning. Their recall of the words was no better when their mood at recall was the same as their mood at learning than when it was different. The reason for this may be similar to that we suggested above. That is, although subjects were put into a happy or sad mood at learning, a concept associated with this mood was irrelevant to the task at hand. Therefore, the concept was not included in the header of the bin in which the to-be-learned information was stored. As a result, emotion concepts that were activated by subjects' mood at the time of retrieval had no influence on the likelihood of identifying the bin and retrieving the information contained in it.

If this interpretation is correct, emotion concepts that are activated at the time of retrieval should affect the recall of information under conditions in which features of the concept *are* likely to be included in the bin headers. A second study by Bower et al. (1978) bears on this possibility. Subjects in this study were asked to learn *two* lists of words, and then to recall the words contained in both lists. Using hypnotic induction, subjects' mood at the time they learned the first list, their mood at the time they learned the second list, and their mood at the time of recall, were manipulated independently.

It seems reasonable to suppose that subjects under these conditions may store the two lists of words in separate bins. Moreover, they may perceive the concepts associated with their mood to be discriminative cues that distinguish the two lists, and therefore may include features of these concepts in the headers of the bins. If this is so, inducing a mood at the time of retrieval should facilitate the recall of words in the list that was learned in this mood, contrary to the results of the first study. This was in fact the case.

The proportion of words recalled under each condition is summarized in Table 12.2. When both lists were learned in the same mood, and also recalled in this mood, the proportion of words recalled in each list was virtually identical. When the lists were learned in different moods, however, inducing a particular mood at the time of retrieval increased subjects' recall of the list that they learned in the same mood but decreased their recall of words that they learned in a different mood.

One aspect of Bower et al.'s mood induction procedure should be noted. That is, subjects, although under hypnosis, are explicitly told to put themselves in either a "happy" or a "sad" mood, and that once they are in this mood, they should try to maintain it during the subsequent learning (or recall) test. This raises the question of whether subjects' emotional (e.g., physiological) reactions cued the retrieval of the to-be-learned material, or only the particular verbal labels ("happy," "sad," etc.) that the experimenter used to describe the emotions that subjects were told to experience during the various phases of the experiment. Although this seems to be a subtle distinction, it also becomes important in understanding other results we discuss.

In the research described above, the associations between the material to be learned and affect-related concepts were formed during the experiment. Similar considerations might be expected to apply when these associations have been established before the experiment takes place. Specifically, if the to-be-learned material has become linked to affect-related concepts prior to the experiment, the material may spontaneously activate these concepts at the time of learning. If this occurs, activating these same concepts at the time of retrieval should facilitate

TABLE 12.2
Proportion of Words Recalled in Each of Two Lists as a Function of Induced
Mood at the Time Each List was Learned and Mood at the Time of Recall
(based on data reported by Bower et al., 1978)

	Learning mood, list 1	Learning mood, list 2	Recall mood	Proportion of words recalled	
				List 1	List 2
a. Mood at recall same as mood at time both lists were learned	Happy	Happy	Happy		
	Sad	Sad	Sad	.54	.57
b. Mood at recall same as mood at time of list 1 learning	Happy	Sad	Happy		
	Sad	Happy	Sad	.66	.48
c. Mood at recall same as mood at time of list 2 learning	Happy	Sad	Sad		
	Sad	Happy	Happy	.46	.90

subjects' recall of the material even though their mood at learning was not manipulated.

According to the proposed formulation, however, this is not necessarily true. That is, for such an effect to occur, the to-be-learned items must not only spontaneously activate an emotion concept at the time of learning, but *they must be stored in a bin that is defined in terms of this concept.* In most studies, this latter condition may not be met. When it is not, the recall of newly learned material should not be affected by subjects' mood at retrieval, regardless of whether the individual items spontaneously elicit affect. In fact, this appears generally to be the case (Blaney, 1986).

A study by Clark and Teasdale (1985) is worth considering in light of the above considerations. Subjects were exposed to words that were likely to elicit either positive affect (considerate, thoughtful, beauty, etc.) or negative affect (rude, cruel, atrocity, misery, etc.). This was done as part of an "unconscious decision making" task in which subjects were given pairs of words and were told to decide which one the experimenter had designated as "correct." They were given no indication of the criterion for correctness, apparently being led to believe that it was projective test. After performing the task, subjects listened to either lively music or gloomy music played at half speed, being told that the study concerned the effects of mood on performance and that they should use the music intentionally to get into either a happy or a sad mood. Finally, they were unexpectedly asked to recall the words that were presented in the decision task.

The results were contingent on gender. Specifically, females recalled more affectively positive words, and fewer negative ones, if they were in a happy mood at the time of recall than if they were in a sad mood. In contrast, males' recall of both types of words was low and was unaffected by their mood. Although this contingency was obviously unexpected, it can be interpreted after the fact in terms of our conceptualization of when retrieval effects of mood should theoretically occur. That is, these effects should only be evident if the initial decision task led subjects to store the words in referent bins that were identified by different affect-related concepts. Perhaps females, unlike males, assumed that the criterion for "correctness" in the decision task was the affective quality of the words presented. Consequently, only females categorized them into bins that were defined in terms of emotion concepts, and so only these subjects' recall of the words was influenced by the activation of concepts at retrieval that led to one or the other of the bins to be identified.

3. Recall of Personal Experiences

The processes that underlie the effect of emotion concepts on the recall of information that is learned during an experiment should also operate when subjects retrieve previously acquired knowledge such as personal experiences. This should be true if the information that subjects are asked to recall elicited affect at the time it was acquired, and if it is stored in a bin whose header contains the probe cues selected at the time of retrieval.

A study cited by Bower (1981) supports this prediction. In this study, subjects who had been put into a hypnotically induced happy or sad mood were asked to recall early childhood experiences. Subjects recalled more pleasant experiences (as inferred from their own posthypnotic ratings of the experiences) when they were happy than when they were sad. Two studies reported by Parrott and Sabini (1989) confirmed this general finding using a different mood-induction procedure. In the first of these studies, subjects were explicitly told to get into a happy or sad mood by listening either to lively up-beat music (e.g., Dixieland) or to gloomy music played at half speed, and were told to maintain this mood while they performed a series of tasks that followed. One of these tasks involved recalling three experiences they had had in high school. Consistent with Bower's findings, happy subjects reported more pleasant experiences than sad subjects. To eliminate an alternative interpretation based on demand compliance, subjects in a second study were told after listening to the music and a subsequent interpolated task that the mood induction part of the experiment was over and that they were no longer required to maintain their mood. The effects of mood induction of the type of experiences recalled persisted despite the instructions.

In principle, the use of music to induce mood should have a methodological advantage over other procedures. That is, it minimizes the likelihood that other descriptive concepts activated by the mood induction will affect the recall of the information. Unfortunately, however, the procedure used in these particular studies may have eliminated this advantage. As noted above, subjects were explicitly instructed to use the music to put themselves in a happy or sad mood. It seems reasonable to suppose that many subjects accomplished this by reminiscing about an event that elicited the emotion they were trying to acquire. This event may have been the one that came easily to mind when subjects were later asked explicitly to recall a past experience.

Another problem is related to the one we noted earlier in our discussion of the list-learning studies. That is, the experimenter's request to use the music to get into a specific mood calls subjects' attention to the verbal label that is used to describe this mood. This *label* may then cue the retrieval of a previous experience that has also been assigned this label, independently of any influence of subjective physiological reactions that subjects happen to be experiencing or other features of the emotion concept with which such reactions are associated. To eliminate this possibility, it is necessary to induce emotions without describing them verbally and without requiring subjects to label the emotions themselves. It turns out that when this is done, the effects of mood states on the type of past experiences that subjects are most likely to recall is not only eliminated, but is actually reversed!

This reversal was identified by Parrott and Sabini (1989) both in the laboratory and in the field. In a laboratory study, subjects listened to music similar to that used to induce mood in the studies described above. However, they were led to believe that the music was being played as part of an experiment on aesthetic judgment, and no indication was given that the music was intended to make them feel happy or sad. In fact, no reference to subjects' mood state was made at all. The manipulation was nonetheless successful in inducing happiness and sadness, as indicated by subjects' self-reports at the end of the experiment. However, when subjects were asked to list three experiences they had, the first experience listed (i.e., the one that came to mind most quickly) was happier if subjects were feeling sad!

Identical findings were obtained in two nonlaboratory studies. In one, students on campus were approached on either sunny or rainy days and simply asked to describe three past experiences they had had in high school. The first experience they reported was more likely to be happy if they were asked on a rainy day than if they were asked on a sunny day. In the second study, students in a class were asked to report experiences after receiving the results of an examination. The first experience they reported was more likely to be happy if they had done badly on the exam than if they had done well. Thus, all three studies showed a tendency for the most accessible past experience to be incongruent with the mood that subjects were in. Interestingly, the second and third experiences that subjects recalled were *not* mood-incongruent, but rather, were affectively consistent with the emotion subjects were experiencing. This tendency was also apparent in all three studies.

These results, which appear to be quite reliable, differ considerably from those obtained in the other studies we described. Why? The main thing that distinguishes Parrott and Sabini's studies from the others is that no explicit indication was given to subjects that they should intentionally get into a happy or sad mood. This suggests that the positive effects observed in the earlier studies were not a result of inducing differences in subjects' subjective physiological reactions. Rather, they may have resulted from the cueing properties of the labels that were made accessible to subjects as a result of the mood-induction procedure and the similarity of these labels to ones that subjects had previously used to describe their past experiences.

This interpretation does not explain the tendency for the first experience that subjects recalled to be incongruent with their emotional state (rather than simply being unrelated to it). Nor does it explain why the second experience that subjects reported was, in fact, mood congruent. Perhaps people who are asked about the past spontaneously think about in in relation to the present. Therefore, if they are asked to recall a past experience when they are in a particularly happy mood, their first reaction may be to the effect that "things are usually not as good as they are today." This though may stimulate them to recall an experience that confirms this opinion. Having done so, their next reaction may be that "things aren't always quite *that* bad, however," and this reaction may cue the recall of a positive experience that corroborates this view.

Correspondingly, subjects who are unhappy at the time they are asked about the past may spontaneously think that "things aren't usually as awful as they seem now," and this may cue the retrieval of a positive experience. Having recalled this experience, however, they may realize that "things aren't always quite that good," and this may lead them to remember a negative experience.

Be that as it may, the general implication of Parrott and Sabini's results is that the effects of subjects' emotional states on the recall of information are not as straightforward as the model we have proposed (or, for that matter, any other existing model) suggests. That is, the results cannot be understood in terms of the cueing properties of emotion concepts per se. Rather, one must take into account the cognitions that are elicited by the emotional state, and the effects that these cognitions have on information retrieval.

Inference Making: Informational Properties of Affective States

It seems obvious that many inferences we make about ourselves and others are based in part on our subjective emotional reactions we have to the object being judged. Anyone who has ever been in love can testify to this fact. Moreover, the influence of emotional reactions on judgments is implied by the language we use to describe these judgments. That is, we say that we "feel" positively or negatively about ourselves, our acquaintances, or various social issues and concepts. Therefore, if we are asked to report our liking for someone or something, we may often interpret this as a request to assess our subjective affective reactions to the object and to base our responses on the implications of these reactions. In short, the emotional reactions we experience and attribute to a stimulus may be used as "information" in making inferences along dimensions to which these reactions are relevant.[2]

To this extent, the affect we may be experiencing for reasons that have nothing to do with the object we are asked to judge may often be misperceived as being a reaction to the object, and it therefore may influence our judgments of the object. This phenomenon is an implication of the model we propose. Specifically, the Work Space is always searched first for judgment-relevant material (Postulate 5.2). Therefore, if subjects happen fortuitously to be experiencing the subjective reactions that are associated with an emotion at the time they are asked to make a judgment to which affective reactions are believed to be relevant, a cognitive representation of these reactions (which is presumably in the Work Space) may be identified and used to make the judgment independently of any other judgment-relevant information.

1. A Definitive Demonstration

One of the most compelling demonstrations of the informational influence of affect on judgments was constructed by Strack, Martin, and Stepper (1988). Their research was based on the assumption that proprioceptive stimulation produced by a person's facial expression are a part of the configuration of internal reactions that activate affect-related concepts, and that these concepts, one activated, may be used as a basis for judgments to which they are relevant. Their studies not only confirm our assumption that features of emotion concepts include clusters of subjective physiological reactions, but also circumscribe the type of evaluative judgments to which affect has informational relevance.

---

2. The notion that an affective reaction to a stimulus is used as a basis for evaluating the stimulus is hardly of recent vintage. In fact, it is one of the oldest notions in social psychology. It was a working assumption underlying the development of attitude scaling techniques. An attitude is often defined as a positive or negative affective reaction to an object or concept (cf. Fishbein & Ajzen, 1975). This assumption led to the development of sophisticated ways of selecting and scaling opinion items, the agreement with which was theoretically based solely on the respondent's affective reactions to the object to which they referred and not on their descriptive implications or objective validity (Edwards, 1957; Thurstone, 1959).

The studies were ostensibly concerned with the ability of physically hand-icapped persons to adjust to alternative modes of motor behavior. On this pretense, subjects rated a series of cartoons using a felt-tip pen that they held either (a) between their teeth, (b) between their lips without touching their teeth, or (c) with their nonpreferred hand. As can be seen in Figure 12.5, the first procedure requires the use of muscles that are typically involved in smiling, whereas the second procedure requires muscles that are involved in more gloomy facial expressions. However, subjects were not aware that the procedure had anything to do at all with a manipulation of these expressions. Therefore, it avoided problems encountered in the interpretation of numerous previous studies of the affect of facial feedback on affect-relevant judgments and behavior. (For a detailed review and evaluation of these studies, see Strack et al., 1988).

In the first study, subjects held the pen as each cartoon was presented in one of the three ways described above, and then rated the cartoon with the pen in this position. Subjects rated the cartoons more positively when they held the pen with their teeth, and less positively when they held it with their lips, than when they held it in their nonpreferred hand. This suggests that proprioceptive cues associated with the pen-holding procedures were among the cluster of subjective physiological reactions that subjects used as a basis for judging the cartoons.

A second study confirmed these findings and, in addition, identified two important contingencies in the occurrence of the effects. As noted earlier, the induction of affect should only affect judgments that are normally based on subjects' perceptions of their affective reactions to the stimuli rather than on descriptive features of the stimuli themselves. To establish this contingency, subjects in this study were asked to indicate both (a) the feelings of amusement that were elicited by the cartoons (along a scale from "not at all amused" to "very much amused") and (b) how funny they would consider the cartoons if they applied an "objective standard." The first judgment requires subjects to assess their affective reactions to the cartoons, whereas the second is more likely to lead them to focus on specific features of the cartoons themselves. Thus, the authors expected that the pen-holding procedure would be more likely to influence the first judgment than the second.

A second factor they considered was whether subjects held the pen in a way that elicited different affective reactions at the time they viewed the cartoons, or only at the time they made their ratings. Presumably subjects are more likely to confuse the affect elicited by the pen-holding procedure with the affect elicited by the cartoons in the first condition than they are in the second.

Results bearing on these possibilities are shown in Table 12.3. The top half of this table presents subjects' reported feelings of amusement as a function of how they held the pen and when they held it. Subjects judged themselves to be more amused by the cartoons when they held the pen in their teeth while they viewed these cartoons than when they held the pen in their lips, confirming the results of

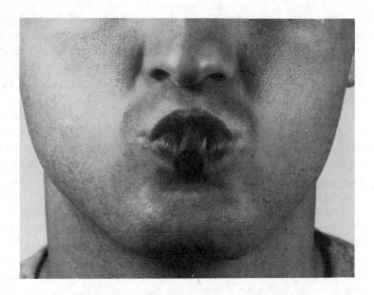

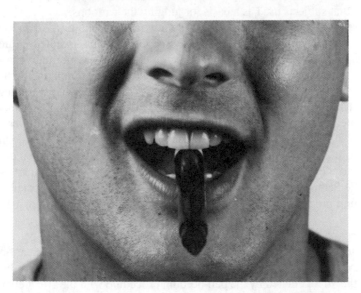

Figure 12.5 Typical facial expressions resulting from holding a felt-tip pen (a) with the lips and (b) with the teeth (reprinted from Strack, Martin, & Stepper, 1987).

TABLE 12.3
Ratings of Amusement and "Objective" Funniness as a Function of How and When the Pen was Held (adapted from Strack, Martin, & Stepper, 1988)

	Pen held during stimulus presentation	Pen held only at time of rating
A. Reported feelings of amusement		
Pen held in teeth	6.43	5.05
Pen held in lips	5.40	6.00
B. "Objective" funniness of cartoons		
Pen held in teeth	5.48	4.95
Pen held in lips	5.65	5.68

the first experiment. When they viewed the cartoons without the pen in their mouth, and only made ratings with the pen in the critical positions, the effect was in the opposite direction.

In fact, this contrast effect might be expected. In these conditions, the affect that subjects experienced as they viewed the cartoons did not systematically differ. However, subjects who held the pen in their teeth or lips at the time they rated the cartoons presumably experienced positive or negative affective reactions, respectively, at the time of judgment. They may therefore have used these reactions as standards of comparison in evaluating the implications of the feelings they remembered having experienced at the time the cartoons were presented. This would produce the sort of contrast effect that the authors observed.

Neither of these effects was expected to occur when subjects rated the "objective" funniness of the cartoons, as these judgments are not based on subjects' affective reactions. Data shown in the bottom half of Table 12.3 confirm this hypothesis as well; no effects of the pen-holding procedure on these judgments were reliable.

Supplementary data collected by the authors eliminated alternative interpretations of these findings. For example, subjects' perceptions of the difficulty of the alternative pen-holding procedures were unrelated to the judgments they reported. Moreover, subjects reported no insight whatsoever into the fact that their facial expressions were being manipulated or that these expressions (and the emotions they reflected) were relevant to the experiment. Thus, the results provide strong support for our conceptualization of emotion concepts (see Figure 12.1) and also for subjects' use of these concepts as information in making judgments to which their affective reactions are relevant.

Strack et al.'s findings make very clear that not *all* evaluative judgments of stimuli are based on the affective or emotional reactions that people have to these stimuli. Many such judgments are based on descriptive features of the stimuli themselves. The question is not *whether* affective reactions are used as information in making judgments of a stimulus, but *when* they are used, and what determines their contribution in relation to other types of judgment-relevant information.

Research on the information properties of affect has focused primarily on three types of judgments that seem intuitively likely to be based in part on subjects' affective reactions. The most definitive and diagnostic experiments have been conducted by Schwarz, Strack and their colleagues in the context of research on the cognitive and affective bases of life satisfaction. The other two types of judgment concern (a) subjects' perceptions of their self-worth, and (b) interpersonal attraction. We discuss these areas of research in turn.

2. Inferences of Life Satisfaction

It seems intuitively likely that if subjects are asked to report their general life satisfaction or state of well-being, they will interpret this as a request to report how they feel about their current life situation, and will base their judgment in part on these feelings. A series of studies by Schwarz, Strack and their colleagues provide compelling support for this hypothesis. In addition, they circumscribe some of the conditions in which affect is likely to have a more predominant influence on judgments than other, descriptive information.

The first and one of the most definitive studies was reported by Schwarz and Clore (1983, Experiment 1). In this experiment, subjects' affective states were manipulated by asking them to recall either a happy or a sad event they had had, and to relive the emotions they had experienced at the time the event occurred. (This was ostensibly done for the purpose of collecting samples of life events for use as stimulus materials in a later study.) The content of the experiences that subjects recall under such conditions are likely to have descriptive implications for their life satisfaction. Considered in isolation, therefore, an effect of these recalled experiences on satisfaction judgments would not necessarily indicate that the judgments were based on affect per se. To circumvent this problem, Schwarz and Clore employed a technique suggested by research on the role of arousal in cognitive dissonance reduction (Zanna & Cooper, 1974, 1976). Specifically, subjects wrote about their experiences, and ultimately made judgments in a soundproof booth. They were led to believe that the booth was necessary for the main part of the study, which involved memory for music. However, they were given an indication that being in the booth for a period of time was likely (a) to make them feel elated, (b) to make them depressed, or (c) to have no effect at all. Upon entering the booth, subjects first performed the music memory task, then wrote about the type of past experience they were assigned, and finally judged their general happiness and life satisfaction.

The descriptive implications of the life events subjects recalled did not appreciably differ in the three booth conditions. Therefore, if subjects base their judgments on these implications rather than on the affect that they experienced as

TABLE 12.4
Judgments of General Happiness and Life Satisfaction as a Function of the
Affective Quality of a Recalled Personal Experience and Ostensible
Characteristic of the Booth (adapted from Schwarz & Clore, 1983)

	Ostensible effects of booth		
	Tense	No affect	Elated
a. Judgments of general happiness (7-point scale)			
Happy recalled experience	6.5	6.4	6.7
Sad recalled experience	6.1	4.1	3.1
b. Judgments of life satisfaction (11-point scale)			
Happy recalled experience	9.6	8.6	9.7
Sad recalled experience	8.6	5.7	4.4

a result of thinking about these events, these judgments should be affected similarly by this cognitive activity regardless of the ostensible effects of the booth on their emotions. However, suppose subjects use their internal affective reactions as bases for inferring their general happiness and life satisfaction. Then, the effects of these reactions should be reduced when an alternative explanation of them (i.e., the booth) is available. Moreover, these effects should be increased when subjects' actual affective reactions differ from the reactions that ostensibly are produced by the booth, thereby indicating to subjects that their feelings about themselves must be particularly intense in order to have offset the booth's influence.

Results bearing on these possibilities are shown in Table 12.4. Several aspects of these data are noteworthy. First, subjects who were not told that the booth would influence their affective state reported less general happiness and life satisfaction when they had written about a sad experience than when they had written about a happy one. As predicted, the satisfaction reported by sad subjects was even less when they were led to believe that the booth they were in typically made people feel elated. However, it was just as high as the satisfaction reported by happy subjects when the booth ostensibly depressed people (thereby providing an explanation for their sadness that had no implications for their feelings about themselves).

The second thing to note is that happy subjects reported generally high life satisfaction regardless of characteristics of the booth. These subjects, then, apparently used their positive affect as a basis for judging their life satisfaction regardless of whether alternative explanations existed for it. Considered more generally, this asymmetric effect of positive and negative affect suggests that subjects use the positive affect they experience as a basis for self-judgments regardless of whether alternative explanations for this affect exist. However, they use the negative affect they experience as a basis for judging themselves only if an alternative explanation for their feelings that has no implications for them personally is not immediately apparent. A similar conclusion can be drawn from other studies (e.g., Arkin, Gleason, & Johnston, 1976; for further discussion of this asymmetry, see Wyer & Carlston, 1979).

Finally, the question arises as to whether the descriptive implications of subjects' recalled experiences *also* affected their judgments of life satisfaction. If this had been the case, a difference in life satisfaction as a function of the type of description they wrote should have been evident in all three booth conditions. As noted above, however, subjects' judgments of their life satisfaction under depressing booth conditions were virtually identical regardless of what type of experience they wrote about. Thus, it appears that in this study, at least, subjects' judgments were based almost exclusively on the affect they experienced and attributed to their feelings about themselves with respect to the characteristic being judged, and were not affected at all by the descriptive features of their past experience.

This does not mean that the descriptive aspects of subjects' life experiences are never considered as a basis for their life satisfaction judgments. Rather, it indicates that when thinking about these experiences elicits affective reactions, the implications of these affective reactions take priority. This interpretation receives additional support from a series of studies by Strack, Schwarz, and Gschneidinger (1985). In one study, subjects recalled life events that occurred in either the present or the past. However, they simply described these events briefly, in a way that did not elicit affective reactions. Subjects' judgments of general life satisfaction increased with the pleasantness of the current life experiences that they had reported. This suggests that subjects based these judgments on the descriptive implications of the particular subset of experiences that happened to be salient to them at the time. However, the quality of the past experiences that subjects recalled had a contrast effect on their judgments of life satisfaction, indicating that subjects used these experiences as a standard of comparison in evaluating their present life circumstances.

The critical results were obtained in a second study in which subjects were asked to recall past experiences in a way that either did nor did not elicit affect. When they did not elicit affect, the recalled experiences had contrast effects on judgments similar to those obtained in the first experiment. When they elicited strong affect, however, they had positive effects similar to those obtained by Schwarz and Clore (1983). It therefore appears that subjects use the descriptive implications of their past experience as a standard of comparison in evaluating their present life situation when no affect is elicited in the course of recalling them. If affect is elicited, however, the implications of these affective reactions override the effects of descriptive considerations.

The effects of laboratory manipulations of affect may seem to have limited generality. Similar effects have been obtained, however, when differences in affect are produced by naturally occurring everyday life events. For example, subjects report greater life satisfaction after a victory by a favorite soccer team than after a tie or defeat (Schwarz, Strack, Kommer, & Wagner, 1987). Moreover, they report greater life satisfaction on sunny days than on rainy days (Schwarz & Clore, 1983, Experiment 2). There is an important contingency in this latter effect. That is, it does not occur if the weather is explicitly mentioned to subjects before asking them to make their estimates. This suggests, as does Schwarz and Clore's other study, that when an alternative explanation for subjects' negative affect (in this case, rainy weather) is made salient to them, they are likely to attribute their affective reactions to this factor rather than to themselves, and, therefore, to base their judgments of life satisfaction on other criteria.

It is extremely important to bear in mind, however, that these effects are likely to occur only when the judgments to be made are ones to which subjects' feelings are directly relevant. When the judgments to be made are typically based on descriptive features of the objects to be judged, subjects may only use their affective reactions as information when these descriptive features do not come easily to mind. Two studies by Schwarz et al. (1987) provide evidence for this contingency. In the study mentioned briefly above, subjects reported greater general life satisfaction after a watching a soccer team's victory than after watching a tie. However, their judgments of satisfaction with particular aspects of their life (e.g., their income, their work, or the national economy) were unaffected.

A second study provided an even clearer demonstration of the contingency. In one condition, the experiment was conducted in a very pleasant room decorated with attractive posters and flowers. In a second condition, it was conducted in a dirty, overheated room with an offensive odor. Subjects reported greater general life satisfaction in the first condition than in the second. However, they reported *less* satisfaction with the apartments in which they were living in the first condition. These latter judgments were apparently based on a comparison of the descriptive features of their apartments with those of their immediate surroundings, producing a contrast effect.

These results, like Strack et al.'s (1988), point out the need to circumscribe the types of evaluative judgments that are typically based on descriptive features of the stimuli being judged and the types that are based on subjective affective reactions to the stimuli. Further evidence bearing on this matter is provided by the research described below.

2. Judgments of Self-Worth

Subjects' perceptions of how satisfied they are with their lives are undoubtedly related to how they feel about themselves as persons. These latter feelings may be reflected more directly in their judgments of self-esteem, or of their competence in specific areas of importance to them. In case of competence judgments, however,

TABLE 12.5
Judgments of Domain-Specific Competence as a Function of the Domain and
Affective Quality of Subjects' Recalled Experiences

Variable	Positive experience recalled	Negative experience recalled
Judgments of competence in the same domain as recalled experience		
Achievement experience recalled, achievement competence judged	4.77	4.37
Social experience recalled, social competence judged	4.38	4.38
Judgments of competence in a different domain than recalled experience		
Achievement experience recalled, social competence judged	4.46	3.46
Social experience recalled, achievement competence judged	4.87	4.60

descriptive aspects of judgment-relevant knowledge (e.g., successes and failures in areas that require the abilities being judged) may have an influence as well.

These possibilities were evaluated in a study by Levine, Wyer, and Schwarz (1987). Subjects first recalled either a happy or sad personal experience that had occurred to them in either an achievement situation or an interpersonal situation. This procedure activated not only emotion concepts but also specific subsets of self-knowledge that was relevant to competence in the types of situations that subjects described. However, content analyses revealed that the descriptive implications of this self knowledge differed in the two domains. Specifically, subjects typically took responsibility for the achievement experiences they recalled. However, they attributed the interpersonal experiences they recalled either to external circumstances or to the other persons involved. In other words, the achievement experiences that subjects recalled had descriptive implications for their achievement competence, whereas the interpersonal experiences they recalled did not have descriptive implications for their social competence.

Subjects after describing these experiences were asked (as part of an ostensibly unrelated experiment) to judge their competence in both achievement and social situations and to report their general feelings of self-esteem. The affective quality of the experience that subjects recalled had a positive effect on their judgments of global self-esteem regardless of the domain of this experience. Its effects on judgments of competence were somewhat more complicated. These judgments are summarized in Table 12.5 as a function of the domain and affective quality of the experiences that subjects recalled. First consider subjects' judgments of competence in the domain to which the experience they recalled was relevant. Subjects' judgments of their achievement competence were influenced by the affective quality of the achievement experience they recalled, but their judgments of their social competence were *not* affected by the quality of the interpersonal experience they recalled. This pattern of results suggests that subjects based their judgments of competence in the same domain as their recalled experiences on the descriptive implications of those experiences.

Now consider subjects' judgments of their competence in the domain to which their recalled experience was not descriptively relevant. These judgments increased with the affective quality of this experience regardless of the domain in which the recalled experience occurred. These judgments, then, seem to have been based on the emotional reactions that subjects were experiencing.

These results suggest a quite plausible hypothesis. When subjects are asked to judge their competence in a particular domain and a specific experience they have had in this domain is easily accessible in memory, subjects use the descriptive implications of this experience as a basis for their judgments. If, however, no such experience comes easily to mind, subjects use the affective reactions they happen to be experiencing as a basis for deciding how they feel about themselves with respect to the attribute they are judging. This hypothesis also accounts for the effects of affective reactions on subjects' judgments of their global self-esteem.

This interpretation must be evaluated in the context of the conclusion we drew from the studies by Strack et al. (1985). That is, Levine et al.'s results suggest that when both subjects' affective reactions and the descriptive implications of their self knowledge are relevant to self-judgments and are easily accessible in memory, the descriptive implications of their self-knowledge take priority. In contrast, results of the earlier studies described suggest that in making judgments of general life satisfaction, the use of affective reactions as a basis for judgments takes priority over descriptive considerations.

Although these two conclusions may appear incompatible at first glance, their inconsistency is more superficial than real. Note that judgments of domain-specific competence, like judgments of the funniness of cartoons in Strack et al.'s (1988) pen-holding study and domain-specific satisfaction judgments in Schwarz et al.'s (1986) studies, are not the sort of inferences that are based *directly* on affect. Rather, they pertain to descriptive aspects of one's ability in the area. Therefore, subjects in making these judgments give priority to descriptive knowledge with implications for the judgments, and may consider how they "feel" about themselves with respect to the ability only if such knowledge is not easily accessible in memory. In contrast, judgments of general life satisfaction more directly concern affective reactions (i.e., how subjects "feel" about their lives). In making these judgments, then, subjects' descriptive self-knowledge may be used only when strong affect is not experienced at the time that judgments are made. Very simply, the relative priorities given to (a) affective reactions and (b) the descriptive implications of information may depend on which type of information is considered more relevant on a priori grounds to the particular judgment to be reported.

3. Interpersonal Attraction

Research on the role of affect in judgments of interpersonal attraction predates by many years the more general concern with the role of affect in social information processing. Much of this research was inspired by Byrne's (1971) similarity-attraction hypothesis. This hypothesis asserts that when subjects learn that another person is either similar or dissimilar to them in attitudes, interests or general personality, they experience positive or negative affect, respectively. This affect then becomes associated with the similar or dissimilar other and, therefore, it is subsequently used as a basis for reporting attraction to this person.

Several studies based on this conceptualization have been performed in an attempt to establish the mediating role of affect in the processes outlined above. As Wyer and Carlston (1979) point out, however, the results of this research are not definitive. The main ambiguity surrounds the difficulty of separating the influence of subjects' affective reactions per se from the contribution of descriptive concepts and knowledge.

The strategy that has been most commonly used to investigate this matter is conceptually similar to that employed in the other studies we have reviewed. That is, affect is induced in a way that is objectively irrelevant to the judgments to be made of the target person, and the influence of this affect on attraction to the target (as well as the effect of attitude- similarity information) is determined.

One of the most provocative studies in this area (for a more complete review, see Clore, 1975), but also one that is representative of the interpretative difficulties noted above, was performed by Griffitt and Veitch (1971). Subjects were given information about their similarity in attitudes to a target person and were asked to report their liking for the person. The study, however, was conducted in either a crowded room or uncrowded one, and at either normal room temperature or a temperature of 90 degrees. Subjects evaluated the target more unfavorably when the room was hot or crowded than in other conditions. Subjects presumably experienced negative affect as a result of being exposed to the unpleasant experimental conditions, and it is reasonable to suppose, based on the considerations outlined earlier, that some proportion of this affect was attributed to the target person. An alternative interpretation, however, is that the room conditions activated thoughts about people in general ("It certainly can be unpleasant to have other people around," "People should have their heads examined for running experiments under conditions like this," etc.), and these thoughts, independently of the affect associated with them, affected judgments of the target person in particular.

The problems that are created by a failure to separate the effects of affective reactions from the effects of other judgment-relevant cognitions are exemplified in a study by Bleda, Bell, and Byrne (1973). In this study, subjects' moods prior to judging a target person were manipulated by exposing them to either humorous or serious television commercials. In some cases, however, the serious commercials depicted social problems that, although successful in putting subjects in a bad mood, simultaneously activated positive thoughts about people and their need for help. In these cases, the serious commercials led subjects to rate the target person favorably despite the negative affect they elicited.

The studies described above attempt to induce qualitatively different affective reactions and then to determine the extent to which judgments were affected by these reactions. A second approach has been based on somewhat different reasoning. Suppose a stimulus person elicits positive or negative affective reactions and subjects use these reactions as a basis for their judgments. Then, an increase in subjects' general level of arousal should increase their perceptions of the intensity of their affective reactions to the stimulus, and this, in turn, should increase the extremity of the judgments they make.

A good example of this approach is provided by White, Fishbein, and Rutstein (1981). In this study, subjects were asked to evaluate a target person who was either quite attractive or quite unattractive. Before doing so, however, they engaged in physical exercise that increased their general arousal level. The time interval between the exercise and the judgment task was such that subjects would still experience arousal but would not attribute it to the exercise (Cantor, Zillmann, & Bryant, 1974; see also Zillmann, 1978). As expected, these subjects rated the attractive target more favorably, and the unattractive target less favorably, than control subjects who were less aroused.

Unfortunately, there are alternative interpretations of this study as well. For example, subjects who are moderately aroused at the time they perform a judgment task may simply be more involved in the task. Therefore, they may be more responsive to the information provided them, than subjects who are less aroused. As a result, they may be relatively more affected by differences in the implications of this information.

In summary, few studies of the role of affect in interpersonal attraction provide compelling evidence that subjects use their affective reactions per se as information about their attraction to other persons. This is quite surprising in light of the intuitive plausibility of the hypothesis. In fact, the hypothesis seems so self-evident that it is probably only a matter of time before a more definitive laboratory demonstration of this influence is constructed.

4. Judgments of Other Concepts and Objects

Research on the influence of affect in judgments has obviously not been restricted to the three domains described above. Johnson and Tversky (1983), for example, found that exposing subjects to a vivid description of a death from one type of cause (e.g., leukemia) increased subjects' subsequent estimates of the likelihood of dying from other causes. Moreover, these increases were similar in magnitude regardless of whether the cause being judged was related to the one that subjects read about (i.e., another illness) or was unrelated (accidents or natural disasters). Comparable effects were also obtained by having subjects read about an unpleasant interpersonal experience that did not involve death. In contrast, reading about positive experiences decreased subjects' estimates of the probability of dying from the various causes they considered. These results argue very strongly that subjects based their probability estimates in part on the affective reactions they had at the time they considered the events being judged, and that their perceptions of these reactions, in turn, were influenced by the story they had read. Moreover, this influence was independent of the descriptive implications of these stories for the judgments they made.

Not all studies are so unequivocal. One of the best known but least clearly interpretable studies of the effects of affect on judgments was reported by Isen, Shalker, Clark, and Karp (1978). In this study, some shoppers were given a small gift as they approached a supermarket. Then, immediately afterwards, these shoppers were asked by someone who was ostensibly conducting a survey of consumer attitudes to evaluate their automobile service. Shoppers who were not given a gift were also interviewed. Subjects who had received a gift evaluated their automobile service more favorably than those who had not. The most obvious interpretation of this finding is that subjects based their evaluation of their automobile service on their perception of how they felt about it, and the affective reactions induced by the gift they received contributed to these perceptions.

Unfortunately, there are several other plausible interpretations as well. For one thing, the effects may have had nothing to do with subjects' affective reactions at all. That is, receiving a gift in a supermarket may activate cognitions (e.g., "Businesses are not always out to get you after all") that have descriptive implications for subjects' judgments of their automobile service, and, therefore, affected subjects' judgments for this reason.

Even assuming that the accessibility of affect-related concepts affected judgments, it is difficult to localize this effect at a particular stage of processing. As noted above, our own interpretation of Isen et al.'s study is that affect had an informational influence on judgments. However, the model we propose calls attention to at least two other possibilities.

1. Affect-related concepts that were activated by the gift were presumably in the Work Space at the time subjects were asked to evaluate their automobile service. In making these evaluations, subjects may have retrieved descriptive knowledge about their automobile service from Permanent Storage, interpreted it in terms of these concepts, and based their judgments on the implications of this interpretation.

2. Subjects may have different referent bins pertaining to good and bad experiences they have had with their automobile service, and the headers of these bins may contain representations of their subjective reactions to these experiences.

If features associated with subjects' positive subjective reactions to the gift were still in the Work Space at the time subjects were interviewed, these features may have been included among the probe cues that were used to identify a judgment-relevant referent bin. As a result, a "good automobile service" bin may have been identified, and so favorable information was retrieved.

Isen et al.'s study is only one of several that has these interpretative ambiguities. One value of the model we propose is that it calls attention to the alternative cognitive mechanisms that underlie the phenomena reported.

5. Summary

Considered as a whole, the research summarized in this section provides good evidence that subjects do use their perceptions of their affective reactions as a basis for judgments. Moreover, it circumscribes the conditions in which this occurs.

1. Affective reactions and their implications are most likely to be used as bases for judgments that pertain directly to one's own "feelings" about a person, object, or event. In these cases, the affect that is experienced at the time of judgment is given priority over other available judgment-relevant information, with the latter information being used as a basis for judgment only if the affective reactions one experiences are not sufficiently intense.

2. When affective reactions are only indirectly related to a judgment, the descriptive implications of judgment-relevant information take precedence. However, one's affective reactions may still be used as a heuristic basis for judgments when information with descriptive implications for these judgments is not easily accessible in memory.

3. Subjects find it difficult to distinguish between the affective reactions that are elicited by the particular stimuli they are asked to judge and the reactions they are experiencing for other reasons. Therefore, these latter, objectively irrelevant reactions may often contribute to judgments as well as relevant ones.

4. Subjects do not appear to use the negative affective reactions they are experiencing as a basis for judging attributes of themselves if nonself-relevant explanations for these reactions are called to their attention. In contrast, they appear to use positive affective reactions as a basis for self-judgments regardless of whether alternative explanations of these reactions are available.

A Recapitulation

The general model of information processing we have proposed provides a viable conceptualization of the way that affect is represented in memory, and offers a theoretical account of its role in several different phases of cognitive processing.

The empirical data bearing on this role, however, are often more equivocal than one would like. The model specifies several a priori contingencies in the effect of emotional reactions on the encoding, organization, and retrieval of information, and the use of affect as information. Moreover, it can account for still other contingencies after the fact. In many instances, however, compelling empirical demonstrations of these contingencies have not been reported. To summarize:

Interpretation of ambiguous information. Few studies have been constructed to demonstrate that the concepts associated with different types of emotional reactions affect subjects' interpretation of information that can be encoded in terms of these concepts. Although one study (Kelly & Wyer, 1987) provides some evidence that these effects occur, the results of the study have not been replicated.

Selective encoding and organization. Emotion concepts appear to influence the selective encoding of information that can be interpreted in terms of these concepts when the information is presented in a narrative (e.g., a story) and subjects have the objective of forming an impression of the situation described or the persons involved in it. However, these effects are much less evident in list learning studies where subjects' objective is simply to learn the material, and an encoding of the material in terms of higher order attribute (e.g., emotion) concepts is not necessary to attain this objective.

Retrieval. When new or previously acquired information has been organized in memory in terms of affect or emotion concepts, the subsequent activation of these concepts may sometimes increase the likelihood of recalling the information. A precondition, however, is that the mood that subjects experience at retrieval be explicitly labeled or otherwise called to their attention (e.g., by asking them explicitly to experience the mood). When this is not the case, the activation of an emotion may sometimes increase the likelihood of recalling information that is affectively inconsistent with this emotion. More generally, it is not clear from the evidence available whether the recall of affect-congruent information is cued by the subjective affective reactions that subjects experience or only the verbal labels that are associated with subjects' mood state, independently of other features of the emotion concepts that are presumably activated.

Inference making. The affective reactions that subjects experience at the time they make an evaluative judgment appear to be used as a basis for judgments to which the reactions are directly relevant (e.g., judgments of how one "feels" about a stimulus). However, emotion judgments that do not directly pertain to feelings may be based on subjects' affective reactions only if information or knowledge with descriptive implications for the judgments is not easily accessible in memory.

Therefore, of the various ways in which affective reactions, or the concepts associated with them, can directly influence different stages of information processing, their role in inference making has received the strongest support to date. In contrast, the influence of emotion concepts on information retrieval, although extensively investigated (cf. Blaney, 1986) is less well established.

It is important to note, however, that emotions may also have indirect influences on information processing. That is, they may affect the amount of cognitive activity that is performed in the pursuit of processing objectives to which these emotions are not directly relevant. The last section of this chapter is devoted to a consideration of these indirect effects.

Indirect Influences of Affect and Emotion on Information Processing

Many early theories of learning and motivation were based on the assumption that organisms behave in ways that eliminate unpleasant internal states. The hypothesis that internal states of affect or arousal influence the efficiency of performing cognitive or motor activity is also not of recent vintage (cf. Easterbrook, 1959). These general notions enter into several different hypotheses concerning the effects of positive and negative emotions on both the motivation and the ability to engage in complex information processing. These hypotheses are typically described in the literature in terms of the influence of motives to engage in "mood repair" and "mood maintenance" (cf. Isen, 1984) and the role of emotion in information processing efficiency. They are stated below in terms that are compatible with the general model we are proposing.

1. Mood repair. The experience of a negative emotion is psychologically unpleasant. Therefore, if a negative emotion concept exists in the Work Space, it may stimulate the retrieval of a goal schema that specifies procedures for decreasing or eliminating the unpleasant reactions that are associated with the concept. There are three general ways in which this may be done.

a. People may engage in cognitive or motor activity that eliminates the source of the negative emotional reactions they experience.

b. People may engage in cognitive or motor activity that places sufficient demands on the information processing system to displace from the Work Space the emotion concepts that give rise to the unpleasant experience. Consequently, these concepts are no longer activated (thought about). Put more simply, people who experience negative emotions may distract themselves from thinking about the conditions that give rise to these emotions by engaging in other, affect-irrelevant activity.

c. People may focus their attention on stimulus information (or previously acquired knowledge) with which positive emotion concepts have been associated. The activation of these concepts leads pleasant reactions to be experienced that override the unpleasant reactions that were produced by the original emotion concept.

2. Mood maintenance. People who experience a positive emotion find it psychologically pleasant. They may therefore avoid engaging in activities that are likely to displace the concept associated with this emotion from active memory (the Work Space). Thus, they avoid engaging in cognitive activity that places high demands on the cognitive system or that runs the risk of disrupting or eliminating the conscious experience of these reactions. For similar reasons, people may avoid thinking about new or previously acquired information with which negative emotion concepts have been associated.

3. Cognitive efficiency. To the extent that negative emotion concepts activate goal schemata that are employed in an attempt to eliminate them, the presence of these schemata in the Goal Specification Box reduces the amount of space available for other goal schemata, and, therefore, reduces the amount of information processing that can be devoted to other goal-directed activity (see chapter 2). Positive affect, which does not activate goal schemata, may not have this effect. This implies that negative emotions, unlike positive ones, may interfere with both the amount and effectiveness of information processing that is performed in the pursuit of other goals.

All of these various effects seem intuitively plausible. However, certain of them have diametrically opposite implications. For example, the assumption that subjects who experience a negative emotion attempt to distract themselves from thinking about it (version 'b' of the mood repair hypothesis) implies that they will more often engage in affect-irrelevant cognitive activity, and devote more time and energy to this activity, than subjects who experience positive emotions. On the other hand, if the activation of goal schemata that are associated with the elimination of negative affect decreases information processing capacity (the cognitive efficiency hypothesis), subjects who experience negative emotions should devote less cognitive activity to affect-irrelevant information processing. To this extent, they should be *less* effective in attaining the goals to which this latter processing is relevant than subjects who experience positive emotions.

The notion that negative affective states give rise to cognitive activity that is directed toward their elimination is, of course, a basic tenet of cognitive dissonance theory (Festinger, 1957). Several impressive studies, beginning with the work of Zanna and Cooper (1972; for summaries, see Cooper & Fazio, 1984; Zanna & Cooper, 1976), have demonstrated that subjects who engage in attitude-discrepant behavior do indeed experience unpleasant physical and cognitive reactions, and that they consequently engage in cognitive activity (e.g., belief change) that eliminates the source of these reactions. However, subjects typically do not perform this cognitive work if they can attribute their negative affect to something other than their attitude-discrepant behavior (cf. Higgins, Rhodewalt, & Zanna, 1979; Croyle & Cooper, 1983; for a review, see Zanna & Cooper, 1976). These results are consistent with part 'a' of the mood repair hypothesis.

There is much less evidence that subjects who experience negative affect intentionally distract themselves from thinking about it by engaging in more extensive processing of other information. Instead, the evidence is more consistent with the cognitive efficiency hypothesis. That is, complex cognitive functioning is more characteristic of persons who experience positive emotions. Isen (1984) cites several examples of her own work that indicate that people who are in an experimentally induced good mood give more unusual responses to neutral words in a word association test, and perform more efficiently on creative problem solving tasks, than do control subjects. Isen also notes that positive mood subjects are more likely to use heuristics in problem-solving situations. However, this behavior may not reflect cognitive inefficiency or simplicity. Rather, like these subjects' success in creative problem solving, it may reflect a tendency for subjects in a good mood to seek imaginative, "elegant" solutions rather than defaulting to established but uninteresting routines.

Unfortunately, conditions in which subjects experienced negative emotions were not run in any of the above studies, and so the general hypothesis that subjects with positive emotions engage in more extensive processing than subjects who experience negative emotions cannot be evaluated. Nevertheless, the data appear to contradict the hypothesis that subjects in a good mood tend to avoid engaging in cognitive activity in order to insure that their mood is maintained.

1. Reactions to Persuasive Communications

It may well be that *both* positive and negative emotions lead subjects to increase the extensiveness with which information is processed. Their effects may differ primarily in terms of the type of cognitive activity they stimulate. Direct evidence bearing on this is provided in a recent study by Bless, Bohner, Schwarz, and Strack (1987) on the role of affect in reactions to persuasive communications. In this study, subjects who had been put into an experimentally induced good or bad mood read a communication advocating an increase in university fees. The communication contained either strong arguments in favor of the increase (e.g., the promise of increased parking facilities for all students) or weak arguments (the promise of only a nominal increase in parking that was unlikely to have much impact on the parking problems that existed). After reading the message, subjects reported their general approval of the fee increase and indicated the amount of increase they considered to be desirable. Then, having done so, they listed the thoughts they had had about the message as they read it (Osterhouse & Brock, 1970; Petty & Brock, 1981).

Indices of subjects' attitudes toward a fee increase are shown in Tables 12.6a and 12.6b as a function of subjects' affective state and the type of arguments contained in the message they read. Weak argument messages had little influence regardless of subjects' affective state. However, the influence of the strong argu-

TABLE 12.6

Mean Approval of a Fee Increase, Amount of Increase Advocated, and Cognitive Responses as a Function of Mood State and the Quality of Arguments Presented (based on data reported by Bless et al., 1987)

	Mood state	
	Positive	Negative
A. Approval of fee increase		
Strong arguments presented	5.00	6.35
Weak arguments presented	3.85	3.00
B. Amount of increase recommended (in Deutsch-marks)		
Strong arguments presented	52.5	56.7
Weak arguments presented	52.1	47.2
C. Cognitive responses		
Strong arguments presented		
Proportion of positive thoughts	.165	.340
Proportion of negative thoughts	.515	.340
Total	.680	.680
Weak arguments presented		
Proportion of positive thoughts	.175	.105
Proportion of negative thoughts	.520	.545
Total	.695	.650

ment messages was greater when subjects were unhappy. Put another way, subjects were significantly more influenced by the quality of the arguments in the message when they were in a bad mood than when they were in a good one.

Considered in isolation, the relatively greater influence of argument quality on the opinions of bad mood subjects might be interpreted as support for part 'b' of the mood repair hypothesis. That is, these subjects may have engaged in more analytic processing of the message than did subjects who were in a good mood. However, two other results argue strongly against this interpretation. First, post-experimental evaluations of the arguments presented indicated that both good mood and bad mood subjects were equally sensitive to differences in the quality of the arguments contained in the two messages. The second piece of evidence concerns subjects' cognitive responses to the message. Table 12.6c shows the proportions of positive and negative thoughts that subjects listed as a function of experimental variables. The overall proportion of judgment-relevant thoughts that subjects reported having was very similar, regardless of their mood or the quality of the arguments they read. Thus, there is no evidence at all that bad mood subjects engaged in any more extensive processing of the message content than good mood subjects.

The difference between good mood and bad mood subjects lies in the *type* of processing that occurred. All subjects listed more negative than positive thoughts in response to weak arguments. In response to strong arguments, however, bad mood subjects engaged in more positive thinking about the issue (e.g., elaboration of the arguments and their personal benefits), but less negative thinking (e.g., counterarguing, or thinking about why the fee increase would not benefit them personally) than did good mood subjects. This difference in the relative proportions of positive and negative thoughts that subjects had in response to the strong message could account for why bad mood subjects were more influenced by this message than were good mood subjects.

This difference in processing can be interpreted in terms of the factors implied by two of the hypotheses we have raised. Specifically, the evidence that good mood subjects have relatively greater tendency to counterargue suggests that they were more highly motivated to think critically about the message and to process it analytically than were bad mood subjects. This difference is consistent with the cognitive efficiency hypothesis. The focus of bad mood subjects on positive thoughts has a different explanation. Note that the strong arguments in the message described benefits to students that, if provided, would be likely to make them very happy. It seems likely, therefore, that bad mood subjects were motivated to think about these benefits, which presumably elicited positive emotional reactions, in order to offset the negative feelings they experienced as a result of the previous mood induction task. This interpretation is consistent with part 'c' of the mood repair hypothesis.

In any event, the results discredit alternative hypotheses concerning the effects of mood state on cognitive processing. First, they contradict version 'b' of the mood repair hypothesis, that subjects who experience negative affect try to distract themselves by engaging in more extensive processing of mood-irrelevant material *in general*. Second, the results disconfirm the mood-maintenance hypothesis concerning the effects of positive emotion. If subjects in a positive mood were motivated to maintain this mood, it seems unlikely that they would have generated negative thoughts about the fee increase (i.e., reasons why the increase would not be beneficial to them). Rather, they should have engaged in positive thinking, much as the bad mood subjects did.

2. "Depressive Realism"

Bless et al.'s (1987) findings suggest that negative emotions lead subjects to engage in less complex information processing than do positive emotions. This conclusion is also suggested by results obtained in a completely different area of research on "depressive realism" (Alloy & Abramson, 1979). Based on the results of several studies, Alloy and Abramson concluded that depressed subjects are more accurate than nondepressed subjects in perceiving contingencies between their behavior and its consequences. To the extent that this is true, it could indicate that persons who experience negative affect do indeed think more critically and analytically about the information to which they are exposed than persons who

TABLE 12.7
Estimated Control Over Outcomes as a Function of Depression Level and
Outcome Contingencies (based on data from Alloy & Abramson, 1979,
Experiments 1 and 2)

Outcome contingencies		$P(L|P)-P(L|\overline{P})$ (Actual control)	Depressed subjects	Nondepressed subjects
$P(L|P)$	$P(L|\overline{P})$			
75	0	75	71.5	74.4
75	25	50	47.1	46.2
75	50	25	35.0	35.3
75	75	0	17.2	40.8
25	25	0	15.4	13.7

experience positive or neutral affect. However, a closer scrutiny of the data reported by Alloy and Abramson suggests a different interpretation.

Two types of studies were performed to investigate the hypothesis. The basic experimental task was the same in all cases. That is, subjects were classified as either mildly depressed or nondepressed, based on their responses to the Beck Depression Inventory. These subjects were then exposed to a series of trials in which they were given a choice of either pressing a button or not doing so. Their decision (to press or not to press) either was or was not followed by a light of a particular color. The conditional probabilities that the light would appear if subjects pressed the button, $P(L|P)$, and that it would appear if they did not press the button, $P(L|\overline{P})$, were systematically varied. The difference between these two conditional probabilities was used as an index of the actual amount of control that subjects had over the light. The main dependent variable in the studies was the amount of control that subjects reported themselves to have.

In two studies (Alloy & Abramson, 1979, Experiments 1 and 2), subjects were told explicitly that their task was to decide how much control they had over whether or not the light came on. The studies differed in the levels of actual control that were used. The results of both studies combined are shown in Table 12.7 as a function of subjects' depression level and the outcome contingency. Depressed subjects' estimates of their control increased consistently with their actual control. With one exception, however, nondepressed subjects' estimates were very similar to those of the depressed subjects. The only exception is due to the fact that nondepressed females in the 75-75 condition reported an inordinately high degree of control (51.4). (Nondepressed male subjects' estimates in this condition ($M = 30.3$) were similar to depressed males' estimates ($M = 21.2$).) This one aberrant cell has no clear explanation and seems likely to be spurious. To this extent, the results clearly indicate that depressed and nondepressed subjects are equally

TABLE 12.8

Estimated Control Over Outcomes as a Function of Depression Level and Outcome Contingencies (based on data from Alloy & Abramson, 1979, Experiments 3 and 4)

Outcome contingencies		Depressed subjects	Nondepressed subjects
$P(L|P)$	$P(L|\bar{P})$		
"Win" conditions			
75	25	56.0	64.5
50	50	36.0	17.2
25	75	40.0	73.5
"Lose" conditions			
75	25	52.5	54.5
50	50	11.4	21.2
25	75	49.5	21.2

capable of estimating the amount of control they have over outcomes when they are told explicitly that the purpose of the experimental task is to make these estimates.

In two additional studies (Alloy & Abramson, 1979, Experiments 3 and 4), the task objective given subjects was different. That is, subjects were told in these studies that their task was to "learn how to turn on the light." Moreover, monetary incentives were introduced in two ways. In "win" conditions, subjects started off with no money, but were given a quarter every time they turned on the light. In "lose" conditions, they started off with $5, and lost a quarter when they failed to turn on the light. This manipulation, therefore, focused subjects' attention on either winning money or losing money. Three outcome contingencies were considered in the two experiments. In two conditions, the actual amount of control was the same. In one condition, however, the probability of turning on the light by pressing the button was higher than the probability of turning it on by not pressing the button (75% vs. 25%). In a second condition, the two probabilities were reversed. In a third condition, the probabilities of turning on the light by pressing or not pressing the button were the same (50%). Subjects' estimates of the control they had in these conditions are summarized in Table 12.8.

The implications of these data can be seen by partitioning them into three sets of orthogonal comparisons, each indicating the contribution to judgments of a different factor: (a) subjects' focus of attention on winning money or losing money, (b) the actual amount of control they had, and (c) the amount of reinforcement they were given for active (button pressing) vs. passive (nonpressing) behavior. The effects of the first factor is reflected by the difference between estimates under "win" conditions and estimates under "lose" conditions. Nondepressed subjects' perceptions of their control were much greater when the procedure focused their attention on winning money (M = 60.5) than when it focused their attention on losing money (M = 22.8). In contrast, depressed subjects' estimates were not influenced by this manipulation (46.2 vs. 38.9 under "win" and "lose" conditions, respectively).

The actual amount of control that subjects had was the same in 75-25 and 25-75 conditions. The influence of actual control on judgments can be inferred from the difference between judgments under these two conditions combined and judgments under 50-50 conditions. This difference was much greater for depressed subjects (53.1 vs. 21.5) than for nondepressed subjects (44.8 vs. 35.4). Note that these data contrast markedly with the first set of data (Table 12.7), which showed that both groups of subjects were equally sensitive to the actual control they had over the light.

The effect of receiving reinforcement for positive (button-pressing) behavior as opposed to passive (nonbutton-pressing) behavior can be inferred from the difference between judgments under 75-25 conditions (where the reinforcement for button pressing was high) and judgments under 25-75 conditions (where the reinforcement for nonpressing was high). Nondepressed subjects typically estimated their control to be higher when they were primarily reinforced for active behavior (M = 59.6) than when they were primarily reinforced for passive behavior (M = 30.0). However, this difference was much less in the case of depressed subjects (56.9 vs. 49.3).

The question is what implications these results have for the influence of negative affect on subjects' perceptions of control in particular, and for their involvement in the experimental task more generally. The results of the first two studies we described show that there is no inherent difference between depressed and nondepressed subjects' estimates of their control when they perceive that the purpose of the task is to make these estimates. When subjects' objective is to "turn on the light," however, nondepressed subjects appear to be much more inclined than depressed subjects to base their control estimates on additional factors that are introduced by the experimental procedure. That is, they are more likely to infer their control from perceptions of themselves as "winning," and from the reinforcement they get for positive behavioral decisions (pressing the button) as opposed to negative ones (not pressing). Because of the relatively greater attention they pay to these factors, the influence of their actual control is correspondingly less than the influence of this factor on depressed subjects' judgments.

There are many interesting interpretations of these differences. In the context of the issues considered in this chapter, however, the most important implication is the following. The greater sensitivity of nondepressed subjects to factors other than the actual contingency of outcomes on their behavior does not in any way indicate that these subjects are less sensitive to the features on the experimental task, or are less inclined to think about it, than are depressed subjects. In fact, nondepressives' greater sensitivity to these (albeit objectively irrelevant) factors suggests that they were *more* involved in the experiment, and were more sensitive to procedural differences, than were the depressives. These data, then, provide little support for the hypothesis that subjects who experience negative affect immerse themselves in the experimental task in order to distract themselves from their negative mood state. If anything, positive (or, at least, neutral) affect appears to have this effect. Thus, the results once again appear consistent with the implications of the cognitive efficiency hypothesis.

In evaluating this conclusion, it is important to note that the differences in affect that Alloy and Abramson's subjects experienced were chronic, and therefore existed prior to the experiment. When affect is induced experimentally, as in Schwarz and Clore's (1983) study described earlier, negative emotions may often lead subjects to search for explanations of these emotions that do not reflect negatively on themselves. Under these conditions, negative affect may stimulate more cognitive activity than positive affect.

3. Conclusions ,

The research we have summarized indicates that categorical conclusions about the relative amounts of cognitive activity that positive and negative emotions are likely to stimulate are inevitably misleading. Whether negative affect stimulates more or less cognitive processing than positive affect appears to depend primarily on the relevance of this activity to subjects' processing objectives at the time. Subjects who experience negative affect may be more likely to engage in extensive information processing if they perceive that this activity may help them to eliminate their unpleasant emotional state. Such activity is directed toward the identification of reasons for the emotion that do not reflect negatively on themselves (Schwarz & Clore, 1983). Or, it may involve thinking about things that generate positive affect, thereby overriding the negative feelings that are being experienced (Bless et al., 1987). Under conditions in which cognitive activity is neither self-relevant nor instrumental in eliminating negative affect, however, the experience of this affect may *decrease* information processing relative to positive affect.

Concluding Remarks

This chapter has covered a lot of ground. We have considered not only the cognitive determinants of affect and emotion but also the effects that affect and emotion may have on both specific types of cognitive activity and on the motivation and capacity to engage in information processing more generally. There are undoubtedly many issues associated with the role of affect in information processing that we have not discussed. However, the work we have cited is sufficiently representative to suggest that the proposed model is a useful device for both conceptually integrating a reasonably large number of these issues and for generating additional hypotheses concerning the role of affect in cognitive processing.

Chapter 13
The Self

People's psychological adjustment to the world in which they live appears to be strongly influenced by the perceptions they have of themselves. Perhaps because of this, the determinants and effects of people's self concepts have been a major focus of psychological inquiry since the turn of the century (James, 1890; see also Cooley, 1902; Mead, 1934). This concern has been an integrative force in many areas of clinical, personality, social, and, more recently, cognitive psychology. The specific issues that have been investigated are too numerous to recount. Indeed, it is hard to think of a social psychological phenomenon in which people's perceptions of themselves are unlikely to have either a direct or an indirect influence. This is partially because "self" is implicated, in one way or another, in virtually all cognitive activity as well as the overt behavior that results from this activity. Almost all of the information we receive is acquired under conditions in which we are more or less aware of ourselves as the receiving agent. Cognitions that we have about ourselves in these situations, as either an observer or active participant, are potentially a part of every mental representation we form (cf. Tulving, 1983).

The role of self knowledge in social information processing has been apparent throughout this volume. Virtually every chapter has devoted at least some attention to this role and how it can be conceptualized within the theoretical framework we have proposed. In Chapter 5, for example, we discussed the spontaneous and goal-directed retrieval of self knowledge in the context of "reminding" phenomena. These processes also came into play in Chapter 12, where we considered the influence of affect and emotion on the recall of personal experiences.

The role of personal values and goals on the interpretation of information was noted in our discussion of encoding effects in Chapter 6. The cognitive representation of personal experiences, and their similarity to the representations that are formed from information about others' experiences, were considered in Chapter 8. The role of self knowledge in response generation was noted in Chapter 11, where we noted the influence of one's own attitudes and opinions on the positioning of one's response scale and, consequently, the ratings that are assigned to other stimuli along this scale.

Our discussion has led us to consider the determinants of people's self concepts as well as their consequences. Our analysis of recency effects of information on memory and judgment (Chapters 5 and 10) contained several examples of how previously acquired self knowledge is used to make inferences about oneself. These effects were further examined in Chapter 11, where we noted the different effects that positive and negative feedback about oneself may have on self evaluations. Finally, Chapter 12 explored the manner in which the blocking and attainment of personal goals can influence the emotions that one experiences and the effects of these and other emotional reactions (along with descriptive self knowledge) on judgments of personal life satisfaction, competence, and self esteem.

We have, therefore, already devoted considerable attention to the role of self in information processing, and have addressed a large number of issues surrounding both the determinants and effects of self knowledge. Moreover, several excellent reviews of research and theory regarding the role of self in information processing exist elsewhere (see in particular Greenwald, 1981; Greenwald & Pratkainis, 1984; Kihlstorm & Cantor, 1984; Kihlstrom, Cantor, Albright, Chew, Klein, & Niedenthal, 1988). Because of this, it may seem unnecessary to devote a separate chapter to "self." However, several issues surrounding the processing of self information that were not raised in our previous discussion deserve attention. First, we review the implications of the model we propose for the representation of self knowledge in memory, and consider them in relation to the implications of alternative formulations. Research bearing on the recall and use of self-relevant information to make self judgments and self descriptions is then discussed in terms of these formulations. Finally, we turn to some selected issues surrounding the role of self knowledge in information processing, focusing primarily on its influence on the organization and retrieval of new information.

The Cognitive Representation of Self

Concepts and knowledge about oneself are stored in referent bins. The referent of these bins, however, is not necessarily the self. The bin in which a given piece of information is stored is determined by processing objectives that exist at the time the information is acquired. A man who interacts with another may construct a representation of the interaction that includes features of both himself and the other. He may store this representation in a self bin if his goal is to make a good impression or if he is otherwise concerned about himself as an object of evaluation. If, however, his goal is to form an impression of the person with whom he is interacting, he may store the representation in a bin that refers to the other.

Self bins. Self bins contain information that has been acquired and thought about with reference to oneself as object. There may be several different self bins, each pertaining to a different domain of experience. Each self bin is identified by a header whose features circumscribe the domain of self knowledge that is contained in it and characterize the nature of the "self" to which it refers. Thus, a general self bin may exist whose header is composed of attributes that have become strongly associated with oneself in general, without regard to situational context. In addition, more restricted bins may exist that refer to oneself in particular types of situations (at work, in social situations, in high school, etc.) or in certain social roles (as a professor, as a husband, as a tennis player, etc.). The characteristics of oneself that compose the headers of these domain-specific bins may differ. Thus, the header of a "self as professor" bin may contain the attribute "intelligent," whereas the header of a "self in social situations" bin may contain "shy" instead. Different information about oneself may consequently be retrieved, and different inferences may be made, depending on which of several alternative self bins happens to be identified by the probe cues that are compiled at the time the information is sought.

The knowledge units that are contained in a self bin may be of several types. They may include abstract characterizations of oneself (e.g., trait descriptions), representations of individual behaviors that one has performed in particular situations, or schemata pertaining to sequences of events that have involved both oneself and others. Self bins may also contain representations of events in which one was not personally involved but that were thought about with reference to oneself as object (e.g., overheard conversations in which one's name was mentioned or one's behavior was discussed). Many of the event schemata contained in a self bin may be similar to those described in Chapter 12. That is, they may specify general sequences of behaviors that one typically performs to attain a specific objective, and can be used as guides in goal attainment. These behavior sequences may be idiosyncratic to the person. That is, they may differ from the prototypic event representations that are stored in other bins, which specify sequences of goal-directed actions that are typically performed by people in general.

The units of information that are contained in a self bin, like those in other referent bins, are typically stored and retrieved independently of one another. This means that which particular subset of self knowledge is retrieved at any given time depends not only on the sort of probe cues that are compiled but also on which units of knowledge happen to be near the top of the bin that is identified on the basis of these cues.

Self knowledge contained in other referent bins. As noted above, self knowledge may also be contained in referent bins that pertain to other persons, objects, and events. This knowledge may be similar in character to the knowledge contained in self bins. At the time the information was acquired, however, it was not thought about with reference to oneself as object, but rather, was considered with reference to another person, object, or event to which the representation is also relevant. Therefore, although information may have implications for one's self description, self evaluation, or behavioral decisions, it will typically not be retrieved when information that is relevant to these judgments or decisions is sought. (This is because self-referent features are not included in the headers of the bins that contain this information. Consequently, these bins are unlikely to be identified by probe cues that govern the search for self-relevant information.) This self knowledge may come to mind only as a result of thinking about objects or situations *other* than oneself. Thus, a person who is asked to describe himself may retrieve information from a general referent bin containing the features "intelligent" and "honest" and be unable to recall any evidence implying otherwise. However, if the person is fortuitously reminded of an undergraduate class in economics, he may recall that he never understood the material and always cheated on the examinations.

These considerations make salient the fact that "self" is not a single representation in memory, nor is it even a circumscribed set of representations. Rather, self knowledge is distributed throughout the memory system. Moreover, the retrieval and use of any particular subset of self-relevant information, and the sort of self judgments and behavioral decisions that result, may depend substantially on the nature of the processing objectives that exist both at the time of information acquisition and at the time of retrieval.

Alternative Conceptualizations of Self

The formulation outlined above differs in several important ways from alternative conceptions of the representation of self in memory. A comprehensive summary of these alternatives is provided by Kihlstrom and Cantor (1984; see also Greenwald & Pratkanis, 1984). They point out several possible conceptualizations of self knowledge, each of which is suggested by a more general theory of categorization and memory. Four representative conceptualizations, and their relevance to the formulation we propose, are noted below.

1. Unified (Single-Representation) Theories

One class of models views "self" as a stable representation in memory. That is, it consists of a multiplicity of features (traits, abilities, interests, behavioral descriptions, etc.) that, once formed, is fairly resistant to change. This view, which has many historical antecedents (cf. Allport, 1955; Snygg & Combs, 1949), is exemplified by the more recent work of Rogers and his colleagues (1981; Rogers, Kuiper, & Kirker, 1977). They assume the existence of a single "self-schema," the features of which are quite stable. Thus, "self" functions as a fixed reference point (Rogers, Kuiper, & Rogers, 1979) that can be used both for organizing new information (cf. Rogers et al., 1977) and as a basis for comparison (cf. Srull & Gaelick, 1983).

The conceptualization we propose obviously differs in several respects from this single-schema view of self. According to our conceptualization, self judgments should appear to be stable only if (a) the different situations in which these judgments are reported activate the same set of probe cues, and therefore lead the same self bin to be identified and (b) the judgments can be made on the basis of the features contained in the bin's header. When different bins are identified each time subjects are asked to judge themselves, or when subjects must search the contents of a self bin for judgment-relevant information (the relative accessibility of which depends on the recency of its acquisition and use), self judgments may appear to be unstable. One implication of this is that self concepts will appear to be more stable if the experimental conditions in which subjects are asked to report them are similar than if they differ.

2. Piecemeal Representations of Self-Knowledge

Quite different assumptions concerning the organization of self knowledge in memory, and its retrieval for use in making self judgments, are exemplified by Bem's (1972) theory of self perception. According to this theory, self judgments are inherently unstable, depending on whatever subset of judgment-relevant information happens to be accessible in memory at the time of judgment. Support for this view comes in part from evidence that after subjects engage in belief-relevant behavior, they change not only their belief in the position advocated but also their estimate of the belief they had held before the behavior occurred (cf. Bem & McConnell; for a summary of relevant research, see Bem, 1972). Thus, both judgments appear to be based on the implications of whatever judgment-relevant behavior happens to be salient at the time the judgments are made. Evidence cited earlier in this volume, showing that activating small subsets of self knowledge can affect self judgments of religiousness (cf. Salancik, 1974; Salancik & Calder, 1974), competence and self esteem (Levine et al., 1987), also testifies to the instability of many self judgments. These data suggest that self judgments are based on a disorganized pool of self-knowledge, and therefore depend on which parts of this pool happen, perhaps fortuitously, to be retrieved.

As we have noted above, however, the model we propose can in principle account for variability in self judgments as well as stability. To reiterate, self judgments are likely to appear unstable if any of three things is true:

1. Judgments are reported only a short time after a selective subset of judgment-relevant self knowledge has been acquired or used, and therefore the knowledge is in the Work Space at the time judgments are made.
2. Different self bins are accessed under different conditions in which self judgments are reported.

3. The attributes being judged are not strongly associated with the referent of a self bin. That is, they are not in the bin header, and so the bin's contents must be searched for judgment-relevant information.

It seems likely that in many of the conditions in which self-perception theory has been tested, the attitudes and beliefs being evaluated are not sufficiently central to subjects to be included in the header of a self-bin. Moreover, in most studies that report experimentally induced changes in self judgments, subjects report these judgments only a short time after a subset of judgment relevant information has been activated. To this extent, the proposed model is capable of accounting for the results of these studies and, moreover, circumscribes the conditions to which these results are likely to generalize.

3. Markus's Self-Schema Theory

A third conceptualization of self representations, which has many implications similar to our own, is proposed by Markus (1977; Markus & Sentis, 1982; Markus & Smith 1981). She postulates the existence of "self- schemata," or knowledge structures pertaining to oneself. Each self-schema is organized around a particular attribute that the individual perceives him or herself to have and considers to be important. Thus, people who consider themselves to be extremely honest and believe that it is important to have this trait are *schematic* with respect to honesty. Correspondingly, people who either do not believe they are honest or who think they are honest but consider honesty to be unimportant are *aschematic*. People who are schematic with respect to an attribute are postulated to have a well- articulated and organized knowledge structure in areas to which the attribute is relevant, and to have self knowledge pertaining to the attribute easily accessible in memory. Consequently, they process self-relevant information bearing on the attribute both rapidly and efficiently.

Markus's conception is generally compatible with the model we propose if one assumes that people are schematic with respect to those attributes that compose the header of a self bin, and are aschematic with respect to attributes that, although perhaps implied by specific information that is contained within the bin, are not included in the header.

Two important distinctions must be made between the conceptualizations, however. First, Markus defines schematicity on the basis of not only the extent to which an attribute is believed to be self descriptive, but also how important a person considers the attribute to be. The model we propose makes no provision for this second criterion. As we will see, the use of this additional criterion sometimes makes it difficult to evaluate the effects of self-schemata on information processing. That is, these effects could often result from differences in the importance that subjects attach to different attributes, independently of whether they believe the attributes to be self-descriptive.

A second difference arises from the fact that, according to the formulation we propose, people may have several different self bins, each pertaining to a different social role or domain of experience. The attributes that are contained in the header of each self bin may differ. This means, in Markus's terms, that whether or not a person is "schematic" with respect to a given attribute may depend on which of several situational contexts the person happens to be thinking about, and, therefore, which of several alternative self bins happens to be identified. (To use our previous example, a person may be schematic with respect to intelligence when he thinks of himself as a university professor but not when he thinks about himself in social situations. Alternatively, he may be schematic with respect to shyness in the latter domain but not the former.)

4. Associative Network Conceptions of Self in Memory

The cognitive representation of self may often be conceptualized in terms of an associative network metaphor, in which "self" is a concept node to which other concepts and features are attached. Kihlstrom and Cantor (1984) describe several alternative types of network representations that might in principle apply. A simplified associative network that incorporates many features of a bin conceptualization is shown in Figure 13.1. In this network, the "self" node is associatively linked to trait concepts (T_1, T_2), behavior concepts (b_3, b_4), a situation concept ("at home"), and a social role concept ("professor"). The trait concepts, in turn, are linked to behaviors that exemplify them. Moreover, both trait and behavior concepts, which may differ from those that are directly connected to the central "self" node, are associated with concepts pertaining to the situation or social role in which the traits and behaviors are manifested.

Given a few reasonable assumptions, a model that postulates such a network can account for many of the phenomena implied by Markus's formulation. For example, suppose a man whose self knowledge is organized in the manner shown in Figure 13.1 is asked if he has trait T_1. His search for information bearing on this question presumably begins at the "self" node. Because T_1 is directly connected to this node, he should answer very quickly. If the person is asked if he has trait T_3, which is not directly associated with the "self" node, judgment time will be longer, as the judgment must either be "computed" on the basis of the implications of b_3 (an exemplar of T_3) or inferred indirectly by accessing a situation-specific self node (e.g, "at home"). Thus, suppose a person is schematic with respect to attributes that are directly connected to "self" and aschematic with respect to others. Then, the person should respond more quickly to questions about schematic traits than to questions about aschematic ones, as Markus also predicts.

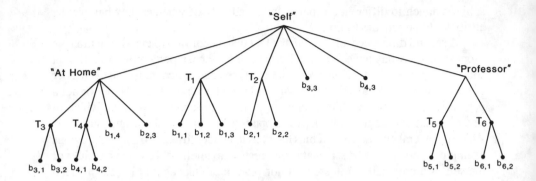

Figure 13.1 Associative network representation of self knowledge. Concepts are denoted by nodes, and associations by pathways connecting them. T_1 - T_6 denote trait concepts, and b_1 - b_6 denote behaviors that exemplify these trait concepts.

At the same time, the conceptualization could account for situation- specific schematicity. Suppose, for example, that the "at home" concept node is activated by calling the person's attention to this particular area of self knowledge. Then, the person's search may begin from this node rather than the general "self" node. If this occurs, the person should take less time to decide if he has T_3 than to decide if he has T_1 (which must be inferred indirectly on the basis of b_1). More generally, the activation of different self nodes theoretically leads to different patterns of self judgments, as the bin model also implies.

The problems with this conception arise primarily when the representation of self knowledge is viewed as part of a more general associative network of semantic concepts and information in memory (cf. Anderson & Bower, 1973; Wyer & Carlston, 1979). In such a network, both concepts that are specific to self and more general semantic concepts are all interconnected. Thus, in Figure 13.1, for example, $b_{3,3}$ which is directly connected to the self but exemplifies T_3, would be semantically linked to this trait in the "at home" cluster. Moreover, trait concepts would presumably be associated not only with the specific behaviors possessed by the person, but also with other behaviors that the person has never performed but that exemplify these concepts or have become associated with them in the past. Similarly, role concepts (e.g., "professor") would be associated not only with the traits that the individual himself possesses in this role but with other traits that characterize the role more generally. Thus, traits and behaviors that characterize the person himself are not clearly distinguished from those that do not.

Some of these problems might be resolved by postulating different concepts for general roles and situations (e.g., "professor") than for self- relevant ones ("self as professor"), and by assuming that different traits and behaviors are directly associated with each. Nevertheless, the high degree of interrelatedness that is implied by a general associative network model makes clear predictions hard to generate. Inasmuch as nothing seems to be gained by postulating a general associative network model of self knowledge, and much is to be lost in terms of parsimony, the conceptualization we propose seems preferable. (For further discussion of the advantages of the bin model over an associative network model, see Wyer & Srull, 1986.)

5. Other Considerations

Procedural vs. declarative self knowledge. Kihlstrom and Cantor (1984) distinguish between declarative self knowledge (knowledge that pertains to oneself as object) and procedural self knowledge (knowledge of oneself as actor, and of how one behaves in certain situations in order to attain certain goals). Both are obviously necessary to consider in any comprehensive formulation of self. As we noted in Chapter 12, the same underlying representations (e.g., event schemata) theoretically serve not only as descriptive knowledge that can be used to interpret and organize new information, but also as a specification of the behavioral steps that are required to attain a given end. These event schemata may sometimes pertain to oneself in a particular type of situation, and may be stored in a self bin where they can be retrieved by the Executor and used (along with the specifications of a goal schema) to attain the behavioral objective in question.

According to our conceptualization, however, procedural self knowledge, like declarative self knowledge, is not located in a particular place. The sequence of behavioral subgoals that are required to attain a particular objective is specified in an event schema that may be stored in a self bin. However, many of the cognitive operations that underlie the use of this schema are specified in a *goal* schema that is stored in the goal bin. Other cognitive operations, and also procedures for generating specific well- learned sequences of motor acts, may be hard-wired into the libraries of the various processing units. All of these sources of procedural knowledge are required in combination to generate a behavior, or series of behaviors.

Self complexity. Linville (1982) postulates individual differences in self complexity, which is conceptualized in terms of the number and degree of independent attribute dimensions that people use to characterize their personality or the social roles they occupy. People with more complex self representations are presumably more adaptable, and are less adversely affected by experiences that thwart the attainment of goals in particular domains of experience. Although the model we propose does not make any specific provision for differences in self-complexity, these differences seem likely to be reflected in the number of different domain-specific self bins that a person has formed and the independence of the attributes that compose the headers of these bins. That is, a cognitively simple person is one who either has few domain-specific self bins, or whose self bins are defined in terms of highly overlapping sets of attributes. Correspondingly, a complex person is one who has many self bins, each defined in terms of a different set of attributes. Complex persons' self judgments are therefore less likely to be based on the implications of self knowledge in any one particular domain, and no single subset of attributes is likely to provide the basis for their self descriptions or self evaluations. As a result, an adverse experience in a particular domain, or negative feedback about a particular attribute, is less likely to influence their general perceptions of themselves or their feelings of self worth.

The Retrieval of Self-Relevant Information

The various conceptualizations of the representation of self knowledge in memory have implications for the manner in which information is recalled. An understanding of this process is of importance both theoretically and practically. As we have noted, much of the traditional research on self has been stimulated by the assumption that a major determinant of one's social adjustment is one's perception of self worth. This perception theoretically depends on the implications of the self-knowledge that one brings to bear on it, and, therefore, may depend on factors that make a particular subset of self-knowledge more or less accessible.

Many of the factors that affect the retrieval of self-knowledge, and the processes that underlie these effects, have been discussed in other chapters. Rather than repeating this material, we limit our present discussion to three bodies of literature that bear on the organization and content of self representations. We first consider the process of retrieving general self knowledge of the sort that presumably underlies people's trait descriptions of themselves. In doing so, we draw primarily on the research that has been performed by Markus, Rogers, and their colleagues to evaluate the theoretical formulations described earlier. Second, we discuss the implications of a quite different body of research conducted by William and Claire McGuire on the spontaneous self concept. Third, we consider the retrieval of situation-specific self knowledge, focusing primarily on the processes that govern its temporal coding and organization.

The Retrieval of General Self Knowledge: The Cognitive Bases of Trait Descriptions

Subjects who are asked to describe themselves, or to judge themselves with respect to a particular attribute, theoretically go through a sequence of steps. First, they search the Work Space for judgment-relevant information. If none is found, they compile a set of features (probe cues) from the material contained in the first compartment of the Work Space, which typically includes a specification of the referent about which information is requested ("self," "self in situation X," etc.). Then, they identify a bin whose header contains these features, and determine if the remaining features of the header have implications for the judgment. If they do not, information that is stored in the bin itself is retrieved and used. One obvious implication of this analysis is that subjects will take less time to decide that they have a particular attribute if the attribute is contained in a self bin header than if it is not.

Two sets of studies bear on this hypothesis. In a study by Rogers, Kuiper, and Rogers (1979), subjects were given pairs of adjectives that varied in self-descriptiveness and were asked in each case to decide which adjective described them better. Subjects responded more quickly if the adjectives being compared differed in self-descriptiveness than if they were similar. The authors interpreted this "symbolic distance" effect as evidence that subjects have a stable self-schema that they use as a fixed reference point to judge the self-descriptiveness of the stimulus adjectives, and that this point does not vary as a function of the particular pair of attributes being judged.

This result is also compatible with the theoretical formulation we have proposed. Under the conditions constructed by Rogers et al., subjects are likely to identify a general "self" bin for use in making their judgments, the header of which is likely to contain only highly self-descriptive features. If this is so, subjects should be able to distinguish between two attributes' self-descriptiveness more quickly if one attribute in the pair is in the bin header (i.e., is self-descriptive) and the other is not (i.e., is generally less self-descriptive) than if either both attributes are in the header or neither are (and therefore cannot be distinguished on the basis of this criterion). Assuming that attribute pairs that differ substantially in self-descriptiveness are most likely to be of the first type, Rogers et al.'s results would be predicted.

There is an additional implication of this interpretation, however. That is, holding constant the difference in self-descriptiveness of the adjectives being compared, it should take less time to distinguish between two highly descriptive adjectives than to distinguish between two highly nondescriptive ones. This is because the information bearing on the first two attributes (which are both in the header) can be identified more quickly than information bearing on the second two. Unfortunately, these data were not reported.

A second series of studies that bear on the conceptualization we have proposed was performed by Markus and her colleagues (Markus, 1977; Markus, Crane, Bernstein, & Siladi, 1982) in the context of self-schema theory. In the study by Markus (1977), subjects were classified on the basis of pretest data as either (a) schematic with respect to independence, (b) schematic with respect to dependence, or (c) aschematic with respect to both attributes. All subjects were asked to decide whether each of several adjectives, some implying independence and others implying dependence, were self descriptive. If subjects who are schematic with respect to an attribute have this attribute in their self bin header, they should confirm that they have this attribute more quickly than should aschematics, who must search the contents of the bin itself for judgment-relevant information.

Although Markus's results are generally consistent with this prediction, some ambiguities arise. Schematic subjects were of course more likely to confirm that they had schema-consistent adjectives, and less likely to confirm that they had schema-inconsistent ones, than were aschematics. The question is how quickly they made these decisions. The times required to make "yes" (confirmatory) and "no" (disconfirmatory) responses were analyzed separately. Pooling over the two types of schematicity, subjects who were schematic with respect to one of the two bipolar attributes (independence or dependence) took less time to confirm that they had an attribute if it was schema-consistent ($M = 2.03$ s)[1] than if it was schema-inconsistent ($M = 2.42$ s). Moreover, they took less time to disconfirm that they had an attribute if it was schema-inconsistent ($M = 2.36$ s) than if it was schema-consistent ($M = 2.54$ s). On the other hand, neither the time that schematics took to confirm the presence of schema-consistent attributes nor the time they took to disconfirm that they had schema-inconsistent attributes (2.03 s and 2.36 s, respectively) was appreciably less than the time that aschematics took to make corresponding judgments of these attributes (2.15 s and 2.41 s, respectively).

The results of a second study (Markus et al., 1982) have similar interpretative problems. Here, subjects who had been classified as schematic with respect to masculinity, schematic with respect to femininity, or aschematic (androgenous) were asked whether they had attributes that were either stereotypically masculine or stereotypically feminine. In this study, only the times to make "yes" (confirmatory) responses were reported. Pooled over the two types of schematicity, subjects were quicker to confirm that they had attributes that were schema-consistent ($M = 1.56$ s) than ones that were schema-inconsistent ($M = 1.83$ s) (see Footnote 1). However, the time that schematics took to confirm that they had schema-consistent attributes ($M = 1.56$ s) was very similar to the time that aschematics took to confirm the presence of these same attributes ($M = 1.52$ s). This was true regardless of whether the aschematics were high in androgeny (i.e., high in both masculinity and femininity, as independently defined) or low.

Therefore, both studies suggest that the time required by schematics to confirm that they have schema-consistent attributes does not differ appreciably from the time required by aschematics to infer the presence of these same attributes. Rather, schematics simply take less time to confirm that they have schema-consistent attributes than to confirm that they have schema-inconsistent ones. This difference is implied by the model we propose. That is, subjects use features of the self bin header both to confirm the presence of attributes that are implied by these features and to disconfirm the presence of attributes that are inconsistent with these features.

---

1. These means are estimated from bar graphs reported in the article, and therefore may be only approximate.

However, some attributes, although schema-inconsistent, may not be sufficiently incompatible with the bin header features to warrant a negative judgment, and so subjects search the bin itself for information bearing on these attributes (often finding information that confirms their presence). A relatively long time is required to perform this search, as Markus's data indicate.

A more rigorous test of the conceptualization we propose would of course involve a systematic variation in the particular self bins that subjects are likely to access and use as a basis for their self judgments. The time to verify an attribute's self descriptiveness should theoretically depend on whether the attribute is contained in the header of the particular self bin that is identified. Thus, to return once again to an earlier example, I should take less time to confirm that that I am "intelligent" than to confirm that I am "shy" if I use my "self as professor" bin as a basis for my decisions. The reverse should be true, however, if I identify and use my "self in social situations" bin.

The Determinants of Spontaneous Self Descriptions

Perhaps the best evidence that subjects identify and use different self bins as sources of knowledge about themselves is provided in research conducted by William and Claire McGuire and their colleagues on the "spontaneous self concept" (cf. McGuire & McGuire, 1980, 1981, 1982, 1986, 1987; McGuire, McGuire, Child, & Fujioka, 1978; McGuire, McGuire, & Winton, 1979; McGuire & Padewar-Singer, 1976). Subjects in this research (usually grade school or high school students) are simply asked by the experimenter to "tell me about yourself." Their verbal responses are recorded and content analyzed for the types of things that they mention. To generate these responses, subjects theoretically identify a self bin and spew out its contents in roughly the order it is encountered. Therefore, subjects should first report features of the bin header. These features should be followed by the contents of the bin itself, beginning with the material on the top. One obvious implication of this (which unfortunately cannot be extracted from the data reported) is that subjects are more likely to provide general self- descriptions (i.e., header features) before more specific (e.g. behavioral) characteristics. A second implication is that the nature of subjects' self descriptions should depend on factors that affect which of several alternative self bins they identify and use as a source of information.

1. The Distinctiveness Effect

It is interesting to consider the second implication in the context of an intriguing phenomenon that the McGuires and their colleagues have labeled the *distinctiveness effect*. Specifically, subjects show a tendency to report features of themselves that distinguish them from others, either in their immediate social environment or in their general life situation. The effect of distinctiveness has been obtained in several different attribute domains. For example, students are more likely to mention physical attributes that distinguish them from their classmates (McGuire & McGuire, 1980, 1981; McGuire & Padewar-Singer, 1976). Thus, for example, they are more apt to describe themselves as short when the majority of their classmates are tall, to mention that they have dark hair when most of their classmates are blonde, and to mention that they wear eyeglasses when their classmates predominantly have normal vision. Students are more likely to refer to their ethnicity if they are in a minority in the class than if they are in the majority (McGuire et al., 1978). Thus, in the predominantly white classes from which subjects were drawn, white children were less apt to mention their ethnicity than were blacks or Hispanics. However, the likelihood that whites and Hispanics mentioned their ethnicity increased as their representation in their class decreased. (Although this was not true of blacks, McGuire et al. attribute this to the unique problems that have historically surrounded the acceptance of blacks in American society. As a result of these problems, blacks may require a certain minimal level of social support in order to feel comfortable about mentioning their race.)

The effects of gender (McGuire et al., 1979) are particularly interesting because they apply in both subjects' immediate social environment and their home environment. That is, children were more likely to mention their gender if they were in the minority in their class than if they were in the majority. In addition, they were also more apt to mention gender if they were in the minority at home. Thus, for example, boys were more apt to refer to their gender if most of their siblings were girls, and were also more apt to do so if they came from a father-absent home than if their home was intact.

Our formulation of self-knowledge does not predict these distinctiveness effects a priori. However, a consideration of the effects in terms of this formulation suggests some hypotheses as to why they occur. Specifically, the effects of one's distinctiveness in one's home environment and the effects of one's distinctiveness in one's immediate social situation may have different explanations. The effect of a person's home environment on the person's spontaneous self description is theoretically attributable to factors in this environment that have led self-descriptive features to be included in the person's general self bin header. It seems reasonable to suppose the distinctive features become part of a person's self description because they are used by *others* to describe the person. For example, a boy from a father-absent home with no male siblings may more often be referred to by others as a male (e.g., "the man of the house"). Or, a minority group member is likely to be confronted with more experiences that make him think of his ethnicity than is a majority group member. Therefore, these distinctive features are more likely to become part of a general self bin header, and consequently are more apt to be reported when the bin is identified as a source of self knowledge.

The features that compose subjects' self bin headers have already been established at the time they generate their self descriptions, however. The above explanation is therefore unable to account for the effects of subjects' distinctiveness in their immediate social environment. These distinctiveness effects must be attributable to two factors. First, persons who have attributes that distinguish them from others in a situation may become conscious of this difference, and so features associated with it may be in the Work Space at the time self descriptions are generated. Because the Work Space is searched first for goal-relevant information, these features may be retrieved and reported. Second, salient features of one's immediate social environment may fortuitously be included among the probe cues that determine the identification of a self bin. For example, a boy who finds himself surrounded by girls may include "girl" along with "self" in the set of probe cues that govern his search for self knowledge. He may therefore identify a bin pertaining to, for example, "self when interacting with girls," the content of which includes "boy" as a dominant feature.

2. General Characteristics of Self Knowledge

Two other lines of work (for a summary, see McGuire & McGuire, 1987) are also noteworthy. One (McGuire & McGuire, 1982) has examined the tendency to mention other people in the narratives that subjects produce when they are asked to describe themselves, and changes in these tendencies with age. For example, the proportion of times that children mention people outside their immediate family increases as they get older, suggesting that their "social self" expands with age. Moreover, girls are more likely to mention other persons, and therefore to have a broader "social self," than are boys. Perhaps more interesting is the finding that children show a tendency to mention their same-sex parent but their opposite-sex sibling. This suggests that their social self is more likely to be formed by identifying with the parent of the same sex, but by using an opposite-sex sibling as a standard of comparison, or negative referent.

A second avenue of investigation (McGuire & McGuire, 1986) focused on the verbs that people use in their spontaneous descriptions of both themselves and other persons. This research is particularly interesting to consider in terms of our conceptualization of how self knowledge is stored in memory. In these studies, subjects were asked to talk (or write) about either their family or about school, rather than about themselves. Thus, unlike the other studies mentioned, knowledge that subjects reported was unlikely to be drawn from self bins. Rather, it was theoretically drawn from bins pertaining to the referent of the question being asked ("the family," or "school"). The contents of these bins may include judgments or general descriptions of other persons that are germane to the given group or situation which the bins refer, and were formed in the course of attaining a processing objective to which they were relevant. In contrast, the self knowledge contained in those bins is unlikely to include general descriptions of oneself as object, as self was not the focus of attention at the time the information was stored. Rather, self knowledge is likely to be extracted from event schemata, and to pertain to one's activities in the course of the events being represented. One implication of this is that the knowledge about others that is drawn from these bins is likely to refer to traits whereas the self-knowledge that is drawn from these bins is likely to refer to behaviors. Consistent with this hypothesis, the McGuires found that subjects were inclined to use "state verbs" (descriptions of what one *is*) in other-referent statements, but to use "action verbs" (descriptions of what one *does*) in self-referent statements. Moreover, when subjects did use state verbs in self-referent statements, the verbs tended to be descriptions of dynamic being states (that is, descriptions of what one is becoming rather than what one is at the time.) These results, then, are quite consistent with the formulation we propose. Note, however, that the formulation predicts that an opposite pattern of self-other differences should emerge when subjects are asked to describe themselves rather than a situation, and, therefore, are likely to draw information from a self bin. If this were so, it would provide strong support for our conception of how self knowledge is stored in memory.

These examples suffice to indicate the potential importance of the approach the McGuires have taken in understanding the sort of information that people have about themselves and its relative accessibility. In addition to the issues noted above, the general approach might be used to understand when self concepts appear stable and when they do not. Subjects who are asked to describe themselves may provide not only general trait descriptions but also descriptions of specific experiences they have had. Both types of responses may vary over situations in which subjects are led to identify and retrieve information from different self bins. In contrast, the general self descriptions that subjects generate in a given type of situation (which are based on the headers of the bin from which it is drawn) may remain constant over time. On the other hand, the specific experiences they mention may nevertheless vary, depending on the recency with which they have been acquired and deposited in the bin itself.

Retrieval of Episodic Self Knowledge

The most common type of self information that we communicate to others concerns particular experiences we have had. Sometimes this information is retrieved in response to a particular question (e.g., to describe why one decided to become a psychologist, or the events that led up to one's divorce). It may also be activated spontaneously by others' descriptions of their experiences, features of which are common to our own. (For a theoretical discussion of the processes that underlie these spontaneous remindings, see Chapter 5.)

The retrieval of personal experiences from self bins is governed by processes identical to those that underlie the retrieval of information from other referent bins. Two steps are theoretically involved. First, a set of probe cues is compiled and used to identify a bin whose header has the features specified in these cues. Second, the contents of the bin are searched. This latter search is presumably top down, with the consequence that the most recently stored knowledge units are typically retrieved first. Evidence that this "recency" assumption applies to the retrieval of personal experiences was obtained by Chew (1983; cited in Kihlstrom et al., 1988). Specifically, when subjects are asked to recall personal experiences that occurred at different times in their lives, they took longer to recall events that occurred early in life than those that occurred later. This suggests that subjects typically begin their search with recent events and work backwards. This process, of course, contrasts with the retrieval of actions that make up any given experience and, therefore, compose a single knowledge unit in the bin (e.g., an event schema). These actions are apt to be recalled chronologically, in the order they occur in the representation (Wyer & Bodenhausen, 1985). Thus, if I am asked what happened to me in high school, I may recall that I got suspended for drinking at a school function before I recall going out on my first date (which occurred much earlier). However, the individual actions that made up each of these experiences are recalled in the order they occured.

The hypothesis that people store their personal experiences independently of one another in several different self bins raises a question. Suppose we are called upon to decide which of two personal experiences occurred sooner. How is this done? In some cases, of course, our representations of the experiences have detailed temporal features that permit their order to be determined directly. More often, however, such features are incomplete, if they exist at all. That is, experiences may contain some temporal features but not others. For example, I can remember having gone to Colorado on vacation in the early summer rather than in the late fall, although I cannot recall whether this occurred in 1980 or 1981. Also, I can remember that a tennis match I played recently was in the morning rather than after work, but I cannot remember what day of the week it was. In still other instances, no distinct temporal features at all may be associated with the events.

Several strategies may conceivably be employed in such circumstances to determine the temporal order in which personal experiences occurred.

1. The temporal order of some events is causally and logically constrained, and so it can be determined on the basis of general world knowledge without regard to any specific self knowledge. I am quite confident, for example, that I had my first date before breaking up with a particular girl friend because I know that breaking up with a girl friend cannot logically occur if one has never gone out on a date. I may make this determination without remembering anything at all about the specific personal experiences being compared.

2. Although events themselves may not be temporally coded, their descriptive features may sometimes permit them to be localized in general periods of life, the coding of which does include temporal features. For example, if I am asked whether I met my wife before or after getting my first paper published, I may determine that the first event occurred in graduate school and that the second occurred when I was an assistant professor at Illinois. I may then compute their order on the basis of my knowledge that I went to graduate school before accepting a job at Illinois.

3. The temporal order of two unrelated events may often be computed by considering their relation to a third, "landmark" event, or particularly important experience. For example, I may initially be unable to remember whether I wrote a particular paper on person memory before or after I gave a colloquium in New York several years ago. However, I know that my wife had a baby in May of that year, and I recall trying to write part of the paper in the waiting room of the hospital. I also remember that the baby later came down with pneumonia and that I called my wife several times during my trip to New York to see how things were going. These considerations may allow me to order the events correctly. (For more general evidence of the role of landmark events in locating other, less salient ones, see Loftus & Marburger, 1983.)

4. Heuristics may often be used to infer the relative order in which life events occur. One such heuristic was noted in Chapter 9. That is, we can typically recall more detailed information about events that occurred recently than about ones that occurred in the more distant past. Recent events may also be more vivid, or may come more easily to mind. Therefore, because we treat conditional relations as biconditionals (see Chapter 9), we may infer that more vivid or detailed events are relatively more recent. Thus, if we find that our memory for one event is more detailed than our memory for another, we may infer in the absence of other criteria that the first event occurred more recently. Support for the use of this heuristic in temporally ordering nonpersonal events (e.g., the death of John Lennon and the eruption of Mount St. Helens) was obtained by Brown, Rips, and Shevell (1985). It seems likely that similar processes operate when making temporal order judgments of unrelated personal experiences.

5. A different heuristic is suggested by research on time estimation (for a review, see McGrath & Kelly, 1986). Fewer life events typically intervene between two experiences that occur close together in time than between two experiences that are temporally distant. Because of this fact and the tendency to treat conditional relations as biconditionals (see Chapter 9), we may infer that an experience took place more recently if we can think of only a few life events that occurred in the interim than if we can think of many. Thus, suppose a person is asked to judge the temporal order of (a) having a wisdom tooth removed and (b) breaking up with his first girl friend. The first experience may be stored in a "self at the dentist" bin, and the second in a "self in romantic relationships" bin. Different numbers of subsequent experiences that occurred in the two domains may have been deposited on

top of the target experiences in the interim. The subjective recency of each target event may therefore depend on the number of intervening events that are stored on top of it *in the particular bin in which the event is contained*, independently of the total number of interpolated events that actually occurred.

A related implication derives from the fact that events may often be represented in more than one bin. For example, a man who met an ex-lover at a party to celebrate his passing qualifying examinations may have a representation of the event both in a "romantic relationships" bin and an "academic accomplishments" bin. To the extent that different numbers of other domain-relevant event representations have since been deposited in the two bins on top of the target experiences, the event may be inferred to have occurred more recently if the person searches for it in one of the bins than if he searches for it in the other. The possibility of manipulating time perceptions by stimulating subjects to search for information in different domains of experience is an intriguing avenue of investigation.

The process of determining the temporal order of personal experiences can be conceptualized more formally in terms of the general model we propose, and may potentially be investigated by applying procedures similar to those we used to determine the temporal coding and organization of hypothetical event sequences (see Chapter 8). Specifically, a subject who is called upon to decide the order of two unrelated experiences may first identify a self bin that contains both experiences. This may be done by using features of the event as probe cues. Sometimes, the header of the bin that is identified will have temporal features. (Thus, for example, "beat Podunk High in football" contains features that may cue the identification of a "high school football games" bin, which locates the event as occurring in high school.) If the headers of the bins containing the events being compared have different temporal features, the order of the events can be determined on the basis of these features. However, suppose the bin headers have the same temporal features, or that one or the other header has no temporal features at all. Then, the subject must compute the order of the events by employing strategies similar to those outlined above.

The processes implied by the above analysis are somewhat analogous to those we outlined in Chapter 8 when discussing the temporal ordering of events that persons read about. Specifically, these processes involve

1. identification of a bin in which each experience is contained;
2. comparison of the temporal features (if any) of the bin header;
3. (if necessary) computation of the temporal order of the experiences on the basis of general knowledge or heuristics; and
4. generation of an overt response.

To this extent, it may be possible to evaluate the temporal coding and organization of personal experiences in memory in much the same way that we have used to evaluate the organization and coding of hypothetical events (Wyer, Shoben, Fuhrman, & Bodenhausen, 1985; see Chapter 8).

This strategy was used with some success by Fuhrman and Wyer (1988, Experiments 2 and 3). In one study, subjects first recalled five personal experiences that occurred in junior high school and five others that occurred in college. In some cases, the events in each time period were thematically related and in other cases they were not. Later, subjects were exposed to all possible pairs of the ten events they reported and asked to judge their temporal order. Several interesting results emerged.

1. Subjects judged events more quickly if they occurred in different time periods than if they occurred in the same time period. This is consistent with the assumption that the events in different time periods were distinguished on the basis of temporal features of the headers of the bins in which they were contained, whereas for events in the same time period, an additional processing step was necessary (i.e., step 3, as enumerated above).

2. If events are discriminated on the basis of the temporal features of the bin headers, the time required to make this discrimination should not depend on the location of the events within the time periods in which they occurred. Data shown in the top of Figure 13.2 indicate that this was in fact the case. That is, the time to compare events in different time periods did not vary with the symbolic temporal distance between them (i.e., the number of other events that separated them in the sequence being judged).

3. In contrast, the time to compare events within a given time period depended substantially on the symbolic temporal distance between them, as shown in the bottom half of Figure 13.2. This indicates that the procedures that are used to distinguish the order of the events within each time period (step 3 above) were easier to apply when the events were temporally distant from one another. This seems intuitively likely to be the case regardless of which computational or heuristic strategy is used.

4. The time required to distinguish events within each time period was a non-monotonic function of their serial position in the time period. Specifically, events were compared more quickly if they both occurred near either the beginning or the end of the time period to which they belonged than if they both occurred near the middle of the period. This provides further evidence that the events were organized according to the time period in which they occurred rather than on the basis of other criteria.

Results of a second study (Fuhrman & Wyer, 1988, Experiment 3) become of interest in light of these considerations. Subjects recalled and ordered events that

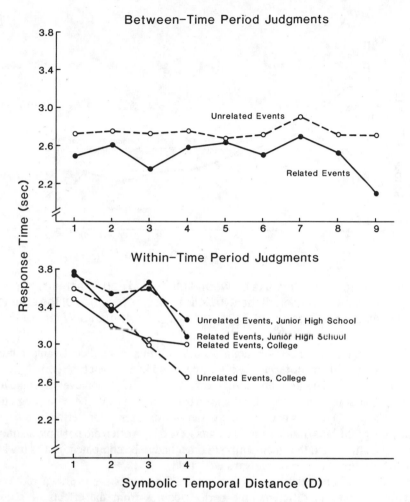

Figure 13.2 Mean time to make between-time period and within-time period comparisons as a function of the symbolic temporal distance of the events being compared—Experiment 2. (from Fuhrman & Wyer, 1988)

had occurred to them either in grade school or in high school. In this study, however, the events they recalled in both time periods pertained to the same domains of life experience (e.g., some events in each time period pertained to social relations, others to class projects, etc.). In this case, we expected that subjects would not always retrieve the events from bins whose headers had temporally coded features. Rather, they would retrieve them from bins that referred to domains of life experience, which cut across the time periods in which the events occurred. When this occurs, the events cannot be distinguished on the basis of the features in the

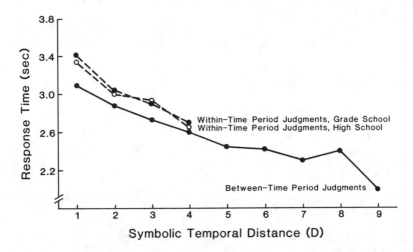

Figure 13.3 Mean time to make between-time period and within-time period comparisons as a function of the symbolic temporal distance of the events being compared—Experiment 3. (reprinted from Fuhrman & Wyer, 1988)

bin headers, and so other computational procedures must be applied. Events in this study were still judged more quickly if they occurred in different time periods than if they occurred in the same period. As shown in Figure 13.3, however, the time to make comparisons decreased as the distance between the events increased, regardless of whether the events occurred in the same or different time periods. Perhaps the headers of the bins from which the events were drawn often did not have distinct temporal features, and thus their temporal order had to be computed, just as it was when within-time period comparisons were made.

Further evidence that the bins in which the events were drawn did not necessarily represent different time periods comes from the effects of serial position. In Experiment 2, response time was a function of the serial position of the events *within* each time period. In this study, it was a non-monotonic function of the serial positions of the events in the *overall sequence*. (Thus, unlike the first study, events that occurred near the end of the first time period or near the beginning of the second period were judged quite slowly.)

In summary, then, the results of the two studies suggest that personal experiences may be drawn from either bins that are temporally coded or bins that are not, and that the procedures for determining their temporal order may depend on which is the case. Some caution should be taken in interpreting these results as reflecting the organization of events in permanent memory. Subjects were asked to recall and order the events they judged before these judgments were made. In the process of doing so, they may have constructed an ad hoc representation of the events that they used as a basis for their judgments without having to determine their location in Permanent Storage. Nevertheless, the general approach, if used in combination with other research methodologies for understanding both the temporal ordering of events (cf. Loftus & Marburger, 1983; Brown et al., 1985; Wyer & Bodenhausen, 1985), and autobiograhpical memory more generally (Rubin, 1986), may ultimately provide insight into the organization of self knowledge in memory.

The Effects of Self Knowledge on Information Processing

To the extent that knowledge about oneself is easily accessible in memory, this knowledge, or concepts associated with it, is likely to influence information processing at all of the stages we have considered. The role of self-knowledge in many of these processes has already been discussed in earlier chapters. In this section, we concentrate on only a few issues that were not fully considered in other contexts.

The Interpretation of Information About Others

If knowledge about oneself has recently been acquired or thought about, concepts associated with this knowledge may still be in the Work Space at the time new information is received. Therefore, these concepts may be used to interpret aspects of the information to which they are applicable. This means, for example, that if a man has recently been thinking about how hostile he is personally, he may be more likely to interpret another's behavior as hostile than he would otherwise.

In fact, there is not much direct evidence to support this hypothesis. A rigorous demonstration of encoding effects would require a design similar to that described in Chapter 6 and employed by Kelly and Wyer (1987) to investigate the role of affect in encoding processes. That is, suppose subjects are induced to think about themselves along specific dimensions either before or after they receive information about another person that could potentially be interpreted in terms of concepts activated by this self knowledge. Evidence that the self knowledge affected judgments of the person when it was activated before the information was presented but not when activated afterwards would provide evidence of encoding effects.

Unfortunately, this procedure is easier to describe than to implement. Attempts to activate specific subsets of self-knowledge experimentally may run into problems similar to those we noted in our discussion of affect. That is, the procedures used (e.g., asking subjects questions about themselves) may activate concepts that could influence the interpretation of information independently of the relevance of these concepts to "self" per se. Moreover, even if the experimental inductions were successful, this would not indicate that persons *spontaneously* apply self-knowledge and its associated concepts in interpreting information. It would only mean that they do so if these concepts (like any other concepts) happen to be easily accessible.

Perhaps the best way to circumvent the problem is to capitalize on individual differences in subjects' a priori self concepts. That is, one could determine if subjects whose self-concepts differ along specific dimensions make different interpretations of ambiguous information in terms of its meaning along these dimensions. Some evidence suggests that this is the case. An early study by Bruner (1951), noted in Chapter 6, indicated that subjects with different values generated interpretations of TAT cards that were consistent with these values. Klinger's (1975) observation that people's "current concerns" color their interpretation of the events they encounter in their daily lives provides another example.

At the same time, other evidence would seem to argue against this hypothesis. For example, the apparent tendency to attribute one's own behavior to different factors than others' behavior (Jones & Nisbett, 1971) suggests that subjects do not always apply the concepts they have about themselves in interpreting others' behavior. Thus, the effects of self-knowledge on the spontaneous encoding of information remains to be established conclusively.

Selective Encoding

A related issue concerns the extent to which subjects *selectively* encode information they receive in terms of concepts associated with themselves as object. Evidence of selective encoding in other domains has come largely from studies of memory. These studies show that information is better remembered if it can be encoded in terms of concepts that are accessible at the time it is received than if it cannot. In the present context, this means that information about a person or object will be better remembered if it can be encoded in terms of concepts or knowledge that one has about oneself. Surprisingly little evidence bears on this hypothesis. This is undoubtedly due to the problem noted earlier. That is, it is hard to know what specific aspects of self knowledge are likely to be spontaneously activated at any given moment. Consequently, it is difficult to predict a priori which features of new information should theoretically be encoded in terms of self-relevant concepts and which should not be.

However, a quite different approach to investigating the selective encoding of self-relevant information, designed by Bargh (1982), convincingly demonstrated the existence of these effects. An anecdotal example of the phenomenon Bargh investigated is the "cocktail party" effect. That is, although people may be intensely involved in a conversation and apparently oblivious to their surroundings, their attention is often captured by the mention of their name in a totally unrelated conversation that takes place across the room.

Bargh devised an empirical demonstration of this phenomenon within the framework of Markus's self-schema theory. Subjects who were either schematic or aschematic with respect to independence performed a dichotic listening task. Specifically, nouns were presented in one ear and adjectives in the other, and subjects were asked to attend to the material of only one of the two types. During one period, most of the adjectives presented pertained to independence. Bargh hypothesized that when schematic subjects were instructed to attend to the nouns, they would be spontaneously distracted by the self-relevant (independence-related) adjectives that were being presented, as evidenced by an increased response latency to a probe stimulus that was presented during this period. This was indeed the case. When subjects were told to attend to the nouns, schematics took longer to respond to the probe stimulus while "independent" adjectives were being played into their other ear than while unselected adjectives were being played. This was not true of aschematics. This indicates that subjects' attention was spontaneously diverted to adjective descriptions that were strongly associated with "self," much as persons' attention is diverted to their names at a cocktail party.

In contrast, when subjects were told to attend to the adjectives, schematic subjects took relatively *less* time to respond to the probe stimulus when it occurred while the "independent" adjectives were being played. This suggests that self-relevant information requires less intensive processing, and therefore increases the cognitive resources that can be allocated to other activities.

Results reported by Markus (summarized by Markus & Sentis, 1982) are also suggestive of selective encoding, although their interpretation is somewhat equivocal. Markus and Fong (1976), for example, found that when independent schematics and aschematics were given information about a target that contained different numbers of independent behaviors, schematic subjects' judgments were more affected by this variation than were aschematics. This could indicate that schematics were more likely to encode self-relevant information and therefore were more influenced by it. Another possibility, however, is that both groups of subjects were equally attentive to the information, but schematics (who by definition consider independence to be more important) simply gave independence-related information greater weight in combining its implications with those of other information during the inference stage of processing (see Chapter 9).

Although subjects may selectively encode information in terms of attributes that they use to describe themselves, this does not necessarily mean that they are always more attentive to the details of this information. Subjects who have more clearly articulated concepts for interpreting self-relevant information can more easily use these concepts to reconstruct the information, and therefore they may need to retain fewer details of the information in the memorial representation they form from it. Evidence reported by Markus, Smith, and Moreland (1979) supports this view. Using Newtson's (1973) procedure for assessing the size of the units into which ongoing behavior sequences are divided (for details, see Chapter 8), they found that subjects broke the sequences into fewer units when the observed behaviors implied schematic rather than nonschematic attributes.

Unfortunately, there is an inherent problem in interpreting all of these studies. Independent schematics, for example, are defined as persons who not only judge themselves to be very independent but also consider independence to be very important. An alternative interpretation of Bargh's findings is simply that subjects are more attentive, and therefore more likely to encode information pertaining to attributes that they consider to be generally important, independently of how self descriptive these attributes are. The other studies cited could be similarly reinterpreted.

Retrieval Processes: The Self-Referent Effect

The most active area of research on the role of self knowledge in information processing has focused on the effect of self-knowledge on memory. This general concern is of course related to the selective encoding effects mentioned above. However, the approach taken has been somewhat different. Rather than looking at individual differences in the type of information that is recalled as a function of its self-relatedness, the approach has been to induce subjects to think intentionally about information with reference to themselves, and to determine if this cognitive activity produces better recall of the information than does other types of activity.

The first evidence of this "self-referent effect" was reported by Rogers, Kuiper, and Kirker (1977). Subjects were given a series of stimulus words (e.g., trait adjectives) with instructions to decide if each word (a) was in capital letters, (b) sounded like another (specified) word, (c) was similar in meaning to another word, or (d) described themselves. Later, they were asked to recall the words they had rated. Subjects recalled almost twice as many words in the fourth (self-referent) condition as they recalled in any of the other three conditions. In other words, thinking about the words in relation to oneself substantially increased their memorability. The question is why this is so.

To answer this question, it is important to note that the effect is not unique to the processing of information with reference to self. Thinking about information with respect to other well-articulated bodies of knowledge has similar effects (Bower & Gilligan, 1979; Keenan & Baillet, 1980). Bower and Gilligan, for example, found that subjects were no better able to recall words after indicating whether the words described themselves than after indicating whether the words described their mother (another person about whom they had a lot of knowledge), whereas their recall was better in both cases than it was after deciding whether the words described Walter Cronkite (a person whose specific characteristics were less well known). Thus, the self-referent effect is not unique to "self." Processing information with reference to other bodies of knowledge appears to have the same effect, provided the knowledge is well articulated.

There are two possible interpretations of the self-referent effect. The interpretation suggested by Bower and Gilligan's research is that the self- referent task leads the words being judged to become associated with features of a highly elaborated, pre-existing knowledge structure, and that these features later serve as a mnemonic device for recalling the stimulus words that have become linked to them. If this is so, however, the words should be recalled better if they are, in fact, self descriptive, and therefore can be easily associated with the features of one's self representation, than if they are not. In contrast, Rogers et al. (1977) found no difference between the probability of recalling words that subjects said were self descriptive (.30) and the probability of recalling words that they said were not self descriptive (.29). One later study (Kuiper & Rogers, 1979, Experiment 1) did in fact detect an appreciable difference in the probabilities or recalling self-descriptive and nonself-descriptive words (.42 vs. .21), but two other studies in the same series yielded much smaller differences (.35 vs. .30, and .39 vs. .29). Thus, although some difference appears to exist, the effect is not as strong or as consistent as one would expect on the basis of the hypothesis.

Another viable account of these effects is not based on the notion that the specific features of self representations serve as retrieval cues. Rather, it assumes that the self-referent task is effective because it leads subjects to organize the words into categories, and that this categorization facilitates their later recall independently of the specific self knowledge that was used as a basis for organizing it. (For a general discussion of the effect of categorization of person information on memory, see Chapter 7.) The simplest organization that is imposed by the self-referent task results from classifying the words as either "self-descriptive" or "not self- descriptive." However, other spontaneous categorizations of the words may occur as well (e.g., "attributes I like" vs. "attributes I don't like," "things that describe me at home" vs. "things that describe me at work"). The mental organization of words into categories may facilitate their later recall for reasons similar to those we described in Chapter 7 in predicting trait-category set-size effects (see also Hamilton, Katz, & Leirer, 1980a). If this is so, it could account for the similar recall of adjectives that subjects reported as self-descriptive and those they reported as not self-descriptive. That is, if "me" and "not me" function as two general categories into which the adjectives were organized, subjects' recall of the words in each category should be facilitated to about the same degree.

The relative merits of these two interpretations have been explored in a series of studies by Stanley Klein and his colleagues (Klein & Kihlstrom, 1986; Klein & Loftus, 1987). Klein and Kihlstrom (1986) reasoned that if the effect of self-referent processing is due to the organization it imposes on the stimulus items, its effects should not be apparent when subjects think about the stimulus items in relation to themselves in ways that do not provide any clear categorization of the information. To investigate this possibility, parallel task conditions were constructed in which the judgment task (self-referent vs. semantic) and the degree of categorical organization imposed by the task were varied independently. One study (Klein & Kihlstrom, 1986, Experiment 5) is illustrative. In *self-referent, organization* conditions, subjects were asked to decide whether each of several occupations was one that they had ever wanted to be (e.g., "Have you ever wanted to be a barber?"). In *self-referent, no-organization* conditions, subjects were asked to agree or disagree with personal statements, each of which mentioned a different occupation (e.g., "I often look as if I could use the services of a good barber"). Because the criterion for agreement with each statement was different, responses to these statements should not induce any categorization of the occupations mentioned.

The two semantic tasks paralleled the self-referent tasks. In *semantic, organization* conditions, subjects were asked whether each occupation required a college education. Thus, this condition was similar to the self-referent, organization condition in that it led subjects to organize the occupations into two categories. However the categories had nothing to do with self-descriptiveness. Finally, in *semantic, no-organization* conditions, subjects were asked if persons in each occupation performed a task that differed for each occupation (e.g., "Does a barber give shampoos?"). This task, like the self-referent, no-organization task, did not impose any clear organization on the stimulus words.

Subjects after performing one of the four tasks were asked to recall the occupations they had considered. The results were very clear. The proportion of occupations that subjects recalled was significantly better when the processing task imposed an organization on the items ($M = .56$) than when it did not ($M = .48$), and these proportions were virtually identical regardless of whether the processing was self-referential (.55 vs. .49) or semantic (.56 vs. .46). There was obviously no difference whatsoever in the effects of self-referent vs. semantic processing per se.

This does not mean, however, that the effect of self-referent processing is *only* a function of the organization it imposes on the items being judged. If this were so, the differences in effects of self-referent and other-referent processing identified by Keenan and Baillet (1980) and Bower and Gilligan (1979) would be difficult to explain. In fact, the *categorization* of the stimulus items that results from self-referent processing, and the cognitive elaboration that produces associations between these items and features of oneself, may both contribute independently to recall. The relative contributions of the two factors may depend on the type of material to be processed. For example, suppose the information items fall into easily recognizable semantic categories. In these conditions, the items may be spontaneously assigned to these categories, and the additional increment in organization that results from self-referent processing may have little observable effect. On the other hand, the formation of associations between the individual information items and features of one's self representation may facilitate the recall of the items over and above the influence of their organization into categories. Alternatively, suppose the information is *not* easily categorized on a priori grounds. Then, the organizational influence of self-referent processing may be more evident.

TABLE 13.1
Mean Number of Words Recalled as a Function of List Type and Orienting
Task (adapted from Klein & Loftus, 1987)

	List type	
Task type	Obscure categories	Obvious categories
Definition generation	11.64	18.36
Categorization	17.07	15.07
Self-reference	18.36	18.07

To investigate these possibilities, Klein and Loftus (1987) selected two sets of 30 stimulus words. In one, *obvious-category* list, six words exemplified each of five clearly recognizable semantic categories (countries, types of music, body parts, etc.). In the other, *obscure-category* list, six words exemplified each of five ad hoc categories that were unlikely to be identified spontaneously by simply reading the words (e.g., things found on the beach, things associated with illness, etc.). Subjects were exposed to the words by performing one of three tasks. In one, *definition-generation* task, subjects defined each word and then rated the ease of defining it. This task presumably led subjects to think of each word in terms of a previously formed concept that was stored as part of general knowledge, without requiring them to think about the words in relation to one another. In the second, *categorization* task, subjects were given the five category labels and asked to sort the words into the categories defined by these labels. In the third, *self-referent* task, subjects were asked to indicate whether each word did or did not refer to an important personal experience. Thus, the self-referent task resembled the definition generation task in that it led subjects to think about each piece of information in terms of a previously acquired piece of knowledge. However, it was like the organizational task in that it stimulated subjects to categorize the words.

Subjects after performing one of the three tasks were given a surprise recall test. The number of words recalled is shown in Table 13.1 as a function of task and list conditions. First consider the recall of words under definition generation and categorization task conditions. When the categories to which the words belonged were obscure, sorting the words into these categories significantly increased recall performance relative to conditions in which subjects considered each word independently. Thus, the organization of the words into categories clearly increased their likelihood of being recalled. However, the recall of the same words under self-referent conditions was even higher. The self-referent task presumably led to an implicit categorization of the words, facilitating the recall of these words in much the same way as the explicit categorization task. However, elaboration (associating the items with previously acquired self knowledge) may have produced an additional increment in their recall, over and above the effect of categorization.

When the schematic categories to which the words belonged were easily identifiable, the recall of the words was generally high. This indicates that subjects spontaneously organized the words into these categories without being told, and that this organization facilitated recall in all task conditions. However, asking subjects for definitions increased their recall of the words relative to categorization conditions. This suggests that elaboration had a facilitating effect on recall over and above the spontaneous categorization of the words that occurred in this condition. In other words, both spontaneous categorization *and* elaboration appeared to facilitate recall in definition-generation conditions. Note, however, that recall of these words under self-referent conditions was virtually identical to their recall under definition generation conditions. This suggests that both factors (associating the words with aspects of previously acquired knowledge and categorization) had facilitating effects on recall in self-referent conditions as well.

In combination, then, it appears that the self-referent effect on recall is due partly to its influence on the organization of information into self-relevant and nonself-relevant categories, and partly to the associations that are formed between the individual items of information and individual pieces of self knowledge. However, unless the items are such clear examples of semantic categories that they are spontaneously organized into these categories without the benefit of self-referent processing, the organizational effects of this processing may play the more dominant role.

Several other investigations of self referent effects on recall are worth nothing in this context. Keenan and Baillet (1980), for example, found that self-referent effects did not occur in the recall of anatomical features, suggesting that these effects may be restricted to words that have evaluative implications. Two other studies (Ferguson, Rule, & Carson, 1983; Friedman & Pollybank, 1982) found that asking subjects to make evaluative judgments of trait terms had effects very similar to those that occurred as a result of self-referent processing. The likelihood that a trait is reported as self descriptive undoubtedly increases with its favorableness. The above studies therefore suggest that the categorization that underlies many self-referent effects may be based on whether the items being considered have favorable or unfavorable implications rather on their self-descriptiveness per se. (Note, however, that this alternative interpretation seems less applicable to Klein's studies, where the words pertained to features of personal experiences, occupations, etc. rather than trait terms.)

The Use of Self in Inference Making

Subjects who are asked to make an inference about a target person or event may identify a previously formed representation that has similar features and may use other features of this representation as a basis for the inference. This process presumably underlies stereotype-based inferences of persons (Chapter 7) and also inferences of the determinants and consequences of events (Chapter 8). Perhaps the biggest single source of information that people have to draw upon in making inferences, however, is the knowledge that they have about themselves. We have noted that people have different "selves," in different roles and situations, and the characteristics of these selves may vary. For this reason, people often find it quite easy to identify similarities between another person and themselves. In addition, they are likely to see a parallel between almost any experience that another person relates and some past experience of their own.

Indeed, when listening to another person's description of an experience, it is often quite difficult *not* to interpret it in terms of a personal experience that contains similar features, and to use this experience as a basis for inferring why the other's experience occurred, what the other is feeling, and what courses of action the other might take as a result of the experience. One person's description of an automobile accident spontaneously elicits a memory of an accident we have had, and another's description of his marital problems inevitably elicits thoughts about our own.

It therefore seems almost self evident that people use information about themselves as a basis for making inferences about others. Because of this, the lack of empirical support for this hypothesis is somewhat surprising. Perhaps the single most convincing evidence comes from clinical studies of projection. In a review of these studies, Holmes (1968) concluded that people are quite likely to attribute their own characteristics to others. For this to occur, however, they must be aware that they personally have these attributes. Subjects who are inferred on the basis of clinical and personality tests to have certain attributes, but are not aware that they have them, do not infer others to have these traits. This means, then, that projection is a conscious process that involves the intentional use of oneself as a basis for judging others.

Ross, Greene, and House (1977) report evidence bearing on the use of self knowledge as a basis for judging others, but their results are susceptible to alternative interpretation. In one study, for example, subjects who had previously either agreed or refused to carry a sandwich board sign around campus were asked to estimate the proportion of other students who would agree to perform this behavior. Subjects who personally agreed to carry the sign predicted that an average of 61.4% of other students would also agree to do so, whereas those who refused estimated that only 30.4% of other students would agree to carry the sign. In addition, both groups of subjects made more extreme trait attributions to hypothetical persons who made the opposite decision than their own (whichever decision this happened to be). These data suggest that subjects not only expect others to behave as they do, but they interpret others' failure to do so as an indication of some extreme (deviant) facet of their personality.

Although this finding is consistent with the hypothesis that subjects use themselves as a basis for inferring attributes of others, there are compelling alternative explanations which do not involve the assumption that self knowledge enters into the inference process at all. In the situation described, it seems likely that subjects' own decisions about whether or not to carry the sandwich board based on evaluations of the costs and benefits of performing the behavior. This information was presumably retrieved from an event bin containing knowledge about this general sort of behavior. It seems reasonable to suppose that this same pool of information was used as a basis for predicting others' decisions as well. In other words, subjects may not have used their own decision per se as a basis for predicting others'. Rather, they may have independently used the same information (about the consequences of performing the requested behavior) both to make their own decision and to infer what others would do. Moreover, they may consider people who would decide otherwise to have deviant personalities. To this extent, the "egocentric bias" detected by Ross et al. is not really egocentric at all.

In any event, it is important to note that although people may use information about themselves as bases for inferences about others, the reverse is also true. That is, subjects may also use information about others as a basis for inferring characteristics of themselves (cf. Goethals & Darley, 1977; Festinger, 1954). It seems reasonable to suppose that the direction of influence depends in part on the relative amounts of judgment-relevant information one already has about oneself and another. When subjects are uncertain about their own behavior and attributes, they may use another's characteristics as a basis for inferring their own. When, on the other hand, subjects are confident of their own attributes and behavior but have very little information about another, they may use themselves as a basis for inferring the other's characteristics. This hypothesis seems self evident. To our knowledge, however, it has not been systematically investigated.

Situational and Individual Differences in Self-Referential Processing

The research we have discussed in preceding sections, and in this volume more generally, provides some insight into the types of effects that self-knowledge is likely to have on social information processing. Yet, there are clearly both situational and individual differences in the extent of this influence. Bargh's (1982) research suggests that specific self-conceptions and knowledge can sometimes intrude spontaneously on information processing. More generally, however, it seems likely that the tendency to involve the self in information processing depends substantially on the extent to which subjects are stimulated to think about themselves as object at the time the information is presented. This, in turn, may depend both on situational factors that call subjects' attention to themselves, and on more general individual differences in self-consciousness that generalize over situations.

These contingencies have not been explored. Nevertheless, certain approaches for doing so seem viable. One of the more promising was developed many years ago by Wicklund (1976). Wicklund was concerned with the effects of objective self awareness, that is, of consciousness of oneself as an object of evaluation. The source of evaluation may be either oneself or another. Although the experimental procedures for inducing self-awareness seem rather contrived, they are extremely effective. Specifically, subjects' consciousness of themselves as an object of self evaluation (*private self consciousness*) can be induced by having them participate in an experiment in front of a mirror that has ostensibly been left in the experimental room by another investigator. Alternatively, subjects' consciousness of themselves as an object of evaluation by others (public self consciousness) can be induced by leading subjects to believe that their actions are being recorded on television or that others may be observing them. Such procedures are likely to induce self consciousness in all subjects. However, individual differences in public and private self consciousness may exist as well. These differences have, in fact, been successfully assessed using questionnaire methods (Fenigstein, Scheier, & Buss, 1976).

A substantial amount of work has been performed on the effects of both private and public self consciousness on subjects' overt behavior. Private self consciousness appears in general to induce subjects to evaluate themselves critically, to accept negative feedback about their performance, and to accept responsibility for undesirable outcomes (Wicklund, 1975). On the other hand, it also leads subjects to feel more responsible for favorable feedback about themselves. In other words, self-conscious subjects appear generally more sensitive to information that has implications for their self esteem.

Self awareness can also influence the type of standards that are used to evaluate one's behavior or its consequences. This contingency was identified in a study by Diener and Srull (1979). Subjects were exposed to a dot judgment task. Before engaging in the task, each subject indicated the level of performance with which he or she would personally be satisfied. Then, on each trial that followed, subjects received feedback about their performance, were reminded of the standard they had personally set for themselves, and were told the performance level that previous subjects had typically attained. This was done in a way that led subjects to believe that their performance level was either above both their own standard and the external standard (others' typical performance), below both standards, or above one standard but below the other. To induce differences in self-awareness, subjects performed the task under distraction conditions which consisted of playing an audio and video tape of either (a) an automobile chase (low self awareness) or (b) subjects themselves (high self awareness). Subjects after each trial reported their satisfaction with their performance, and were given an opportunity to "reward" themselves with tokens.

In low self awareness conditions, subjects' satisfaction and reward allocations were primarily a function of how well they had performed in relation to their personal standard. In high self awareness conditions, however, it was determined primarily by how well their performance compared to that of other persons. Therefore, self awareness in this case appeared to make subjects more sensitive to indications of how well they were doing in relation to a socially defined criterion for evaluation.

It is interesting to view these results in the context of research on deindividuation (for a review, see Diener, 1980). In one extremely innovative study (Diener, Fraser, Beaman, & Kelem, 1976), Halloween trick-or-treaters (residents of the experimenter's neighborhood) were met at the door by the experimenter who either greeted them by name or did not. The children were then directed to a bowl of candies but told that they should take only one candy apiece. The experimenter then left the room on a pretense, and the number of candies that each child actually took was unobtrusively observed. Children were significantly less likely to take more than one candy if they had been greeted by name than if they had been greeted anonymously. This study suggests that self awareness increases conformity to internalized standards of social responsibility, even in the absence of observation or of any repercussions for noncompliance. To the extent that the use of others' performance as a basis for evaluating one's own performance reflects the adoption of a social responsibility norm (e.g., equity), Diener and Srull's results would also be compatible with this conclusion.

What effect does self awareness have on social information processing, or on cognitive functioning more generally? Unfortunately, no research that we know of provides direct evidence concerning this matter. A tangentially relevant study is an intriguing one, however. It shows that the way in which people deal with the unpleasant emotions that result from attitude-discrepant behavior may depend on which aspects of self-knowledge they attend to. In this study (Scheier & Carver, 1980), subjects were asked to write a counterattitudinal essay. In critical conditions, they were given a choice over whether to write the essay or not, so that their agreement to do so was voluntary. In one (*private self consciousness*) condition, they wrote their essay in front of a mirror. In another (*public self consciousness*) condition, they did so in front of a television monitor. In a third (*low self consciousness*) condition, neither of these conditions existed. After writing the essay under one of the above conditions, subjects were asked both to estimate the extremity of the position they had advocated in the essay and to assess their personal attitude toward the position.

According to dissonance theory (Festinger, 1957), subjects attempt to eliminate the discomfort produced by an attitude-behavior discrepancy by decreasing the magnitude of this discrepancy. In Scheier and Carver's study, this could be done either by changing one's attitude toward the position advocated or by convincing oneself that the essay one had written (i.e., the behavior) was not, in fact, attitude discrepant. The authors reasoned that private self consciousness would increase subjects' commitment to their internal standard (i.e., their initial attitude), and therefore should increase their tendency to reduce dissonance by altering their perception of their behavior. In contrast, public self consciousness should increase subjects' commitment to their public (essay writing) behavior, and therefore should increase the tendency to reduce dissonance through attitude change. Consistent with this reasoning, privately self conscious subjects reported less change in their attitudes, but rated their behavior as having less extreme implications, than did publicly self conscious subjects. A second study, in which individual differences in public and private self consciousness were assessed through questionnaire methods, produced parallel results. Thus, situationally induced self awareness and chronic self awareness appear to have similar effects.

In summary, the techniques developed by Wicklund and his colleagues to induce differences in self-focused attention appear to be quite successful in producing differences in social behavior and in reactions to the consequences of this behavior. However, the technique has not yet been applied in determining the degree to which self awareness determines the influence of self-knowledge on specific types of information processing. This would seem easy to do. Subjects who are induced to be self aware should be more likely to encode information in terms of concepts they apply to themselves, to respond more quickly to information about attributes for which they are "schematic," to use self-knowledge as retrieval cues in recalling information, and to use themselves as a basis for judging others. Evidence that this is the case would help to eliminate many ambiguities that currently surround the role of self in social cognition.

Appendix
Summary of Postulates

The Structure and Function of the Work Space

3.1 The Work Space is of limited capacity.

3.2 The displacement of information from the Work Space may be either automatic or volitional.

3.3 Under conditions of high information load, the material in the Work Space that has been least recently involved in processing (either as input to a processing unit or as output from the unit) is most likely to be displaced.

3.4 Once the Work Space is cleared, any material that has not been transmitted to a bin in Permanent Storage is irretrievably lost.

3.5 When information relevant to a processing objective is required, the Work Space is searched first, before goal-relevant information is retrieved from Permanent Storage.

3.6 The search for information in the Work Space is random. The probability of retrieving a given unit of information from the Work Space increases with the number of times the unit is represented there at the time information is sought.

The Organization of Information in Permanent Storage

4.1 The Permanent Storage Unit consists of a set of content-addressable storage bins. Each bin is identified by a header whose features define the bin and circumscribe its contents.

4.2 The retrieval of information from the semantic bin is under the direct control of the Comprehender as well as the Executor.

4.3 Semantic concepts are not applied to input information by the Comprehender unless they are necessary to understand the denotative meaning of this information.

445

4.4 Only the output of processing information in pursuit of a specific objective is transmitted to Permanent Storage.

4.5 The output of processing at each stage is transmitted to, and stored in, a referent bin as a separate unit of information. The output of each stage is transmitted and stored in the order it is generated.

4.6 Information is transmitted to a bin pertaining to the referent to which processing objectives are relevant. If no previously formed bin pertaining to the referent exists, a new bin is formed.

4.7 The header of a referent bin consists of (a) a name that specifies the referent and (b) a set of features that are strongly associated with it.

4.8 The features of a bin header are applicable to all of the individual units of information contained in the bin.

Retrieval Processes

5.1 No more information is retrieved for use in attaining a processing objective than is sufficient to allow the objective to be attained. When this minimal amount of information has been retrieved, the search terminates.

5.2 When information relevant to a processing objective is required, the contents of the Work Space are searched first.

5.3 The search for information in the Work Space is random.

5.4 The relevance of a referent bin to a particular processing objective is determined by comparing the features of its header with a set of probe cues compiled by the Executor. These cues are a subset of the features contained in Compartment 1 of the Work Space at the time the information is sought.

5.5 The bin identified for use in attaining a particular objective is the one whose header (a) contains all of the features specified in the probe set and (b) maximizes the quantity

$$\frac{\Sigma S_{h \cap p}(i)}{\Sigma S_h(j)}$$

where $S_{h \cap p}(i)$ = the strength of the association between the referent and the ith feature that is common to both the header and the probe set, and $S_h(j)$ is the strength of the association between the referent and the jth feature of the header.

5.6 When no bin is found that contains all of the features in a set of probe cues, the set is randomly subdivided into smaller subsets, and the search is repeated using these subsets as probe cues until a bin is found.

5.7 Once a bin is identified, the remaining features of its header are searched for information relevant to the processing objectives being pursued. If these features and their implications are sufficient to attain the objectives, they are used without retrieving information from the bin itself.

5.8 When the contents of a bin are searched for information relevant to a processing objective, the search proceeds from the top down. A unit of information is identified as potentially relevant if its features include the probe cues governing the search. The probability of retrieving any particular unit, given that units stored on top of it have not been used, is a constant value.

5.9 (Copy Postulate) When a unit of information in a bin is identified as potentially relevant for attaining a processing objective, a copy of this unit is sent to the Work Space. Thus, the original position of the information in the bin is preserved. When the use of the information is completed, this copy of it is returned to the top of the bin from which it was drawn.

5.10 (Stopping Rule) A referent bin will be searched for goal-relevant information until either (a) information sufficient for attaining the processing objective has been found, (b) a total of n units have been retrieved that are inapplicable for attaining these objectives, or (c) a total of k identical units of information have been retrieved, whichever comes first.

The Cognitive Representation of Persons

7.1 People who learn about a person's behaviors for the purpose of forming an impression of the person will spontaneously interpret these behaviors in terms of the trait concepts they exemplify.

a. These trait encodings are performed by the Encoder/Organizer by comparing the behavior descriptions with features of trait concepts that are stored in the semantic bin.

b. When a behavior can be encoded in terms of more than one trait concept, the concept that is most easily accessible in memory is the most likely one to be applied.

7.2 (a.) If people do not have trait-based expectations for a person at the time they learn about the person's behaviors, they encode all of the behaviors in terms of trait concepts. (b.) If people do have expectations for a person's traits at the time they learn about the person's behaviors, only behaviors that exemplify these traits are encoded and organized in terms of them. In this case, behaviors with implications for other attributes of the person are not encoded in trait terms.

7.3 People who are asked to form a general impression of a person will attempt to construct a general concept of the person as likeable or dislikeable. This concept, although based on the trait concepts used to interpret the person's behavior, is primarily evaluative in nature.

7.4 The evaluative concept of a person is typically based on only a subset of the information available about the person. This is most often the first subset of information that permits an evaluatively coherent concept to be formed.

7.5 Once an evaluative person concept is formed, individual behaviors of the person are interpreted in terms of it. The ease of interpreting behaviors in terms of the concept, and therefore the strength of their association with it, is an increasing function of the behaviors' evaluative consistency with this concept.

7.6 If a clear evaluative person concept cannot be formed on the basis of the initial information presented (e.g., if the initial implications of the information differ in favorableness), subjects who are uncertain about the person's traits review the behaviors they have encoded in terms of each trait to insure that they have interpreted these behaviors correctly. This cognitive activity leads associations to be formed among the behaviors that have been encoded in terms of each concept (e.g., the behaviors contained in each trait-behavior cluster).

7.7 Once an evaluative person concept has been formed, individual behaviors are evaluatively inconsistent with the concept are thought about in relation to other behaviors that have evaluative implications in an attempt to reconcile their occurrence. This leads to the formation of associations among these behaviors. In contrast, behaviors that are either evaluatively neutral or evaluatively consistent with the person concept do not stimulate this cognitive activity.

7.8 If people who have formed an evaluative concept of a person learn about specific behaviors of the person that are inconsistent with this concept, they mentally review and think about other behaviors the person has performed that support its validity. This cognitive activity further strengthens the associations between the concept and behaviors that are evaluatively consistent with it.

7.9 The trait-behavior clusters that are formed as a result of encoding a person's behaviors in terms of trait concepts, and the evaluation-based representation that is ultimately formed of the person, each functions as a separate unit of information. These representations are stored independently of one another in a referent bin that pertains to the person.

7.10 The recall of the specific behaviors contained in a representation is the result of a sequential search process. The search begins at the central concept node and progresses along the various pathways in the network. Behaviors are recalled in the order they are identified in the course of this search.

    a. When more than one pathway emanates from a particular node, the most likely path to be traversed is the one that reflects the strongest association between the nodes it connects.

    b. When the only path emanating from a behavior node is the one by which it was accessed, the search is reinitiated at the central concept node.

7.11 Traversing a pathway between two nodes increases the strength of the association between them. It therefore increases the probability that recalling one of the concepts (behaviors) will cue the retrieval of the other.

7.12 When a search activates *n* successive features, all of which have been retrieved previously, the search is terminated.

The Cognitive Representation of Social Events

8.1 A person who learns about a specific sequence of actions or events with the objective of comprehending them divides the sequence into one or more units, each corresponding to a different action or event concept.

8.2 The number of subjective units into which a sequence is divided (a) increases with the level of detail at which one believes the sequence may later need to be reconstructed, and (b) decreases with the redundancy of the sequence with general world knowledge.

8.3 Each action unit into which an event sequence is divided is assigned both (a) a descriptive code that identifies the concept used to interpret it, and (b) a temporal code that denotes its time of occurrence in relation to other units.

8.4 The actions contained in a unit become associated with the concept that is used to define the unit, but are not themselves assigned individual temporal codes.

Inference Making

9.1 People who believe that one stimulus condition implies another (that X implies Y) will also believe that the second condition implies the first (that Y implies X) and, therefore, will infer X from the existence of Y.

10.1 People who are asked to judge a characteristic of a person will search memory for a representation of the person whose central concept specifically pertains to this characteristic. If such a representation is found, they base their judgments on the implications of its central concept without reviewing the individual behaviors contained in it.

10.2 If a representation whose central concept has direct implications for a judgment cannot be found, people will retrieve and use the general evaluation-based person representation as a basis for the judgment. This judgment will be based on both (a) the evaluative implications of the central person concept defining the representation, and (b) behaviors contained in the representation that have direct implications for the judgment.

References

Abelson, R. P. (1976). Script processing in attitude formation and decision-making. In J. S. Carroll & J. W. Payne (Eds.), *Cognition and social behavior*. Hillsdale, NJ: Lawrence Erlbaum Associates.

Abelson, R. P. (1981). The psychological status of the script concept. *American Psychologist, 36*, 715-729.

Abelson, R. P. (1983). Whatever became of consistency theory? *Personality and Social Psychology Bulletin, 9*, 37-54.

Abelson, R. P., Aronson, E., McGuire, W. J., Newcomb, T. N., Rosenberg, M. J., & Tannenbaum, P. (Eds.). (1968). *Theories of cognitive consistency: A sourcebook*. Chicago: Rand-McNally.

Abelson, R. P., & Reich, C. M. (1969). Implicational molecules: A method for extracting meaning from input sentences. In D. E. Walker & L. M. Norton (Eds.), *Proceedings of the International Joint Conference on Artificial Intelligence*.

Abelson, R. P., & Rosenberg, M. J. (1958). Symbolic psycho-logic: A model of attitudinal cognition. *Behavioral Science, 3*, 1-13.

Allen, R. B., & Ebbesen, E. B. (1981). Cognitive processes in person perception: Retrieval of personality trait and behavioral information. *Journal of Experimental Social Psychology, 17*, 119-141.

Alloy, L. B., & Abramson, L. Y. (1979). Judgment of contingency in depressed and nondepressed students: Sadder but wiser? *Journal of Experimental Psychology: General, 108*, 441-485.

Allport, G.W. (1955). *Becoming*. New Haven, CT: Yale University Press.

Anderson, J. R. (1976). *Language, memory and thought*. Hillsdale, NJ: Lawrence Erlbaum Associates.

Anderson, J. R. (1980). *Cognitive psychology and its implications*. San Francisco: Freeman.

Anderson, J. R. (1983). *The architecture of cognition*. Cambridge, MA: Harvard University Press.

Anderson, J. R., & Bower, G. H. (1979). *Human associative memory*. Hillsdale, NJ: Lawrence Erlbaum Associates. (Originally published 1973)

Anderson, J. R., & Hastie, R. (1974). Individuation and reference in memory: Proper names and definite descriptions. *Cognitive Psychology, 6*, 495-514.

Anderson, N. H. (1965). Averaging versus adding as a stimulus-combination rule in impression formation. *Journal of Experimental Psychology, 70*, 394-400.

Anderson, N. H. (1970). Functional measurement and psychological judgment. *Psychological Review, 77*, 153-170.

Anderson, N. H. (1971). Integration theory and attitude change. *Psychological Review, 78*, 171-206.

Anderson, N. H. (1974). Cognitive algebra: Integration theory applied to social attribution. In L. Berkowitz (Ed.), *Advances in experimental social psychology* (Vol. 7). New York: Academic Press.

Anderson, N. H. (1981). *Foundations of information integration theory.* New York: Academic Press.

Anderson, N. H., & Hubert, S. (1963). Effects of concomitant verbal recall on order effects in personality impression formation. *Journal of Verbal Learning and Verbal Behavior, 2*, 379-391.

Anderson, R. C., & Pichert, J. W. (1978). Recall of previously unrecallable information following a shift in perspective. *Journal of Verbal Learning and Verbal Behavior, 17*, 1-12.

Anderson, R. C., Reynolds, R. E., Schallert, D. L., & Goetz, E. T. (1976). *Frameworks for comprehending discourse* (Tech. Rep. No. 12). Urbana, IL: Laboratory for Cognitive studies in Education, University of Illinois at Urbana-Champaign.

Arkin, R. M., Gleason, J. M., & Johnston, S. (1976). Effect of perceived choice, expected outcome, and observed outcome of an action on the causal attributions of actors. *Journal of Experimental Social Psychology, 12*, 151-158.

Asch, S. E. (1946). Forming impressions of personality. *Journal of Abnormal and Social Psychology, 41*, 258-290.

Atkinson, R. C., & Shiffrin, R. M. (1968). Human memory: A proposed system and its control processes. In K. W. Spence & J. T. Spence (Eds.), *The psychology of learning and motivation* (Vol. 2). New York: Academic Press.

Baddeley, A. D. (1976). *The psychology of memory.* New York: Basic Books.

Baddeley, A. D., Cuccaro, W. J., Egstrom, G., & Willis, M. A. (1975). Cognitive efficiency of divers working in cold water. *Human Factors, 17*, 446-454.

Baddeley, A. D., & Hitch, G. J. (1974). Working memory. In G. H. Bower (Ed.), *The psychology of learning and motivation* (Vol. 8). New York: Academic Press.

Baddeley, A. D., & Hitch, G. J. (1977). Recency reexamined. In S. Dornie (Ed.), *Attention and performance* (Vol. 6). Hillsdale, NJ: Lawrence Erlbaum Associates.

Bahrick, H. P. (1984). Semantic memory content in permastore: Fifty years of memory for Spanish learned in school. *Journal of Experimental Psychology: General, 113*, 1-29.

Baker, L. (1978). Processing temporal relationships in simple stories: Effects of input sequence. *Journal of Verbal Learning and Verbal Behavior, 17*, 559-572.

Banks, W. P. (1977). Encoding and processing of symbolic information in comparative judgments. In G. H. Bower (Ed.), *The psychology of learning and motivation* (Vol. 11). New York: Academic Press.

Barclay, J. R., Bransford, J. D., Franks, J. J., McCarrell, N. S., & Nitsch, K. (1974). Comprehension and semantic flexibility. *Journal of Verbal Learning and Verbal Behavior, 13*, 471-481.

Bargh, J. A. (1982). Attention and automaticity in the processing of self-relevant information. *Journal of Personality and Social Psychology, 43*, 425-436.

Bargh, J. A. (1984). Automatic and conscious processing of social information. In R. S. Wyer & T. K. Srull (Eds)., *Handbook of social cognition* (Vol. 3). Hillsdale, NJ: Lawrence Erlbaum Associates.

Bargh, J. A., Bond, R. N., Lombardi, W., & Tota, M. E. (1986). The additive nature of chronic and temporary sources of construct accessibility. *Journal of Personality and Social Psychology, 50,* 869-878.

Bargh, J. A., & Pietromonaco, P. (1982). Automatic information processing and social perception: The influence of trait information presented outside of conscious awareness on impression formation. *Journal of Personality and Social Psychology, 43,* 437-449.

Bargh, J. A., & Thein, R. D. (1985). Individual construct accessibility, person memory, and the recall-judgment link: The case of information overload. *Journal of Personality and Social Psychology, 49,* 1129-1146.

Barsalou, L. W., & Sewell, D. R. (1985). Contrasting the representation of scripts and categories. *Journal of Memory and Language, 24,* 646-665.

Bear, G., & Hodun, A. (1975). Implicational principles and the cognition of confirmatory, contradictory, incomplete, and irrelevant information. *Journal of Personality and Social Psychology, 32,* 594-604.

Bellezza, F. S., & Bower, G. H. (1981). Person stereotypes and memory for people. *Journal of Personality and Social Psychology, 41,* 856-865.

Bem, D. J. (1965). An experimental analysis of self-persuasion. *Journal of Experimental Social Psychology, 1,* 199-218.

Bem, D. J. (1967). Self-perception: An alternative interpretation of cognitive dissonance phenomena. *Psychological Review, 74,* 183-200.

Bem, D. J. (1972). Self-perception theory. In L. Berkowitz (Ed.), *Advances in experimental social psychology* (Vol. 6). New York: Academic Press.

Bem, D. J., & McConnell, H. K. (1970). Testing the self-perception explanation of dissonance phenomena: On the salience of premanipulation attitudes. *Journal of Personality and Social Psychology, 14,* 23-31.

Berkowitz, L., & Lepage, A. (1967). Weapons as aggression-eliciting stimuli. *Journal of Personality and Social Psychology, 7,* 202-207.

Berlyne, D. E. (1967). Arousal and reinforcement. In W. J. Arnold (Ed.), *Nebraska symposium on motivation* (Vol. 15). Lincoln: University of Nebraska Press.

Berlyne, D. E. (1971). *Aesthetics and psychology.* New York: Appleton.

Birnbaum, M. H. (1974). The nonadditivity of personality impressions. *Journal of Experimental Psychology, 102,* 543-561.

Birnbaum, M. H. (1981). Thinking and feeling: A skeptical review. *American Psychologist, 36,* 99-101.

Birnbaum, M. H., & Mellers, B. A. (1979a). One-mediator model of exposure effects is still viable. *Journal of Personality and Social Psychology, 27,* 1090-1096.

Birnbaum, M. H., & Mellers, B. A. (1979b). Stimulus recognition may mediate exposure effects. *Journal of Personality and Social Psychology, 37,* 391-394.

Bjork, R. A., & Whitten, W. B. (1974). Recency-sensitive retrieval processes in long-term free recall. *Cognitive Psychology, 6,* 173-189.

Black, J. B., Galambos, J. A., & Read, S. (1984). Comprehending stories and social situations. In R. S. Wyer & T. K. Srull (Eds.), *Handbook of social cognition* (Vol. 3). Hillsdale, NJ: Lawrence Erlbaum Associates.

Blaney, P. H. (1986). Affect and memory: A review. *Psychological Bulletin, 99,* 229-246.

Bleda, P. R., Bell, P. A., & Byrne, D. (1973). Prior induced affect and sex differences in attraction. *Memory and Cognition, 1,* 435-438.

Bless, H., Bohner, G., Schwarz, N., & Strack, F. (1987). *Happy and mindless? Moods and the processing of persuasive communications*. Unpublished manuscript, University of Mannheim, Germany.

Bobrow, D. G., & Norman, D. A. (1975). Some principles of memory schemata. In D. G. Bobrow & A. Collins (Eds.), *Representation and understanding: Studies in cognitive science*. New York: Academic Press.

Bodenhausen, G. V. (1987). *Effects of social stereotypes on evidence processing: The cognitive basis of discrimination in juridic decision making*. Unpublished doctoral dissertation, University of Illinois, Urbana-Champaign.

Bodenhausen, G. V., & Lichtenstein, M. (1987). Social stereotypes and information processing strategies: The impact of task complexity. *Journal of Personality and Social Psychology, 52*, 871-880.

Bodenhausen, G. V., & Wyer, R. S. (1985). Effects of stereotypes on decision-making and information-processing strategies. *Journal of Personality and Social Psychology, 48*, 267-282.

Bower, G. H. (1975). Cognitive psychology: An introduction. In W. K. Estes (Ed.), *Handbook of learning and cognitive processes* (Vol. 1). Hillsdale, NJ: Lawrence Erlbaum Associates.

Bower, G. H. (1981). Mood and memory. *American Psychologist, 36*, 129-148.

Bower, G. H., Black, J. B., & Turner, T. J. (1979). Scripts in memory for text. *Cognitive Psychology, 11*, 177-220.

Bower, G. H., & Gilligan, S. G. (1979). Remembering information related to one's self. *Journal of Research in Personality, 13*, 420-432.

Bower, G. H., Gilligan, S. G., & Monteiro, K. P. (1981). Selectivity of learning caused by affective states. *Journal of Experimental Psychology: General, 110*, 451-483.

Bower, G. H., Monteiro, K. P., & Gilligan, S. G. (1978). Emotional mood as a context for learning and recall. *Journal of Verbal Learning and Verbal Behavior, 17*, 573-585.

Bradburn, N. M. (1969). *The structure of psychological well-being*. Chicago: Aldine.

Bransford, J. D., & Stein, B. S. (1984). *The ideal problem solver: A guide to improving thinking, learning, and creativity*. New York: W. H. Freeman.

Brewer, M. (1988). A dual process model of impression formation. In T. K. Srull & R. S. Wyer (Eds.), *Advances in social cognition, Volume I: A dual-process model of impression formation*. Hillsdale, NJ: Lawrence Erlbaum Associates.

Brewer, W. B., & Dupree, D. A. (1983). Use of plan schemata in the recall and recognition of goal-directed actions. *Journal of Experimental Psychology: Learning, Memory and Cognition, 9*, 117-129.

Brown, D. R. (1953). Stimulus-similarity and the anchoring of subjective scales. *American Journal of Psychology, 66*, 99-214.

Brown, N. R., Rips, L. J., & Shevell, S. K. (1985). The subjective dates of natural events in very-long-term memory. *Cognitive Psychology, 17*, 139-177.

Bruner, J. S. (1951). Personality dynamics and the process of perceiving. In R. Blake & G. Ramsey (Eds.), *Perception: An approach to personality*. New York: Ronald.

Bruner, J. S. (1957). On perceptual readiness. *Psychological Review, 64*, 123-152.

Burnstein, E., & Schul, Y. (1983). The informational basis of social judgments: Memory for integrated and nonintegrated trait descriptions. *Journal of Experimental Social Psychology, 19*, 49-57.

Byrne, D. (1971). *The attraction paradigm*. New York: Academic Press.

Cantor, J., Zillmann, D., & Bryant, J. (1974). Enhancement of experienced sexual arousal in response to erotic stimuli through misattribution of unrelated residual excitation. *Journal of Personality and Social Psychology, 32,* 69-75.

Cantor, N., & Kihlstrom, J. (Eds.). (1981). *Personality, cognition and social interaction.* Hillsdale, NJ: Lawrence Erlbaum Associates.

Cantor, N., & Mischel, W. (1977). Traits as prototypes: Effects on recognition memory. *Journal of Personality and Social Psychology, 35,* 38-48.

Carlston, D. E. (1980a). Events, inferences and impression formation. In R. Hastie, T. Ostrom, E. Ebbesen, R. Wyer, D. Hamilton, & D. Carlston (Eds.), *Person memory: The cognitive basis of social perception.* Hillsdale, NJ: Lawrence Erlbaum Associates.

Carlston, D. E. (1980b). The recall and use of traits and events in social inference processes. *Journal of Experimental Social Psychology, 16,* 303-328.

Carlston, D. E., & Skowronski, J. J. (1986). Trait memory and behavior memory: The effects of alternative pathways on impression judgment response times. *Journal of Personality and Social Psychology, 50,* 5-13.

Carver, C. S., Ganellen, R. J., Froming, W. J., & Chambers, W. (1983). Modelling: An analysis in terms of category accessibility. *Journal of Experimental Social Psychology, 16,* 779-804.

Chew, B. R. (1983). *Selective recall of self- and other-referenced information.* Unpublished doctoral dissertation, Harvard University, Cambridge.

Clark, D. M., & Teasdale, J. D. (1985). Constraints on the effects of mood on memory. *Journal of Personality and Social Psychology, 48,* 1595-1608.

Clark, H. (1985). Language use and language users. In G. Lindsey & E. Aronson (Eds.), *Handbook of social psychology* (Vol. 2, pp. 179-232). Reading, MA: Addison-Wesley.

Clore, G. L. (1975). *Interpersonal attraction: An overview.* Morristown, NJ: General Learning Press.

Cohen, C. E., & Ebbesen, E. B. (1979). Observational goals and schema activation: A theoretical framework for behavior perception. *Journal of Experimental Social Psychology, 15,* 305-339.

Collins, A. M., & Loftus, E. G. (1975). A spreading-activation theory of semantic processing. *Psychological Review, 83,* 407-428.

Cooley, C. H. (1902). *Human nature and the social order.* New York: Scribner's.

Cooper, J., & Fazio, R. H. (1984). A new look at dissonance theory. In L. Berkowitz (Ed.), *Advances in experimental social psychology* (Vol. 17). New York: Academic Press.

Craik, F. I. M., & Lockhart, R. S. (1972). Levels of processing: A framework for memory research. *Journal of Verbal Learning and Verbal Behavior, 11,* 671-684.

Crocker, J., Hannah, D. B., & Weber, R. (1983). Person memory and causal attribution. *Journal of Personality and Social Psychology, 44,* 55-66.

Crowder, R. B. (1976). *Principles of learning and memory.* Hillsdale, NJ: Lawrence Erlbaum Associates.

Croyle, R. T., & Cooper, J. (1983). Dissonance arousal: Physiological evidence. *Journal of Personality and Social Psychology, 46,* 782-791.

Csikszentmihalyi, M. (1975). *Beyond boredom and anxiety.* San Francisco: Jossey-Bass.

Csikszentmihalyi, M., & Bennet, S. (1971). An exploratory model of play. *American Anthropologist, 73,* 45-58.

Davis, F. M., Baddeley, A. D., & Hancock, T. R. (1975). Diver performance: The effect of cold. *Undersea Biometical Research, 2,* 195-213.

Deci, E. L. (1975). *Intrinsic motivation.* New York: Plenum.

Diener, E. (1980). Deindividuation: The absence of self-awareness and self-regulation in group members. In P. Paulus (Ed.), *The psychology of group influence.* Hillsdale, NJ: Lawrence Erlbaum Associates.

Diener, E., & Emmons, R. A. (1984). The independences of positive and negative affect. *Journal of Personality and Social Psychology, 47,* 1105-1117.

Diener, E., Fraser, S. C., Beaman, A. L., & Kelem, R. T. (1976). Effects of deindividuation variables on stealing among Halloween trick-or-treaters. *Journal of Personality and Social Psychology, 33,* 178-183.

Diener, E., & Srull, T. K. (1979). Self-awareness, psychological perspective, and self-reinforcement in relation to personal and social standards. *Journal of Personality and Social Psychology, 37,* 413-423.

Dooling, D. J., & Christiaansen, R. E. (1977). Episodic and semantic aspects of memory for prose. *Journal of Experimental Psychology: Human Learning and Memory, 3,* 428-436.

Dreben, E. K., Fiske, S. T., Hastie, R. (1979). The independence of item and evaluative information: Impression and recall order effects in behavior-based impression formation. *Journal of Personality and Social Psychology, 37,* 1758-1768.

Duval, S., & Wicklund, R. A. (1972). *A theory of objective self-awareness.* New York: Academic Press.

Dweck, C. S., & Gilliard, D. (1975). Expectancy statements as determinants of reactions to failure: Sex differences in persistence and expectancy change. *Journal of Personality and Social Psychology, 32,* 1077-1084.

Easterbrook, J. A. (1959). The effect of emotion on cue utilization and the organization of behavior. *Psychological Review, 66,* 183-201.

Ebbesen, E. B. (1980). Cognitive processes in understanding ongoing behavior. In R. Hastie, T. Ostrom, E. Ebbesen, R. Wyer, D. Hamilton, & D. Carlston (Eds.), *Person memory: Cognitive basis of social perception.* Hillsdale, NJ: Lawrence Erlbaum Associates.

Ebbesen, E. B., & Allen, R. B. (1979). Cognitive processes in implicit personality trait inferences. *Journal of Personality and Social Psychology, 37,* 471-488.

Edwards, A. L. (1957). *Techniques of attitude scale construction.* New York: Appleton-Century Crofts.

Erdelyi, M. H., & Appelbaum, G. A. (1973). Cognitive masking: The disruptive effects of an emotional stimulus upon the perception of contiguous neutral items. *Bulletin of the Psychonomic Society, 1,* 56-61.

Erdley, C., & D'Agostino, P. R. (1988). Cognitive and affective components of automatic priming effects. *Journal of Personality and Social Psychology, 54,* 741-747.

Ericsson, K. A., & Simon, H. A. (1980). Verbal reports as data. *Psychological Review, 87,* 215-251.

Fazio, R. H., Sherman, S. J., & Herr, P. M. (1982). The feature-positive effect in the self-perception process: Does not doing matter as much as doing? *Journal of Personality and Social Psychology, 42,* 404-411.

Fenigstein, A., Scheier, M. F., & Buss, A. H. (1975). Public and private self-consciousness: Assessment and theory. *Journal of Consulting and Clinical Psychology, 43,* 522-527.

Ferguson, T. J., Rule, B. G., & Carlson, D. (1983). Memory for personally relevant information. *Journal of Personality and Social Psychology, 44,* 251-261.

Festinger, L. (1954). A theory of social comparison processes. *Human Relations, 7,* 117-140.

Festinger, L. (1957). *A theory of cognitive dissonance.* Stanford: Stanford University Press.

Festinger, L., & Carlsmith, J. M. (1959). Cognitive consequences of forced compliance. *Journal of Abnormal and Social Psychology*, *58*, 203-210.

Festinger, L., & Maccoby, E. (1964). On resistance to persuasive communications. *Journal of Abnormal and Social Psychology*, *68*, 359-366.

Fishbein, M., & Ajzen, I. (1975). *Belief, attitude, intention and behavior: An introduction to theory and research*. Reading, MA: Addison-Wesley.

Fishbein, M., & Hunter, R. (1964). Summation versus balance in attitude organization and change. *Journal of Abnormal and Social Psychology*, *69*, 505-510.

Fiske, D. W., & Maddi, S. R. (1961). *Functions of varied experience*. Homewood, IL: Dorsey Press.

Fiske, S. T. (1988). Compare and contrast: Brewer's dual process model and Fiske et al.'s continuum model. In T. K. Srull & R. S. Wyer (Eds.), *Advances in social cognition, Volume I: A dual-process model of impression formation*. Hillsdale, NJ: Lawrence Erlbaum Associates.

Fiske, S. T., & Pavelchak, M. A. (1986). Category-based vs. piecemeal-based affective responses: Developments in schema-triggered affect. In R. M. Sorrentino & E. T. Higgins (Eds.), *Handbook of motivation and cognition*. New York: Guilford Press.

Fiske, S. T., & Taylor, S. E. (1984). *Social cognition*. Reading, MA: Addison-Wesley.

Fiske, S. T., Taylor, S. E., Etcoff, N. L., & Laufer, J. K. (1979). Imaging, empathy, and causal attribution. *Journal of Experimental Social Psychology*, *15*, 356-377.

Forgas, J. P., & Bower, G. H. (1987). Mood effects of person-perception judgments. *Journal of Personality and Social Psychology*, *53*, 53-60.

Friedman, A., & Pollybank, J. (1982). *Remembering information about oneself and others*. Paper presented at Psychonomic Society, Minneapolis, MN.

Fuhrman, R. W., & Wyer, R. S. (1988). Event memory: Temporal-order judgments of personal life experiences. *Journal of Personality and Social Psychology*, *54*, 365-384.

Fuhrman, R. W., & Wyer, R. S. (1989). *Event memory: The role of scripts in the mental representation of context-specific information*. Unpublished manuscript, University of Illinois at Urbana-Champaign.

Futoran, G. C., & Wyer, R. S. (1986). Effects of traits and gender stereotypes on occupational suitability judgments and the recall of judgment-relevant information. *Journal of Experimental Social Psychology*, *22*, 475-503.

Gaelick, L., Bodenhausen, G. V., & Wyer, R. S. (1985). Emotional communication in close relationships. *Journal of Personality and Social Psychology*, *49*, 1246-1265.

Galambos, J. A., & Rips, L. J. (1982). Memory for routines. *Journal of Verbal Learning and Verbal Behavior*, *21*, 260-281.

Gick, M. L., & Holyoak, K. J. (1980). Analogical problem solving. *Cognitive Psychology*, *12*, 306-355.

Gick, M. L., & Holyoak, K. J. (1983). Schema induction and analogical transfer. *Cognitive Psychology*, *14*, 1-38.

Gillund, G., & Shiffrin, R. M. (1984). A retrieval model for both recognition and recall. *Psychological Review*, *91*, 1-67.

Goethals, G. R., & Darley, J. M. (1977). Social comparison theory: An attributional approach. In J. Suls & R. Miller (Eds.), *Social comparison processes: Theoretical and empirical perspectives*. Washington, DC: Hemisphere-Halsted.

Goodhart, D. E. (1985). Some psychological effects associated with positive and negative thinking about stressful life events: Was Pollyanna right? *Journal of Personality and Social Psychology, 48*, 216-232.

Goodhart, D. E. (1986). The effects of positive and negative thinking on performance in an achievement situation. *Journal of Personality and Social Psychology, 51*, 117-124.

Gordon, S. E., & Wyer, R. S. (1987). Person memory: Category-set-size effects on the recall of a person's behaviors. *Journal of Personality and Social Psychology, 53*, 648-662.

Graesser, A. C. (1981). *Prose comprehesion beyond the word.* New York: Springer-Verlag.

Graesser, A. C., & Clark, L. F. (1985). *The structures and procedures of implicit knowledge.* Norwood, NJ: Ablex.

Graesser, A. C., Gordon, S. E., & Sawyer, J. D. (1979). Memory for typical and atypical actions in scripted activities: Test of a script pointer + tag hypothesis. *Journal of Verbal Learning and Verbal Behavior, 18*, 319-332.

Graesser, A. C., & Nakamura, G. V. (1982). The impact of a schema on comprehension and memory. In G. H. Bower (Ed.), *The psychology of learning and motivation: Advances in research and theory* (Vol. 16). New York: Academic Press.

Graesser, A. C., Woll, S. B., Kowalski, D. J., & Smith, D. A. (1980). Memory for typical and atypical actions in scripted activities. *Journal of Experimental Psychology: Human Learning and Memory, 6*, 503-513.

Greenwald, A. G. (1968). Cognitive learning, cognitive responses to persuasion and attitude change. In A. G. Greenwald, T. C. Brock, & T. M. Ostrom (Eds.), *Psychological foundations of attitudes.* New York: Academic Press.

Greenwald, A. G. (1981). Self and memory. In G. H. Bower (Ed.), *The psychology of learning and motivation* (Vol. 15). New York: Academic Press.

Greenwald, A. G., & Pratkanis, A. R. (1984). The self. In R. S. Wyer & T. K. Srull (Eds.), *Handbook of social cognition* (Vol. 3). Hillsdale, NJ: Lawrence Erlbaum Associates.

Grice, H. (1975). Logic and conversation. In P. Cole & J. Morgan (Eds.), *Syntax and semantics, Vol. 3: Speech acts* (pp. 68-134). New York: Academic Press.

Griffitt, W., & Veitch, R. (1971). Hot and crowded: Influences of population density and temperature on interpersonal affective behavior. *Journal of Personality and Social Psychology, 17*, 92-98.

Hamilton, D. L. (Ed.). (1981). *Cognitive processes in stereotyping and intergroup behavior.* Hillsdale, NJ: Lawrence Erlbaum Associates.

Hamilton, D. L., Katz, L. B., & Leirer, V. O. (1980a). Cognitive representation of personality impressions: Organizational processes in first impression formation. *Journal of Personality and Social Psychology, 39*, 1050-1063.

Hamilton, D. L., Katz, L. B., & Leirer, V. O. (1980b). Organizational processes in impression formation. In R. Hastie, T. Ostrom, E. Ebbesen, R. Wyer, D. Hamilton, & D. Carlston (Eds.), *Person memory: The cognitive basis of social perception.* Hillsdale, NJ: Lawrence Erlbaum Associates.

Hartwick, J. (1979). Memory for trait information: A signal detection analysis. *Journal of Experimental Social Psychology, 15*, 533-552.

Harvey, J., Ickes, W., & Kidd, R. (Eds.). (1976). *New directions in attribution research* (Vol. 1). Hillsdale, NJ: Lawrence Erlbaum Associates.

Harvey, O. J., Hunt, D., & Schroder, H. (1961). *Conceptual systems and personality organization.* New York: Wiley.

Hastie, R. (1980). Memory for behavioral information that confirms or contradicts a personality impression. In R. Hastie, T. Ostrom, E. Ebbesen, R. Wyer, D. Hamilton, & D. Carlston (Eds.), *Person memory: The cognitive basis of social perception*. Hillsdale, NJ: Lawrence Erlbaum Associates.

Hastie, R. (1983). Social inference. *Annual Review of Psychology, 34*, 511-542.

Hastie, R. (1984). Causes and effects of causal attribution. *Journal of Personality and Social Psychology, 46*, 44-56.

Hastie, R., & Carlston, D. E. (1980). Theoretical issues in person memory. In R. Hastie, T. Ostrom, E. Ebbesen, R. Wyer, D. Hamilton, & D. Carlston (Eds.), *Person memory: The cognitive basis of social perception*. Hillsdale, NJ: Lawrence Erlbaum Associates.

Hastie, R., & Kumar, P. A. (1979). Person memory: Personality traits as organizing principles in memory for behaviors. *Journal of Personality and Social Psychology, 37*, 25-38.

Hastie, R. Ostrom, T. M., Ebbesen, E. B., Wyer, R. S., Hamilton, D. L., & Carlston, D. E. (Eds.) (1980). *Person memory: Cognitive basis of social perception*. Hillsdale, NJ: Lawrence Erlbaum Associates.

Hastie, R., & Park, B. (1986). The relationship between memory and judgment depends on whether the judgment task is memory-based or on-line. *Psychological Review, 93*, 258-268.

Heider, F. (1946). Attitudes and cognitive organization. *Journal of Psychology, 21*, 107-112.

Heider, F. (1982). *The psychology of interpersonal relations*. Hillsdale, NJ: Lawrence Erlbaum Associates. (Originally published 1958)

Helson, H. (1964). *Adaptation-level theory*. New York: Harper & Row.

Henninger, M., & Wyer, R. S. (1976). The recognition and elimination of inconsistencies among syllogistically-related beliefs: Some new light on the "Socratic effect." *Journal of Personality and Social Psychology, 34*, 680-693.

Herr, P. M., Sherman, S. J., & Fazio, R. (1983). On the consequences of priming: Assimilation and contrast effects. *Journal of Experimental Social Psychology, 19*, 323-340.

Higgins, E. T. (1981). The "communication game": Implications for social cognition and persuasion. In E. T. Higgins, C. P. Herman, & M. P. Zanna (Eds.), *Social cognition: The Ontario Symposium* (Vol. 1). Hillsdale, NJ: Lawrence Erlbaum Associates.

Higgins, E. T. (1987). Self-discrepancy: A theory relating self and affect. *Psychological Review, 94*, 319-340.

Higgins, E. T., Bargh, J. A., & Lombardi, W. (1985). The nature of priming effects on categorization. *Journal of Experimental Psychology: Learning, Memory, and Cognition, 11*, 59-69.

Higgins, E. T., & Chaires, W. M. (1980). Accessibility of interrelational constructs: Implications for stimulus encoding and creativity. *Journal of Experimental Social Psychology, 16*, 348-361.

Higgins, E. T., Herman, P. C., Zanna, M. P. (Eds.) (1981). *Social cognition: The Ontario Symposium* (Vol. 1). Hillsdale, NJ: Lawrence Erlbaum Associates.

Higgins, E. T., King, G. (1981). Accessibility of social constructs: Information processing consequences of individual and contextual variability. In N. Cantor & J. F. Kihlstrom (Eds.), *Personality, cognition and social interaction*. Hillsdale, NJ: Lawrence Erlbaum Associates.

Higgins, E. T., & Lurie, L. (1983). Context, categorization and recall: The "change-of-standard" effect. *Cognitive Psychology, 15*, 525-547.

Higgins, E. T., & McCann, C. D. (1984). Social encoding and subsequent attitudes, impressions and memory: "Context-driven" and motivational aspects of processing. *Journal of Personality and Social Psychology, 47*, 26-39.

Higgins, E. T., McCann, C. D., & Fondacaro, R. (1982). The "communication game": Goal-directed encoding and cognitive consequences. *Social Cognition, 1*, 21-37.

Higgins, E. T., Rhodewalt, F., & Zanna, M. P. (1979). Dissonance motivation: Its nature, persistence, and reinstatement. *Journal of Experimental Social Psychology, 15*, 16-34.

Higgins, E. T., & Rholes, W. S. (1976). Impression formation and role fulfillment: A "holistic reference" approach. *Journal of Experimental Social Psychology, 12*, 422-435.

Higgins, E. T., & Rholes, W. S. (1978). "Saying is believing": Effects of message modification on memory and liking for the person described. *Journal of Experimental Social Psychology, 14*, 363-378.

Higgins, E. T., Rholes, W. S., & Jones, C. R. (1977). Category accessibility and impression formation. *Journal of Experimental Social Psychology, 13*, 141-154.

Holmes, D. S. (1968). Dimensions of projection. *Psychological Bulletin, 69*, 248-268.

Holtgraves, T., Srull, T. K., & Socall, D. (1989). Conversation memory: The effects of speaker status on memory for the assertiveness of conversation remarks. *Journal of Personality and Social Psychology, 56*, 149-160.

Holyoak, K. J., & Gordon, P. C. (1984). Information processing and social cognition. In R. S. Wyer & T. K. Srull (Eds.), *Handbook of social cognition* (Vol. 1). Hillsdale, NJ: Lawrence Erlbaum Associates.

Hong, S., & Wyer, R. S. (1989). *Determinants of product evaluations: Country of origin, attributes, and time delay between information and judgments.* Unpublished manuscript, University of Missouri at Columbia.

Hovland, C. E., Janis, I. L., & Kelley, H. H. (1953). *Communication and persuasion.* New Haven: Yale University Press.

Ingram, R. E., Smith, T. W., & Brehm, S. S. (1983). Depression and information processing: Self-schemata and the encoding of self-referent information. *Journal of Personality and Social Psychology, 45*, 412-420.

Insko, C. A. (1967). *Theories of attitude change.* New York: Appleton-Century Crofts.

Insko, C. A. (1984). Balance theory, the Jordan paradigm, and the Wiest tetrahedrom. In L. Berkowitz (Ed.), *Advances in experimental social psychology* (Vol. 18). New York: Academic Press.

Isen, A. M. (1984). Affect, cognition, and social behavior. In R. S. Wyer & T. K. Srull (Eds.), *Handbook of social cognition* (Vol. 3). Hillsdale, NJ: Lawrence Erlbaum Associates.

Isen, A. M., Shalker, T. E., Clark, M., & Karp, L. (1978). Affect, accessibility of material in memory, and behavior: A cognitive loop? *Journal of Personality and Social Psychology, 36*, 1-12.

Jacoby, L. L., & Witherspoon, D. (1982). Remembering without awareness. *Canadian Journal of Psychology, 36*, 300-324.

James, W. (1890). *Principles of psychology.* New York: Holt.

Janis, I. L., & Feshbach, S. (1953). Effects of fear-arousing communications. *Journal of Abnormal and Social Psychology, 48*, 78-92.

Johnson, E. J., & Tversky, A. (1983). Affect, generalization and the perception of risk. *Journal of Personality and Social Psychology, 45*, 20-31.

Jones, E. E., Kanouse, D., Kelley, H., Nisbett, R., Valins, S., & Weiner, B. (Eds.). (1987). *Attribution: Perceiving the causes of behavior*. Hillsdale, NJ: Lawrence Erlbaum Associates. (Originally published 1971)

Jones, E. E., & Davis, K. E. (1965). From acts to dispositions: The attributional process in person perception. In L. Berkowitz (Ed.), *Advances in experimental social psychology* (Vol. 2). New York: Academic Press.

Jones, E. E., & Nisbett, R. E. (1971). *The actor and the observer: Divergent perceptions of the causes of behavior*. Morristown, NJ: General Learning Press.

Kahneman, D., Slovic, P., & Tversky, A. (Eds.). (1982). *Judgment under uncertainty: Heuristics and biases*. New York: Cambridge University Press.

Kahneman, D., & Tversky, A. (1971). Subjective probability: A judgment of representativeness. *Cognitive Psychology, 3*, 430-454.

Kahneman, D., & Tversky, A. (1973). On the psychology of prediction. *Psychological Review, 80*, 237-251.

Kahneman, D., & Tversky, A. (1982). The simulation heuristic. In D. Kahneman, P. Slovic, & A. Tversky (Eds.), *Judgments under uncertainty: Heuristics and biases*. New York: Cambridge University Press.

Kanouse, D. E., & Hanson, L. R. (1971). Negativity in evaluations. In E. Jones, D. Kanouse, H. Kelley, R. Nisbett, S. Valins, & B. Weiner (Eds.), *Attribution: Perceiving the causes of behavior*. Morristown, NJ: General Learning Press.

Keenan, J. M., & Baillet, S. D. (1980). Memory for personally and socially significant events. In R. S. Nickerson (Ed.), *Attention and performance* (Vol. 7). Hillsdale, NJ: Lawrence Erlbaum Associates.

Kelley, H. H. (1967). Attribution theory in social psychology. In D. Levine (Ed.), *Nebraska symposium on motivation, 15*, 192-238.

Kelley, H. H. (1987). Causal schemata and the attribution process. In E. Jones, D. Kanouse, H. Kelley, R. Nisbett, S. Valins, & B. Weiner (Eds.), *Attribution: Perceiving the causes of behavior*. Hillsdale, NJ: Lawrence Erlbaum Associates. (Originally published 1971)

Kelly, J., & Wyer, R. S. (1987). *Emotional communication: The effects of recalling personal experiences in reaction to another's experience*. Unpublished manuscript, University of Illinois at Urbana-Champaign.

Kihlstrom, J. F., & Cantor, N. (1984). Mental representations of the self. In L. Berkowitz (Ed.), *Advances in experimental social psychology* (Vol. 15). New York: Academic Press.

Kihlstrom, J. F., Cantor, N., Albright, J. S., Chew, B. R., Klein, S. B., & Niedenthal, P. M. (1988). Information processing and the study of the self. In L. Berkowitz (Ed.), *Advances in experimental social psychology* (Vol. 19). New York: Academic Press.

Klatzky, R. L. (1975). *Human memory: Structures and processes*. San Francisco: W. H. Freeman.

Klatsky, R. L. (1984). Visual memory: Definitions and functions. In R. S. Wyer & T. K. Srull (Eds.), *Handbook of social cognition* (Vol. 2). Hillsdale, NJ: Lawrence Erlbaum Associates.

Klein, S. B., & Kihlstrom, J. F. (1986). Elaboration, organization and the self-reference effect in memory. *Journal of Experimental Psychology: General, 115*, 26-38.

Klein, S. B., & Loftus, J. B. (1987). *The nature of self-referent encoding: The contributions of elaborative and organizational processes*. Unpublished manuscript, Trinity University, San Antonio, TX.

Klinger, E. (1971). *Structure and functions of fantasy*. New York: Wiley.

Klinger, E. (1975). Consequences of commitment to and disengagement from incentives. *Psychological Review, 82*, 1-25.

Klinger, E. (1977). *Meaning and void: Inner experience and the incentives in people's lives*. Minneapolis: University of Minnesota Press.

Kosslyn, S. M. (1980). *Image and mind*. Cambridge, MA: Harvard University Press.

Kosslyn, S. M., & Pomerantz, J. R. (1977). Imagery, propositions and the form of internal representations. *Cognitive Psychology, 9*, 52-76.

Kraut, R. E., & Higgins, E. T. (1984). Communication and social cognition. In R. S. Wyer & T. K. Srull (Eds.), *Handbook of social cognition* (Vol. 3). Hillsdale, NJ: Lawrence Erlbaum Associates.

Kruglanski, A. (1980). Lay epistemo-logic—process and contents: Another look at attribution theory. *Psychological Review, 87*, 70-87.

Kuiper, N. A., & Rogers, T. B. (1979). Encoding of personal information: Self-other differences. *Journal of Personality and Social Psychology, 37*, 499-512.

Kunst-Wilson, W. R., & Zajonc, R. B. (1980). Affective discrimination of stimuli that cannot be recognized. *Science, 207*, 557-558.

Lachman, R., Lachman, J. L., & Butterfield, E. C. (1979). *Cognitive psychology and information processing*. Hillsdale, NJ: Lawrence Erlbaum Associates.

Lambert, A. J. (1987). *The effects of stereotypes on social judgments*. Unpublished masters thesis, University of Illinois at Urbana-Champaign.

Lampel, A. K., & Anderson, N. H. (1968). Combining visual and verbal information in an impression-formation task. *Journal of Personality and Social Psychology, 9*, 1-6.

Langer, E. (1978). Rethinking the role of thought in social interaction. In J. Harvey, W. Ickes, & R. Kidd (Eds.), *New directions in attribution research* (Vol. 2). Hillsdale, NJ: Lawrence Erlbaum Associates.

Langer, E., & Abelson, R. P. (1972). The semantics of asking a favor: How to succeed in getting help without really dying. *Journal of Personality and Social Psychology, 24*, 26-32.

Lazarus, R. S. (1982). Thoughts on the relations between emotion and cognition. *American Psychologist, 37*, 1019-1024.

Leary, T. (1957). *Interpersonal diagnosis of personality*. New York: Ronald.

Lerner, M. J., & Simmons, C. H. (1966). Observer's reaction to the "innocent victim": Compassion or rejection. *Journal of Personality and Social Psychology, 4*, 203-210.

Levine, S. R., Wyer, R. S., & Schwarz, N. (1987). *Are you what you feel? The affective and cognitive determinants of self-esteem*. Unpublished manuscript, University of Illinois at Urbana-Champaign.

Lichtenstein, E., & Brewer, W. F. (1980). Memory for goal-directed events. *Cognitive Psychology, 12*, 412-445.

Lichtenstein, M., & Srull, T. K. (1985). Conceptual and methodological issues in examining the relationship between consumer memory and judgment. In L. F. Alwitt & A. A. Mitchell (Eds.), *Psychological processes and advertising effects: Theory, research and application*. Hillsdale, NJ: Lawrence Erlbaum Associates.

Lichtenstein, M., & Srull, T. K. (1987). Processing objectives as a determinant of the relationship between recall and judgment. *Journal of Experimental Social Psychology, 23*, 93-118.

Lichtenstein, S., Slovic, P., Fischoff, B., Layman, M., & Combs, B. (1978). Judged frequency of lethal events. *Journal of Experimental Psychology: Human Learning and Memory, 4*, 551-578.

Lindsay, P. H., & Norman, D. A. (1977). *Human information processing.* New York: Academic Press.

Lingle, J. H., Altom, M., & Medin, D. L. (1984). Of cabbages and kings: Assessing the extendability of natural object concept models to social things. In R. S. Wyer & T. K. Srull (Eds.), *Handbook of social cognition* (Vol. 1). Hillsdale, NJ: Lawrence Erlbaum Associates.

Lingle, J. H., & Ostrom, T. M. (1979). Retrieval selectivity in memory-based impression judgments. *Journal of Personality and Social Psychology, 37*, 180-194.

Linville, P. W. (1982). Affective consequences of complexity regarding the self and others. In M. S. Clark & S. T. Fiske (Eds.), *Affect and cognition.* Hillsdale, NJ: Lawrence Erlbaum Associates.

Locksley, A., Hepburn, C., & Ortiz, V. (1982). Social stereotypes and judgments of individuals: An instance of the base-rate fallacy. *Journal of Experimental Social Psychology, 18*, 23-42.

Loftus, E. F., & Marburger, W. (1983). Since the eruption of Mt. St. Helens, has anyone beaten you up? Improving the accuracy of retrospective reports with landmark events. *Memory & Cognition, 11*, 114-120.

Loken, B. A. (1984). Attitude processing strategies. *Journal of Experimental Social Psychology, 20*, 272-296.

Loken, B. A., & Wyer, R., S. (1983). Effects of reporting beliefs in syllogistically related propositions on the recognition of unmentioned propositions. *Journal of Personality and Social Psychology, 45*, 306-322.

Lombardi, W. J., Higgins, E. T., & Bargh, J. A. (1987). The role of consciousness in priming effects on categorization. *Personality and Social Psychology Bulletin, 13*, 411-429.

Malamuth, N. M., & Donnerstein, E. (1982). The effects of aggressive-pornographic mass media stimuli. In L. Berkowitz (Ed.), *Advances in experimental social psychology* (Vol. 15). New York: Academic Press.

Mandler, G. (1975). Consciousness: Respectable, useful, and probably necessary. In R. Solso (Ed.), *Information processing and cognition: The Loyola Symposium.* Hillsdale, NJ: Lawrence Erlbaum Associates.

Mandler, G. (1984). *Mind and body.* New York: Norton.

Mandler, J. M., & Johnson, N. S. (1977). Remembrance of things parsed: Story structure and recall. *Cognitive Psychology, 9*, 111-151.

Markus, H. (1977). Self-schemas and processing information about the self. *Journal of Personality and Social Psychology, 35*, 63-78.

Markus, H., Crane, M., Bernstein, S., & Siladi, M. (1982). Self-schemas and gender. *Journal of Personality and Social Psychology, 42*, 38-50.

Markus, H., & Fong, G. (1976). *The role of self in other perceptions.* Unpublished manuscript, University of Michigan, Ann Arbor, MI.

Markus, H., & Sentis, K. (1982). *The self in social information processing. In J. Suls (Ed.), Psychological perspectives on the self* (Vol. 1). Hillsdale, NJ: Lawrence Erlbaum Associates.

Markus, M., & Smith, J. (1981). The influence of self-schemata on the perception of others. In N. Cantor & J. F. Kihlstrom (Eds.), *Personality, cognition, and social interaction.* Hillsdale, NJ: Lawrence Erlbaum Associates.

Markus, H., Smith, J., & Moreland, R. L. (1979). *Self schemas and other perceptions.* Paper presented at the American Psychological Association Convention, New York.

Martin, L. L. (1985). *Categorization and differentiation: A set, reset, comparison analysis of the effects of context on person perception.* New York: Springer-Verlag.

Martin, L. L. (1986). Set/Reset: The use and disuse of concepts in impression formation. *Journal of Personality and Social Psychology, 51,* 493-504.

Massad, C. M., Hubbard, M., & Newtson, D. (1979). Perceptual selectivity: Contributing process and possible cure for impression perseverance. *Journal of Experimental Social Psychology, 15,* 513-532.

McClelland, D. C., Atkinson, J. W., Clark, R. A., & Lowell, E. L. (1953). *The achievement motive.* New York: Appleton-Century Crofts.

McGrath, J. E., & Kelly, J. E. (1986). *Time and human interaction: Toward a social psychology of time.* New York: Guilford.

McGuire, W. J. (1960). A syllogistic analysis of cognitive relationships. In M. J. Rosenberg, C. I. Hovland, W. J. McGuire, R. P. Abelson, J. W. Brehm (Eds.), *Attitude organization and change.* New Haven: Yale University Press.

McGuire, W. J. (1964). Inducing resistance to persuasion: Some contemporary approaches. In L. Berkowitz (Ed.), *Advances in experimental social psychology* (Vol. 1). New York: Academic Press.

McGuire, W. J. (1968). The nature of attitudes and attitude change. In G. Lindzey & E. Aronson (Eds.), *Handbook of social psychology* (Vol. 3). Reading, MA: Addison-Wesley.

McGuire, W. J. (1972). Attitude change: An information processing paradigm. In C. G. McClintock (Ed.), *Experimental social psychology.* New York: Holt, Rinehart, and Winston.

McGuire, W. J. (1981). The probabilogical model of cognitive structure and attitude change. In R. Petty, T. Brock, & T. Ostrom (Eds.), *Cognitive responses in persuasion.* Hillsdale, NJ: Lawrence Erlbaum Associates.

McGuire, W. J. (1985). Attitudes and attitude change. In G. Lindsey & E. Aronson (Eds.), *Handbook of social psychology* (Vol. 2, 3rd ed.). Reading, MA: Addison-Wesley.

McGuire, W. J., & McGuire, C. V. (1980). Salience of handedness in the spontaneous self-concept. *Perceptual and Motor Skills, 50,* 3-7.

McGuire, W. J., & McGuire, C. V. (1981). The spontaneous self-concept as affected by personal distinctiveness. In M. D. Lynch, A. Norem-Hebeisen, & K. Gergen (Eds.)., *The self-concept.* New York: Ballinger.

McGuire, W. J., & McGuire, C. V. (1982). Significant others in self-space: Sex differences and developmental trends in the self. In J. Suls (Ed.), *Social psychological perspectives on the self.* Hillsdale, NJ: Lawrence Erlbaum Associates.

McGuire, W. J., & McGuire, C. V. (1986). Differences in conceptualizing self versus conceptualizing other people as manifested in contrasting verb types used in natural speech. *Journal of Personality and Social Psychology, 51,* 1135-1143.

McGuire, W. J., & McGuire, C. V. (1987). Content and process in the experience of self. In L. Berkowitz (Ed.), *Advances in experimental social psychology* (Vol. 20). New York: Academic Press.

McGuire, W. J., McGuire, C. V., Child, P., & Fujioka, T. (1978). Salience of ethnicity in the spontaneous self-concept as a function of one's ethnic distinctiveness in the social environment. *Journal of Personality and Social Psychology, 36*, 511-520.

McGuire, W. J., McGuire, C. V., & Winton, W. (1979). Effects of household sex composition on the salience of one's gender in the spontaneous self-concept. *Journal of Experimental Social Psychology, 15*, 77-90.

McGuire, W. J., & Padawer-Singer, A. (1976). Trait salience in the spontaneous self-concept. *Journal of Personality and Social Psychology, 33*, 743-754.

Mead, G. H. (1934). *Mind, self, and society.* Chicago: University of Chicago Press.

Medin, D. L., & Smith, E. E. (1981). Strategies and classification learning. *Journal of Experimental Psychology: Human Learning and Memory, 7*, 241-253.

Miller, G. A., Galanter, E., & Pribram, K. (1960). *Plans and the structure of behavior.* New York: Holt, Rinehart and Winston.

Miller, N. E., & Campbell, D. T. (1959). Recency and primacy in persuasion as a function of the timing of speeches and measurements. *Journal of Abnormal and Social Psychology, 59*, 1-9.

Miller, N. E. (1959). Liberalization of basic S-R concepts: Extensions to conflict behavior, motivation, and social learning. In S. Koch (Ed.), *Psychology: Study of a science* (Vol. 2). New York: McGraw-Hill.

Monson, T. C., & Snyder, M. (1977). Actors, observers and the attribution process: Toward a reconceptualization. *Journal of Experimental Social Psychology, 13*, 89-111.

Moreland, R. L., & Zajonc, R. B. (1977). Is stimulus recognition a necessary condition for the occurrence of exposure effects? *Journal of Personality and Social Psychology, 35*, 191-199.

Moreland, R., & Zajonc, R. (1979). Exposure effects may not depend on stimulus recognition. *Journal of Personality and Social Psychology, 37*, 1085-1089.

Newman, J., Wolff, W. T., & Hearst, E. (1980). The feature-positive effect in adult human subjects. *Journal of Experimental Psychology: Human Learning and Memory, 6*, 630-650.

Newtson, D. A. (1973). Attribution and the unit of perception of ongoing behavior. *Journal of Personality and Social Psychology, 28*, 28-38.

Newtson, D. A. (1976). Foundations of attribution: The perception of ongoing behavior. In J. Harvey, W. Ickes, & R. Kidd (Eds.), *New directions in attribution research* (Vol. 1). Hillsdale, NJ: Lawrence Erlbaum Associates.

Newtson, D. A., & Engquist, G. (1976). The perceptual organization of ongoing behavior. *Journal of Experimental Social Psychology, 12*, 436-450.

Newtson, D. A., Engquist, G., & Bois, J. (1977). The objective basis of behavior units. *Journal of Personality and Social Psychology, 35*, 847-862.

Nisbett, R. E., Caputo, C., Legant, P., & Maracek, J. (1973). Behavior as seen by the actor and as seen by the observer. *Journal of Personality and Social Psychology, 27*, 154-164.

Nisbett, R. E., & Ross, L. (1980). *Human inference: Strategies and shortcomings of social judgment.* Englewood Cliffs, NJ: Prentice-Hall.

Nisbett, R. E., & Wilson, T. D. (1977). Telling more than we can know: Verbal reports on mental processes. *Psychological Review, 84*, 231-259.

Norman, D. A., & Bobrow, D. G. (1976). On the role of active memory processes in perception and cognition. In C. W. Cofer (Ed.), *The structure of human memory.* San Francisco: W. H. Freeman.

Norman, D. A., & Bobrow, D. G. (1979). Descriptions: An intermediate stage in memory retrieval. *Cognitive Psychology, 11,* 107-123.

Nottenburg, G., & Shoben, E. J. (1980). Scripts as linear orders. *Journal of Experimental Social Psychology, 16,* 329-347.

Orne, M. T. (1962). On the social psychology of the psychological experiment: With particular reference to demand characteristics and their implications. *American Psychologist, 17,* 776-783.

Ortony, A., Clore, G. L., & Collins, A. M. (1988). *The cognitive structure of emotions.* New York: Cambridge University Press.

Osgood, C. E., & Tannenbaum, P. H. (1955). The principle of congruity in the prediction of attitude change. *Psychological Review, 62,* 42-55.

Osterhouse, R. A., & Brock, T. C. (1970). Distraction increases yielding to propaganda by inhibiting counterarguing. *Journal of Personality and Social Psychology, 15,* 344-358.

Ostrom, T. M., Pryor, J. B., & Simpson, D. D. (1981). The organization of social information. In E. T. Higgins, C. P. Herman, & M. P. Zanna (Eds.), *Social cognition: The Ontario Symposium.* Hillsdale, NJ: Lawrence Erlbaum Associates.

Ostrom, T. M., & Upshaw, H. S. (1968). Psychological perspective and attitude change. In A. G. Greenwald, T. C. Brock, & T. M. Ostrom (Eds.), *Psychological foundations of attitudes.* New York: Academic Press.

Ottati, V., Riggle, E., Wyer, R. S., Schwarz, N., & Kuklinski, J. (1989). The cognitive and effective bases of opinion survey responses. *Journal of Personality and Social Psychology,* in press.

Parducci, A. (1965). Category judgment: A range-frequency model. *Psychological Review, 72,* 407-418.

Park, B., & Rothbart, M. (1982). Perception of out-group homogeneity and levels of social categorization: Memory for the subordinate attributes of in-group and out-group members. *Journal of Personality and Social Psychology, 42,* 1051-1068.

Parrott, G., & Sabini, J. (1989). *Mood and memory under natural conditions.* Unpublished manuscript, Georgetown University.

Pennington, N. (1986). *Story structures in evidence evaluation.* Paper presented at the Conference on juror decision making, Northwestern University, Evanston, IL.

Pennington, N., & Hastie, R. (1985). *Causal reasoning in decision making.* Unpublished manuscript, University of Chicago, Chicago, IL.

Pennington, N., & Hastie, R. (1986a). Evidence evaluation in complex decision making. *Journal of Personality and Social Psychology, 51,* 242-258.

Pennington, N., & Hastie, R. (1986b). *Explaining the evidence: Tests of the story model for juror decision making.* Unpublished manuscript, University of Chicago, Chicago, IL.

Petty, R. E., & Brock, T. C. (1981). Thought disruption of persuasion: Assessing the validity of attitude change experiments. In R. E. Petty, T. M. Ostrom, & T. C. Brock (Eds.), *Cognitive responses in persuasion.* Hillsdale, NJ: Lawrence Erlbaum Associates.

Petty, R. E., & Cacioppo, J. T. (1981). *Attitudes and persuasion: Classic and contemporary approaches.* Dubuque, IA: W. C. Brown.

Petty, R. E., & Cacioppo, J. T. (1986). *Communication and persuasion: Central and peripheral routes to attitude change.* New York: Springer-Verlag.

Petty, R. E., Ostrom, T. M., & Brock, T. C. (Eds.). (1981). *Cognitive responses in persuasion.* Hillsdale, NJ: Lawrence Erlbaum Associates.

Picek, J. S., Sherman, S. J., & Shiffrin, R. M. (1975). Cognitive organization and coding of social structures. *Journal of Personality and Social Psychology, 31*, 758-768.

Pryor, J. B., Simpson, D. D., Mitchell, M., Ostrom, T. M., & Lydon, J. (1982). Structural selectivity in the retrieval of social information. *Social Cognition, 1*, 336-357.

Raaijmakers, J. G. W., & Shiffrin, R. M. (1980). SAM: A theory of probabilistic search of associative memory. In G. H. Bower (Ed.), *The psychology of learning and motivation* (Vol. 14). New York: Academic Press.

Raaijmakers, J. G. W., & Shiffrin, R. M. (1981). Search of associative memory. *Psychological Review, 88*, 93-134.

Read, S. (1987). Constructing causal scenarios: A knowledge structure approach to causal reasoning. *Journal of Personality and Social Psychology, 52*, 288-302.

Read, S., Druian, P., & Miller, L. (1985). The role of causal sequence in the meaning of actions. Unpublished manuscript, University of Southern California.

Reed, S. K. (1973). *Psychological processes in pattern recognition*. New York: Academic Press.

Regan, D., & Totten, J. (1975). Empathy and attribution: Turning observers into actors. *Journal of Personality and Social Psychology, 32*, 850-856.

Revlin, R., & Mayer, R. E. (1978). *Human reasoning*. Washington, DC: Winston.

Riggle, E. D., Ottati, V. C., Wyer, R. S., Kuklinski, J., & Schwarz, N. (1989). *Bases of political judgments: The role of a candidate's physical attractiveness, party membership, and voting record*. Unpublished manuscript, University of Illinios at Urbana-Champaign.

Rogers, T. B. (1981). A model of the self as an aspect of the human information processing system. In N. Cantor & J. F. Kihlstrom (Eds.), *Personality, cognition, and social interaction*. Hillsdale, NJ: Lawrence Erlbaum Associates.

Rogers, T. B., Kuiper, N. A., & Kirker, W. S. (1977). Self-reference and the encoding of personal information. *Journal of Personality and Social Psychology, 35*, 677-688.

Rogers, T. B., Kuiper, N. A., & Rogers, P. J. (1979). Symbolic distance and congruity effects for paired-comparison judgments of degree of self-reference. *Journal of Research in Personality, 13*, 433-449.

Rokeach, M. (1960). *The open and closed mind*. New York: Basic Books.

Rosch, E. H. (1973). On the internal structure of perceptual and semantic categories. In T. E. Moore (Ed.), *Cognitive development and the acquisition of language*. New York: Academic Press.

Rosch, E. H., & Lloyd, B. B. (Eds.). (1978). *Cognition and categorization*. Hillsdale, NJ: Lawrence Erlbaum Associates.

Roseman, I. (1979). *Cognitive aspects of emotion and emotional behavior*. Paper presented at the annual meeting of the American Psychological Association, New York.

Rosen, N. A., & Wyer, R. S. (1972). Some further evidence for the "Socratic effect" using a subjective probability model of cognitive organization. *Journal of Personality and Social Psychology, 24*, 420-424.

Rosenberg, S., & Sedlak, A. (1972). Structural representations of implicit personality theory. In L. Berkowitz (Ed.), *Advances in experimental social psychology* (Vol. 10). New York: Academic Press.

Rosenthal, R., & Rosnow, R. L. (Eds.). (1969). *Artifact in behavioral research*. New York: Academic Press.

Ross, B. H. (1984). Remindings and their effects in learning a familiar skill. *Cognitive Psychology, 16*, 371-416.

Ross, B. H. (1986). *Remindings in learning and instruction.* Unpublished manuscript, University of Illinois, Urbana-Champaign.

Ross, L., Greene, D., & House, P. (1977). The "false consensus effect": An egocentric bias in social perception asnd attribution processes. *Journal of Experimental Social Psychology, 13*, 279-301.

Ross, L., Lepper, M., & Hubbard, M. (1975). Perseverance in self-perception and social perception: Biased attributional processes in the debriefing paradigm. *Journal of Personality and Social Psychology, 32*, 880-892.

Ross, L., Lepper, M. R., Strack, F., & Steinmetz, J. (1977). Social explanation and social expectation: Effects of real and hypothetical explanations on subjective likelihood. *Journal of Personality and Social Psychology, 35*, 817-829.

Rubin, D. S. (Ed.). (1986). *Autobiographical memory.* New York: Cambridge University Press.

Rumelhart, D. E. (1977). *Introduction to human information processing.* New York: Wiley.

Rumelhart, D. E. (1984). Schemata and the cognitive system. In R. S. Wyer & T. K. Srull (Eds.), *Handbook of social cognition* (Vol. 1). Hillsdale, NJ: Lawrence Erlbaum Associates.

Rumelhart, D. E., & Ortony, A. (1977). The representation of knowledge in memory. In R. C. Anderson, R. J. Spiro, & W. E. Montague (Eds.), *Schooling and the acquisition of knowledge.* Hillsdale, NJ: Lawrence Erlbaum Associates.

Rundus, D. (1971). Analysis of rehearsal processes in free recall. *Journal of Experimental Psychology, 89*, 63-77.

Rundus, D. (1973). Negative effects of using list items as recall cues. *Journal of Verbal Learning and Verbal Behavior, 12*, 43-50.

Salancik, G. R. (1974). Inference of one's attitude from behavior recalled under linguistically manipulated cognitive sets. *Journal of Experimental Social Psychology, 10*, 415-427.

Salancik, G. R., & Calder, B. J. (1974). *A non-predispositional information analysis of attitude expressions.* Unpublished manuscript, University of Illinois, Urbana-Champaign, IL.

Salancik, G. R., & Conway, M. (1975). Attitude inferences from salient and relevant cognitive content about behavior. *Journal of Personality and Social Psychology, 32*, 829-840.

Schachter, S. (1964). The interaction of cognitive and physiological determinants of emotional state. In L. Berkowitz (Ed.), *Advances in Experimental social psychology* (Vol. 1). New York: Academic Press.

Schachter, S., & Singer, J. E. (1962). Cognitive, social and physiological determinants of emotional state. *Psychological Review, 69*, 379-399.

Schank, R. C. (1972). Conceptual dependency: A theory of natural language understanding. *Cognitive Psychology, 3*, 552-631.

Schank, R. C. (1975). The structure of episodes in memory. In D. G. Bobrow & A. Collins (Eds.), *Representation and understanding: Studies in cognitive science.* New York: Academic Press.

Schank, R. C. (1982). *Dynamic memory: A theory of reminding in computers and people.* Cambridge, England: Cambridge University Press.

Schank, R. C., & Ableson, R. P. (1977). Scripts, plans, goals, and understanding. Hillsdale, NJ: Lawrence Erlbaum Associates.

Scheier, M. F., & Carver, C. S. (1980). Private and public self-attention, resistance to change, and dissonance reduction. *Journal of Personality and Social Psychology, 39,* 390-405.

Schneider, W., & Shiffrin, R. M. (1977). Controlled and automatic human information processing: I. Detection, research and attention. *Psychological Review, 84,* 1-66.

Schul, Y., & Burnstein, E. (1985). When discounting fails: Conditions under which individuals use discredited information in making a judgment. *Journal of Personality and Social Psychology, 49,* 894-903.

Schwarz, N., & Clore, G. L. (1983). Mood, misattribution, and judgments of well-being. Informative and directive functions of affective states. *Journal of Personality and Social Psychology, 45,* 513-523.

Schwarz, N., & Clore, G. L. (1987). How do I feel about it? The informative function of affective states. In K. Fiedler & J. Forgas (Eds.), *Affect, cognition and social behavior.* Toronto: Hogrefe International.

Schwarz, N., Hippler, H. J., Deutsch, B., & Strack, F. (1985). Response scales: Effects on behavioral reports and comparative judgments. *Public Opinion Quarterly, 49,* 388-395.

Schwarz, N., & Scheuring, B. (1986). *Inter- and intraindividual comparisons: A function of questionnaire structure?* Paper presented at meetings of the American Psychological Association, Washington, DC.

Schwarz, N., & Strack, F. (1981). Manipulating salience: Causal assessment in natural settings. *Personality and Social Psychology Bulletin, 6,* 554-558.

Schwarz, N., Strack, F., Kommer, D., & Wagner, D. (1987). Soccer, rooms, and the quality of your life: Mood effects on judgments of satisfaction with life in general and with specific life domains. *European Journal of Social Psychology, 17,* 69-79.

Schwarz, N., & Wyer, R. S. (1985). Effects of rank ordering stimuli on magnitude ratings of these and other stimuli. *Journal of Experimental Social Psychology, 21,* 30-46.

Scott, W. A. (1963). Conceptualizing and measuring structural properties of cognition. In O. J. Harvey (Ed.), *Motivation and social interaction.* New York: Ronald Press.

Scott, W. A. (1969). Structure of natural cognitions. *Journal of Personality and Social Psychology, 12,* 261-278.

Selfridge, O. (1959). Pandemonium: A paradigm for learning. In *Symposium on the mechanization of thought processes.* London: HM Stationary Office.

Sentis, K. P., & Burnstein, E. (1979). Remembering schema-consistent information: Effects on a balance schema on recognition memory. *Journal of Personality and Social Psychology, 37,* 2200-2212.

Sherif, M., & Hovland, C. I. (1961). *Social judgment.* New Haven: Yale University Press.

Sherman, S. J., Ahlm, K., Berman, L., & Lynn, S. (1978). Contrast effects and the relationship to subsequent behavior. *Journal of Experimental Social Psychology, 14,* 340-350.

Sherman, S. J., Cialdini, R. B., Schwartzman, D. F., & Reynolds, K. D. (1982). *Imagining can heighten or lower the perceived likelihood of contracting a disease: The mediating effect of ease of imagery.* Unpublished manuscript, Arizona State University, Tempe, AZ.

Sherman, S. J., & Corty, E. (1984). Cognitive heuristics. In R. S. Wyer & T. K. Srull (Eds.), *Handbook of social cognition* (Vol. 1). Hillsdale, NJ: Lawrence Erlbaum Associates.

Sherman, S. J., Skov, R. B., Hervitz, E. F., & Stock, C. B. (1981). The effects of explaining hypothetical future events: From possibility to probability to actuality and beyond. *Journal of Experimental Social Psychology, 17*, 142-158.

Sherman, S. J., Zehner, K. S., Johnson, J., & Hirt, E. R. (1983). Social explanation: The role of timing, set, and recall on subjective likelihood estimates. *Journal of Personality and Social Psychology, 44*, 1127-1143.

Smith, E. E. (1978). Theories of semantic memory. In W. K. Estes (Ed.), *Handbook of learning and cognitive processes* (Vol. 6). Hillsdale, NJ: Lawrence Erlbaum Associates.

Smith, E. E., Adams, N., & Schorr, D. (1978). Fact retrieval and the paradox of interference. *Cognitive Psychology, 10*, 438-464.

Smith, E. E., & Medin, D. L. (1981). Categories and concepts. Cambridge, MA: Harvard University Press.

Smith, E. E., Shoben, E. J., & Rips, L. J. (1974). Structure and process in semantic memory: A featural model for semantic decisions. *Psychological Review, 81*, 214-241.

Smith, E. R. (1984). Models of social inference processes. *Psychological Review, 91*, 392-413.

Smith, S. M., Glenberg, A., & Bjork, R. A. (1978). Environmental context and human memory. *Memory & Cognition, 6*, 342-353.

Snyder, M., & Cantor, N. (1979). Testing hypotheses about other people: The use of historical knowledge. *Journal of Experimental Social Psychology, 15*, 330-342.

Snyder, M., & Swann, W. B. (1978). Hypothesis-testing processes in social interaction. *Journal of Personality and Social Psychology, 36*, 1201-1212.

Snyder, M., & Uranowitz, S. W. (1978). Reconstructing the past: Some cognitive consequences of person perception. *Journal of Personality and Social Psychology, 36*, 941-950.

Snygg, R. L., & Combs, A. W. (1949). *Individual behavior*. New York: Harper & Row.

Solomon, R. L., & Corbit, J. D. (1974). An opponent-process theory of motivation: I. Temporal dynamics of affect. *Psychological Review, 81*, 119-145.

Sorrentino, R., & Higgins, E. T. (Eds.). (1986). *Handbook of motivation and cognition*. New York: Guilford Press.

Sperling, G. (1960). The information available in brief visual presentations. *Psychological Monographs, 74*, 1-29.

Spiro, R. J. (1977). Remembering information from text: The "state of schema" approach. In R. C. Anderson, R. J. Spiro, & W. E. Montague (Eds.), *Schooling and the acquisition of knowledge*. Hillsdale, NJ: Lawrence Erlbaum Associates.

Srull, T. K. (1981). Person memory: Some tests of associative storage and retrieval models. *Journal of Experimental Psychology: Human Learning and Memory, 7*, 440-463.

Srull, T. K. (1983). Organizational and retrieval processes in person memory: An examination of processing objectives, presentation format, and the possible role of self-generated retrieval cues. *Journal of Personality and Social Psychology, 44*, 1157-1170.

Srull, T. K. (1984). Methodological techniques for the study of person memory and social cognition. In R. S. Wyer & T. K. Srull (Eds.), *Handbook of social cognition* (Vol. 2). Hillsdale, NJ: Lawrence Erlbaum Associates.

Srull, T. K., & Brand, J. F. (1983). Memory for information about persons: The effect of encoding operations on subsequent retrieval. *Journal of Verbal Learning and Verbal Behavior, 22*, 219-230.

Srull, T. K., & Gaelick, L. (1983). General principles and individual differences in the self as a habitual reference point: An examination of self-other judgments of similarity. *Social Cognition, 2*, 108-121.

Srull, T. K., Lichtenstein, M., & Rothbart, M. (1985). Associative storage and retrieval processes in person memory. *Journal of Experimental Psychology: Learning, Memory, and Cognition, 11*, 316-345.

Srull, T. K., & Wyer, R. S. (1979). The role of category accessibility in the interpretation of information about persons: Some determinants and implications. *Journal of Personality and Social Psychology, 37*, 1660-1672.

Srull, T. K., & Wyer, R. S. (1980). Category accessibility and social perception: Some implications for the study of person memory and interpersonal judgment. *Journal of Personality and Social Psychology, 38*, 841-856.

Srull, T. K., & Wyer, R. S. (1983). The role of control processes and structural constraints in models of memory and social judgment. *Journal of Experimental Social Psychology, 19*, 497-521.

Srull, T. K., & Wyer, R. S. (1986). The role of chronic and temporary goals in social information processing. In R. M. Sorrentino & E. T. Higgins (Eds.), *Handbook of motivation and cognition.* New York: Guilford.

Stein, N. L., & Glenn, C. G. (1979). An analysis of story comprehension in elementary school children. In R. O. Freedle (Ed.), *New directions in discourse processing.* Norwood, NJ: Ablex.

Steiner, I. D. (1968). Reaction to adverse and favorable evaluation of one's self. *Journal of Personality, 36*, 553-563.

Stern, L. D., Marrs, S., Millar, M. G., & Cole, E. (1984). Processing time and the recall of inconsistent and consistent behaviors of individuals and groups. *Journal of Personality and Social Psychology, 47*, 253-262.

Storms, M. (1973). Videotape and the attribution process: Reversing actors' and observers' point of view. *Journal of Personality and Social Psychology, 27*, 165-175.

Strack, F., & Martin, L. L. (1987). Thinking, judging, and communicating: A process account of context effects in attitude surveys. In H. J. Hippler, N. Schwarz, & S. Sudman (Eds.), *Cognitive aspects of survey methodology.* New York: Springer-Verlag.

Strack, F., Martin, L. L., & Schwarz, N. (1987). *The context paradox in attitude surveys: Assimilation or contrast?* Unpublished manuscript, University of Mannheim, Germany.

Strack, F., Martin, L. L., & Stepper, S. (1988). Inhibiting and facilitating conditions of the human smile: A non-obtrusive test of the facial-feedback hypothesis. *Journal of Personality and Social Psychology, 54*, 768-777.

Strack, F., Schwarz, N., & Gschneidinger, E. (1985). Happiness and reminiscing: The role of time perspective, affect, and mode of thinking. *Journal of Personality and Social Psychology, 49*, 1460-1469.

Tannenbaum, P. H. (1967). The congruity principle revisited: Studies in the reduction, induction and generalization of persuasion. In L. Berkowitz (Ed.), *Advances in experimental social psychology* (Vol. 3). New York: Academic Press.

Taylor, S. E., & Fiske, S. T. (1978). Salience, attention, and attribution: Top of the head phenomena. In L. Berkowitz (Ed.), *Advances in experimental social psychology* (Vol. 11). New York: Academic Press.

Taylor, S. E., Fiske, S. T., Close, M. M., Anderson, C. E., & Ruderman, A. (1974). *Solo status as a psychological variable.* Unpublished manuscript, University of California, Los Angeles, CA.

Thompson, W. C., Fong, G. T., & Rosenhan, D. L. (1981). Inadmissible evidence and juror verdicts. *Journal of Personality and Social Psychology, 3,* 453-463.

Thurstone, L. L. (1959). *The measurement of values.* Chicago: University of Chicago Press.

Trafimow, D., & Srull, T. K. (1986). *The situation specificity of mental representations of another.* Unpublished manuscript, University of Illinois, Urbana-Champaign, IL.

Tulving, E. (1972). *Episodic and semantic memory.* In E. Tulving & W. Donaldson (Eds.), Organization and memory. New York: Academic Press.

Tulving, E. (1983). *Elements of episodic memory.* Oxford: Clarendon Press.

Tulving, E., Schacter, D. L., & Stark, H. A. (1982). Priming effects in word-fragment completion are independent of recognition memory. *Journal of Experimental Psychology: Learning, Memory, and Cognition, 8,* 336-342.

Tversky, A. (1977). Features of similarity. *Psychological Review, 84,* 327-352.

Tversky, A., & Gati, I. (1978). Studies of similarity. In E. Rosch & B. B. Lloyd (Eds.), *Cognition and categorization.* Hillsdale, NJ: Lawrence Erlbaum Associates.

Tversky, A., & Kahneman, D. (1973). Availability: A heuristic for judging frequency and probability. *Cognitive Psychology, 5,* 207-232.

Tversky, A., & Kahneman, D. (1974). Judgment under uncertainty: Heuristics and biases. *Science, 185,* 1124-1131.

Tzeng, O. J. L. (1973). Positive recency effect in delayed free recall. *Journal of Verbal Learning and Verbal Behavior, 12,* 436-493.

Upshaw, H. S. (1962). Own attitude as an anchor in equal-appearing intervals. *Journal of Abnormal and Social Psychology, 64,* 85-96.

Upshaw, H. S. (1965). The effect of variable perspectives on judgments of opinion statements for Thurstone scales: Equal-appearing intervals. *Journal of Abnormal and Social Psychology, 64,* 85-96.

Upshaw, H. S. (1969). The personal reference scale: An approach to social judgment. In L. Berkowitz (Ed.), *Advances in experimental social psychology* (Vol. 4). New York: Academic Press.

Upshaw, H. S. (1978). Social influence on attitudes and on anchoring of congeneric attitude scales. *Journal of Experimental Social Psychology, 14,* 327-339.

Warr, P., Barter, J., & Brownbridge, G. (1983). On the independence of positive and negative attitudes. *Journal of Personality and Social Psychology, 44,* 644-651.

Warrington, E. K., & Weiskrantz, L. (1974). The effect of prior learning on subsequent retention in amnesic patients. *Neuropsychologia, 6,* 283-291.

Wason, P. C. (1968). Reasoning about a rule. *Quarterly Journal of Experimental Psychology, 20,* 273-281.

Watkins, M. J., & Peynicrioglu, Z. F. (1983). Three recency effects at the same time. *Journal of Verbal Learning and Verbal Behavior, 22,* 275-384.

Weber, R., & Crocker, J. (1983). Cognitive processes in the revision of stereotypic beliefs. *Journal of Personality and Social Psychology, 45,* 961-977.

White, G. L., Fishbein, S., & Rutstein, J. (1981). Passionate love and the misattribution of arousal. *Journal of Personality and Social Psychology, 41,* 56-62.

Wicklund, R. A. (1975). Objective self-awareness. In L. Berkowitz (Ed.), *Advances in experimental social psychology* (Vol. 8). New York: Academic Press.

Wicklund, R. A., & Brehm, J. W. (1976). *Perspectives on cognitive dissonance*. Hillsdale, NJ: Lawrence Erlbaum Associates.

Williams, M., & Hollan, J. D. (1981). The process of retrieval from very long-term memory. *Cognitive Science, 5*, 87-119.

Wilson, W. R. (1979). Feeling more than we can know: Exposure effects without learning. *Journal of Personality and Social Psychology, 37*, 811-821.

Wilson, T. D., & Nisbett, R. E. (1978). The accuracy of verbal reports about the effects of stimuli on evaluations and behavior. Social Psychology, 41, 118-131.

Winter, L., & Uleman, J. S. (1984). When are social judgments made? Evidence for the spontaneousness of trait inferences. *Journal of Personality and Social Psychology, 47*, 237-252.

Winter, L., & Uleman, J. S., & Cunniff, C. (1985). How automatic are social judgments? *Journal of Personality and Social Psychology, 49*, 904-917.

Wyer, R. S. (1970a). Information redundancy, inconsistency and novelty and their role in impression formation. *Journal of Experimental Social Psychology, 6*, 111-127.

Wyer, R. S. (1970b). The prediction of evaluations of social role occupants as a function of the favorableness, relevance and probability associated with attributes of these occupants. *Sociometry, 33*, 79-96.

Wyer, R. S. (1970c). The quantitative prediction of belief and opinion change: A further test of a subjective probability model. *Journal of Personality and Social Psychology, 16*, 559-571.

Wyer, R. S. (1972). Test of a subjective probability model of social evaluation processes. *Journal of Personality and Social Psychology, 22*, 279-286.

Wyer, R. S. (1973). Category ratings as "subjective expected values": Implications for attitude formation and change. *Psychological Review, 80*, 446-467.

Wyer, R. S. (1974). *Cognitive organization and change: An information-processing approach*. Hillsdale, NJ: Lawrence Erlbaum Associates.

Wyer, R. S. (1975). Functional measurement analysis of a subjective probability model of cognitive functioning. *Journal of Personality and Social Psychology, 31*, 94-100.

Wyer, R. S. (1976). An investigation of the relations among probability estimates. *Organizational Behavior and Human Performance, 15*, 1-18.

Wyer, R. S. (1977). The role of logical and nonlogical factors in making inferences about category membership. *Journal of Experimental Social Psychology, 13*, 577-595.

Wyer, R. S. (1981). An information-processing perspective on social attribution. In J. Harvey, W. Ickes, & R. Kidd (Eds.), *New directions in attribution research* (Vol. 3). Hillsdale, NJ: Lawrence Erlbaum Associates.

Wyer, R. S., & Bodenhausen, G. V. (1985). Event memory: The effects of processing objectives and time delay on memory for action sequences. *Journal of Personality and Social Psychology, 49*, 304-316.

Wyer, R. S., Bodenhausen, G. V., & Gorman, T. F. (1985). Cognitive mediators of reactions to rape. *Journal of Personality and Social Psychology, 48*, 324-338.

Wyer, R. S., Bodenhausen, G. V., & Srull, T. K. (1984). The cognitive representation of persons and groups and its effect on recall and recognition memory. *Journal of Experimental Social Psychology, 20*, 445-469.

Wyer, R. S., & Budesheim, T. L. (1987). Person memory and judgments: The impact of information that one is told to disregard. *Journal of Personality and Social Psychology, 53*, 14-29.

Wyer, R. S., Budesheim, T. L., & Lambert, A. J. (1989). *Person memory and judgment: The cognitive representation of informal conversation.* Unpublished manuscript, University of Illinois at Urbana-Champaign.

Wyer, R. S., Budesheim, T. L., Lambert, A. J., & Martin, L. L. (1989). *Person memory: The priorities that govern the cognitive activities involved in person impression formation.* Unpublished manuscript, University of Illinois, Urbana-Champaign, IL.

Wyer, R. S., & Carlston, D. E. (1979). *Social cognition, inference and attribution.* Hillsdale, NJ: Lawrence Erlbaum Associates.

Wyer, R. S., & Goldberg, L. (1970). A probabilistic analysis of the relationships among beliefs and attitudes. *Psychological Review, 77,* 100-120.

Wyer, R. S., & Gordon, S. E. (1982). The recall of information about persons and groups. *Journal of Experimental Social Psychology, 18,* 128-164.

Wyer, R. S., & Gordon, S. E. (1984). The cognitive representation of social information. In R. S. Wyer & T. K. Srull (Eds.), *Handbook of social cognition* (Vol. 2). Hillsdale, NJ: Lawrence Erlbaum Associates.

Wyer, R. S., & Hartwick, J. (1980). The role of information retrieval and conditional inference processes in belief formation and change. In L. Berkowitz (Ed.), *Advances in experimental social psychology* (Vol. 13). New York: Academic Press.

Wyer, R. S., & Hartwick, J. (1984). The recall and use of belief statements as bases for judgments: Some determinants and implications. *Journal of Experimental Social Psychology, 20,* 65-85.

Wyer, R. S., & Martin, L. L. (1986). Person memory: The role of traits, group stereotypes and specific behaviors in the cognitive representation of persons. *Journal of Personality and Social Psychology, 50,* 661-675.

Wyer, R. S., & Ottati, V. C. (in press). Political information processing. In S. Iyengar & W. J. McGuire (Eds.), *Current approaches to political psychology.* Urbana, IL: University of Illinois Press.

Wyer, R. S., & Schwartz, S. (1969). Some contingencies in the effects of the source of a communication upon the evaluation of that communication. *Journal of Personality and Social Psychology, 11,* 1-9.

Wyer, R. S., Shoben, E. J., Fuhrman, R. F., & Bodenhausen, G. V. (1985). Event memory: The cognitive representation of social action sequences. *Journal of Personality and Social Psychology, 49,* 857-877.

Wyer, R. S., & Srull, T. K. (1980). The processing of social stimulus information: A conceptual integration. In R. Hastie, T. Ostrom, E. Ebbesen, R. Wyer, D. Hamilton, & D. Carlston (Eds.), *Person memory: The cognitive basis of social perception.* Hillsdale, NJ: Lawrence Erlbaum Associates.

Wyer, R. S., & Srull, T. K. (Eds.). (1984). *Handbook of social cognition* (Vols. 1, 2, and 3). Hillsdale, NJ: Lawrence Erlbaum Associates.

Wyer, R. S., & Srull, T. K. (1986). Human cognition in its social context. *Psychological Review, 93,* 322-359.

Wyer, R. S., & Srull, T. K. (1988). Understanding social knowledge: if only the data could speak for themselves. In D. Bar-tal & A., Kruglanski (Eds.), *Social psychology at knowledge.* Cambridge: Cambridge University Press.

Wyer, R. S., & Srull, T. K., & Gordon, S. E. (1984). The effects of predicting a person's behavior on subsequent trait judgments. *Journal of Experimental Social Psychology, 20,* 29-46.

Wyer, R. S., Srull, T. K., & Gordon, S. E., & Hartwick, J. (1982). The effects of taking a perspective on the recall of prose material. *Journal of Personality and Social Psychology, 43*, 674-688.

Wyer, R. S., Strack, F., & Fuhrman, R. W. (1988). Erwerb von Informationen uber Personen: Einflusse von Aufgabenstellung und personlichen Erwartungen. *Zeitschrift fur experimentelle und angewandte Psychologie, 35*, 657-688.

Wyer, R. S., & Unverzagt, W. H. (1985). The effects of instructions to disregard information on its subsequent recall and use in making judgments. *Journal of Personality and Social Psychology, 48*, 533-549.

Zajonc, R. B. (1980). Feeling and thinking: Preferences need no inferences. *American Psychologist, 35*, 151-175.

Zajonc, R. B., & Markus, H. (1984). Affect and cognition: The hard interface. In C. E. Izard, J. Kagan, & R. B. Zajonc (Eds.), *Emotion, cognition and behavior*. New York: Cambridge University Press.

Zanna, M. P., & Cooper, J. (1974). Dissonance and the pill: An attribution approach to studying the arousal properties of dissonance. *Journal of Personality and Social Psychology, 29*, 703-709.

Zanna, M. P., & Cooper, J. (1976). Dissonance and the attribution process. In J. Harvey, W. Ickes, & R. Kidd (Eds.), *New directions in attribution research* (Vol. 1). Hillsdale, NJ: Lawrence Erlbaum Associates.

Zillmann, D. (1983). *Connections between sex and aggression*. Hillsdale, NJ: Lawrence Erlbaum Associates.

Zillmann, D. (1978). Attribution and misattribution of excitatory reactions. In J. H. Harvey, W. Ickes, & R. Kidd (Eds.), *New directions in attribution research* (Vol. 2). Hillsdale, NJ: Lawrence Erlbaum Associates.

Author Index

Numbers in *italics* denote pages with complete bibliographic information.

Subject Index